Attorney-Client Privilege in the Americas: Professional Secrecy of Lawyers

One of the major challenges facing the legal profession today is how to adapt and apply the concept of attorney-client privilege (or professional secrecy) in an increasingly globalised world. Rules on attorney-client privilege differ significantly from country to country. This book explores such differences within 32 jurisdictions in North, Central and South America and the Caribbean. Together with its complementary volume *Professional Secrecy of Lawyers in Europe* (2013), this book explores the creation of a common definition for attorney-client privilege that can be accepted by a wide variety of countries and international institutions. Practice and interpretation within each jurisdiction are mapped and explored, including reference to local laws, ethical rules and case law. This book is a useful resource for those working on transactions or litigation which involve several countries.

This book is the second volume in a project intended to provide an overview and better understanding of professional secrecy (also known as the attorney-client privilege) around the world. The first volume examined professional secrecy in the member states of the European Union, the member states of the European Economic Area and Switzerland.

The book is written by representatives of bar associations and law firms in the relevant countries. James R. Silkenat and Dirk Van Gerven are respectively past president of the American Bar Association and the Bar of Brussels and in this capacity are professionals who have a good knowledge of attorney-client privilege or professional secrecy, as they have been asked to solve issues and reply to queries with respect to professional secrecy during their mandate as President of the Bar.

Attorney-Client Privilege in the Americas

Professional Secrecy of Lawyers

The Countries of North, Central and South America and the Caribbean

Edited by

JAMES R. SILKENAT AND DIRK VAN GERVEN

CAMBRIDGE
UNIVERSITY PRESS

University Printing House, Cambridge CB2 8BS, United Kingdom

Cambridge University Press is part of the University of Cambridge.

It furthers the University's mission by disseminating knowledge in the pursuit of education, learning, and research at the highest international levels of excellence.

www.cambridge.org
Information on this title: www.cambridge.org/9781107171282
DOI: 10.1017/9781316759882

© Cambridge University Press 2017

First published 2017

Printed in the United States of America by Sheridan Books, Inc.

A catalogue record for this publication is available from the British Library.

Library of Congress Cataloging-in-Publication Data
Silkenat, James R., editor. | Gerven, Dirk van, editor.
Attorney-client privilege in the Americas : professional secrecy of lawyers / edited by James Silkenat, Dirk Van Gerven.
Cambridge [UK] : Cambridge University Press, 2016.
LCCN 2016026622 | ISBN 9781107171282 (hardback)
LCSH: Confidential communications – Lawyers. | Attorney and client. | Confidential communications – Lawyers – America.
LCC K2281.A7 A78 2016 | DDC 347.7/06–dc23
LC record available at https://lccn.loc.gov/2016026622

ISBN 978-1-107-17128-2 Hardback

Contents

Contributors

General
JAMES R. SILKENAT *Sullivan & Worcester LLP*
DIRK VAN GERVEN *NautaDutilh BVBA/SPRL*

Anguilla
YVETTE A. WALLACE ANGELA A. MULLIX *Keithley Lake & Associates*

Antigua & Barbuda
SAFIYA L. ROBERTS *Roberts & Co.*

Argentina
MARCELO BOMBAU *M. & M. Bomchil*

Bahamas
VANN P. GAITOR, LASHAY A.S. THOMPSON, ANDREA A. MOULTRIE, FELIX F.L.
BENEBY JR., CAMRYN A. CARTWRIGHT *Higgs & Johnson*

Barbados
GILES A.M. CARMICHAEL, SHARALEE M.J. GITTENS *Chancery Chambers*

Belize
EAMON H. COURTENAY SC, ILIANA N. SWIFT *Courtenay Coye LLP*

Bermuda
GRANT SPURLING, KIERNAN BELL *Appleby*

Bolivia
FERNANDO AGUIRRE B. *Bufete Aguirre Soc. Civ.*

Brazil
FLAVIO OLIMPIO DE AZEVEDO *Olimpio de Azevedo Advogados*

British Virgin Islands
CLAIRE GOLDSTEIN *Harney Westwood & Riegels*

Canada
MALCOLM M. MERCER *McCarthy Tétrault LLP*

Chile
RAIMUNDO MORENO, MONICA VANDER SCHRAFT *Cariola Díez Pérez-Cotapos & Cía. Ltda.*

Colombia
CARLOS URRUTIA-VALENZUELA *Brigard & Urrutia*

Costa Rica
ANDREA SITTENFELD, ADRIANA CASTRO, KARLA GONZÁLEZ, EDUARDO CALDERON *BLP Legal*

Cuba
MARIA ANTONIETA LANDA MARTI, MIGUEL FRANCISCO SARDIÑAS ARCE *Bufete Internacional S.A.*

IMARA FRANCISCA BETANCOURT SUAREZ *Lupicinio International Law Firm*

Curaçao
BOUKE BOERSMA *Houthoff Buruma*

Dominican Republic
LUIS RAFAEL PELLERANO, RICARDO PELLERANO *Pellerano & Herrera*

Ecuador
SEBASTIAN CAICEDO RICAURTE BRUCE HOROWITZ *Paz Horowitz Robalino Garces Abogados*

El Salvador
RICARDO CEVALLOS *BLP Abogados*

Guatemala
ALFONSO CARRILLO M. *Carrillo y Asociados*

Honduras
J. HUMBERTO MEDINA ALVA, MARCELA AGUILAR *Central Law Honduras*

Jamaica
PETER S. GOLDSON, RENÉ C.K. GAYLE *Myers, Fletcher & Gordon*

Mexico
SAMUEL GARCÍA-CUÉLLAR MICHEL NARCIA MARTÍNEZ *Creel, García-Cuéllar, Aiza y Enríquez, S.C.*

Panama
JOSÉ AGUSTÍN PRECIADO M., MARIO A. PRECIADO MIRÓ *Fabrega Molino Mulino*

Paraguay
ROSA ELENA DIMARTINO *Berkemeyer Law Firm*

Peru
JEAN PAUL CHABANEIX, LUIS BEDOYA *Rodrigo, Elías & Medrano Abogados*

Puerto Rico
RICHARD GRAFFAM-RODRÍGUEZ *McConnell Valdés LLC*

Trinidad and Tobago
MARK JAMES MORGAN *Fitzwilliam Stone, Furness – Smith & Morgan*

United States
GERRY SILVER *Sullivan & Worcester LLP*

Uruguay
SANTIAGO GATICA, JOSÉ JUAN GARI, JUAN BONET, SANTIAGO MURGUÍA, DANIEL MOSCO, CAMILA UMPIÉRREZ *Guyer & Regules*

U.S. Virgin Islands
XAVERIE L. BAXLEY-HULL *Dudley Rich Davis LLP*

Venezuela
FERNANDO PELÁEZ-PIER, ALEJANDRO GALLOTTI *Hoet Peláez Castillo & Duque*

Preface

Every lawyer is bound by a duty of professional secrecy. Professional secrecy is not only a duty but also a right, to ensure that everyone receives the best legal advice and, consequently, the best legal representation, be it before or outside a court of law. Communications between lawyers and their clients benefit from the attorney-client privilege. To ensure the best advice or defense, a client must be able to speak freely to his or her lawyer, which will only be possible if the lawyer can, under no circumstances, disclose the information received from the client to the authorities or to other parties to the proceedings. If the lawyer could be forced to do so, the information could be used against the client. This fear often makes people reluctant to seek legal advice, and we all know that the worst defense is one mounted without the advice and assistance of a lawyer.

The attorney-client privilege ensures the confidentiality of discussions between lawyers and their clients so that no third party can gain access to the information exchanged. Lawyers are not entitled to disclose information provided by their clients and should never be forced to do so. The information exchanged is privileged. In general, the authorities and the courts should not be able to access information protected by the attorney-client privilege and should refuse to take privileged information into account if it is disclosed in violation of the professional secrecy rules. This is essential to ensure that everyone enjoys the same rights, is bound by the same obligations and is able to defend himself or herself adequately.

This book examines how the attorney-client privilege and professional secrecy are applied in the various jurisdictions in North, Central and South America and the Caribbean. In most (civil law) European countries, the term professional secrecy is used. In common law countries, however, this concept is known as the attorney-client privilege or legal professional privilege. In general, these terms refer to the same concept.

Lawyers and law associations are obliged to work together to make the world a better place by ensuring that all individuals can exercise their rights, including the right to assistance in understanding and defining rights and obligations. Legal assistance will be effective, however, only if clients can speak freely with their lawyers. This means the lawyer cannot disclose (or be obliged to disclose) information provided by the client. Because people are traveling more than ever before and engaging in international relations, they should be able to obtain legal advice (and benefit from the attorney-client privilege) anywhere in the world. Hence, a proper understanding of how professional secrecy and the attorney-client privilege operate in other countries is necessary.

It is hoped that this volume, as well as related books on other geographical regions, will help to define a common definition of professional secrecy that can be accepted by all countries and international institutions. Such a definition is indeed necessary in an increasingly globalized world, where people cross borders with increasing frequency and can be virtually present in several countries simultaneously, through electronic means. Adapting the concept of professional secrecy and attorney-client privilege to meet the realities of this new world, while safeguarding the rights of citizens, is one of the major challenges facing the legal profession.

We wish to thank Bianca Porcelli and Michele Thompson for helping us to put the different chapters in the appropriate format.

James R. Silkenat
Sullivan & Worcester LLP
New York, New York

Dirk Van Gerven
NautaDutilh BVBA/SPRL
Brussels, Belgium

1

Attorney-Client Privilege in the Americas

JAMES R. SILKENAT

Sullivan & Worcester LLP
Former President of the American Bar Association

DIRK VAN GERVEN

NautaDutilh BVBA/SPRL
Former President of the Brussels Bar (Dutch-speaking section)

1. Concepts

1. People seeking legal advice should be assured, when discussing their rights or obligations with a lawyer, that the latter will not disclose to third parties the information provided. Only if this duty of confidentiality is respected will people feel free to consult lawyers and provide the information required for the lawyer to prepare the client's defense or ascertain the client's legal position. Regardless of the type of information disclosed, clients must be certain that it will not be used against them in a court of law, by the authorities or by any other party. It is generally considered to be a condition of the good functioning of the legal system and, thus, in the general interest. Legal professional privilege is much more than an ordinary rule of evidence, limited in its application to the facts of a particular case. It is a fundamental condition on which the administration of justice as a whole rests.[1]

    Lawyers, representing clients, are generally bound by a duty to treat any information received from the client or any advice given as confidential. This obligation not to reveal applies to all information relating to the representation of the client (American Bar Association [ABA] Model Rule 1.6(a)). In this

---

[1] *Regina v. Derby Magistrates Court ex parte B*, House of Lords UK, Oct. 19, 1995.

1

respect, a lawyer shall make reasonable efforts to prevent the inadvertent or unauthorized disclosure of, or unauthorized access to, information relating to the representation of a client (ABA Model Rule 1.6(c)). Clients should be entitled to hold the lawyer liable in the event of breach of this duty.

In common law jurisdictions, this secrecy is part of the attorney-client privilege. It generally implies that the communications between lawyers and their clients are confidential and that no authority should be empowered to order disclosure of such information. *Professional secrecy* is the term generally used in continental legal (i.e., civil law) systems to refer to the common law concept of legal professional privilege or the attorney-client privilege – that is, the lawyer's duty to refuse to disclose, and the client's right to prevent the lawyer from disclosing, any information received from the client to prepare the latter's defense. In any case, regardless of the term used, the underlying goal is the same, namely to protect information exchanged between the client and the lawyer with respect to the client's legal position in relation to a specific matter.

2.   Privileged information cannot be used against the client, and the lawyer cannot be forced to disclose it. To qualify as such, however, the information must have been provided to the lawyer or by the lawyer to the client for the purpose of legal advice or general assistance in defining the client's legal position toward authorities or other parties. It covers all information that is relevant to the legal representation.

If privileged information is nonetheless disclosed in violation of the applicable rules, it may not be used in court or otherwise against the client. However, if the information is disclosed pursuant to a derogation provided for by law (see "Limitations and Derogations," later in this chapter), it can be used in court.

3.   In several jurisdictions, litigation privilege is distinguished from attorney-client privilege. Litigation privilege applies to matters in litigation and the information exchanged between the lawyer and the client in relation to this litigation. The distinction has a historic explanation, as the English House of Lords first recognized in 1577 privilege of communication to clients in anticipation of or pending litigation[2] and extended it later (in 1833) to advice outside court litigation.[3] The distinction is made in Anguilla, Bahamas, Barbados, Bermuda, British Virgin Islands, Canada, Jamaica, and Trinidad and Tobago, even though litigation privilege is part of the broader attorney-client privilege. Nevertheless, litigation privilege may apply to communications between a lawyer and third parties if it is for the purpose of obtaining advice in connection with the litigation, such as gathering evidence.[4]

---

[2] *Berd v. Lovelace, EngR* 10, (1957–77) *Cary 61*, 1576 21 ER 33(E).

[3] *Greenough v. Gaskell* (1833) *EngR* 333.

[4] *See* Chapter 2, no. 10 (Anguilla); Chapter 5, no. 3 (Bahamas); Chapter 6, no. 4 (Barbados); Chapter 8, no. 4 (Bermuda); Chapter 11, no. 10 (British Virgin Islands).

Litigation privilege may, in certain U.S. states such as California, refer to a type of immunity for things said in court when defending one's position and presenting legal arguments. In the heat of debate and to defend themselves, parties are entitled to speak more freely and to openly attack the other party without fear of a defamation suit.

2. Basis

4.   Typically in common law jurisdictions, the attorney-client privilege has been developed by case law originating in the United Kingdom (see no. 3 in the preceding section). The legal basis for the privilege in those countries is still the case law and part of the common law. This is the case in Anguilla, Bermuda, British Virgin Islands and the United States. In several countries in which common law or case law provides for the basis of the privilege, specific statutes, such as a criminal code, may define the secrecy duty of lawyers. This is the case in Bahamas, Belize, Canada and Jamaica. Also, in several civil law countries, case law is the basis of the attorney-client privilege, even though confirmed by several statutes and more particularly in the criminal code. This is the case in Argentina, Brazil, Chile, Curaçao, Dominican Republic, El Salvador, Mexico, Paraguay and Uruguay. In certain countries, the privilege is found in professional codes and not in the law, such as in Costa Rica, Cuba and Puerto Rico (but additionally in the judicial code).

In other countries, the attorney-client privilege and the duty of professional secrecy have been enshrined in statutes specifically applicable to the attorney-client privilege. In several countries, this is the legislation applicable to lawyers. This is the case in Antigua and Barbuda, Barbados, Bolivia, Guatemala, Honduras, Panama, Trinidad and Tobago, U.S. Virgin Islands and Venezuela. In other countries, it is laid down in the constitution or other legislation on rights and freedoms, such as in Québec (Canada), Colombia, Ecuador and Peru.

5.   In a large number of countries, the duty of professional secrecy or attorney-client privilege is enshrined in the bar association's code of ethics. Violations will result in disciplinary sanctions, in accordance with local procedures.

In addition, it appears that the duty of professional secrecy is generally considered to result from or at least to be part of the contract between the lawyer and the client, as part of the representation of the client by the lawyer. Consequently, any violation of the privilege constitutes a breach of contract, allowing the injured party to claim the appropriate remedies and damages. This is explicitly accepted in Anguilla, Argentina, Bahamas, Barbados, Bermuda, Bolivia, Brazil, British Virgin Islands, Colombia, Costa Rica, Curaçao, Ecuador, El Salvador, Guatemala, Mexico, Peru, Puerto Rico, Trinidad and Tobago, and Uruguay.

3. Scope

A. Information Protected by Attorney-Client Privilege and Professional Secrecy

6.   In general, professional secrecy protects all information a lawyer receives or obtains in the context of assisting a client. Under European law, this encompasses all information received in relation to legal proceedings or any conflict in general, or to determine whether the rights and obligations of the client benefit from the attorney-client privilege.[5] Similarly, attorney-client privilege protects any information the client gives to the lawyer to get legal advice, and the lawyer gives to the client as part of the legal advice. This includes any exchange to facilitate the advice[6] and assistance in determining a legal position whether in or pending litigation or outside litigation. Indeed, effective representation of a client's interests requires that clients be able to speak freely to their lawyers and that the information exchanged be kept confidential. The protected information cannot be disclosed and, if so, cannot be used as evidence in litigation.

    The advice is generally protected if it is given by the lawyer as part of a professional relation, even if the lawyer is not paid for it. This is generally referred to as information communicated to the lawyer or by the lawyer in his or her capacity as an attorney. Consequently, when a personal opinion is given outside any legal advice, the information is not protected.[7] In general, any information exchanged outside the professional relation of the lawyer is not protected. Also, information given to third parties (who are not employees or agents of the lawyer) will not be protected unless, in certain countries, by the litigation privilege (see no. 7). The privilege generally applies to any documents and notes prepared by the lawyer and any communications, in particular correspondence, between the lawyer and the client. Communications may be in writing or oral, including electronically exchanged information.

7.   The litigation privilege applies to all information exchanged by a lawyer with third parties – that is, parties who are not clients of such lawyer – with the dominant purpose of providing or receiving legal services in actual, anticipated or pending proceedings in which the client is or may be a party. It relates to all confidential communications and documents where "the dominant purpose in creating the document (or making the communication) is to use it or its contents to obtain legal advice or help in the conduct of litigation which at that time was at least reasonably in prospect."[8]

---

[5] European Court of Justice, June 26, 2007, case C-305/05 (Belgian Bar Associations). *See* Dirk Van Gerven, "Professional Secrecy in Europe," in *Professional Secrecy of Lawyers in Europe*, Bar of Brussels (ed.), Cambridge University Press, Cambridge, 2013, 11–12.

[6] *See* Chapter 30, no. 3 (United States).

[7] *See* Chapter 2, no. 8 (Anguilla); Chapter 28, no. 6 (Puerto Rico).

[8] Virginia Dunn, *Be Civil! A Guide to Learning Civil Litigation and Evidence*, Worth Publishing Ltd, 2014, 219; *see* Chapter 6, no. 4 (Barbados).

B. The Advisers Subject to Professional Secrecy

8. When defending the interests of their clients, that is, advising on the client's rights and obligations or representing the client in legal proceedings challenging such rights and obligations, lawyers are subject to a duty of professional secrecy. This is the case regardless of where the lawyer or the client is situated. In general, foreign lawyers working in the country benefit from attorney-client privilege only if duly registered to practice in such country.

    The duty of professional secrecy and the attorney-client privilege apply in most countries to the lawyer's associates, staff and employees working within the law firm or working for the lawyer representing a client. The information made available to these persons, or gleaned by them in the course of assisting the client, is subject to the attorney-client privilege. Exceptionally, this is not the case in countries such as Antigua and Barbuda. Further, it is advisable to provide for an obligation to keep all information confidential in the employment contract. It is useful to include clear provisions in the employment agreements with staff informing them of the duty of professional secrecy applicable to the law firm.

    In most countries, external service providers who perform services on behalf of the lawyer in representation of a client also benefit from the attorney-client privilege. In some countries, such as Jamaica and Panama, this may be subject to certain doubt, or it may not be the case, such as in Antigua and Barbuda and the British Virgin Islands. In several countries, it is generally recommended to sign confidentiality agreements with independent service providers when disclosing confidential information to them. Finally, in countries that distinguish attorney-client privilege from litigation privilege, the latter will apply to information shared with external service providers in relation to preparing litigation (see no. 7 in the preceding section).

9. In the Americas, legal advice of in-house counsel benefits from attorney-client privilege. When practicing law in their work, in-house counsel are considered lawyers and therefore also subject to a duty of professional secrecy. Lord Denning said in this respect that the only difference between in-house counsel and a lawyer in private practice is that in-house counsel act for one client, not for several clients.[9] The privilege applies only with respect to queries for legal advice and thus information provided as part of this legal advice. Furthermore, in some countries, the in-house counsel must be guaranteed an independent position in the company to qualify for the privilege.

    In Europe, the matter of whether in-house counsel benefit from attorney-client privilege is challenged. The European Court of Justice is of the opinion that exchanges within a company with in-house lawyers are not covered by professional secrecy in European legal proceedings governed by European law,

---

[9] *See* Chapter 6, no. 13 (Barbados).

such as antitrust proceedings against the European Commission. This court based its decision on the fact that in-house counsel are, further to their employment, not sufficiently independent from their employer.[10] In this respect, held the court, independent lawyers are bound by professional rules that ensure their independence, while lawyers employed by companies are not. However, as the European Court of Justice recognized, this is for national proceedings a matter of state law, and state law may provide otherwise.

C. Limitations and Derogations

10. The attorney-client privilege is linked to the lawyer's duty to defend a client's interests in law. Consequently, it does not apply when the lawyer acts outside this context – for example, when the lawyer acts as a company director or a court-appointed representative, such as a trustee in bankruptcy. In such cases, the information gathered by lawyers in the exercise of their functions is not protected by the duty of professional secrecy (unless the lawyer in question consults a lawyer to assist him or her with respect to the exercise of such functions).

11. Furthermore, a number of limitations and derogations apply, which refer in general to cases in which the lawyer cannot rely on the attorney-client privilege or is even forced to disclose certain information. In some of these cases, the authorities are entitled to break through the attorney-client privilege; in others, it is up to the lawyer to decide whether to disclose the confidential information without the authorities being entitled to force the lawyer.

Rule 1.6(b) of the Model Rules of the American Bar Association list the following cases in which a lawyer is entitled to reveal confidential information, but only to the extent the lawyer reasonably believes necessary:

(1) to prevent reasonably certain death or substantial bodily harm;
(2) to prevent the client from committing a crime or fraud that is reasonably certain to result in substantial injury to the financial interests or property of another and in furtherance of which the client has used or is using the lawyer's services;
(3) to prevent, mitigate or rectify substantial injury to the financial interests or property of another that is reasonably certain to result or has resulted from the client's commission of a crime or fraud in furtherance of which the client has used the lawyer's services;
(4) to secure legal advice about the lawyer's compliance with these Rules;
(5) to establish a claim or defense on behalf of the lawyer in a controversy between the lawyer and the client, to establish a defense to a criminal charge or civil claim against the lawyer based upon conduct in which the

---

[10] ECJ May 18, 1982, case 155/79 *AM&S Europe v. Commission, Eur. Court Reports* 1982, 1575; Sept. 14, 2010, case C-550/07, *Akzo and Ackros, Eur. Court Reports* 2010, I-8301.

client was involved, or to respond to allegations in any proceeding concerning the lawyer's representation of the client;

(6) to comply with other law or a court order; and

(7) to detect and resolve conflicts of interest arising from the lawyer's change of employment or from changes in the composition or ownership of a firm, but only if the revealed information would not compromise the attorney-client privilege or otherwise prejudice the client.

12. The prevention of bodily harm or, in a number of countries, a greater damage is generally recognized as an exception authorizing the lawyer to contact authorities to prevent the harm. In such cases, the information to be communicated should be limited to what is required to prevent such harm (or damage). The lawyer will have to assess the information when deciding to step forward and disclose information. Also, specific matters of public interest, such as money laundering, terrorism or abuse of children, can be reasons provided by the law to refuse to invoke professional secrecy and force lawyers to disclose confidential information.

Furthermore, it is generally accepted that attorney-client privilege cannot be used to commit a crime. Communications made for the purpose of getting advice for the commission of fraud or other crime are not protected.[11] In some countries, this is also the case if the information is used to commit a wrongful act in general. This is the case in Anguilla, Bahamas, Belize and possibly in the British Virgin Islands.

Lawyers should be able to defend themselves against claims based on negligence or malpractice and may, to the extent required to argue their defense, disclose confidential information. The same applies generally to a lawyer's claim to obtain payment of fees.

D. Waiver by the Client

13. The attorney-client privilege is intended to protect the client's interests.[12] In general, it is accepted in the Americas that a client can waive the attorney-client privilege. Only in Guatemala is the attorney-client privilege a matter of public law and cannot be waived, not even by the client.

The client's consent to waive must be informed, that is, the client must be aware of the consequences of the consent. Also, the initiation of civil or disciplinary proceedings against a lawyer because of negligence or malpractice is in some countries construed as an implicit waiver, permitting the lawyer to defend himself by disclosing confidential information. However, in Curaçao, only the lawyer can waive the attorney-client privilege (with consent of the client).

---

[11] *See* Chapter 30, no. 5 (United States).

[12] Lord Denning, *The Due Process of Law*, Butterworths, London, 1980, 29.

4. No International Supervision

14.   Contrary to the situation in Europe,[13] many countries in the Americas are not a party to an international convention that institutes an international court ensuring the application of human rights and freedoms, such as a right to a fair trial, and legal assistance and professional secrecy of any information exchanged between lawyer and client. While the Inter-American Court of Human Rights and the Inter-American Commission on Human Rights have certain responsibilities in this area, they are not typically cited as controlling on issues of attorney-client privilege. Furthermore, contrary to the European Court of Human Rights, citizens do not have access to the Inter-American Court on Human Rights.

---

[13] The European Court of Human Rights has confirmed in several decisions that the attorney-client privilege is part of the rights of defense and the right to a fair trial. *See* Dirk Van Gerven, "Professional Secrecy in Europe," in *Professional Secrecy of Lawyers in Europe*, Bar of Brussels (ed.), Cambridge University Press, Cambridge, 2013, 6 *et seq.*

2

Anguilla

YVETTE A. WALLACE
ANGELA A. MULLIX
Keithley Lake & Associates

Preliminary Note

1.   In Anguilla, the court admits lawyers to practice either as barristers or solicitors. However, every person enrolled as a barrister is entitled to practice as a solicitor. Lawyers are subject to a duty of attorney-client privilege, which is also known as professional secrecy or legal professional privilege.

Under Section 65 of the Eastern Caribbean Supreme Court (Anguilla) Act (ECSCA), a judge of the High Court may admit a person who fulfills the admission criteria to practice as a barrister or solicitor at the bar. In accordance with Section 66 of the ECSCA, all lawyers must be duly registered in the Court Roll maintained by the Registrar, and only lawyers who are duly registered are entitled to appear before the courts. Lawyers may be self-employed, partners or associates in a law firm.

Anguilla's judicial system is administered by the Magistrate's Court, the High Court and the Court of Appeal of the Eastern Caribbean Supreme Court, with the appeal process culminating with the Judicial Committee of the Privy Council (JCPC).

In Anguilla, there is one bar association, which is presided over by the president. The Anguilla Bar Association (ABA) is a voluntary association of legal practitioners admitted to practice in Anguilla, and membership is available to all lawyers in private and public practice. The ABA has its own rules and ethical standards to uphold, and its main objectives are to support and protect the character of the legal profession, promote and undertake activities to familiarize the community with the legal system, and protect the administration of justice in Anguilla.

The ABA is a constituent member of the Organization of Eastern Caribbean States Bar Association (OECS BA), and as such the ABA, its members and OECS BA members are bound by the rules and Code of Ethics of the OECS BA. The OECS BA is a regional professional umbrella association, of which the bar associations of nine of the member territories and states of the Eastern Caribbean are member organizations.

The member associations voluntarily adopted the OECS BA Code of Ethics in 1991 to govern the practice of all barristers, solicitors and attorneys in the region. As such, the ABA is governed by it, to the extent permitted by law. The OECS BA is a voluntary body, not recognized by any statute and without the authority to alter the general law. With that being said, it does appear from case law within the jurisdiction that the provisions of the Code of Ethics may be taken into consideration and therefore are not completely without weight. In matters of ethics and in the absence of applicable law, the OECS BA is largely responsible for setting the standards for the profession.

2.   This chapter focuses on the professional secrecy, legal professional privilege or attorney-client privilege of lawyers who are admitted to practice law in Anguilla. Unless indicated otherwise, for the purposes of this chapter, the term "lawyer" refers to a barrister or solicitor duly recorded on the Court Roll in Anguilla.

1 Scope of and Limitations on the Duty of Professional Secrecy/Attorney-Client Privilege

A Statutory Basis and Implications

3.   There is no statutory basis in Anguilla for attorney-client privilege. Under the Common Law (Declaration of Application) Act,[1] the common law of England is directly applicable in Anguilla, subject to statute. The doctrines of attorney-client privilege and the duty of confidentiality are well entrenched in the common law.

In Anguilla, the duty of confidentiality is also codified, where business of a professional nature either arises in or is brought to Anguilla. The Confidential Relationships Act[2] (CRA) applies to all the confidential information generated and to all persons who come into possession of that information at any time, whether inside or outside of Anguilla. Under the CRA, a professional person includes an accountant, an attorney (or other legal practitioner by whatever name called), a broker, commercial agent or adviser, a bank or other financial institution, any public officer or other government official or employee, and other such persons as may be prescribed by law.

4.   Business of a professional nature connotes a relationship between a professional person and a principal, in whatever form that relationship may take. Confidential information may include information about any property, business of a professional nature or a commercial transaction that either has taken place or is contemplated. Additionally, the recipient of that information is not, other than in the normal course of business or professional practice, authorized by the principal to divulge that information.

Historically, the lawyer-client relationship has been characterized as one of confidence, and it is also a part of lawyers' fiduciary duty to their clients. The arrangement for legal services between clients and their lawyers constitutes a contract, and as such the obligation to keep confidential information

---

[1]   Chapter C60, Revised Statutes of Anguilla.   [2]   Ibid., Chapter C85.

provided by the client or by a third party on the client's behalf is implied in the contract. Any disclosure without the client's consent or waiver of the right constitutes a breach of contract. The duty of confidentiality also has some origins in equity, and the principles are largely enshrined in the Code of Ethics.

5.   When a lawyer is employed, the lawyer is in a position of confidence. Accordingly, the lawyer bears the following duties with respect to the information acquired as counsel: (i) the lawyer must not communicate that information to any third party, (ii) the lawyer must not use that information to the client's detriment, and (iii) the lawyer must not use that information for the lawyer's own benefit.

This duty continues after the relationship between lawyer and client has ceased.[3] This principle is illustrated by the common law rule wherein a lawyer, in certain circumstances, ought not accept a brief from a new client to act against a former client, even where that former client is no longer desirous of using the lawyer's services. The reason behind this rule is that the lawyer may hold information that could become prejudicial to the former client throughout the course of litigation.

Where confidential information is divulged, the courts may grant an injunction to contain the spread of the information and may also set aside any transaction from which a lawyer stands to benefit from his or her breach of confidentiality. If a lawyer receives a document from a party other than the client that is confidential but not privileged, the lawyer may be compelled by injunction to return it to the owner and may be prevented from using the information contained therein.[4] The same is also true of privileged documents, where privilege has not been waived.[5]

6.   The duty of confidentiality and attorney-client privilege are similar. However, they are distinct in some ways. First, privilege is based on arguments of public policy. Second, communications protected by confidentiality are more numerous than those protected by privilege. Finally, privileged information is protected from compulsory disclosure, unless abrogated by statute or waived. Non-privileged confidential information, on the other hand, may still have to be disclosed in certain circumstances.

The duty of confidentiality is enshrined in the Code of Ethics. Rule 23(2) Part A provides: "An attorney-at-law shall scrupulously guard and never divulge his clients' secrets and confidences."

Rule 15 Part B provides:

> An attorney-at-law shall never disclose unless lawfully ordered to do so by the court or required by statute, what has been communicated to him in his capacity as an attorney-at-law by his client, or which he has acquired in his

---

[3] *Carter v. Palmer* (1839) 1 Dr & Wal 722.
[4] *Goddard v. Nationwide Building Society* [1987] QB 670.   [5] Ibid.

capacity as his client's ~ and this duty not to disclose extends to his partners, to junior attorneys-at law assisting him, and to his employees provided however that an attorney-at-law may reveal confidences or secrets necessary to establish or collect his fee or to defend himself or his employees or associates against an accusation of wrongful conduct.

Attorney-client privilege is designed solely to protect the client, and it is underpinned by confidentiality. The rationale is that, owing to the complexity and difficulty of the law, litigation can be conducted only by professional lawyers, and therefore the layperson has limited alternatives other than to instruct a lawyer if the layperson is to be properly represented. In light of this, it is of paramount importance that clients feel they may consult freely with their lawyers; have complete, unrestricted and unbounded confidence in their lawyers; and, fundamentally, that the communications with their lawyer will remain confidential.[6] If a person confiding in a lawyer feels that confidence will be easily broken and the contents of the communications divulged, then the client may approach the lawyer in a circumspect manner and may even withhold necessary disclosures. Trust in the lawyer may be affected in circumstances where a client knows that communications may be revealed without restraint.[7]

B Scope

7. There are two kinds of attorney-client privilege. First is advice privilege, which arises irrespective of whether litigation is contemplated. Second is litigation privilege, which surrounds communications connected with contemplated or intended litigation. Attorney-client privilege does not extend to everything that lawyers have a duty to keep confidential. Attorney-client privilege protects only those confidential communications falling under advice privilege or litigation privilege – such communication will be protected from production. The privilege belongs to the client, and the lawyer is under a duty to maintain it unless the client waives it.

Attorney-client privilege creates an absolute rule that entitles the client to refuse to disclose documents or answer questions, and it also requires the client's advisers and others to do the same.[8] The privilege must be respected by the court and any other party to the proceedings.

a Attorney-Client Privilege

8. Attorney-client privilege extends to all oral and written communications that pass between a lawyer and the client that are made for the purpose of giving or

---

[6] *Anderson v. Bank of British Columbia* (1876) 2 Ch D 644.
[7] *Regina v. Derby's Magistrates Court ex parte B* (1996) AC 487.
[8] *R (on the application of Prudential plc and another) v. Special Commissioner of Income Tax and Another* [2011] 1 All ER 316.

receiving legal advice. For privilege to attach to a communication, it must be confidential, and it must be made with the purpose and intention of obtaining or giving legal advice.[9] As such, advice from a lawyer to a client must be given in professional circumstances – that is, it must occur in the performance of the lawyer's professional duties as a lawyer retained to give professional advice, as compared to some other capacity that is far removed from professional advice.[10] In other words, no privilege attaches to communications made between a lawyer and an acquaintance who seeks the lawyer's mere opinion rather than legal advice or in circumstances that cannot be described as professional.[11] Whether the legal advice is given in contemplation of actual or impending litigation has no bearing on the application of advice privilege, as it does with litigation privilege.

Provided that any communication is directly related to the performance of the lawyer's professional duty as a legal adviser, where a lawyer is instructed to give legal advice in relation to a particular transaction or series of transactions, privilege will attach to all communications between the lawyer and client relating to that particular transaction, notwithstanding that they do not specifically contain matters of law or construction.[12]

Attorney-client privilege is not limited to specific requests from clients for advice from lawyers and documents containing legal advice. This, together with another issue, was considered in *Balabel v. Air India*.[13] The Court of Appeal stated that documents requesting or sharing legal advice are not the only documents to which privilege attaches. There will often be situations in which there is a "continuum of communication," where information is passed between lawyer and client as part of this continuum, which keeps both parties informed so that advice may be sought and given. In such instances, privilege will attach. It was also held that legal advice is not limited to only telling the client the law but also extends to advice about what should sensibly be done in the relevant legal context. Privilege extends to all that passes between a client and a lawyer on matters that fall within the realm and ordinary business of a lawyer and are referable to that relationship. While privilege may extend to advice given on the commercial wisdom of a transaction, the privilege does not extend to all work that may be undertaken by lawyers, such as investment advice and advice given as a patent or estate agent.

9.   Privilege applies with respect to communications made by and through an agent of the lawyer or client. Privilege also applies to communications that

---

[9] *Sheikh Mohamed Ali M. Alhamrani and Others v. Sheikh Abdullah Ali Alhamrani* HCVAP 2012/026.

[10] *Nederlandse Reassurantie Groep Holding NV v. Bacon & Woodrow (a firm) and Others* [1995] 1 All ER 976.

[11] *Smith v. Daniell* (1874) LR 18 Eq 649.   [12] *Minter v. Priest* [1930] All ER Rep 431.

[13] [1988] Ch 317, CA.

are received by the lawyer from third parties[14] that are necessary to provide the legal advice to the client or that relate to that legal advice. Further, where a lawyer has a corporate client, communication between the lawyer and the employees of a corporate client may not be protected by the privilege if the employee cannot be considered "the client" for the purposes of the retainer. As such, some employees will be clients, while others will not.[15]

Privilege also attaches to copies or translations of privileged documents, but the same does not apply to non-privileged documents unless the documents in question fall within an exception – that is, if the documents are obtained from a third party and disclosing them would betray the trend of advice given by the lawyer to the client.

b Litigation Privilege

10. Litigation privilege is broader than advice privilege and protects confidential communications made after litigation has started, or is reasonably expected, between (i) a lawyer and a client; (ii) a lawyer and an agent, whether or not that agent is a lawyer; (iii) a lawyer and non-professional agent or a third party; or (iv) in certain circumstances, a client and a non-professional agent, employee or third party.

These communications must be for the sole or dominant purpose of litigation, either (i) for seeking or giving advice in relation to it, (ii) for obtaining evidence to be used in it, or (iii) for obtaining information that may in turn lead to obtaining such evidence.

Documents that came into existence for a purpose other than litigation, but are subsequently obtained by a lawyer for use in litigation, are not privileged and may have to be disclosed to the other side for inspection.[16] An original document not brought into existence for privileged purposes and so is not already privileged does not become privileged merely by being given to a lawyer for advice or for any other privileged purpose.

C Persons Subject to the Duty of Professional Secrecy

11. The attorney-client privilege attaching to communications between lawyer and client also extends to the employees of lawyers, as well as supervised trainees, in-house lawyers and appropriately qualified foreign lawyers. It does not attach to advice given by other professionals or persons with whom one may share confidences, such as priests, doctors, accountants, or tax advisers – and this is so even in circumstances where legal advice is given by the adviser.

---

[14] *Re Sarah Getty Trust* [1985] 2 All ER 809.
[15] *Three Rivers District Council v. The Governor and Company of the Bank of England* (no 5) [2003] QB 1556.
[16] *Ventouris v. Mountain* [1991] 1 WLR 607.

In *R (on the application of Prudential plc and another) v. Special Commissioner of Income Tax and another*,[17] the Court of Appeal held that attorney-client privilege is strictly limited to legal professionals and could not be extended by the judiciary to any other professionals (this could only be achieved through the enactment of legislation). The court further stated that the existing duty had to be clear and certain and that opening up the duty to other categories of professionals would only raise questions as to the scope and application of the common law duty. The duty of professional privilege also extends to foreign lawyers who are properly admitted in their home jurisdictions and properly recognized as lawyers.[18]

In *Anderson v. Bank of British Columbia*, the court attributed a principal with the knowledge of the agent in matters of the agency. The rationale is that the thoughts and knowledge of the agent should also be attributed to the principal. In law, if a principal asks the agent to undertake certain acts on the principal's behalf, those acts are truly the actions of the principal; thus, the principal is deemed to know the facts, even before the principal has the information. The fact that one's agent carried out the task, transaction or matter cannot be used as a defense to a request for disclosure, and thus no privilege attached to communications between the agent and principal.

Attorney-client privilege must be respected by prisons, the courts, prosecutors (Attorney-General Chambers or police) and any party to the proceedings.

D Exceptions to and Optional Derogations from the Duty of Professional Secrecy

12.   Subject to recognized exceptions, communications concerning professional legal advice, whether or not in connection with pending court proceedings, are absolutely and permanently privileged from disclosure even if that means they cannot be used in court proceedings in which they might be important evidence.

The three recognized exceptions are communications made for a fraudulent or illegal purpose, when the client waives the privilege and permits disclosure, and communications made for the purpose of being repeated, such as instructions to settle a claim.

a Limitations

13.   No privilege will attach where communications between a client and a lawyer are made for the purposes of committing a crime, fraud or wrongful act.

---

[17] [2011] 1 All ER 316.

[18] *Lawrence v. Campbell* March 7, 1859; the same privilege with respect to the non-production of confidential communications as between an English solicitor and his client was extended to like communications as between a Scottish solicitor and law agent practicing in London, though not admitted as an English solicitor, and his client in Scotland.

Attorney-client privilege still protects the advice that a lawyer gives to a client on avoiding the commission of a crime or warning the client that the lawyer's proposed actions could attract prosecution. Privilege will normally still apply to legal advice that is given after the commission of a crime.

It is not just the client's intention that is relevant for the purpose of ascertaining whether information was communicated for the furtherance of a criminal purpose. It is also sufficient that a third party intends the lawyer–client communication to be made with that purpose[19] (e.g., where the innocent client is being used by a third party).

No privilege will attach even in circumstances where the lawyer is unaware of the alleged crime, as the furtherance of such activities cannot properly be described as falling within the duties of a lawyer, and therefore no confidentiality attaches to the communication.

However, a bare allegation is insufficient to remove the privilege from what would otherwise be considered a privileged communication. It is necessary to establish prima facie evidence of the crime, fraud or wrongdoing, and the allegation must have a finding in fact.

Courts are reluctant to deprive parties of their privilege, and as such the facts of each case will be carefully considered, with a view to striking a balance between the policy considerations that underpin privilege and the seriousness of the allegation made.

14. A person who is entitled to privilege may waive it[20]. Privilege can be waived by placing privileged material before the Court, by loss of confidentiality in the material or by express or implied waiver[21].

Privileged material may be placed before the court by reading it, cross-examining a witness on it, or referencing it in a witness statement, expert chapter and statement of the case, or exhibit. When waiver actually occurs is arguable, but the preferred view is that waiver happens not by mere reference alone but when the privileged material is summarized, quoted or described. Waiver is also implicit where a client initiates proceedings against a former lawyer, as the very proceedings put in issue the contents of the advice provided. The caveat, however, is that waiver only applies to a communication that is specifically relevant to the dispute in question.[22]

Privileged documents can lose their confidentiality as a result of voluntary and unintentional disclosures. Where disclosure happens inadvertently, the evidence may still be admissible even if obtained illegally or unethically. However, it may be possible to apply for a court order seeking injunctive relief, which may be granted at the discretion of the court. Under the Eastern Caribbean Supreme Court Civil Procedure Rule (ECSC CPR) 28.15,

---

[19] *R v. Central Criminal Court ex p Francis & Francis* [1989] 1 AC 346.
[20] *Minter v. Priest* [1930] AC 558, *Paragon Finance plc v. Freshfields* [1999] 1WLR 1183.
[21] *Lillicrap v. Nalder & Son* [1993] 1 WLR 94.   [22] *Lillicrap v. Nalder & Son.*

inadvertently disclosed privileged documents may not be used except with the permission of the court or the disclosing party's agreement.

Waiver may be partial or complete, but the court will consider whether the document or partial document that has been disclosed is properly severable from the rest of the materials or whether it must be read with other documents or as a whole document to be best placed in context. Another factor the court will consider is whether the disclosure is complete in terms of the provision of all material that is relevant to the issue in question.

15. Privilege will not attach to communications that are disclosed between the lawyers for opposing parties or between the lawyer for one party and the opposing party, as the communications are not confidential, except by agreement.

16. Exceptions to privilege are rare even in circumstances where a higher value or a public interest may be served by making an exception to the duty.[23] Where legal professional privilege exists and it is not waived, it is paramount and absolute and not subject to the balancing exercises of weighing competing public interests as in the field of public interest immunity.

The Privy Council in *B v. Auckland District Law Society*[24] considered whether privilege may be overridden by a competing public interest. The court determined that it would be a travesty of justice to allow communications that were clearly privileged, and that occurred on the understanding that they were never to be disclosed or used by others, to then be used in a manner that was detrimental to the party.

The common law care or wardship proceedings involving children is one area in which the courts have recognized an overriding public interest or overarching duty that justifies an exception to privilege. In *Re D & M*,[25] it was held that children's cases fall into a special category where the court is bound to undertake all necessary steps to arrive at an appropriate result in the paramount interests of the welfare of the child. The general privilege attaching to an expert's chapter must therefore yield to the higher legislative purpose of making the child's welfare the sole criterion in care proceedings.

b Derogations

17. The statutory modification or removal of attorney-client privilege is rare; one exception is the Anti-Money Laundering (AML) and Counter Financing of Terrorism (CFT) legislation. There is no legislation that by necessary implication overrides privilege. However, please see section 5(A) of this chapter for further information on this.

---

[23] *R v Derby Magistrates' Court, ex parte B* [1995] 4 All ER 526; *Ansol Limited v. Elleray Management Limited and another* BVIHCV2007/0316.
[24] [2003] UKPC 38.   [25] 18 BMLR 71.

E Law Firms

18.   In undertaking their retainers with clients, lawyers in law firms tend to share privileged information with one another. It is commonly accepted that, when a client engages the services of a firm, all or some of the lawyers of the firm will equally be able and may be required to perform the terms of the retainer. The attorney-client privilege applies to all information provided to any lawyer within the firm, and each lawyer is under a duty to maintain privilege.

F Legal Assistants and Staff

19.   Law firms employ other staff such as assistants, secretaries and administrators to assist in their work. These employees are not qualified lawyers. The duty of attorney-client privilege also extends to such employees in their capacity as representatives of the firm, in the work undertaken in relation to client matters.

G External Service Providers

20.   Outsourcing work such as secretarial tasks or even legal work is not commonplace in Anguilla, as most work is undertaken within the law firm. To the extent that any work is conducted with external non-legal professionals that would require the firm to share communications, the client's consent should be obtained. The duty of maintaining attorney-client privilege still remains, and the lawyer should take steps to see that this privilege is preserved. The non-legal professional should proceed to work within the terms of the agreement made with the lawyer.

H Multidisciplinary Associations

21.   With the client's consent, a lawyer may cooperate and share information with another professional who is not a lawyer. Any information that is shared should be done sensitively and proportionately, so that only the information that is necessary to properly advise and protect the client is divulged. A lawyer should observe the duty of maintaining privilege at all times, and any information shared should also remain privileged.

I In-House Counsel

22.   In Anguilla, the use of in-house counsel is not commonplace in private practice, and only a few companies employ qualified lawyers in diverse and varied roles. Some of these lawyers working within companies may undertake tasks of a legal nature within their job functions, though they may not occupy the role of or carry out the functions typically associated with in-house counsel, whereas others may well do so. Moreover, in the public service, the Attorney-General Chambers (lawyers employed by the Government of Anguilla (GOA))

provides legal services for the GOA. Accordingly, attorney-client privilege is likely to attach to communications generated where there is a professional relationship with legal advice being provided to the employer by the in-house counsel or employee.

2 History of the Duty of Professional Secrecy in Anguilla

23. The common law principle of professional secrecy, or attorney-client privilege, is extremely longstanding in English common law. The earliest recorded instance of the principle in English case law dates from 1577 in the case of *Berd v. Lovelace*.[26] The principle of attorney-client privilege and its applicability to cases where legal proceedings had not been commenced was clearly and comprehensively established in *Greenough v Gaskell*[27] in 1833. By virtue of the Common Law Declaration of Application Act, in the absence of a statute, the decision immediately formed a part of Anguilla law.

The case law shows a bold attempt by the judiciary to dampen the absolute nature of attorney-client privilege, particularly in scenarios where it perhaps seems attractive for the rule to yield to some other important consideration. Any relaxation to the all-or-nothing approach would engage the judiciary in a complex balancing exercise wherein the competing interests of one party would have to be weighed against another, for example, the prejudice to one party of disclosure versus the seeming prejudice to another party of nondisclosure. It was envisaged that the exercise of such discretion would present an impossible task fraught with potential issues.

Any judicial extension or modification to the rule of attorney-client privilege laid down in the 16th century was found to be quite inappropriate; the responsibility was adjudged to fall squarely within the ambit of the legislature. As such, for at least 180 years after *Greenough v. Gaskell*, subject to the recognized exceptions, privileged communications, whether or not created in connection with pending court proceedings, have been absolutely and permanently privileged from disclosure, even though as a direct consequence they will not be available in court proceedings for which they may constitute important evidence.

3 Supervision

A The Bar Associations

24. The supervisory capacity of the bar associations is limited. At the time of writing, Anguilla does not have a Legal Profession Act or similar legislation.

---

[26] [1577] Cary 62.   [27] [1833] 1 M & K 98.

The ABA, without statutory power, has a limited role, outside of its advisory function, guidance and conciliatory contribution.

The ABA is a voluntary organization and, according to its website, aims to, among other things: "promote honourable practice, to repress malpractice, to settle disputed points of practice, and to decide at questions of professional usage or courtesy."

The president of the ABA may, at the invitation of a party or a lawyer, be asked to offer guidance on or consider an issue, with a view to assisting with its resolution. There is somewhat of a balance to be struck as it relates to any intervention or assistance given, as there are no investigatory powers or disciplinary powers vested in the president.

The OECS BA also has a limited supervisory role in the region, in relation to the supervision of breaches of the Code of Ethics. It is a voluntary organization that is not created by statue and therefore has limited disciplinary power.

B The Courts

25.   Under Section 70 of the ECSCA, any judge of the High Court may, for reasonable cause, suspend any lawyer from practicing in Anguilla during any specified period and may order the lawyer's name to be struck off the Court Roll. In any proceeding under this section, a minute of the order of the court shall be made to record its decision, and an appeal against any decision may be made to the Court of Appeal. As the High Court is charged with this power, the supervisory element is implied.

All lawyers must abide by the laws of Anguilla. The High Court has the jurisdiction to hear any claim for professional liability brought against a lawyer by a client. The courts have jurisdiction over crimes committed by lawyers in the exercise of their profession. There are no special rules applicable to lawyers.

4 Sanctions

A Proceedings and Sanctions

a Disciplinary Proceedings and Sanctions

26.   In accordance with Section 70 of the ECSCA, lawyers are officers of the court, and their regulation and discipline lies within the purview of the High Court.[28]

Disciplinary proceedings against a lawyer cannot be categorized as either criminal or civil proceedings. This was endorsed by the Court of Appeal decision in *Hansraj Matadial v. John Bayliss Frederick.*[29] It followed that

---

[28] *Simeon Fleming (In his capacity as Administrator of the Estates of Sarah Ann Connor aka Richardson and Catherine Fleming) v. Jenny Lindsay dba Jenny Lindsay & Associates* AXAHCV2015/0032.

[29] St. Vincent and the Grenadines Civil Appeal No. 23 of 2001.

because there is no claimant and no defendant in such proceedings, there are no parties and therefore no litigation. The terms of Anguilla's ECSCA are on all fours with the St. Vincent provisions; and while Anguilla may lack regulations that are on all fours with that jurisdiction, it is clear from Section 70 of the ECSCA that the process is judge-led.

b Criminal Proceedings

27.   In relation to professionals, a general duty of confidence is enshrined in the CRA. Under the CRA, a professional person commits an offence if he or she, being in possession of confidential information, however obtained, (i) divulges it to any person who is not entitled to possess it; (ii) attempts, offers or threatens to divulge it to any person not entitled to possess it; (iii) obtains or attempts to obtain confidential information to which he or she is not entitled; or (iv) being in possession of information that he or she knows or has reason to suppose is confidential information, makes use of that information without the consent of the principal to benefit herself or any other person.

A professional person charged with any of the aforementioned offences may establish a defense if he or she can prove to the court's satisfaction that, when the offence was committed, he or she did not know, and did not have reasonable grounds to suspect, that his or her actions would be a breach of an express or implied duty to preserve confidentiality or would be contrary to the CRA. Any professional person who commits an offence is liable on summary conviction for a fine of EC$25,000 and/or imprisonment for 12 months, or, in the case of a corporation, a fine of $250,000. Where a person receives a reward by virtue of the commission of an offence, a further fine equivalent to the amount or value of the reward solicited, received or offered is levied, and he or she must forfeit any reward actually received.

28.   The CRA does not require lawyers not to disclose confidential information entrusted to them by their clients, but it makes available sanctions when they act outside the parameters outlined above. The written consent of the Attorney General must be obtained before commencing proceedings under the CRA. The Magistrate's Court has jurisdiction, appeal lies with the High Court for any reason stated in Section 197(2) of the Magistrate's Code of Procedure Act (MCPA) and thereafter there is recourse to the Court of Appeal and the JCPC.

c Civil Proceedings

29.   The violation of attorney-client privilege is a breach of contract with the client, and as such damages may be awarded where there is loss or damage to the client. The usual civil burden of proof applies, and the claimant must prove that the weight of the evidence shows that the facts necessary to support a judgment in the claimant's favor are probably true. The client may in certain circumstances also be able to formulate a claim grounded in the tort of professional

negligence. The value and nature of the claim determines whether the Magistrate or High Court has jurisdiction over the proceedings, and appeal is possible to the Court of Appeal and the JCPC.

B Relationship between Criminal Sanctions and Disciplinary Sanctions

30. Disciplinary and criminal sanctions are imposed independently and have no effect on one another. There is no rule of law prohibiting the imposition of both criminal and disciplinary sanctions arising out of the same facts.

5 Duty to Provide Information to the Authorities

a Money Laundering and Terrorism

31. Certain types of conduct are prohibited by criminal statute, such as the Proceeds of Crime Act 2009[30] (POCA), Proceeds of Crime Amendment Act 2013[31] and the anti-terrorist financing laws that are applicable to all persons, including lawyers. Additionally, the AML legislation creates a framework of prohibited conduct and lays down specific requirements for service providers.

The Externally and Non-Regulated Service Providers Regulations (Regulations) were approved by the Governor-in-Council on September 23, 2013, and are aimed at regulating non-regulated service providers (NRSPs), which includes lawyers engaged in (i) the buying and selling of real estate and business entities; (ii) the managing of client money, securities or other assets; (iii) the opening or management of bank, savings or securities accounts; (iv) the organization of contributions necessary for the creation, operation or management of companies; or (v) the creation, operation or management of trusts, foundations, companies or similar structures, excluding any activity that requires a license under the Trust Companies and Offshore Banking Act or the Company Management Act.

However, pursuant to a court order (a stay) obtained through litigation that challenged the constitutionality of the legislation as applicable to legal practitioners, these Regulations do not currently apply to barristers, solicitors and notaries public. As such, there is currently a stay on the requirement that lawyers register with the Financial Services Commission (FSC), and they are not required to comply with certain AML/CFT laws.

32. Section 128 of POCA imposes a duty on a person to disclose any information pertaining to knowledge or suspicion of money laundering that comes to the person in the course of relevant business. The disclosure then becomes a protected disclosure.

---

[30] Act No. 13/2009.   [31] Act No. 3/2013.

POCA provides an exception to the duty to disclose. Lawyers are exempt from the requirement to disclose as it relates to material imparted in privileged circumstances. This exception also extends to the employees providing assistance to a lawyer. However, the exception does not apply to any information that is communicated or given with the intent of furthering a criminal purpose, in which case disclosure must be made. It is therefore reasonable to believe that, in instances where information does not come to a lawyer in privileged circumstances, lawyers are not exempt from the duty to disclose.

b Collective Settlement of Debts

33. To gather information about a debtor's financial situation, the courts are bound by the applicable rules of evidence. There are no special rules concerning the collective settlement of debts. In the Magistrate's Court, the judge has the power to compel a party or witness to produce documentation that is necessary for the proper determination of the dispute.[32] In the High Court, a party may ask the court to compel the disclosure of documentation that has been withheld by a party.[33] Where a lawyer who is asked to give evidence with respect to the debtor's transactions and assets, or to provide documentation, claims attorney-client privilege, it is a matter for the court as to whether to compel disclosure. The court may be reluctant to do so, given the absolute nature of the rule and the limited exceptions to it.

6 Treatment of Lawyers' Documents and Correspondence in the Context of Judicial or Police Investigations

34. When, in the course of an investigation, the authorities come upon documents prepared by a lawyer, or letters to or from a lawyer, these documents should be treated as privileged.

In the case of police investigations, if privileged communications are discovered, they should not be used. They should be placed in sealed envelopes, and if necessary the direction of the court should be sought.

In the context of High Court civil proceedings, the parties will have identified all documents including privileged documents in the list of documents or in accordance with the ECSC CPR 28. If a party wishes to see or rely on a document for which privilege is claimed by another party, an application can be made to the court, and the judge will determine whether the material is covered by privilege and whether it should be disclosed. The court may ask to see the document in question and may invite any person to make representations as to whether the document should be disclosed. See section 1(D) earlier in this chapter for further details on the treatment of privileged material.

---

[32] Section 168, Magistrate's Code of Procedure Act RSA c. M5.
[33] Eastern Caribbean Supreme Court Civil Procedure Rule 28.14(5).

7 Search of a Lawyer's Office

35. The principle of legal professional privilege allows for only one exception, that being where the lawyer is himself implicated in a crime and there is reasonable cause to suspect that evidence of the lawyer's crimes may be found in the lawyer's office. Even so, the search must be conducted in such a way as to protect the privilege of the attorney's clients.

Under the Anguilla Constitution Order 1982[34] (Constitution), no person shall be subjected to the search of his or her person or his or her property or the entry by others on his or her premises without his or her consent, save and except in certain prescribed circumstances,[35] when a search will be permitted with cause.

Section 38 of the Anguilla MCPA provides:

> Where the Magistrate is satisfied on evidence on oath that there is reasonable cause to believe that any property whatsoever or with respect to which an offence has been committed is in any place, he may grant a warrant:
> (a) To search that place for the property; and
> (b) If the property or any part of it is found there, to bring it before the Magistrate.

A magistrate may issue a search warrant. Section 7 of the MCPA also gives authority to a justice of the peace to issue a search warrant.

36. A search of a lawyer's office is therefore possible, provided that a search warrant is obtained, in accordance with the aforementioned procedure and requirements of the MCPA. The execution of the warrant should be very exact.[36] In relation to computers and cell phones that may be recovered, case law suggests that any warrant issued should state expressly what searches may be conducted on any cell phones and computers that are recovered.[37]

8 Tapping Telephone Conversations with a Lawyer

37. At the time of writing this chapter, there are no express statutory provisions for the tapping of telephone conversations in Anguilla.

Under Section 1 of the Constitution, every person in Anguilla is entitled to the fundamental rights and freedoms of the individual, whatever his or her race, place of origin, political opinions, color, creed or sex. The rights are at all times subject to respect for the rights and freedoms of others and for the public

---

[34] S.I. 1982 No. 334.   [35] Section 8, Anguilla Constitution Order.
[36] *The Jamaica Bar Association & others v. The Attorney General and DPP*, Jamaica Court of Appeal, Dec. 14, 2007, SCCA Nos. 96,102 &108/2003.
[37] *In the matter of . . . Shankiell v. Myland v. COP et al.*, GDAHCV2012/0045.

interest. The rights granted include freedom of expression and "respect for his private and family life."

Under Section 11(1): "Except with his own consent, no person shall be hindered in the enjoyment of his freedom of expression, and for the purposes of this Section the said freedom includes the freedom to hold opinions and to receive and impart ideas and information without interference, and freedom from interference with his correspondence and other means of communication."

The right to privacy is implicit in this section, and it is arguable that the right to privacy would involve the freedom not to have one's correspondence perused or interfered with. There shall be no breach of Section 11(1) where the act in question is permissible by a law that is reasonably required in the public interest on the grounds of defense, public safety, public order, public morality or public health, or that is reasonably required for the purpose of protecting the reputations, rights and freedoms of other persons or the private lives of persons concerned in legal proceedings; preventing the disclosure of information received in confidence; maintaining the authority and independence of the courts; or regulating telephony, telegraphy, posts, wireless, broadcasting or television.

When taking into consideration the fundamental freedoms provided by the Constitution, the tapping of lawyers' conversations must be considered prohibited in circumstances where there is no express statutory provision that allows it. Even if there was a justifiable reason to intercept communications, based on the aforementioned criteria, there is no statutory framework in Anguilla to authorize and set the parameters for it.

At common law (and under the MCPA), the police have the power to search, seize and retain property that may contain evidence of the commission of a crime.[38] However, this does not extend to phone tapping. Lastly, the European Convention on Human Rights[39] is extended to Anguilla, and issues pertaining to privacy may arise under Article 8 of this convention.

Unlawful recording or monitoring of communications is not criminalized under the Criminal Code and thus may constitute a tort, allowing civil action in the courts.

9 The Lawyer as Witness

38. The court will not at the bare request of a third party compel the client or allow the lawyer to give evidence of privileged oral communications or disclose privileged written communications.

A lawyer may be called to testify in court as a witness. Lawyers must take the oath and may raise attorney-client privilege when refusing to answer

---

[38] *Francis v. Marston and Others* (1965) 8 WIR 311, 313.   [39] ROME 4 November 1950.

26

questions pertaining to privileged material. Lawyers cannot refuse to testify on the basis of privilege in matters in which they did not act as lawyer. The difference between a lawyer and every other witness is that a lawyer does not have to give evidence of matters to which attorney-client privilege attaches, and the lawyer must not give evidence voluntarily on confidential matters without the consent of the client.

When a lawyer is privy to information heard in court in earlier proceedings, the information is not deemed confidential nor is it covered by privilege, so it may be given in evidence. While there is no rule of law that prohibits a lawyer from conducting a case in which the lawyer is giving evidence, it is undesirable. The Code of Ethics states that the attorney should recuse himself or herself, and it is accepted that this is an appropriate course of action.

Under Rule 35(1) Part A of the Code of Ethics: "An attorney-at-law should not appear as a witness for his own client except as to merely formal matters or where such appearance is essential to the ends of justice."

Rule 35(2) Part A states: "If an attorney-at-law is a necessary witness for his client with respect to matters other than such as are merely formal, he should entrust the case to another attorney-at-law of his client's choice."

10 The Lawyer and the Press

39. Privileged information should not be disclosed to the press. Where the client consents, a lawyer can speak to the press to express the client's view on a matter, within set parameters. However, lawyers should be cautious in their associations with the press, and a case should certainly not be conducted in the media. A lawyer should therefore remember that the client's interest is paramount and that there may be ramifications depending on the specific context for associating with the press. It may be the case that engaging with the press is not the optimal course of action for the advancement of the client's case.

11 Powers of the Tax and Other Authorities

40. It is generally accepted that no authority has the power to compel lawyers to disclose privileged documents. Where some form of disclosure is required in the natural course of business and with the client's consent, documentation sufficient to satisfy the authority can be given, for example, where proof of the underlying transaction must be given to a bank to prove how funds will be used. It is generally accepted that the information disclosed should be adequate to meet the desired ends, but no more, and it may be appropriate in certain circumstances to redact the documentation that is to be shared.

12 National Security Issues

41. Attorney-client privilege must be respected by the Government of Anguilla even when it comes to matters of national security. However, there may be circumstances in which this privilege may be penetrated in the public interest. See section 8 of this chapter for the derogations from the implied right of privacy. Generally, provided that there is a specific law protecting the public interest and that the breach is reasonably required on public interest grounds, there will be no contravention or breach of the right to privacy. Where there is no law providing for the interference with the right to privacy, there could potentially be a breach of a constitutional right.

3

Antigua & Barbuda

SAFIYA L. ROBERTS

Roberts & Co.

Preliminary Note

1.   Antigua & Barbuda is an island located in the Caribbean with a population of approximately 100,000. Prior to gaining its independence in 1981, Antigua & Barbuda was a British colony; therefore, its legislation is similar to that of the United Kingdom. However, Antigua has adopted legal practices that differ from those of the UK. For instance, although attorneys who attend court and are called to the bar in Antigua wear the long black robe that is innate to UK practice, there is no distinction between barristers and solicitors in Antigua. Legal practitioners, both those attending court and conducting solicitor work, are referred to as attorneys-at-law.

     Attorneys-at-law can practice in Antigua only if they have complied with the requirements of the Legal Profession Act of 2008 and have been admitted to the Roll of Attorneys. Such admission entitles the attorneys to practice law and have a right of audience before any court in Antigua. These requirements apply to attorneys practicing as either in-house counsel or external counsel.

     Attorneys-at-law in Antigua are bound by a statutory code of ethics and a code of ethics that has developed within the profession. Amongst these ethical obligations, and some would say the most important, is an attorney's duty of professional secrecy (also known as attorney-client privilege). This chapter focuses on an attorney's duty to keep a client's information privileged and explores the application of this duty to different areas of the law.

1 Scope of and Limitations on the Duty of Professional Secrecy/ Attorney-Client Privilege

A Statutory Basis and Implications

2.   Attorneys-at-law who practice in Antigua are bound by the Code of Ethics Rules set out in Schedule 4 of the Legal Profession Act of 2008 (hereinafter "Code of Ethics" or "Code"). These rules regulate the professional practice, etiquette, conduct and discipline of attorneys-at-law.

     The Code of Ethics provides the statutory basis for attorney-client privilege. Article 22(2), Part B, of the Code of Ethic states, "an attorney-at-law shall scrupulously guard and never divulge the secrets and confidence of his client except with his client's consent." Further, Article 15, Part B, of the Code of Ethics states:

> An attorney-at-law shall never disclose, unless ordered to do so by the Court or required by statute, what has been communicated to him in his capacity as an attorney-at-law by his client or the attorney-at-law of his client and this duty not to disclose extends to his partners and to any junior attorney-at-law assisting him, however, an attorney-at-law may reveal confidences or secrets necessary to establish or collect his fee or to defend himself or associates against an accusation of wrongful conduct.

The Code also has provisions relating to breach of an attorney's duty to keep a client's secrets and confidence. Breach of Part A of the Code, which provides for general guidelines, may constitute professional misconduct depending on the circumstances of the particular case. On the other hand, breach of the rules in Part B containing the mandatory provisions and specific prohibitions, constitutes professional misconduct, and an attorney-at-law who commits a breach of Part B is subject to any of the penalties that the Disciplinary Committee and the court are empowered to impose. These penalties include suspension from practice, fines and disbarment, among others.

The inclusion of the attorney-client privilege provision in Part B of the Code confirms the significance and ethical ramifications of an attorney's duty not to disclose a client's secrets or confidences. The attorney-client relationship is based on trust, and the public must feel assured that attorneys will not divulge information provided to them in confidence. As a result, attorney-client privilege is protected by statute in Antigua & Barbuda.

B Scope

3. An attorney's duty is not to divulge what has been communicated to the lawyer by a client in his or her capacity as an attorney-at-law. First, there must be an attorney-client relationship. Second, the communication must have been provided to the attorney in his or her capacity as an attorney-at-law.

Once these factors are satisfied, then any information provided by the client (or the client's representative) will be deemed confidential. This information may be communicated in writing or orally and may take the form of correspondence, external information, account statements, maps, drawings or plans, and personal notes taken by the attorney. In this sense, the duty is far reaching, as any communication received from a client (or the client's representative) is privileged.

The requirement may seem straightforward; however, a practicing attorney must be cautious when acting in another capacity with a client. For instance, if a practicing attorney acts as a company director or secretary, or as an executor of a deceased's estate, such communication with the attorney in the above-mentioned capacities will not be privileged. An attorney-at-law in such situations must therefore ensure that the client understands the capacity in which the lawyer is engaged and that such relationship will not result in privileged communication.

C Persons Subject to the Duty of Professional Secrecy

4. As noted above, every attorney-at-law practicing in Antigua is bound by the duty of professional secrecy. The Legal Profession Act expressly provides that the duty extends to an attorney's partners and any junior attorneys assisting the attorney. However, the duty can also extend to the wider society.

The courts and tribunals have a duty to respect attorney-client privilege and should disregard any information that has come to light inadvertently and that is clearly privileged. Attorneys will undoubtedly object to any use of privileged information by an opponent in court proceedings. The practice of the courts in Antigua has been to strike a balance between guarding the attorney-client privilege and the administration of justice and right to a fair trial in deciding issues concerning the disclosure of privileged information.

5.   It is anticipated that the wider public receiving privileged information in error should respect the attorney-client privilege and disregard such information immediately. Attorneys often put precautionary measures in place, such as a disclaimer at the footing of email communications, putting the public on notice that the communication may be privileged and confidential. However, the extent that the general public adheres to such measures may never be accurately known.

Similarly, those bodies or personnel who routinely come into contact with attorneys and their clients should also be knowledgeable and respectful of the ethical duty of an attorney to protect a client's information. Prison officers and guards and other law enforcement personnel must be respectful of a client's right to communicate in confidence with an attorney when making arrangements for attorney-client telephone conversations or meetings. Unfortunately, in practice, lack of resources and training can hinder the public's respect for attorney-client privilege.

D Exceptions to and Optional Derogations from the Duty of Professional Secrecy

6.   The express provisions of the Code provide for certain exceptions to the attorney-client privilege rule. The client can consent to the disclosure of certain information, which would make such disclosure not adverse to the application of the rule. Furthermore, an attorney can divulge confidential information if ordered to do so by a court or statute. Finally, an attorney can break privilege if necessary to collect the attorney's fee or to defend the attorney against an accusation of wrongful conduct.

Under the Code, an attorney is allowed to break privilege with the client's consent. This consent must be clear and unequivocal, and the client must be made aware of the effect of such instructions. The instructions for an attorney to break privilege must also be narrowed to refer specifically to the information that can be disclosed, particularly where the attorney is instructed on more than one matter.

7.   There is judicial guidance on what amounts to waiver of privilege. In the case of *R v. A*,[1] the Court of Appeal had to decide whether the complainant had

---

[1] [2007] All ER (D) 491 (Nov).

waived her right to claim privilege through her conduct in respect of the entire contents of her attorney's file. The Court of Appeal held:

> On settled law, documents might be disclosed for a limited purpose without waiving privilege, generally. However, if a document or communication was disclosed voluntarily, privilege would normally be lost generally and with it the right to withhold production of other documents or communications relating to the same subject matter, or "transaction." The principle governing the loss of privilege in the transaction generally was one of fairness. It was contrary to the interests of justice to allow a person to disclose a limited range of material relating to a particular matter, perhaps chosen to serve his own interests, whilst depriving the other party to the litigation of the full picture which the remainder of the material relating to that matter would disclose. However, the importance of legal professional privilege to the proper administration of justice was such that it should be jealously guarded and it followed that courts should not be astute to hold that a litigant had lost the right to claim privilege save to the extent that justice and the right to a fair trial made that necessary. It was necessary to identify the confidential communications which the person chose to disclose and see to what extent fairness demanded that other documents or communications should also be disclosed.[2]

This dicta was adopted by the Eastern Caribbean Supreme Court in *Jeffers v. Maynard*.[3] In *Jeffers*, an attorney who previously acted for both parties gave evidence for the defendant in the litigation proceedings after a dispute arose. The court considered whether the attorney had breached attorney-client privilege and held that the claimant had impliedly waived her privilege. The Court of Appeal held:

> [S]ince Ms. Jeffers [the claimant] disclosed the documents relating to the transaction in which she claims undue influence it is in the interests of Justice and fairness to allow Mrs. Maynard an opportunity to present her side of the events to which transpired and which lead to the Transfer of property and execution of the Last Will and Testament. In the circumstances I make no finding that Mr. Hobson breached Attorney/Client privilege in the matter.

Therefore, the Court's interpretation of consent to disclosure of information makes it clear that a client can waive privilege not only expressly but also impliedly through the client's conduct.

8.   The Code provides that the attorney-client privilege may be waived by order of the court. However, the courts would intervene only in the interest of justice. The High Court of Justice in the British Virgin Islands[4] highlighted the dicta of Lord Millett in Bolkai:

---

[2] Ibid. para. 3.   [3] [2015] ECSCJ No. 60.

[4] *In the High Court of Justice v. In the Matter of the International Business Act* (Cap. 291) – [2000] ECSCJ No. 98.

It is of overriding importance for the proper administration of justice that a client should be able to have complete confidence that what he tells his lawyer will remain secret. This is a matter of perception as well as substance. It is of the highest importance to the administration of justice that a solicitor or other person in possession of confidential and privileged information should not act in any way that might appear to put that information at risk of coming into the hands of someone with an adverse interest.

It is clear that the courts in Antigua & Barbuda have a high regard for the attorney-client privilege and will allow for breach of the privilege only after balancing the prejudice to both parties.

E Law Firms

9. An attorney's duty not to divulge a client's secrets and confidences is an obligation that an attorney will be held liable for personally under the Legal Profession Act. However, when an attorney works in a firm, it is quite common for an attorney to share information about a case with colleagues in the firm. There may be more than one attorney on a matter, or a junior attorney may seek advice from a senior attorney. In such scenarios, the attorney-client privilege will extend from the individual attorney who was the recipient of the confidential information to each attorney practicing in the firm.

F Legal Assistants and Staff

10. Legal assistants and staff are not covered by the statutory obligations laid out in the Code of Ethics of the Legal Profession Act. Therefore, clients should be aware that information communicated directly to a legal assistant or staff member is not privileged.

    However, such legal assistants and staff are made aware of the attorney's duty to keep a client's information confidential from the onset of the employment. Employment contracts would therefore provide for legal assistants and staff working in a law firm to keep confidential all information to which they are made privy. Breaches of such provisions would be dealt with in the employment contract and may result in suspension without pay or termination.

G External Service Providers

11. Similarly, external service providers are not covered by professional secrecy obligations unless they are practicing attorneys-at-law in Antigua. Obligations for confidentiality will be detailed in the individual service provider contract to protect the attorney and client from any misuse of information to which any such service provider may become privy.

H Multidisciplinary Associations

12. An attorney-at-law may need to seek information or assistance from a non-lawyer. However, attorneys must be cautious in that regard, as non-lawyers are not bound by the duty to protect the client's information. The client must therefore consent to the disclosure of such information and must be made aware of the risk that such disclosure may not be protected once in the hands of the third party.

I In-House Counsel

13. As noted previously, there is no distinction between the obligations of in-house counsel and external counsel. All practicing attorneys-at-law are bound by the duty of professional secrecy enshrined in the Code of Ethics of the Legal Profession Act.

2 History of the Duty of Professional Secrecy in Antigua & Barbuda

14. The concept of attorney-client privilege is enshrined in the history of the legal profession in Antigua. As a British colony prior to its independence in 1981, Antigua followed British law and judicial precedents, which guided lawmakers and society as a whole. The courts highlighted the importance of the rule in 1876 in *Anderson v. Bank of British Colombia*:

> [T]he object and meaning of the rule is this: that as, by reason of the complexity and difficulty of our law, litigation can only be properly conducted by professional men, it is absolutely necessary that a man, in order to prosecute his rights or to defend himself from an improper claim, should have recourse to the assistance of professional lawyers, ... to use a vulgar phrase, that he should be able to make a clean breast of it to the gentleman who he consults with a view to the prosecution of his claim, or the substantiating of his defence ... that he should be able to place unrestricted and unbounded confidence in the professional agent, and that the communications he so makes to him should be kept secret, unless with his consent (for it is his privilege, and not the privilege of the confidential agent), that he should be enabled properly to conduct his litigation.

This concept has been applied in the practice of law in Antigua and has been upheld by the courts since that time. The duty to protect attorney-client privilege is now laid out in statute, with the basis of the rule still underlying an attorney's duty to his or her client.

3 Supervision

A The Bar Association

15. The Legal Profession Act governs the operation and structure of the bar association. The affairs of the association are managed by the council as

constituted under the act.[5] The aims of the association are, among others, to maintain and improve the standards of professional conduct of attorneys-at-law in Antigua and Barbuda; promote, maintain and support the administration of justice and the rule of law; and to represent and protect the interests of the legal profession in Antigua and Barbuda. To become a member of the association, you must have a practicing certificate and pay the requisite dues.

Although the association is entrusted to maintain the standards of professional conduct, the Disciplinary Committee is charged with disciplining attorneys-at-law in the face of professional misconduct. Therefore, the bar association takes a supervisory role in ensuring attorneys comply with their duties, including the duty of professional secrecy. Any breach of attorney-client privilege could result in disciplinary sanctions as detailed in the section on "Sanctions."

The Disciplinary Committee consists of the president of the bar association and six other people appointed by the chief justice after consultation with the council and the attorney general. The appointed members shall include two members of the council. The chair and the vice chair shall be people who have held judicial office or have been practicing attorneys for at least 10 years. The other appointed members shall be practicing attorneys for at least six years and at least two non-attorneys.

B The Courts

16. An attorney's duty to maintain a client's secrets, among other professional codes of conduct, are policed by the courts. An aggrieved client has access to the courts by way of a civil claim for professional negligence. The client will have to prove the general requirements for succeeding in a negligence case, that is, that the attorney breached the duty to maintain the client's secrets and confidences and the client suffered loss or damage as a result.

The Legal Profession Act also empowers the attorney general to commence proceedings before the court against an attorney where the attorney general receives a report from the Disciplinary Committee (see no. 15) suggesting punishment more severe than the committee is able to impose, such as suspension from practice or removal from the Roll.[6]

4 Sanctions

A Proceedings and Sanctions

17. Any person who claims to have been aggrieved by an attorney in such attorney's practice of law may apply to the Disciplinary Committee, requiring the attorney to answer allegations contained in an affidavit made by that

---

[5] Art. 4, Legal Profession Act.   [6] Art. 39(3), Legal Profession Act.

person.[7] A complaint against an attorney-at-law for misconduct shall not be brought more than three years after (a) the date of occurrence of the facts giving rise to the complaint or (b) the date of knowledge of the facts giving rise to the complaint.[8]

The Legal Profession Act also provides the procedure for disciplinary hearings. The Disciplinary Committee has proceedings similar to those of the court, with powers to summon witnesses, call for the production of books and documents, and examine witnesses and parties under oath.[9] On hearing of the application, the Disciplinary Committee is empowered to (a) dismiss the application, (b) impose on the attorney-at-law to whom the application relates a fine as it thinks proper, (c) reprimand the attorney-at-law to whom the application relates and (d) award costs as it thinks fit.[10]

18.   An attorney does have a right to appeal a decision of the Disciplinary Committee to the Court of Appeal. The Court of Appeal may affirm or set aside the decision or penalty, it may substitute any other decision or penalty that the Committee could have made or imposed, or it may resubmit the matter to the committee for a rehearing.[11]

The Court of Appeal can also impose further sanctions in cases where the Disciplinary Committee is of the opinion that the case justifies more severe sanctions. Where the attorney general commences proceedings under Article 39(3) before the court, the court may impose any one or more of the following sanctions: (a) remove from the Roll the name of the attorney-at-law against whom disciplinary proceedings have been instituted; (b) suspend the attorney-at-law from practice for a time that the court considers fit; (c) award costs for both the proceedings before it and the proceedings before the committee, as the court considers fit; and (d) any further order as the circumstances of the case may require.

B Relationship between Criminal Sanctions and Disciplinary Sanctions

19.   There is no standalone criminal sanction for professional misconduct, particularly breach of attorney-client privilege. A criminal sanction would have to be based on a criminal action that may consist of a breach of professional misconduct, such as fraud. Furthermore, although a complaint could be made to the police or law enforcement personnel in regard to a criminal allegation, it is still within the purview of the Director of Public Prosecutors to prosecute a criminal allegation against an attorney-at-law.

Disciplinary sanctions can be imposed for breaches of professional misconduct under the Legal Profession Act. Unlike with a criminal sanction, the aggrieved client has control over pursuing the complaint with the Disciplinary Committee. Nevertheless, the sanctions that can be imposed under the

---

[7] Ibid., Art. 37.   [8] Ibid., Art. 37(3).   [9] Ibid., Art. 38(2).   [10] Ibid., Art. 39(1).
[11] Ibid., Art. 40(2).

Disciplinary Committee or the courts by way of report from the Attorney General are not as stringent as the sanctions attaching to criminal actions, particularly imprisonment.

There is no direct relationship between the criminal sanctions and disciplinary sanctions, and both sanctions would be the result of separate proceedings. The Legal Profession Act does allow for a conviction of an attorney of a criminal offense to be accepted by the committee as proof of the attorney having committed the offense, for the purpose of the disciplinary proceedings.[12]

5 Duty to Provide Information to the Authorities

A Money Laundering and Terrorism

20. There are money laundering provisions that could impede an attorney's duty to keep a client's information secret. The Money Laundering Act states, "subject to the provisions of the Constitution, the provisions of this Act shall have effect notwithstanding any obligation as to secrecy or other restriction upon the disclosure of information imposed by any law or otherwise."[13] The Money Laundering Act contemplates the wide-sweeping and potentially harmful effect of this provision when dealing with information provided to a professional in confidence, particularly attorneys. Therefore, Article 26(2) further states:

> [I]t shall be unlawful for any person to disclose any information relating to the business affairs of a customer of a financial institution that he has acquired as an officer, employee, agent, auditor, or attorney of the financial institution, or otherwise in the performance of his duties of the exercise of his functions, except in the performance or exercise of those duties or functions, in compliance with a requirement of this Act or any other statute, in response to a request from a competent authority, or pursuant to an order of a court of competent jurisdiction in Antigua and Barbuda.

Therefore, the statute makes it a legal requirement to disclose a client's confidences should the relevant authorities require information to assist in an investigation or if such disclosure is ordered by a court in relation to any allegation of money laundering or like offenses. It must be noted that these requirements are "subject to the provisions of the Constitution," and therefore a breach of attorney-client privilege can be challenged under this basis.

6 Treatment of Lawyers' Documents and Correspondence in the Context of Judicial or Police Investigations

21. Attorney-client privilege prevails even in the context of judicial or police investigations. If an investigation uncovers a document covered by

---

[12] Ibid., Art. 38(3). [13] Art. 23, The Money Laundering Act.

privilege, it should not be used to advance the investigations. The same principle applies should the investigators ask the attorney to produce documents and correspondence that are privileged. The only way a lawyer can be compelled to produce documents or correspondence in judicial or police investigations is by way of order of the court. The court will take into account the allegation against the client and the prejudice that would result for both parties if an order for production of documents is not made.

7 Search of a Lawyer's Office

22.   Similarly, a lawyer's office cannot be searched without requisite legal authority. A search warrant for a lawyer's office must be obtained pursuant to a rule that allows for breach of secrecy rules (for instance, the Money Laundering Act) and must be specific to the client who is under investigation.

A wide-sweeping search of a lawyer's office without the necessary authority will put the lawyer's duty to keep clients' confidences in jeopardy and will undoubtedly be opposed by the law firm in question.

8 Tapping of Telephone Conversations with a Lawyer

23.   There is no general statutory provision allowing telephone conversations to be tapped in Antigua & Barbuda, and any attempt to tap phone conversations by any authority would be illegal. This principle applies to an even greater extent for telephone conversations between a lawyer and a client. The attorney-client privilege extends to any form of communication between a lawyer and a client. This include meetings, emails, written communication and telephone conversations. Therefore, the attorney-client privilege would still apply to telephone conversations, and an attorney must ensure that telephone conversations with clients are not being tapped.

9 The Lawyer as Witness

24.   The Code of Ethics states that a lawyer should not act as a witness in a matter in which the lawyer represents a party. On this basis, no affidavit or witness statement should be entered that could force the attorney to divulge confidential information of a client.

A lawyer could be summoned to act as a witness in a matter involving a client with the aim of piercing the attorney-client privilege. However, the attorney would be bound by attorney-client privilege unless specifically ordered to breach the privilege by order of the court.

10 The Lawyer and the Press

25. The media's aims and duties are most often running counter to that of an attorney who has a duty to maintain a client's confidences. The attorney-client privilege will still exist in connection with any interaction with the media in Antigua. It is even more necessary to keep client confidences, as any information divulged to the press will reach a wider audience with more damaging effects. The media has no special rules or practices that allow them to pierce the attorney-client privilege enshrined in and protected by the Legal Professions Act.

11 Powers of the Tax and Other Authorities

26. At this time, a tax or other authority cannot compel a lawyer to disclose a client's privileged information. The long arm of the anti–money laundering legislation, licensing requirements for various corporate services providers and the application of Foreign Account Tax Compliance Act (FATCA) in Antigua may result in changes and challenges to the status quo in this regard.

12 National Security Issues

27. National security, like in most territories, can have sweeping jurisdiction. This jurisdiction could compel an attorney to divulge client information if such disclosure is in the interest of national security. Such actions by an attorney will not be regarded as a breach of the attorney's duty under the legal code, because an attorney under the code also has a duty to the state. However, to pierce the attorney-client privilege in the interest of national security, it must be by way of an order of the court. There must also be compelling evidence that the issues requiring an attorney to disclose information are, in fact, necessary to protect national security.

4

Argentina

MARCELO BOMBAU

M. & M. Bomchil

Preliminary Note

1. In Argentina, lawyers are subject to the duty of professional secrecy, one of the basic pillars of the legal profession. Although lawyers must be licensed to practice and be members of a bar association to appear in court, professional secrecy – also referred to as attorney-client privilege – is not imposed by a lawyer's membership in a bar association. Every lawyer, member or not, is legally bound by the same rules. Whether in public service, in a law firm or self-employed, lawyers must comply with the ethics code of the bar association to which they belong.

1 Scope of and Limitations on the Duty of Professional Secrecy/ Attorney-Client Privilege

A Statutory Basis and Implications

2. There is no specific statutory basis for the attorney-client privilege in Argentina.

   The local Criminal Code[1] imposes a duty of professional secrecy upon every person who gains knowledge – based on his or her condition, occupation, employment, profession or art – of a secret the disclosure of which could cause harm. Disclosure of such secrets without just cause is prohibited. Violation of this duty can be sanctioned with a fine and, where appropriate, professional disqualification for six months to three years. This rule certainly includes lawyers.[2]

   The information covered by the attorney-client privilege is that acquired through professional performance. There is no need for the client to specify that the information is confidential; it is sufficient for the information to be received in the course of rendering professional services.

   Furthermore, the code requires that disclosure of the secret be capable of causing harm, and this includes the potential to produce damage, whether economic, physical or moral. Breach of professional secrecy is the disclosure of a secret without just cause. This can occur through an action or omission that allows an unauthorized person to acquire knowledge of the secret.[3] In addition, disclosure must involve true information. A disclosure of false information may constitute defamation, but it is not a violation of the attorney-client privilege.

   The National Code of Criminal Procedure[4] states that people cannot be called as witnesses in court regarding secrets obtained through their

---

[1] Art. 156, Argentine Criminal Code.

[2] Sebastián Soler, *Argentine Criminal Law*, book IV, Tipográfica Editora, Argentina, Buenos Aires, 1976.

[3] Ibid.   [4] Art. 244, National Code of Criminal Procedure.

professional performance. Any such testimony will be deemed null (see no. 26 of this chapter). This regulation does, however, allow the interested party to waive this duty, allowing the confidential information to be be disclosed.

3. The duty of professional secrecy is closely connected with the constitutional rights of proper judicial defense and protection against self-incrimination. Compelling lawyers to disclose confidential information would violate these constitutional rights and compromise essential aspects of the rule of law.

As mentioned previously, lawyers must comply with the ethics code of their respective bar association. The Ethics Code of the Buenos Aires Bar Association provides:

> [T]he practice of the legal profession entails the following inherent duties: . . . the lawyer must firmly respect professional secrecy and oppose before judges or other authority the disclosure of professional secrecy, refusing to answer questions that expose him to violate it. Only the following cases are excluded: a) when the client so authorizes; b) in the case of self-defense.[5]

Likewise, the law that regulates the exercise of the legal profession states that, "notwithstanding other duties set forth in special laws, lawyers have the following specific duties: . . . faithfully comply with professional secrecy, except when having express authorization granted by the interested party."[6] Similar provisions are established in the other Argentine jurisdictions.

B Scope

4. Professional secrecy protects all information, either written or oral, provided by the client to a lawyer, related to the client's rights and obligations, or in the course of soliciting advice regarding the client's legal rights and obligations. It includes all information that comes to the lawyer's attention in this context, including information provided by the opposing party, a third party or colleagues in the course of the lawyer's professional performance.

Local case law has consistently affirmed that intercepting an attorney's telephone communications (of course, such interception should have been ordered by a competent judge) shall be undertaken with serious caution, ensuring that the evidence obtained does not infringe third parties' rights or result in a breach of professional trust.

Moreover, the National Court of Appeals for Federal and Administrative Matters has held that attorney-client privilege not only protects information entrusted by the client but also that which the lawyer has obtained due to his or her professional performance.[7]

---

[5] Art. 10, Ethics Code of Buenos Aires Bar Association.
[6] Art. 6, Law no. 23,187, governing legal practice in the City of Buenos Aires.
[7] *S., C. L. y otro c. Colegio Público de Abogados en la Capital Federal*, National Court of Appeals for Federal and Administrative Matters, Sept. 6, 2005.

C Persons Subject to the Duty of Professional Secrecy

5. Being considered as a matter of public policy, attorney-client privilege must be respected by the court, by the public prosecutor and any party to the proceedings.

    In accordance with the Argentine Criminal Code, any person who gains knowledge – based on such person's condition, occupation, employment, profession or art – of a secret whose disclosure could cause harm is subject to the duty of professional secrecy. Disclosure of such secrets without just cause is prohibited. Lawyers, accountants, doctors, notaries and psychologists, among others, are subject to this duty. Notwithstanding the foregoing, the duty of professional secrecy is not in all cases equal, for example, doctors are mandated to report to the authorities when they become aware, by virtue of their profession, that a crime has been committed.

D Exceptions to and Optional Derogations from the Duty of Professional Secrecy

6. Because professional secrecy is an important public policy matter, attorney-client privilege protection is interpreted broadly while limitations and exceptions are interpreted narrowly. The general principle is to preserve the duty and right of professional secrecy and, when in doubt, maintain confidentiality. Furthermore, even when revealing professional secrets is permitted, attorneys must limit such exposure to only what is strictly necessary.

    Under the rules of the Argentine Criminal Code, professional secrets can be revealed based only on a just cause. Just cause generally involves necessity, which entitles the attorney to expose confidential information to avoid a greater damage. If a lawyer is mistaken with regard to such necessity, the court must determine whether the lawyer reasonably and honestly believed in the necessity.[8]

    Furthermore, per the Ethics Code of the Buenos Aires Bar Association, disclosure is allowed only in two specific situations: (i) when the attorney is released from the duty by the owner of the secret and (ii) when it is necessary for defending attorneys against accusations brought by their own clients, and even then, limited to information that is essential for the attorney's defense.

E Law Firms

7. The attorney-client privilege applies to all information provided by a client to lawyers at a firm, whether they are partners or associates.

    Lawyers working in a law firm tend to share privileged information, and it is generally accepted that no restrictions apply to this type of information sharing.

---

[8] Sebastián Soler, *Argentine Criminal Law*, book IV, Tipográfica Editora, Argentina, Buenos Aires, 1976, 124–25.

F Legal Assistants and Staff

8. Information covered by confidentiality is not only that acquired through professional performance but also by virtue of employment. Some legal scholars consider that this category includes the employees of law firms to the extent they have access to the secrets that concern the principal. It would be illogical that an attorney could not be required to testify, but a typist who the lawyer employs could.[9]

   Under this approach, lawyers must maintain the confidentiality of client matters and documents and make sure that all their employees, whether they are lawyers or not, adopt the same measures of confidentiality and care.[10] Likewise, the firm may be civilly liable if employees of a law firm disclose privileged information.

G External Service Providers

9. Parties working as external service providers to a firm carry confidentiality obligations within the limit of their particular assignment. If a breach occurs, both the service provider and the lawyer or firm that surrendered the information to the service provider will be liable (to the extent either had not taken reasonable measures to protect the confidentiality of the information).

H Multidisciplinary Associations

10. Lawyers can share confidential information with non-lawyers if the client remains anonymous and disclosure is necessary to safeguard the client's interests. Likewise, if the client agrees, the lawyer is entitled to consult with a person who is not a lawyer, but only to the extent necessary.

    However, lawyers should be careful not to share privileged information with some professionals, such as accountants, who are subject to the duty to report suspicious transactions to the local authorities. In this regard, in accordance with the Ethics Code of the Buenos Aires Bar Association, it is considered serious misconduct to share attorney fees with non-lawyer professionals, such as notaries, accountants and auctioneers, among others.

    Regardless of the foregoing, the same rules allow attorneys to form associations among themselves and also with other professionals, provided that the attorney retains the independence to advise his or her clients on legal issues.

I In-House Counsel

11. A particular case is the one dealing with in-house counsel, whose labor status does not release them from the duty of professional secrecy. Insofar as labor conditions do not affect the technical autonomy of employed professionals,

---

[9] Ibid., 117 et seq.   [10] Ethics Code of the Bar Association of the City of Buenos Aires.

they must comply at all times with legal and ethical obligations, regardless of how they are employed.

2 History of the Duty of Professional Secrecy in Argentina

12. Precursors to the current legal provision on professional secrecy (see nos. 1 and 2 of this chapter) include the Argentine Criminal Code of 1887 and the Tejedor Project.[11]

    The section on professional secrecy in the Tejedor Project established that "lawyers, doctors, surgeons and everybody who discloses the secrets with which they are entrusted due to the profession they practice will suffer a fine . . . except in the cases in which the law may oblige them to disclose those secrets."[12]

    The first Argentine Criminal Code (1887) referred to the breach of professional secrecy, establishing that "those practicing a profession that requires a title, who disclose secrets revealed to them because of their profession, will be punished with suspension."

    In contrast with the current legislation, the old criminal laws required that the revealed secret be a "trusted" one. Considering the legislation currently in force, one can see that this obligation became more general, without establishing which specific professions were affected by the secrecy obligation.

    Since 1985, and within its jurisdiction, the Bar of the City of Buenos Aires established a Disciplinary Court for the evaluation and sanctioning of professional ethics breaches.

3 Supervision

A The Bar Associations

13. As mentioned at the beginning of this chapter, lawyers in Argentina must be members of the bar association of the jurisdiction where they want to appear in court. They are nonetheless able to provide legal advice to clients even if they are not members of the bar. But they need to be registered members to submit pleadings as a lawyer, file lawsuits and, in general, to perform their profession before a court.

    Each bar association has its own ethics rules and disciplinary tribunals that have to be respected by lawyers who are members of the same. They are subject to the authority of the bar association to which they belong, although this

---

[11] The first attempt for general criminal codification was prepared at the request of the National Executive Power, by Carlos Tejedor, professor at the University of Buenos Aires. The project followed in large part the Criminal Code of Baviera of 1813 and to a lesser extent Spanish doctrine through Joaquín Francisco Pacheco.

[12] Carlos Parma, "Violation of the professional secret."

authority is limited to the imposition of disciplinary sanctions when lawyers breach their ethical duties.

B The Courts

14. Breach of professional secrecy may lead to the intervention of civil or criminal courts. Criminal courts have jurisdiction to impose criminal sanctions for the violation of professional secrecy when it rises to the level of "criminal law" status, while civil courts have jurisdiction to impose economic sanctions for damages derived from the breach of attorney-client privilege. However, there are no specific rules in this respect for lawyers.

4 Sanctions

A Proceedings and Sanctions

a Disciplinary Proceedings and Sanctions

15. The Buenos Aires Bar Association has a Disciplinary Tribunal, the powers of which include investigating cases of ethical violations and imposing sanctions when necessary. Additionally, the bar association has exclusive authority to enforce proper practice rules concerning the legal profession. This disciplinary authority exists independently of the potential civil or criminal liability of its members.[13]

Cases are brought before the Disciplinary Tribunal by complaint or *ex officio*. The complaint may be brought by any party who feels affected by the professional conduct of a lawyer. Anonymous complaints are not allowed.

The complaint must be in writing with a clear statement of facts specifying details of the complaint and the accused. The complaint must be grounded in specific facts and contain all relevant evidence.

Complaints are first reviewed by an investigative unit that meets with the plaintiff to certify the complaint. At the meeting, the investigative unit may request additional information and produce a brief summary of the case. Performance of preliminary fact-finding measures is also possible.

After the preliminary hearing, the investigative unit sends the case to the Disciplinary Tribunal, which can in turn dismiss it when, for example, the claim is manifestly unsupported or the alleged facts are not covered by the bar association's rules.

If the Disciplinary Tribunal decides to try the case, it grants the accused 15 days to respond to the complaint. During this term, the lawyer or the lawyer's counsel can file a written defense admitting or denying the alleged facts and the authenticity of the documents presented, arguing against the unlawfulness of the alleged conduct and presenting evidence.

---

[13] Art. 39, Law no. 23,187.

After an evidentiary hearing, the Disciplinary Tribunal will issue a judgment within 30 days. Sanctions may include (a) admonition; (b) warning in the presence of the Board of Directors; (c) a fine that cannot exceed the monthly salary of a first-instance judge; (d) suspension from professional activity up to one year; or (e) disbarment if (i) the accused has been suspended five or more times in the previous ten years or (ii) the accused has been convicted of an intentional crime, punishable by imprisonment, under circumstances that affect professional ethics and decorum. In determining the appropriate sanctions, the Disciplinary Tribunal shall consider the background of the accused. The judgment of the Disciplinary Tribunal is subject to court review. A ruling imposing suspension or disbarment is published by the bar association. Other sanctions do not need to be published. Access to the records of the Disciplinary Tribunal is reserved to the plaintiff, the accused, their counsel and others who may be duly authorized by the former. The accused may also request publication of acquittals.

The following principles apply to the disciplinary process: (1) innocent until proven otherwise; (2) any doubt will be adjudicated in favor of the accused; (3) *non bis in idem* – no individual shall be prosecuted twice for the same act; (4) no broad interpretation nor by analogy and no interpretation based exclusively on assumptions; (5) the Disciplinary Tribunal will always adopt the interpretation of the rules in the manner most favorable to the accused; and (6) the Disciplinary Tribunal will not apply laws retroactively unless they are benign for the accused.

b Criminal Proceedings and Sanctions

16. Violation of professional secrecy is punishable in accordance with the Criminal Code[14] with a fine and, when appropriate, professional disqualification between six months and three years. The criminal court's decision can be appealed before the competent court of appeals.

In Argentina, violation of professional secrecy from a criminal law perspective is a crime of private action, which means that the process cannot be initiated *ex officio* without a formal criminal complaint brought before the court by the injured party.

c Civil Proceedings and Damages

17. Parallel to criminal and disciplinary proceedings, the injured party may also bring a civil action to obtain compensation for damages, and the plaintiff has the burden of proof. Likewise, if a criminal judgment has been handed down pending the civil claim, the facts proven in the criminal case cannot be overturned by the civil court.

---

[14] Art. 156, Argentine Criminal Code.

B Relationship between Criminal and Disciplinary Sanctions

18.　The disciplinary rules indicate that, when the same facts give way to both disciplinary and criminal cases, the process before the Disciplinary Tribunal will be parallel to the criminal case, although a decision by the latter will be binding on the Disciplinary Tribunal as to the facts and their qualification. The Disciplinary Tribunal has the power to order a stay of the disciplinary procedure if the decision in the criminal action is still pending.

In all cases where a guilty verdict is imposed, the intervening tribunal is obligated to notify the professional organization about the verdict, providing a full copy of the ruling.

Disciplinary sanctions have no effect on criminal procedures. However, many of the criminal sanctions established by Article 156 of the Criminal Code entail professional disbarment.

5 Duty to Provide Information to the Authorities

A Money Laundering and Terrorism

19.　With the enactment of Law no. 25,246 (Anti-Money Laundering Act), the main concepts of the 40 Recommendations[15] of the Financial Action Task Force[16] (FATF) were incorporated into local law. This law also defines the concept of suspicious transactions and establishes the legal obligation to disclose information about them while creating a sanctions regime.

Recommendation 16 includes lawyers and their duty to inform the authorities about unusual or suspicious transactions when, "in the name and on behalf of a client, they participate in a transaction which activities are those described in Recommendation 12(d)." Recommendation 12(d) refers to the purchase and sale of real property; management of income, bank or savings accounts, securities, or other assets; organization of contributions for the creation, operation and administration of companies; and the purchase and sale of commercial entities.

However, Recommendation 16 notes that "it is not a requirement for lawyers ... to report their suspicions if the relevant information has been obtained under circumstances in which they were subject to the privilege of professional secrecy or legal secrecy."

---

[15] The 40 Recommendations constitute the basic framework of the struggle against money laundering and have been conceived for universal application. They comprise the police and criminal legal system, the financial system and its regulation, and international cooperation.

[16] During the XV Economic Summit held in Paris in July 1989, the Organization for Economic Cooperation and Development (OECD) created the Financial Action Task Force, even though it is not a formal part of the OECD or of any other international organization. It is an ad hoc group, the purpose of which is to develop common strategies regarding the crime of money laundering, based on international cooperation.

The Interpretative Note of Recommendation 16 explains:

> It is the responsibility of each jurisdiction to determine the issues that should be considered as privileged. Usually, this would include information the lawyers . . . receive from their clients or through them: (a) within the course of determining the legal position of their client; or (b) within the task of defending or representing that client in proceedings in judicial, administrative, arbitration or mediation matters, or related to the client.

Therefore, the specific obligation to inform the Financial Information Unit applies to certain individuals, but not to lawyers.

20. A recent draft law presented before the Argentine Congress suggests, as indicated by the aforementioned Recommendation 16, that lawyers should be included in the obligation to inform the Financial Information Unit about "suspicious transactions" arising from the professional relationship with their clients. As of August 2015, this draft had still not been approved.

B Collective Settlement of Debts

21. In Argentina, professional secrecy prevails over a collective settlement of debts. Therefore, it cannot be set aside to obtain information about the debtor's assets, which, as a matter of fact, are covered by the attorney-client privilege.

6 Treatment of Lawyers' Documents and Correspondence in the Context of Judicial or Police Investigations

22. No person's correspondence can be subject to search or scrutiny unless authorized by a judicial order. This requirement exists to safeguard the constitutional right to privacy, which is also considered a human right.

Lawyers' documents and correspondence are specially protected insofar as any judicial investigation or proceedings not complying with this requirement will be deemed null.

Moreover, the constitutional right refers not only to correspondence but also to private documents. Documents generated by lawyers within the performance of their profession are private and therefore privileged.

7 Search of a Lawyer's Office

23. Similarly to most Argentine jurisdictions, the rules on professional procedure of the city of Buenos Aires provide lawyers with "the inviolability of their professional office, by virtue of the constitutional guarantee of proper defense. In case of search, the competent authority that had issued the order shall give notice to the professional organization when executing the same and the lawyer shall have the right to require the presence of a member of the Board of Directors during the procedure."

Furthermore, the Ethics Code of the Buenos Aires Bar Association provides that "the lawyer must defend the right to the inviolability of his office and the documents entrusted to him."

There are two principles stemming from these provisions. The first one strengthens a person's right to defense in court, as the individual is able to trust that documents are secure in the attorney's office. The second one ensures that individuals are also protected by professional secrecy rules.

It must also be noted that a judge who issues a search warrant for a lawyer's office has the duty to communicate the activity to the lawyer's bar association. The bar association will appoint an observer, who will observe the judicial action and control how it is conducted so as to prevent irregularities.

If this person observes irregularities, he or she is obliged to record the opposition to such behavior in the minutes. The lawyer whose office is being searched has the same right.

8 Tapping of Telephone Conversations with a Lawyer

24. Tapping a lawyer's communications is prohibited in Argentina unless the lawyer is the person being investigated or accused. The National Criminal Court of Appeals[17] ruled that such recordings would damage the sphere of privacy required to prepare a criminal defense and constituted a clear violation of the guarantees of proper defense and due process. Communications and other records exchanged between the accused and his or her defense counsel are inadmissible in a criminal procedure.

Likewise, a ruling by the National Supreme Court[18] declared unconstitutional a regulation that allowed interception of telephone and online conversations in which the subject party was a lawyer. The court based its decision on the fact that it affected the privilege of confidentiality in conversations with the lawyer's clients.

The interception of a lawyer's telephone communications must be decided with caution and conducted carefully. The judge must make sure that the evidence obtained does not infringe on third-party rights or violate professional secrecy.

9 The Lawyer as Witness

25. In principle, Argentine law does not allow lawyers to be called as witnesses in cases involving their clients, given that it may constitute a breach of professional secrecy.

However, some legal scholars believe that, even if the attorney can rely on the duty of professional secrecy, such attorney cannot refuse to testify prior to being

---

[17] Case no. 30,932 of Feb. 15, 2012.
[18] *Halabi, Ernesto c/ P.E.N. s/amparo*, National Supreme Court, Feb. 24, 2009.

informed of the matters to be questioned upon. An attorney cannot rely on professional secrecy to avoid appearing at court. The attorney must raise the existence of such duty, if applicable, in response to each question being asked.[19]

Additionally, the Argentine Federation of Bar Associations considers professional secrecy to be both a duty and a right of the attorney. It is a duty with respect to clients, and it is a right with respect to judges. After all, attorneys would not be suitable parties to trust if they could be required at any time to reveal clients' information.

There is disagreement among legal scholars as to whether the attorney is required to disclose confidential information when the client has consented to such disclosure.

26.   The Argentine Code of Criminal Procedure provides that attorneys, among other parties, "cannot decline to testify when released from the duty of confidentiality by the interested party."[20] Therefore, this rule can be construed as providing the "just cause" by which attorneys can be required to testify regarding confidential information.

Attorneys who wish to maintain the confidentiality of the information entrusted to them, despite the client's consent to divulge the information, shall be required to testify nonetheless. If they refuse, they carry the risk of being punished under the Criminal Code with imprisonment from 15 days to one month.[21]

Under this system, the Code of Criminal Procedure grants the client the sole discretion to determine whether confidential information continues to be kept secret or revealed.

It is important to bear in mind that the obligation of the attorney to testify when released from the duty of confidentiality arises from procedural rules, whereas the obligation to maintain professional secrecy is established by substantive law, which carries greater weight in Argentina. Even so, if the client has released the attorney from the duty of professional secrecy, the attorney cannot decline to testify, and such testimony will not be a criminal violation of professional secrecy due to the just cause exception.

Along this line of thinking that confidentiality belongs solely to the client, the National Court of Appeals in criminal matters decided:

> [T]he conduct of the investigating judge violates the guarantee of due process by relieving defense attorneys of professional secrecy when they are deposed as witnesses in clear contravention of the provisions of Article 244 of the Code of Criminal Procedure, which provides that the duty to refrain from testifying can only be relieved by the interested party.[22]

[19] *El Derecho, jurisprudencia general*, book 2, Universidad Católica de Argentina, Buenos Aires, 1962, 188–91.
[20] Art. 244, National Code of Criminal Procedure.   [21] Art. 243, Criminal Code.
[22] *Telleldin Carlos A. and others/ appeal*, National Criminal Court of Appeals, room II, May 19, 2006.

27. On the other hand, other scholars firmly believe that the obligation to maintain secrecy is absolute. Therefore, they believe the attorney shall not be exempt from it by any authority or person, nor by the confidants themselves. Such scholars believe this obligation entitles the attorney to invoke professional secrecy and refuse to answer any questions that might challenge that secrecy.

10 The Lawyer and the Press

28. Lawyers can speak to the press only with the client's consent. They must limit themselves to reveal what it is essential to inform the press, withholding privileged information and always safeguarding the client's interests.

11 Powers of the Tax and Other Authorities

29. Professional secrecy is one of the limits to the broad powers of tax authorities. In tax proceedings, when professionals are called to testify as witnesses, they cannot refuse to attend the hearing. However, they may decline to answer questions the answers of which may result in the disclosure of secrets.[23]

There is a debate about the conflict between professional secrecy and the law that regulates tax proceedings insofar as the latter grants the right to the Federal Tax Administration to request a national judge to order the search of offices in order to verify compliance with tax laws.

Those who consider this right unconstitutional argue that, since the law does not enumerate the cases in which a search can be ordered, it violates Article 18 of the National Constitution, which states that "a law shall determine in which cases and for what reasons" a location may be searched.

However, those who consider this right constitutional argue that, when searches are ordered against the client but are to be performed at the attorney's office, the order can authorize the review, examination or seizure of specific documents.

12 National Security Issues

30. In Argentina, there is no specific regulation related to professional secrecy and its interaction with national security. There is, however, a dispute between legal scholars as to which of the following principles should prevail in case of a conflict between them.

---

[23] Sara Diana Telias, "Allanamiento de domicilio-secreto- secreto profesional," *La ley* 1991-E, 1513, online quote: AR/ DOC/ 12294/ 2001.

One line of thinking is that the Argentine intelligence agencies must respect professional secrecy and that a breach of professional secrecy when investigating potential threats to national security requires a previous judicial order.

Others believe that, when national intelligence agencies have serious indications of a potential threat to national security, such belief constitutes a just cause to allow a breach of professional secrecy rules.

5

Bahamas

VANN P. GAITOR

LASHAY A.S. THOMPSON

ANDREA A. MOULTRIE

FELIX F.L. BENEBY JR.

CAMRYN A. CARTWRIGHT

Higgs & Johnson

Preliminary Note

1.   The terms *professional secrecy, lawyer-client privilege*, and *attorney-client privilege*, otherwise known as *legal professional privilege*, refer to a doctrine that forms part of the common law observed in the Bahamas since 1799, when the Declaratory Act No. 2 of 1799 declared the common law of England to be in full force within the Bahamas, except where altered by certain acts of England, among other things.

    The privilege is the client's and once the conditions are fulfilled for its application, it can only be waived by the client or overridden by statute. As will be seen in this chapter, statutes have made inroads on the doctrine of legal professional privilege. Questions often arise as to whether a particular provision in a statute overrides the privilege. But unless the statute expressly or by necessary implication overrides the protection afforded by legal professional privilege, the privilege will be deemed absolute if the conditions exist for its application.

2.   The topics of this chapter demonstrate that legal professional privilege gives rise to many challenges in the Bahamas, as this society tries to address or provide remedies for many issues that warrant an intervention by statute. At the same time, it is obvious that lawmakers understand why the privilege has survived for so long and the desire for its retention, both as an important part of the law of the Bahamas and as a matter of public policy.

1 Scope of and Limitations on the Duty of Professional Secrecy/ Attorney-Client Privilege

3.   The Bahamian lawyer's duty of professional secrecy is defined as "a duty to hold in strict confidence all information received in the course of the professional relationship with or concerning a client or a client's affairs, which information should not be divulged by the attorney unless the attorney is expressly or impliedly authorized by the client or required by the laws of the Commonwealth of The Bahamas so to do."[1] Professional secrecy, otherwise known as attorney-client privilege,[2] refers to the protection from disclosure of

---

[1] Rule IV, Schedule to the Bahamas Bar (Code of Professional Conduct) Regulations.

[2] *Paragon Finance plc (formerly known as National Home Loans Corp plc) and others v. Freshfields (a firm)* [1999] All ER (D) 251 (CA).

communications, whether oral or written, passing between (i) a lawyer and a client, or a client or his or her lawyer and a third party, made for the purpose of litigious proceedings, which is known as litigation privilege; and (ii) a lawyer and a client for the purpose of giving or receiving legal advice, which is known as legal advice privilege.[3]

The purpose of this chapter is to provide a discussion of the scope of and limitations to the Bahamian lawyer's duty of professional secrecy. The focus will be on attorney-client privilege, which is a privilege enjoyed by the client and not the lawyer.[4] Attorney-client privilege will be referred to as "client privilege" for the purposes of this chapter.

A Statutory Basis and Implications

4.   A lawyer has an obligation of professional secrecy with regard to the confidential information of a client. The recognition of professional secrecy and the right of an individual to have certain information kept confidential are evident in the following Bahamian statutes:

(i) Evidence Act (Chapter 65, Statute Laws of The Bahamas, 2009 Edition). Section 136 provides: "No one shall be compelled to disclose to the court any confidential communication which has taken place between himself and his counsel and attorney."

(ii) Proceeds of Crime Act (Chapter 93, Statute Laws of The Bahamas, 2009 Edition)

Under Section 35(2), if a court has reasonable cause to believe that a person may possess material, information or other matter that is involved with drug trafficking or other offense, it may order production from that individual of such material. Notwithstanding the power to make such an order, Section 35(5)(a) specifically states that

---

[3] *Three Rivers District Council v. Governor and Company of the Bank of England* [2004] UKHL 48 (HL). Lord Scott of Foscote describes the relationship between litigation privilege and legal advice privilege at para. 27:

"[L]egal advice privilege has an undoubted relationship with litigation privilege. Legal advice is frequently sought or given in connection with current or contemplated litigation. But it may equally well be sought or given in circumstances and for purposes that have nothing to do with litigation. If it is sought or given in connection with litigation, then the advice would fall into both of the two categories. But it is long settled that a connection with litigation is not a necessary condition for privilege to be attracted . . . . On the other hand it has been held that litigation privilege can extend to communications between a lawyer or the lawyer's client and a third party or to any document brought into existence for the dominant purpose of being used in litigation. The connection between legal advice sought or given and the affording of privilege to the communication has thereby been cut."

[4] *Ventouris v. Mountain; The Italia Express* [1991] 3 All ER 472 (CA).

a production order "shall not confer any right to production of, or access to, items subject to legal privilege."[5]

Section 43 places a duty on an attorney to notify or report to the Financial Intelligence Unit a suspicious transaction if the attorney has reasonable grounds to believe that a client is involved in money laundering that may relate to drug trafficking.

Section 43(2) provides that a person shall not be required to disclose information or to produce a document that he or she would be entitled to refuse to disclose or to produce on the grounds of legal professional privilege, except that an attorney may be required to provide the name and address of a client or principal.

Section 43(6) specifically references client privileges. It states that any information or other matter that comes to an attorney in privileged circumstances if it is communicated or given to the attorney (a) by a client, or by a representative of a client, in connection with the legal advice given by the attorney to the client; (b) by a person, or by a representative of a person, seeking legal advice from the attorney; or (c) by any person in contemplation of, or in connection with, legal proceedings, and for the purpose of those proceedings. However, no information or other matter shall be treated as coming to an attorney in privileged circumstances if it relates to criminal conduct or is communicated or given with a view to furthering any criminal purpose.

(iii) Central Bank of The Bahamas Act (Chapter 351, Statute Laws of The Bahamas, 2009 Edition)

Under Section 35, the Central Bank may, by notice in writing, require any financial institution, trust company, Registered Representative, money transmission service provider or money transmission agent – or any director, officer or servant of such entity, or a person reasonably believed to have information relevant to an inquiry – to supply to the bank such information as the bank considers necessary.

However, Subsection (8) of the act provides: "A person shall not be required under this Section to disclose information or to produce

---

[5] Section 7 of the Proceeds of Crime Act defines "items subject to legal privilege" as:

    (a) communications between a counsel and attorney and his client made in connection with the giving of legal advice to the client; and

    (b) communications between a counsel and attorney and his client or between such counsel and attorney and any other person made in connection with or in contemplation of legal proceedings and for the purpose of such proceedings,

when they are in the possession of a person who is entitled to possession of them; but items held resulting from criminal conduct or with the intention of furthering a criminal purpose are not items subject to legal privilege:

    Provided that the legal privilege shall not extend to information regarding the identity and address of the client or principal.

a document which he would be entitled to refuse to disclose or to produce on the grounds of legal professional privilege in court proceedings."

(iv) Financial Transactions Reporting Act (Chapter 368, Statute Laws of The Bahamas, 2009 Edition)

This statute imposes an obligation, among other things, on financial institutions to report suspicious transactions to the Financial Intelligence Unit. Section 17 of the Act, titled "Legal Professional Privilege," preserves and recognizes an individual's right to confidentiality of his or her information and an attorney's professional secrecy obligation. Having regard to the importance of Section 17 and its language, the entire section is reproduced as follows:

17. (1) Nothing in Section 14 requires any counsel and attorney to disclose any privileged communication.

(2) For the purposes of this Section, a communication is a privileged communication only if —

(a) it is a confidential communication, whether oral or written, passing between —

(i) a counsel and attorney in his or her professional capacity and another counsel and attorney in such capacity; or

(ii) a counsel and attorney in his or her professional capacity and his or her client, whether made directly or indirectly through an agent of either;

(b) it is communicated or given to a counsel and attorney by, or by a representative of, a client of his or her in connection with the giving by the counsel and attorney of legal advice to the client;

(c) it is made or brought into existence for the purpose of obtaining or giving legal advice or assistance; and

(d) it is not made or brought into existence for the purpose of committing or furthering the commission of some illegal or wrongful act.

(3) Where the information consists wholly or partly of, or relates wholly or partly to, the receipts, payments, income, expenditure or financial transactions of a specified person (whether a counsel and attorney, his or her client or any other person), it shall not be a privileged communication if it is contained in, or comprises the whole or part of, any book, account, statement or other record prepared or kept by the counsel and attorney in connection with a client's account of the counsel and attorney.

(4) For the purposes of this Section, references to a counsel and attorney include a firm in which he or she is a partner or an associate or is held out to be a partner or an associate."

59

(v) Data Protection (Privacy of Personal Information) Act (Chapter 324A, Statute Laws of The Bahamas, 2009 Edition)

The statute was enacted to protect the privacy of individuals' personal data and to regulate the collection, processing, keeping, use and disclosure of certain information relating to individuals, among other things.

Section 8 provides that certain data can and will be provided in certain circumstances, but Section 9 exempts personal data "in respect of which a claim of privilege could be maintained in proceedings in a court in relation to communications between a client and his professional legal advisers or between those advisers."

(vi) Securities Industry Act, 2011 (No. 10 of 2011)

The Securities Industry Act of 2011 requires the disclosure of some confidential information while preventing disclosure of communications generally protected by client privilege. The Act gives with one hand and takes with the other. Section 37 provides that assistance may be given by the Securities Commission (the "Commission") to an overseas regulatory authority, notwithstanding "the provisions of any prescribed written law or any requirement imposed thereunder, or any rule of law, in relation to a request by an overseas regulatory authority for assistance." The Commission may, under Section 37(1), (a) transmit to the overseas regulatory authority any material in the possession of the Commission that is requested by the authority; (b) order any person to furnish to the Commission any material that is requested by the overseas regulatory authority, which the Commission may then transmit to that authority; (c) order any person to give the Commission assistance in connection with a request made by an overseas regulatory authority; or (d) order any person to make an oral statement to the Commission on any information requested by the overseas regulatory authority, record such statement and transmit the recorded statement to the authority.

Section 37(2) provides that an order under Subsection (1)(b), (c) or (d) shall have effect notwithstanding any obligations as to secrecy or other restrictions on the disclosure of information imposed by any prescribed written law or any requirement imposed thereunder, any rule of law, any contract or any rule of professional conduct.

Section 37(3) provides that a person shall not be required under the section to disclose information or to produce a document that the person would be entitled to refuse to disclose or to produce on the grounds of legal professional privilege in court proceedings.

To avoid doubt and to emphasize the professional secrecy protection afforded to an individual, the remainder of Section 37 provides as follows:

(4) For the purposes of this Section, any information or other matter comes to a professional legal adviser in privileged circumstances if it is communicated or given to the legal adviser —

(a) by, or by a representative of, a client of the adviser in connection with the giving by the adviser of legal advice to the client;

(b) by, or by a representative of, a person seeking legal advice from the adviser; or

(c) by any person —

(i) in contemplation of, or in connection with, legal proceedings; and

(ii) for the purpose of those proceedings.

(5) No information or other matter shall be treated as coming to a professional legal adviser in privileged circumstances if it is communicated or given with a view to furthering any criminal purpose.

B Scope

5. A lawyer's duty of professional secrecy is an unqualified duty to keep a client's information confidential, not merely to take all reasonable steps to do so. This duty survives the termination of the retainer and the death of the client.[6]

Lord Millett discusses the extent of a lawyer's duty of confidentiality in the case of *Prince Jefri Bolkiah v. KPMG (A Firm)* [1999] 2 AC 222, 235–36 (HL), where he states:

> Whether founded on contract or equity, the duty to preserve confidentiality is unqualified. It is a duty to keep the information confidential, not merely to take all reasonable steps to do so. Moreover, it is not merely a duty not to communicate the information to a third party . . .
>
> It is of overriding importance for the proper administration of justice that a client should be able to have complete confidence that what he tells his lawyer will remain secret. This is a matter of perception as well as substance. It is of the highest importance to the administration of justice that a solicitor or other person in possession of confidential and privileged information should not act in any way that might appear to put that information at risk of coming into the hands of someone with an adverse interest.

For a lawyer to owe a client a duty of professional secrecy (other than a duty arising out of contract or statute), "the information in question must be of a nature and obtained in circumstances such that any reasonable person in the position of the recipient ought to recognize that it should be treated as confidential."[7]

---

[6] *Prince Jefri Bolkiah v. KPMG (A Firm)* [1999] 2 AC 222 (HL).

[7] *Napier and another v. Pressdram Ltd* [2009] EWCA Civ 443 (CA) at para. 42.

Given that the lawyer's duty of professional secrecy survives the termination of the retainer, the lawyer should ensure that he or she does not put a former client at risk that confidential information obtained from the relationship may be used against the former client in any circumstances. In the case of *Prince Jefri Bolkiah v. KPMG (A Firm)*, Lord Hope of Craighead states at page 227:

> A solicitor is under a duty not to communicate to others any information in his possession which is confidential to the former client. But the duty extends well beyond that of refraining from deliberate disclosure. It is the solicitor's duty to ensure that the former client is not put at risk that confidential information which the solicitor has obtained from that relationship may be used against him in any circumstances.

6.   For communications to be privileged, the relationship of lawyer and client must exist, and the communications must be fairly referable to the aforesaid relationship. Furthermore, client privilege survives the death of the client.[8]

According to Lord Millett in *B v. Auckland District Law Society* [2004] 4 All ER 269 (PC), the following principles relating to client privilege are well established: (i) the privilege remains after the occasion for it has passed unless waived; (ii) the privilege is the same whether the documents are sought for the purpose of civil or criminal proceedings and whether by the prosecution or the defense; (iii) the refusal of the claimant to waive his or her privilege for any reason or none cannot be questioned or investigated by the court; and (iv) save in cases where the privileged communication is itself the means of carrying out a fraud, the privilege is absolute.[9]

Client privilege extends to "[l]etters written and oral communications made during a dispute between the parties, which are written or made for the purpose of settling the dispute, and which are expressed or otherwise proved to have been made 'without prejudice.'"[10] This privilege (i) protects both the lawyer and the client and (ii) covers both the letter and subsequent related correspondence on both sides, even if the subsequent correspondence is not expressed as "without prejudice," except where there is a clear break in the chain of correspondence to show that ensuing letters are open.[11] Parties who use the substance of "without prejudice" communications in support of their case may not object to their opponents' use of admissions made in those "without prejudice" communications.[12]

---

[8] *Minter v. Priest* [1930] AC 558, 568 (HL) *per* Lord Buckmaster; *Bullivant v. Attorney-General for Victoria* [1901] AC 196.

[9] *B v. Auckland District Law Society* [2004] 4 All ER 269, 280 *per* Lord Millett.

[10] "Civil Procedure" in *Halsbury's Laws of England*, Volume 11 (2009), paras. 1–1108; Volume 12 (2009), paras. 1109–836. Evidence/(2) 'Without Prejudice' Communications/804, "Communications 'without prejudice.'"

[11] Ibid.   [12] Ibid. at 805, "Limits of the rule."

C Persons Subject to the Duty of Professional Secrecy

7.   As previously stated, only lawyers are subject to the duty of professional secrecy; however, as will be seen in no. 10 of this chapter, a lawyer is required to take reasonable care to prevent other lawyers within the law firm and non-legal staff from disclosing or using any information that the lawyer is bound to keep confidential.

The common law doctrine of client privilege does not extend to any professional other than a lawyer.[13] In *R (on the application of Prudential plc and another) v. Special Commissioner of Income Tax and another*, the English Supreme Court held that the common law doctrine of legal professional privilege does not extend to legal advice received from a non-legal professional, such as an accountant, except where allowed by statute.[14] However, there are currently no statutory provisions in the Bahamas that extend the application of the doctrine of legal professional privilege to communications with professionals other than qualified lawyers or to other disciplines. Yet there may be instances when a person's information and records are to be kept confidential, provided such information and records do not pertain to the commission of criminal offenses.

D Exceptions to and Optional Derogations from the Duty of Professional Secrecy

8.   A lawyer's duty of professional secrecy does not apply in the following circumstances:

(i)   Where communications are made in furtherance of a criminal or fraudulent purpose or in preparation of it or a part of it. If it were otherwise, a person intending to commit a crime or fraud could obtain legal advice for the purpose of enabling such person to commit a crime with impunity.[15]

(ii) Where a client expressly or impliedly waives the lawyer's duty of confidentiality.[16]

(iii) Where a court orders the lawyer to disclose the information. In the case of *Finers (a firm) and others v. Miro*, [1991] 1 All ER 182, the English Court of Appeal held:

> Where a solicitor had strong evidence of suspected fraud on the part of a client he was entitled, under the rule that fraud unravelled all obligations

---

[13] *R (on the application of Prudential plc and another) v. Special Commissioner of Income Tax and another* [2013] UKSC 1 (SC).

[14] *Three Rivers District Council v. Governor and Company of the Bank of England* [2004] UKHL 48 (HL).

[15] *R v. Cox and Railton* (1884) 14 QBD 153 (CCR); *Butler v. Board of Trade* [1971] Ch. 680 (Ch D).

[16] *Paragon Finance plc (formerly known as National Home Loans Corp plc) and others v. Freshfields (a firm)* [1999] All ER (D) 251 (CA).

of confidence, to apply to the court either under its inherent jurisdiction or under RSC Ord 85 [Order 74 of the Rules of the Supreme Court of The Bahamas] for directions as to how to deal with the client's assets under his control notwithstanding the inevitable breach of the solicitor's duty of confidence to his client, and, because the solicitor was potentially liable as a constructive trustee at the suit of those entitled to assets misappropriated by the fraud, the court could direct the solicitor to notify interested persons of the existence of the proceedings.

(iv) Where it is necessary for lawyers to disclose confidential information to establish or collect their fee or to defend themselves or their associates or employees against an allegation of malpractice or misconduct (but only to the extent necessary for such purpose).[17]

E Law Firms

9. Based on the foregoing, each lawyer in a law firm owes a duty of professional secrecy to the firm's clients. This duty survives termination of the retainer. Nevertheless, there is no rule that a lawyer who has acted for a client before could not act for the opposing party. Accordingly, lawyers in the same law firm may act against the interests of another lawyer's former client. In those circumstances and if made an issue in proceedings, a court may consider whether an effective barrier (commonly known as an ethical wall) was erected within the law firm to prevent improper or inadvertent disclosure of confidential information among lawyers.

In *Prince Jefri Bolkiah v. KPMG (A Firm)*, Lord Millett states that, for ethical walls to be effective, a law firm must have "established organisational arrangements which preclude the passing of information in the possession of one part of the business to other parts of the business."[18] Ethical walls or other similar arrangements may or may not be sufficient to eliminate the risk of disclosing confidential information. But unless a firm takes special measures with regard to information movement within the firm, a court may restrain a law firm from representing a new client unless the court is satisfied on clear and convincing evidence that effective measures are in place to ensure confidential information won't be disclosed.

Lord Millett states that ethical walls normally involve some combination of the following organizational arrangements: (i) the physical separation of the various departments within a law firm to insulate them from each other; (ii) an educational program, normally recurring, to emphasize the importance of not

---

[17] Commentary 10 to Rule IV of the Bahamas Bar (Code of Professional Conduct) Regulations.

Note: Regulation 2 of the Bahamas Bar (Code of Professional Conduct) Regulations provides that the commentary to the rules is intended only as general guidelines as to the meaning, scope, requirements and purpose of the respective rule and do not form part of the rule.

[18] *Prince Jefri Bolkiah v. KPMG (A Firm)* [1999] 2 AC 222, 238 (HL) *per* Lord Millett.

improperly or inadvertently divulging confidential information; (iii) strict and carefully defined procedures for dealing with a situation where it is felt that the ethical wall should be crossed and maintaining proper records where this occurs; (iv) monitoring by compliance officers of the ethical wall's effectiveness; and (v) disciplinary sanctions where there has been a breach of the ethical wall.[19]

F Legal Assistants and Staff

10. There is an implied authority that a lawyer, to the extent necessary, may disclose a client's affairs to partners or associates within the law firm, as well as to non-legal staff such as secretaries and filing clerks. However, this implied authority imposes a duty on lawyers to impress upon their partners, associates, employees and even students under their supervision the importance of non-disclosure during and after their employment. Lawyers must also take reasonable care to prevent such individuals from disclosing or using any information that the lawyer is bound to keep confidential.[20]

G External Service Providers

11. A lawyer must keep confidential all information received in the course of the professional relationship from or concerning a client or a client's affairs received from external service providers. However, the duty of professional secrecy does not extend to information passing directly between a client and an external service provider.

Communications between a client or the client's lawyer and a third party may or may not be privileged, depending on the circumstances. For communications between a client or the client's lawyer and a third party to be privileged, they must be made for the purpose of obtaining information or advice in connection with existing or contemplated litigation. The following conditions must be satisfied: (i) litigation must be in progress or in contemplation; (ii) the communications must have been made for the sole or dominant purpose of conducting that litigation; and (iii) the litigation must be adversarial, not investigative or inquisitorial.[21]

H Multidisciplinary Associations

12. Only lawyers acting in the capacity of giving legal advice or preparing for or engaging in litigation within a multidisciplinary association will be subject to

---

[19] Ibid.

[20] Commentary 9 to Rule IV of the Bahamas Bar (Code of Professional Conduct) Regulations.
  Note: Regulation 2 of the Bahamas Bar (Code of Professional Conduct) Regulations provides that commentary to the rules is intended only as guidance and is not part of the rule.

[21] *Three Rivers District Council v. Governor and Company of the Bank of England* [2004] UKHL 48, para. 102 (HL) *per* Lord Scott.

the duty of professional secrecy. A lawyer is required to take reasonable care to prevent other lawyers and non-legal staff within the multidisciplinary association from disclosing or using any information that the lawyer is bound to keep confidential for any other purpose than for which it was given or obtained.

I In-House Counsel

13.   In the Bahamas, the common law doctrine of legal professional privilege extends to communications of in-house lawyers when such communications fall within the scope of legal advice privilege and litigation privilege.

Determining when communications by in-house lawyers are protected by legal professional privilege can be challenging at times. Lawyers working as in-house counsel usually consult with various persons within the organization. They may be from different parts of the organization and also from different companies within a group structure. In such circumstances, it may be difficult to discern a lawyer-client relationship among the various persons or entities and the in-house lawyer. It is impractical for an in-house lawyer to confirm the engagement of everyone within the organization or group structure who requests advice, particularly because in-house lawyers are often called on to address urgent requests.

While the privilege generally does extend to communications exchanged with in-house counsel, difficulties may arise in identifying who exactly is the in-house lawyer's client. The court has held that only those employees of an organization who were given the task of obtaining or receiving legal advice from a lawyer could be considered the client for the purpose of legal advice; however, there is a dearth of case law on the issue.[22] Accordingly, a helpful means by which an organization may ensure that communications with its in-house lawyer are privileged is to (i) clearly establish who can make requests of the in-house lawyer and under what circumstances such requests may be made; (ii) make it clear to whom the in-house lawyer must render his or her advice; (iii) ensure that, whenever possible, the person or entity within the group structure making a request of the in-house lawyer is engaged for the purpose of seeking or receiving legal advice; and (iv) ensure communications with the in-house lawyer that attract privilege are kept separately from communications relating to other matters.[23]

---

[22] *Three Rivers District Council and Others v. The Governor and Company of the Bank of England (no 5)* [2004] 3 All ER 168.

[23] Jean-Pierre Douglas-Henry, Paul Smith, Dorsey and Whitney, "Legal Professional Privilege," *Tax Journal*, 897, 12 (2007); Huw Wallis and Mary Dodwell, "Three Rivers Meet at the House of Lords: An Opportunity Missed," *Journal of International Banking and Financial Law*, 20.2 (2005).

2 History of the Duty of Professional Secrecy in the Bahamas

14. Legal professional privilege arises out of the common law. Lord Hoffman articulated the basis of a client's privilege in *R (on the application of Morgan Grenfell & Co Ltd) v. Special Comr of Income Tax*, [2002] 3 All ER 1 (HL) at paragraph 7:

> [L]egal professional privilege is a fundamental human right long established in the common law. It is a necessary corollary of the right of any person to obtain skilled advice about the law. Such advice cannot be effectively obtained unless the client is able to put all the facts before the adviser without fear that they may afterwards be disclosed and used to his prejudice.

The principle was recorded in English law as early as 1577 in the case of *Berd v. Lovelace*, (1576) 21 ER 33. The full report thereof states:

> A solicitor served with process to testify, ordered not to be examined. – Thomas Hawtry, gentleman, was served with a subpoena to testify his knowledge touching the cause in variance; and made oath that he hath been, and yet is a solicitor in this suit, and hath received several fees of the defendant; which being informed to the Master of the Rolls, it is ordered that the said Thomas Hawtry shall not be compelled to be deposed, touching the same; and that he shall be in no danger of any contempt, touching the not executing of the same process.

As noted in no. 4 of this chapter, the common law doctrine of privilege has been recognized in various Bahamian statutes.

3 Supervision

A The Bar Associations

15. Each attorney admitted to practice in the Bahamas is a member of the Bahamas Bar Association (BBA), and officers are elected and appointed from among the members to function as the Bar Council.

Under the Legal Profession Act, 1993, the Bar Council has responsibility for the direction, control and governance of the BBA. These general powers and duties extend to the supervision of standards of etiquette and professional conduct required of members in relation to professional secrecy and attorney-client privilege as contained in Rule IV of the Bar Code. Rule IV specifically states that attorneys have a duty to hold in strict confidence all information received in the course of the professional relationship from or concerning a client or a client's affairs, which information should not be divulged by the attorney unless the attorney is expressly or impliedly authorized by the client or required by the laws of the Bahamas to do so.

The Bar Council is aided with supervision by the Ethics Committee and the Disciplinary Tribunal. The Ethics Committee is composed of members appointed by the Bar Council to receive complaints about the conduct of counsel, attorneys, registered associates and legal executives and to determine whether there are reasonable grounds for referring such complaints to the Disciplinary Tribunal. The function of the Disciplinary Tribunal is to hear complaints referred to it by the Ethics Committee.

If an attorney discloses confidential information protected by attorney-client privilege in breach of the Code, the client may lodge a complaint with the Ethics Committee of the BBA.

B The Courts

16.   The courts may hear and determine any action against attorneys relating to professional misconduct, and attorneys may face criminal or civil liability for any professional misconduct in connection with a breach of their duty to maintain attorney-client privilege.

4 Sanctions

A Proceedings and Sanctions

a The Bar Association

17.   The Ethics Committee will consider whether there are reasonable grounds for a complaint against an attorney for improper conduct. Improper conduct includes contravention by counsel and attorneys of any regulation as to professional practice, conduct or etiquette. If there are reasonable grounds for the complaint, the Ethics Committee may reprimand the attorney for the improper conduct or refer the complaint to the Disciplinary Tribunal if it warrants a penalty or any order other than a reprimand.

Any complaint by or on behalf of a client or former client of a counsel and an attorney must be substantiated under oath by or on behalf of the complainant before disciplinary action may be taken by the Disciplinary Tribunal.

The hearing of the complaint is heard in private unless the attorney whose conduct is being investigated requests otherwise. At the hearing, the attorney has the right to be represented by counsel, to adduce evidence and to make submissions. If the attorney fails to appear at the hearing or fails to answer to a notice issued by the Disciplinary Tribunal or Ethics Committee, the Disciplinary Tribunal may proceed with the hearing in the attorney's absence if it is satisfied that there is no reasonable excuse for the absence. The Disciplinary Tribunal or Ethics Committee may also proceed with the hearing of a complaint in the absence of the complainant. This applies even in cases where the complainant is no longer desirous of proceeding and the Committee considers the improper conduct alleged in the complaint to be of such nature or frequency that it is in the interest of the legal profession to proceed with a hearing.

At the hearing, the Disciplinary Tribunal and Ethics Committee have jurisdiction to certify as an offense any conduct that would be deemed contempt in a court of law. For example, the Disciplinary Tribunal or Ethics Committee may certify the offense of an attorney being duly summoned to appear to give evidence before the Disciplinary Tribunal or Ethics Committee who does not appear, an attorney who attends the hearing to give evidence but refuses to be sworn or to make solemn affirmation as may be legally required, or an attorney who refuses to produce any document in his or her power or control legally required to be produced. The court may inquire into the certified offense and hear any witness against or on behalf of the attorney charged with the offense. The court may also punish or take steps to punish that attorney as if the attorney had been guilty of contempt of court.

The Disciplinary Tribunal and Ethics Committee also have powers exercisable by a judge of the court in relation to summoning and examining witnesses and production of books and documents.[24]

Following the hearing of the complaint, the Disciplinary Tribunal may either dismiss the complaint against the attorney or make such order of a disciplinary nature as it sees fit. The decision of the Disciplinary Tribunal is pronounced in public and may be enforceable in the same manner as a judgment or order of the court. The order may include any of the following actions: (i) striking off the roll the name of the counsel and attorney to whom the complaint relates, effectively disbarring the attorney; (ii) suspending the counsel and attorney from practice for a period not exceeding three years; (iii) requiring payment by the counsel and attorney of a penalty not exceeding $1,000, which shall be forfeited to the Crown; (iv) requiring payment by the counsel and attorney of compensation for any personal injury, loss or damage resulting from the improper conduct that is the subject matter of the complaint; or (v) requiring payment by any party of costs or of such sum as the tribunal may consider a reasonable contribution toward costs.

The attorney may appeal the decision of the Ethics Committee or Disciplinary Tribunal to the Court of Appeal. No further appeal shall lie from the decision of the Court of Appeal.

b The Courts

18.   Civil proceedings may be commenced against an attorney to recover damages associated with breach of the attorney's duty to maintain attorney-client privilege. The matter may be tried before a judge of the Magistrate's Court or the Supreme Court. However, the Magistrate's Court may hear and determine only a matter where the amount sought does not exceed $5,000.

There are no express provisions relating to attorney-client privilege in the Penal Code of the Bahamas. However, the Data Protection (Privacy of Personal Information) Act provides a general framework for privacy of individuals in

---

[24] Section 36(2), Legal Profession Act.

69

relation to personal data and protection against the disclosure of certain information. As previously discussed, Section 8 of the Data Protection (Privacy of Personal Information) Act exempts personal data for which a claim for privilege could be asserted under the doctrine of attorney-client privilege.

Under the Data Protection (Privacy of Personal Information) Act, any disclosure of personal data without prior authority is an offense punishable by a fine not exceeding $2,000 on summary conviction and not exceeding $100,000 on a conviction on information. Summary proceedings for an offense may be commenced and prosecuted by the Data Protection Commissioner appointed under the Data Protection (Privacy of Personal Information) Act to ensure compliance with the provisions of the act and to investigate complaints to the commissioner regarding any contravention of the provisions of the Data Protection (Privacy of Personal Information) Act. Summary proceedings should be instituted within one year from the date of the offense. The exception to the rule is cases where disclosure is required for the purpose of obtaining legal advice or for the purpose of, or in the course of, legal proceedings in which the person making the disclosure is a party or a witness.[25]

B Relationship between Criminal Sanctions and Disciplinary Sanctions

19.   Criminal and disciplinary sanctions operate independently and may be instituted concurrently. The most severe sanction in the case of disciplinary proceedings is disbarment, in contrast with a fine of $100,000 under the Data Protection (Privacy of Personal Information) Act in criminal proceedings.

5 Duty to Provide Information to the Authorities

A Money Laundering and Terrorism

20.   Money laundering is an offense under the Proceeds of Crime Act. As previously discussed in Section 1(A), "Statutory Basis and Implications," the Proceeds of Crime Act requires that any person who, in the course of his or her employment or profession, comes across information that suggests that another person is engaged in money laundering, he or she is to disclose such information to the Financial Intelligence Unit or to a police officer.[26] A person who fails to do so is guilty of an offense.

The foregoing requirement to disclose information does not extend to information or documents that would be precluded from such disclosure or production on the grounds of legal professional privilege; however, a lawyer may be required to provide the name and address of the client or principal.[27] Further, information that relates to criminal conduct, or is communicated or

---

[25] Section 13(f), Data Protection (Privacy of Personal Information) Act.
[26] Section 43, Proceeds of Crime Act.   [27] Ibid.

given with a view to furthering any criminal purpose, is not treated as privileged information and is therefore subject to disclosure.

21.   As noted in no. 4 (iv) of this chapter, pursuant to the Financial Transactions Reporting Act, "financial institutions" are obligated to report to the Financial Intelligence Unit any financial transactions that they suspect may involve the proceeds of a crime. Lawyers are considered "financial institutions" under the Financial Transactions Reporting Act, but only to the extent that they receive funds, in the course of business, for the purposes of deposit or investment, settling real estate transactions, or to be held in a client account.[28]

The reporting obligation imposed on lawyers under the Financial Transactions Reporting Act does not require a lawyer to disclose privileged communications. However, where the information in question consists of, or relates wholly or partly to, the receipts, payments, income, expenditure or financial transactions of a specified person (whether that be a lawyer, a client, or another person), the information will not be treated as privileged if it is contained in any record prepared or kept by the lawyer, in connection with a client's account.[29]

22.   Pursuant to the Anti-Terrorism Act (Chapter 107, Statute Laws of The Bahamas, 2009 Edition), where any person has reasonable grounds to suspect that funds or financial services are related to or being used to facilitate terrorism, that person is obligated to report the matter to the Commissioner of Police.[30] The Anti-Terrorism Act does not provide that lawyers are exempt from such reporting on the grounds of legal professional privilege.

B Collective Settlement of Debts

23.   The collective settlement of debts is not regulated in the Bahamas. There are no laws that relate to this practice, unlike several other jurisdictions, and so the concept of legal professional privilege will operate in the normal fashion with regards to any attempt to settle or otherwise mediate indebtedness.

6 Treatment of Lawyers' Documents and Correspondence in the Context of Judicial or Police Investigations

24.   As discussed in no. 6 of this chapter, communications between lawyers and their clients are privileged, having regard to the purpose for which they are made; therefore, the courts will offer protection from disclosure of communications. If legal proceedings are taking place, then privilege attaches to documents and correspondence pertaining to or that came into existence in

---

[28] Section 3, Financial Transactions Reporting Act.   [29] Ibid., Section 17.
[30] Section 7, Anti-Terrorism Act.

connection with or in contemplation of proceedings or with the giving of legal advice. This will include all manner of correspondence, including but not limited to letters, emails, faxes, phone text messages and the like.

The treatment of lawyers' documents in the context of judicial or police investigations regularly gives rise to several legal issues. Such issues include the protection for privacy of home and other property, one of the fundamental rights of an individual guaranteed by The Constitution of the Commonwealth of The Bahamas (Chapter 1, Statute Laws of The Bahamas, 2009 Edition) ("the Constitution"), in addition to the privilege derived from a lawyer-client relationship.[31] The challenge for investigators lies in balancing the protection of a client's rights under the attorney-client privilege, the client's fundamental rights and the need to secure evidence that may ensure an investigation is conducted in the interest of justice or to prevent unlawful activity. The privilege cannot be relied on to protect an individual whose intent is to facilitate unlawful activities.

7 Search of a Lawyer's Office

25. The Constitution affords protection to everyone for the privacy of home and property. Article 21(1) provides that, except with one's consent, no person shall be subjected to the search of his or her person or property, or the entry by others on his or her premises.

Article 21(2) provides that nothing done under the authority of any law shall be held to be inconsistent with or in contravention of this article to the extent that the law in question makes provision:

  (a) which is reasonably required –
  (ii) for the purpose of protecting the rights and freedoms of other persons.

26. Notwithstanding the protection afforded the individual by Article 21, if a search of an individual's person or property, or entry upon the individual's premises, under any law is considered "reasonably justifiable in a democratic society," such search will not be deemed to have violated a person's funda-mental right guaranteed by Article 21.

Notwithstanding the protection of individual rights guaranteed by the Constitution, Section 70 of the Criminal Procedure Code Act (Chapter 91, Statute Laws of The Bahamas, 2009 Edition) empowers a court to issue search warrants to any peace officer to effect a search in any place where the court is satisfied by evidence, given under oath, that there is reasonable cause to believe that property involved in the commission of an offense is present. Such a warrant will grant a police officer the power to enter any place, at any time, with or without permission and by force, if deemed necessary. The term "place"

---

[31] Art. 21, The Constitution.

in the section refers to a number of locations, including buildings, ships, vehicles, aircrafts or any locality situated in the Bahamas as specified in the search warrant. This will also include a lawyer's premises. The extent, however, of the police search would exclude documents protected by attorney-client privilege, unless there is reason to believe a crime is contemplated or has been committed.

Members of the Royal Bahamas Police Force also possess an inherent power, outside the ambit of section 70 of the Criminal Procedure Code, that allows a place to be searched without the procurement of a warrant issued by a magistrate.

Under Section 41 of the Police Force Act, 2009 (No. 3 of 2009), a member of the Police Force may, with the authority granted by another member of the force, no less than the rank of Inspector, enter upon any premises to exercise the power of search any time of the day or night, with or without consent, and also with the use of force, if required. The premises, however, must be occupied by a person known to have been convicted within the past five years of an offense involving fraud or dishonesty and on whose premises there is a reasonable belief that stolen or unlawfully obtained property exists on the premises. This authority is given, provided that there is good reason to believe that the delay involved in obtaining a search warrant under Section 70 of the Criminal Procedure Code would seriously hamper an investigation. The authority for the search should be obtained in writing, except in cases of extreme urgency.

8 Tapping of Telephone Conversations with a Lawyer

27.   The circumstances giving rise to legal professional privilege has been outlined in no. 6 of this chapter. But for limited exceptions, the privilege is absolute. Examples of such exceptions are (i) where the privileged communication is itself the means of carrying out a fraud[32] and (ii) where legal professional privilege is overridden by express words of a statute or by implication.[33]

The exercise of certain powers under the provisions of the Listening Devices Act, 1972 (Chapter 90, Statute Laws of The Bahamas, 2009 Edition) enables certain government authorities to carry out activities that override legal professional privilege in some instances. The Listening Devices Act, 1972 governs the use of listening devices in the Bahamas. The general position is that any

---

[32] *B and Others v. Auckland District Law Society and Another* [2003] 2 AC 736 *per* Lord Millett at para. 44 of his opinion: "save in cases where the privileged communication is itself the means of carrying out a fraud, the privilege is absolute."

[33] *Three Rivers District Council and Other, supra,* per Lord Scott at para. 25 of his opinion, citing with approval the decision of the House of Lords in *R (Morgan Grenfell & Co. Ltd) v. Special Commissioner of Income Tax and Another* [2003] 1 AC 563, and where he stated that legal professional privilege could be overridden by statute but only by express words of the statute or by implication.

person who uses a listening device to hear, listen to or record a private conversation to which he or she is not a party is guilty of an offense. Anyone convicted of an offense shall be subject either to a fine not exceeding $2,000 or to imprisonment for a term not exceeding six months, or both.[34]

Under Section 5 of the Listening Devices Act, 1972, the Minister responsible for National Security has the power to authorize the use of listening devices where the minister is sufficiently satisfied that such use is required in the interests of defense or the internal security of the Bahamas.[35] Additionally, the Commissioner of Police, after consultation with the Attorney General, may authorize the use of a listening device for the purpose of investigating an offense that has already been committed, is believed to have been committed, is about to be committed or is reasonably likely to be committed to obtain evidence of the commission of the offense or of the identity of the offender.[36]

In the Bahamian case of *Taylor v. Commissioner of the Police*, [2010] 1 BHS J No. 72, police officers obtained evidence to possess and distribute dangerous drugs through covert monitoring and listening to the appellant's cell phone conversations with persons subsequently deemed co-conspirators after being authorized by the appropriate authorities to carry out their surveillance. The issue of legal professional privilege did not arise in the case. The Court of Appeal upheld a Magistrate's Court finding that the phone intercepts were lawfully obtained and therefore admissible into evidence. The court was satisfied that the law enforcement's efforts to discourage the supply of dangerous drugs outweighed the appellant's individual rights, taking into account the broader interest of the community at large. The judgment affirms the position that, regardless of the presence of liberties and rights normally afforded to an individual, such rights may be overridden if access to such communication is necessary to prevent illicit activities and to enforce the law.

The Listening Devices Act, 1972 makes no reference to legal professional privilege, but given the decision in *Taylor v. Commissioner of the Police*, properly authorized covert telephone surveillance of a lawyer's telephone conversation with a client may not be protected by legal professional privilege. Depending on the nature and purpose of the telephone communication, the evidence obtained through listening devices may or may not be protected by legal professional privilege.

9 The Lawyer as Witness

28. In accordance with Rule VIII of the Bahamas Bar (Code of Professional Conduct) Regulations (the "Bar Code"), attorneys acting as advocates must represent their clients resolutely, honorably and within the limits of the law while treating the tribunal with courtesy and respect. One facet of this

---

[34] Section 9, Listening Devices Act, 1972.   [35] Ibid., Section 5.   [36] Ibid.

obligation is that, if the attorney is a necessary witness, the attorney should testify, and the conduct of the case should be entrusted to another attorney.

In circumstances where attorneys are called upon as witnesses to testify, such attorneys cannot disclose communications that are fairly referable to the existing relationship of lawyer and client (i.e., communications that they learned in their capacity as an attorney). For example, where an attorney makes himself or herself a subscribing witness, such attorney assumes another character for such occasion and adopts the duties it imposes and is therefore bound to give evidence of all that a subscribing witness can be required to provide.[37]

10 The Lawyer and the Press

29.   Attorneys in the Bahamas are not permitted to engage in unregulated competitive advertising that (in accordance with Rule XIII of the Bar Code) is incompatible with the integrity of the profession and may be detrimental to the public interest. Accordingly, attorneys can advertise through the press only in limited circumstances, such as publication of announcements of persons joining or being promoted in the firm.

Additionally, the Bahamian press reports on high-profile matters that are before the court and open to the public. In these instances, an attorney should not solicit an appearance but may speak to the press with respect to a client's matter. However, the attorney should be extremely careful not to disclose confidential or privileged information unless authorized to do so.

11 Powers of the Tax and Other Authorities

30.   Mention has already been made of the impact of the powers that other government authorities have on legal professional privilege. Therefore, only the powers of the tax authorities are addressed in this section.

The Value Added Tax Act, 2014 (No. 32 of 2014) of the Bahamas came into force on January 1, 2015. A value-added tax (VAT) rate of 7.5% is applied to goods purchased and services provided within The Bahamas. The VAT department of the Ministry of Finance holds the responsibility of managing the collection of incoming taxes and ensuring that all businesses are tax compliant.

The Comptroller and VAT officers have extensive investigative powers. The Comptroller may, by notice, require any person to furnish specified information concerning such person or any other person, attend and be examined under oath before the Comptroller or any VAT officer, produce any record or computer in his or her control that the Comptroller requires, and provide access to premises and books, of which the Comptroller may take

---

[37] *Greenough v. Gaskell* [1824–34] All ER Rep 767 (Lord Chancellor's Court).

possession.[38] The Comptroller may require a bank or other financial institution to furnish details of a banking account or other assets held by or on behalf of a taxable or related person or permit inspection of the records of books, among other things.[39]

The investigative powers pertaining to bank or other financial institutions have effect notwithstanding any other law relating to "privilege, public interest, bank confidentiality or bank secrecy."[40] Financial institutions include offices of counsel and attorneys, depending on the purpose for which they receive funds in the course of their business as stipulated under Section 3 of the Financial Transaction Reporting Act. Legal professional privilege is acknowledged when it comes to reporting suspicious transactions in certain circumstances by an attorney under the Financial Transactions Reporting Act and in some circumstances under the Value Added Tax Act, 2014.

12 National Security Issues

31.   Where matters of national security are concerned, a matter can hardly be envisioned where legal professional privilege can be asserted for any act that is preparatory for or involves the commission of a serious crime.

As stated previously, the Minister responsible for National Security and the Commissioner of Police have the power to authorize the tapping of a lawyer's telephone conversation once certain prerequisites of the Listening Devices Act, 1972 are satisfied. Such conversations are deemed privileged, except if such conversation is for the purpose of carrying out a criminal offense.

Legal professional privilege is a common law doctrine that has been upheld for so long in the Bahamas and other nations of the British Commonwealth of Nations that circumstances warranting an override of the principles of legal professional privilege will be viewed with great scrutiny.

[38] Section 62, Value Added Tax Act, 2014.   [39] Ibid.   [40] Ibid., Section 62(6).

Preliminary Note

1. The Barbadian legal system, like that of other Commonwealth Caribbean territories and many of Barbados' post-colonial counterparts, is principally derived from the adaption and development of British legal systems. As such, much of the legislation and case law applied in Barbados follows the British precedents. Up until 2002, the House of Lords (before being replaced by the Caribbean Court of Justice) was still the highest forum of appeal for Barbadian cases. Unlike in Britain, however, since 1973 the legal profession in Barbados no longer distinguishes between the two British categories of advocates (barristers) and legal advisers (solicitors). All legal professionals seeking to practice law in Barbados are now required to apply to the High Court for admission and have their names entered on the roll – that is, the register of attorneys-at-law kept by the Registrar of the Supreme Court of Barbados pursuant to the Legal Profession Act[1] (the "Act"). The Barbados lawyer, therefore, acts as both an advocate of the court and as a legal adviser.

   Like many legal professionals, Barbados' attorneys-at-law ("attorneys") owe a duty to keep confidential and secret their communications with clients. It is out of this relationship between attorney and client that the principle of legal professional privilege, also known as attorney-client privilege, is born. This chapter will focus on the doctrine of legal professional privilege as it applied in Barbados in both civil and criminal practice.

1 Scope of and Limitations on the Duty of Professional Secrecy/ Attorney-Client Privilege

A Statutory Basis and Implications

2. Although the Act governs the procedures and qualifications for a person to be admitted as an attorney in Barbados, the Act itself does not set out the principles of legal professional privilege. A duty of confidentiality is imposed under Rule 26(2) of the Legal Profession Code of Ethics 1988[2] (the "Code"), which stipulates that in their dealings with clients, Barbadian attorneys are required to "scrupulously guard and never divulge [their] client's secrets and confidences." It is also a mandatory and specific provision of the Code that, unless ordered to do so by the court or via legislation, an attorney should never disclose any communication undertaken with a client. This duty not to disclose extends to an attorney's partners, junior attorneys and other employees.[3]

   The duty of confidentiality, while universally shared in varying degrees, is not enough to give security to a client that any communications between the client and the attorney would not be compelled to come to light by a court of

---

[1] Section 3, Legal Profession Act, Cap. 370A of the laws of Barbados.
[2] Legal Profession Code of Ethics 1988, Cap. 370A of the laws of Barbados.   [3] Ibid., Rule 71.

law. For this reason, the principle of legal professional privilege was developed by the common law to accompany the rules of evidence relating to the disclosure of documents in legal proceedings. In Barbados, authority for the exclusion of communications between attorneys and their clients on the grounds of legal professional privilege is found in the Evidence Act, Cap. 121 of the laws of Barbados. Under the Evidence Act, a client can seek the permission of the court for evidence to be excluded on the basis of legal professional privilege in circumstances where that evidence would involve the disclosure of confidential information.[4] The Evidence Act also provides for the exclusion of communications between the client and the attorney, or two or more attorneys for the client, as well as communications between employees or agents of the attorney.[5]

3. There is no automatic right of exclusion of all confidential communications between a client and an attorney – the client must object to the admission of the confidential communications, and the court must be satisfied that the objection is well founded. The test to determine whether a particular document or piece of communication can be accorded legal professional privilege developed around the notion that the dominant purpose of the communication must be for the purposes of legal advice, as expressed in the English case of *Balabel v. Air India* [1988] 2 All ER 246 per Taylor LJ at 330:

> In my judgment, therefore, the test is whether the communication or other document was made confidentially for the purposes of legal advice. Those purposes have to be construed broadly. Privilege obviously attaches to a document conveying legal advice from solicitor to client and to a specific request from the client for such advice. But it does not follow that all other communications between them lack privilege. In most solicitor and client relationships, especially where a transaction involves protracted dealings, advice may be required or appropriate on matters great or small at various stages. There will be a continuum of communication and meetings between the solicitor and client.

These sentiments are echoed in Section 104 of the Evidence Act, such that the communication must have been made for the dominant purpose of the attorney, or one of the attorneys, providing legal advice to the client, or providing or receiving professional legal services in relation to a legal or administrative proceeding or an anticipated or pending administrative or legal proceeding in which the client is or may be a party. The Evidence Act also provides for the principle to be applied to parties without legal representation in legal proceedings where there has been confidential communication between that party and a third party or documents prepared by or on behalf of that party "for the dominant purpose of preparing for or conducting the proceeding[s]."[6]

---

[4] Section 104, Evidence Act, Cap. 121 of the laws of Barbados.   [5] Ibid., Section 104(1).
[6] Ibid., Section 104(3).

For civil cases, the Supreme Court (Civil Procedure) Rules, 2008 (the "Rules") outline the procedure for seeking to exclude confidential information on the grounds of legal professional privilege where a request for disclosure has been made. This feature is governed by Part 28 of the Rules, which provides that, where reliance is being made on the nondisclosure or non-inspection of documents, due to attorney-client privilege, the individual must "make that claim for the document; and state the grounds on which such a right or privilege is claimed . . . in writing to the person wishing to inspect the document."[7] Part 28 imposes a further requirement for attorneys facing a request for the disclosure of privileged documents to "explain . . . the necessity of making full disclosure in accordance with the terms of the order for disclosure and of [the] Rules; and the possible consequences of failing to do so . . . ."[8]

B Scope

4. The duty of legal professional privilege pertains to all communications between attorneys and their clients. Whether the communications are oral or written, they are protected by this duty and are deemed confidential. Legal professional privilege can be divided into two categories: legal advice privilege and litigation privilege. Regardless of the category of legal professional privilege, an attorney will be bound by the privilege, and because it is a privilege enjoyed by the client and not the attorney, only the client can waive this privilege during legal representation.

As it relates to legal advice privilege, the duty applies not only to communications between the attorney and the client, but also communications between two or more attorneys for the client and communications among employees or agents of the attorneys.[9] Where a document containing or seeking legal advice is prepared by the client or the attorney, the contents of that document will benefit from the privilege, even if the document was never delivered to the intended recipient.[10] Within the ambit of litigation privilege, documents or communications that would be deemed privileged under legal advice privilege would also be privileged. However, additionally, confidential communications between the client, the attorney(s), and the attorney's employees or agents and (a) a third party or (b) the employees or agents of the client will also be deemed privileged, provided that the dominant purpose of the documents or communications was for providing or receiving legal services in actual, anticipated or pending administrative or legal proceedings in which the client is or may be a party.[11]

Litigation privilege introduces a third party (e.g., an expert) into the equation, and such confidential communications and documents are privileged

---

[7] Rule 28.14(1), Supreme Court (Civil Procedure) Rules 2008, Cap. 117A of the laws of Barbados.
[8] Ibid., Rule 28.8.   [9] Section 104(1)(a), Evidence Act.   [10] Ibid., Section 104(1)(b).
[11] Ibid., Section 104(2).

where "the dominant purpose in creating the document (or making the communication) is to use it or its contents to obtain legal advice or help in the conduct of litigation which at that time was at least reasonably in prospect."[12] Further, where a party in legal proceedings is not represented by a legal team and the court is satisfied that there had been confidential communications between that party and a third person or where documents had been prepared by that party or under the party's instructions or request, the court may exclude the communication or documents as privileged.[13]

Section 106 of the Evidence Act further extends the scope of legal professional privilege to cover situations where an interested party would be harmed, if such confidential documents or communications are disclosed during court proceedings. Section 106 provides:

> Where, on the application of a person who is an interested person in relation to a confidential communication or a confidential document, the court finds that, if evidence of the communication or document were to be adduced in the proceedings, the likelihood of harm to an interested person; harm to the relationship in the course of which the confidential communication was made or the confidential document prepared; or harm to relationships of the kind concerned, together with the extent of that harm, outweigh the desirability of admitting the evidence, the court may direct that the evidence not be adduced.[14]

5. In the Barbadian case *Duboff, Edwards, Haight & Schachter v. Crisdar (Barbados) Trade Corporation*,[15] the court was given the additional task of determining whether legal professional privilege could be applied in the case of an attorney compelled to produce confidential communications under an application for the court to assist in obtaining evidence required for proceedings in a foreign jurisdiction.[16] Kentish J, while determining that the attorney in that case could not, based on the facts of that case, be compelled to produce the required documents, also highlighted that an attorney could not be compelled to give evidence that the attorney could not otherwise be compelled to give in civil proceedings in Barbados, as this position would destroy the client's right to claim legal professional privilege and would circumvent the law relating to legal professional privilege.[17]

---

[12] Virginia Dunn, *Be Civil! A Guide to Learning Civil Litigation and Evidence*, Worth Publishing Ltd., p. 219.

[13] Section 104(3), Evidence Act.

[14] Section 106, Evidence Act, Cap. 121 of the laws of Barbados.

[15] *Duboff, Edwards, Haight & Schachter v. Crisdar (Barbados) Trade Corporation*, BB 2002 HC 27.

[16] Section 4, Evidence (Proceedings in Other Jurisdictions) Act, Cap. 121A of the laws of Barbados.

[17] *Duboff, Edwards, Haight & Schachter v. Crisdar (Barbados) Trade Corporation, per* Kentish J at 21.

In recent years, the principle of privilege has been expanded past legal professional privilege and covers communications among attorneys, their clients and a third party – usually the other side – regarding their attempts to reach a settlement between the parties before litigation commences. Communications such as these are generally not accorded legal professional privilege because they are not communications between the client and the attorney. However, the English courts found it necessary to apply a special form of privilege to these pre-action communications to ensure that any concessions made during an attempt to settle would not be admissible as evidence of the respondent's acceptance of liability. This form of evolved privilege has been labeled "without prejudice" privilege, and it covers letters, documents and negotiations (including failed ones) between the parties prior to the start of formal legal proceedings. English authority for "without prejudice" communications is found in *South Shropshire District Council v. Amos*, where it was held that documents prefaced with the words "without prejudice" suggested that the communications were intended to be part of the negotiations and, as such, should be privileged unless there was some other contrary ground for their exclusion.[18]

This principle has been incorporated into legislation by way of Section 110 of the Evidence Act and has been directly applied in Barbados through the 2014 case *Mapp (Nee Callendar) v. Pile and Springer*, where Cornelius J stated;

> In order to determine whether the "without prejudice" privilege attaches to a particular document, the Court is entitled to examine it. ... The Court must then consider whether this communication can be regarded as a bona fide part of or attempt to promote negotiations between the parties. ... The test for determining whether the privilege applies is clearly objective; the subjective intent of the party responsible for the communication in question is understandably of no concern. ... It is the communication itself and the relevant surrounding circumstances as examined by the Court from the perspective of a reasonable recipient that are conclusive. ... The protection given to communication made with the purpose of settling a dispute is, however, itself not absolute, being subject to a number of exceptions."[19]

6. In more recent cases, however, the courts have been less inclined to presume legal privilege solely on the basis of a document being titled "without prejudice" and have decided that there must be a genuine dispute and a genuine attempt to resolve the dispute.[20] Cornelius J also explored this in *Mapp v. Pile and Springer*, where she stated that "[t]he 'without prejudice' rule developed under common law provides that communication made with the genuine intent

---

[18] [1986] 1 WLR 1271, *per* Parker LJ.   [19] BB 2014 HC2 *per* Cornelius J at 28–31.
[20] *Avonwick Holdings Ltd. v. Webinvest Ltd. and Another* [2014] EWHC 3322 (Ch), *per* David Richards J.

of seeking the settlement of a dispute between two or more parties is, as a general rule, privileged from disclosure and cannot be adduced into evidence in subsequent litigation relating to the same subject matter except in certain specific instances."[21] Therefore, although the court held that the "without prejudice" letter was admissible at that stage in the proceedings, it was noted that:

> marking a document with the clause "without prejudice" does not in itself make the letter privileged ... [a]ttaching the clause does not operate to shield those documents from being adduced in litigation. While the Court may take note of any designation placed upon letters that are sought to be admitted into evidence, it must examine the entire content and context of the letter to determine whether it is privileged from admission in a particular case.[22]

This protection, however, generally does not cover any discussions or issues in relation to costs or the parties.

C Persons Subject to the Duty of Professional Secrecy

7.   As noted above, all Barbados attorneys are bound by a duty of confidentiality and secrecy to their clients under the Code. However, given the provisions of the Evidence Act, which extends privileged communications to those between the client and the attorney's employees and agents, it will be necessary to highlight a mandatory provision of the Code that prohibits attorneys from disclosing communications with clients unless lawfully ordered to do so by the court or pursuant to statute and extends the duty of nondisclosure to attorneys' partners, junior attorneys assisting them and their employees.[23] The Code states that, unless lawfully ordered to do so by the court or required to do so by statute, attorneys-at-law shall never disclose what has been communicated by clients to attorneys in their capacity as attorneys. This duty not to disclose extends to partners, assisting junior attorneys and employees. However, attorneys may reveal confidences or secrets necessary to establish or collect fees or to defend themselves or their employees or associates against accusations of wrongful conduct. Attorneys' employees or agents are subject to the duty of legal professional privilege.

D Exceptions to and Optional Derogations from the Duty of Professional Secrecy

8.   Legal professional privilege is generally considered to be an absolute duty on the part of the attorney, with the client being the only party with the right to

---

[21] Ibid., per Cornelius J at 22.   [22] Ibid., per Cornelius J at 54.
[23] Rule 71, Legal Professional Code of Ethics 1988, Cap. 370A of the laws of Barbados.

waive the duty and allow confidential communications or documents to be disclosed.[24] However, there are several exceptions to the rule of legal professional privilege whereby documents or communications will still be admissible despite their confidential nature. For example, where the purpose of adducing evidence is to show the legal competence or intentions of a deceased client or party[25] or to enable the court to enforce a court order,[26] the evidence would be admissible. Other examples of instances where privileged communications will be admissible into evidence include documents affecting the rights of a third party or communications made in the furtherance of the commission of a criminal offense or a civil wrong, or in the furtherance of a deliberate abuse of a power.[27] The rationale for the latter examples is that the attorney-client relationship and any duty of confidentiality accorded thereunder is broken by any illegality.

The above exceptions also apply to the extended principle of without prejudice communications. Unlike standard legal professional privilege, however, which only requires the consent of the client to be waived, without prejudice communications require the consent of all the parties to the communications.[28] Further guidance can be found in common law cases such as the unreported Barbadian case *Wendy Newton v. Barbados Transport Board*,[29] where it was held that the principle of estoppel was an exception to the duty of legal professional privilege. In that case, the plaintiff had sought to rely on a "without prejudice" letter from the defendant in which the defendant had accepted liability for the accident giving rise to her claim, as well as the defendant's subsequent conduct, to argue that the defendant was estopped from raising the limitation point at trial. Walrond J (acting) examined the contents of the "without prejudice" letter and held that it was admissible. She appeared to do so on the basis that it contained a clear statement made by one party that was intended to be and was in fact relied upon by the other and therefore operated as an estoppel.

A more recent example of the ability of an attorney to disclose confidential communications between the attorney and a client would be where the attorney is legally obligated to do so by statute. The main source of this "legislative override" is derived from the *Money Laundering and Financing of Terrorism (Prevention and Control) Act*, 2011–23, which will be discussed later in this chapter.

E Law Firms

9. Confidential information and documents are often passed among members of a law firm. Because of the nature of legal practice in a firm and the reality that any member of a firm can be assigned to a client's file, all attorneys will be

---

[24] Section 105(1), Evidence Act. [25] Ibid., Section 105(2). [26] Ibid., Section 105(3).
[27] Ibid., Sections 105(5), (12). [28] Ibid., Section 110(2)(a), (b).
[29] *Wendy Newton v. Barbados Transport Board* (unreported) High Court of Barbados Civil Suit No. 2297 of 2001.

jointly bound by the duty of confidentiality to all of the firm's clients, whether they have immediate contact with the particular client or not.[30]

F Legal Assistants and Staff

10. Although the Code applies principally to attorneys, so as to outline the expected duties and obligations, the duty of confidentiality mandated by the Code is extended to the attorney's employees.[31] As previously mentioned in this chapter, the Evidence Act also contemplates communications of the attorney's employees and agents within the ambit of communications and documents governed by legal professional privilege. It could therefore be implied that all legal staff assisting the attorney on a client's file, be they junior attorneys, paralegals, clerks, legal secretaries and the like, would be bound by legal professional privilege. However, as noted above, the test for whether communications with the attorney's employees will be privileged will depend on whether the dominant purpose of the communication is for legal advice or the provision of legal services.

G External Service Providers

11. Attorneys are not permitted to enter into partnerships or fee-sharing arrangements with non-legal professionals.[32] However, as the world of business and the demands of clients have evolved, so too have the interactions between attorneys and external service providers. Hence, attorneys are now required to engage the services of many external service providers to remain competitive and effective in their fields of practice. External bodies that work in conjunction with attorneys, or on behalf of attorneys, are bound by legal professional privilege. Although there is no express authority, it is presumed that any confidential communications or documents in the possession of external bodies is considered privileged. However, under Rule 73 of the Code,[33] "an attorney-at-law shall not delegate to a person not legally qualified and not in his employ or under his control, any functions which are by the laws of Barbados only to be performed by a qualified attorney-at-law."

H Multidisciplinary Associations

12. As previously noted, attorneys are restricted from partnering with non-legal professionals. However, in many instances, the attorney will need to work closely with such other professionals to properly advise the client. For example, an attorney engaged to assist a client with multijurisdictional matters may need to engage or correspond with legal counsel abroad. Or, in complex global structures, an attorney may need to correspond with banking, business and

---

[30] Section 104, Evidence Act.   [31] Rule 71, Legal Professional Code of Ethics, 1988.
[32] Ibid., Rule 65.   [33] Ibid., Rule 73.

85

accounting personnel acting for the client both locally and abroad. In these cases, there is likely to be information transmitted between the attorney and these parties that is confidential to the client's business. Whether such correspondence will be held to be privileged or not will depend on the dominant purpose of the communications, as outlined above. Authority for the privilege being extended to foreign lawyers can be found in the English case *Re Duncan, Garfield v. Fay*, where Ormrod J (as he was at the time) did not find that the existing case law was intended to limit the rule of legal professional privilege to lawyers registered in England but was rather apt to cover foreign legal advisers as local lawyers.[34] However, the courts were reluctant to extend the privilege to non-legal professionals giving legal advice where there had been correspondence from tax advisers to the client giving legal advice.[35]

I In-House Counsel

13.   There is no distinction in Barbados between attorneys who work exclusively for a company, known as in-house attorneys, and other attorneys in private practice. Much of the common law relating to legal professional privilege was developed with private practice attorneys in mind. However, as the profession has developed, so too has the law developed and the concept of legal professional privilege now equally extends to counsel both in-house and in private practice. Lord Denning in *Alfred Crompton Amusement Machines Ltd. v. Customs and Excise Commissioners (No. 2)* gave the following statement of in-house lawyers who, despite being a servant or agent of a single employer, were:

> regarded by the law as in every respect in the same position as those who practice for their own account. The only difference is that they act for one client only, and not for several clients. They must uphold the same standards of honour and etiquette. They are subject to the same duties to their client and to the court. They must respect the same confidences. They and their clients have the same privileges. ... I speak, of course [only] of their communications in the capacity of legal advisers.[36]

2 History of the Duty of Professional Secrecy in Barbados

14.   Prior to 1973, there was no legislation in place in Barbados that sought to govern the admissibility into evidence of communications or documents held in confidence between attorneys and their clients. As an inheritor of the English common law rules, the duty of legal professional privilege in Barbados was

---

[34] [1968] at 311.

[35] *R v. Special Commissioner and Another, ex parte Morgan Grenfell & Co Limited* [2002] UKHL 21; *R (on the application of Prudential plc and another) (Appellants) v. Special Commissioner of Income Tax and another (Respondents)* [2013] UKSC 1.

[36] [1979] 2 QB 102, *per* Lord Denning MR at 129.

derived from much of the English case law and, in particular, the case of *Minter v. Priest*,[37] decided by the House of Lords. In *Minter*, the court held that "communications passing between a solicitor and a prospective client with a view to the client retaining the solicitor on professional business are privileged from disclosure, even if the solicitor does not accept the retainer."[38] The case further stated that "where the relation of solicitor and client is established, any conversation passing between them, to be protected from disclosure, must be fairly referable to that relation; it must be for the purpose of giving or receiving professional advice."[39]

The basis for implementing the privilege was a policy decision focused on ensuring that a client was "able to consult his lawyer in confidence, since otherwise he might hold back half the truth."[40] The English courts recognized that clients were more likely to provide their attorney with enough information to properly represent them if they could do so "without fear that they may afterwards be disclosed and used to [their] prejudice."[41] The courts went further in stating that legal professional privilege exceeded the bounds of merely an ordinary rule of evidence and was " ... a fundamental condition on which the administration of justice as a whole rest[ed]."[42] As such, it should not be "confined to telling the client the law ... [but] must include advice as to what should prudently and sensibly be done in the relevant legal context ...."[43]

However, it was noted early on that it was important to find a balance between "making the maximum relevant material available to the court of trial and avoiding unfairness to individuals by revealing confidential communications between their lawyers and themselves."[44] This view led the courts to develop the rule of examining the dominant purpose of the communications as the best method of resolving the competing principles – namely, whether there should be full disclosure of relevant material during litigation and whether there must be effective maintenance of legal professional privilege.[45]

15. Initially, the privilege was restricted only to communications concerning litigation. However, the English courts took it a step further in deciding that "subject to recognised exceptions, communications seeking professional legal advice, whether or not in connection with pending court proceedings, are absolutely and permanently privileged from disclosure."[46] Thus, the courts further developed the principle so that legal professional privilege could be divided into two

---

[37] [1930] AC 558.   [38] Ibid.   [39] Ibid.
[40] *R v. Derby Magistrates' Court Ex p. B* [1996] AC 487, *per* Lord Taylor of Gosforth CJ at 507, quoting *Belabel v. Air India* [1988] Ch. 317.
[41] *R v. Special Commissioner of Income Tax Ex. p Morgan Grenfell & Co Limited* [2002] UKHL 21, *per* Lord Hoffman at 7.
[42] Ibid., *per* Lord Taylor at 507.   [43] *Balabel v. Air India* [1988] 1 Ch 317, *per* Taylor LJ at 330.
[44] *Seabrook v. British Transport Commission* [1959] 1 WLR 509, *per* Havers J at 513.
[45] *Waugh v. British Railways Board* [1980] AC 521, *per* Lord Edmund-Davies at 543.
[46] *R v. Derby Magistrates' Court Ex p. B* [1996] AC 487, *per* Lord Nicholls of Birkenhead at 510.

categories: litigation privilege (legal advice given in anticipation of legal proceedings or pending legal proceedings) and legal advice privilege (legal advice given irrespective of the existence of litigation, contemplated litigation or pending litigation).

The justification for implementing this privilege was supported by Lord Scott in the *Three Rivers* case, where he set out four main policy reasons for retaining legal advice privilege:

> First, legal advice privilege arises out of a relationship of confidence between lawyer and client. Unless the communication or document for which privilege is sought is a confidential one, there can be no question of legal advice privilege arising. The confidential character of the communication or document is not by itself enough to enable privilege to be claimed but is an essential requirement. Second, if a communication or document qualifies for legal professional privilege, the privilege is absolute. It cannot be overridden by some supposedly greater public interest. It can be waived by the person, the client, entitled to it and it can be overridden by statute . . . but it is otherwise absolute. . . . Third, legal advice privilege gives the person entitled to it the right to decline to disclose or to allow to be disclosed the confidential communication or document in question. . . . Fourth, legal advice privilege has an undoubted relationship with litigation privilege. Legal advice is frequently sought or given in connection with current or contemplated litigation. But it may equally well be sought or given in circumstances and for purposes that have nothing to do with litigation. If it is sought or given in connection with litigation, then the advice would fall into both the two categories. . . . On the other hand it has been held that litigation and privilege can extend to communications between a lawyer or the lawyer's client and a third party or to any document brought into existence for the dominant purpose of the litigation. The connection between legal advice sought or given and the affording of privilege to the communication has thereby been cut.[47]

16.   With the passing of the Act and the Code, the duty of legal professional privilege has been governed by Barbadian law. Under Rule 71 of the Code:

> An attorney-at-law shall never disclose, unless lawfully ordered to do so by the Court or required by statute, what has been communicated to him in his capacity as an attorney-at-law by his client and this duty not to disclose extends to his partners, to junior attorneys-at-law assisting him and to his employees provided however that an attorney-at-law may reveal confidences or secrets necessary to establish or collect his fee or to defend himself or his employees or associates against an accusation of wrongful conduct.[48]

---

[47] *Three Rivers District Council and Others (Respondents) v. Governor and Company of the Bank of England (Appellants)* [2004] UKHL 48, *per* Lord Scott of Foscote at 24–27.

[48] Rule 71, Legal Professional Code of Ethics 1988, Cap. 370A of the laws of Barbados.

3 Supervision

A The Bar Associations

17.   The Barbados Bar Association (the "Bar Association") is tasked with the governance and supervision of the conduct and duties of attorneys and derives its disciplinary powers from the Bar Association Act[49] and the Act. The Bar Association, together with the committee established by the Act and known as the Disciplinary Committee (the "Committee"), are responsible for upholding the standards of professional conduct within the legal profession. The Committee is the body responsible for issuing the Code and acts as the tribunal for hearing disciplinary matters.[50] The Disciplinary Committee is composed of seven attorneys-at-law who are nominated by the Barbados Bar Association in writing and addressed to the Registrar of the Supreme Court. At least three of the members of the Disciplinary Committee must have no less than 10 years' standing in the legal profession, and, from this senior group, a chair and a deputy chair must be elected by the Disciplinary Committee. Members can serve for up to two years but are eligible for re-nomination.

B The Courts

18.   A client can bring a claim in the Barbados courts against an attorney for breach of legal professional privilege accorded by legislation. A breach of the mandatory rules of the Code constitutes professional misconduct. An attorney who commits such a breach shall be liable to any of the penalties that the Disciplinary Committee recommends and that the Court of Appeal is empowered to impose.[51] The other provisions of the Code, while not mandatory, may still amount to professional misconduct.[52]

4 Sanctions

A Proceedings and Sanctions

19.   As noted above, the Committee was set up to deal with disciplinary issues pertaining to members of the Bar of Barbados. Accordingly, pursuant to Section 19 of the Act, a client, or a third party granted leave by the Committee, who alleges to have been aggrieved by an act of professional misconduct (including any default) on the part of an attorney may apply to the Committee to require the attorney to answer allegations contained in an affidavit made by such person. The Registrar of the Supreme Court of Barbados or any member of the Committee may also make a similar application to the Committee with respect to any allegations concerning professional

---

[49] Cap. 363 of the laws of Barbados.   [50] Section 18, Legal Profession Act.
[51] Rule 90(1), Legal Profession Code of Ethics, 1988.   [52] Ibid., Rule 90(2).

misconduct against an attorney, including misconduct that would constitute grave professional misconduct. The latter would include specified criminal offenses. During any court proceedings, if the court is of the opinion that an act of professional misconduct has been committed by an attorney other than the Attorney-General or the Director of Public Prosecutions, the court has discretion to cause the Registrar of the Supreme Court to make an application to the Committee with respect to that attorney.[53]

Where an application for misconduct is made to the Committee under the Act, the Committee has the powers of the High Court with respect to its power to summon witnesses, call for the production of books and documents, and examine witnesses and parties concerned under oath.[54] Pursuant to Section 21 of the Act, after a hearing, where the Committee decides that a case of professional misconduct has been made out against an attorney, the Committee has 21 days to issue its decision and forward it to the Chief Justice with reasons for its decision as well as any recommendations. These recommendations may include the removal of the attorney's name from the roll, suspension of the attorney subject to conditions determined by the Committee, the imposition of a fine on the attorney, imprisonment or the payment of the costs of any party to the misconduct proceedings.[55]

Once the Chief Justice has received the Committee's report of its decision, the Court of Appeal is required to consider the decision and any recommendations listed therein. The Court of Appeal may refer the report back to the Committee for its findings on any point, and it also has the authority to dismiss any application. Alternatively, the Court of Appeal has the discretionary power to grant an order for pecuniary measures against the attorney, as previously noted.[56] Under Rule 90 of the Code, where an attorney has been found in breach of the duty of professional conduct, the attorney will be liable for any other penalties that the Disciplinary Committee recommends and that the Court of Appeal is empowered to impose.[57]

B Relationship between Criminal Sanctions and Disciplinary Sanctions

20.   While there is no express link between criminal sanctions and disciplinary sanctions imposed on attorneys, given that the proceedings for each are kept separate, there is a link between the commencement of disciplinary action and the threat of actual, pending or suspected proceedings for a criminal offense against the attorney. This view is supported since an attorney may be found in breach of the Code where that attorney has committed a criminal offense that the Committee considers is likely to bring the legal profession into disrepute.[58]

---

[53] Section 19, Legal Profession Act.   [54] Ibid., Section 20.   [55] Ibid., Section 21.
[56] Section 22, Legal Profession Act.
[57] Rule 90, Legal Profession Code of Ethics 1988, Cap. 370A of the laws of Barbados.
[58] Ibid., Rule 63.

Furthermore, the principle applies even if the attorney has been convicted of any offense by a Barbados court or a foreign court of competent jurisdiction or where the attorney has not been prosecuted, but the Committee is satisfied of the facts constituting the criminal offense. The Committee may also find that the attorney is in breach of the conduct provisions of the Code where (a) the attorney had been prosecuted for a criminal offense and was subsequently acquitted or (b) where the attorney was convicted but the conviction was subsequently quashed, by reason of a technical defense.[59]

5 Duty to Provide Information to the Authorities

A Money Laundering and Terrorism

21.　The Money Laundering and Financing of Terrorism (Prevention and Control) Act, 2011–23 (MLFTA) is Barbados' main legislative instrument geared toward combatting money laundering and the financing of terrorism. Apart from the obligations to collect and maintain adequate information on clients for due diligence purposes, the MLFTA also contains reporting requirements that interfere with the otherwise absolute nature of legal professional privilege. Independent attorneys who are engaged in the purchase, sale or disposal of real property; the management of money, securities or other assets of a client; the management of bank savings or securities accounts; the organization of contributions for the creation, operation or management of bodies corporate; the creation, operation or management of legal persons or arrangements; or the purchase or sale of business entities are deemed nonfinancial institutions for the purposes of the MLFTA.[60]

Where caught, attorneys are required to monitor and report to the Financial Intelligence Unit (FIU) of the Anti-Money Laundering Authority on transactions for which there are reasonable grounds to suspect that the transaction involves the proceeds of a crime or the financing of terrorist activity or is of a suspicious nature.[61] In addition, these attorneys are required to report to the director of the FIU on any currency exchanges or wire transfer instructions that appear to be of a suspicious or unusual nature.[62] Failure to comply with these provisions is an indictable offense, punishable on conviction by a fine. There are additional reporting requirements outlined in Sections 30 and 48(5) of the MLFTA.

It is clear that there will be instances where complying with the MLFTA's reporting provisions will require an attorney to disclose information that would otherwise be subject to legal professional privilege. However, the MLFTA

---

[59] Ibid., Section 63 Legal Profession Code of Ethics 1988.
[60] Second Schedule, para. 3, Money Laundering and Financing of Terrorism (Prevention and Control) Act, 2011–23.
[61] Ibid., Section 23(1)(a).　　[62] Ibid., Section 23(1)(b).

provides a form of immunity from suit for breach of confidence through Section 48(6), where it states that no action, suit or proceeding would lie against attorneys or their officers, employees or agents acting in the course of their employment in relation to their complying with the reporting requirements under the MLFTA.

B Collective Settlement of Debts

22.   There is currently no express provision under the laws of Barbados that governs an attorney's duty in relation to the collective settlement of debts from clients, by a third party.

6 Treatment of Lawyers' Documents and Correspondence in the Context of Judicial or Police Investigations

23.   Under the Constitution of Barbados, citizens of Barbados are afforded the right to have freedom from deprivation of their property. Article 16 provides that "No property of any description shall be compulsorily taken possession of, and no interest or right over property of any description shall be compulsorily acquired, except by or under the authority of a written law, and where provision applying to that acquisition or taking of possession is made by a written law." In *R v. Leeds CC ex parte Switalski*,[63] the documents belonging to a lawyer that were used for criminal purposes, were not covered by legal professional privilege. Here, it was held that the firm was under investigation. Fraud on the legal aid fund and conspiracy to pervert the course of justice were alleged. Exceptionally, it was unnecessary to exclude items subject to legal privilege since it was impossible to anticipate which items were excluded from privilege. Bearing in mind these two contrasting outcomes, it is safe to presume that in Barbados the two differing situations are likely to produce the intended consequences as above stated.

7 Search of a Lawyer's Office

24.   Under the Constitution of Barbados, citizens of Barbados are afforded the right to have freedom from unlawful search. As a citizen of Barbados, an attorney also shares the same rights and freedoms as every other citizen. Article 17 of the Constitution provides:

> Except with his own consent, no person shall be subjected to the search of his person or his property or the entry by others on his premises . . . for the purpose of authorising an officer or agent of the Government, or of a local government authority or of a body corporate established directly by law

---

[63]   [1991] CLR 559.

for public purposes ... for the purpose of authorising the entry upon any premises in pursuance of an order of a court for the purpose of enforcing the judgment or order of a court in any proceedings ... or ... for the purpose of authorising the entry upon any premises for the purpose of preventing or detecting criminal offences.

However, there are certain situations that render it possible for an attorney's office to be searched. Such situations include that of suspected criminal activity and situations arising out of public interest immunity.

The magistrate's court has wide powers to issue a warrant to order the search and seizure of any premises that belong to, or are in the possession or control of, an attorney or any officer or employee of an attorney. The warrant may be issued where the magistrate is satisfied by evidence under oath that there are reasonable grounds to believe that an attorney has not complied with the records-keeping or reporting requirements under the MLFTA or where an officer or employee of the attorney is involved in an act of money laundering or terrorist financing.[64] Where a magistrate is satisfied by evidence under oath that there are reasonable grounds to believe that an attorney has committed an offense under the MLFTA or that the attorney's premises or any other place may be housing a document or other article that may provide proof of the commission of an offense under the MLFTA, the magistrate may issue a general warrant for search and seizure.[65]

The MLFTA provides for an interested party to request the return of any document or article that was seized. However, the MLFTA only allows for the return where the document or article will not be required for investigations or proceedings under that piece of legislation.[66] It is not clear how the courts in Barbados will balance the objection of a seized document being entered into evidence under the MLFTA where that seized document would otherwise be accorded protection under legal professional privilege.

8 Tapping of Telephone Conversations with a Lawyer

25.   There are certain situations that render it possible for an attorney's telephone to be tapped. Such situations include cases of suspected criminal activity and situations arising out of public interest immunity.

9 The Lawyer as Witness

26.   Under the Code, attorneys are restricted from appearing as a witness for their own client, except where the evidence to be given is in relation to a merely

---

[64] Section 39, Money Laundering and Financing of Terrorism (Prevention and Control) Act 2011–23.
[65] Ibid., Section 40.   [66] Ibid., Section 41.

formal matter or where the attorney's appearance is essential to the ends of justice.[67] However, there is no express exemption accorded to attorneys under the Evidence Act against being compelled to give evidence. An attorney would therefore be required to attend to give evidence but would object to answering certain questions or disclosing certain information on the grounds of his protection under legal professional privilege.

10 The Lawyer and the Press

27.   Attorneys are prohibited under the Code from divulging their client's secrets and confidences and should therefore refrain from discussing their client's cases in the media, except where the client gives consent.[68] It is also a mandatory provision of the Code that attorneys should not advertise for business indirectly by involving themselves in newspaper comment about cases or causes with which the attorney has been or is connected.[69]

11 Powers of the Tax Administration and Other Authorities

28.   Under Section 76 of the Income Tax Act[70] (ITA), the Commissioner of Inland Revenue (the "Commissioner") and any person authorized by the Commissioner have wide powers relating to the administration or enforcement of the provisions of the ITA. They may, at any reasonable time, enter into a person's premises or place of business or place where business records are kept to, among other things, audit or examine the books and records and any other document that would assist in ascertaining a person's tax liability under the ITA.[71] As part of the audit powers granted under the ITA, the Commissioner may require persons, including an attorney, to produce information by way of a registered letter request or a personally served demand.

The ITA recognizes that in some instances an attorney may be required to disclose information that is privileged. Accordingly, by way of Section 77 of the ITA, the legislation provides that, where attorneys are prosecuted for failure to comply with a requirement under Section 76 of the ITA to give information or produce a document, attorneys would be acquitted provided that they could satisfy the Court that (a) they had reasonable grounds for believing that the information or document was privileged in connection with a named client and (b) that they informed the Commissioner within the required seven-day deadline of their belief that the requested document or information was privileged.

Where the Commissioner exercises the power of seizure under the ITA and, in the process of examining or seizing a document, the officer of the

---

[67] Rule 39(1), Legal Profession Code of Ethics 1988, Cap. 370A of the laws of Barbados.
[68] Ibid., Rule 26(2).   [69] Ibid., Rule 62(3).   [70] Cap. 73 of the laws of Barbados.
[71] Section 76(1), Income Tax Act, Cap. 73 of the laws of Barbados.

Commissioner is advised that the document is protected by legal professional privilege, that person is required to cease examining the document and is restricted from making any copies of the document. However, the examining person still has the power to seize the document and to forward it for safe-keeping by the Registrar of the Supreme Court. This allows the Registrar to accept an application by the attorney to a Judge in Chambers for an order determining whether the document is indeed privileged. Only the judge presiding over the hearing will have the power to inspect the document that was seized. To protect the client's interests, the attorney is required to make the application within 30 days of its being lodged with the Registrar, failing which, it will be deemed that the legal privilege accorded to the document in question had been waived. Notwithstanding the above, the client still has the right to waive any legal professional privilege accorded to a document being inspected by the Commissioner or authorized staff.[72]

12 National Security Issues

29.   The legal professional privilege between an attorney and a client is protected only where the admission of the confidential information is deemed to be outweighed by the preservation of such information. Section 109(1) of the Evidence Act provides that the preservation of the privilege must be in the public interest. However, where such information concerns "matters of state," which includes evidence relating to "the security or defence of Barbados . . . or the prevention or detection of offences or contraventions of the law," the information will be admissible notwithstanding Section 104 of the Evidence Act.[73]

---

[72] Ibid., Section 77.   [73] Section 109, Evidence Act 1995, Cap. 121 of the laws of Barbados.

7

Belize

EAMON H. COURTENAY SC
ILIANA N. SWIFT
Courtenay Coye LLP

Preliminary Note

1.   Individuals are qualified to practice as attorneys in Belize after being admitted to practice law and after their names have been enrolled on the roll of attorneys-at-law kept by the Registrar of the Supreme Court.[1] At common law, an attorney's client has the right to attorney-client privilege in relation to legal advice and documents prepared in anticipation or during the course of litigation.[2] This common law right is further protected as a fundamental right under the Belize Constitution, which guarantees individuals protection from arbitrary search or unlawful interference with their correspondence.[3]

However, the privilege is not absolute; it may be waived by the client or limited by statute. Where a communication with an attorney is made to further some criminal purpose, a wrongful act or fraud, attorney-client privilege would not apply.[4] If a complaint of professional misconduct is made, attorneys may rely on an otherwise privileged communication to defend themselves.[5]

1 Scope of and Limitations on the Duty of Professional Secrecy/ Attorney-Client Privilege

A Statutory Basis and Implications

2.   The basis for attorney-client privilege is found both in statute and common law. Attorneys-at-law have both a legal and professional ethical duty to keep confidential all communications with clients in their capacity as attorneys. This ethical obligation extends to other attorneys-at-law and administrative staff in their firms.

The Belize Constitution provides two important protections that relate to attorney-client privilege. The first can be found in Section 14 of the Belize Constitution, the supreme law of Belize.[6] That section provides:

(1) A person shall not be subjected to arbitrary or unlawful interference with his privacy, family, home or correspondence, nor to unlawful attacks on his honour and reputation. The private and family life, the home or correspondence of every person shall be respected.

(2) Nothing contained in or done under the authority of any law shall be held to be inconsistent with or in contravention of this Section to the extent that the law in question makes provision of the kind specified in Subsection (2) of Section 9 of this Constitution.

---

[1] Sections 5–8, Legal Profession Act, Cap. 320 as amended by Acts No. 22 of 2004 and No. 22 of 2014.
[2] The Caribbean Civil Court Practice, 2nd ed., Note 24.25.
[3] Sections 9, 14, Belize Constitution, Cap. 4.   [4] Section 61(3), Evidence Act, Cap. 94.
[5] Rule 66, Legal Profession Regulations.   [6] Section 2, Belize Constitution.

The Constitution therefore provides strong protection of an individual's, including a client's, right to privacy of his or her correspondence. As discussed later in this chapter, this fundamental right is not absolute but subject to derogations set out in the Constitution.

Secondly, Section 9 of the Belize Constitution guarantees protection against the search of a person or such person's property or the entry by others on such person's premises. Section 9 of the Belize Constitution states:

(1) Except with his own consent, a person shall not be subjected to the search of his person or his property or the entry by others on his premises.

(2) Nothing contained in or done under the authority of any law shall be held to be inconsistent with or in contravention of this Section to the extent that the law in question makes reasonable provision–

    (a) that is required in the interests of defence, public safety, public order, public morality, public health, town and country planning, the development and utilisation of mineral resources of the development or utilisation of any property for a purpose beneficial to the community;

    (b) that is required for the purpose of protecting the rights or freedoms of other persons;

    (c) that authorises an officer or agent of the Government, a local government authority or a body corporate established by law for public purposes to enter on the premises of any person in order to inspect those premises or anything thereon for the purpose of any tax, rate or due or in order to carry out work connected with any property that is lawful on those premises and that belongs to the Government or to that authority or body corporate, as the case may be; or

    (d) that authorises, for the purpose of enforcing the judgment or order of the court in any civil proceedings, the search of any person or property by order of a court or entry upon any premises by such order.

The primary purpose of this fundamental right, as it relates to the attorney-client relationship, is that it provides strong protection against the search of the person, the property and the premises of both the attorney and the client.

3.   Attorney-client privilege is also recognized by Section 61 of the Evidence Act, which limits the admissibility of confidential communications between an attorney and a client. The section provides a shield against disclosure – whether it is compulsory or voluntary – with respect to the oral or written confidential communications between the attorney and a client. Importantly, the privilege attaches to communications, oral or written, given by the client to the attorney, and to the advice given by the attorney to the client. Section 61(1) provides:

> A legal adviser or his client shall not be compelled to disclose any confidential communication, oral or written, which passed between them, directly or indirectly through an agent of either, and such communication was made for the purposed of obtaining or giving legal advice.

The critical factor for the applicability of this privilege is the existence of an attorney-client relationship. For the privilege to apply, it is not necessary that litigation be contemplated or pending.[7] The privilege does not apply if the communication was made for the purpose of committing a fraud, crime or other wrongful act. This privilege provides strong protection to the client and the attorney-at-law. It is broad and likely to be defeated in very limited circumstances.

The client's protection under the Evidence Act operates in conjunction with the attorney's professional ethical obligation. Pursuant to Rule 66 of the Legal Profession (Code of Conduct) Rules, attorneys should not disclose any communications between themselves and their clients. Rule 66 states:

> An attorney shall never disclose, unless lawfully ordered to do so by the Court or required by statute, what has been communicated to him in his capacity as an attorney by his client and this duty not to disclose extends to his partners to junior attorneys assisting him and to his employees provided however that an attorney may reveal confidences or secrets necessary to establish or collect his fees or to defend himself or his employees or associates against an accusation of wrongful conduct.

4. The rules governing civil procedure in the Supreme Court also recognize a client's right to withhold from disclosure privileged information.[8] If such privileged information has been inadvertently disclosed, the party inspecting the document cannot rely on it without the permission of the court or the party disclosing the document.[9]

B Scope

5. An attorney's duty of confidentiality covers a wide scope of communications. Rule 66 of the Legal Profession (Code of Conduct) Rules states rather generally that an attorney is prohibited from disclosing "what has been communicated to him in his capacity as an attorney by his client." Therefore, an attorney is obligated to keep confidential written and oral communications, unless required to disclose such communications by way of court order or statutory requirement.

The scope of an attorney's professional obligation is mirrored by the protection afforded the client pursuant to Section 61 of the Evidence Act. Section 61 provides that a client may claim legal professional privilege in

---

[7] Section 61(2), Evidence Act. [8] Rule 28.14, Supreme Court (Civil Procedure) Rules, 2005.
[9] Ibid., Rule 28.15.

relation to any confidential written or oral communications between the client and the attorney if the communication was made for the purpose of obtaining or giving legal advice, whether or not litigation was pending or contemplated.

The privilege, however, does not apply to communications made for the purpose of committing a fraud, crime or other wrongful act. Therefore, an attorney may be legally compelled to disclose any communications with a client made for the purpose of committing an offence or wrongful act.

C Persons Subject to the Duty of Professional Secrecy

6. The duty to maintain client confidentiality is one of the main professional and ethical duties of attorneys-at-law practicing law in Belize. The legal professional privilege belongs to the client, not the attorney or a third party. Therefore, unless lawfully compelled, only the client can waive the privilege.[10] The confidentiality of a client's communications ought to be respected by any third party, including the judiciary, opposing parties, their legal representatives and public authorities.

An attorney's duty to preserve the confidentiality of a client's communication subsists even after the attorney-client relationship has ended. In *Narda Garcia v. Senator Godwin Hulse et al.*,[11] the claimant had challenged *inter alia* the appointment of a Special Senate Select Committee. Counsel for the claimant was previously the Solicitor General of Belize. While representing the claimant, counsel filed an affidavit indicating that, as Solicitor General, he had advised the Attorney General regarding the appointment of the Committee and had met with members of the Committee on several occasions. The court was of the view that he had breached his duty to preserve the confidentiality of information that had been imparted to him while he was the Solicitor General.

Similarly, in *Belize Telemedia Ltd. v. Lois M. Young doing business as Lois Young Barrow & Co.*,[12] the respondent was the appellant's legal adviser between 1987 and 2001 and the company secretary from 1987 to 2004. The Court of Appeal of Belize found that it was improper for the respondent to represent a former employee of the appellant against the appellant in a claim for unlawful termination of her employment. In its unanimous decision, the Court held that the core issue was not the conduct of the attorney or the conflict of interest, but the mere risk of disclosure of confidential information. The court affirmed[13] *Prince Jefri Bolkiah v. KPMG*[14], where it was held:

> [W]here it was established that solicitors or accountants providing litigation services were in possession of information confidential to a former client which might be relevant to a matter in which they were

---

[10] The Caribbean Civil Court Practice, 2nd ed., Note 24.30.
[11] Action No. 496 of 2006 at para. 23.   [12] Civil Appeal No. 19 of 2008.   [13] Ibid., para. 3.
[14] [1999] 2 A C 222

instructed by a subsequent client the court should intervene to prevent the information from coming into the hands of anyone with an adverse interest unless it was satisfied that there was no real risk of disclosure.

Statutes also mandate that certain public authorities must respect legal professional privilege while conducting searches and seizures. The Money Laundering and Terrorism (Prevention) Act[15] provides that a person shall not be required to disclose, and the inspecting officer cannot inspect, documents subject to legal professional privilege. The Freedom of Information Act[16] also provides that the government is not required to disclose any information that is covered by legal professional privilege. Additionally, the judiciary is limited by the Evidence Act[17] from admitting into evidence in legal proceedings any communications that are protected by legal professional privilege.

D Exceptions to and Optional Derogations from the Duty of Professional Secrecy

a Exceptions

7. Attorney-client privilege is not an absolute privilege and is therefore subject to several statutory exceptions that are, in essence, a codification of the common law position.

A client's protection of privacy and protection from arbitrary search and seizure and entry is subject to the exception of laws enacted in the public interest. There are a number of statutes that recognize attorney-client privilege but also recognize exceptions to such privilege.

The Evidence Act[18] sets out the specific instances in which a claim of privilege from disclosure does not apply. Section 61(3) of the act stipulates that communications made for the purposes of committing a crime, fraud or other wrongful act would not be covered by legal professional privilege.[19] A similar exception can be found in the Money Laundering and Terrorism (Prevention) Act,[20] which obliges an attorney to disclose privileged information if the information was communicated for some criminal purpose.

Under the Money Laundering and Terrorism (Prevention) Act, attorneys-at-law are designated reporting entities[21] and, as such, are required to take preventative measures against crimes such as money laundering and terrorist financing. This act assigns duties to attorneys that are not normally associated with their profession. These duties, which include having to report the particulars of a client to external authorities on the mere suspicion of an illicit transaction,[22] leave attorneys in precarious positions because the legislation effectively binds them both to their clients and to the state.

---

[15] Section 17(9). [16] Section 28(2). [17] Section 61(3). [18] Cap. 95, 2000. [19] Ibid.
[20] Act No. 18 of 2008. [21] Ibid., First Schedule of the Act, No. 26. [22] Ibid., Section 17(4).

Additionally, if clients accuse their attorneys of professional misconduct pursuant to the Legal Profession Act of Belize,[23] the attorneys may disclose privileged information to defend themselves. In the application, an affidavit alleging the facts of the misconduct ought to be submitted to the General Legal Council. It follows that, in answer, attorneys may disclose privileged information when defending themselves as a part of those proceedings. Pursuant to the Legal Profession Act, the Council is empowered to summon witnesses and "call for the production of books and documents."[24] However, it would seem that this exception generally applies to clients acting against their attorneys; this would not apply to third parties seeking to establish professional misconduct, except in extraordinary circumstances for a specific purpose.

b Derogations

8. While the release of privileged information may occur as a result of statutory exceptions, at common law the privilege may also be lifted.

The privilege belongs to the client and not the attorney.[25] Therefore, a client may waive such privilege by consenting to disclosure of the communication. This position in common law is also recognized in the Supreme Court (Civil Procedure) Rules, 2005, in which Rule 28.14 gives the litigant the option to determine whether to withhold disclosure of documents, and Rule 29.15 provides that a litigant may agree to the use of a document that has been inadvertently disclosed. The privilege may also be deemed to have lapsed where the client has disclosed the contents of communications to the same parties in another proceeding. In such circumstances, the client cannot refuse disclosure of the document on the basis of legal professional privilege.

E Law Firms

9. It is not uncommon for attorneys working in the same firm to share information with each other; this may also apply to privileged information. Most often, this occurs in the context of attorneys working together on a given case. This is an accepted practice because, in engaging the service of an attorney, a relationship is forged between the client and the firm, not a particular attorney. This would also be true in the case of a senior attorney delegating work to junior attorneys. Consequently, as recognized in Rule 66 of the Legal Profession (Code of Conduct) Rules, co-counsel on a case would be bound by the same duty of confidentiality to the client. The same principle applies where multiple firms are representing a client in the same matter.

The Bar Association in Belize is relatively small. Therefore, it is very likely that, whenever an attorney migrates to a new firm, that firm might have several matters in opposition to the old firm. The duty of confidentiality subsists, and

---

[23] Section 15, Cap. 320.   [24] Section 16(4), No. 22 of 2014.

[25] *Belize Telemedia Ltd. v. Young (doing business as Lois Young Barrow & Co.)*, at 19.

the practice in Belize is to fully disclose the situation to the respective clients and, if acceptable to the clients, to create an ethical wall. Attorneys would therefore not have any interaction or communications at their new firm regarding any pending matters at their previous firm. The courts have frowned upon attorneys acting in matters against former clients whose confidential information they may have. In the case of *Belize Telemedia Ltd.*, mentioned earlier, the Court of Appeal granted an injunction restraining an attorney from proceeding against her former client, Belize Telemedia Ltd., where it was likely that she was in possession of confidential information and there was a risk of disclosure.

F Legal Assistants and Staff

10. Law firms in Belize employ administrative staff to carry out the firm's daily operations. This includes, but is not limited to, secretaries, paralegals and messengers. Members of the administrative staff are not allowed to practice as attorneys-at-law under the Legal Profession Act.[26] However, they may occasionally have access to confidential client information to facilitate the attorney's work for the client. They are likewise obliged to keep such information confidential in the interest of maintaining attorney-client privilege. The current practice is to familiarize administrative staff during the orientation period of the need to maintain confidentiality regarding all communications at the firm. The administrative staff is therefore both legally and professionally bound to keep the information confidential.

Pursuant to Section 61(1) of the Evidence Act, legal professional privilege also attaches to communications passed through the administrative staff between the attorney and a client. The section provides that an attorney is not obliged to disclose any communications between the attorney and a client if it is communicated "directly or indirectly through an agent of either."

G External Service Providers

11. Although attorney-client privilege is confined to the legal profession, it may extend to other non-legal personnel when an attorney or a firm outsources work. This is especially applicable in Belize, where most firms operate as small businesses. Thus, any communication passing, directly or through an agent, between an attorney and a non-professional agent or a third party that comes into existence after litigation is contemplated or commenced, and that is made in relation to such litigation, either for the purpose of obtaining legal advice or obtaining information or evidence to be used in those proceedings, is privileged.[27] As such, documents obtained or prepared confidentially under like circumstances are similarly privileged, other than copies of unprivileged documents.[28]

---

[26] Section 2(1), Cap. 320.   [27] *Anderson v. Bank of British Columbia* (1876) 2 Ch D 644.
[28] *Chadwick v. Bowman* (1886) 16 QBD 561.

H Multidisciplinary Associations

12.　At present, there is no legislation in Belize that specifically authorizes the establishment of multidisciplinary firms. There is therefore no instance of legal firms offering services in partnership with other professionals.

I In-House Counsel

13.　There is no different treatment in relation to in-house counsel. The law regarding attorney-client privilege is applicable to all attorneys-at-law and therefore applies to in-house counsel.

2 History of the Duty of Professional Secrecy in Belize

14.　Section 61 of the Evidence Act, which places legal professional privilege on a statutory footing in Belize, was enacted in 1953. Prior to that, legal professional privilege would have been governed by the common law duty of confidentiality, which would have applied to legal practitioners in Belize.

　　The Legal Profession Act was enacted in 1980. It introduced a statutory scheme to discipline attorneys-at-law in the event that they breached their professional duties, generally, and specifically in relation to the confidentiality of the attorney-client relationship.

3 Supervision

A Bar Association of Belize

15.　While membership in the Bar Association of Belize is no longer compulsory,[29] the Bar Association remains a functioning organization, and among its objectives is ensuring rules of etiquette, ethics and practice are made and enforced.[30] Furthermore, the Bar Association also has a mandate to ensure the "highest standards of learning, integrity, honour and courtesy among its members in the legal profession."[31]

　　While the association has compulsory standards for its members to abide by, the only body that can impose disciplinary sanctions against an attorney-at-law is the General Legal Council. This council is composed of the Chief Justice, the Attorney General of Belize, three attorneys elected by the Bar Association and two attorneys appointed by the Attorney General.[32] Despite it becoming non-compulsory, the bar continues to play an important function in the administration of the practice of law in Belize.

---

[29] Legal Profession (Amendment) Act, Act No. 22 of 2014.　　[30] Ibid., Section 40.　　[31] Ibid.
[32] Ibid., Section 3(2).

B The Courts

16. All attorneys must abide by the laws of Belize and, generally, have a duty to practice in an ethical and honest manner. Failure to do so may result in disciplinary sanctions by the General Legal Council under the Legal Profession Act.[33]

    Where a judge is of the view that an attorney has violated the Legal Profession (Code of Conduct) Rules, the judge may cause the Registrar of the Supreme Court to apply to the to the General Legal Council requesting that disciplinary action be taken.

4 Sanctions

A Professional Misconduct Proceedings

17. The most serious professional sanction an attorney-at-law can face in Belize is disciplinary action for professional misconduct. The Legal Profession Act governs this process. An aggrieved person who alleges that an act or omission by an attorney that has adversely affected the individual amounts to professional misconduct may make an application to the Council for disciplinary action to be taken.[34] This application must be supported by an affidavit containing the particular facts of the alleged misconduct. The wide range of acts that may constitute professional misconduct are listed in the Legal Profession (Code of Conduct) Rules,[35] and this includes disclosing privileged information.[36]

    In the event that such an application is made, the Council may choose to ask the applicant to provide further evidence of misconduct, including documents and information. At that point, if there is no prima facie case of misconduct, the application may be dismissed.[37] However, if there is enough support for the application, the Council will fix a date for a hearing, and both parties may supply information to support their respective positions.

    If the Council is satisfied that an attorney's actions constitute professional misconduct or grave professional misconduct, a report is made to the Chief Justice of Belize. Therein, the Council may make recommendations as to the disciplinary action to be taken including, but not limited to, removing the attorney's name from the roll, imposing a fine and subjecting the attorney to a reprimand.[38] The Chief Justice may then choose to dismiss the complaint or, if there is sufficient evidence, summon the attorney to refute the recommendations. If the attorney cannot show just cause, or shows insufficient cause, then the Chief Justice may choose to adopt the recommendations of the Council or impose such other punishment as provided by Section 16(2) of the Legal Profession Act.[39] An attorney has a right of appeal to the Court of Appeal

---

[33] Ibid., Section 15(1).   [34] Ibid., Section 15(1).   [35] Statutory Instrument No. 42 of 1991.
[36] Ibid., Rule 66.   [37] Ibid., Rule 88.
[38] Section 16, Legal Profession Act of Belize, Cap. 320.   [39] Ibid.

against an order of the Chief Justice, and this shall be done through a rehearing.[40] The Court of Appeal may dismiss or allow the appeal. However, Section 20(2) of the Legal Profession Act provides that the court cannot inflict a greater punishment than was given by the Chief Justice in the original hearing.

The consequence of these disciplinary measures may include the revocation of an attorney's practicing certificate or a suspension from practicing law in Belize.[41] However, an attorney may petition the Chief Justice to be restored to the roll or have the suspension lifted.[42] For this to occur, the Chief Justice must refer the petition to the Council, and the Council will determine whether the applicant is once again eligible to practice law in Belize. The attorney's name may be restored to the roll, or the suspension may be lifted.[43]

However, unless and until such a petition is granted, that individual would be expressly prohibited from practicing as an attorney, making representations that he or she is entitled to practice law or doing work in connection with practicing attorneys.[44] Furthermore, attorneys who act as agents for any person not entitled to practice law as an attorney may be subject to fines in relation to furthering this prohibited conduct.[45]

B The Relationship between Criminal Sanctions and Disciplinary Sanctions

18. In Belize, criminal and disciplinary sanctions are enforced separately and are dealt with in their own respective proceedings. In the event that criminal proceedings are brought against an attorney for crimes such as fraud, it may be adduced as evidence of professional misconduct, but the proceedings would still operate apart from each other. Criminal matters are heard by the court that has jurisdiction over the particular crime listed in the Belize Criminal Code.[46]

5 Duty to Provide Information to the Authorities

A Money Laundering and Terrorism

19. Belize is a jurisdiction that offers commercial and corporate services to non-residents who require no-tax corporations with a high level of confidentiality, that is, an offshore jurisdiction. Recently, offshore jurisdictions have been heavily scrutinized to ensure that the services provided are being used lawfully. Offshore jurisdictions have commonly been misrepresented as being used for illegitimate purposes, such as tax evasion, money laundering and financing terrorism. In an attempt to comply with international standards and requirements,[47] Belize has

---

[40] Ibid., Section 19 (1).   [41] Ibid., Section 21(1).   [42] Ibid.   [43] Ibid., Section 24(2).
[44] Ibid., Section 26.   [45] Ibid., Section 26(5).   [46] Section 4(1), Cap. 101, 2000.
[47] Specially the Financial Action Task Force (FATF) and the Caribbean Financial Action Task Force (CFATF).

implemented the Money Laundering and Terrorism (Prevention) Act[48] to provide additional safeguards against the misuse of the services being offered by Belize's offshore industry. This legislation mandates disclosure by financial institutions, trusts or company service providers, among other bodies corporate.

The Financial Intelligence Unit, a statutory body established by the Financial Intelligence Unit Act,[49] administers the Money Laundering and Terrorism (Prevention) Act. The Financial Intelligence Unit is empowered to investigate and prosecute money laundering offences. It may also investigate for the purpose of providing information to foreign regulatory bodies.

Apart from the requirement to report suspicious transactions, all legal persons or entities conducting transactions are required to collect information on that legal person or legal arrangement. The information must adequately identify the company, the beneficial owner and ultimate natural persons providing the funds of such legal person or legal arrangement. One must also take reasonable measures to identify and verify the legal status, ownership and control structure, including measures for (i) verifying proof of incorporation or similar evidence of establishment or existence; (ii) identifying and verifying the customer's name, name of trustee and ultimate settler (for trusts) and identifying persons providing funds and council members (for foundations), legal form, head office address and identities of directors (for legal persons) and source of funds; (iii) verifying that any person purporting to act on behalf of the customer is authorized to do so, identifying that person and verifying the identity of that person; and (iv) where the reporting entity engages in insurance business, identifying each beneficiary under any long-term or investment-linked policy issued or to be issued by the reporting entity, and verifying the identity of each beneficiary.[50]

It is manifest that the requirements of the Money Laundering and Terrorism (Prevention) Act are very onerous and may ostensibly seem to erode the attorney-client privilege. However, Section 17(10) of the act preserves privileged communication if it is to a person who is a professional legal adviser and the disclosure falls within subsection (b). A disclosure falls within this subsection if it is a disclosure:

> by or by a representative of a client of the professional legal adviser in the course of ascertaining the legal position of the client; from or through a client in connection with the performing by the legal adviser of the task of defending or representing that client in, or concerning judicial, administrative, arbitration or mediation proceedings, provided that a disclosure does not fall within Subsection (b) if it is made with the intention of furthering a criminal purpose.[51]

---

[48] Act No. 18 of 2008. [49] Act No. 35 of 2002.
[50] Section 15(3)(c), Money Laundering and Terrorism (Prevention) Act.
[51] Section 17 (10), Money Laundering and Terrorism (Prevention) Act.

This provision is in accordance with the cardinal elements of attorney-client privilege, that is, the privilege encapsulates all information provided in pursuance of advice in relation to legal proceedings, but it excludes information disclosed with the intention of committing a crime.

The provision, prima facie, seems to preserve the tenets of attorney-client privilege. However, as will be discussed in the "Search of a Lawyer's Office" section, it is questionable whether the privilege is truly safeguarded, having regard to the arbitrary inspections that may be conducted by the Financial Intelligence Unit in the Fifth Schedule Section 11(1)(g) of the Money Laundering and Terrorism (Prevention) Act.

6 Treatment of Lawyers' Documents and Correspondence in the Context of Judicial or Police Investigations

20.   Correspondence between an attorney and a client is deemed privileged information in Belize. The effect of this privilege extends to both criminal and civil proceedings. Rule 66 of the Legal Profession (Code of Conduct) Rules provides that exceptions to the protection of privilege are court orders and statutory obligations.[52] An example of legislation compelling attorneys to reveal information about clients is Belize's Money Laundering and Terrorism (Prevention) Act.[53] However, the act also contains a provision that attorneys would not be required to disclose information protected by attorney-client privilege.[54] Section 17(4) states that attorneys should report clients suspected of illicit activities such as money laundering to the Financial Intelligence Unit. Therefore, a court may order that an attorney's documents be disclosed if there is reasonable suspicion that the purpose of the communication was for a criminal act.

If the communication was not for the purpose of a criminal act, the communication would be inadmissible in any proceedings. However, if the communication was made for the purpose of "committing a fraud, crime or other wrongful act," it would not be privileged.[55] No privilege attaches to the communication, and it may be admitted into evidence.

7 Search of a Lawyer's Office

21.   For the purposes of the Summary Jurisdiction (Procedure) Act, a magistrate may order the police to search any premises on the reasonable belief that illicit activities have occurred or may occur there.[56] There is other legislation that allows the search of buildings, which may include attorneys' offices, such as the Money Laundering and Terrorism (Prevention) Act.[57] Inspections of

[52] Statutory Instrument No. 42 of 1991.   [53] Act No. 18 of 2008.   [54] Ibid., Section 17(9).
[55] Ibid., Section 61(3).   [56] Section 23(1), Cap. 99, 2000.   [57] Section 28(2), Cap. 104.

attorneys' offices by the Financial Intelligence Unit is sanctioned by Section 4 of the Fifth Schedule of that act for the purposes of assessing or enforcing compliance with the objectives of the act against illicit activities. However, it must be noted that the aforementioned statutory protections for privileged information should still apply in those situations.[58]

The most notable exception to this protection would be a court order. However, the courts in Belize would more than likely apply the common law and constitutional principle of proportionality when choosing to limit this right, as is the case in other jurisdictions. The test of proportionality from *R (Daly) v. Secretary of State for Home Development*[59] would be applied to determine whether authorities could have access to attorneys' confidential information in the process of a search.[60] In other common law jurisdictions, such as Jamaica, the application of this rule has shown that even for the purposes of disciplinary proceedings against an attorney, the courts are still reluctant to allow the disclosure of privileged information.[61] This is reflected in Rule 66 of the Legal Profession (Code of Conduct) Rules.[62] An attorney could possibly face professional misconduct proceedings if any privileged information is disclosed to third parties without the express consent of the client.

8 Tapping of Telephone Conversations with a Lawyer

22. The Interception of Communications Act of Belize[63] was a somewhat controversial piece of legislation when it was introduced because of the powers of access it seemed to grant. An authorized officer may intercept communications upon application to the Supreme Court for an interception direction. An application must be supported by an affidavit including, inter alia, supporting facts or allegations, information on the subject of the interception, and the period of time in which the surveillance will be carried out.[64] A judge may grant the order if the judge is satisfied that there is sufficient interest in public safety, national security or even reasonable belief that offenses will be committed.[65] These wide grounds on which an interception direction may be granted would suggest that the court may grant a direction to intercept an attorney's communication. It is to be noted that, while Section 20(1) of the act states that the intercepted communications shall be admissible in proceedings in accordance with the Evidence Act, Section 20(4) of the Communications Act provides for the admissibility of otherwise privileged communications on much wider grounds. Section 20(4) states:

[58] Ibid., Fifth Schedule, Section 5.   [59] [2001] 1 AC 532.
[60] Rule 28.14, Supreme Court (Civil Procedure) Rules, 2005.
[61] Rule 66, Statutory Instrument No. 42 of 1991.   [62] Statutory Instrument No. 42 of 1991.
[63] Act No. 25 of 2010.   [64] Ibid., Section 5(1).   [65] Ibid., Section 6(1).

Any communication, information or data discovered during the execution of an interception direction or entry warrant or through the disclosure of protected information or communication data between a client and his attorney shall not be produced as evidence in court unless this communication, information or data refers to an offence that has been, is being or may being committed.

Section 20(4) is therefore in apparent conflict with the Evidence Act and the Legal Profession (Code of Conduct) Rules, which provide that the purpose of the communication must be to commit an offence. The communication must not merely "refer to an offence."

A prisoner's protection of privacy and protection from arbitrary search and seizure has been significantly eroded by the Interception of Communications Act. The investigating officer is merely required to obtain written authorization from the National Security Council to intercept communications made from the Central Prison or any detention facility.[66] However, Section 20 of the Interception of Communications Act regarding admissibility of the communication, as aforementioned, is equally applicable to the admissibility of communications intercepted from a detention facility.

9 The Lawyer as Witness

23.   Pursuant to Rule 37(1) of the Legal Profession (Code of Conduct) Rules, an attorney cannot appear as a witness for the attorney's own client, save for merely formal matters. If the information to be given by the witness is of a more onerous nature, the attorney should entrust the conduct of the case to another attorney chosen by the client.

With respect to proceedings brought by a third party, an attorney may appear as a witness in a trial; however, the court cannot compel that attorney to disclose any confidential information in relation to a matter the attorney is advising or has advised a client on, pursuant to Section 61 of the Evidence Act of Belize.[67]

Therefore, information passed between an attorney and a client is not protected if such information or communication was not made to the attorney in the attorney's professional capacity, or if the client provided the information outside the scope of the legal relationship with the attorney, notwithstanding whether litigation was pending or contemplated. However, documents and information remain protected after the termination of the relationship between the attorney and the client. All information previously gathered from a client cannot be released.[68]

---

[66] Legal Profession (Amendment) Act, Act No. 22 of 2014.

[67] Rule 16, Legal Profession (Code of Conduct) Rules.

[68] Legal Profession (Amendment) Act, Act No. 22 of 2014.

An exception is that the privilege does not exist where the communication between the client and the attorney was made for an unlawful purpose, such as committing a fraud, a crime or other wrongful act.

10 The Lawyer and the Press

24.   The Legal Profession (Code of Conduct) Rules do not address the scope of attorney-client privilege in relation to the press. However, the wide prohibition provided by Rule 66 of the Legal Profession (Code of Conduct) Rules would likewise apply to communications between an attorney and the press. Communications with a client remain confidential unless the client instructs that the lawyer may disclose such communications. Nevertheless, one of the traditions of the profession is that trial of the matter ought not be held in the press but in the court.

11 Powers of the Tax and Other Authorities

25.   Belize has no statute or case law in this respect.

12 National Security Issues

26.   As aforementioned, a client's right to protection of privacy and protection from arbitrary search and seizure is subject to the public interest, that is, the "interests of defence, public safety, public order, public morality." Therefore, an act may derogate a client's right to attorney-client privilege if it is necessary for national security. An attorney also "owes a duty to the State to maintain its integrity, its constitution and its laws and not to aid, abet, counsel or assist anyone 'to act in any way contrary to those laws.'"[69]

27.   The state may also claim privilege from disclosure of certain documents where it is in the interest of national security. In such instances, privilege is claimed on the basis that it is protected by public interest immunity. It is not necessary for the document to be a communication between the state and its legal adviser. In *Minister of Finance and Home Affairs et al. v. Belize Printers Associations Ltd. et al.*,[70] Morrison JA summarized the principle as follows:

> It is common ground between the parties that this is an accurate statement of the modern law of discovery. It is also common ground that what Lord Radcliffe once described as a "weighty public reason" (referred to in the dictum of Lord Edmund-Davies set out in the preceding paragraph) may operate to curtail the operation of the correlative right to and duty of disclosure. It is in this sense that there can be in this branch of the law

[69] Rule 16, Legal Profession (Code of Conduct) Rules.
[70] Civil Appeal No. 7 of 2004, para. 15.

111

a tension between competing public interest requirements. As Lord Reid observed in *Conway v. Rimmer* (at page 940):

"it is universally recognized that there are two kinds of public interest which may clash. There is the public interest that harm shall not be done to the nation or the public service by disclosure of certain documents and there is the public interest that the administration of justice shall not be frustrated by withholding of documents which must be produced if justice is to be done" (and see, to similar effect, Lord Morris at pages 955–956, where he speaks of the "balance of desirabilities".).

Therefore, where it may be prejudicial to national security to disclose a document, privilege would attach to such document, and the state is protected from disclosing it.

8

Bermuda

GRANT SPURLING
KIERNAN BELL

Appleby

Preliminary Note

1.   In Bermuda, lawyers are required to act in accordance with the provisions of the Barristers' Code of Professional Conduct 1981 ("Barristers' Code"). This includes an obligation to hold all information acquired in the course of their professional relationship with their clients strictly confidential, unless the client agrees to the release of such information or the barrister is required by law to divulge it.[1] Infractions of the Barristers' Code are dealt with by the Professional Conduct Committee, a committee set up under the Bermuda Bar Act 1974 to conduct inquiries when a barrister's professional conduct is called into question and, where appropriate, impose such sanctions or take such other action as is deemed appropriate.[2]

    Bermuda derives a substantial portion of its law from England, owing to its historical roots as an English colony and subsequently as a United Kingdom Overseas Territory. Section 15 of the Supreme Court Act 1905 provides:

> Subject to the provisions of any Acts which have been passed in any way altering, amending or modifying the same, and of this Act, the common law, the doctrines of equity, and the Acts of Parliament of England of general application which were in force in England at the date when these Islands were settled, that is to say on the 11th day of July 1612, shall be, and hereby declared to be in force within Bermuda.

    Since 1612, local refinements, adapting English law to local conditions and enacting legislation through the Bermudian Parliament, have shaped Bermudian law into a discrete system of legislation and common law. As to the interpretation of statutes, Bermuda courts will apply decisions of English courts where Bermuda's legislature has adopted identical statutory language from England.

    Bermuda's courts are not, strictly speaking, hierarchically subordinate to the English House of Lords or other English courts. Nonetheless, because Bermuda's common law derives from the common law of England, "generally it can be said that the Courts of Bermuda will accept as binding decisions of the House of Lords in common law matters."[3]

    The final court of appeal for actions brought in the courts of Bermuda is the Judicial Committee of the Privy Council, which sits in London, England, and is composed of members of the Supreme Court of the United Kingdom (the highest court of Appeal for England).

2.   In contrast to the system in England and Wales, the legal profession in Bermuda operates as a "fused profession": whereas the profession in England has traditionally been divided into barristers and solicitors, all lawyers in Bermuda are admitted to the Bar of Bermuda. Similarly, all lawyers in

---

[1] Section 15, Barristers' Code of Professional Conduct 1981.
[2] Section 15, Bermuda Bar Act 1974.   [3] *Crockwell v. Haley* [1993] Bda LR.

Bermuda are regulated by the Bermuda Bar Association. Although lawyers called to the Bar of Bermuda may have trained in overseas jurisdictions that distinguish between barristers and solicitors, once called to the Bermuda Bar, they can appear before Bermuda's courts and are not restricted in the legal work they can carry out on behalf of clients.

1 Scope of and Limitations on the Duty of Professional Secrecy/ Attorney-Client Privilege

A Statutory Basis and Implications

3.   Attorney-client privilege in Bermuda (generally referred to as legal professional privilege) is based on common law as applied in Bermuda.

While Bermuda courts reserve the capacity to deviate from English House of Lords (now Supreme Court) authorities if the social conditions of Bermuda make inappropriate the particular path of development taken by the House of Lords,[4] for present purposes Bermuda common law on attorney-client privilege is the same as the common law of England and Wales.

The Barristers' Code was drafted by the Bar Council under Section 9 of the Bermuda Bar Act 1974 and thus has the force of law as secondary legislation. Therefore, a barrister's duty to treat client information confidentially is both a professional requirement and a legal obligation derived from statute.

B Scope

4.   Legal professional privilege falls into two categories in Bermuda: legal advice privilege, which applies only to professional legal advice between a lawyer and client, and litigation privilege, where litigation is pending or contemplated and communications take place between a client or a lawyer (or both) and a third party for the purposes of that litigation.[5]

Legal advice privilege arises where a lawyer enters information into a document that the lawyer came to know only because of the lawyer's professional relationship with the client. This includes communications sent from a client to the lawyer. However, information procured outside of the course of a lawyer's professional practice will not be privileged.

Litigation privilege arises where litigation is proceeding, pending or reasonably contemplated, and the document comprises a confidential communication between a lawyer or a client and a third party, where the dominant purpose of that communication is to assist or advise with respect to that litigation.

---

[4] Ibid.   [5] *Stiftung Salle Modulable v. Butterfield Trust (Bermuda) Ltd* [2012] Bda LR 78.

5. Legal professional privilege is considered to be "a fundamental human right"[6] and as such will be protected by the Bermuda courts. In *Fubler and others v. Attorney General and Commissioner of Police*,[7] Ground J said, "legal professional privilege is a common law concept which forms part of the cluster of rights which together make up the concept of a fair trial in accordance with the common law notion of that expression. As such I consider that it is part of, and ancillary to, the right to a fair hearing."

    Although a document or information protected by legal professional privilege enjoys a fundamental right to be withheld by the lawyer, client or (in certain circumstances) third party, that does not mean that its very existence may be concealed. Where disclosure is ordered in pre-trial preparations, a document subject to legal professional privilege must be included on the exchanged list of documents, though it should be indicated on the list that privilege is being asserted with respect to that document's contents. The tribunal is not permitted to derive an adverse inference from the fact that privilege is asserted.

    Legal professional privilege, though strongly protected, is also narrowly applied. Thus, the courts of Bermuda will not preserve privilege in a document that has been created to further a criminal or fraudulent purpose, whether the purpose is conceived between the parties directly or a third party is manipulating an innocent client.

    Where the confidentiality of a document covered by legal professional privilege has been compromised by the information becoming available to the general public, a party loses the right to claim privilege in that information.

    Similarly, where a party divulges part of a privileged document, the court may require that the entire contents of the document relevant to that issue be disclosed, to prevent lawyers from cherry-picking helpful passages from a document while keeping uncertainties or damaging statements concealed.[8] However, where a portion of a privileged document has merely lost its confidentiality, this will not require the production of the entire document (though may do so if the party asserting privilege subsequently relies on the leaked portion).

    Where a document is disclosed with express terms that privilege in that document is not being waived, then the privilege in that document will be preserved as against other parties.[9] Although this was decided in the context of an appeal from the Court of Appeal of New Zealand, it is a decision by the Judicial Committee of the Privy Council (also Bermuda's highest appellate

---

[6] *Quinn Direct Insurance Ltd v. The Law Society* [2009] EWHC 2588 (Ch); *Morgan Grenfell & Co Ltd v. Special Commissioner of Income Tax* [2002] UKHL 21.

[7] [1994] Bda LR 64.

[8] *Stiftung Salle Modulable v. Butterfield Trust (Bermuda) Ltd* [2012] Bda LR 78; *Trustees 1 – 4 v. The Attorney General and Respondent 2–3* [2014] Bda LR 19.

[9] *B v. Auckland District Law Society* [2003] UKPC 38.

court) on a matter of common law, and the Bermuda courts would follow the decision.

If advice protected by legal professional privilege is circulated to third parties, this will likely be construed as a waiver of privilege. However, if the advice is kept confidential between the parties, and all parties have a common interest in the subject matter of the advice, a "common interest privilege" may be deemed to exist, meaning that the overarching legal professional privilege will be preserved.

In proceedings between a client and a lawyer, privilege in documents passing between the two will be waived by implication, as it would be unjust to ask lawyers to justify their actions or to particularize a claim for fees while denying lawyers the right to refer to the documents passing between lawyers and clients, being the only, or substantially the only, evidence on which lawyers would be able to defend themselves or prove a claim.[10] However, this waiver is limited to actions between lawyer and client. In the general course of litigation, the fact that a document is relevant to a particular issue in the proceedings does not waive any privilege attaching to it.[11]

Legal professional privilege belongs to the client, and the client is therefore the only party entitled to waive that right, unless the client expressly authorizes the lawyer to do so.

C Persons Subject to the Duty of Professional Secrecy

6. Legal professional privilege attaches to communications with lawyers, registered associates and legal executives. Communications with in-house lawyers are protected by legal professional privilege in the same way as communications with external counsel. However, due to the integrated nature of an in-house legal department, great care should be taken to identify communications that are for the purpose of legal advice in the in-house lawyer's capacity as a legal adviser. Communications with in-house lawyers in relation to business advice or administrative matters will not be covered by legal professional privilege.

The question of whether advice has been provided in an attorney's professional capacity as a lawyer will depend on "whether the advice relates to the rights, liabilities, obligations or remedies of the client either under private law or under public law."[12]

As legal professional privilege is derived from the principle that clients should be able to communicate freely with their lawyers when seeking legal

---

[10] *Digicel v. Cable & Wireless Plc* [2009] EWHC 373 (Ch).

[11] *FarmAssist v. Secretary of State for the Environment, Food and Rural Affairs* [2008] EWHC 3079 (TCC).

[12] *Three Rivers District Council v. Bank of England* [2004] UKHL 48.

advice, no privilege will attach where clients knew their lawyer was in fact not a qualified practitioner or had been disqualified from practice.

D Exceptions to and Optional Derogations from the Duty of Professional Secrecy

7.   The circumstances under which a lawyer may disclose confidential client information are limited. Under Section 18 of the Barristers' Code, barristers may be obliged to reveal client information to recover fees; defend themselves, an associate or an employee in legal or disciplinary proceedings; prevent the commission of a crime; or if ordered to reveal such information by an order of a court.

However, where legal professional privilege arises, as a strongly protected fundamental right, the circumstances where the corresponding duty of confidentiality can be penetrated are rare. As indicated previously in the section on "Scope," there are limited circumstances where the client will be deemed to have waived (or lost) privilege in information or documents due to the client's conduct or the loss of confidentiality in such information or document. Aside from this, legal professional privilege will not apply where the information or documents are created for the furtherance of a criminal purpose.

Finally, there is a limited exception in circumstances where the Information Commissioner, pursuant to powers under the Public Access to Information Act 2010 ("PATI"), is conducting a review. In such circumstances, the Information Commissioner may examine any record under the control of a public authority. PATI stipulates that no such record may be withheld from the Information Commissioner on any grounds.[13] However, this exception is of very limited scope in that the power vests solely in the Information Commissioner with respect to records held by a public authority, and the Information Commissioner cannot be required to give evidence in judicial proceedings with respect to anything that came into the Information Commissioner's knowledge as a result of the exercise of official functions as Information Commissioner.

E Law Firms

8.   Communications with a qualified attorney's department are deemed to fall under the individual attorney's obligations with respect to legal professional privilege. As with conventional privilege between a client and an attorney, privilege will attach only where such communications are for the purpose of providing legal advice in the context of the professional relationship between the supervising lawyer and the client. Unless the client expressly forbids it, a lawyer is permitted to disclose such information as may be necessary to employees and other members of the lawyer's firm.[14]

---

[13] Public Access to Information Act 2010 s.56(2).
[14] Section 15, Barristers' Code of Professional Conduct 1981.

F Legal Assistants and Staff

9. Similarly, communications with trainee lawyers, paralegals and executive assistants will be privileged where their work is supervised by a qualified attorney. This is because such communications are deemed to be communications with the qualified attorney's department. As with conventional privilege between a client and an attorney, privilege will attach only where such communications are for the purpose of providing legal advice in the context of the professional relationship between the supervising lawyer and the client.

G External Service Providers

10. Where external service providers work on behalf of an attorney or a firm, information received will be subject to legal professional privilege in the same manner as members of staff in a law firm as outlined above.

    However, where a consultant or accounting professional provides advice, even if that advice in substance would be identical to that given by a lawyer, legal advice privilege will not apply. While other professions may be subject to duties of confidentiality as imposed by their respective regulatory bodies or by contract, such obligations may be overridden by the courts and will not be afforded the same level of protection as information or documents subject to legal professional privilege.

    In *Prudential Plc and Prudential (Gibraltar) Ltd. v. Special Commissioner of Income Tax and Philip Pandolfo (HM Inspector of Taxes)*,[15] the Supreme Court of the United Kingdom was divided on the question of whether legal advice provided by accountants ought to be afforded the same protection under legal advice privilege as advice provided by lawyers. The dissenting minority held that, as legal professional privilege is a common law concept, it would be improper for the court to interpret such a fundamental right on the basis of a "capricious distinction."[16] Rather, the minority held that it would be proper to extend legal advice privilege to ensure that the common law reflected legal, social and commercial practice: legal professional privilege ought to attach to the advice of skilled professional legal advisers, not merely to "members of any particular professional body."[17] However, the majority of the court held that ultimately the extension of legal professional privilege was a parliamentary policy decision, particularly as many professions beyond accountants are regulated by a governing body and provide legal advice to clients. Such a sweeping change to the law ought to be determined by the elected members of Parliament.

    The Bermuda courts would almost certainly apply *Prudential*, and it is unlikely that the courts of Bermuda would extend legal advice privilege to non-lawyer advisers.

[15] [2013] UKSC 1.   [16] Ibid., *per* Lord Sumption.   [17] Ibid., *per* Lord Clarke.

Nevertheless, if an external service provider is contacted in confidence by the client or the client's lawyer (or both) where litigation is proceeding, pending or reasonably contemplated, where the dominant purpose of that communication is to assist or advise in respect of that litigation, then the document will fall under the protection of litigation privilege. Best practice, however, is to ensure that the legal adviser is the direct sender or recipient of such communications.

H Multidisciplinary Associations

11. As with external service providers, a lawyer may engage the services of a non-legal professional where litigation is proceeding, pending or reasonably contemplated for assistance or advice with respect to that litigation. Such communications will be protected from disclosure under litigation privilege.

I In-House Counsel

12. As noted in the "Persons Subject to the Duty of Professional Secrecy" section, in-house counsel are treated the same as external counsel by Bermuda law.

2 History of the Duty of Professional Secrecy in Bermuda

13. The history of the duty of professional secrecy[18] reflects the common legal history of England and Bermuda, given that Bermuda common law is derived from the common law of England and Wales.

The common law principles of legal professional privilege, encompassing legal advice privilege and litigation privilege, have been applied by the courts of Bermuda entirely consistently with the common law of England and Wales. When issues of legal professional privilege have been raised in proceedings before the courts of Bermuda, English principles of common law, decided cases and authoritative texts have been referred to and adopted without comment. Therefore, English case law outlining the development of the common law concept of legal professional privilege is the most appropriate elucidation of the history of legal professional privilege as it is applied in Bermuda.

As early as 1577, it was recognized that lawyers could not be called to give evidence of matters that came to their knowledge in the course of their professional service, and "such a refusal would not bear any danger to the lawyer of being charged with contempt."[19]

Subsequently, in *Wilson v. Rastall*,[20] it was determined that privilege belongs to the client and not the attorney. In *Wilson*, the former attorney of the accused actively sought to give evidence in the proceedings but was sternly

---

[18] The authors' research on the history of the duty was assisted by Bankim Thanki, *The Law of Privilege*, Oxford University Press, New York, 2006.

[19] *Berd v. Lovelace* (1577) Cary 62.   [20] [1792] 4 TR 753.

rebuked by Buller J, who "strongly animadverted on his conduct, and would not suffer him to be examined . . . the mouth of such a person is shut forever."[21]

In 1833 the principle was extended from cases where legal proceedings were already in contemplation to simple advice on legal affairs (the modern legal advice privilege). As Lord Brougham (Lord Chancellor of Great Britain) explained in *Greenough v. Gaskell*,[22] "[i]f the privilege did not exist at all, everyone would be thrown upon his own legal resources; deprived of all professional assistance, a man would not venture to consult any skillful person, or would only dare to tell his counsellor half his case."[23]

In *R v. Derby Magistrates' Court, Ex Parte B*,[24] Lord Nicholls was able to proclaim that "[t]he law has been established for at least 150 years . . . subject to recognized exceptions, communications seeking professional legal advice, whether or not in connection with pending court proceedings, are absolutely and permanently privileged from disclosure even though, in consequence, the communications will not be available in court proceedings in which they might be important evidence."[25]

By 2002, legal professional privilege was declared to be "a fundamental human right long established in the common law."[26]

3 Supervision

A The Bar Association

14. The Bermuda Bar Association is composed of all barristers admitted to practice in Bermuda. Out of the membership of the Bermuda Bar Association, a Bar Council is elected to manage the affairs of the Bermuda Bar Association and related professional duties. Matters of discipline are considered and dealt with by a Professional Conduct Committee, which has powers designed to ensure proper professional conduct by members of the Bermuda Bar Association, including the power to conduct inquiries into and investigations of complaints of improper conduct made against a barrister.[27] This includes breaches of confidentiality as required under Section 15 of the Barristers' Code and violation of legal professional privilege.

B The Courts

15. The courts will hear an action in contract against an attorney where it is claimed that such attorney failed to exercise due care and skill in the performance of duties to the client.[28] If an attorney conspired with a client to further a criminal

---

[21] Ibid.   [22] (1833) 1 M.&K. 98.   [23] Ibid.   [24] [1996] 1 AC 487 (UKHL).   [25] Ibid.
[26] *R (Morgan Grenfell & Co Ltd) v. Special Commissioner of Income Tax* [2002] UKHL 21.
[27] Section 18A(a), Bermuda Bar Act 1974.
[28] *White v. Conyers, Dill & Pearman* [1994] Bda LR 9.

purpose, the attorney will be liable to criminal prosecution. In the context of a proposed disclosure in breach of legal professional privilege, the courts could restrain such disclosure with injunctive relief.

4 Sanctions

A Proceedings and Sanctions

16.   A complaint of a breach of the Barrister's Code may be made to the Bar Council in writing or may be made against an attorney by the Bar Council itself of its own motion. The complaint is then referred to the Professional Conduct Committee, which may either dismiss a complaint in accordance with Section 3 of the Bar Professional Conduct Committee Rules 1997 on the basis that it is trivial, frivolous or lacking in merit, or, if a prima facie case exists, formulate charges and convene a disciplinary tribunal. The chief justice of Bermuda appoints the members of the disciplinary tribunal to determine the complaint. The tribunal must consist of a judge of the Supreme Court and two other members of the Bermuda Bar Association. A complaint of improper conduct must be proven beyond all reasonable doubt (the criminal burden of proof). The tribunal may summon witnesses, examine witnesses under oath or otherwise compel the production of relevant documents. A decision of the disciplinary tribunal may be decided by a majority.[29]

     The disciplinary tribunal has the power to impose the following sentences on a respondent: (i) admonition or reprimand, (ii) disbarment, (iii) striking off the roll of the court or removal from the Register of Associates, (iv) suspension, (v) suspension or revocation of a professional company's certificate of recognition or (vi) a fine.[30]

     A barrister, professional company or a registered associate aggrieved by the disciplinary tribunal's determination may appeal to the Court of Appeal within 21 days of being notified of such determination.[31]

17.   An attorney is bound by legal professional privilege, and breaching that obligation is a breach of the duty of care and skill implied if not express in the terms of engagement. If the breach causes damage to the client, an attorney may be liable for damages. The burden of proof is on the client to prove loss. Such proceedings can be commenced in the Magistrates' Court (where the amount claimed does not exceed $25,000) or the Supreme Court of Bermuda. Appeals of Magistrates' Court decisions lie with the Supreme Court of Bermuda, and appeals of Supreme Court decisions (including in its appellate jurisdiction) lie with the Court of Appeal. Appeals from the Court of Appeal lie with the Judicial Committee of the Privy Council.

---

[29] Section 19, Bermuda Bar Act 1974.   [30] Section 18, Bar Disciplinary Tribunal Rules 1997.
[31] Ibid., Section 23.

B Relationship between Civil Sanctions and Disciplinary Sanctions

18.   Disciplinary and civil sanctions are imposed independently and have no effect on each other. (If there are disciplinary and criminal proceedings, the disciplinary proceedings are typically stayed pending the outcome of the criminal proceedings.) Where a civil action bears an inference of impropriety, an individual may make a complaint to the Bar Council in writing, or the Bar Council may make a complaint of its own motion. The disciplinary proceedings and civil action may proceed in tandem, as they arise from different violations: violations of the Barristers' Code on the one hand and breach of contract on the other.

5 Duty to Provide Information to the Authorities

A Money Laundering and Terrorism

19.   Money laundering and anti-terrorist financing are regulated by statute. However, these provisions do not override the protection afforded to documents subject to legal professional privilege. Rather, the limitation that legal professional privilege cannot attach to documents that are intended to further a criminal purpose operates so that privilege ought not be asserted with respect to such documents.

        Under the Anti-Terrorism (Financial and Other Measures) Act 2004, Anti-Money Laundering and Anti-Terrorist Financing-regulated institutions are under a duty to disclose information to the Financial Intelligence Authority where they believe or suspect that an offence under the Anti-Terrorism (Financial and Other Measures) Act 2004 has been committed.[32] However, this does not apply where such information has been received by a professional legal adviser (other than with a view to furthering a criminal purpose) in connection with the provision of legal advice by a professional legal adviser to a client, from a person seeking legal advice or for the purpose of actual or contemplated legal proceedings. Furthermore, Anti-Money Laundering and Anti-Terrorist Financing-regulated institutions are under a duty to provide information relating to transactions or business relationships.[33] However, this duty does not apply to documents or information to which a claim of legal professional privilege could be maintained in legal proceedings.

        The Financial Intelligence Agency Act 2007 imposes similar requirements on Anti-Money Laundering and Anti-Terrorist Financing-regulated institutions. In the course of inquiring into a suspicious transaction relating to a money laundering offence or a terrorist finance offence, the Financial Intelligence Authority may serve a notice requiring a person to provide such information as the Financial Intelligence Agency may reasonably require for

---

[32] Section 9, Anti-Terrorism (Financial and Other Measures) Act 2004.   [33] Ibid., Section 12H.

the purpose of its inquiry, in such format as it may require.[34] However, the Financial Intelligence Authority cannot require the disclosure of information subject to legal professional privilege. Indeed, Section 20 of the Financial Intelligence Act 2007, which eases restrictions (however imposed) on provision of information to the Financial Intelligence Agency to aid in the discharge of its functions, expressly forbids disclosure of information subject to legal professional privilege.

Similarly, the Proceeds of Crime (Anti-Money Laundering and Anti-Terrorist Financing Supervision and Enforcement) Act 2008 authorizes an officer of a designated professional body or a competent authority to require a person, entity or connected person to provide information and answer questions.[35] Yet, again, this duty is subject to the stipulation that a person may not be required to disclose information subject to legal professional privilege. The same applies to site visits, where a designated professional body may inspect, make copies, require an individual to provide an explanation or state where any recorded information may be found, unless such item is subject to legal professional privilege.[36] In both cases, however, individuals may be required to provide the name and address of their clients.

20.   There are a number of other acts that provide for searches of premises for materials relevant to investigations. However, these search powers are uniformly restricted from application to information subject to legal professional privilege:

(i)   The Attorney General may decline a request for assistance under Section 11E of the Criminal Justice (International Co-Operation) (Bermuda) Act 1994 where legal professional privilege would apply;

(ii) The Minister of Finance may decline a request for assistance under Section 4(2)(d) of the International Cooperation (Tax Information Exchange Agreements) Act 2005 where the requested information is protected from disclosure under Bermuda law on the ground of legal professional privilege;

(iii) A warrant under Section 11M of the Criminal Justice (International Co-Operation) (Bermuda) Act 1994 is conditional on the item not consisting of or including items subject to legal professional privilege;

(iv) The court will not grant access under the Proceeds of Crime Act 1997 to material consisting of or including items subject to legal professional privilege;[37]

---

[34] Section 16, Financial Intelligence Agency Act 2007.
[35] Section 30D, Proceeds of Crime (Anti-Money Laundering and Anti-Terrorist Financing Supervision and Enforcement) Act 2008.
[36] Ibid., Section 30E.   [37] Section 37(4)(b)(ii), Proceeds of Crime Act 1997.

(v) Search warrants issued under the Proceeds of Crime Act 1997 specifically exclude seizure of items subject to Legal Professional privilege;[38]

(vi) Section 49F of the Proceeds of Crime Act 1997 specifically stipulates that systematic reporting by Anti-Money Laundering and Anti-Terrorist Financing-regulated financial institutions may not be exercised to require the production of documents that would be subject to legal professional privilege in court proceedings;

(vii) Search warrants under the Police and Criminal Evidence Act 2006 authorizing a police officer to enter and search premises where a magistrate is satisfied that there are reasonable grounds to do so may not include access to documents or information covered by legal professional privilege;[39]

(viii) The Police and Criminal Evidence Act 2006 expressly excludes authorizations made under any earlier act for the search of premises for the purposes of a criminal investigation from applying to items subject to legal privilege;[40] and

(ix) Finally, Section 19(6) of the Police and Criminal Evidence Act 2006 states that no power of seizure contained in any act, even an act passed after the Police and Criminal Evidence Act 2006, authorizes seizure of an item that a police officer exercising such power has reasonable grounds for suspecting to be subject to legal professional privilege. Thus, an objective test is applied to the judgment of the executing officer, and any legislative attempt to alter this provision would have to expressly supersede Section 19(6) of the Police and Criminal Evidence Act 2006.

6 Treatment of Lawyers' Documents and Correspondence in the Context of Judicial or Police Investigations

21. A lawyer's documents may be searched in the context of a police investigation, but such a search ought to be conducted at the lawyer's offices with an associate present. Where any questions arise, the documents should be handed over to the investigating officer but sealed until such time as the court may determine whether the documents are required to be disclosed. This can be done before the relevant proceedings by application or at the start of the proceedings themselves.[41]

7 Search of a Lawyer's Office

22. Officers are permitted to search a lawyer's office but must be sensitive to the fact that a number of privileged and irrelevant documents will also be housed

---

[38] Ibid., Section 39.   [39] Section 8, Police and Criminal Evidence Act 2006.
[40] Ibid., Section 9.
[41] *Fubler and others v. Attorney General and Commissioner of Police* [1994] Bda LR 64.

there. Documents not covered by the warrant authorizing the search must not be seized nor read, and the same applies to any documents subject to legal professional privilege. However, to ascertain whether a document falls under the scope of the authorizing warrant and may be seized, officers will necessarily have to "glance" at documents. This is not a violation of legal professional privilege.[42]

8 Tapping of Telephone Conversations with a Lawyer

23.   Although the United Kingdom has enacted legislation authorizing surveillance of conversations between lawyers and their clients where national security so requires, Bermuda has not enacted replicating legislation. Although the matter has not been determined by the courts of Bermuda, it is unlikely that a court would hold such a violation to be justified even where it was shown that national security outweighed the client's right to confidential legal advice. In *R v. Derby Magistrates' Court*, Lord Lloyd of Berwick held: "the courts have for very many years regarded legal professional privilege as the predominant public interest. A balancing exercise is not required in individual cases, because the balance must always come down in favour of upholding the privilege."[43] In general terms, it is prohibited by the Telecommunications Act Sections 61(5) and (6) to record any telephone conversation without knowledge of the parties, and Section 54 of the act makes it a statutory offence to do so.

9 The Lawyer as Witness

24.   As indicated above, legal professional privilege belongs to the client and not the lawyer. Thus, as in *Wilson v. Rastall*, a lawyer may not be compelled to reveal matters subject to legal professional privilege. However, lawyers may be compelled to testify on matters that came to their knowledge outside the context of their professional relationship with their clients. Where a client seeks to instruct a lawyer and the lawyer believes he or she may be required to testify, the lawyer ought to refuse the instruction.

10 The Lawyer and the Press

25.   With the client's consent, a lawyer may speak to the press to defend a client against allegations made in the press. However, the lawyer should refrain from conducting the case in the press rather than the courtroom. In any case,

---

[42] Ibid.   [43] [1996] AC 487, at 509.

the lawyer must not disclose privileged information to the press. This would likely cause the information to lose its privilege, having ceased to be confidential. Moreover, the lawyer would be liable to disciplinary sanctions under the Barristers' Code and an action for breach of contract, as discussed above.

11 Powers of the Tax and Other Authorities

26.   The Bermuda Monetary Authority has wide regulatory powers as chiefly conferred by the Bermuda Monetary Act 1969. The Bermuda Monetary Authority may appoint investigators and compel information from a company's past and present controller, officer, employee, agent, banker, auditor, accountant, or barrister and attorney under the BMA Act 1969, the Corporate Service Provider Business Act 2012, the Insurance Act 1978, the Investment Business Act 2003, the Investment Funds Act 2006 and the Trusts (Regulation of Trust Business) Act 2001. However, in each of these circumstances, the Bermuda Monetary Authority's power is expressly excluded from applying to documents or information subject to legal professional privilege.

Under the Public Access to Information Act 2010, a record held by a public authority is exempt from being published or provided by a public authority if legal professional privilege would apply in legal proceedings. However, Section 35(2) of the Public Access to Information Act 2010 stipulates, "a record shall be disclosed if disclosure of it is in the public interest." Though this issue has not been before the courts, it is possible that this provision would be held to override legal professional privilege in limited circumstances where the public interest relied on was greater than the public's interest in preserving legal professional privilege. Additionally, as explained above, the Information Commissioner's powers under the act may require disclosure of all documents, including those subject to legal professional privilege, as a public authority is required to produce any record for inspection by the Information Commissioner, and no such record may be withheld from the Information Commissioner on any grounds. Of course, this disclosure is limited to the Information Commissioner alone, and it is unlikely that such disclosure would be held to have destroyed the confidentiality of such documents so that any legal professional privilege attaching to them would be lost.

12 National Security Issues

27.   There are no Bermuda authorities that would support overriding legal professional privilege in the interests of national security. This is a matter of competing public interests, and there is a long line of authorities ending in the Privy

Council decision of *B. v. Auckland District Law Society*[44] that have rejected the argument that legal professional privilege can be balanced against competing public interests. This leads to the likely result that, should there be a competing public policy argument around disclosure of communications otherwise subject to legal professional privilege, such communications would remain privileged and disclosure could not be compelled.

---

[44] [2003] 2AC 736, at 756–57.

9

Bolivia

FERNANDO AGUIRRE B.

Bufete Aguirre Soc. Civ.

Preliminary Note

1. Professional secrecy in general has a long tradition of legal regulation and protection in Bolivia, not only for the legal profession, but for others as well, including other non-professional activities. It has been reflected in different kinds of rules, of which those in the Bolivian Criminal Code are most relevant when proposing a general principle. Said Code provides the general framework, which states that if individuals in possession of secrets by virtue of their state, ministry, profession, employment, art, activity or commission reveal them without just cause or use them for their own benefit or the benefit of others, they are to be sanctioned by imprisonment.[1]

    The purpose of professional secrecy, broadly considered, is to allow a professional or similar activity involving secrets or private matters to be conducted in an environment of privacy and trust. This encourages proper knowledge of the facts and subject matter for an efficient and more truthful service. More particularly, if damages (either material or moral) can be triggered by revelation, secrecy should be respected even in trials and legal processes.

    The exact meaning and scope of "just cause" is a matter of interpretation and legal controversy. There are those who consider that, to be legally protected, the person whose secret may be revealed must have expressly stated that certain information is not to be revealed. Also, if the person consented to the revelation, then there would not be an offense resulting from disclosure of it[2] (this is the prevailing legal criteria).

    But placing the condition that the protected person must state what information is not to be revealed may defeat the purpose of secrecy (and is not a requirement in Bolivian law), which results from the general private nature of the service involved – the reason why the law creates protections. The creation of confidentiality under contract arises in a different context. Confidentiality is in the common interest of the parties essentially for commercial reasons, not necessarily because of the nature of one of the party's obligations (like lawyers, for example). So parties under contract may create a broad range of information to be treated confidentially, triggering responsibility for civil damages in case of breach, while a lawyer's (or similar) breach of general duty may trigger criminal responsibility.

1 Scope and Limitations on the Duty of Professional Secrecy/ Attorney-Client Privilege

A Statutory Basis and Implications

2. Within the general framework described in no. 1 of this chapter, a new Law for the Exercise of the Legal Profession was enacted on July 9, 2013, followed by

---

[1] Art. 302, Bolivia's Criminal Code.

[2] Fore more, see "Secreto profesional," *La guía de Derecho*, http://derecho.laguia2000.com/derecho-penal/secreto-profesional#ixzz3fcOdIlDy.

regulations enacted by means of Supreme Decree no. 1760 of October 9, 2013.[3] This law cancels all previous laws and regulations on the legal profession, though of course the rules of the Criminal Code and the Code of Criminal Procedure continue to apply. One very important feature of the reform is that affiliation with bar associations is no longer compulsory, as had been the case up until then, having thus become voluntary. On the other hand, the new law creates a public registration of lawyers and law companies under the care and responsibility of the Ministry of Justice. With this reform, if a lawyer continues to be associated with a bar association,[4] such lawyer can be subject to the bar's code of conduct and ethical tribunals, which internally prosecute violations of the duties of the profession. In addition, under the Ministry of Justice, a system of state professional prosecution for such violations has been established as a new feature of the law.

B Scope of the Duty

3. The 2013 law establishes general principles and specific duties. Under its Article 4, one of the principles for the exercise of the profession is that of confidentiality, under which lawyers must keep to themselves revelations of the sponsored client. Article 9 includes the duty to maintain professional secrecy, though it creates exceptions, as will be discussed in no. 5 of this chapter.

C Persons Subject to the Duty of Professional Secrecy

4. Within the framework of the regulations on the legal profession, specific rules are stated in respect of lawyers. These rules include lawyers with an individual practice and lawyers in law firms. No distinction is made between in-house counsel or independent practitioners, all of whom would be reached by essentially the same rules.

D Exceptions to and Optional Derogations from the Duty of Professional Secrecy

5. Article 9 of the 2013 law includes the following exceptions: cases involving the lawyer's own safety, defense of the truth, if the client expressly authorizes revelation or by judicial order. The foregoing language has been found to be imprecise, especially with respect to "defense of the truth" and "judicial order," and is likely to trigger controversy in practice if not properly understood, since

---

[3] *See* Gaceta Oficial de Bolivia No. 570.
[4] There are nine departmental bar associations, one for each of the nine departments into which the territory of the Plurinational State of Bolivia is divided. There is also a National Bar Association, which acts, among other functions, as an appeal body against resolutions of the departmental courts of honor, which have the power of prosecuting lawyers for breach of their professional duties. In the past, lawyers needed to be associated with each departmental bar association of the departments in which they intended to practice.

such provisions could appear to contradict the nature of confidentiality.[5] A situation could exist where a lawyer is accused of committing a felony together with others described as "clients." This would not properly be considered an attorney-client relationship triggering the privilege and so, by order of the court, the attorney could have to disclose information despite the "client" relationship.

E Law Firms

6. The legal framework allows the incorporation of law firms by way of civil companies to be properly incorporated, registered and formally recognized by the Ministry of Justice. With law firms being composed of lawyers, it is to each individual lawyer to whom the rules on confidentiality apply. There are no rules relating to the firms themselves as separate entities from their members. Members of the firm generally have a joint and several responsibility as between them personally, which can trigger joint and several obligations of a civil nature for all other members when one of them is found to have broken his or her duties when sponsoring clients of the firm, including those of confidentiality.

F Legal Assistants and Staff

7. There is no specific rule pertaining to legal assistants and staff, unless a legal assistant is a lawyer. The obligations of legal assistants and staff are to be governed by labor laws to which they are subject. Labor contracts or written rules and regulations applicable to them would normally contain specific and customary provisions relating to their own duties of confidentiality – that is, an obligation not to reveal any information to any third parties unless such information is in the public domain or when it must be revealed by order of an authority with competent jurisdiction. If an investigation of an alleged felony is conducted, which could require that legal assistants and staff appear as witnesses, then the general rules of the Criminal Code and of the Code of Criminal Procedure, as explained above, would be applicable.

G External Service Providers

8. These are governed by contract, the scope of which in connection with professional secrecy would depend on the nature of the contract. In any event, one will commonly look at standard confidentiality clauses. On the other hand, an external service provider could be bound to keep confidential information that it acquires by performing its services that in turn is confidential information under the rules of professional secrecy. If information of such nature is disclosed to a service provider because of the scope of its work, then professional secrecy rules ought to apply. One would also need to look into the specific rules

---

[5] On this subject, see sections 5 and 6 of this chapter.

that apply to the service provider, for example, if there is an investigation of an alleged felony, which could require appearances as witnesses, then the rules of the Criminal Code and of the Code of Criminal Procedure as explained above would be applicable.

H Multidisciplinary Associations

9. Law firms, organized as civil companies, are supposed to have rendering of legal services as their only purpose. They cannot be organized simultaneously for other, non-legal services. In turn, only lawyers qualify to create companies that render legal services. In practice, however, there are companies, even organized under commercial law rules, that render multidisciplinary services. These may be subject to penalties under corresponding rules. One of the problems they would face is the absence of specific secrecy rules for multidisciplinary entities. In theory, when rendering legal services, rules of the legal profession would apply, as rules of other professions would apply for services other than legal.

This concurrence of different professional rules may trigger controversies and contradictions as to what rule is to apply and with what scope and effect are the rules to be applied. For example, secrecy or reservation rules for services by auditors and lawyers differ because of the distinct nature of each service. It is a common practice that auditing companies conducting the audit of a company that may be required for public registration purposes require that outside counsel of the company confirm certain matters or cases under their care or of which they have information.

Lawyers and law firms might be under the obligation, because of confidentially or secrecy rules, to refrain from providing certain information to the auditors. The authorization by a client, however, would represent a release of liability, but sometimes this is not clearly understood or established in the client-attorney relationship, and sensitive disclosures could trigger controversy. When dealing with potentially confidential information, responsible lawyers or law firms should first obtain specific approval or consent from the client. In any event, this remains a sensitive matter.

I In-House Counsel

10. General rules for lawyers apply to in-house counsel. There is no provision distinguishing between in-house and outside counsel or providing a particular treatment.

2 History of the Duty of Professional Secrecy in Bolivia

11. The most relevant period during which broad rules governing the ethics of lawyers and secrecy for the legal profession, now substituted by the 2013 law, was from September 1974 to August 1979, during military rule in Bolivia.

By Decree No. 11782 of September 12, 1974, compulsory affiliation for lawyers with their departmental bar association was established. A Code of Professional Ethics for Lawyers was enacted by means of Supreme Decree No. 11788 of September 9, 1974.[6] Article 10 of said law provided that lawyers must keep professional secrets both as a right as well as an obligation, the most important obligation to a client. With respect to the courts, lawyers had the right not to disclose confidential information given by a client. If called as a witness, lawyers would have to appear and, using their own independent judgment, respond or not to the questioning by the court, but in no event violating the duty of secrecy.

This Decree had extended the obligation of secrecy to information supplied by a third party or learned or heard during negotiations for a settlement that did not materialize. It was also extended to confidential information supplied by other lawyers. If a lawyer was accused of wrongdoing by a client, the lawyer had the duty to reveal the secret in defense of the truth, even if by doing so the lawyer was compelled to disclose secrets given by the client. It is in this context that the exception of "truth" in the current 2013 law should be understood as well.

The Decree also provided that, when a client informs his or her lawyer of the client's intent to commit a felony or other crime, such confidence was not protected by professional secrecy. The lawyer had the obligation to reveal the client's intentions to avoid the occurrence of the felony or other crime.

By means of Decree Law No. 16793 of July 19, 1979, a Law of the Legal Profession had been enacted, canceling the previous one of 1941.[7] Its Article 24 confirmed that lawyers, individually or as members of a company of lawyers, have the duty to keep professional secrecy.

By Decree Law No. 17023 of August 3, 1979,[8] rules governing the rendering of services by procurators appearing before administrative and judicial authorities within all kinds of processes and procedures (ancillary to the legal profession) were approved. *Procuradores* had to have concluded the third degree of a law school and be approved by a School of *Procuradores*. They were subject to the duty of professional secrecy.[9]

3 Supervision

A The Bar Associations and Ethical Courts

12.   As mentioned in no. 2 of this chapter, under the new 2013 law, affiliation with bar associations is no longer compulsory, and a new public registry of lawyers and

---

[6] *See* publication containing this and other decrees and regulations: Servando Serrano Torrico, Editorial Serrano Ltda., Cochabamba, Bolivia, June 1, 1992.

[7] Ibid.

[8] Published at *Legislación del Abogado*, Colegio de Abogados de La Paz, AVF Productions, La Paz, Bolivia, October 1999.

[9] Ibid., at 185.

law companies under the care and responsibility of the Ministry of Justice has been created. With this reform, if a lawyer continues to be associated with a bar association, the lawyer is subject to the bar's code of conduct, the bar itself and ethical tribunals that internally supervise the profession and prosecute violations to the duties of the profession, in accordance with the bar's internal rules.

The 2013 law establishes follow-up and supervision by means of a number of authorities and entities with the powers of substantiating and resolving complaints that might be filed against lawyers for infraction of their ethical duties. Responsibility for such infractions does not preclude civil, criminal or administrative responsibility, if any, to be processed under applicable rules. Lawyers' responsibility applies not only to those who are in private practice, law firms or acting as in-house counsel, but also to lawyers with a public function or state administrative function of any kind.

Competent authorities are divided in the two probable supervisory bodies: (1) at the Ministry of Justice, for lawyers not affiliated with a bar association, for which there are departmental ethics courts and the National Ethics Court, and (2) at the bar associations, for lawyers affiliated with them, for which there are the same two kinds of ethics courts.

The national courts for both instances are composed of nine members and their alternates. In the case of departmental courts, the number depends on the respective number of affiliates. To be a member of such courts, certain pre-requisites are fixed in the law. Lawyers can individually apply to become such members. Universities, law firms and any other form of lawyers' associations can also sponsor candidates. Procedures at the ministerial level are to be fixed by special regulations.

13.   Bar associations establish their own rules, based on the framework fixed by the law and its regulations. Taking as a reference the relatively well-established Bar Association of La Paz, its rules broadly include organizational bylaws and regulations and procedural rules for prosecution due to infringement of the Code of Conduct. The same structure is found at the other bars, both departmental and national.

B The Courts

14.   Ordinary courts do not properly exercise supervision over lawyers on professional secrecy matters.

4 Sanctions

A Proceedings and Sanctions

15.   Sanctions that ethical courts can apply depend on the degree of seriousness or gravity of the infraction: these may be minor, grave and very grave. The law

contains extensive detail of the respective infractions (Articles 40, 41 and 42), running from the infraction not to favor conciliation to that of illegal practice. This graduation is quite subjective. For example, a very grave infraction is charging fees beyond what has been contracted, while not defending the interest or mandate of the sponsored client is a minor infraction.

The sanction for minor infractions is a written reprimand and a fine equivalent to one minimum monthly salary (approximately $230); for a grave infraction, temporary suspension from one to twelve months and a fine from two to six minimum monthly wages; for a very grave infraction, temporary suspension from one year to two years and a fine of six minimum monthly wages. The statute of limitations is, respectively, six months, one year and two years. Abandonment of process for six months also extinguishes the sanction.

The law provides detailed rules governing the sanction procedure, which is always triggered by a denunciation filed by any individual with legitimate interest or "ex officio" before the Prosecutors' Offices or the corresponding bar associations. Conciliation is fostered. The process consists of a summary proceeding at the departmental level, ending with a first-instance ruling, which can be appealed to the corresponding national court. The Ministry of Justice or the corresponding bar association is entrusted with enforcement.

B Relationship between Criminal Sanctions and Disciplinary Process

16. The law provides that, if during the disciplinary process there are indications that a felony has occurred, the corresponding ethical court is to report the information to the Prosecutors' Office, which will then open an investigation and, if indications are confirmed, file for prosecution before a criminal court. The court will impose the corresponding criminal sanctions, all in accordance with the Criminal Code and the Code of Criminal Procedure.

There may also be a civil responsibility involving pecuniary compensation for damages, which can be prosecuted in accordance with the applicable rules of the Civil Code and the Code of Civil Process. Administrative responsibility can apply to all those lawyers in any public function pursuant to the relevant rules, depending on the area of public responsibility. Administrative process can derive itself in civil or criminal prosecution and responsibility.

5 Duty to Provide Information to the Authorities

17. Law 387 includes among the obligations of lawyers the duty to denounce all actions contrary to the legal order committed by judicial public servants, prosecutors, support or administrative staff, or other lawyers. Complaints are to be filed with competent authorities, depending on the illegal action. Lawyers are also bound to denounce the illegal exercise of the profession by individuals in general.

Separate from the foregoing are the exceptions to the obligation of confidentiality, as has been discussed before, which because of the ambiguities is a gray zone and delicate area for lawyers. In a broader context, the Code of Criminal Procedure provides that every individual who becomes aware of a felony of a public character *may* denounce it to the corresponding prosecutors' office. So there is no obligation to denounce. The Code provides such obligation only in two cases: by public servants who become aware of such facts or felonies and medical professionals becoming aware of them in the exercise of their profession, except if they have become aware under professional secret.[10] So, with respect to lawyers, the exceptions on confidentiality are to be taken into account as they might relate to a duty to provide information to authorities.

6 Treatment of Lawyers' Documents and Correspondence in the Context of Judicial or Police Investigations and Search of a Lawyer's Office

18. Law 387 includes among the rights of the legal profession, in addition to the inviolability of their opinions, whether oral or written, the right of the inviolability of their offices, as well as of documents and objects that have been placed there by their clients, except if otherwise instructed by a competent authority.

The Constitution recognizes the general right of inviolability of domicile and of secrecy of private communications in all of their forms, which cannot be confiscated except in cases provided for in the law and based on a written and justified order by a competent authority for purposes of criminal investigation. Stolen private documents have no legal effect.[11]

Articles 190 and 191 of the Code of Criminal Procedure establish that, provided this is considered useful for investigating the truth, the judge or court shall instruct by means of a reasoned resolution the sequestration of public or private correspondence, documents and papers. This resolution can be appealed. Once reviewed, the documents will be retained by the court only if they are found to be useful. With respect to all the rest, the court is to ensure and maintain their confidentiality and shall instruct they be returned to the owner or beneficiary.[12] In an investigation, prosecutors would require a proper court order to sequestrate documents and correspondence in general, subject to the foregoing rules. For a search of a lawyer's office, the same rules and procedures would apply.

---

[10] Arts. 284, 286, Bolivia's Criminal Code.   [11] Art. 25, Bolivian Constitution.

[12] This is an area of debate within courts and the legal profession; *see, for example, Guía de Actuaciones Para la Aplicación del Nuevo Código de Procedimiento Penal, Alberto J. Morales Vargas, 1ª Edición, La Paz – 2004. Derechos Reservados GTZ – Proyecto de Apoyo a la Reforma Procesal Penal.*

7 Tapping of Telephone Conversations with a Lawyer

19.   Article 25 of the Constitution also includes the following among the rights of citizens: no public authority, individual or entity can intercept private conversations or communications. Proof and information obtained in violation of one's privacy of communications in any of their forms shall have no legal effect. This rule against tapping or recording private conversations in general, including of course lawyers, so far has no exception.

8 The Lawyer as Witness

20.   In connection with the investigation and prosecution of crimes, the Bolivian Code of Criminal Procedure provides that individuals who are called to testify must abstain from revealing facts that have become known to them by reason of their occupation or profession related to legally established duties of secrecy and reservation. This rule includes lawyers. Such individuals, however, cannot refuse to testify when freed from the duty of secrecy by the protected person. Individuals not freed from the duty must in any event appear before the court and explain the reasons for their abstention. If the court considers that the witness is erroneously invoking the right to maintain secrecy, by means of a reasoned and justified resolution, it must order that the deposition be taken.[13] This decision is subject to appeal.

9 The Lawyer and the Press

21.   It is not uncommon that lawyers, especially those defending criminal cases, make statements to the press as part of their function or activity. There is no legal restriction to do so, except for the general duty of confidentiality to the client.

10 Powers of the Tax and Other Authorities

22.   The primary substantive tax law in Bolivia is the Tax Code.[14] On this subject matter, it provides that the entity entrusted with investigating and controlling compliance with tax obligations (for example, the Bolivian IRS for the national taxation system) has ample and unlimited powers to demand disclosure of books, documents and commercial correspondence. It may also require personal appearances before the administrative authorities for individuals to provide information; obtain documents that have been inspected and take security measures for their preservation; seize books and documents when the

---

[13] Art. 197, Bolivia's Code of Criminal Procedure.
[14] See updated version at: http://boliviaimpuestos.com/codigo-tributario-actual.

seriousness of the case so requires; request information from third parties, individuals or entities who know (or should have known) of the facts forming part of the taxpayer's obligations; as well as demand that such parties disclose documentation relating to those situations to the extent related to taxation.

However, the Code expressly provides that professionals (like lawyers) who have the right to uphold the obligation of professional secrecy cannot be required to provide information to the tax authorities. The same privilege applies to persons in general, including lawyers, who are bound to respect secrecy of correspondence and of communications in general.[15]

It should be understood that the exercise of such right of secrecy is within the general framework of the law as described above, for example, in connection with criminal investigations, since tax fraud is a criminal offense. Tax administrative authorities, who as part of their controlling and sanctioning process identify that there are indications or elements of criminal offenses of a tax nature (fraud), are bound to send the corresponding background information and documentation to the public prosecutors for criminal prosecution separate from administrative process.

More generally, all public servants have a duty to similarly denounce felonies subject to public prosecution when facts that may constitute a possible criminal offense have become known to them in the exercise of their functions.[16]

11 National Security Issues

23. Relating to a lawyer's confidentiality duties and exceptions as discussed earlier in this chapter, there are no special national security rules. Even though Article 139 of the Constitution authorizes that a state of exception (legal reserve) can be declared by means of a law of Parliament (which could be justified for security reasons), in no case can such law suspend the rights and guarantees recognized by the Constitution.

---

[15] Art. 129, Tax Code.
[16] SAFCO Law (Law No. 1178 and related regulations), which generally governs responsibility of public servants (of which there are four kinds: executive, administrative, civil and criminal). *See* http://magistratura.organojudicial.gob.bo.

10

Brazil

FLAVIO OLIMPIO DE AZEVEDO

Olimpio de Azevedo Advogados

Preliminary Note

1.   In Brazil, only lawyers registered with the Bar Association of Brazil (OAB) and not otherwise impeded from legal practice (suspended or unlicensed) have pleading capacity before any organ of the judiciary, in any jurisdiction or authority in the country. Such capacity is essential to file lawsuits, appeals, and request court procedures.

Under Article 4 of the Bar Association Charter, lawyering by unregistered third parties is an absolute nullity of the acts carried out. In addition to the civil and administrative penalties, such action also constitutes the crime of illegal practice of a regulated profession (Art. 47 of the Criminal Misdemeanor Act).

Carlos Henrique Soares[1] considers that "Without the lawyer, the construction of the ruling constitutes an illegitimate act, due to the lack of constitutional

---

[1] Carlos Henrique Soares, *O Advogado e o Processo Constitucional*, Belo Horizonte, Decálogo, 2004, at 174.

support, as established in Article 133, and Article 1 of the Constitution of 1988, which determines the choice by the Brazilian state of the democratic paradigm of the Law." And he concludes in the following terms: "The lawyer is the guarantor of the effective exercise of the right to the adversary system and broad defense, of the structuring of legal proceedings, be they ordinary, summary, special, or extraordinary; as well as the performance of the adjudication."[2]

The lawyer's indispensability to the administration of justice is enshrined in the Constitution of 1988 (Art. 133), by which the lawyer exercises the function of guardian of the rule of law, because "legality and freedom is the tablet of the calling of a lawyer." (Ruy Barbosa). Within the constitutional framework, the participation of a lawyer is the guarantee of due process and of the exercise of a broad and unrestricted defense of the accused.

The lawyer is the protagonist of the adjudication, since the lawyer is the first judge of the case, the intermediary between the party and the judge. The lawyer is, therefore, essential to the proper functioning of the judiciary, the main scope of which is to give all parties what belongs to them.

2. Brazilian lawyers can work autonomously as a partner or associate of a law firm, or work in a company or public agency, but all must respect the rules of the statute, regulation and Code of Ethics of Law Practice. One of the main tenets set out in the ethical provisions is the lawyer's obligation to keep the professional secrecy inherent in the attorney-client relationship.

1 Scope of and Limitations on the Duty of Professional Secrecy/ Attorney-Client Privilege

A Statutory Basis and Implications

3. Secrecy is inherent in the legal profession. It is the imperative duty in the attorney-client relation established in Article 25 of the Code of Ethics of the Bar Association of Brazil and is, likewise, provided for in Article 35 of the draft of the new code under discussion in the Federal Council of the Bar Association of Brazil.

Besides covering the facts disclosed by reason of the professional involvement, this secrecy is important also for information provided in confidence, or known through third parties (witnesses, family members or employees of the client), and all information derived from letters, email messages, recordings and the like, without exception. The office or the lawyer's workplace, files and data stored on the lawyer's computers, correspondence and telephone communications are also inviolable.

---

[2] Ibid.

The respect for the confidentiality, in addition to covering all client's information, extends to partners, associates, or law firm clerks who should, therefore, also await the two-year interregnum to advocate against the firm's clients, after revocation of the powers of attorney resulting from termination of a contract linking the lawyer to the law firm, while preserving at any time unwavering ethical commitment of professional secrecy.[3]

This interval of two years before advocating against a former client or former employer, provided that professional confidentiality and privileged information are respected forever, is stipulated repeatedly by the ethical jurisprudence of the Brazilian Bar Association in these terms:

> The lawyer should respect the time lapse of two years as of the completion of the mandate to advocate against former clients, and even after that period, it should always respect the professional confidentiality and the privileged information entrusted to it, as this is the construction of the final part of the Article 19 of the Code of Ethics and Discipline (CED). This council has advised the two-year term as of the end of the last mandate, so as not to characterize unethical conduct, as a way to release the lawyer, not from the allegiance and secrecy, but from the impediment to advocate against the person for whom he worked.[4]

However, in a friendly consensual separation, provided that the professional secrecy of the attorney sponsoring the interest of one of the parties is respected, a waiver is possible:

> Under Article 18 of the CED, it is the attorney's right, in case of conflicts of interest between its clients, and the parties not agreeing, to choose one of the mandates, with due prudence and discernment, giving up the other, and protecting the professional secrecy. It is not, however, this Council's duty to endorse the attorney's behavior in this case. It is up to the Consulter, after weighing its election of one of the clients, to formalize in writing the resignation to the sponsorship of the other party. Thereafter, it will be up to it to ensure the professional secrecy, not using insider information, a task that, as it is very well highlighted in the Ethics Court (TED-I)'s case law, requires discernment and prudence, and is subject to disciplinary sanctions.[5]

---

[3] Jornal Tribuna do Direito SP, March 2002, Flavio Olímpio de Azevedo.

[4] Court of Ethics and Discipline of the São Paulo Bar Association, May 17, 2001, case nr. E-2. 360/01 Rapporteur's opinion and summary, Dr. Luiz Antônio Gambelli, Review by Dr. Claudio Felippe Zalaf, Chairman Dr. Robison Baroni.

[5] Court of Ethics and Discipline of the São Paulo Bar Association, November 12, 2009, case nr. E-1.867/99, n. E-2160/00 (2nd Summary), n. E-2914/2004, and n. E-3320/2006 opinion and summary of the Rapporteur Dr. Luiz Francisco Torquato Avolio, with dissenting vote Judge Dr. Mary Grün, Reviewed by Dr. Fabio Plantulli, Incumbent Chairman Dr. Fabio Kalil Vilela Leite.

4.   The requirement of professional secrecy reaches the attorney employed with a private or public company (Art. 19 of the CED). Thus, after the break of the employment relation, the confidentiality of all information provided and obtained by the employee through confidences or otherwise, documents, internal company communications and opinions must be respected.

       Of course, there is no secret if the fact is public and notorious, and the entire society knows it, or if it is disclosed by the client or third parties, where it is meaningless for the lawyer to bear the ethical duty of secrecy.

5.   Hélcio Maciel points out that the primary duty of a "lawyer in relation to its client is to be faithful to it. The litigant trusts him with its secrets and leaves in his or her hands the defense of its interests. If the lawyer wants, he may refuse the case, as he is free to do it, but if he accepts it, he should be worthy of the trust placed on him."[6]

       The lawyer shall keep client information confidential by all means, during or after the sponsorship or provision of services, taking precautions in different respects, either by private and public statements, or through written, spoken or television communication, and should proceed with discretion in dealing with issues inherent to the client, subject to infringement of the ethical principles being protected. This duty extends jointly to all the lawyers included in the powers of attorney granted to a law firm.

       An effective statement of this issue is as follows:

> "[T]he secret does not the result from an agreement between the client and the lawyer. It is mandatory and inherent in the profession, imposing in any circumstances, even if the client expressly authorizes the lawyer to disclose it. It, as a principle of public policy, is established in the public interest, namely the society itself, ensuring, ultimately, the right of defense.[7]

6.   In the same vein is Rafael Bielsa: "The professional secrecy and its extensive application to the inviolability of the 'office' is no exceptional attribute in a personal capacity, but an objective and impersonal principle established in the public interest, and considering a logical consequence of the professional practice."[8]

       Article 19 of the Code of Ethics of the Bar Association of Brazil allows a lawyer to represent a new client against a former client. The lawyer, in postulating on behalf of others, against a former client or former employer,

---

[6] Hélcio Maciel França Madeira, *História da advocacia: origem da profissão e advogado no direito romano*, São Paulo, Editora Revista dos Tribunais, 2002, at 77.

[7] Ruy de Azevedo Sodré, *A ética profissional e o Estatuto do Advogado*, at 398, http://www.direitocom.com/estatuto-da-advocacia-comentado/titulo-i-da-advocacia-do-artigo-1-ao-43/capitulo-ix-das-infracoes-e-sancoes-disciplinares-do-artigo-34-ao-artigo-43/artigo-34o-ao-43o-_ftn17.

[8] Rafael Bielsa, *La abogacía*, Buenos Aires, 1934, at 192.

judicially and extra judicially, must protect the confidentiality of proprietary or privileged information that has been entrusted to it.

7. The Brazilian legislature ensured that the lawyer is a servant of society by endowing the lawyer with pleading capacity, an essential element to the administration of justice. The lawyer is a guardian of the rule of law through Article 133 of the Constitution. This means the inviolability and immunity of the professional practice, subject only to the ethical rules stemming from the Code of Ethics and Discipline of the Brazilian Bar Association, and from the Bar Association charter.

    The disclosure of professional secrets, beyond being a serious ethical fault, is considered in the Brazilian law a civil and criminal offense regulated by the Constitution (Art. 5, items XII and XIV), by the Civil Code (Art. 144) and Civil Procedure Code (Art. 363), by the Criminal Code (Art. 154), and by the Statute of the Brazilian Bar Association – OAB (Art. 34), among other legislation of the Brazilian legal system.

    The protection of the lawyer and the lawyer's office is supported for the benefit of society, as pointed out by Paulo Sérgio Leite Fernandes and Alberto Rollo: "There is no reason for the lawyer not receiving such prerogatives as well, because the lawyer is the intermediary between the people and the judge, requiring independence and untouchability not to be destroyed during the rough path of the defense of individual rights against the public authority."[9]

    Rafael Bielsa recalls the public interest involved in the inviolability of professional secrecy: "The professional secrecy and its extensive application to the inviolability of the 'office' is no exceptional attribute in a personal capacity, but an objective and impersonal principle established in the public interest, and considering a logical consequence of the professional practice."[10]

B Scope of the Duty

8. The duty to maintain professional secrecy reaches any judicial, civil litigation or other legal advice. A simple query from a client to a lawyer is protected by the attorney-client privilege; in short, all information disclosed under the attorney-client relationship is protected by secrecy. Professional secrecy refers to facts about which the lawyer becomes knowledgeable during the attorney-client relationship. This duty of confidentiality reaches documents, letters, email and the like.

    This duty of secrecy does not stem from the client's express request, because professional secrecy is a matter of public interest and constitutes an essential element of the privacy of certain professionals to whom people entrust their personal privacy and businesses.

---

[9] Fernandes, Paulo Sérgio Leite and Rollo, Alberto, excerpt copied from article in the National Bar Association Conference, 18, Annals, São Paulo, 2003, p. 1839.

[10] Bielsa, Rafael, *La abogacía*, Buenos Aires, 1934, p. 192.

Professional secrecy is an essential tool to ensure the fulfillment of the citizen's rights of defense, because it ensures to the client the inviolability of facts entrusted to the lawyer. Consequently, it is assigned the status of general interest and a matter of public policy. The lawyer who becomes aware of facts exposed by the client cannot disclose them or use them for the benefit of other clients, or in the lawyer's own interest, and should remain silent and abstain forever.[11]

In another case, if the Internal Revenue Service is assessing the client and asks the lawyer to provide information about the business and financial position of the client, the information is considered confidential, and the lawyer should refuse to provide such information, basing his or her decision on Articles 25 to 27 of the Code of Ethics and Discipline of the Brazilian Bar Association.

In addition, judgments passed by ethical courts forbid even the provision of information to the IRS office that is assessing the client and asks the lawyer for information concerning the client's business:

> Item LXIII of the Article 5 of the Constitution addresses the apparent conflict between the duty to inform and the right to silence. In this antinomy, prevails the understanding that the passive subject of the tax obligation cannot be compelled to provide information that might incriminate itself. (Equivalent to the Fifth Amendment in the USA.) Confidentiality is a mandatory precept, and is based on the principle of trust between the lawyer and the client, and is above the mere contractual relationship "inter parties," and should be preserved, under penalty of committing the disciplinary offense provided for in the Law Nr. 8906/94. Interpretation of the Articles 5, item LXIII of the Constitution, 34, item VII of the Law Nr. 8.906/94, and Articles 25 and 26 of the Code of Ethics and Discipline.[12]

C Law Firms

9. Lawyers regularly enrolled with the Brazilian Bar Association may associate for mutual professional cooperation to combine efforts and expertise in a partnership to provide advocacy services. This partnership's charter is registered and approved by the OAB. These legal entities, in accordance with Brazilian law, cannot commit disciplinary ethical infractions. So, if a disclosure of professional secrecy on behalf of the firm occurs, the law firm punishment applies to all its members.

---

[11] Court of Ethics and Discipline of the São Paulo Bar Association, March 17, 2011, opinion and summary of the Rapporteur Dr. Mary Grün, Reviewer Dr. Fabio de Souza Ramacciotti, Chairman Dr. José Carlos Santos da Silva.

[12] Court of Ethics and Discipline of the São Paulo Bar Association, March 20, 2003, opinion and summary of the Rapporteur Dr. José Roberto Bottino, Reviewed by Dr. Ernesto Lopes Ramos, Chairman Dr. Robison Baroni, case nr. E-2. 709/03.

Likewise, if other ethical misconduct is committed by the partners or associates using the name of the law firm (for instance, immoderate advertisement, lack of accountability in contracts signed on behalf of the firm or customer acquisition), all partners and associates will be punished by the Ethics Courts of the sectional offices.

Also, under penalty of committing an ethical violation, lawyers from a particular firm may not represent clients in court with opposing interests, especially when there is breach of professional secrecy. In this light, the ethics precepts included in the Attorney's Statute and the Code of Ethics and Discipline apply to law firms.

A typical form of breach of confidentiality is the practice of law concurrent with unrelated activities in the same place, without operational segregation. This results in the possibility of violation of the lawyer's files, a breach of privacy and thus offending the secrecy principle of the profession, which is to respect the privacy and the confidentiality of all information provided by the client.

There is no impediment to lawyers being partners in different businesses, performing other activities and being a partner in a law firm. What violates ethical requirements is to have the seat of different companies at the same premises where the law firm is based, without any protection of confidentiality. The confusion between the practices of concurrent activities on the same site, including the display of advertising of different activities with law firms, all commingled, offends the principle of inviolability of the law practice and professional secrecy.

10.   In Brazil, violations of this ethical precept are sometimes made by lawyers who form a law firm along with accountants, realtors, industrial property agents and real estate management, in an effort to attract clients. For example, a client hires a firm's accounting services, and at some point the client needs a lawyer to submit a defense to the IRS. This union of professions greatly facilitates the acquisition of clients, but it violates ethical principles in Brazil.

An effective statement of this principle is as follows:

> [T]here is no way to guarantee the confidentiality of the relationship between the client and the lawyer – a secret similar to the confessional secrecy – when other non-lawyer professionals circulate in the same environment; when secretaries or receptionists work jointly for all activities performed. On the other hand, it is clear the possibility of clients' acquisition, considering the legal issues existing in the other activities, which the lawyer learns through the joint activity.[13]

---

[13] Court of Ethics and Discipline of the São Paulo Bar Association, opinion and summary of the Rapporteur Dr. Zanon de Paula Barros, Reviewed by Dr. Maria do Carmo Whitaker, Chairman Dr. João Teixeira Grande.

The obligation of keeping the confidentiality of documents filed in the office and its computers and disclosures occurring within the law firm are not limited to the lawyer but include the employees and collaborators in that office. If professional secrets are disclosed, employment termination with cause is applicable for serious misconduct.

11. There is a quarantine of two years for a lawyer being adverse to a former client, provided that the lawyer does not disclose information covered by professional secrecy. This applies to the law firm, as well, but only to those partners or employees directly involved with the former client, mainly those who received powers of attorney, as stated in the solution to questions resolved by the Ethics Court of the Bar Association, Sectional Office of São Paulo:

> The attorney-client relationship and representation being governed by the individual granting of mandate, and not by the fee contract with the law firm (Art. 15 of the CED), there is no ethical impediment of its members to advocate against a person with whom they have not had any relation. Only regarding the former client's lawyer, an ethical impediment applies (called "quarantine," for two years), as well as the compliance "ad eternum" with the professional secrecy, in the light of the interpretation long given by this Council to the provision in the Articles 19 and 25 of the CED, consolidated in the Case nr. E-3481/2007. As a result, it is mandatory that the Consulter's name will not appear in the said case, on the instrument of powers of attorney granted by the bank, or on the letterhead of the law firm.[14]

12. A new reality emerges with the operation of foreign lawyers in Brazil, as consultants on foreign law. They are also subjected to the rigors of the protection of professional confidentiality and other ethical rules applicable to lawyers and law firms, as provided for in Ordinance nr. 91-2000 of the Federal Council of the Brazilian Bar Association – OAB, which provides in Article 8:

> [T]he provisions of the Federal Law nr. 8906 of July 4, 1994, the General Regulation of the Statute of Law Practice and of the Bar Association of Brazil-OAB, the Code of Ethics and Discipline of the OAB, the Internal Regulations of the Sectional Offices, the Resolutions and Ordinances of the OAB, especially this Ordinance apply to consultancy firms on foreign law and consultants on foreign law.

D The Lawyer as Witness

13. In the name of protecting professional secrecy, Brazilian law provides as follows, regarding the lack of obligation of the lawyer to testify in court

---

[14] Court of Ethics and Discipline of the São Paulo Bar Association, June 19, 2008, case nr. E-3630/2008; opinion and summary of Judge Dr. Luiz Francisco Torquato Avolio, against the vote of Rapporteur Dr. Diogenes Madeu, Reviewed by Dr. Carlos José Santos da Silva, Chairman Dr. Carlos Roberto F. Mateucci.

concerning facts known because of the lawyer's professional relationship with the client. The *mens leges* is to protect the inviolability of the professional secrecy:

(i) Statute of the Law Practice of the Bar Association of Brazil – OAB (Law nr. 8906/94, as amended by Law nr. 11.767/08, Article 7, Paragraph XIX: "It is the lawyer's right . . . to refuse to testify as a witness in a case where it worked or should work; or about facts related to the person of whom it is, or has been a lawyer, even if authorized or required by the client, as well as facts that constitute professional secrecy."

(ii) Code of Ethics and Discipline of the Bar Association of Brazil (Art. 25): "The professional confidentiality is inherent in the profession, imposing the compliance with it, except in case of serious threat to the right to life, honor; or when the lawyer is affronted by the client and, in self-defense, has to disclose a secret, but always restricted the interest of the case. Article 26. The lawyer should keep the confidentiality even in court testimony about what it knows because of its office, and should refuse to testify as a witness in a case where it worked or should work, or about facts related to a person of whom it is or has been a lawyer, even if authorized or required by the client. Article 39 of the draft of the new Code of Ethics maintained the release of obligation: The lawyer is not required to testify in judicial or administrative proceedings, on facts about which it should keep the professional secret."

(iii) Brazilian Civil Code (Art. 229), "No one may be compelled to testify on a fact: I – About which, due to status or profession, it should keep secret."

(iv) Code of Civil Procedure (Art. 347), "The party is not required to testify on facts: . . . II – About which, due to status or profession, it should keep secret."

(v) Code of Criminal Procedure (Art. 207), "People who, because of function, ministry, trade, or profession are required to keep secrecy are forbidden to testify, unless they are released from the obligation by the interested party, and want to give their testimony."

The protection of professional secrecy is of interest to the entire society, not exhausting itself as a prerogative inherent in a profession, and is essential to the fulfillment of a citizen's right of defense. This way, the lawyer cannot be a witness of facts the lawyer learned during the attorney-client relationship, since this would violate the pact of silence.

The point is made by Fernando da Costa Tourinho, by quoting Tornaghi:

> The protection of professional secrecy, in accordance with Tornaghi, stems from the interests of all, from the need that one has to trust, and be sure that its secret will not be revealed, and its disclosure may even constitute a criminal offense pursuant to the Article 154 of the Criminal Code.

The law forbids the testimony of people who, because of their function, ministry, trade, or profession must keep a secret.[15]

14. The lawyer subpoenaed to testify concerning a client either before a police authority or in court should not even attend on the appointed day, informing the court or the authority, by petition, the impediment, as already enshrined in the case law: "The Lawyer can and should refuse to appear, and to testify as a witness in investigation related to alleged false documents, originated from its client, which it attached to the judicial dockets."[16]

However, the judgments of the Court of Ethics indicate that the facts witnessed must have a direct relationship with the client representation.

15. An example is the resolution of the First Court of Ethics of the Bar Association – Sectional São Paulo, which released a lawyer to testify in a case of sexual harassment between a client and an employee of the client's company. The decisive opinion by Ricardo Cholbi Tepedino puts very properly the question, and resolves the issue:

> The consulter declares that it witnessed the harassment by its client (that it does not clarify whether it was an employer or client) of the employee of the company for which it worked, and that this situation bears no relation whatsoever to the purpose for which the consulter was hired, because, as explained above, this consulter rendered its services to this company only in the civil area.

That is, the consulter says that it did not deliver any service (*rectius* did not practice law, either by counseling or by issuing a value judgment about the client's behavior) related to the illicit facts at hand. Rather, it should be repeated, he claims to have witnessed them, and on this factual premise, and on no other premise originated from cogitations of the Court, should an attorney be allowed to testify about a client. So, the answer is to be based on this premise and will be considered if it is true: Would facts coming to the attorney's knowledge because of the attorney's physical proximity to the client be covered by professional secrecy (which is, we should insist on this *ad nauseam*, the situation described in the query), or are only those facts that the client discloses to the lawyer as a result of the professional practice covered?

It is worth mentioning the provision of Section 1 of Article 1 of the Resolution Nr. 17/2000 of this Court:

> Client information is guarded by the cloak of secrecy, not only the secrets entrusted by the client to the lawyer, and the insider information, but all that becomes known to the lawyer resulting from the professional practice,

---

[15] Fernando da Costa Tourinho, Criminal Procedures Code, commented, São Paulo, Editora Saraiva, 1998, at 411.
[16] Revista dos Tribunais nr. 531/401.

either revelations made by word of mouth by the client, or those in documents or communication letters, and also those known from other sources.

It should be noted that the provision refers to disclosures made by the client or documents and communication letters, and not facts merely witnessed by the lawyer, just because the lawyer was in the company of the client.

If the lawyer witnesses the client perpetrating an illegal act that has nothing to do with the object of the advice it lends, but the lawyer witnessed it only because the lawyer was providing this assistance (such as in the case of a tax lawyer invited to have lunch with a client, who witnesses the client committing a crime of racism at the restaurant), can the lawyer testify about that fact?

Still to give a broader understanding of what is *professional practice*, the mere physical proximity that the professional relationship provides alone is not sufficient to constitute professional practice. So, in the example of the restaurant mentioned above, the professional would have witnessed the act of racism only because the lawyer was the offender's lawyer, but that conduct, entirely unrelated to the lawyer's service, cannot be taken as professional secrecy. "In this particular case, the same occurs: the sexual and moral harassment would have only been witnessed by the Consulter, who regarding it did not provide any legal advice, so there is no professional secrecy to protect."[17]

The case had the following summary:

> The duty to keep the confidentiality of the facts that come to the lawyer's knowledge because of the practice of law is one of the fundamental principles of the profession, and only exceptionally can be mitigated. It is not included in this duty, however, the facts witnessed by the lawyer that have no relation to the exercise of its occupation, and that have not been the subject of consultation or counseling, reason why, in this case and on these specific facts, the lawyer can testify in court.[18]

But the lawyer may never denounce the client to the authorities, as indicated by the First Ethics Court of the Bar Association of São Paulo:

> In times when the law practice is mobilized by their peers and representatives in defending the right and duty of confidentiality against violations of professional prerogatives, with indiscriminate invasion of offices by the police, it sounds at least strange a desire of denunciation by a lawyer. The denouncing lawyer, with its reprehensible act taints not only itself, but the law practice as a whole, sowing a sense of widespread

---

[17] Court of Ethics and Discipline of the São Paulo Bar Association, December 15, 2011, case nr. 4061/2011, opinion and summary of the judge Dr. Ricardo Cholbi Tepedino, defeated the Rapporteur, Dr. Fabio Kalil Vilela Leite, with convergent voting statement of the judge, Dr. Fábio de Souza Ramacciotti, Review by Dr. Luiz Francisco Torquato Avolio, Chairman Dr. José Carlos Santos Da Silva.

[18] Ibid.

distrust of the profession. The lawyer has the right to silence and the duty to silence. Regardless of the statutory penalty to be applied, the accusing lawyer shall have from its peers and from the Order itself not only contempt, but shall carry the stigma of a denouncer.[19]

E Exceptions to and Optional Derogations from the Duty of Professional Secrecy

16.   There are two exceptions set forth in the Code of Ethics and Discipline of the Bar Association of Brazil regarding the breach of secrecy.

The first exception is embodied in Article 25:

> The professional confidentiality is inherent in the profession, imposing the compliance with it, except in case of serious threat to the right to life, honor; or when the lawyer is affronted by the client and, in self-defense, needs to disclose a secret, but always restricted by the interest of the case.

The second exception is in Article 27: "The confidences made by the client to the lawyer may be used at the limits of the need for defense, as long as it is authorized by the client."

Article 37 of the draft of the new Code of Ethics upholds the exception: "The professional secrecy will yield in the face of compelling circumstances that lead the lawyer to disclose secrets in its defense, especially when forced to do so by a hostile attitude of the client."

The Ethical Courts of the Brazilian Bar Association interpret the rule in exceptional cases:

> The professional secret is an essential tool to ensure the fulfilment of the citizen's rights of defense, because it ensures the client the inviolability of facts entrusted to the lawyer. So it is assigned the status of general interest and a matter of public policy. The lawyer who becomes aware of facts exposed by the client cannot disclose them, or use them for the benefit of other clients, or in his own interest, and should remain silent and abstain forever. The professional who violates this principle is subject to disciplinary penalty (Art. 34, item VII of the EOAB), and subject to the definition of crime of violation of professional secrecy as provided in the Article 154 of the Criminal Code. However, if the lawyer was wrongly accused by the client of having committed acts it did not commit, and that will bring it harm, or when it is unjustly threatened, it is imperative that it may be able to defend against such accusations, and it is not acceptable that the lawyer's right of defense is hampered by ethical principles. A lawyer cannot have its right of defense harmed, or guaranteed in a lesser extent than the right of defense of other citizens. If it suffers accusation or attack, it could disclose facts covered by the professional

---

[19] Court of Ethics and Discipline of the São Paulo Bar Association, August 18, 2005, case nr. E-3. 200/2005, opinion and summary of the Rapporteur, Dr. Fábio Kalil Vilela Leite, Reviewed by Dr. Maria do Carmo Whitaker, Chairman Dr. João Teixeira Grande.

secrecy cloak, based on the Arts. 25 of the CED, and 3 of the Resolution 17/2000 of the TED-I SP. However, the lawyer only profits from the exclusion of illegality if the disclosures are made within the strict limit and interest of its defense, and if the lawyer who takes personal responsibility for the violation (Art. 4 of Resolution 17/2000) is admonished.[20]

In the face of accusations and vilification suffered by the lawyer by former clients, it does not impose on it the duty to preserve the professional secrecy "in totum," and it may make disclosures in the necessary limits and very restricted to the interest of its own defense, and provided that they are useful to it (Resolution No. 17/2000 of the TED-I). A lawyer affronted by another lawyer should resort to the Ethics and Discipline Court to resolve the issues related to professional rights, as provided in the Ordinance nr. 83/96 of the Federal Council.[21]

Professional secrecy in legal practice is quite strict, but not absolute, and can be broken in cases of threat to life or honor, or when the lawyer is affronted by the client and needs to disclose secrets or exhibit documents that have been entrusted to the lawyer and that are indispensable for the lawyer's defense. The disclosure of professional secrets and exhibition of documents should be confined exclusively to the limits of the case, its transmission for the benefit of third parties or to protect the lawyer from unfair attack by the client. In this case, not having occurred any of the exceptions of the Article 25 of the CED, the Consulters must refrain from using, in their defense, the documents belonging to the former client, which are in their power.[22]

F In-House Counsel

17. In-house counsel in Brazil enjoy the same prerogatives, in all areas of the law, as extended to lawyers in external law firms. All client communications with in-house lawyers are similarly protected.

2 Supervision and Sanctions

18. A lawyer who violates professional secrecy regulations will be subject to the legal consequences discussed in the following sections.

---

[20] Court of Ethics and Discipline of the São Paulo Bar Association, March 17, 2011, case nr. 3965/2010, opinion and summary of Rapporteur Dr. Mary Grün, Reviewer Dr. Fábio de Souza Ramacciotti, Chairman Dr. José Carlos Santos da Silva.

[21] Court of Ethics and Discipline of the São Paulo Bar Association, October 19, 2006, case nr. E-3.388/2006, opinion and summary nr. 1, Dr. Fábio Kalil Vilela Leite, defeated vote of the Rapporteur Dr. João Luiz Lopes.

[22] Court of Ethics and Discipline of the São Paulo Bar Association, March 18, 2004, cases nr. E-1447/97, E-543/97, E- 1669/98, E-2810/03, E-2. 899/04, and Resolution Nr. 17/2000 of this Court, opinion and summary of the Rapporteur, Dr. Guilherme Figueiredo Florindo, Reviewed by Dr. Claudio Felippe Zalaf, Chairman Dr. João Teixeira Grande.

A Ethical-Disciplinary Liability

19.　Article 34, Section VII of the Statute of the Law Practice – Law 8906 of 1994, provides, "Violating professional secrecy without cause is a disciplinary offense."

Expected sanction: reserved censure is accomplished by sending an official letter to the wrongful lawyer, without publicity of the fact. In case of relapse, the applicable penalty is suspension from professional practice throughout the country, for a period of 30 days to 12 months.

In case of an extremely serious disciplinary offense in violation of professional secrecy, the Ethics Court of the Bar Association of Brazil can apply the accessory penalty of censure or suspension, cumulative with a monetary fine in an amount corresponding to one annuity (one year's bar association dues) charged in the year of the sentence, up to a maximum of 10 times that amount, payable to the lawyers' council.

An example of an extremely serious professional secrecy breach is the following sentence of the Ethics Court of the Sectional Office of the São Paulo Bar Association, which applied the maximum penalty to a lawyer:

> A Lawyer who, due to disagreements in the collection of attorneys' fees uses information obtained while in the exercise of the mandate to offer tax denunciation against a former client. Breach of professional confidentiality duty. Representation accepted. Examined, reported, and discussed these dockets of disciplinary proceedings Nr. 4.277/01, the members of the Fourth Disciplinary Panel agree unanimously, in accordance with the vote of the Rapporteur, to accept the representation, and apply to the Respondent the penalty of censure, combined with a fine equivalent to the value of ten (10) annuities, as the violations of Articles 31 and 33 and paragraph VII of Article 34 of the Statute were characterized, in accordance with Article 36, Sections I and II, and 39 of Law Nr. 8.906/94.[23]

The application of a penalty of an ethical nature is a lengthy procedure, and the lawyer is granted legal defense and appeals of the decision to the Appeal's Chamber and to the Federal Council in disciplinary proceedings before the Ethics Courts of the Bar Association of Brazil.

B Criminal Law

20.　The violation of professional secrecy by a lawyer is considered a crime in accordance with Article 154 of the Criminal Code: "Disclose to third parties, without cause, a secret that one knows as a consequence of its function, ministry, trade, or profession, and the disclosure of which could cause harm

---

[23] Court of Ethics and Discipline of the São Paulo Bar Association, Sept. 24, 2004, disciplinary case nr. 4.277 / 01, Chairman Reynaldo Fransozo Cardoso, Rapporteur ad hoc Marcelo Pereira Gômara.

to others. Penalty – detention of three months to one year, or a fine. Sole Paragraph – Subject to complaint."

The protection for the client is the inviolability of professional secrecy. It is the people's right to hire professionals, doctors, lawyers, psychologists and the so-called necessary confidants to whom they reveal secrets of their personal life and business, and to have their secrets preserved.

The rule of Article 7, section XIX of the Brazilian Bar Association Charter goes against the inviolability of the professional secrecy, in case the client consents.

It also does not depend on any losses because it is a formal crime. The law describes an action and a result; the offense will be consummated at the time of taking the action, regardless of the outcome.

C Civil Illicit Actions

21. The Brazilian courts apply monetary compensation for reimbursement of material and moral damages by a lawyer who discloses secrets originating from the attorney-client relationship.

An example of a concrete case: In the town of Cocheira, a lawyer during an interview offered the press details of family litigation of a prominent person in the region who was arrested for nonpayment of child support, causing damage to the image of the client. The lawyer was sentenced to pay compensation in the civil appeal 718109-7-6, Court of Justice of the State of Parana.

3 Duty to Provide Information to the Authorities

A Money Laundering and Terrorism

22. The Money Laundering Fighting Law nr. 12.683 / 2012, which requires individuals or legal entities knowledgeable of financial crime due to their profession to report the operations to the authorities, does not expressly mention lawyers. In October 2001, the Brazilian president of the Council for Financial Activities Control (COAF), Adrienne de Senna, referring to lawyers and accountants, proclaimed that: "No big money laundering operation is done without the help of these professionals."

In accordance with what was reported on the website of the *Revista Consultor Jurídico* on October 31, 2001 (www.conjur.com.br), Senna said:

> [T]he lawyers and accountants became a target of the government in the repressive measures against money laundering. ... The President of the COAF did not specify the measures to be adopted, but it is known that the goal of the government agency is to dismantle the professional secrecy invoked by those who do not cooperate with the investigation. ... Lawyers and accountants are important in money laundering activity because they

open the doors for the businesses, and provide the map for opening offshore accounts and other activities. Companies use lawyers for tax evasion, study legal ways to pay less tax, and also assist in money laundering practices.[24]

The OAB was asked for guidance following the controversy regarding the breach of confidentiality by the Financial Intelligence Unit of Brazil. The OAB stated:

From the Constitutional text quoted (Art. 133), what can be inferred is that the lawyer is indispensable to the administration of justice, but not as "denouncer of its client," but as a defender of the interests of those who are suspected or accused of being involved in a crime, or as an assistant to different subjects (legal or not legal), when, then, he performs services of consulting, assistance, counseling, etc.;

The jurisdictional role of the State revolves around a series of principles of indisputable relevance. Among them is the guarantee of self-defense and technical defense, broad defense, the adversary system, etc. All of these principles and guarantees must be strictly preserved, especially by those who have a duty to ensure them;

When the Constitution says that the lawyer is indispensable to the administration of justice, in short, what is intended is that the interests of the suspect or accused are properly defended, so that in the end, justice prevails, and nothing else. There is no due process without the necessary participation of a technical defense.

Any intent to reverse this constitutional position of the lawyer in the wide spectrum of the structure of Justice, demanding from it the performance of a role other than of defender – if not diametrically opposite – of denouncing those who entrusted professional secrets to it, seems, therefore, absolutely unconstitutional.

The following summary put an end to any discussion:

Law nr. 12.683/12, amended the Law nr. 9.613/98 to make more efficient the criminal prosecution of money laundering offenses. Inapplicability to lawyers and law firms. Special Law, Statute of the Bar Association (Law nr. 8.906/94), cannot be implicitly revoked by law that addresses generally other professions. Lawyers and law firms should not enroll with the COAF (Financial Activities Control Council), and they do not have a duty to disclose sensitive data of their clients that has been delivered to them in the professional practice. Obligation of national and state offices and commissions of prerogatives supporting lawyers who are illegally urged to make that disclosure. Sentence: Examined, reported, and discussed the dockets of the case at hand, the members of the Special Body of Plenum Council of the CFOAB agree unanimously

---

[24] Luiz Flavio Gomes, *Capital laundering and breach of professional secrecy of the lawyer*, http://ww3.lfg.com.br/.

to acknowledge and respond to the query in accordance with the vote of the Rapporteur, an integral part of this sentence.[25]

In the final version of the draft of the newly proposed Code of Ethics of the Bar Association of Brazil, it was discussed recently whether lawyers should be required to report suspicious transactions of their clients to the authorities, as desired by the Financial Activities Control Council.[26] But this breach of confidentiality was not approved.[27]

The chair of the Federal Council of the OAB asserted, regarding the applicability of the breach of confidentiality of lawyers based on the Law nr. 12.683/ 12, "that secrecy is a constitutional guarantee, and that the Attorney General's Office has already spoken out in favor of it at the Supreme Court. The inviolability of legal practice, pursuant to the Constitution, presupposes the confidentiality of information between lawyers and their clients. This constitutional guarantee is in favor of the citizen, who cannot see its defense turned into an instrument of accusation."[28]

The trend in Brazil is to ensure professional secrecy, which is inviolable in money laundering crimes, whatever the action of consultancy or litigation, within the general principle that the lawyer cannot be a denouncer of a client.

B Tapping of Telephone Conversations with a Lawyer

23. The telephone conversations of lawyers and clients can be tapped by the government or by police officials if a court order is obtained in advance. It is not permitted, however, for a lawyer to record a conversations with a client unless the client has agreed to such recording.

C National Security Issues

24. At the time of the military dictatorship in Brazil, Law No. 7,170,14 was enacted in December 1983. This law defines crimes against national security and political and social order. It establishes procedures for prosecution and trial for violations in these areas. However, with the advent of democracy in Brazil, the rule of law has prevailed, and this law has never been applied. The application of it to attorney-client privilege issues is unclear because of its limited application to cases other than a limitation on attorney-client contact during a brief initial period of detention during investigations by the government.

---

[25] Sectional Council of the São Paulo Bar Association, OAB / SP, August 20, 2012, query nr. 49.0000.2012.006678-6 / EPO, Rapporteur Daniela Rodrigues Teixeira, Chairman Alberto de Paula Machado.

[26] *Conjur*, June 28, 2014, http://www.conjur.com.br/2014-jun-28/oab-votara-regra-obrigacao-advogado-delatar-cliente.

[27] *Conjur*, April 12, 2015, http://www.conjur.com.br/2015-abr-12/codigo-etica-oab-comeca-votado-neste.

[28] Ibid.

11

British Virgin Islands

CLAIRE GOLDSTEIN

Harney Westwood & Riegels

Preliminary Note

1.　British Virgin Islands (BVI) law is derived from statutes enacted by the BVI legislature and from the English common law, which applies by virtue of the Common Law (Declaration of Application) Act 1705. This means that English case law is followed in the BVI, although strictly speaking only decisions of the Privy Council are binding. In practice, however, decisions of lower courts in England are highly persuasive and are generally followed. English decisions on confidentiality and legal professional privilege are therefore highly relevant in the BVI. Indeed, BVI law on legal professional privilege is essentially derived from English case law, although the concept has now been incorporated into statutory law in the BVI.

　　The English rules of equity also apply in the BVI by virtue of the West Indies Associated Supreme Court (Virgin Islands) Act 1969, although the terms of the act make it clear that the rules of equity were applied in the territory before that date. The rules of equity are also relevant to considerations of confidentiality.

1　Scope and Limitations on Professional Secrecy

A　Statutory Basis and Implications

2.　There is no specific statutory protection in the BVI for confidential information (although there is statutory protection for information that is covered by legal professional privilege). There is also no data-protection legislation, although the BVI recently passed the Computer Misuse and Cybercrime Act 2014, which incorporates some limited data-protection provisions. There are, however, three different sources of the lawyers' duty to keep their clients' information secret: (i) contractual obligations, which generally arise out of provisions in the retainer letter; (ii) an equitable duty of confidentiality; and (iii) legal professional privilege.

a　Contract

3.　The most straightforward obligation to keep information confidential is likely to arise from the provisions of the retainer letter, which typically clearly spell out a lawyer's duty in relation to the client's information. Where an obligation to keep information secret arises as a result of a contract, this contract remains in force even if the information has become public.[1] This is important to bear in mind because a contractual obligation is different in this regard from an equitable duty of confidentiality and from legal professional privilege. Clearly, however, if information has already become public, then this might limit any damages that may be recoverable for breach of contract. Further, the courts will not usually issue an injunction to restrain a breach of contract if the

---

[1]　*AG v. Barker* [1990] 3 All ER 257.

information has already become public because such an injunction would serve no purpose.[2]

b Equitable Duty of Confidentiality

4.   An equitable duty of confidentiality generally arises either because the relationship between the parties is one that the law imposes a duty of confidentiality or because the nature and circumstances in which the information was received make it such that the law will require the recipient to keep the information confidential. When a lawyer receives information from a client, it is clear that such receipt is impressed with the requirement of confidentiality for both of the above reasons. It has also been stated that, for the law to protect confidential information, it must be clear and identifiable as confidential information.[3] The burden of proof will be on the party asserting that the information is confidential to prove that the information was clearly intended to be confidential.[4]

c Legal Professional Privilege

5.   Legal professional privilege can be seen as an aspect of the lawyer's duty of confidentiality toward a client. It, however, goes further than confidentiality. In certain circumstances, clients will be required to disclose confidential information, but they will not be required to disclose information that is covered by legal professional privilege.

The statutory basis in the BVI for legal professional privilege is found in Section 22 of the Evidence Act, which provides:

(1) Subject to this Act, a legal practitioner or his client shall not be compelled to disclose any confidential communication, oral or written, which passed between them directly or indirectly through an agent of either, if such communication was made for the purpose of obtaining or giving legal advice.

(2) Subsection (1) does not apply unless the communication was made to or by the legal practitioner in his professional capacity or by the client while the relationship of client and legal practitioner subsisted, whether or not litigation was pending or contemplated.

(3) No claim of privilege shall be allowed if the communication between a client and his legal practitioner was made for the purpose of committing a fraud, crime or other wrongful act.

The word "client" is defined in Section 113 of the Evidence Act as:

(a) an employee or agent of a client,

(b) a person acting, for the time being as a manager, committee or other person however described, under a law that relates to persons of unsound mind, if

---

[2] *AG v. Blake* [1998] Ch 439.   [3] *Fraser v. Thames Television Ltd* [1984] QB 44.
[4] Colin Riegels and Ian Mann, *British Virgin Islands Commercial Law*, Sweet & Maxwell Asia Ltd, Hong Kong, 2015, 13.010.

the client is of unsound mind and in respect of whose person, estate or property, the person is so acting, and

(c) if the client had died, a personal representative of the client, and in relation to a confidential communication made by a client in respect of property in which the client had an interest, also includes a successor in title to that interest.

The idea behind legal professional privilege is that clients should be able to go to lawyers to obtain legal advice without fear of subsequently having to disclose information discussed with their lawyers. In this regard, Lord Taylor of Gosforth CJ stated in *R v. Derby Magistrates' Court, Ex p B* [1996] AC 487:

> In *Balabel v Air India* [1988] Ch 317 the basic principle justifying legal professional privilege was again said to be that a client should be able to obtain legal advice in confidence. The principle which runs through all these cases ... is that a man must be able to consult his lawyer in confidence, since otherwise he might hold back half the truth. The client must be sure that what he tells his lawyer in confidence will never be revealed without his consent ... once any exception to the general rule is allowed, the client's confidence is necessarily lost.

Similarly in *R (Morgan Grenfell & Co Ltd) v. Special Comr of Income Tax* [2003] 1 AC 563, Lord Hoffman said that legal advice could not be "effectively obtained unless the client is able to put all the facts before the adviser without fear that they may afterwards be disclosed without his consent."

In *Ventouris v. Mountain* [1991] 1 WLR 607, Bingham LJ also noted that:

> The doctrine of legal professional privilege is rooted in the public interest, which requires that hopeless and exaggerated claims and unsound and spurious defences be so far as possible discouraged, and civil disputes so far as possible settled without resort to judicial decision. To this end it is necessary that actual and potential litigants, be they claimants or respondents, should be free to unburden themselves without reserve to their legal advisers, and their legal advisers be free to give honest and candid advice on a sound factual basis, without fear that these communications may be relied upon by an opposing party if the dispute comes before the court for decision.

6. Another important point in relation to privilege generally is that it is the client's privilege, not the lawyer's privilege.[5] This means that only the client (not the lawyer) can waive privilege. This can lead to difficult situations for lawyers who are accused of negligence and want to rely upon privileged documents to defend themselves.

The concept of legal professional privilege is also recognized in a number of BVI statutes that would otherwise require disclosures to be made to the relevant authorities. These statutes include the Proliferation Financing (Prohibition) Act

---

[5] *Wilson v. Rastall* (1792) 4 TR 753.

2009 Section 18(2); the Financial Investigation Agency Act 2003, Section 4(2) (d); the Mutual Legal Assistance (Tax matters) Act 2003, Section 5(2); and the Financial Services Commission Act 2012, Section 48A(1). Where information is privileged, the lawyer will not have to make the necessary disclosure. As discussed later in this chapter, however, there are some situations when information may be confidential but not privileged, where lawyers may still have to report to the authorities about their clients.

B Scope

7. There are two forms of legal professional privilege: legal advice privilege and litigation privilege. This was accepted in *Three Rivers District Council v. The Governor and Company of the Bank of England* [2005] 1 AC 610 (*Three Rivers*) by Lord Carswell, where he noted that "legal professional privilege is a single integral privilege, whose sub-heads are legal advice privilege and litigation privilege."

a Legal Advice Privilege

8. Legal advice privilege may be claimed whenever a person seeks advice from a lawyer. The leading case on legal advice privilege is *Three Rivers*. In this case, Lord Scott of Foscote helpfully set out a number of features of legal advice privilege:

   (i) To be privileged, a document must be confidential. This is not, by itself, enough, but it is an essential requirement.
   (ii) Privilege is absolute. This means that it "cannot be overridden by some supposedly greater public interest." This is in contrast to some other jurisdictions such as Canada. This principle was also expressed in *In re L (A Minor) (Police Investigation: Privilege)*, [1997] AC 16, 32 by Lord Nicholls of Birkenhead when he said, "the public interest in a party being able to obtain informed legal advice in confidence prevails over the public interest in all relevant material being available to courts when deciding cases."
   (iii) Legal advice privilege has a relationship with litigation privilege because legal advice is often sought when litigation is contemplated. To attract legal advice privilege, however, litigation is not a necessary condition.

In *Three Rivers*, it was made clear that the scope of legal advice privilege extends beyond advice given to clients specifically about their legal rights and obligations. Accordingly, it was held in *Three Rivers* that legal advice privilege extends to advice given in relation to the presentation of material to an inquiry. It was, however, noted that there are some limits to this category of legal professional privilege. In this regard, Lord Scott noted that "if a solicitor becomes the client's 'man of business,' and some solicitors do, responsible for advising the client on all matters of business, including investment policy,

161

finance policy and other business matters, the advice may lack a relevant legal context."

Lord Scott considered that there was no way of avoiding marginal cases but stated that they should be decided in accordance with the following principle:

> In cases of doubt the judge called upon to make the decision should ask whether the advice related to the rights, liabilities, obligations or remedies of the client either under private law or under public law. If it does not, then in my opinion, legal advice privilege would not apply.

Lord Carswell in *Three Rivers* expressed the situation thus:

> '[A]ll communications between a solicitor and his client relating to a transaction in which the solicitor has been instructed for the purpose of obtaining legal advice will be privileged, notwithstanding that they do not contain advice on matters of law or construction, provided that they are directly related to the performance by the solicitor of his professional duty as legal adviser of his client.'

9. Even if information is not considered to be privileged, the information may still be covered by the lawyer's duty of confidentiality. It is also to be noted that the burden of proof is for the party refusing disclosure to establish that the information is privileged.[6]

Legal advice privilege extends only to communications between lawyers and their clients. It does not extend to communications between third parties unless the third party can be considered the client's agent. If, however, information is given to or from, for example, a client's accountant that is intended to be considered by the accountant, then it may not be covered. This situation was explained by Lord Loreburn in *Jones v. Great Central Railway* [1910] AC 4:

> Both client and solicitor may act through an agent, and therefore communication to or through the agent are within the privilege. But if communications are made to him as a person who has himself to consider and act upon them, then the privilege is gone; and this is because the principle which protects communications only between solicitor and client no longer applies.

b Litigation Privilege

10. Litigation privilege, as opposed to legal advice privilege, requires litigation to be clearly in prospect or already in existence. The modern test for just how likely litigation needs to be was stated by Oliver LJ in *Re Highgrade Traders Ltd* [1984] BCLC 151, 172, as "if litigation is reasonably in prospect."

It was also noted in *Waugh* that litigation privilege can be claimed only where the dominant purpose of the document or advice was litigation. In *Waugh*, a report had been prepared after a railway accident. Lord

---

[6] *Waugh v. British Railways Board* [1980] AC 521, 541–42.

Wilberforce considered that the report had been prepared "for a dual purpose; for what may be called railway operation and safety purposes and for the purpose of obtaining legal advice in anticipation of litigation."[7] It was, however, held that the report was not privileged because the dominant purpose was not the litigation.

Litigation privilege is wider than legal advice privilege because it applies to communications between lawyers and third parties. Litigation privilege applies to all communications and documents that are generated for the main purpose of obtaining advice in connection with litigation or gathering or generating evidence for use in litigation.

C Persons Subject to the Duty of Professional Secrecy

11.   Lawyers in the BVI are subject to the duty of professional secrecy both as a result of the principle of legal professional privilege and as a result of the duty of confidentiality, which, as noted previously, is generally included in the lawyer's engagement letter. The OECS Bar Association, which is an organization for legal practitioners acting within the jurisdiction of the Eastern Caribbean Supreme Court, has also published a Code of Ethics for practitioners. It states, "An attorney-at–law shall scrupulously guard and never divulge his client's secrets and confidences." There is, however, currently no body to which breaches of the Code of Ethics can be reported, and there are no sanctions for breach.

Along with lawyers, other practitioners also have to respect the confidentiality of client documents. This duty arises because of the nature of the relationship. As noted in *British Virgin Islands Commercial Law*, "there are a wide variety of relationships which the law regards as giving rise to a duty of confidentiality. They include accountants, agents, arbitrators, bankers, clergy, directors, employees, lawyers, mediators, certain types of professionals, various holders of public offices, spouses and a variety of others."[8] There is, however, no comprehensive list of all of the relationships as a result of which a duty of confidentiality will be imposed. In the case of non-lawyers, the information may also be confidential because of the provisions of a retainer letter or because the information itself is clearly of a confidential nature (for example, if an accountant is retained by a client to assist with preparing evidence for court proceedings). This will obviously be the case, for example, in circumstances where an accountant is assisting a client with a case for litigation purposes. In this situation, the information may be covered by litigation privilege, and it will also be impressed with a duty of confidence.

---

[7] Ibid. at 541.
[8] Colin Riegels and Ian Mann, *British Virgin Islands Commercial Law*, Sweet & Maxwell Asia Ltd, Hong Kong, 2015, 13.029.

D Exceptions to and Optional Derogations from the Duty of Professional Secrecy

12. If a document or communication is privileged, it will not need to be disclosed in litigation. There are, however, some limits. The main limit has become known as the crime or fraud exception. As a result of this exception, information will not be privileged if it has been generated as part of a crime or fraud or if the lawyer's advice has been sought to assist with the commission of a crime or fraud.[9] The exception is derived from the common law, but it is now mirrored in the Proceeds of Criminal Conduct Act 1997, Section 30A(9) and in the Evidence Act 2006.

The fraud or crime exception also extends to civil fraud cases.[10] There is also some indication that wrongful conduct that falls short of a crime or a fraud may be included in this exception. This suggestion comes from *Barclays Bank v. Eustice* [1995] 1 WLR 1238, although this decision conflicts with the approach in *Gamelen Chemical Co. (UK) Ltd v. Rochem Ltd* (no 2) Dec. 7, 1979 (CA) (1980) 124 SJ 276, where Schiemann LJ approached the issue by considering whether the purpose was "sufficiently iniquitous for public policy to require that communications between him and his solicitor in relation to the setting up of these transactions be discoverable."

The courts will not easily hold that legal professional privilege has been lost. When it is lost, however, then confidentiality will also be lost, and documents will be subject to the duty of disclosure.[11]

13. Clients can waive confidentiality or legal professional privilege either to allow another person to use a document or because they want to use it themselves in proceedings. Once a document is disclosed or becomes public, privilege is lost, although confidentiality may not be lost for all purposes. Courts will not, however, generally restrain publication of something that has already been published.[12] There are some exceptions to this. For example, it was held in *Coco v. A.N. Clark (Engineers) Ltd* [1969] RPC 41 that "something that has been constructed solely from materials in the public domain may possess the necessary quality of confidence." It is also a matter of degree as to how "public" information may be, and it was recognized in *Franchi v. Franchi* [1967] RPC 149 that:

> [A] claim that disclosure of some information would be a breach of confidence is not defeated simply by proving that there are other people in the world who knew the facts in question ... it must be a question of degree depending on the particular case, but if relative secrecy remains, the plaintiff can still succeed.

[9] *R v. Cox and Railton* (1884) 14 QBD 153; *see also Kuwait Airways Corp. v. Iraqi Airways Corp.* [2005] 1 WLR 2734 CA for a more modern exposition of the principle.
[10] *Bullivant v. Attorney-General for Victoria* [1901] AC 196; *O'Rourke v. Darbishire* [1920] AC 581.
[11] *R v. Central Criminal Court ex p Francis & Francis* [1989] AC 346.
[12] *AG v. Guardian Newspapers Ltd (no 2)* [1990] 1 AC 109.

14.   The issue of what constitutes the "public domain" has also never been clearly defined. This is particularly problematic in the BVI where the only court documents that are available for public inspection as a matter of course are the claim form, any notice of appeal and any judgments or orders.[13] This means that documents such as witness statements, affidavits and the documents attached thereto, although filed in court, are not publicly available. It is, however, generally accepted that once a document has been referred to in court, it becomes public. This does not mean that a member of the public is automatically entitled to receive a copy of the document, but Civil Procedure Rule 3.14 does provide for members of the public to apply to the court to see documents that were filed with the court. If a document has been referred to in open proceedings, it is much more likely that such an application would be granted.

It was made clear in *Prince Jefri Bolkiah v. KPMG* [1999] 2 AC 222 that confidential information is protected to prevent the misuse of the information. This not only encompasses cases where the issue is disclosure of information, but it also covers cases where the issue is not disclosure but rather use of confidential information for the disclosing person's own gain. In this context, information will still be protected even when it has become public, but only to the limited extent that the disclosing person will not be able to continue to profit from the disclosure.[14]

15.   Another exception to legal professional privilege is if the document has been obtained by another party or if that party has access to the document. In that case, it will not matter that the document is privileged.[15]

16.   Finally, the law will not protect information that is trivial. This arises from the fact that confidentiality is protected by the rules of equity, and equity will not intervene unless the circumstances are of sufficient gravity. In this regard, however, what may seem trivial to one person may be very important to another. In *Stephens v. Avery* [1988] Ch 449, the court was prepared to protect disclosure of someone's sexual conduct.

E   Law Firms

17.   Lawyers in the BVI tend to work in law firms. It is accepted that there is no limit to the sharing of information among lawyers, and information that comes in to one lawyer will remain privileged if it is then seen by another lawyer within the firm. This makes sense from a confidentiality perspective, as the engagement letter will generally be between the client and the law firm.

The law firm, however, will need to make sure that information is not inadvertently disclosed. Obviously, the more people who know the information, the more likely it is that it will accidentally become public. It is clear from

---

[13]   Civil Procedure Rules 3.14.   [14]   *AG v. Guardian Newspapers (no 2)* [1990] 1 AC 109.

[15]   *O'Rourke v. Darbishire* [1919] 1 Ch 320.

Swinney v. Chief Constable of Northumbria [1997] QB 464 that a duty of care is owed under the common law to ensure that information is properly secured. If, therefore, a law firm does not take care to make sure that a proper security policy is in place with regard to client documents and the documents become public, it might find itself liable for negligence.

An issue arises in the BVI because the BVI is such a small jurisdiction, and it can be difficult for clients to find law firms that are not conflicted. There is no law to prevent law firms from acting against former clients, but it is assumed that unless it is restrained, information will flow freely within a firm. The issue has been dealt with by putting ethical walls in place, but law firms need to make sure that these are sufficiently robust. If an issue arises, the law firm will have to satisfy the court that effective measures have been taken to ensure that no disclosure of confidential information will occur.[16]

F Legal Assistants and Staff

18. Communications between clients and other people employed in a law firm such as secretaries and trainees will also be privileged.[17]

G External Service Providers

19. Legal professional privilege extends only to lawyers. It does not extend to advice provided by accountants, actuaries or other persons outside the legal profession.

H Multidisciplinary Associations

20. In England, it is now possible, as a result of the Legal Services Act 2007, for lawyers to form multidisciplinary practices with other professionals to provide legal services. In the BVI, however, this is still not possible, so the issue as to whether this affects the scope of legal professional privilege does not arise.

I In-House Counsel

21. Communications with in-house lawyers are subject to legal professional privilege.[18] To be protected, the information must have been provided for the purpose of obtaining legal advice and not, for example, for advice on commercial matters. In *United States v. Philip Morris Inc (No.1)* [2003] EWHC 3028 (Comm), Moore-Bick J noted:

---

[16] *Prince Jefri Bolkiah v. KPMG* [1999] 2 AC 222.

[17] *Taylor v. Forster* (1825) 2 Car &P 195; *Wheeler v. Le Marchant* (1881) 17 Ch D 675, 682 (CA).

[18] *Alfred Crompton Amusement Machines Ltd v. Customs & Excise Comms (No.2)* [1972] 2 QB 102, 129.

Lawyers do not cease to be regarded as professional legal advisers simply because they are employed by their clients, for example in a company's legal department, but in the nature of things those who are employed in that capacity are more likely than independent practitioners to become involved in aspects of the business that are essentially managerial or administrative in nature. To that extent it is less easy to maintain that all communications passing between them and the company's management attracts privilege.

2 History of the Duty of Professional Secrecy in the BVI

22.   As noted previously, BVI law is based on English law. The English common law has been incorporated into BVI law, and the BVI therefore generally follows English case law. With regard to professional secrecy, the applicable law in the BVI was, until the Evidence Act was passed, derived from English case law in this area.

In 2007, the BVI Constitution also recognized that "every person has the right to respect for his or her private and family life, his or her home and his or her correspondence, including business and professional communications."[19]

3 Supervision

A The Bar Associations

23.   As noted in no. 11 of this chapter, although the OECS has promulgated a Code of Ethics, it does not currently police the Code of Ethics, and there are no disciplinary sanctions for breach. The BVI is, however, a small jurisdiction, and in reality practitioners are concerned about acting in breach of the OECS Code of Ethics for this reason. Reputational risk is therefore a powerful tool.

The Legal Professionals Act 2015 (LPA) has recently been gazetted in the BVI. The LPA is, however, not currently in force. The LPA contains in Schedule 4 a new Code of Ethics, and it is proposed that this will be policed more effectively, as outlined in the section on "Sanctions."

B The Courts

24.   As there are no disciplinary sanctions for breach of the duty of legal professional privilege, the only real sanction would be a claim for breach of confidentiality against the lawyer said to be in breach. Of course, the problem at this stage is that the damage would be likely to have already been done (the information would have been made public), and damages would therefore probably not be an adequate remedy, and, in any event, loss may be difficult to quantify.

---

[19] Art. 19, The Virgin Islands Constitution Order 2007.

A more effective remedy is therefore likely to be an injunction against the lawyer before information said to confidential or subject to the duty of legal professional privilege has been disclosed.

A question that has bothered the courts in a number of cases is whether a claimant in a case involving breach of confidence (or a proposed breach of confidence where an injunction is sought) needs to show damage. In the *British Virgin Islands Commercial Law*, it is suggested that although the damage may not need to be material, there "must be an interest for the law to protect, even if it is ephemeral like a person's reputation or self esteem."[20]

4 Sanctions

A Proceedings and Sanctions

25. There are currently no sanctions for breach of the Code of Ethics or for any other failing on the part of a legal practitioner, including breach of confidence. It appears, however, that this is about to change as a result of the LPA. As noted previously, at the time of writing, the LPA has not yet come into force. But when it comes into force, it will include a new Code of Ethics, which includes a provision that states, "A legal practitioner shall scrupulously guard and never divulge his or her client's secrets and confidences, except as provided by law."[21] Section 26 of the LPA then provides:

(1) The rules contained in the Code of Ethics set out in Schedule 4 shall regulate the professional practice, etiquette, conduct and discipline of a legal practitioner.
(2) A breach of the rules in part A of Schedule 4 may constitute professional misconduct and in part B shall constitute professional misconduct.

LPA Section 18(2) is in Section A of the Code of Ethics, so breach of the client's confidence "may" (or presumably may not) constitute professional misconduct, depending on the specifics of the breach.

LPA Section 27 establishes a "Disciplinary Tribunal," which is "charged with the duty of upholding standards of professional conduct and enforcing the Code of Ethics set out in Schedule 4 and exercising disciplinary control over any legal practitioner."

A complaint can be made to the Disciplinary Tribunal about a legal practitioner by one of the following: (i) a client[22]; (ii) the Attorney General[23]; (iii) any other person who is "aggrieved by an act of professional misconduct"[24]; or (iv) the Court if, in any hearing before it, the judge considers that the legal practitioner is guilty of professional misconduct or a crime.[25]

---

[20] Colin Riegels and Ian Mann, *British Virgin Islands Commercial Law*, Sweet & Maxwell Asia Ltd, Hong Kong, 2015, 13.020.
[21] Section 18(2), LPA.   [22] Ibid., Section 28(1).   [23] Ibid.   [24] Ibid.
[25] Ibid., Section 28(3).

LPA Section 30 then provides that, if a case of professional misconduct is made out against a legal practitioner, the Disciplinary Tribunal has the power to impose any of the following remedies: (i) remove the legal practitioner's name from the roll, (ii) suspend the legal practitioner, (iii) impose fines not exceeding $20,000 for breach of a provision in Part A of the Code of Ethics, (iv) subjecting the legal practitioner to a reprimand or requiring the practitioner to provide a written apology, (v) requiring the legal practitioner to pay the complainant's costs or a portion thereof, (vi) requiring the legal practitioner to pay a sum to the complainant by way of compensation or reimbursement, or (vii) adopting any other course of action not prescribed but that is no more severe than the penalties outlined above.[26]

B Relationship between Criminal Sanctions and Disciplinary Sanctions

26. There are currently no criminal or disciplinary sanctions against lawyers for breach of their duty of confidentiality in the BVI.

As noted in the preceding section, the LPA will impose disciplinary sanctions on legal practitioners who are guilty of professional misconduct, which may include acting in breach of confidence in relation to their clients. Section 28 of the LPA provides that complaints can be made to the Disciplinary Tribunal about professional misconduct or where legal practitioners have committed criminal offences. The two may indeed overlap, and a legal practitioner may be guilty of a crime and, as a result, of professional misconduct. There is, however, no crime in the BVI that covers breach of confidence. If any legal practitioner was to be found guilty of this by the Disciplinary Tribunal, he or she would therefore only be guilty of professional misconduct.

5 Duty to Provide Information to the Authorities

27. There are now a number of statutes in the BVI that either permit or compel the disclosure of information to the authorities. For lawyers, the most relevant are the statutes that deal with money laundering and terrorist financing. These include the Proceeds of Criminal Conduct Act 1997, the Anti-Money Laundering and Terrorist Financing Code of Practice 2008 and the Anti-Money Laundering Regulations 2008.

Under the Proceeds of Criminal Conduct Act 1997, a person who knows or suspects or has reasonable grounds for knowing or suspecting that a person is engaged in money laundering is obliged to report it.[27] This includes confidential information given to a lawyer by a client, and failure to report it is a criminal offence.[28] The legislation makes it clear that any disclosure required under this legislation will not amount to an actionable breach of confidence.

---

[26] All penalties are laid out in Section 30(2) of the LPA.
[27] Section 30A(1), Criminal Conduct Act 1997.   [28] Ibid.

The important exception to this obligation, however, is information covered by legal professional privilege.[29] Individuals will not commit a criminal offence if they have made an internal disclosure to their Money Laundering Reporting Officer. People must also be careful when planning to report to the authorities that they do not commit the offence of "tipping off," or otherwise warning their clients.[30]

As the BVI is a jurisdiction in which the nature of most of its business is cross-border, there are also issues about whether disclosure should be made to courts, regulators and other enforcement authorities in other jurisdictions. To assist, the BVI has enacted a number of statutes that regulate disclosure to foreign courts and agencies. These include the Evidence (Proceedings in Foreign Jurisdictions) Act 1988 ("Evidence Act"), which is the BVI statute implementing the Hague Convention on the Taking of Evidence Abroad in Civil or Commercial Matters 1970 (more commonly referred to as the Hague Evidence Convention). This legislation provides the main mechanism by which foreign courts can seek the assistance of the BVI court to obtain information from people or companies within the BVI that is needed for foreign proceedings. In keeping with the Hague Convention, however, legal professional privilege is expressly preserved.[31] Moreover, the BVI court cannot issue an order that requires steps to be taken to assist the foreign proceedings that could not be taken with respect to BVI proceedings.[32] This means that, if information could not be disclosed because of confidentiality concerns if the proceedings were BVI proceedings, the information will not be disclosable simply because a request has been made from a foreign court. Where, however, a request has been made under the Evidence Act, and if a legal practitioner has been ordered to disclose the information (presumably it having been decided that the information is not covered by legal professional privilege), then the legal practitioner will not be considered to be acting in breach of confidence if he or she discloses the information.

The Evidence Act does not extend to criminal matters. Criminal matters are governed by the Criminal Justice (International Co-operation) Act 1993, under which a request has to be made to the governor rather than to the BVI court. Requests under this act need to be made to the governor who may, after consultation with a High Court judge, nominate a court in the BVI to receive evidence to which the request relates.

6 Search of a Lawyer's Office

28. There have been no statutes enacted that entitle the police to search a lawyer's office. In any event, even in criminal proceedings, the principle of legal professional privilege applies.

[29] Ibid., Section 30A(2).   [30] Ibid., Section 31.   [31] Section 7(1), Evidence Act.
[32] Ibid., Section 5(1).

170

7 Tapping of Telephone Conversations with a Lawyer

29.   Section 90 of the Telecommunications Act of 2006 provides that "the Governor may make written requests and issue orders to operators of telecommunications networks and providers of telecommunications services requiring them, at their expense, to intercept communications for law enforcement purposes or provide any user information or otherwise in aid of his authority." While there is no specific carve out for conversations between lawyers and their clients, in England it is accepted that legal professional privilege should be protected from phone tapping because people should be able to freely converse with their lawyers without fear of their conversations being intercepted.

8 The Lawyer as Witness

30.   There are situations where a lawyer may need to give evidence as a witness, except where the relevant information is covered by legal professional privilege. The lawyer cannot waive this privilege because, as noted previously, the privilege is the client's privilege, not the lawyer's privilege. Where, however, a client has brought a claim against a lawyer, for example, for negligence, and the lawyer needs to refer to privileged information to defend against the claim, then this will generally be permitted.[33] This will not, however, be the case where the claim is brought by a third party unless the client consents.[34] Moreover, where an application is made against a lawyer for a wasted costs order (alleging incurrence of improper costs by an attorney), the lawyer will not be able to use privileged information to defend himself or herself against the application.[35]

9 The Lawyer and the Press

31.   Lawyers have to be very careful when talking to reporters about cases so that they do not breach their general duty of confidentiality or divulge privileged information. Generally, lawyers are free to talk about any information that has been presented in open court. This includes all documents to which reference has been made in open court, even if the entire document has not been read aloud. At this point, the information will no longer be confidential. With regard to privileged information, however, the assumption is that it should never have been disclosed or mentioned in court. If information that was privileged is divulged, then privilege will have been lost, and it can be freely reported in the press.

---

[33] *Paragon Finance Plc v. Freshfields* [1999] 1 WLR 1183.

[34] *R v. Derby Magistrate's Court ex p B* [1996] AC 487, 508.

[35] *Medcalf v. Mardell* [2003] 1 AC 120.

10 Powers of the Tax and Other Authorities

32. There is little tax payable in the BVI, but what is payable is regulated by the Ministry of Finance. The BVI has, however, entered into a number of tax information exchange agreements with various foreign authorities. Under these agreements, a person or company in the BVI can be required, upon request, to provide information regarding such issues as the beneficial ownership of companies or other entities. The Mutual Legal Assistance (Tax matter) Act 2003, which has become the framework for the tax information exchange agreements, provides in Article 7 that the agreement "shall not impose upon a Contracting Party any obligation to provide items subject to legal privilege or information which would disclose any trade, business, industrial, commercial or professional secret or process."

11 National Security Issues

33. There are no known cases in the BVI in which legal practitioners have been required to disclose client information for reasons of national security. There are, however, two exceptions to the general duty of confidentiality: (i) the defense of iniquity and (ii) to prevent serious harm to the public.[36] In reality, the two defenses would seem to overlap and certainly must cover the situation in which disclosure is necessary for reasons of national security. In reality, disclosures for national security reasons are very rare.

---

[36] Colin Riegels and Ian Mann, *British Virgin Islands Commercial Law*, Sweet & Maxwell Asia Ltd, Hong Kong, 2015, 13.109–13.114.

12

Canada

MALCOLM M. MERCER

McCarthy Tétrault LLP

Preliminary Note

1.   Canada operates under a federal system. The province of Québec is a civil law jurisdiction while all other Canadian provinces and territories are common law jurisdictions. Canadian lawyers elect their regulators (the "governing bodies")

in each province and territory.[1] Lawyers in the common law jurisdictions, who are both barristers and solicitors in a fused profession, are regulated by the law society of their jurisdictions. In Québec, advocates and notaries are regulated by the Barreau du Québec and *Chambre des notaires du Québec*, respectively.[2]

Lawyers are subject to codes of professional conduct established by their governing bodies. Breach of these conduct codes can result in disciplinary proceedings. Lawyers are also subject to the law of solicitor-client privilege in common law jurisdictions and to the law of professional secrecy in Québec. Outside of Québec, solicitor-client privilege is based in the common law. In Québec, professional secrecy arises from the Civil Code and other legislative provisions. Despite these different bases, the law of professional secrecy in Québec is applied similarly to the law of solicitor-client privilege in the rest of Canada.

The Canadian understanding of solicitor-client privilege has evolved in recent decades. While solicitor-client privilege and litigation privilege are now seen as different privileges, both have a common origin and were once addressed collectively as solicitor-client privilege.

The nature of solicitor-client privilege has also evolved. While solicitor-client privilege was previously understood as being an evidentiary privilege, it is now a substantive and quasi-constitutional right.[3]

1 Scope of and Limitations on the Privilege and Duty

A Basis and Implications

a Under Canadian Common Law

2.   In Canadian common law jurisdictions, solicitor-client privilege is a common law class privilege.[4] Judicial decisions regarding solicitor-client privilege from one Canadian common law jurisdiction are influential in other common law jurisdictions, and decisions of the Supreme Court of Canada are binding across Canadian common law jurisdictions. As a result, the law of solicitor-client privilege across Canadian common law provinces develops in a consistent way over time.

---

[1] The phrase "governing bodies" is not in common usage but is a convenient phrase when speaking of both the common law and civil law jurisdictions.

[2] Unlike in the rest of Canada, the Barreau du Québec and Chambre des notaires du Québec are subject to the Office des professions du Québec, which supervises the regulation of all Québec professions. Professional Code, CQLR c C-26.

[3] The Ethics and Professional Responsibility Committee of the Canadian Bar Association provides resources with respect to privilege and confidentiality at www.cba.org/CBA/activities/code/. A leading Canadian text on this subject is Adam M. Dodek, *Solicitor-Client Privilege*, 2014, Lexis Nexis, Toronto, Canada.

[4] *Globe and Mail v. Canada (Attorney General)* [2010] 2 SCR 592, 2010 SCC 41, at para. 50; *Ontario (Public Safety and Security) v. Criminal Lawyers' Association* [2010] 1 SCR 815, 2010 SCC 23, at para. 39.

Canadian common law and statutes must conform to the Canadian Charter of Rights and Freedoms (the "Canadian Charter").[5] While legislatures may revise the common law, including the common law of solicitor-client privilege, legislative revisions must conform to the Canadian Charter. Section 8 of the Canadian Charter provides that "[e]veryone has the right to be secure against unreasonable search or seizure." Section 8 applies to state searches and seizures of solicitor-client privileged documents. The courts have held that solicitor-client privilege must be as close to absolute as possible to ensure public confidence and retain relevance and that any legislative provision will be considered unreasonable when it interferes with solicitor-client privilege more than is absolutely necessary.[6]

The courts have clearly determined that solicitor-client privilege is a substantive rule, rather than an evidentiary privilege that merely prohibits legal advisers from giving evidence as to privileged communications in judicial proceedings and entitles clients not to give such evidence.[7]

Solicitor-client privilege is a fundamental civil and legal right, founded upon the unique relationship of solicitor and client.[8] Accordingly, legislative language that may (if broadly construed) allow incursions on solicitor-client privilege must be interpreted restrictively. The privilege cannot be legislatively abrogated by inference.[9]

b Under Québec Civil Law

3.   Section 9 of the Québec Charter of Rights and Freedoms[10] (the "Québec Charter") declares professional secrecy to be a fundamental human right. It provides that persons bound to professional secrecy by law may not disclose protected information absent authorization or express provision of law and that tribunals must respect professional secrecy.

Both the Professional Code[11] and the Act Respecting the Barreau du Québec[12] address professional secrecy. In Québec, professional secrecy applies generally to regulated professionals and not just to lawyers. However, it has been held that the scope and intensity of professional secrecy varies and that the particularly sensitive nature of the solicitor-client relationship is not to be overlooked.[13]

---

[5] *Ontario (Public Safety and Security) v. Criminal Lawyers' Association* [2010] 1 SCR 815, 2010 SCC 23, at para. 39.

[6] *Lavallee, Rackel & Heintz v. Canada (Attorney General)* [2002] 3 SCR 209 ("Lavallee"), at para. 36.

[7] *Descôteaux et al. v. Mierzwinski* [1982] 1 SCR 860, 876 ("Descôteaux").

[8] *Solosky v. The Queen* [1980] 1 SCR 821, 839.

[9] *Canada (Privacy Commissioner) v. Blood Tribe Department of Health*, [2008] 2 SCR 574, at para. 11.

[10] Section 9, Charter of Human Rights and Freedoms, CQLR c C-12.

[11] Section 60.4, Professional Code, CQLR c C-26.

[12] Section 131, Act Respecting the Barreau du Québec, CQLR c B-1.

[13] *Foster Wheeler Power Co. v. Société intermunicipale de gestion et d'élimination des déchets (SIGED) Inc.* [2004] 1 SCR 456 ("Foster Wheeler"), at para. 35.

B Scope

a Under Canadian Common Law

4.   Solicitor-client privilege protects communications between solicitor and client that entail seeking or giving legal advice and that the parties intend to be confidential. Generally, solicitor-client privilege will apply as long as the communication falls within the usual and ordinary scope of the professional relationship. The privilege, once established, is considerably broad and all-encompassing.[14] It is recognized that lawyers, particularly in-house and government lawyers, often have both legal and non-legal responsibilities. While solicitor-client privilege has been held to arise when in-house lawyers provide legal advice to their clients, advice provided outside the realm of their legal responsibilities is not protected by the privilege.[15]

    As solicitor-client communications are protected by the privilege, some Canadian courts have distinguished between facts and communications holding that only communications are protected by solicitor-client privilege. On that basis, some courts have held that the amount of a lawyer's account is not privileged information. Canadian jurisprudence now holds that records of legal fees and other similar records are presumptively considered to be privileged with it being for the court to determine whether the information is neutral information.[16]

    Solicitor-client privilege and litigation privilege must be distinguished, given that solicitor-client privilege is the stronger privilege. Unlike solicitor-client privilege, litigation privilege arises and operates even in the absence of a solicitor-client relationship, and it applies to all litigants, whether or not they are represented by counsel. Confidentiality, the *sine qua non* of the solicitor-client privilege, is not required for litigation privilege.[17]

b Under Québec Civil Law

5.   The Québec Charter protects confidential information revealed to persons bound by professional secrecy by reason of their position or profession. The Professional Code provides that professionals must preserve the secrecy of all confidential information that becomes known to them in the practice of their profession. The Act Respecting the Barreau du Québec provides that advocates must keep absolutely secret the confidences made to them by reason of their profession.[18]

---

[14] *Pritchard v. Ontario (Human Rights Commission)* [2004] 1 SCR 809, 2004 SCC 31 ("*Pritchard*"), at paras. 15–16.

[15] Ibid., paras. 19–20.

[16] *Maranda v. Richer* [2003] 3 SCR 193, 2003 SCC 67, at paras. 32–34; *Donell v. GJB Enterprises Inc.*, 2012 BCCA 135, at paras. 59–60; *Kaiser (Re)*, 2012 ONCA 838.

[17] *Blank v. Canada (Minister of Justice)* [2006] 2 SCR 319, 2006 SCC 39, at para. 32; *General Accident Assurance Co. v. Chrusz*, 45 OR (3d) 321 (OCA) ("Chrusz").

[18] *Foster Wheeler, supra*, at paras. 19–21.

Accordingly, information that is confidential and that becomes known to lawyers in the practice of their profession is protected by professional secrecy. The scope of professional secrecy may be broader than solicitor-client privilege, although it may be expected that the scope and intensity of professional secrecy protection will most closely mirror solicitor-client privilege where the same information would be protected under both regimes.

C In-House Counsel

6. In principle, in-house lawyers and government lawyers are treated no differently from external lawyers for the purpose of solicitor-client privilege. Where communication with an in-house lawyer would otherwise be privileged, the fact that the lawyer is "in-house" does not remove the privilege or change its nature. As in-house counsel often have both legal and non-legal responsibilities, a case-by-case assessment is required to determine if solicitor-client privilege arose. Whether the privilege will attach depends on the nature of the relationship, the subject matter of the advice and the circumstances in which it is sought and rendered.[19]

D Exceptions to the Privilege and Duty

7. Solicitor-client privilege is all but absolute in recognition of the high public interest in maintaining the confidentiality of the solicitor-client relationship. The only recognized exceptions are the narrowly guarded public safety and innocence-at-stake exceptions.[20]

    The public safety exception applies where the facts raise real concerns that an identifiable individual or group is in imminent danger of death or serious bodily harm. When the exception applies, the permitted disclosure is limited so that it includes only the information necessary to protect public safety.[21]

    The Canadian Charter provides that persons are not to be deprived of life, liberty or security of the person except in accordance with principles of fundamental justice. The right to fully answer and defend oneself is a principle of fundamental justice. On this foundation, the innocence-at-stake exception applies where privileged information is required with respect to core issues going to the guilt of an accused and there is a genuine risk of a wrongful conviction.[22]

---

[19] *Pritchard, supra*, at paras. 19–21. The Ethics and Professional Responsibility Committee of the Canadian Bar Association has provided FAQs about privilege and confidentiality for in-house counsel at www.cba.org/CBA/activities/code/.

[20] *Ontario (Public Safety and Security) v. Criminal Lawyers' Association* [2010] 1 SCR 815, 2010 SCC 23, at para. 53.

[21] *Smith v. Jones* [1999] 1 SCR 455, at para. 85.

[22] *R. v. McClure* [2001] 1 SCR 445, 2001 SCC 14, at paras. 38–42, 47.

While not strictly speaking an exception, solicitor-client privilege does not apply where a client seeks guidance from a lawyer to facilitate the commission of a crime or a fraud, whether the lawyer is an unwitting dupe or knowing participant.[23]

Section 9 of the *Québec Charter* provides that the professional secrecy non-disclosure obligation applies absent authorization by the confider or an express provision of law. The Supreme Court of Canada has determined that the common law exceptions to solicitor-client privilege are the express provisions of law for the lawyer's professional secrecy obligation. The Court thereby harmonized the exceptions under common law and civil law.[24]

E Codes of Professional Conduct

8. The governing bodies regulate lawyer conduct. The Codes of Professional Conduct (the "Conduct Codes") generally follow the Model Code of Professional Conduct ("Model Code," composed of the "Model Rules") of the Federation of Law Societies of Canada. Lawyers may be disciplined for breaching the Conduct Code applicable in their jurisdiction.

Model Rule 3.3-1 provides:

> A lawyer at all times must hold in strict confidence all information concerning the business and affairs of a client acquired in the course of the professional relationship and must not divulge any such information unless (a) expressly or impliedly authorized by the client; (b) required by law or a court to do so; (c) required to deliver the information to the Society; or (d) otherwise permitted by this rule.

The information protected by this broad conduct rule, which is adopted in all Canadian jurisdictions, includes information that is protected by solicitor-client privilege and professional secrecy, but it also protects other information including information that is not confidential. The exceptions under the Conduct Codes are broader than the exceptions to solicitor-client privilege and professional secrecy. However, the exceptions under the Conduct Codes cannot provide exceptions to solicitor-client privilege or professional secrecy. The jurisdiction of the governing bodies is with respect to lawyer conduct, rather than the legal rights of their clients.

F Communications with Non-Canadian Lawyers

9. Solicitor-client privilege has long been held to attach to communications with non-Canadian lawyers where the privilege would attach to a communication with a Canadian lawyer. The basis for this conclusion has been conflict-of-laws principles and that solicitor-client privilege was considered to be procedural law rather than substantive law with the result that the law of the forum

---

[23] *Solosky v. The Queen* [1980] 1 SCR 821, 835–36.   [24] *Foster Wheeler, supra*, at para. 37.

governed. As a result, the law of privilege of the non-Canadian jurisdiction was not considered to be relevant.[25]

On this basis, it is necessary in determining whether solicitor-client privilege protects communications with non-Canadian lawyers to determine the nature and reason for the communication.

The Canadian courts have not yet expressly considered whether this approach continues to apply now that solicitor-client privilege has been determined to be substantive law and not merely procedural. However, thoughtful commentary suggests that the approach should not be changed on public policy grounds.[26]

G Law Firms, Legal Assistants and Staff

10.　Communications between clients and the non-lawyer staff of a law firm may be protected by solicitor-client privilege. Lawyer-client communications made through a messenger, translator or amanuensis are protected just as if made directly.[27] Accordingly, where non-lawyer staff simply convey information from the client to the lawyer or the lawyer to the client, the result is not different than if the communication was made directly.

It is increasingly common for law firms to provide non-legal services. For example, a number of law firms have retired politicians and senior public servants on staff to provide government relations advice or assistance. Similarly, some law firms have urban planners on staff to assist in municipal planning matters or scientists on staff to assist with intellectual property matters. The courts have not yet addressed whether sharing information with internal non-legal service providers within a law firm should be analyzed differently from with external service providers. There does not appear to be a principled basis for differential treatment.

In Québec, lawyers and other regulated professionals are permitted to be partners together in multidisciplinary firms and shareholders together in professional corporations. As professional secrecy applies to all regulated professionals (albeit with different scope and intensity), information sharing may not raise the same waiver issues as in the common law jurisdictions.

H External Service Providers

11.　Information obtained for the purpose of providing legal advice other than from a client is not protected by solicitor-client privilege. For example, information obtained from a surveyor based on survey information for the purpose of

---

[25] *Morrison-Knudsen Co. v. British Columbia Hydro and Power Authority* (1971), 19 DLR (3d) 726, 729–31 (BCSC).

[26] Brandon Kain, "Solicitor-client privilege and the conflict of laws," 90 CBR 243, 2011.

[27] *Chrusz, supra.*

obtaining legal advice will not be protected by solicitor-client privilege. Such information might, however, be protected by litigation privilege, which is another matter.[28]

Solicitor-client privilege is ordinarily lost where privileged information is disclosed to third parties. This follows from the essential requirement of confidentiality. Ordinarily, disclosure to an external service provider will result in privilege not arising in the first instance or being lost by waiver.

As noted previously, lawyer-client privileged communication can be through messengers or translators. This can include external service providers. For example, where accountants obtain legal advice for their clients, solicitor-client privilege arises including where the accountant provides expert analysis of the information provided by the client that is required for the purpose of the legal advice.[29]

There is emerging jurisprudence to the effect that external service providers may be considered not to be third parties, and privilege therefore would not be waived where the client requires external expertise to give effect to legal advice and the external expert must have access to that legal advice for that purpose. This has been called "deal team privilege."[30]

While perhaps not strictly an external service provider, communication of solicitor-client privileged information to an external auditor may not result in loss of privilege by waiver. Where disclosure is a result of legal compulsion, Canadian law provides for "limited waiver" rather than full waiver. This principle has been applied in Canadian jurisprudence to communications with auditors where there is a legal requirement to provide audit information. However, the result in these cases has been questioned on the basis that the legislative obligations to provide audit evidence would not include solicitor-client privileged information where the legislation does not explicitly so require.[31]

I Common Interest

12. While sometimes called "common interest privilege," common interest is better understood as being an exception to the general rule that disclosure to a third party operates as waiver of solicitor-client privilege. The common-interest exception to waiver by disclosure originally arose in the context of two parties jointly consulting one solicitor.[32]

---

[28] *Wheeler v. Le Marchant* (1881) 17 Ch. D. 675 (ECA).

[29] *Susan Hosiery Ltd. v. MNR.* [1969] 2 Ex. C.R. 27, 36; *Chrusz, supra.*

[30] *Camp Development Corp. v. South Coast Greater Vancouver Transportation Authority,* 2011 BCSC 88, at paras. 49–65; *Barrick Gold Corp. v. Goldcorp Inc.,* 2011 ONSC 1325.

[31] *Philip Services Corp. v. Ontario Securities Commission* (2005) 77 OR (3d) 209 (OSCDC), at paras. 57–58; *British Columbia (Auditor General) v. British Columbia (Attorney General),* 2013 BCSC 98, at paras. 140–47.

[32] *Pritchard, supra,* at paras. 23–24.

The earliest application of the common interest exception allowed parties in litigation, or its prospect, to share privileged information without waiver in furtherance of their common interest in the conduct of the litigation.[33]

The common interest exception has been extended in Canada to apply to commercial transactions. Where legal opinions are shared by parties with mutual interests in commercial transactions, courts have held that there may be a sufficient interest in common to protect disclosure of opinions even in circumstances where no litigation is in existence or contemplated. One provincial appellate court has held that the common interest exception applies only where it is clearly established that the documents were exchanged in furtherance of a joint interest against a third party.[34]

The Supreme Court of Canada has not yet directly considered this jurisprudence. However, the court has indicated that the common interest exception has been "narrowly expanded to cover those situations in which a fiduciary or like duty has been found to exist between the parties so as to create common interest. These include trustee-beneficiary relations ... and certain types of contractual or agency relations."[35]

2 Supervision

A The Courts

13. The courts have primary jurisdiction with respect to solicitor-client privilege and professional secrecy. In common law jurisdictions, the principle jurisdiction exercised by the courts is their jurisdiction over the administration of justice and the Canadian constitution, although fiduciary law is sometimes invoked.[36] In addition to controlling court proceedings to ensure that privileged information is protected, the supervisory authority of the courts is commonly invoked to disqualify lawyers from continuing to act in circumstances where protection of privileged information is put at risk.[37]

However, there are other judicial remedies available, particularly injunctive power to prevent misuse of privileged information outside of the courts as well as compensatory and punitive financial remedies. The courts could punish

---

[33] *Buttes Gas & Oil Co. v. Hammer (No. 3)* [1980] 3 All ER 475, 483 (ECA).

[34] *Pitney Bowes of Canada Ltd. v. Canada*, 2003 FCT 214, at paras. 16–20; *Maximum Ventures Inc. v. De Graaf*, 2007 BCCA 510, at para. 14; *Canmore Mountain Villas Inc. v. Alberta (Minister of Seniors and Community Supports)*, 2009 ABQB 348, at paras. 5–8; *Sable Offshore Energy Project v. Ameron International Corp.*, 2015 NSCA 8.

[35] *Pritchard, supra*, at para. 24.

[36] *Canadian National Railway Co. v. McKercher LLP* [2013] 2 SCR 649 ("McKercher"), at paras. 13–14; *Canada (Attorney General) v. Federation of Law Societies of Canada* [2015] 1 SCR 401 ("Federation of Law Societies"), at para. 82.

[37] *MacDonald Estate v. Martin* [1990] 3 SCR 1235; *Celanese Canada Inc. v. Murray Demolition Corp.* [2006] 2 SCR 189.

lawyers as officers of the court by way of contempt proceedings. However, recourse to remedies other than disqualification and injunctive protection is rarely sought.

B The Law Societies and the Barreau

14. The courts' purpose in exercising supervisory powers over lawyers has traditionally been to protect clients from prejudice and to preserve the repute of the administration of justice, not to discipline or punish lawyers. Ordinarily, discipline and punishment is the responsibility of the governing bodies.[38]

As mentioned previously, the scope of the Conduct Codes of the governing bodies with respect to client information is broader than solicitor-client privilege. The conduct rules protect solicitor-client privileged information but extend to information that is not privileged and to information that is not confidential. Because the scope of the conduct rule with respect to client information includes solicitor-client privileged information, lawyers can be disciplined for misuse of solicitor-client privileged information under those rules.

Further, the Conduct Codes have general provisions that could also be engaged where lawyers misuse solicitor-client privileged information. Model Rule 2.1-1 provides that a lawyer has a duty to carry on the practice of law and discharge all responsibilities to clients, tribunals, the public and other members of the profession honorably and with integrity. Further, while the express test for professional misconduct may differ among jurisdictions, engaging in conduct that is prejudicial to the administration of justice can be treated as professional misconduct.[39]

Where a lawyer has been found to engage in professional misconduct, the lawyer may be disciplined by reprimand, suspension, fine or loss of license to practice law.[40]

3 Duty to Provide Information to Authorities

A Powers of Police, Tax and Other Authorities

15. In 1982, the Supreme Court of Canada decided *Descôteaux*, which is a foundational authority in Canada with respect to solicitor-client privilege. The court considered a search warrant issued to obtain proof that an applicant

---

[38] *R. v. Cunningham* [2010] 1 SCR 331, at paras. 35–39; *McKercher, supra*, at paras. 13–16.

[39] For example, the definition of professional misconduct in Ontario in the Rules of Professional Conduct expressly includes engaging in conduct that is prejudicial to the administration of justice.

[40] The language used – professional misconduct or conduct worthy of sanction, for example – may differ from jurisdiction to jurisdiction, but there appears to be little practical difference between the tests applied. Other sanctions may be available, but the primary sanctions are reprimand, suspension and loss of license.

for legal aid committed an indictable offence by incorrectly reporting a lower income to be eligible for such services. The court held that there was no jurisdiction to order the seizure of documents that would not be admissible in court on the ground that they are privileged. The court held that a warrant to search a law office should be refused unless there is no reasonable alternative to the law office search. If issued, the warrant should include terms of execution designed to protect the right to confidentiality of the lawyer's clients as much as possible.[41]

In 2002, the Supreme Court of Canada again considered law office searches in *Lavallee*, taking into account the Canadian Charter, which was enacted after *Descôteaux*. The court held unconstitutional legislation that mandated that material seized from law offices be sealed at the time of the search; that the lawyer make application within strict timelines for a determination whether the material is protected by solicitor-client privilege; and allowed the prosecution, with permission of the court, to examine the material to assist on the issue of the existence of privilege. The court held that, given that solicitor-client privilege must remain as close to absolute as possible to retain its relevance, the court must adopt stringent norms to ensure its protection.[42]

As the court forcefully stated in *Lavallee* at para. 24:

> It is critical to emphasize here that all information protected by the solicitor-client privilege is out of reach for the state. It cannot be forcibly discovered or disclosed and it is inadmissible in court. It is the privilege of the client and the lawyer acts as a gatekeeper, ethically bound to protect the privileged information that belongs to his or her client. Therefore, any privileged information acquired by the state without the consent of the privilege holder is information that the state is not entitled to as a rule of fundamental justice.

B Money Laundering and Terrorism

16.   The Proceeds of Crime (Money Laundering) and Terrorist Financing Act, S.C. 2000, c. 17, was enacted to detect and deter money laundering and terrorist financing and to facilitate their investigation and prosecution. The act established record-keeping and client-identification standards; requires reporting from financial intermediaries; and established FINTRAC, an agency to oversee compliance. Regulations made under the act provide how the legislative scheme was to apply to lawyers.[43]

In the face of this legislative scheme, the governing bodies established their own client identification and verification rules and obtained injunctive relief restraining the application of the legislative scheme to lawyers.

---

[41] *Descôteaux, supra*, at 893–94.   [42] *Lavallee, supra*, at paras. 34–46.
[43] *Federation of Law Societies, supra*, at para. 1.

In 2015, the Supreme Court of Canada concluded in the *Federation of Law Societies* that the provisions of this act, which authorized "sweeping searches" of law offices, inherently risked breaching solicitor-client privilege and were therefore unconstitutional violations against the right to be free from unreasonable search and seizure.[44]

Significantly, the court also held that legislation requiring lawyers to comply with the act breached their constitutional right not to be deprived of life, liberty or security of the person except in accordance with principles of fundamental justice on the basis that the principles of fundamental justice include that the state cannot impose duties on lawyers that undermine their duty of commitment to their clients' causes.[45]

As a result, Canadian lawyers are required by the governing bodies to obtain client identification information and to verify client identity in certain contexts. However, such information is to be maintained by the lawyer and not routinely turned over to the state. Where and to the extent appropriate, lawyers can be compelled to disclose this information. And of course, lawyers are not permitted to participate in illegal transactions.[46]

C Collective Settlement of Debts

17. Under the Bankruptcy and Insolvency Act, the property of a bankrupt is vested in the trustee in bankruptcy subject to certain limited exceptions. However, the courts have held that solicitor-client privilege is not lost to a bankrupt and cannot be waived by a trustee in bankruptcy, even where doing so might reveal the whereabouts of some of the bankrupt's property.[47]

D Search of a Lawyer's Office

18. The Supreme Court of Canada addressed the constitutionality of law office searches in *Lavallee* and in *Federation of Law Societies*.[48] The court in *Lavallee* set out guidelines meant to reflect constitutional imperatives for the protection of solicitor-client privilege and to govern both the search authorization process and the general manner in which the search must be carried out.[49]

In a number of Canadian jurisdictions, the website of the governing body provides guidelines to lawyers with respect to law office searches.[50]

---

[44] Ibid., paras. 31–68.   [45] Ibid., paras. 74–115.

[46] In 2008, the Federation of Law Societies adopted a Model Rule on Client Identification and Verification Requirements, versions of which have been adopted across Canada.

[47] Section 71, Bankruptcy and Insolvency Act, RSC 1985, c B-3; *Wong v. Luu*, 2015 BCCA 159, at para. 33

[48] *Lavallee, supra; Federation of Law Societies, supra.*

[49] *Lavallee, supra*, at para. 49; *Federation of Law Societies, supra*, at paras. 35, 43–56.

[50] For example, see www.lsuc.on.ca/searches/.

E Tapping of Telephone Conversations with a Lawyer

19. Part VI of the Canadian Criminal Code, titled "Invasion of Privacy," creates an offence for willful interception of private communications by means of any electromagnetic, acoustic, mechanical or other device except in certain circumstances.[51] There are provisions addressing particular circumstances including interception to prevent bodily harm, interception with consent and imminent harm.[52] Sections 185 and 186 provide for judicial authorization of interception of private communications in certain circumstances. However, Section 186(2) provides that:

> No authorization may be given to intercept a private communication at the office or residence of a solicitor, or at any other place ordinarily used by a solicitor and by other solicitors for the purpose of consultation with clients, unless the judge to whom the application is made is satisfied that there are reasonable grounds to believe that the solicitor, any other solicitor practicing with him, any person employed by him or any other such solicitor or a member of the solicitor's household has been or is about to become a party to an offence.

Section 189(6) of the Criminal Code provides that information that is privileged and inadmissible as evidence remains as such despite interception absent consent of the person enjoying the privilege.

F The Lawyer as Witness

20. Lawyers are compellable witnesses. However, the rules of the governing bodies and procedural law limit the circumstances in which a lawyer may testify where the lawyer appears as an advocate.[53]

Model Rule 3.3-1 provides that, except in certain circumstances, a lawyer at all times must hold in strict confidence all information concerning the business and affairs of a client acquired in the course of the professional relationship and must not divulge any such information.[54] However, lawyers are permitted to divulge information where required by law or a court to do so. Separate from this conduct rule, lawyers are not permitted to disclose information protected by solicitor-client privilege. Where evidence is sought from a lawyer (other than by the privilege holder) that may be protected, the lawyer should advise the court that the information may be protected and provide the basis for the protection so that the court can properly determine whether to require that the information be given in evidence.

---

[51] Section 184, Criminal Code, RSC 1985, c C-46. [52] Ibid., Sections 184.1, 184.2, 184.4.
[53] Model Rule 5.2, Model Code of Professional Conduct. [54] Ibid., Model Rule 3.3-1.

G The Lawyer and the Press

21. The Conduct Codes and the law of solicitor-client privilege limit a lawyer's ability to provide information to the press in the same way that lawyers are limited from disclosing protected information generally. No distinction is made between communication with the press and with others.

H National Security Issues

22. Sections 21 through 24 of the Canadian Security Intelligence Service Act allow the Canadian Security Intelligence Service (CSIS) to obtain warrants from the Federal Court to investigate threats to the security of Canada.[55] In *Atwal* in 1988, the Federal Court of Appeal found a national security exception to solicitor-client privilege in the narrow context of a prospective investigation by CSIS of a national security threat authorized by a Section 21 warrant.[56] The Supreme Court has not yet determined whether a national security exception to solicitor-client privilege should be recognized, although the Court has indicated that such an exception is not foreclosed.[57]

Part VI of the Criminal Code, including Section 189(6), mentioned previously, applies to terrorism offences and certain offences related to criminal organizations. While privilege remains protected where privileged information is intercepted in these circumstances, a judicial authorization for interception is more easily available than with respect to other offences.[58]

---

[55] Canadian Security Intelligence Service Act, RSC 1985, c C-23.

[56] *Atwal v. Canada* [1988] 1 FC 107 (CA); *see also Re Mahjoub*, 2013 FC 1096, at paras. 66–89.

[57] *Smith v. Jones* [1999] SCR 455, at para. 53; *see also* Dodek, *Solicitor-Client Privilege*, *supra*, at paras. 8.53–8.62.

[58] Criminal Code *supra*, Sections 185(1.1), 186(1.1).

13

Chile

RAIMUNDO MORENO
MONICA VANDER SCHRAFT
Cariola Díez Pérez-Cotapos & Cía. Ltda.

Preliminary Note

1. Professional secrecy and attorney-client privilege are not clearly distinguished in Chile's legal or ethical rules, as is the case in other jurisdictions. Both terms will be treated here as equivalents, because, although there are some differences between them, they do not affect the subjects discussed here.

    Professional secrecy and attorney-client privilege are subject to legal and ethical regulation in Chile.

    Legal regulation in Chile incorporates both duties and rights for lawyers. The enforcement of such duties and the protection of these rights are controlled by the corresponding criminal or civil court.

    Regarding ethical regulation, to practice law in Chile, it is not mandatory to be a member of the Chilean Bar Association (hereinafter "the Bar"). The Chilean Political Constitution protects the freedom to voluntarily elect between affiliating or not into a trade association. Under such provision, Chilean lawyers often decide not to affiliate with the Bar and therefore are not subject to its control. As a result, ethical regulation is applied by courts for attorneys who are not affiliated with the Bar and by the Bar for its members.

1 Scope of and Limitations on the Duty of Professional Secrecy/Attorney-Client Privilege

A Statutory Basis and Implications

2. Professional secrecy has been construed as an element of due process, which is protected under Article 19(3) of the Chilean Political Constitution.[1]

    Legal regulation, applicable to all lawyers in Chile, can be found mainly in Articles 231 and 232 of the Chilean Criminal Code; Articles 217, 220, 303 and 304 of the Chilean Criminal Procedure Code; and Article 360(1) of the Chilean Civil Procedure Code.

    Ethical regulation is different for those lawyers affiliated with the Bar and for those who are not. For those affiliated with the Bar, ethical rules are found in the Code of Ethics issued by the Bar in 2011 (hereinafter, the "Code of Ethics") and the Bylaws of the Bar. For lawyers who are not affiliated with the Bar, ethical rules are contained in Decree Law number 3621, the Code of Ethics issued by the Bar in 1948 and the Organic Law of the Bar number 4409, which contains the sanctions that might be applied in these cases.

---

[1] Supreme Court Ruling, Oct. 29, 2013, case no. 5337–2013: "Ninth: that even if our Political Constitution does not have a clear reference of professional secrecy, such right-duty is included as a presupposition of due process. Specifically, it is related with the right to defense guaranteed in Art. 19 number 3 of the Constitution ... without a lawful prospect of confidentiality from the client, the trust in which such relation is grounded would be seriously prejudiced, and consequently, its right to a technical defense seriously damaged."

B Scope

3. The Chilean legal system does not define professional secrecy or confidentiality. Jurisprudence has filled the legal void regarding a definition by repeatedly establishing[2] that "professional secrecy extends to all background information with which the lawyer deals and that is related with the purpose of his services. Such extension has already been acknowledged by a judgment of this Court dated May 13th, 1954, in case Guttman vs. Guttman (Revista de Derecho y Jurisprudencia, T. I, pág. 128, Vol. 51, 1954)."[3]

Professional secrecy's content and limitations can be construed from the regulations identified in the preceding section. Based on them, professional secrecy is legally considered a duty and a right of the lawyer. Lawyers are obliged not to disclose anything that has been entrusted to them in that capacity, and due to this, lawyers also have the right to refuse to testify if such statement infringes this professional secrecy obligation.

The law expressly protects confidentiality, at least regarding the following: (i) client secrets,[4] (ii) communications between a client and lawyer, (iii) notes taken by a lawyer, and (iv) communications or any other object or document entrusted by the client to the lawyer.[5]

Regarding (iii) and (iv), the notes, communications, objects or documents referred to are protected only if they remain in the custody of the lawyer, which is expressly extended to the office where the lawyer practices law. The abovementioned protection does not apply if the lawyer is under investigation for a criminal act, nor does it apply to objects or documents that could be subject to confiscation because they are the product of a criminal act or instrumental to its commission.

The law establishes criminal sanctions for lawyers in case of breach of the prohibition against disclosure of a client's secrets.

4. Besides the duties stated by the law, the Code of Ethics[6] establishes the following obligations:[7]

---

[2] Another quote that is common on professional secrecy in Chilean Supreme Court rulings is the following: "that professional secrecy is a legal obligation, which passive subject is a professional, and it matters that the same cannot reveal what the client is hiding and has only disclosed to him for the best performance of his duties." Eduardo Novoa Monreal, *RDJ Volume XLI*, March to December 1944, no. 10, 85–100.

[3] Supreme Court Ruling, Nov. 28, 2012, case no. 2788–2012.   [4] Art. 231, Criminal Code.

[5] Art. 220(ii)–(iv), Criminal Code.

[6] Notwithstanding the identified obligation that is part of professional secrecy, the Code of Ethics regulates professional secrecy in its Article 7, establishing that: "The lawyer owes strict confidentiality to its client. In order to comply with his or her obligation, it shall demand for its legal right of professional secrecy to be acknowledged. Confidentiality extends to all information regarding the business of the client and to which the lawyer has had access due to the exercise of his or her profession . . .."

[7] Art. 46, Code of Ethics.

(i) Prohibition of revelation. The lawyer must neither reveal information covered by the lawyer's obligation of confidentiality, nor hand over, exhibit or facilitate access to material, electronic or any other type of storage containing information being under the lawyer's custody.

(ii) Obligation of care. The lawyer must adopt reasonable provisions to make sure that the conditions of receiving, obtaining or revealing information subject to the obligation of confidentiality, preserve the confidential character of such information; and

(iii) Obligation of care referring to actions of collaborators. The lawyer must make reasonable provisions to make sure that the confidentiality the lawyer is obliged to maintain is also maintained by those who collaborate with him or her.

The Code of Ethics widens the professional secrecy obligation by means of Article 60, which states that the lawyer must ensure that the right to professional secrecy is observed when such lawyer is required by the law or by the competent authority to provide information on or to declare facts that are subject to confidentiality.

To meet this obligation, the lawyer must act in accordance with the following ethical rules, found in Article 60 of the Code of Ethics:

(i) Interpret the law in the most favorable way concerning confidentiality.

(ii) Limit any communication of facts that are covered by professional secrecy, without explaining why, if the explanation might compromise professional secrecy.

(iii) Carry out any actions or means provided by the law to challenge the decisions of an authority that would constitute a breach of professional secrecy.

Finally, the same Code of Ethics, in Article 47, states that the duty of professional secrecy has an indefinite duration, because it does not expire at the end of the professional relationship, upon the death of the client or by the lapse of time.

C Persons Subject to the Duty of Professional Secrecy

5.   The lawyer is subject to professional secrecy both as a legal and an ethical obligation. In Chile, the law refers only to the lawyer or lawyers who handle the case or client. But under the Code of Ethics, such duty does not only burden the lawyer who has a direct relationship with the client or the case, but, as discussed later in this chapter, it also extends to the other lawyers working at the lawyer's office. The lawyer is responsible for the protection of the confidential information by any other person who might have access to protected documents or information that are under the lawyer's custody.[8]

---

[8] Ibid., Arts. 115, 116.

D Exceptions to and Optional Derogations from the Duty of Professional Secrecy

6. Authorization by the client: professional secrecy exists not only for the individual benefit of the client, but there is also a general interest in its protection. That is why, even if it is not stated in the law, the Code of Ethics establishes that the lawyer might be authorized by the client to disclose confidential information, but such authorization is not binding on the lawyer.[9]

    The authorization granted by the client to disclose confidential information might be express or implied, and such authorization may be revoked at any time. The authorization will be implied[10] when the disclosure of the information is convenient for the successful fulfillment of the professional services of the client, unless the client expressly states the opposite. In case of doubt, the lawyer must always choose to protect the professional secret.

7. Duty to disclose: there are cases in which the lawyer has the duty to disclose confidential information, namely, when the disclosure has the purpose of avoiding the commission of a crime. This exception is explicitly established by Article 53 of the Code of Ethics, and it is also implied in the criminal law common principles.

8. Power to disclose: in certain other cases, the lawyer has the power to disclose information that is protected by professional secrecy. Articles 54 and 63 of the Code of Ethics mention the following circumstances:

    (i)   To avoid a serious danger of death or serious injury for one or several persons.
    (ii) To avoid the commission or consummation of a simple felony punishable with a penalty of over three years and one day of jail.
    (iii) To obtain professional ethical advice. The disclosure in relation to another lawyer must always preserve the confidentiality.
    (iv) To contradict a severe allegation against a lawyer or such lawyer's collaborators, in relation to the professional service offered, or in relation to facts in which the client is involved.
    (v)   To collect fees owed to the lawyer.
    (vi) If the lawyer has reason to believe that the professional service provided was used by the client to commit a crime or felony, or another serious action that the law sanctions and orders to investigate.
    (vii) If the information refers to a deceased client and its revelation may avoid that a charged defendant may be wrongly sentenced for a crime or felony.
    (viii) In other cases explicitly allowed by the rules of professional ethics.

    In the previously mentioned cases, the lawyer will be entitled to disclose confidential information only if it meets reasonability and proportionality

---

[9] Ibid., Art. 51.   [10] Ibid., Art. 52.

standards. This means that the disclosure must be necessary to accomplish the purpose that justifies it, that there is no other possible and less prejudicial way to produce the same result, and when the wrong that is meant to be avoided through the disclosure is materially higher than the one caused by the revelation.

9. General or professional interest: The last exception refers to disclosures made in the general or professional interest. It authorizes disclosure if such disclosure favors juridical culture or the formation of future lawyers. Notwithstanding the foregoing, the lawyer shall always adopt the measures needed to avoid the identification of the client and of the specific case.[11]

E Law Firms

10. Even if the Criminal Procedure Code, when protecting the disclosure of documents under the lawyer's custody, does not refer specifically to law firms, but to the lawyer's physical offices, it should be interpreted that the obligation extends to the whole law firm. Otherwise, the legal protection could easily be lost.

Article 11 of the Code of Ethics has a general provision by means of which every right or duty stated in connection with a lawyer is naturally extended to the corresponding law firm. As a consequence, professional secrecy is not only applicable to the lawyer handling the client but also to any other lawyer working at the same law firm. This is particularly relevant when law firms are composed of independent lawyers who share offices but not clients.

F Legal Assistants and Staff

11. The law does not contain any regulation about legal assistants or staff.

Under Article 9 of the Code of Ethics, lawyers must make sure that the conduct of those third parties who collaborate directly with the execution of the legal matter is compatible with the rules and principles of the Code of Ethics. This provision has general application and therefore is also applicable to following sections, G and H.

In addition, Article 115 of the Code of Ethics contains a provision that states that lawyers are obliged to adopt all reasonable measures that are deemed necessary for legal assistants and staff under their control to comply with the obligations of professional secrecy.

G External Service Providers

12. The law does not contain any regulation concerning external service providers.

Article 116 of the Code of Ethics requests the lawyer to make all necessary efforts to ensure all internal and external service providers act

---

[11] Ibid., Art. 59.

in accordance with professional secrecy regulations under the Code of Ethics. Such obligation does not conflict with any personal liability that the third party might have.

H Multidisciplinary Associations

13.   The law does not contain any regulation concerning multidisciplinary associations.

Article 113 of the Code of Ethics states that partners of a law firm, lawyers who have supervisory responsibilities and solo practitioners "shall make all reasonable efforts in order to ensure that all members of the organization, including administrative personnel, interns and non-lawyers" act in accordance with the Code of Ethics.

Additionally, the same provision states that, if the above-referenced lawyers have information regarding a contravention of professional ethics committed by any member of their organization, the lawyers "shall adopt all reasonable measures in order to avoid or minimize its consequences."

I In-House Counsel

14.   No legal or ethical rule explicitly refers to in-house lawyers. In addition, the issue has not been yet a matter of legal or ethical discussion. In principle, there is no reason to exclude in-house lawyers from the general duty and protection of professional secrecy granted by the law and the Code of Ethics. Client communications with in-house lawyers are most likely covered by attorney-client privilege in Chile.

2 History of the Duty of Professional Secrecy in Chile

15.   Professional secrecy has always been one of the lawyer's main obligations in Chile, as this duty is not only stated in favor of the client but is also in the public interest, based on the institutional role that lawyers play within the legal system. Administration of justice requires a continuous and uninhibited flow of information between the client and the lawyer. Professional secrecy is the way the law protects this flow of information.

The Chilean Criminal Code has sanctioned breaches of professional secrecy since its enactment in 1874. The law has also always protected the right to refuse to testify at trial regarding matters covered by professional secrecy, through provisions contained in both the Criminal Procedure Code and Civil Procedure Code.

As to ethical protection and sanctions for its violation, at the beginning of Chile's republican history, it was mandatory to be a member of the Bar to practice law. Hence, all ethical disciplinary powers resided with the Bar.

In 1980 a new Political Constitution was enacted, which included the freedom to affiliate or not with the corresponding trade association. Decree Law number 3621 of 1981 establishes that the courts would have disciplinary jurisdiction over all lawyers accused of ethical misconduct. However, the Bar continued to supervise ethical trials against its members, invoking the powers granted by Article 553 of the Civil Code, which allows people to associate with nonprofit corporations and to approve their own ethical rules.

Finally, by means of a constitutional amendment introduced in 2005, a new paragraph was added to Article 19(16) of the Chilean Political Constitution, which expressly introduces the distinction between affiliated and non-affiliated members of professional associations regarding the sanctioning of ethical misconduct.

3 Supervision

16.   The Chilean ordinary courts are charged with protecting the rights and duties relating to professional secrecy established by the law and sanctioning in case of breach.

As previously mentioned, with the amendment introduced in 2005, disciplinary control of ethical misconduct was legally returned to the Bar, but only with regard to its members. Article 19(16) of the Chilean Political Constitution establishes that "Professional associations created in accordance with the law, will be empowered to know the claims filed against the ethical misconduct of their members, their judgments might be appealed before the corresponding Court of Appeals. The professionals who are not affiliated will be judged by special courts established by law."

As a consequence, to analyze the supervision of this ethical duty, the following sections distinguish between lawyers who are affiliated with the Bar and those who are not.

A The Bar Associations

17.   The Bar protects professional secrecy in two different ways. On the one hand, all lawyers who are affiliated with the Bar and who find their rights threatened or violated by any circumstance or authority can request professional protection from the Bar. If the Bar rules in favor of the petitioner, it may adopt all measures that are deemed necessary by all the Bar's available means, which typically consists of communicating with the corresponding authority or people to try to stop the violation by notifying them of the Bar's ruling. Nevertheless, the rulings of the Bar are not enforceable against third parties, so it will be up to the notified authority or person to comply with the Bar's decision.

On the other hand, if a third party claims that an affiliated lawyer breached such lawyer's duty of professional secrecy, the Bar has the power to sanction said lawyer in accordance with the rules in the Code of Ethics.

B The Courts

18.   The supervision performed by the courts is also carried out in two ways. First, the courts rule on the corresponding criminal act established in Article 231 of the Criminal Code, which contains a legal duty of professional secrecy and is applicable to all lawyers, no matter whether they are affiliated with the Bar or not. Second, the courts control the ethical misconduct of lawyers who are not affiliated with the Bar.

4 Sanctions

A Proceedings and Sanctions

19.   Proceedings and sanctions applicable to all lawyers: As noted previously, Article 231 of the Criminal Code is applicable to all lawyers. The applicable sanction depends on the extent of the damage caused by the breach of professional secrecy, and it ranges from suspension of the practice of law for 61 days to prohibition of the practice of law for life, plus a fine that ranges from 11 to 20 UTM[12] (between approximately USD $700 and $1,300). The proceeding is the same established in the Criminal Procedure Code for all criminal acts.

Proceedings and sanctions applicable to lawyers affiliated with the Bar: The proceeding for violation of professional secrecy applicable to members of the Bar is established in the Bar's Disciplinary Regulation. It is an oral procedure held before the Court of Ethics of the Bar, which can be initiated by any person filing a claim or by request of the General Counsel of the Bar. In the first case, the Secretary Attorney will act as a mediator and will conduct a friendly mediation between the parties. In the second case, or if mediation fails, an instructor will analyze the admissibility of the claim and will conduct an investigation. If the instructor admits the claim, the instructor will press charges. Consequently, the claimant can either agree with the charges or present charges on its own, after which the defendant must present a defense in writing.

Once all of the above mentioned steps have occurred, the members of the Court of Ethics will be appointed. Such Court will be composed of three or five judges, depending on the sanction proposed by the instructor. Afterwards, an oral hearing will be held, in which the instructor and the parties can present their arguments and file their evidence. After the hearing, the Court of Ethics issues a ruling. This ruling can be appealed before the corresponding Court of Appeals.

The sanctions that the Court of Ethics may apply are established in Article 7 of the Bar Bylaws and include the following: (i) oral admonishment, (ii) written censorship, (iv) fine, (v) suspension for a maximum of one year and

---

[12] UTM stands for *Unidad Tributaria Mensual*, which is a Chilean indexed rate.

(vi) disbarment.[13] In all these cases, the Court of Ethics can also make public the application of the sanction.

20. Proceedings and sanctions applicable to non-affiliated lawyers: The Chilean Political Constitution establishes that non-affiliated lawyers will be judged by special courts, which have not been created yet. A transitional article establishes that, until those courts have been created, these issues will be considered by common courts.

Because it is the usual practice in the Chilean legal system to establish a special procedure when creating a new court, when (or if) those courts are created, it might be expected that a special procedure will also be established. As long as those courts are not created, two plausible interpretations of the applicable proceedings and sanctions can be found, based on the court's decisions.

The first possible interpretation is to consider that the Political Constitution, when establishing that non-affiliated lawyers will be judged by special courts, is referring to the actions contained in Article 4 of Decree Law 3621. Article 4 establishes that "Any person affected by any abusive or unethical act, committed by a professional in the practice of his profession, might file a claim in the Courts asking the application of the sanctions that are currently considered for such acts in the Organic Law of the corresponding trade association, or the valid ethical regulations at that time."

The applicable procedure under such Decree Law would be the one stated for a civil summary trial, to be put before an ordinary judge. The ruling issued by the judge will not be subject to any remedy, not even an appeal.

The applicable sanctions are a troublesome issue, because Article 4 states that the applicable regulation is the one valid "at that time," and transitional Article 2 of the same Decree Law enabled the president of Chile to issue the corresponding ethical regulations within a term of six months. Such authorization was never exercised; therefore, ethical regulations were never issued.

Courts have interpreted[14] that the only plausible way to construe these provisions is by applying the Code of Ethics and Organic Law of the Bar valid at the time of the publication of Decree Law 3621.[15] Hence, under this interpretation, for non-affiliated lawyers, the applicable Code of Ethics would be the Code from 1948 and Organic Law of the Bar number 4409.[16]

---

[13] Disbarment does not imply that the lawyer cannot practice law but only that the lawyer will not be considered a member of the Bar.

[14] At least on one occasion, the court has ruled that there is no applicable sanction, since the sanctions are not incorporated in the Code of Ethics valid at that time but in the Organic Law of the Bar, which establishes that the sanctions shall be applied by the General Counsel of the Bar. Since that General Counsel does not currently exist, the court ruled that there was no applicable sanction. *Vid* Sentencia del 2 Juzgado Civil de Valdivia de fecha 17 de julio de 2012, case no. C-3276–2011.

[15] Feb. 7, 1981.

[16] Ruling of the 2° Civil Court of Antofagasta, Oct. 4, 2013, case no. C-1137–2012 and arguments quoted in ruling of the 2° Civil Court of Valparaíso, June 9, 2014, case no C-1020–2013.

That would mean that the sanctions and ethical rules would be different between affiliated and non-affiliated lawyers.[17] The sanctions established in Articles 16 and 18 of Law 4409 are (i) admonishment; (ii) censorship; (iii) suspension of no more than six months, giving notice to the corresponding Court of Appeals and to the Supreme Court, and (iv) loss of the lawyer degree. Only in the latter case may the ruling be appealed to the Supreme Court.

The second plausible interpretation has been adopted by the Supreme Court in several rulings regarding information requirements, which are not meant to apply sanctions but instead interpret the boundaries of professional secrecy. The second interpretation is that the Code of Ethics of 2011, even if it is not formally a law, materially should be considered as such, since it imposes general regulations of conduct, which are the minimum standards expected from any lawyer. Therefore, they can be considered mandatory for all lawyers.[18]

B Relationship between Criminal Sanctions and Disciplinary Sanctions

21.　　As in most legal systems, Chilean law recognizes the general principle known as *non bis in idem*, or double jeopardy. Under this principle, a person cannot be judged or sanctioned more than once for the same act.

Based on this principle, it could be inferred that criminal sanctions and disciplinary sanctions cannot be applied jointly in connection with the same act

---

[17]　In Antonio Bascuñan Rodriguez, "Deber de Confidencialidad y Secreto Profesional del Abogado," *Revista de Estudios de la Justicia* N° 15, año 2011, at 221–63, it is stated that, notwithstanding that the Code of Ethics of 1948 is the code that should be applied by the courts, the regulations of the Code of Ethics of 2011 are relevant for interpreting the previously mentioned Code of Ethics.

[18]　This has been repeated in several Supreme Court rulings, for example, Supreme Court Ruling, Nov. 28, 2012, case no. 2423–2012: "Fifteenth: That even if the Code of Ethics, approved by the General Counsel of the Chilean Bar Association and valid as of August 1st, 2011, cannot be deemed as law formally, since it has not been issued by the corresponding legislative body in accordance with the requirements and procedures established by the Political Constitution for the value of a law, materially, it can be deemed as one, since substantively it imposes general, permanent, abstract, and certainly mandatory conduct rules for all the lawyers of the country, affiliated or not with the corresponding association, notwithstanding that for each specific case, the ethical control is made by the Professional College in accordance with the corresponding Disciplinary Regulation or the special court that Constitution commands the legislator to incorporate in order for it to judge nonaffiliated professionals as long as those are not created by ordinary justice. Sixteenth: That understanding with the mentioned force the rules regarding the ethical conduct with which university professionals shall act, beyond their affiliation with the corresponding professional college, since such rules are legitimate because of the minimal ethical conduct expected for those who have gained a professional degree that enables them – lawyers even give an oath in accordance with Art. 522 of the Courts Organic Code, with the corresponding implications. It shall also be understood that the rules of the Code of Ethics that oblige lawyers, have for all of them binding force, that this maximum Court, as all judges of the Republic, shall demand in strict compliance and in its maximum strength."

or conduct. However, this conclusion is arguable, by way of stating that criminal sanctions and disciplinary sanctions are of a different nature. This is a debatable and still unsolved matter in Chile, so it is not possible to give a conclusive opinion regarding this issue at this time.

5 Duty to Provide Information to the Authorities

A Money Laundering and Terrorism

22. The regulation of this subject can be found in two special laws: (i) Law number 19913, which creates the Unit of Financial Analysis and amends the provisions regarding money laundering, and (ii) Law number 18314, which defines terrorist acts.

Both laws have a special provision regarding the protection of professional secrecy. The law regarding money laundering states that individuals bound by professional secrecy will not be forced to disclose information.[19] In case of terrorism, even if the law authorizes the general wiretapping of communications, it is expressly stated that this cannot affect the confidentiality of communications between a client and lawyer. In case a court authorizes it, such decision might be appealed.[20]

As a consequence, the general protection of professional secrecy is not modified for money laundering or terrorism under Chilean regulation.

B Collective Settlement of Debts

23. Law number 20720[21] regulates reorganization or liquidation procedures and establishes that the debtor must present statements regarding all assets owned by the debtor or received under another title, the debt status, pending trials and balances. Such obligation is established for the debtor. Therefore, there is no exception to professional secrecy regarding the lawyer.

6 Treatment of Lawyers' Documents and Correspondence in the Context of Judicial or Police Investigations

24. The only legal provision about these matters under Chilean law is a provision in the Criminal Procedure Code that exempts from search only communications, notes and registries that lawyers have under their custody or in their offices. Chilean law does not have general provisions that might be applied in other cases, such as civil procedures, administrative procedures and negotiations.

Notwithstanding the foregoing, the protection of lawyers' documents and correspondence is a topic that has been widely reviewed by Chile's Supreme Court in relation to public requirements of information provided to lawyers

---

[19] Art. 2, Law no. 19913.   [20] Art. 14, of Law no. 18314.   [21] Arts. 55, 115, Law no. 20720.

who act on behalf of the state. In these cases, when professional secrecy might be considered challenged, the Supreme Court has repeatedly ruled in favor of the protection of attorney-client privilege, as transparency of public institutions is protected in favor of the general interest and is a constitutional principle.

Ethical regulation is more comprehensive than the regulations established for criminal procedure. Article 43 of the Code of Ethics expressly states that documents delivered to lawyers, as well as documents produced by lawyers in providing their services, are protected.

The same provision also establishes the obligation of the lawyer to have permanently available for the client all documents, either copies or originals, that are under the lawyer's custody. Once the provided service has ended, the lawyer must return such documents to the client, unless there is an agreement to the contrary.

Finally, Article 43 forbids the lawyer from withholding any documents in order to guarantee the payment of fees, with two exceptions:

(i) Documents that are only for internal use of the lawyer or the lawyer's law firm; and

(ii) Reports or opinions prepared by the lawyer, for which the lawyer has not been paid, as long as the entrusted work is limited exclusively to the preparation of such report or opinion, unless an imminent and irreversible damage to the client might derive from withholding the document.

7 Search of a Lawyer's Office

25. The Criminal Procedure Code contains a general rule regarding entry and search and a special provision applicable only to the offices of a lawyer.

The general rule regarding entry and search establishes that, for closed premises, the search might proceed with the authorization of the owner, and, if denied, a court order will be needed. There is no particular reference to lawyers under this rule, but since a lawyer's office is a closed premise, this general rule applies.

In addition, the seizure of documents and objects that are in the custody of a lawyer or in a lawyer's office is subject to a specific rule[22] that identifies which documents cannot be subject to seizure. Under the law, the following documents or objects are excluded from seizure, as long as they are in the custody of a lawyer or in a lawyer's office: (i) communications between the client and the lawyer, (ii) notes taken by the lawyer, (iii) communication entrusted by the client and (iv) any circumstance protected under the right to remain silent.

[22] Art. 220, Criminal Procedure Code.

The only exception to the aforementioned rules is when the lawyer is directly under investigation for the commission of a criminal act.

Regarding documents protected by professional secrecy, Chilean law does not distinguish among documents issued either directly by the client, between the client and the lawyer, or between a third party and the client, as long as they have been entrusted by the client to the lawyer and are in the lawyer's custody.

The Code of Ethics[23] specifies that the protection of professional secrecy covers all documents in physical, electronic or any other form that contain information subject to confidentiality. It also extends the protection to information with a confidential nature produced by the lawyer, even if it is not in the lawyer's custody, but instead in the client's custody.

8 Tapping of Telephone Conversations with a Lawyer

26.   Neither the law nor the Code of Ethics contains specific rules regarding tapping telephone conversations in connection with professional secrecy. Therefore, general rules apply, giving full protection to communications between a client and a lawyer.

Case law shows that evidence consisting of tapping conversations between a lawyer and a client have been declared illegal and excluded as evidence.

9 The Lawyer as Witness

27.   Both the Civil Procedure Code and the Criminal Procedure Code, which are subsidiarily applicable in any judicial or administrative procedure in Chile, expressly establish the right of the lawyer who appears in court to remain silent and not answer questions that may affect professional secrecy.

Article 360 of the Civil Procedure Code states: "The following [individuals] are not bound to render testimony: 1st. Priests, lawyers, notaries, lawyers, physicians and midwives, on matters that they have been told in confidence, as a result of their status, profession or trade."

Article 303 of the Criminal Procedure Code states:

> Power to abstain from making statements for purposes of secrecy. Those individuals, who, due to their status, profession or legal function, such as a lawyer, physician or confessor, would have the obligation to keep secret anything they have confided, shall not be obliged to render testimony, but only in what relates to said secret. The individuals indicated in the foregoing paragraph cannot invoke the right herein when released from the obligation to keep secret by those who would have thus entrusted to them.

---

[23] Art. 64, Code of Ethics.

Article 62 of the Code of Ethics contains a similar provision, which acknowledges the refusal to testify or to inform about issues subject to confidentiality. However, unlike the Criminal Procedure Code's provision, the Code of Ethics provides limits to a lawyer's testimony, even in a case where the client has liberated the lawyer of the duty of confidentiality.

On the other hand, Article 63 of the Code of Ethics establishes the following cases in which a lawyer has an ethical duty to testify, even if the law does not force the lawyer to do so:

(i)   If the lawyer has founded reasons to believe that the professional service provided was used by the client to commit a crime or felony, or another serious action that the law sanctions; and

(ii) If the information refers to a deceased client and the release of such information may help a charged defendant avoid being wrongly sentenced for a crime or felony.

10 The Lawyer and the Press

28.   The law does not contain specific provisions regarding lawyers and the press. Nevertheless, there are some related legal provisions about judges and public prosecutors.

Regarding the conduct of judges, the Court's Organic Code establishes that it is forbidden for judges to "publish, without authorization of the President of the Supreme Court, writs defending their official conduct or attacking in any way the conduct of other judges or magistrates."[24]

Likewise, the Public Prosecutors Office Organic Law[25] states that public prosecutors must withhold from commenting on their cases, even more, evidently, if the investigation has been declared temporarily secret.

The ethical regulation of the Bar also contains some behavioral standards for the lawyers and the press. First, it establishes that the lawyer must act with veracity and moderation in dealing with the press and get the express or implied consent of the client with regard to such dealing.[26]

Second, this regulation establishes that a lawyer who is currently taking part in or who has taken part in a procedure or pending investigation must refrain from making statements or delivering information outside the procedure or the investigation, when such action might seriously affect the impartiality of those deciding the issue or conducting the investigation.[27]

This provision also covers other lawyers who belong to the same law firm or public office and to any other non-lawyer collaborators who are under the lawyer's direction.[28]

---

[24] Art. 323(4), Court's Organic Code.
[25] Art. 64, Organic Law of the Prosecution Office, law no. 19640.
[26] Art. 101, Code of Ethics.   [27] Ibid., Art. 102.   [28] Ibid., Arts. 104, 105.

Nevertheless, a lawyer is allowed to make statements when necessary to rectify information that has become public and that might have prejudicial effects on the client.[29]

11 Powers of the Tax and Other Authorities

29. The Tax Code[30] states that tax law does not modify legal provisions regarding professional secrecy, unless it is specifically stated otherwise.

An exception to professional secrecy in tax matters arises in cases related to the compliance of tax duties of the lawyer, and it extends to accounting books, invoices and all documents that are related to elements that need to be used to establish the tax itself or to information that has to be included in the lawyer's tax filing.

Another exception is contained in Article 34 of the Chilean Tax Code, which states that the advisers who participated in the preparation of a tax filing, in its preparation or in the preparation of its background, are obliged to testify under oath about the matters contained in the tax declaration. This provision limits the exception to those matters that are included in the tax filing. In case of any other matter, the general rule applies, and the lawyer can refuse to provide testimony.

The Tax Code also states that lawyers are not forced to issue sworn affidavits that the Chilean IRS is entitled to request as inspection measures.

12 National Security Issues

30. There is no special mention of professional secrecy in Chilean law dealing with national security issues. Notwithstanding this, the Chilean Political Constitution states that, in case of war, the president is entitled to intercept, open or register documents and all kinds of communications. This provision has not been applied, but it could theoretically affect professional secrecy.

---

[29] Ibid., Art. 103.   [30] Art. 61, Tax Code.

14

Colombia

CARLOS URRUTIA-VALENZUELA

Brigard & Urrutia

Preliminary Note

1.   In Colombia, all lawyers are subject to the duty of professional secrecy. The practice of law is strictly reserved for lawyers who have fulfilled the requirements prescribed by law, including registration at the Superior Council of the Judiciary ("Superior Council"), the body charged with regulating and supervising the profession, including disciplinary actions against lawyers.

The nature and scope of professional secrecy was defined by the Constitutional Court, which in a 1996 judgment concluded that it entails a duty as well as a right and does not imply simple discretion concerning information acquired in the course of practicing law, but a complete confidentiality with respect to such information, in light of the interpersonal bond that brings together the attorney and the client.[1]

For purposes of professional secrecy, there is no distinction as to the type of practice in which a lawyer is engaged. Indeed, the secrecy principle applies to litigators, solo practitioners, partners and salaried associates at law firms, as well as to lawyers working as attorneys within government agencies or inside public as well as private entities, so long as the performance of their activities involves providing representation or legal advice and assistance to their clients or employers. Of course, this means that lawyers engaged in activities outside the law would not be subject to professional secrecy with respect to matters unrelated to the exercise of the legal profession. As is true everywhere, there are many lawyers in Colombia who have chosen to pursue other paths, such as working inside government agencies or in private business activities, in functions that do not involve providing legal services.

The regulations that govern the legal profession provide that the duty of professional secrecy extends even beyond the completion of the service.

1 Scope and Limitations on the Duty of Professional Secrecy/Attorney-Client Privilege

A Statutory Basis and Implications

2.   Professional secrecy has a statutory basis in Colombia's Constitution.[2] The said principle is not limited to lawyers' attorney-client privilege but applies to all professions that, by virtue of statutes that implement the Constitution, are also entitled to professional secrecy (including medical doctors, accountants, psychologists and the like).

As far as lawyers are concerned, Law 1123 of 2007 ("Law 1123," or the "Disciplinary Code"), which regulates the legal profession, provides the statutory grounds for professional secrecy for the legal profession. Article 28 sets

---

[1] Colombia, Constitutional Court. Ruling no. T-073A of 1996.

[2] Art. 74 of the 1991 Constitution provides that "[t]he professional secret shall be inviolable."

forth the duties to which lawyers are subject and includes in numeral 9 thereof a specific obligation to keep and uphold professional secrecy, even after the rendering of the service has ceased.

Furthermore, Article 34 of Law 1123 defines certain types of breaches to the loyalty that lawyers owe their clients. In accordance with Article 34(f), it is a breach of loyalty to reveal any secret that a client has confided to a lawyer, even in the event of a request from an authority, unless expressly authorized by the client or if it is indispensable to avoid the commission of a crime. In that context, the term "authority" should be construed to mean any governmental or judicial authority.

On the other hand, Article 22 of Law 1123 defines the various causes of exclusion from disciplinary liability. Among them, Article 22(4)[3] provides that lawyers are exempt from liability if they have acted to safeguard a personal right or a right of a third party that must be subordinate to the duty (secrecy), in light of the necessity, adequacy, proportionality and reasonableness of the action. Additionally, in accordance with Article 22(2), lawyers are likewise exempt from professional liability if they have acted in strict compliance with a constitutional or legal duty of higher importance than the sacrificed duty.

B Scope

3.   There has been substantial debate concerning the scope of professional secrecy. However, there is a general consensus that, because the Constitution provides that professional secrecy is inviolable, lawyers are subject to a strict standard that only in extreme circumstances would excuse them from abiding by their secrecy obligation. The matter was brought to the attention of the Constitutional Court (the "Constitutional Court" or the "Court"). A citizen commenced an action to strike down, on the grounds of violating the Constitution, the phrase contained in Article 34 of the Disciplinary Code that enables lawyers to disclose secrets to avoid the commission of a crime. The Court[4] examined the issue and found that the term "inviolable" implies that, absent consent from the client, professional secrecy can be excused only in very extreme circumstances that imply a state of necessity, where lawyers face the dilemma of having to breach their duty to avoid the commission of a grave crime or to prevent a significant risk arising from a potential crime that would affect a third party. The Court rejected the argument that there is a close relationship between professional secrecy and the client's right to privacy. Rather, the Court argued that the rule provides the criteria that must be applied

[3] Art. 22 of the Disciplinary Code provides seven instances in which "there shall be no disciplinary liability."

[4] In judgment no. C-301/12, the Constitutional Court found that the phrase "or that is required to make disclosures to avoid the commission of a crime" does not violate the constitutional right and duty of professional secrecy.

when determining whether lawyers have breached their secrecy obligations in disclosing information covered by professional secrecy.

The Court made a careful comparative analysis of similar statutes contained in the rules of professional ethics in force in various jurisdictions, including Italy, Argentina, Chile, France, the United States, Germany and Spain. The Court concluded that, where the lawyer is under a state of extreme necessity to prevent a crime, the exemption to the duty of secrecy is legitimate and reasonable. Therefore, the Court decided to uphold as constitutional the provision contained in Law 1123.

C Persons Subject to the Duty of Professional Secrecy

4.   The constitutional principle concerning the inviolability of professional secrecy applies to all professions that by virtue of law are required to observe such standard of conduct. Of course, the scope of the secrecy duty varies depending on the nature of the profession. Each individual profession is regulated by statutes that define the extent and scope of the duty of secrecy.

In the case of the legal profession, all practicing lawyers in the exercise of their activities must abide by the duty of professional secrecy. As mentioned previously, the duty of secrecy does not apply to attorneys engaged in activities that do not involve acting as a lawyer.

D Exceptions to and Derogations from the Duty of Professional Secrecy

5.   Lawyers employed as public servants are generally subject to a limited scope of secrecy duty. Indeed, although in principle they must abide by the duty of secrecy with respect to any legal advice and assistance they provide to the entity, including in the context of administrative or judicial proceedings, there are laws and regulations that require government agencies to disclose to the public any information and documents that are not subject to reserve. In that respect, a government lawyer may be excused from the duty to maintain secrecy of information that must otherwise be disclosed to the public or made available to the public upon request. For that purpose, a government lawyer would be exempt from professional liability pursuant to Article 22(2) of the Disciplinary Code.[5]

Likewise, lawyers employed in the judiciary are subject to a different standard. Generally, judges and other judicial employees are exempt from the duty of professional secrecy, as their activities do not involve a lawyer-client relationship.

Furthermore, in the context of proceedings before the courts as well as in administrative proceedings, information that is in the court's docket is usually

---

[5] Art. 22(2) provides that lawyers maybe excused from their secrecy obligation where they are acting pursuant to a constitutional or legal duty of higher ranking.

public information to which anyone can have access. There are, however, certain exceptions; for example, during the investigation phase of criminal proceedings, prosecutors as well counsel are subject to a specific duty to maintain under strict reserve any information gathered. The duty of reserve is different from the professional secrecy obligation and arises under specific statutes in the Criminal Code and the Code of Criminal Proceedings. Of course, counsel to a person charged with a crime is subject to professional secrecy rules, in addition to the duty of reserve. In the context of other areas of law, particularly in matters involving personal taxes and financial transactions, government lawyers are subject to special duties to keep information confidential.

E Law Firms

6.   The rules contained in the Disciplinary Code do not directly address law firms and do not regulate their activities. There are indirect references to lawyers working as members of a law firm, specifically to spell out matters involving liability for actions or inactions that may carry sanctions. However, generally speaking, the regulations that govern the legal profession in Colombia focus on the individual lawyer. Historically, lawyers in Colombia have stayed away from adopting formal associations to practice law in the form of law firms. More than 99 percent of lawyers practice as solo practitioners who in certain cases may share premises with colleagues or even manage jointly certain client affairs.

There are a limited number of law firms, organized under the model that originated in Anglo-Saxon jurisdictions. Matters of liability are addressed assuming that the individual lawyers are responsible, rather than the law firm itself. For this reason, there are no rules that expressly determine whether a law firm and its partners are jointly or severally responsible for a breach of the professional secrecy duty attributable to a firm partner or associate.

To resolve the lack of specific regulation, local law firms tend to adopt rules and standards that are more demanding and that specifically address issues such as professional secrecy, liability and attorney-client privilege, similar to the professional ethics rules of the International Bar Association.

F Legal Assistants and Staff

7.   The Disciplinary Code does not address the issue of whether legal assistants and staff are subject to the same duties of professional secrecy that apply to lawyers. However, the rules imply that each lawyer – and in the case of a law firm, its partners and associates – are responsible for ensuring that legal assistants and staff understand the nature and the scope of the professional secrecy duty and abide by the obligations that apply to their employers.

Accordingly, any disclosure by an employee concerning information that is subject to professional secrecy would expose the attorney to professional liability, in the manner of the sanctions provided by the Disciplinary Code, as well as to civil liability, which may extend to a law firm, if the lawyer practices as member of a firm. Civil liability implies that lawyers would have to compensate their clients for damages and losses resulting from a breach of the secrecy duty.

G External Service Providers

8.   As is the case with respect to staff and legal assistants, the Disciplinary Code is silent on whether external services providers of lawyers and law firms are subject to professional secrecy regulations. As a result, in the event that a service provider unlawfully discloses information deemed to be covered by professional secrecy rules, the lawyer who is responsible for maintaining the confidentiality of the relevant information would personally be exposed to professional liability and to the sanctions that may apply, as well as to civil liability jointly with the service provider.

H Multidisciplinary Associations

9.   The Disciplinary Code does not regulate multidisciplinary associations, and there is no legal impediment that would prevent a multidisciplinary firm from employing lawyers and providing legal services. As a result, there are a number of accounting and auditing firms that have gone into the business of offering legal advice in areas such as taxation, competition, labor and exchange control regulations.

Therefore, the same situation explained above with respect to law firms would, in principle, apply to consequences of a breach of the duty of secrecy by a member of the multidisciplinary association. That is, the lawyer responsible for the attorney-client relationship would be professionally liable for the breach of duty, as well as jointly liable with the multidisciplinary firm for any damages suffered by the client.

I In-House Counsel

10.   As mentioned earlier, in-house counsel are subject to the professional secrecy duty. Lawyers working inside departments devoted to providing legal advice and support to management in public and private entities, including governmental and nongovernmental organizations, must abide by the disciplinary and ethics rules that regulate the profession. In that context, in-house lawyers cannot disclose or otherwise reveal information that they acquire within the organization or that is confided to them by employees who seek legal advice and assistance.

There are, however, exceptions. Lawyers often come into contact with matters that may involve criminal conduct on the part of members of their organization. To the extent that an in-house lawyer finds that management is willfully engaged in criminal activities such as money laundering or actions that support terrorism, the lawyer would be required to report such actions to the Prosecutor's General Office and facilitate the investigation. Likewise, a lawyer working for a company the securities of which are listed on the Colombian Stock Exchange would have to report an employee's activity that might involve wrongful use of so-called privileged information (insider trading).

In that context, the in-house lawyer who discloses information to prevent the commission of a crime would be exempted from sanctions arising from potential violations of the professional secrecy duties, in accordance with Articles 34 (f) and 22(2) of the Disciplinary Code.

2 History of the Duty of Professional Secrecy in Colombia

11.   In Colombia, professional secrecy has constitutional protection since the issuance of the Constitution of 1991. However, laws regulating professional secrecy were first enacted in the second half of the past century, when regulations were issued to protect the secrecy of information in the legal, medical, accounting and other professions.

The duty of professional secrecy for the medical physician was established in Articles 37 to 39 of Law 23 of 1981, and those of the related professions such as dentistry, bacteriology, nursing and psychology were regulated, respectively, by Law 35 of 1989, Law 36 of 1993, Law 266 of 1993 and Law 1090 of 2006. The secrecy duty of these professions has been widely discussed by the Constitutional Court.[6]

In the case of lawyers, the duty of professional secrecy was first established by virtue of Article 47 of the Decree 196 of 1971, which provided rules that governed the profession. Article 47 established the principle that attorneys were mandated to "keep the professional secrecy." Decree 196 of 1971 was mostly repealed by Law 1123. As mentioned previously, Article 28 of the Disciplinary Code now governs the notion of professional secrecy.[7]

The duty of secrecy has also been widely discussed by the Constitutional Court as both an obligation and as a right.[8]

---

[6] For instance, the court addressed the issue of the duty of secrecy of other professions in judgment nos. C-264 of 1996, T-151 of 1996 and T-824 of 2005.

[7] Art. 28(9), Law 1123 of 2007.

[8] The most relevant rulings of the court concerning professional secrecy are judgment nos. C-411 of 1993, T-708 of 2008 and C-301 of 2012.

3 Supervision

A The Bar Associations

12. The legal profession in Colombia is not organized in bar associations. Although permitted by the Disciplinary Code, bar associations (*colegios de abogados*) are not mandatory and have an insignificant role in the affairs of the profession. Generally, lawyers do not become affiliated with bar associations. As a result, bar associations have virtually no influence on how the profession is regulated or in matters such as the appointment of judges and magistrates. Local bar associations are authorized to issue resolutions that provide guidelines concerning fees for legal services. Certain bar associations issue such guidelines from time to time. However, the guidelines are not mandatory, although they provide support to lawyers in their relationships with clients concerning the level of fees to be charged for matters entrusted to them.

B The Courts

13. The legal profession in Colombia is governed by laws approved by Congress and is supervised by the Superior Council. The Council is part of the Judicial Branch. Its most important role is to administer the entire Judicial Branch, with authority to appoint judges and magistrates at all levels, with the exception of the justices of the Supreme Court and of the Constitutional Court, as well as the members of the Council of State, who are subject to different rules for appointment. The Council is also charged with the authority to supervise the legal profession through the Disciplinary Chamber.

In matters regarding the supervision of the activities of lawyers, the Superior Council is the competent court to hear complaints against lawyers. For purposes of the proceedings involving disciplinary actions against lawyers, there are sectional councils (*Consejos Seccionales*) that act as courts of first instance in such proceedings. Certain interlocutory decisions, as well as all judgments handed down by sectional councils, may be appealed to the Disciplinary Chamber of the Council, thus affording a right of appeal in disciplinary actions. Each sectional council is assigned a certain territory over which it has jurisdiction.

In a constitutional amendment approved by Congress in June 2015, the Superior Council created a new body, the National Commission of Judicial Discipline, to supervise and regulate the legal profession. The said commission is not yet operational. For the time being and until 2017, the regulatory and disciplinary function regarding the legal profession will remain with the Superior Council.

The Superior Council hears disciplinary complaints filed against lawyers, as well as against judges and other high-level employees of the judiciary. Lawyers are subject to the ethics and conduct rules contained in the Disciplinary Code. The profession is not self-regulated.

4 Sanctions

A Proceedings and Sanctions

14. As mentioned previously, proceedings against lawyers and judges for violation of their professional duties take place in two instances. The first is before the sectional council that has jurisdiction over the place where the alleged breach occurred, and the second is before the Superior Council.

The proceedings are governed by the provisions of the Disciplinary Code;[9] certain procedural matters not regulated by said code are subject to the rules of the Sole Disciplinary Code (*Código Disciplinario Único*), which governs disciplinary proceedings involving public servants generally and regulates the proceedings in a very detailed manner.

The proceedings are based on rules that emphasize the due process rights of the individuals charged with breaching their professional duties. Individuals have the right to appoint counsel of their choice. Failure to appoint counsel means the court (the competent sectional council) must designate *officio* counsel. The proceedings are carried out orally in hearings. The investigated individuals have the right to be informed as to the charges against them, so as to warrant their right of defense.

Sanctions to be imposed on lawyers for failure to abide by the professional secrecy duty are of a disciplinary nature and are regulated by the Disciplinary Code. Sanctions depend on the seriousness of the offense, taking into account the criteria set forth in Article 45 of the Disciplinary Code.[10]

In accordance with Article 40, a lawyer who has breached a duty, such as the duty of professional secrecy, should be sanctioned as follows, depending on the

---

[9] The Third Book of the Disciplinary Code is devoted to disciplinary proceedings. The guiding principles of the proceedings are set forth in Arts. 43 through 58. They include the prevalence of substantive law over procedural provisions; the principle that the proceedings are oral in nature, gratuitous and should be expeditious, efficient and subject to a right of appeal to a higher court; and the principle that the investigated party has the right to contradict the evidence and that the proceedings should be public.

[10] Art. 45 provides: "(a) certain general criteria, including the type of conduct, the social importance of the conduct, the damage inflicted, the circumstances in which the breach occurred, which must be examined taking into account the care employed in its preparation and the determining motives of the conduct; (b) certain criteria for leniency, including a confession prior to charges being made, the act of having attempted to repair and indemnify the damage inflicted; and (c) certain criteria that aggravate the sanction, including any impact on human rights and on the fundamental rights defined by the Constitution, whether there was the intention to attribute the breach to a third person, the fact that other individuals or public servants may have participated, whether the lawyer had previously been the subject of disciplinary sanctions within the previous 5 years."

criteria defined for purposes of grading the breach: (i) a reprimand (*censura*), which implies a public reprimand for the breach incurred; (ii) a fine equivalent to not less than 100 minimum monthly legal wages, depending on the seriousness of the breach; (iii) a suspension from the practice of law for periods between two months and three years (between six months and five years if the breach originates from actions taken by the lawyer in representing or acting as a counterpart of a public entity); and (iv) exclusion, which includes cancellation of the license and prohibition to practice law.

B Relationship between Criminal Sanctions and Disciplinary Sanctions

15. Disciplinary sanctions are separate and apart from any criminal sanctions that may be attributable to the breach of professional secrecy. Indeed, in certain circumstances, the act of disclosing information subject to professional secrecy may imply, aside from disciplinary sanctions, the commission of a crime.

The principle of *non bis in idem* is established in the Constitution; it means that no one can be tried twice for the same matter. Nevertheless, concerning disciplinary and criminal sanctions, the Constitutional Court stated in judgment C-244 of 1996[11] that criminal and disciplinary proceedings are compatible with respect to a person who may have participated in actions that involve a crime, on the one hand, and a breach of a disciplinary duty, on the other.

This duality of sanctions was recognized by the Superior Council in the case of Álvaro Sánchez Martínez, by means of a ruling dated February 23, 2005. Although the Superior Council absolved Mr. Sánchez of the disciplinary liability, because the accusation made against him by his client did not imply a violation of professional secrecy, the court concluded that he could be tried in disciplinary proceedings and, separately, criminal proceedings for not having reported the action of his client earlier.[12]

For instance, a lawyer who provides to another person privileged information concerning a client whose shares are listed in public markets, and thereafter profits from such information by buying or selling those shares, has participated in a crime that would be subject to severe penalties that include prison. Those prison penalties would be imposed on the lawyer in addition to, and not in substitution for, the disciplinary sanctions that might attach to the lawyer.

---

[11] The court said: "When a disciplinary proceeding and a criminal proceeding involving the same person takes place involving the same facts, it cannot be validly concluded that there is identity on the matter or identity of the cause, since the objective of each proceeding is different and so are the judicial values and interests protected by each. Indeed, in each of these proceedings the conduct of the person involved under rules of content and length of their own."

[12] Superior Council of the Judiciary. Disciplinary Committee. Disciplinary Proceeding against Álvaro Sánchez, Feb. 23, 2005, File no. 200200721 01 (107-I-05).

5 Duty to Provide Information to the Authorities

A Money Laundering

16. Lawyers who, in furtherance of an attorney-client relationship, come into contact with information that clearly indicates that their clients are involved in the commission of a crime involving money laundering are required to denounce such activity. Failure to report money laundering activities is considered a felony pursuant to Article 441 of the Penal Code.

   Any disclosure by the lawyer would imply a breach of the duty of professional secrecy, but the attorney would be excused from liability, as provided in Article 34(f) of the Disciplinary Code.

B Collective Settlement of Debts (Insolvency Proceedings)

17. Lawyers usually play an important role in providing advice and assistance to distressed debtors and often are privy to information that may imply, for instance, that the debtor has transferred or hidden assets that would otherwise be available to pay the debts owed to creditors. Depending on whether the conduct of the debtor involves the commission of a crime, the debtor's counsel may be instrumental in assisting the bankruptcy court in finding assets and making them available to pay the debt.

   However, applicable law does not provide to the bankruptcy court the power to compel the debtor's lawyer to disclose the information. Nevertheless, if the conduct of the debtor involves the commission of fraud or other crime, the debtor's lawyer would be able to voluntarily disclose the information. In that scenario, lawyers who proceed in that manner would be able to argue that they should be exempted from sanctions for breach of their professional duty, in light of the fact that the purpose of such disclosure is to avoid the commission of a grave crime.

6 Treatment of Lawyers' Documents and Correspondence in the Context of Judicial or Police Investigations

18. Lawyers' documents and correspondence with their clients are protected by professional secrecy. However, in the context of a judicial or police investigation, prosecutors may order the seizure of otherwise privileged information contained in a database during seizure procedures. To that end, prosecutors must obtain a prior judicial order to access the documents and correspondence at issue.

7 Search of a Lawyer's Office

19. The search of a lawyer's office may entail the disclosure of protected information of several clients. Therefore, as in the case of seizure of lawyers'

documents and correspondence, the search of a lawyer's office usually requires a prior judicial order. The judicial order should specify what kind of information can be searched in the lawyer's office and what measures should be taken to protect the privacy of the clients involved.

8 Tapping of Telephone Conversations with a Lawyer

20.   In Colombia, the right and duty of professional secrecy is closely related to the fundamental right to privacy and the inviolability of private communications.

The Court, in a Constitutional action against the Ministry of National Defense, concluded that tapping telephone conversations of an attorney can be done only under very restrictive conditions, clearly and carefully weighing the fundamental right to privacy and the inviolability of private communications vis-à-vis the legal value that may be achieved by the intrusion of the police investigation.[13]

9 The Lawyer as Witness

21.   As a general rule, lawyers cannot be compelled to provide testimony that would implicitly violate their duty of secrecy to a client. Article 214 of the Code of Civil Procedure and Article 209 of the General Code of Procedure (which will soon fully replace the Code of Civil Procedure) provide that lawyers, doctors, accountants and other professionals who are subject to a duty of secrecy are excused from giving testimony in respect of matters that have come to their knowledge by reason of their professional activity.

In certain cases involving matters such as national security, however, a lawyer who possesses information acquired from a client that may be important to protect national security and prevent an act of terrorism may be interrogated. In that context, lawyers would be required to disclose the information that may be in their possession and would be excused from any breach of their professional duty of secrecy.

10 The Lawyer and the Press

22.   Lawyers as well as journalists are subject to similar duties of secrecy. A lawyer is not required to provide confidential information to the press regardless of the

---

[13] Constitutional Court, Judgment no. T-708 of 2008: "The connection between the professional secrecy and other fundamental rights strengthen, even more, the right to privacy and the mandate of the inviolability of private communications. In the case that a conversation takes place within a profession that implies deposit of trust and highly personal services, the requisites in order to be able to execute a restriction or intervention of privacy will become more severe and strict. Even more, when it takes place in the relation between the attorney and the client, since in this case, it will have an additional and direct link to the right of defense."

nature of the information that the lawyer may possess and the interest that such information would have to the public. Failure to observe such duty would not be excusable on grounds that the information may have a special interest that should be divulged to the public.

Likewise, journalists are entitled to the right to protect their sources. Regardless of the origin or the nature of the relevant information, a lawyer would not be able to compel a journalist to disclose a source.

11 Powers of the Tax and Other Authorities

23. Colombian law does not treat the breach of tax regulations as a crime. However, certain actions incurred by taxpayers in the course of preparing tax returns or paying taxes may imply the commission of other crimes, such as falsifying documents and fraud.

Tax authorities do not have the power to compel a lawyer to provide testimony in proceedings to challenge matters related to the taxes paid or payable by the lawyer's client. Likewise, tax authorities do not have the power to search the files and information in the possession of a lawyer regarding clients of such lawyer.

A lawyer's breach of confidentiality owed to his or her client concerning information that may be relevant for purposes of a tax investigation would not be excusable from the perspective of the lawyer's professional liability.

12 National Security Issues

24. In Colombia, the Statutory Law of Intelligence allows the state's specialized agencies to collect, process, analyze and disseminate information to protect human rights and to prevent and fight internal or external threats to the national security.[14] Therefore, attorney-client privileged information may be subject to intelligence or counterintelligence processes to protect national security interests.

However, pursuant to the Statutory Law of Intelligence, the specialized agencies' functions of intelligence and counterintelligence are limited to human rights, constitutional rights, international humanitarian law and international human rights law. Accordingly, the Statutory Law of Intelligence provides that the constitutional right to privacy, which is closely related to the duty of professional secrecy, must be protected through the principle of legal reserve of the information.[15]

[14] Art. 2, Statutory Law 1621 of 2013.
[15] Ibid., Art. 4. In accordance with the Constitutional Court (Judgment no. C-301/12), the principle of legal reserve of information constitutes a sufficient means for the protection of the right to privacy, as it requires public officials of specialized agencies to maintain the secrecy of all the information to which they may have access in the exercise of their duties.

15

Costa Rica

ANDREA SITTENFELD
ADRIANA CASTRO
KARLA GONZÁLEZ
EDUARDO CALDERON

BLP Legal

Preliminary Note

1. To practice law in Costa Rica, after graduating from law school, the student has to undergo the admission process to the Costa Rican Bar Association. This admission is a requirement that all lawyers have to fulfill.

    Every lawyer is subject to a duty known as attorney-client privilege, by which lawyers must maintain the secrecy of the information that the lawyers receive from their clients during the legal services the lawyers render. This obligation is extended to those who work with and assist lawyers, such as paralegals and staff who work at law firms or who have contact with the client's information.

    The Costa Rican Bar Association is the only institution in Costa Rica in charge of admitting new lawyers and ensuring compliance with ethics regulations for lawyers.

    This chapter describes the professional secrecy regulations applicable to lawyers in accordance with Costa Rican legislation.

1 Scope of and Limitations on the Duty of Professional Secrecy/Attorney-Client Privilege

A Statutory Basis and Implications

2. Professional secrecy, or the attorney-client privilege, in Costa Rica comprises the obligation that the lawyer has regarding the information and secrets known because of the legal services rendered to a client. This obligation is extended to the knowledge acquired from the perusal of private documents, conversations and participation in hearings or any type of meetings.

    Professional secrecy is regulated by law to ensure that legal advice is provided under the principle of confidentiality, meaning that the information exchanged with the client will not be used to affect other areas of the client's life that are not related to the issue that is being handled by the lawyer.[1]

    The internal regulations of the Costa Rican Bar Association state that all lawyers are obliged to follow in their practice the general ethical and moral principles contained in the Code of Legal Duties, Moral and Professional Ethics of the Lawyer (*Código de Deberes Jurídicos, Morales y Éticos de los Profesionales en Derecho*), hereinafter referred to as the "Code."

---

[1] Barahona Vargas, *The Duty of the Lawyer and Notary Public of Professional Secrecy in Costa Rica*, Graduation Thesis, University of Costa Rica, 2012, at 84–85.

The purpose of the Code is to establish the main duties and obligations that the lawyer has, not only legally, but also in accordance with basic moral and ethical principles. The Code also provides the respective sanctions, if the lawyer does not abide by the rules, in accordance with the general sanctions included in the internal regulations of the Costa Rican Bar Association.

The lawyer's duty of professional secrecy is clearly established in Article 41 of the Code, which defines the duty of professional secrecy as the proper use of the confidential information known by attorneys from their legal practice. This information includes any information given by the client, any counterpart of the client, and any colleagues, or any information acquired during an administrative or judiciary process. It also includes the information obtained from the perusal of private documents reviewed by the lawyer during legal counseling. The duty of professional secrecy prohibits the lawyer from disclosing or transferring confidential information to any third party. The exceptions to this duty are stated in Articles 42 and 43 of the Code and are described in Section 1(D) of this chapter. Furthermore, Article 47 establishes that the lawyer must keep in strict custody all documents and materials obtained as a result of the legal services rendered. Article 47 states that the lawyer must keep client's documents and materials separate from the lawyer's own and is precluded from withholding them to ensure the payment of legal fees.[2]

If a lawyer becomes aware of certain confidential information as the result of an inquiry made by another colleague, the lawyer must maintain confidentiality regarding such information as well. Attorneys must warn their staff, paralegals and any other employees working for them of the duty of confidentiality.

B Scope

3. The lawyer's obligation to maintain the secrecy of certain information is based on the trust relationship the lawyer maintains with the client by which the lawyer will give advice and guard the client's interests.

To provide a complete and correct defense to the client, the lawyer must know all the information regarding a certain case and must refrain from transferring or sharing such information with third parties.

The duty to maintain professional secrecy remains after the lawyer-client relationship is terminated. Furthermore, the duty to maintain professional secrecy is a right of the lawyer, since no authority can oblige the lawyer to disclose the information kept under this protection as long as no superior interest is being violated.

---

[2] Colegio de Abogados y Abogadas, *Código de Deberes Jurídicos, Morales y Éticos de los Profesionales en Derecho*, 2013.

C Persons Subject to the Duty of Professional Secrecy

4.   This obligation of professional secrecy extends to the staff working for the lawyer, including third parties, such as a financial adviser or any other professionals.[3]

D Exceptions to and Optional Derogations from the Duty of Professional Secrecy

5.   When two legal duties come into conflict, the one that protects a more highly ranked right prevails. For example, the public interest to protect life, public health and the like will prevail over the client's personal interests or the lawyers' duty of professional secrecy.

The Code includes some exceptions to the duty of professional secrecy. They are[4] (i) if the lawyer is accused of committing a crime; (ii) if the lawyer is collecting the legal fees that the client owes, in which case the information that can be disclosed is only the information relevant to determining the amount of the pending legal fees; (iii) if revealing the information would avoid the possible conviction of an innocent person; and (iv) if the client communicates to the attorney the intention to commit a crime. In this case, if the attorney cannot persuade the client to desist, the attorney is obliged to reveal the information to prevent the crime (Arts. 42 and 43).

Another exception to the duty of professional secrecy is that an attorney can reveal information obtained through research or for teaching purposes. In this scenario, it is important that the attorney does not share or communicate to the students specific details, such as personal information about the client.[5]

E Law Firms

6.   In accordance with Article 41 of the Code, all of the lawyers who work at a law firm are obliged to maintain their duty of professional secrecy regarding not only their clients but also the clients of other colleagues in the firm. A client needs to know that the information that client shares with the lawyer is going to be protected under the same conditions by all of those who have access to it.

F Legal Assistants and Staff

7.   Lawyers who coordinate work with legal assistants or other professionals in the firm are obligated to warn them about the conditions in which they will work and handle the information.

---

[3] Ibid.   [4] Ibid.
[5] Barahona Vargas, *The Duty of the Lawyer and Notary Public of Professional Secrecy in Costa Rica*, Graduation Thesis, University of Costa Rica, 2012, at 109.

G External Service Providers

8. The duty of professional secrecy extends to all of the external service providers that the lawyer uses or might need to service a client. The lawyer should alert the external service provider of the duty of professional secrecy and that all information must be treated as privileged.

H Multidisciplinary Associations

9. In some cases, the lawyer may require the help of professionals from other organizations. These professionals are also obliged to the duty of professional secrecy regarding the information that the lawyer shared with them in connection with the required services. The authorization of the client in this situation is not required because Article 41 of the Code extends the duty of professional secrecy to all of the professionals or persons who in any way help the lawyer in providing legal services, meaning that they have to manage the information under the same conditions as the lawyer. Nevertheless, lawyers should remind any of those with whom they share the client's information that they are also obliged under the duty of professional secrecy to keep all information confidential.[6]

I In-House Counsel

10. An in-house counsel is a lawyer and therefore is subject to the duty of professional secrecy established in Article 41 of the Code. The information protected by the duty of professional secrecy in relation to in-house counsel includes any information given by the company regarding legal issues or any information acquired during an administrative or judiciary process in which the in-house counsel participates or coordinates. It also includes the information obtained from the perusal of private documents reviewed by the lawyer during legal counseling. The duty of professional secrecy prohibits the in-house lawyer from disclosing or transferring confidential information to any third party. The exceptions to the in-house counsel duty are stated in Articles 42 and 43 of the Code and are described in Section 1(D) of this chapter.

2 History of the Duty of Professional Secrecy in Costa Rica

11. The first regulation that Costa Rica adopted regarding the duty of professional secrecy dates back to the General Code of 1841, which was based on Spanish regulations. Article 314 established professional secrecy as a duty not only for lawyers, doctors and other professionals but also for priests or any other people

---

[6] Colegio de Abogados y Abogadas, *Código de Deberes Jurídicos, Morales y Éticos de los Profesionales en Derecho*, 2013.

who, because of their position, would have access to confidential information from third parties. Article 314 also established sanctions for violating the duty, which included from two months to three years in prison and the possibility of not being able to practice their profession.

Later on, other regulations were enacted regarding this obligation. For example, the Criminal Code of 1880 made it a crime for a professional to violate confidentiality and make public the information that the professional had obtained because of his or her position. This Criminal Code was based on the Spanish Criminal Code of 1822.

Also, the Criminal Code of 1918 introduced prison sentences and the suspension of the lawyer's license as punishment for violating the secrecy of the information that the lawyer had obtained because of the practice of law.

Article 203 of the Criminal Code of 1971 regulates the duty of professional secrecy up to today. This regulation establishes prison from one month to one year, or a fine, to the person who makes public, with no justification, the secret information that the lawyer has received because of the lawyer's position and that causes irreparable damages. Additionally, if the person who violates this duty of secrecy is a professional, his or her license can also be suspended from six months to two years.

The Criminal Procedure Code of 1910 and its reforms stated that lawyers and other professionals could not be witnesses concerning any information that had been communicated to them because of their profession. In 1973, the Criminal Procedure Code was amended, indicating that lawyers and other professionals should abstain from being witnesses with regard to any information related to their profession. Then in 1998, the Criminal Procedure Code underwent yet another reform, and it is currently the statutory regulation in place. Such regulation provides that the exception of the duty to serve as a witness in the Court's Office applies to all persons regarding the information that they obtained because of their profession, unless their clients authorize the disclosure. Consequently, if called to the Court's Office as a witness, the lawyer shall inform the judge prior to the court hearing that the lawyer is protected under the duty of professional secrecy. If the judge considers that the witness is not protected by the exception to the duty to be a witness, the judge can issue an order indicating the reasons why the judge considers that such person should serve as a witness.

The duty of professional secrecy is included in Articles 41 through 43 of the Code. It is one of the basic principles that regulates the practice of law and that "allows that any person who needs legal guidance to be protected by the principle that his/her information will be secret and confidential. If this duty is not maintained society cannot function because the person seeks legal counsel instead of taking any other action that might be harmful to society."[7]

---

[7] Barahona Vargas, *The Duty of the Lawyer and Notary Public of Professional Secrecy in Costa Rica*, Graduation Thesis, University of Costa Rica, 2012, at 150.

Regulations that are directly connected with the human right of defense are protected by the Constitution and international human rights agreements and treaties.

3 Supervision

A The Bar Associations

12. The state has the duty to ensure the proper and efficient exercise of the legal profession. This duty of supervision is delegated to the Bar Association. It includes the duty to supervise the provision of proper legal services and to impose the corrective sanctions for any behavior that breaches the duties imposed by the law.[8]

    One of the multiple duties that the *Ley Orgánica del Colegio de Abogados* establishes for the Bar Association is to guard the academic excellency of its members and the proper provision of the legal counsel that they offer through their services.[9]

B The Courts

13. Articles 39 and 41 of the Constitution establish that, for a sanction or penalty to be imposed, a person has the right to a trial before a judge. In the event of a violation of the duty of professional secrecy, the client has the right to file a claim with the Bar Association or the courts.

    The civil courts have jurisdiction regarding any claim for professional liability filed by a client against a lawyer. The criminal courts have jurisdiction to oversee the crimes committed by lawyers in the exercise of their profession.

4 Sanctions

A Proceedings and Sanctions

14. In accordance with Article 1 of the Regulations of the Disciplinary Proceedings of the Costa Rican Bar Association, the Board of Directors of the Bar Association, in coordination with the Internal Prosecution Department, will constitute a Disciplinary Board in charge of the internal process that should be followed to apply an administrative sanction in cases of breach of an attorney's duties and responsibilities. The administrative process can result in the suspension of the lawyer from the practice of law.

    Once the complaint is filed, the Internal Prosecution Department prepares a file to submit to the Board of Directors of the Bar Association. The Board of Directors will decide if there are sufficient grounds for

---

[8] Administrative Contentious Court, IV Section, Dec. 17, 2013, No. 150–2013.
[9] Legislative Assembly, Ley Orgánica del Colegio de Abogados, 2014.

disciplinary sanctions and therefore whether an internal investigation should be opened. The Internal Prosecution Department should appoint an instructor, who will lead the administrative process and coordinate the internal process, ultimately preparing a report that is submitted to the Board of Directors for it to issue the final resolution.

Lawyers are given eight days to respond to the claim filed against them. Before having the private hearing, in which all evidence is received, the instructor will give both the lawyer and the complainant the opportunity to sign a conciliatory agreement. It is relevant to mention that the complainant can withdraw the complaint at any time during the proceedings, but the Board of Directors can choose to continue the investigation to find the truth regarding the situation.

If no agreement is reached, a private hearing will take place. After the hearing, the complainant and the defendant will have a five-day period to file their conclusions and final arguments. Then the report by the Internal Prosecution Department is submitted to the Board of Directors for a final decision. Decisions of the Internal Prosecution Department and any final resolution issued during the investigation and administrative process can be appealed to the Board of Directors.

The disciplinary sanctions that can be imposed by the Disciplinary Board regarding the violation of the duty of professional secrecy consist of a 3- to 10-year suspension from the practice of law.

a Criminal Proceedings and Sanctions

15.   The Criminal Court has jurisdiction to impose the sanctions established by Articles 203, 292 and 345 of the Criminal Code. The criminal sanction consists of one month to one year in prison or a fine. The court's decision can be appealed to the competent court of appeals, the decision of which can in turn be appealed, although only on legal grounds, to the Third Chamber of the Supreme Court.

A lawyer can be convicted by the administrative and criminal proceedings and also be held responsible for civil damages.

b Civil Proceedings and Damages

16.   The violation of the duty of professional secrecy of the attorney can be considered a breach of contract with the client, and damages may be awarded if any are caused by the attorney's actions. However, the client will have the burden of proof in this case. The civil courts of first instance will have jurisdiction, and appeal is possible to the courts of appeal and finally to the First Chamber of the Supreme Court.

B Relationship between Criminal Sanctions and Disciplinary Sanctions

17.   Article 11 of the Code establishes that disciplinary and criminal sanctions are imposed independently and have no effect on each other. If there is a criminal

proceeding against a lawyer in the criminal court regarding a criminal sanction that is directly related with the practice of law, the Board of Directors of the Bar Association can initiate disciplinary proceeding against the lawyer on the basis of the same facts. If the same facts form the basis for both disciplinary and criminal sanctions, the statute of limitations applicable to both is the one regarding the criminal sanction.

Under Costa Rican law, the imposition of both criminal and disciplinary sanctions on the basis of the same facts does not violate the general principle of *non bis in idem*, because the reason for each of the sanctions results from the infringement of different rules, and each proceeding imposes different types of sanctions. The criminal sanction can be prison, while administrative proceedings cannot impose such sanction.[10]

For the *non bis in idem* principle to apply, the Constitutional Court[11] has stated in its resolutions that the lawyer must be declared by the Court as not guilty either because of insufficient evidence or certainty that the lawyer did not commit the crime. In other situations, both disciplinary and criminal proceedings can be held simultaneously on the basis of the same facts.

5 Duty to Provide Information to the Authorities

A Money Laundering and Terrorism

18.   There are no specific regulations regarding the duty of professional secrecy and how it applies to money laundering and terrorism.

This means that the duty of professional secrecy established in Article 41 of the Code prevails even in cases of money laundering and terrorism when the information is obtained because of the lawyer-client relationship.

As stated in Section 9 of this chapter, Law Number 7425, "Registration, abduction and examination of private documents and intervention of communications," excludes the possibility of asking a judge for permission to tape a conversation between a lawyer and the lawyer's client, even when related to money laundering and terrorism, because of the right of defense of the person who seeks legal counsel. Therefore, the client is protected by the duty of professional secrecy of the lawyer.

Also, international human rights instruments and principles, which stand above the Constitution and the law, establish the prohibition against recording a conversation between a lawyer and a client. Both the Constitution and the law guarantee, under all possible situations, that clients will be able to tell their lawyers all that they consider necessary for their defense. This protection for the duty of professional secrecy between lawyer and client prevails even in situations in which money laundering and terrorism are being investigated.

---

[10] Constitutional Court, Aug. 11, 1999, 6290–99.

[11] Administrative Court of Appeal, April 23, 2012, 00065.

The only exception in which the duty of professional secrecy will not apply is if the client communicates to the lawyer the client's intention of committing a crime related to money laundering or terrorism. In this case, the lawyer will be able to communicate the information that the lawyer has to the authorities to prevent the commission of the crime.

B Collective Settlement of Debts

19. In accordance with Costa Rican law, the curator is in charge of the administration of all of the assets of the debtor and represents the interests of the creditor. The law establishes as one of the requirements that the curator must be a lawyer. However, it does not specifically regulate the professional secrecy of the curator. But because curators are lawyers, they are obliged to keep confidential, under the duty of professional secrecy, the information that they have obtained because of their role as curator, for the best interests of the creditors and for the correct administration of the assets of the debtor. Nonetheless, the curator has to fulfill the obligations of the law, while complying with the duty of professional secrecy, which can affect the interests and the assets of the entity the curator is representing, in this case the debtor and creditors.

The curator is the legal representative of the debtor and is capable of executing all of the contracts on behalf of the debtor. Therefore, the civil courts have not required that the curator be called to testify against the entity the curator represents.[12]

6 Treatment of Lawyers' Documents and Correspondence in the Context of Judicial or Police Investigations

20. Article 24 of the Constitution states that only a judge can authorize the intervention into private documents and communications. Law No. 7425, "Registration, abduction and examination of private documents and intervention of communications," states that private documents can be examined by the authorities, with the previous resolution of a judge, only when they are needed as evidence of the commission of a crime.

Also, Article 9 of Law No. 7425 establishes that, during a police or judicial investigation, a judge can authorize the intervention into private communications of any type in cases in which any of the following crimes are being investigated: kidnapping, aggravated corruption, aggravated pimping, fabrication or production of pornography, trafficking, homicide, genocide, terrorism and crimes related to money laundering and drug trafficking.

Nevertheless, it is important to mention that Article 27 of Law No. 7425 establishes an exception to the registration, taking and examination of private

---

[12] Civil Court, Jan. 19, 2001, 104-L.

documents and intervention into communications between the lawyer and the client that are directly related to the exercise of the right of defense. This means that professional secrecy will be protected from the application of this law if the document or communication has to do with the defense of the client and a judge cannot authorize its registration or intervention.

The only scenario in which a lawyer's documents and communications can be reviewed by an authority is when the lawyer is being accused of or investigated for the commission of a crime that is not directly related to the lawyer's duty of professional secrecy, which precludes any possibility of the intervention of the documents and communications held for the lawyer's clients.

7 Search of a Lawyer's Office

21. As seen throughout this chapter, professional secrecy is a manifestation of the human rights of defense and privacy that are protected not only by the Constitution but also by human rights and other international instruments.

Therefore, the lawyer's office is the place where the private documents that the lawyer keeps for the client are stored and cannot be searched by any authority, unless the lawyer is being investigated for or accused of the commission of a crime that is related to the lawyer's own conduct. This exception does not apply to any conduct or situation related to the attorney-client relationship, because that is protected by professional secrecy in Costa Rica.

Even in this exceptional situation in which the lawyer is being investigated by the authorities regarding private documents that are not accounting books, a judge has to authorize the search of the lawyer's office. However, the authorization of the judge to search the lawyer's office can be done only to obtain private documents that have nothing to do with clients' cases but rather are related to the lawyer's own conduct or possible issues with the law.

Also, the lawyer's office can be searched with the previous authorization of a judge in accordance with the following exceptions to the duty of professional secrecy stated in Article 42 of the Code. That is, a lawyer does not have to comply with the lawyer's duty of professional secrecy when the lawyer is being accused of committing a crime, when the information is required to determine the fees for services or when it is required to avoid an innocent's conviction.

Notwithstanding, in recent years, there have been some cases in which a law firm was searched by the Judiciary authorities in connection with an investigation of a fraud committed by one of its clients. Typically, in this situation, the shelf company that the client used to commit the crime was chartered by the law firm. This procedural action has been accepted by the Constitutional's Court's jurisprudence as long as the criminal trial judge supervises the investigation process in order to guarantee that the professional secrecy is maintained regarding the documents of the other clients. Related to this topic, author Antonio Fernández Serrano has stated that, "when the necessities of Justice establish the search of a lawyer's office because of a criminal case or investigation being held against him, there should be a resolution that authorizes and justifies such diligence and all of the possible guarantees to protect his duty of professional secrecy should be adopted."[13]

8 Tapping of Telephone Conversations with a Lawyer

22.   In accordance with the constitutional right of privacy of conversations, only a judge can authorize the tapping of any type of conversation, and the law will determine in which cases the judicial authorization proceeds.

Law Number 7425, "Registration, abduction and examination of private documents and intervention of communications," which regulates the specific cases in which a private conversation can be tapped, excludes, in Article 27, the possibility of asking a judge for the permission to tap a conversation held between a lawyer and a client because it is directly related to the right of the person's defense and therefore is protected by the professional's duty of professional secrecy.

In Costa Rica, the international human rights instruments and principles, which stand above the Constitution[14] and the law, all coincide in the prohibition of the tapping of a conversation between a lawyer and client under the justification that it is protected by the attorney-client privilege, an important part of the right of defense and privacy that every person has. The only situation in which a conversation with a lawyer can be tapped is if the lawyer is being investigated for or accused of one of the crimes established in Article 9 of Law No. 7425 (kidnapping, corruption, aggravated pimping, fabrication or production of pornography, trafficking, homicide, genocide, terrorism and crimes related to money laundering and drug trafficking).

However, it is important to note that this exception can proceed only with a judge's authorization and that the conversation with the lawyer that is authorized to be tapped must not be related to the professional secrecy between the lawyer and the client. Rather, the conversation must relate to conduct strictly by the lawyer and not from the lawyer's relation with the person who consults the lawyer or who is the lawyer's client.

9 The Lawyer as Witness

23.   A lawyer can be called by the court as a witness. However, the lawyer has a duty to abstain from testifying about any information related to the lawyer's client because of the attorney-client privilege. If the client releases the attorney from such duty, then the lawyer is obliged to testify. Once the court calls the lawyer as a witness, the attorney can refer to the attorney-client privilege when refusing to answer. If the lawyer discloses information to the court that is

---

[13] Antonio Fernández Serrano, "The Professional Secrecy/Attorney Client," JT 1968, at 238.
[14] Constitutional Court 13313–2010, Aug. 10, 2010, 2010–2010013313.

protected by the attorney-client privilege, the lawyer may be subject to a disciplinary sanction.

If the court considers that the witness is using the attorney-client privilege improperly, then the court will issue a resolution justifying why it considers that the person is not under the duty of abstention to testify and will order the lawyer to testify.

The lawyer also will have to testify on issues that are not related to the lawyer's position as a lawyer and cannot refuse to testify on the basis of the attorney-client privilege. The attorney-client privilege will not apply if the lawyer's client tells the lawyer about the client's intention to commit a crime. Also, the duty of abstention to testify will not apply if the lawyer is called as a witness in the lawyer's capacity as a Notary Public.[15]

10 The Lawyer and the Press

24.   The original version of Article 64 of the Code prohibited lawyers from referring publically to any of the cases or issues that were being counseled at the Court's Office or to publish any of the documents related to them. Once the process was over, lawyers could make public what they considered relevant but keep the confidentiality of certain information that was inappropriate to share.

However, this prohibition was declared null and void by the Administrative Tribunal.[16] The argument of the Court was that such prohibition was against Costa Rica's regulations and international human rights instruments because it violated the right of freedom of expression. Also, the resolution indicated that the Costa Rican Bar Association did not have the authority to issue a regulation that established a restriction on the human right of freedom of expression.

11 Powers of the Tax and Other Authorities

25.   Article 105 of the Code of Tax Rules and Procedures states that every person has the duty to provide significant tax information to the Tax Authority. An exception to this duty applies to professionals who, in accordance with the law, are subject to the duty of professional secrecy, like an attorney. However, such professionals cannot allege the duty of professional secrecy as an excuse to avoid the corroboration of such professional's own tax status.

In accordance with this article, the Tax Authority cannot ask attorneys to deliver information that their clients have given to their lawyers as part of the attorney-client privilege, nor can the Tax Authority ask attorneys to submit the significant tax information of their clients where the lawyers are being investigated concerning their own tax status.

---

[15] Third Chamber of the Supreme Court, March 23, 2012, 00571.
[16] Administrative Court of Appeal, Aug. 7, 2009, No. 1542–2009.

The duty of professional secrecy protects the significant tax information that attorneys have of their clients, and the authorities cannot ask for this information. They can only ask for the significant information of the attorney as a professional, who must pay taxes for legal services rendered, but this power does not include the data of the lawyer's clients.

Article 24 of Costa Rica's Constitution clearly protects the person's right to confidentiality and therefore states that private documents can be registered or examined by the authorities only with the permission of a judge. This same article also establishes that the Tax Authorities can only ask, without a judge's authorization, for the accounting books of a person or company for tax purposes. In accordance with the above, professional secrecy is not only a manifestation of the right of confidentiality of the person but also involves the duty of the lawyer to protect it from the powers of the authority. Therefore,

> if the tax status of a lawyer is being investigated, it is not legal to ask for the private documents that he or she has of his/her clients as a result of his/her professional relation with them, since this is protected by the Constitutional basis of the duty of professional secrecy, that include the right of confidentiality that has to be observed not only by the attorney as part of his obligations but also by the Authorities.[17]

26. Also related to this topic, it is necessary to mention the Basic Principles Regarding the Legal Profession, adopted by Costa Rica in the Congress of the United Nations for the Prevention of Crime and Treatment of the Offender, celebrated in La Habana (Cuba) on August 27, 1990. This international human rights instrument is in accordance with Costa Rica's Constitutional Court and forms part of the regulations of that country's law, even if it has not been approved by Congress, because such regulations protect fundamental human rights. In this case, the regulations protect the rights of defense and confidentiality that every person has and that are strictly related to the justification of the protection of professional secrecy.[18]

This means that the tax and other authorities cannot ask for private documents that are part of the attorney-client relationship because such documents are specially protected by professional secrecy as part of the right of confidentiality and defense of the person. If the lawyer's tax status is being investigated, the documents or any type of information regarding the lawyer's clients, even if it is significant tax information, cannot be acquired by the tax or other authority.

The Constitutional Court[19] has indicated that, when the information that the Tax Authority claims from the lawyer is protected by the duty of professional secrecy, asking for such information can put at risk the basic human rights of

---

[17] A. Aguallo, *The Contributor and Tax Authorities, Jurisprudence of the Constitutional Court (1981–1989)*, Editorial Tecnos, Madrid, 1990, at 233.

[18] Constitutional Court, May 9, 1995, 2313–95.

[19] Constitutional Court, July 18, 1995, 3929–95.

the client, so the professional should not deliver such information to the authority, unless it has asked the criminal judge for permission to do so. This is the exception that will apply if the Tax Authority considers that it is relevant to have access to the information protected by the duty of professional secrecy. But the authority has to ask permission from a criminal judge, who will act as the representative of the human rights that can be violated by such action and will determine if the lawyer should deliver the information based on a principle of public interest.

12 National Security Issues

27. Articles 292 and 345 of the Criminal Code consider it a crime if someone reveals information regarding national security issues like political secrets related to the protection of the nation or its diplomatic relations. The criminal sanction consists of one to six years in prison. Article 345 refers to the case of the civil servant who reveals information related to national security issues, in which case the sanction is three months to two years in prison and suspension from such civil servant's professional duties.

Lawyers, as any other person, cannot reveal any information that is related to national security issues, or they can be sanctioned with prison. This sanction will mostly apply to those situations in which the lawyer is a civil servant and manages national security issues as per the lawyer's position. However, the law has not defined what should be considered national security issues, making it very difficult for the above sanctions to be applied by the criminal courts because there is no certainty as to the information that can be considered national security issues.

16

Cuba

MARIA ANTONIETA LANDA MARTI
MIGUEL FRANCISCO SARDIÑAS ARCE
Bufete Internacional S.A.

IMARA FRANCISCA BETANCOURT SUAREZ
Lupicinio International Law Firm

Preliminary Note

1. An ongoing challenge for entrepreneurs, foreign lawyers and clients has been whether the Cuban lawyer can observe professional secrecy considering the private practice of the profession is not allowed in Cuba, nor is the *Colegiatura de Abogados* (the Cuban equivalent of a bar association) present, as in other jurisdictions. However, the existence of a hybrid model, *sui generis*, which on the one hand permits the practice of law in law firms and, on the other, establishes that the lawyer is subordinate only to the law, allows lawyers to assert the existence of legal guarantees regarding attorney-client confidentiality.

   The regulatory framework governing the practice of law is Decree-Law No. 81, issued in 1984 by the State Council of the Republic of Cuba, which remains in force and establishes the creation of an *Organización Nacional de Bufetes Colectivos* (National Organization of Collective Law Offices, hereinafter ONBC). The law determines that only lawyers who are members of the ONBC or the Civil Societies of Legal Services recognized by law[1] are authorized to provide consultation and lead, represent and defend the rights of a natural or legal person before the courts, arbitration bodies and administrative authorities of the country, as well as before foreign or international bodies, authorities and organizations.

   These firms[2] are independent entities with their own legal identity and patrimony, and they are composed of jurists who are authorized to practice law as members.

   The ONBC provides, as an exception, that another group of legal professionals who are not linked to the aforementioned ONBC or Civil Societies of Legal Service may practice law circumstantially, such as in the following cases:

   (i) those who take on the management or representation of issues in their own right, such as those with their spouse or their relatives to the fourth degree of consanguinity or the second degree of affinity;

   (ii) those employed by a state entity, cooperative or mass social organization who manage or represent that entity in a party in proceedings; or their

---

[1] See the website of the Ministry of Justice of Cuba (www.minjus.cu) Bufete Internacional SA, Consultoría Jurídica Internacional SA, Consultores y Abogados Internacionales (CONABI), LEX SA, CLAIM SA, on existing societies. The Civil Societies intended for the practice of law came under Decree Law No. 77, "On Civil Service Companies," dated January 20, 1984, and published in the Extraordinary Official Gazette No. 1 of January 21, 1984. These societies are also referred to as firms by the law and are used to provide legal services, including notary services to foreign persons or entities and to Cuban citizens in foreign countries, as well as any legal form of foreign investment in Cuba. The provision of services has now been extended to Cuban citizens residing in the country regarding certain legal areas (e.g., intellectual property), to legal persons within the state sector and new forms of non-state business management (e.g., non-agricultural cooperatives).

[2] In this chapter, the generic term "firms" refers to the firms in the ONBC and Civil Societies of Legal Services legally authorized to practice law.

managers when dealing with events corresponding to their professional duties;

(iii) those who have been granted exceptional authorization by the Minister of Justice to act in certain proceedings; and

(iv) those who teach in law schools. This exception seeks to connect teachers with professional practice and is regulated by the higher education institution where the teacher works.

In Cuba, there is also an organization called the *Unión Nacional de Juristas de Cuba* (National Union of Cuban Jurists, or UNJC), uniting jurists and representing them both within the country and abroad. It is formed not just by lawyers but also by academics, researchers, judges, prosecutors, notaries and legal advisers, and therefore it does not constitute a bar association due to the diversity of its members and the objectives it pursues.

2.   To conclude, when this chapter refers to "lawyers," it focuses specifically on members of the ONBC and the Civil Societies of Legal Services authorized by law.

1 Scope of and Limitations on the Duty of Professional Secrecy/ Attorney-Client Privilege

A Statutory Basis and Implications

3.   The practice of law in Cuba is conceived as a free and independent profession and is subject only to the law. Lawyers enjoy all rights and legal guarantees to present their arguments in relation to the law they defend, guaranteeing its practice and the right of citizens to effective representation and defense to ensure their access to justice.[3]

With regard to the professional secrecy of the lawyer, there exists a regulatory vacuum. Although the 1976 Constitution established the right to defense[4] as a fundamental prerogative of everyone in the country, it was not until 1997, with the approval of the Code of Ethics of the National Organization of Collective Law Offices (ONBC), that it was expressly regulated as a duty of lawyers "to maintain the strictest discretion on the issues in which they are involved, due to the nature of such professional activity," as well as the obligation "to maintain the secrecy of the issues they are aware of and which may affect their client, even if they cease to provide the client with their services."[5]

---

[3] *See* Arts. 1, 2, Decree Law No. 81, "On the Practice of Law and the National Organization of Collective Law Offices," of June 8, 1984. State Council of the Republic of Cuba.

[4] *See* Art. 59, Constitution of the Republic of Cuba.

[5] *See* Art. 10, Code of Ethics of the National Organization of Collective Law Offices of Feb. 8, 1987.

From this first regulatory ethical standard of lawyers' professional secrecy,[6] the successive Codes of Ethics of Civil Societies of Legal Services authorized to practice law made a brief reference to the secrecy of the lawyer in their precepts. These Codes of Ethics essentially allude to three aspects: a) that the duty of discretion relates to all matters in which the lawyer is involved for professional reasons – advice and consultation; b) that the secrecy is limited only to what affects or may affect the client; and c) the confidentiality obligation extends beyond the term of the professional relationship, remaining even when such relationship is concluded.[7]

Moreover, members of the firms or Civil Societies of Legal Services authorized to practice law agree to the Internal Disciplinary Regulations document containing the rights and responsibilities of lawyers and other technical and administrative staff within these entities. In these regulations, the outline of the lawyer-client privilege emerges.

Specifically, the service provided by a lawyer is established in a contract signed for this purpose by the client and the law firm or society to which the chosen lawyer is bound. The contract has the substance of the mandate at its core and constitutes the law between the parties. Although the contractual initiative is institutional, it prioritizes the principle of autonomous will in the sense that, in its provisions, the client can determine the scope of the selected lawyer's secrecy and the confidentiality of information provided, which enjoys full protection, provided that legal regulations are not violated.

4.   In the Republic of Cuba, neither Decree Law No. 81 on the Exercise of Law and the National Organization of Collective Law Offices nor its regulations – Resolution 142 of 1984 of the Ministry of Justice – contains an express or direct reference to the professional secrecy of lawyers. It provides only an overview of its regulation in Article 19(a): "to receive the guarantees and respect due to the social importance of their work from the authorities and their agents." Hence, there is a lack of conceptualization and definition of its scope in the abovementioned legislation, which is still fully in force.

Current Cuban criminal law, including proceedings in the military courts, recognizes this privilege, albeit in an incomplete manner. It offers only direct protection for lawyers and the interests of the client, excluding them from the obligation to report the accused regarding the events under investigation revealed in confidence by clients to lawyers in their capacity as defenders, as well as from testifying against them. However, it does not explicitly prohibit obtaining and disclosing confidential information by a third party generated

---

[6] This refers specifically to 1984 onwards, with the elimination of the Bar Association and the creation of the ONBC.

[7] Y. Muñoz Juvera Yainelis and P. Peterssen Padrón, "The regulation of lawyers' professional secrecy in the Republic of Cuba. An analysis of criminal protection and potential conflicts between the accused and the defence," 2015.

through communication between them, nor does it protect the client from the eventual disclosure of information by the client's own lawyer, a breach that can only be categorized as a violation of professional discipline. As such there might be a conflict in practice between lawyer and client that as of yet has not been provided for by any regulation. Furthermore, the solution to these potential problems has not previously been explored locally, which would have provided useful guidance to standardize the stance that could and should be adopted in this regard.

In other areas of law, the peculiar nature of lawyer-client relations has been respected so far as to waive the obligation of anyone with a direct interest in the lawsuit[8] to testify as an expert or witness in any civil proceedings, and statutory procedures essentially provide for the same. However, in civil law, appellate courts will not consider whether the evidence was illegally obtained, that is, evidence that is obtained by a third party violating fundamental rights or lawyer-client professional secrecy.

B Scope

5. Ethical standards (meaning the aforementioned Code of Ethics and Internal Disciplinary Regulations of the ONBC Civil Societies of Legal Services) and the Cuban practice of law establish the scope of the lawyer's professional secrecy as being:

 (i) To maintain confidentiality regarding information provided by the client, including confessions and proposals that will involve the client or third parties in the case.

 (ii) To not provide the police, prosecutors or courts, or anyone else, with letters, emails, messages, notes or any other form of communication sent to or by the client.

 (iii) To not listen to other lawyer-client conversations without prior authorization and, in the case of the latter, to not reveal their contents.

 (iv) To extend these duties to other lawyers; technical, administrative or service personnel; and any other person in the same office with knowledge of the case.

 (v) That the same lawyer may not act as a representative for two or more clients who have conflicting interests, or accept cases in which a former client appears as a legal opponent, if the information provided to the latter as advice may cause damages.

 (vi) That publicity in relation to professional performance cannot implicate the direct or indirect disclosure of facts, data or situations covered by secrecy.

---

[8] *See* Arts. 306(3), 328(a), Law on Civil, Administrative, Labour and Economic Procedure.

C Persons Subject to the Duty of Professional Secrecy

6. Lawyers belonging to the ONBC or the Civil Societies of Legal Services are subject to the obligation of lawyers' professional secrecy regarding their clients and any information that they become aware of through their profession, including by means of their coworkers, managers, colleagues, technical support staff, and administrative and service personnel.

    Furthermore, judges should respect the lawyer-client privilege and can even be challenged, if at some point previously they assumed the defense of a particular defendant.[9] Along with police, prosecutors and prison officials are obliged to respect and guarantee the exercise of professional secrecy. The Law on Criminal Procedure in Article 249(1) provides for the right of defendants to communicate with their lawyers and be interviewed by their lawyers with due privacy. This guarantee is also backed by the rights to defense and privacy enshrined in the Cuban Constitution.

D Exceptions to and Optional Derogations from the Duty of Professional Secrecy

7. The Cuban Law on Criminal Procedure places limits on professional secrecy. Lawyers are obliged to appear before the authorities should they be called and can only be excused from testifying to facts that are being investigated and about which the accused told them in confidence in their capacity as a defender in relation to the proceedings in which they are assisting or representing their clients. It can be inferred that they are obliged to disclose information provided to them by their clients concerning events that are unrelated to the case and that contravene any rule of law.

E Law Firms

8. It is obligatory that the law be exercised by lawyers of the ONBC and the Civil Societies of Legal Services, save for the exceptions set out in Decree Law No. 81, and these are required to safeguard professional secrecy. Although legal service is provided by the selected lawyer, the contract protecting secrecy is between the office and the client, so the responsibility for the confidential information provided extends to the firm.

    It often happens that complex cases are analyzed by a legal team. In this case, all lawyers involved are aware of the confidential information provided by the client, and all are required to maintain absolute discretion.

    In most Cuban law firms, there is an internal monitoring system to ensure quality of service. The directors of these firms can monitor their members regarding the conduct of duties, having access to all information, including that which is confidential, which does not breach professional secrecy, as legal

---

[9] *See* Art. 26(6), Law on Criminal Procedure.

representatives of the firm are accountable for safeguarding confidential information.

F Legal Assistants and Staff

9.   In Cuba, unlike other jurisdictions, the role of a lawyer's aide is performed by a trained technician who is specifically qualified, differing substantially from the figure of the solicitor that existed before the creation of collective law offices, among other things, because the lawyer's aide lacks the capacity to directly represent the parties in legal proceedings.

This technical assistant lawyer is recognized in the law as an entity that acts in the courts, bodies and organizations of Central State Administration by delegation and performs procedures and operations on behalf of the lawyer. Nevertheless, responsibility for the conduct of the legal proceedings is ultimately the lawyer's.

The technical assistant lawyer has the express obligation, in the disciplinary regulations of the Internal Disciplinary Regulations of the ONBC and Civil Societies of Legal Services, not to disclose information obtained while assisting the lawyer. If these rules are violated, this may warrant disciplinary action, including expulsion from the firm or union.

G External Services Providers

10.   Cuban law is not exempt from the realities of the national and international environments that require greater synergy in work from lawyers, increasingly demanding that they be more organized, work in teams and use the complementary services of specialists that address different areas, including secretaries, translators and lawyers from foreign firms. To this is added the fact that the services of law firms and Civil Societies of Local Services are required more and more frequently by foreign clients. This reality demands a universal vision, a mastery of other languages and a knowledge of the international dynamics and environments that was not common in earlier times. This in turn has generated significant advances and changes in terms of protecting professional secrecy in the confidentiality clauses of contracts signed with service providers, and in confidentiality agreements signed with foreign firms with whom working relationships are established. This means that there will be a possibility of recourse to the civil courts in case of a breach.

H Multidisciplinary Associations

11.   It is common in legal practice for lawyers to have the help of experts and other consultants to bring a case to a successful conclusion. Cuban law firms sometimes sign cooperation agreements with other consulting companies or hire consultants for financial audits or other complementary services. In civil and criminal

proceedings, too, specialized professionals are required, who then act as experts in court. In any case, the lawyer is obliged to refer its decision to the client and obtain consent, especially if a third party is exposed to confidential information.

1 In-House Counsel

12.   In Cuba, in addition to lawyers in the ONBC and public service companies, other legal professionals can provide legal advice to legal persons. They carry out this work either as a full-time employee for a business or as part of a legal consultancy group, working under local government with the purpose of providing legal services to state-owned businesses and other entities. In the latter case, the connection is established through a specific contract. The regulations governing the practice of legal counsel in state entities are set out in Decree 138 of March 20, 1987, and include the following functions: (i) represent and defend the interests of the entity against the authorities, businesses and other national and international entities; (ii) advise the main directors of the entity; and (iii) draw up agreements, contracts and legal documents of various kinds.

    The lawyer-client privilege exists for members of the legal consultancy, who must maintain discretion regarding the matters that are under their consideration. However, the legislation fails to address the matter of responsibility in the event of a violation by the legal professional.

2 History of the Duty of Professional Secrecy in Cuba

13.   The right to, and duty of, professional secrecy law dates back to the Spanish legal tradition, which must be mentioned as it has always been an important influence in Cuba, including the *Partidas* (Castilian statutory code) and the Royal Charter of Alfonso the Tenth. In the Royal Charter, the right to and duty of secrecy is not openly discussed, but lawyers were indeed prevented from using the confidences bestowed on them by their clients against such clients. In contrast to the laws of the *Partidas*, not only was the duty of confidentiality established, but there was also a penalty for those who violated this obligation, namely regarding the prohibition of practicing as a lawyer in the case of malicious deception imposed upon one's client, and even making it possible for the judge to penalize the lawyer. It is the third *Partida* in which the vast regulation on the matter can be found and which contains an express prohibition against revealing the secrets of the client.[10]

    The history of the professional secrecy of lawyers dates from the moment where written rules emerged, which, upon being codified into laws, led to the proliferation of law and the creation of the a*colegiatura* (Bar Association) in Cuba.

---

[10] Taken from E. Arribas, *On the limits of professional secrecy of the lawyer*, 2009.

It was in 1799 that the town of Santa María del Puerto del Principe (today known as Camaguey) held the Royal Hearing of Santo Domingo. This event marked the origin of law in Cuba.

An order by Spanish King Fernando VII in 1819 established the creation of Cuban law schools in Havana and Port-au-Prince as part of a process to introduce management structures for colonial justice in Cuba, inspired by its counterpart in Madrid. By 1842, the schools in Santiago de Cuba and Trinidad-Remedios-Santi Spiritus had been constituted.

Ten years later, the Bar Association of Havana was closed by decision of the Captain General of the Island, halting its activity until 1879, when it was once again restored.

The U.S. government, which intervened in the war between Cuba and Spain, dissolved law schools in December 1900 under Military Order No. 500. However, by 1909, the provisional governor decreed the Bar Association to be a prerequisite for professional practice, and so it was ratified in the 1940 Constituent Assembly.

Between December 27 and 30, 1916, the Bar Association of Havana held the First National Legal Congress, which was intended to propose legislative reforms to modernize the legal system, resulting in a Cuban law with Spanish influences. Hence, the regulatory standards of ethics in Cuba corresponded with those that existed at the time in Spain.

A significant fact is that, in July 1948, the General Assembly of Lawyers approved a Code of Ethics, uniform for all the schools in the country.

14. Since January 1959, as a reflection on the process of radicalization in the central structures of the new government, the bar was restructured. In 1965, the first collective law office was established, based in the capital, subject to the bar's jurisdiction but under the guidance of the Ministry of Justice. These changes had an effect on the ethical standards that existed thus far.

Under Act No. 1189 of April 25, 1966, the registration of lawyers was placed in a register of persons in charge of that body of Cuban Central State Administration. In June 1973, Act No. 1250 on the Organization of the Legal System established the obligation to belong to a group practice as an indispensable requirement to act as a lawyer.

Private lawyers and law firms existed in Cuba until 14 years after the triumph of the Revolution. Through a series of steps taken in that period of time – during which the creation of the country's first collective law office came about in 1965 at the request of the lawyers at the College of Havana – in 1973 the collective model of law practice was approved. The creation of the National Organization of Collective Law Offices in 1984 finalized the process of implementing an organizational and practical framework, which marginalized the modes of psychology and thinking that had allowed lawyers to privately practice their profession. The ONBC was joined by Civil Societies of Legal Services with ethical standards that, although specific to each firm, agree on the scope and limits of the lawyer's professional secrecy laid out in this chapter.

3 Supervision

A The Bar Associations

15. In Cuba there are no bar associations; instead, there is the ONBC and Civil Societies of Legal Services, which are authorized by law. These firms have an organizational structure and a form of management. Regarding the monitoring system of the technical quality of the lawyer, the ONBC has a team conducting national, provincial and firm-level supervision. In the rest of the Civil Societies of Legal Services are the General and Legal Services Directors, who oversee the professional work carried out individually or collectively by their members.

With this monitoring system, it is intended for clients to receive the best technical service, the assessment of which is beyond the scope of their knowledge, since it is assumed that they cannot appreciate the technical quality of their lawyers in terms of their professional duties, since they have no expertise in the profession.

Lawyers are required to comply with the approved ethical standards, as well as parameters of quality for performing their duties. In case of a violation of the parameters of quality and professional ethics of the lawyer, the responsible professional will be administratively sanctioned under the Internal Disciplinary Rules of the entity. Additionally, the lawyer will be analyzed by the Commission of Ethics, which exists in each office, as an advisory body to the Directors in order to impose the disciplinary measures on the lawyer in question.

B The Courts

16. In the Republic of Cuba, the criminal courts have no jurisdiction to punish breaches of ethics by the lawyer. Decisions on the implementation of measures derived from these breaches remain in the field of administrative law. Only the courts will know the crimes committed by lawyers in the exercise of their duties and which relate to the failure to observe the scope and limits of professional secrecy. For example, a lawyer who assumes the representation of a client accused of a crime and learns that the client has committed another crime, separate from the case in which the lawyer is representing the client, will incur a breach of the lawyer's duty to report by not making the crime known to the law enforcement authorities.

In the civil courts, although there is no precedent for this, civil proceedings could be commenced if a client is affected economically by a breach of professional secrecy and the lawyer has not agreed to repair the damage and pay compensation.

4 Sanctions

A Proceedings and Sanctions

17. The ONBC and Civil Societies of Legal Services have a commissions system in each of their units or agencies to systematically assess the ethical conduct of their members, without being able to propose, and much less impose, disciplinary measures with administrative criteria. One such procedure concludes with the classification of the improper conduct as "mild," "severe" or "very severe," to allow the competent authority to determine the corresponding penalty that could be applied according to law.

    The disciplinary procedure requires, in all cases, that a preliminary report be issued by the professional ethics committees, which have a consulting role. The report should include evidence, and, if the breach of ethics is proven, it should recommend a sanction. The measures to be imposed, and the authorities with the power to do so, generally appear in the internal Disciplinary Regulations. Failing that, the highest ranking regulation on the matter applicable to all workers in the country is applied, which is currently Act No. 116 of 2013, the Labour Code, and its subsidiary legislation. Penalties can range from a simple private reprimand of the accused to separation from the sector or activity, public warning before the collective where they work, a fine of up to 25 percent of one month's salary, a temporary transfer of up to one year or permanent placement to another position with lower pay or different working conditions, and definitive exclusion from the lawyer's current workplace.

    In all cases, at least one instance is established to be able to appeal in a timely manner the penalty imposed by the administrative authority, and, in the most serious cases, it exceptionally provides for the possibility to request a review of the procedure.

B Relationship between Criminal Sanctions and Disciplinary Sanctions

18. General labor legislation orders the administrative authority to impose a measure for a violation that may in turn qualify as a reportable crime, which applies to internal procedures adopted by the ONBC and Civil Societies of Legal Services, even though this decision should not be subject to that which is adopted by a criminal court, because it is a recognized principle of law that every jurisdiction is independent of the other.

    The violation of professional secrecy by a lawyer in Cuba, even if it affects the interests of the client, will not find any punitive response before a criminal court while it can and should be corrected administratively. This does not prejudice the victim of such a violation, who may demand compensation for the tangible damage caused to the victim before the courts of civil jurisdiction.

5 Duty to Provide Information to the Authorities

A Money Laundering and Terrorism

19.   In line with the international commitments taken on by Cuba to prevent and combat money laundering and terrorism, the Cuban government has issued a set of laws that are complemented by Resolutions of the Central Bank of Cuba and the Ministry of Justice. These laws expressly establish the obligation of lawyers and other legal professionals to report "possible suspicious transactions related to the introduction of illicit assets, to be used in terrorist activities or money laundering, the proliferation of arms and activities of a similar gravity in the Cuban market."[11]

    This duty applies to lawyers in the provision of advice or representation in property-trading activities and in the creation, operation or management of companies or other forms of organization authorized by law. When legal practitioners detect a suspected money laundering operation, the financing of terrorism, weapons proliferation or activities of a similar nature and gravity, they are obliged to report to the Directorate General of the Investigation of Financial Operations of the Central Bank of Cuba. Failure to do so will lead to the implementation of measures stipulated by the administrative, disciplinary and penal fields. This is true even if this information was learned from a client of the lawyer. Lawyers are also obliged to provide any information requested by the Directorate General in their area of competence and to collaborate with it.

    It is understood that, in this case, there is no conflict of legal interests, since the right to life and the integrity of people prevail over the rights to privacy and defense. In such cases, it is understood that the lawyer is communicating data or information pertaining to professional secrecy to avoid a greater evil – one of the limits on the scope of the lawyer-client privilege. The law itself excuses lawyers and others from disclosing information under these circumstances.

20.   In the event that money laundering, the financing of terrorism, arms sales or other offences of a similar gravity are made known to a Cuban lawyer, the law stipulates that the lawyer may be required to supply all such information to the authorities should they request it. This does not require special permission from jurisdictional authorities, institutions or others. These cases constitute an exception to the lawyer-client privilege.

6 Treatment of Lawyers' Documents and Correspondence in the Context of Judicial or Police Investigations

21.   The Cuban Criminal Procedure Act regulates the registering of books and documents, as well as the withholding and opening of written, telegraphic or

---

[11] Decree Law No. 317 of the State Council and Decree Law No. 322 of the Cabinet, of Dec. 7, 2013, published in Extraordinary Official Gazette No. 8 of Jan. 23, 2014. The Ministry of Justice issued Resolution No. 175/2014, published in Extraordinary Official Gazette No. 36 of Aug. 15, 2014.

cabled correspondence during the course of a police investigation. It also regulates the way in which the court will examine the documentary evidence it has in sight during the trial – without distinguishing any quality of the person to whom the evidence belongs. Consequently, the treatment of documents and correspondence of the lawyer in Cuba is governed by the same standards.

The procedure establishes that the registering of documents and correspondence of the accused and others shall take place only when there is sufficient evidence to allow discovery and verification of the crime investigated or important circumstances relating to the same.

It also establishes a number of formalities that must be observed by researchers when carrying out this type of procedure. With the exception of printed books, documents that are collected must be signed on every page by the official carrying out the register, the person or persons who represent them and others attending the register. A reasoned decision is required from the instructor where it is necessary to retain postal correspondence, or telegraph, radiotelegraph or cable transfer correspondence, of which copies must be issued. For the opening and revision of postal correspondence, the relevant person must be named, whether he or she is there in person or represented by a designated witness to the operation.

7 Search of a Lawyer's Office

22. Lawful requests by police or prosecutors may arise in the course of police investigations where it is necessary to enter and search, whether during the day or night, all public buildings and places, specifically a law firm. This refers to investigations where lawyers, or their clients, are suspects in a crime. These records interfere, logically, with lawyer-client professional secrecy, and this procedure is regulated by the Law on Criminal Procedure, Articles 215 to 231.

There are no regulations on the ethical standards of Cuban law practice regarding the behavior to be followed in such cases, so only the rules of law on criminal matters apply.

If records are requested, the law firm cannot make any objection. The resolution that provides for police action expresses the precise aim of verifying, in the place where it must be verified, the name of the official. It requires that the search be conducted in the least disruptive way possible, avoiding non-necessary work and not extending it to ends that do not fall within the strict objective of the search.

In this way, confidential information provided by other clients, and even information provided by the client being investigated that is not strictly related to the investigation, are protected from the search.

Criminal procedure law refers, in the case of the search of documents or books, to the provisions of civil law.

8 Tapping of Telephone Conversations with a Lawyer

23.   Article 57 of the Cuban Constitution provides for the inviolability of telephone communications, except in certain exceptions provided for by law, preserving the confidentiality of matters other than those specifically targeted by the recordings.

The cases covered by the act are those in which sufficient incriminating elements are accumulated in order for a person to become a suspect in a crime, especially if it comes to crimes against the internal or external security of the Cuban state, which is the most important objective protected in substantive criminal law.

However, there has been no legislation establishing what actions may be taken with these recordings once they are made – that is, how they are transcribed, preserved and analyzed, and what their ultimate purpose might be.

9 The Lawyer as Witness

24.   Lawyers may be called to testify in civil and criminal proceedings as witnesses. To appear at the request of the penal authority is mandatory, but not in the civil courts. However, the laws of civil and criminal procedures safeguard the lawyer's right not to testify in cases that violate professional secrecy.[12]

However, if lawyers decide in both jurisdictions to opt to give evidence, they should adhere to the strictest truth. In the case where they decide to sacrifice professional secrecy for the sake of a police investigation, professionally they assume responsibility for a lack of ethics.

10 The Lawyer and the Press

25.   The Cuban Constitution, in Article 53, provides that the press is state or social property and cannot, in any case, be private property, ensuring its service for the exclusive use of the working people and in the social interest.

Therefore, rules that may apply in other countries or jurisdictions may not be applicable to the Cuban model. The press does not provide space to lawyers to intervene in cases in which they are acting, with the exception of those in the national interest.

11 Powers of the Tax System and Other Authorities

26.   In Cuba, fiscal matters are governed by Law 113 of July 23, 2012, and its regulations, Decree 308 of October 31, 2012, which entered into force

---

[12] *See* Art. 170, Criminal Procedure; Art. 328(1), Code of Civil, Administrative, Labour and Economic Procedure.

on January 1, 2013. It decrees that the tax administration must establish a relationship of administrative aid in collaboration and coordination with the state, its authorities and organizations; secondary or associated entities; and other state institutions, in line with their corresponding fiscal functions. Among these, the National Office of Tax and Administration (ONAT) – Article 12 of the aforementioned regulations – requires that local legal professionals submit any current data or information pertaining to their taxes, as well as a record of their fiscal history, derived from their financial and professional relationships. In such a way, should lawyers engage in tax evasion, they will be obliged to submit all the fiscal data requested by the tax authorities.

Article 344.1 of the Cuban Penal Code, Law 62, defines the crime of tax evasion in the following terms: when a person who has the responsibility to register and offer information relating to the calculation, determination and paying of taxes, fees, contributions or any other obligation of a fiscal nature, hides, omits or alters the truthful information, and especially if the person does so knowing of the criminal act or having planned it, or benefits from the act, for himself, herself or for a third party.

12 National Security Issues

27.   The Department of Criminal Investigation and Instruction of the Body of State Security, affiliated with the Ministry of the Interior of the Republic of Cuba, is governed by the same regulations that have been noted throughout this chapter with regard to the inviolability of professional secrecy by defense lawyers for people who are accused of crimes against the internal or external security of the Cuban state. This does not prevent, however, when enough indicators are found, the ONBC or Civil Societies for Legal Services from taking action to determine whether the lawyer in question is guilty of committing a crime. This may include recording all conversations (including those held with clients) and a search of their homes, as well as access to their computers and correspondence. This inevitably places another limit on lawyer-client privilege but is justified by the need to protect this important objective.

17

Curaçao

BOUKE BOERSMA

Houthoff Buruma

Preliminary Note

1. Curaçao is an independent country within the Kingdom of the Netherlands. The Kingdom of the Netherlands further consists of the Netherlands (which includes the Caribbean islands Bonaire, St. Eustatius and Saba), St. Maarten and Aruba. Curaçao has its own set of laws, though the Dutch Supreme Court acts as the final court of appeals for each country within the Kingdom of the Netherlands. As will be discussed in this chapter, the attorney-client privilege as it is understood in Curaçao today is primarily a product of case law from the Dutch Supreme Court. Curaçao laws are not always clear or comprehensive. It is therefore customary to look at applicable Dutch law for guidance on the meaning of similar terms under Curaçao law or to fill gaps when relevant Curaçao law precedents are absent.

    In Curaçao, persons who have been admitted to practice as attorneys by the Joint Court for Aruba, Curaçao, St. Maarten and Bonaire, St. Eustatius and Saba (*Gemeenschappelijk Hof van Justitie van Aruba, Curaçao, Sint Maarten en van Bonaire, Sint Eustatius en Saba*) (hereinafter, "the Court of Appeals for the Dutch Caribbean") are granted the attorney-client privilege (*verschonings-recht*). Pursuant to the attorney-client privilege, admitted attorneys may refuse to produce documents or testify on matters that were entrusted to them in their professional capacity. Curaçao law does not require that parties in commercial legal proceedings be represented by an admitted attorney. Please note that the attorney-client privilege does not extend to such other representatives. Admitted attorneys must comply with a Code of Conduct for Attorneys, which was adopted by the Curaçao Bar Association on February 24, 1999. Attorneys who engage in professional misconduct or otherwise damage the reputation of the legal profession can be subject to disciplinary sanctions imposed by the Board of Supervisors (*Raad van Toezicht*). Although it is not mandatory, most attorneys are members of the Curaçao Bar Association.

2. This chapter primarily focuses on attorney-client privilege of attorneys who have been admitted by the Court of Appeals for the Dutch Caribbean. Unless otherwise indicated, for the purposes of this chapter, the term "attorney" refers to a person admitted by the Court of Appeals for the Dutch Caribbean (*advocaat*).

1 Scope of and Limitations on the Duty of Professional Secrecy/Attorney-Client Privilege

A Statutory Basis

3. Under Curaçao law, the attorney-client privilege should be distinguished from the duty of professional secrecy. The legal privilege is the right of certain professionals who have a duty of professional secrecy by virtue of their

247

profession to refuse to give testimony in court or to provide information that has been entrusted to them by their clients in their professional capacity. The attorney-client privilege is based on the generally accepted legal principle that persons should have the right to freely consult an attorney to determine their legal position or to assist them in legal proceedings, without fear that confidential information shared by a client with the attorney will later be disclosed. This principle outweighs in most cases the public's interest that the truth be established in legal proceedings.[1]

The attorney-client privilege primarily serves the interest of the public and not the interest of the client. Consequently, the right to invoke the privilege pertains to the attorney, not the client; even if the client waives the privilege, the attorney has the right to invoke the privilege. Conversely, the duty of professional secrecy is primarily owed by the attorney to the client. The attorney, subject to the duty of secrecy, cannot waive the privilege without the consent of the client. The privilege and the duty of professional secrecy are in most cases two sides of the same coin. Under Curaçao law, only persons who are bound by a duty of professional secrecy can be granted the privilege not to disclose privileged information, provided that the duty is based on statute or case law (merely a contractual duty of secrecy is not sufficient).

The attorney-client privilege in Curaçao is almost entirely a product of case law. In other words, there is no all-encompassing statutory basis for the attorney-client privilege under Curaçao law. Article 144(1) of the Curaçao Code of Civil Procedure (*Wetboek van Burgerlijke Rechtsvordering*) ("Code of Civil Procedure") provides that everyone who has been duly summoned to appear in court is obliged to testify. However, those who by virtue of their profession are under a duty of professional secrecy may refuse to testify with respect to information that was received in a professional capacity (Art. 144(2) (b), Code of Civil Procedure). Article 252(1) of the Curaçao Code of Criminal Procedure (*Wetboek van Burgerlijke Strafvordering*) ("Code of Criminal Procedure") provides substantially the same for criminal proceedings. A law requiring attorneys to disclose confidential information that has been entrusted to them by their clients in connection with their case could violate Article 6 (right to counsel in criminal cases) of the European Convention on Human Rights ("ECHR"), which also applies to Curaçao. Dutch case law dating as far back as the first half of the nineteenth century has recognized privileges for only limited categories of professionals, primarily medical practitioners, civil law notaries, clerics and attorneys.[2] Consequently, many other professionals were denied the privilege, including accountants, tax advisers and bankers.

---

[1] Dutch Supreme Court, March 1, 1985, NJ 1986, 173. The Court of Appeals for the Dutch Caribbean has confirmed (Dec. 20, 1994, TAR 1996, 53) that this legal principle also applies to the Dutch Caribbean.

[2] J.J.I. Verburg, *Het Verschoningsrecht in Strafzaken*, Groningen, 1975, at 101, 106.

The duty of professional secrecy for admitted attorneys is set out in Rule 9(1) of the Curaçao Code of Conduct for Attorneys, which requires that attorneys keep confidential all information that is entrusted to them in the exercise of their profession by their clients. A duty to keep information confidential will customarily be included in a retainer agreement or engagement letter entered into between the attorney and a client, and it will otherwise be implied in the contract between the attorney and the client. As is explicitly stated in Rule 9(2) of the Curaçao Code of Conduct for Attorneys, this duty of the attorney continues after the relationship with the client ends. Violation of the duty of professional secrecy can constitute a breach of contract and lead to disciplinary sanctions on the basis of Article 20(1) of the Curaçao Attorneys Act (*Advocatenlandsverordening 1959*) (the "Curaçao Attorneys Act"). In addition, Article 2:232(1) of the Curaçao Criminal Code (*Wetboek van Strafrecht*) imposes a duty of secrecy on all who have been entrusted with "secrets" that they know or should know must be kept confidential pursuant to their profession. A person who intentionally violates this duty can be sent to prison for up to a year or be subject to a criminal fine.

4. Foreign attorneys who are admitted in their home country can invoke the attorney-client privilege in the same way as Curaçao attorneys, if they are requested to give evidence before the Curaçao courts, since Curaçao civil procedure applies to such proceedings. In this author's view, admitted foreign attorneys can also refuse to provide copies of correspondence with the client and any other documents that are covered by the attorney-client privilege.

B Scope

5. Under Curaçao law, the scope of the attorney-client privilege is broad and covers all confidential information that has been received by an attorney in the exercise of a professional capacity.[3] The information can be in any form, oral or written, and even consist of impressions or thoughts attorneys have formed with respect to their clients.

In commercial matters, the most important provision for compulsory document disclosure is Article 843a of the Code of Civil Procedure. This article provides that a court may, upon the request of one party, compel the production of a specific document by any person who has possession of such document, provided that the document relates to the legal relationship at issue and such party has a legitimate interest in obtaining that document. Attorneys, however, may invoke the legal privilege if and to the extent they retain possession of a document in their professional capacity.

It is generally accepted that most, although not all, documents that are in the possession of an attorney are privileged. Any notes or documents the attorney

---

[3] Dutch Supreme Court, Aug. 9, 2002, NJ 2004, 47.

generates in the course of preparing the client's case are privileged. In addition, any advice the attorney gives the client and any correspondence between them is also privileged. Communications between the attorney and third parties or between the client and a third party, even if the attorney is copied on that correspondence, will in most cases not be privileged. However, an exception exists if the attorney deems it necessary for the proper handling of the case to engage the services of an adviser, for example, an accountant. If that is the case, the adviser can benefit from the derived privilege (see no. 13 of this chapter). Information that attorneys discover by conducting their own research may also be protected.[4] The privilege extends to invoices and specifications of the services rendered by the attorney,[5] the specific date and time of an appointment between the client and the attorney, when the client has asked the attorney for legal advice,[6] and the name and contact details of the client.[7]

The information must be entrusted to attorneys in the exercise of their profession. Information is privileged if it was given to the attorney for the purpose of rendering legal advice or providing legal assistance to the client. It is generally assumed that this should not be construed narrowly: all information that is in any way entrusted to the attorney in the exercise of his or her professional tasks is privileged, whether the information comes from the client or from third parties, and whether the information was provided intentionally or coincidently.

However, if the attorney is a witness to a crime committed by a client, the attorney cannot invoke the privilege with regards to this observation, as this information was not entrusted to the attorney in connection with providing legal advice or assistance. An attorney who participates in the consummation of fraudulent acts can also not invoke the privilege, as these acts do not pertain to the practice of an attorney.[8] Likewise, if the attorney acts in a different capacity, for example, as trustee in bankruptcy,[9] the attorney cannot invoke the attorney-client privilege. The Dutch Supreme Court has ruled that, unless exceptional circumstances apply, mediators can also not invoke the privilege, even when the mediator is an attorney and therefore required by virtue of his or her profession to observe secrecy.[10] Please note that the parties to the proceedings can agree to exclude statements of the mediator as evidence in legal proceedings.

---

[4] Dutch Supreme Court, April 21, 1913, NJ 1913, 958.
[5] Dutch Supreme Court, May 24, 2011, ECLI:NL:HR:2011:BP4663.
[6] District Court of Amsterdam, Sept. 4, 1991, NJ 1992, 351.
[7] Dutch Supreme Court, April 27, 2012, NJ 2012, 408.
[8] Spronken, *Verdediging: Een onderzoek naar de normering van het optreden van advocaten in strafzaken*, Maastricht, 2001, 394.
[9] Amsterdam District Court, April 17, 1941, NJ 1942, 345.
[10] Dutch Supreme Court, April 10, 2009, NJ 2010, 471.

C Persons Subject to the Duty of Professional Secrecy

6. As discussed previously, the duty of professional secrecy is based on
statute and case law and is also enshrined in the Code of Conduct that
applies to attorneys in Curaçao. Consequently, any breach of the duty of
professional secrecy constitutes a violation of the ethical rules and can
result in the imposition of disciplinary sanctions. The duty of professional
secrecy is also a contractual obligation that is primarily owed by the
attorney to the client. If a client fears that the attorney will disclose
privileged information, the client may request the court to order the attorney to refrain from doing so.

   The attorney-client privilege in Curaçao is primarily based on case law.
The privilege must be respected by the court, the police, the public prosecutor
and any party to legal proceedings. It is the attorney who holds the privilege,
not the client. The client only has a derived legal privilege. This means that the
attorney can invoke the privilege, even if the client would want the attorney to
waive it. If the attorney has invoked the privilege, it is presumed that the
attorney has done so correctly, and a court will only marginally test that
decision. The court will uphold the privilege as long as there would be reasonable doubt that an attorney cannot truthfully testify without disclosing privileged information.[11] If the court denies the privilege, only the attorney can
appeal this decision.[12] However, if the court agrees with the attorney and
upholds the privilege, the parties to the legal proceedings can appeal the
decision. To safeguard that clients can speak freely to the attorney without
having to worry whether or not information is privileged, Curaçao law makes
no distinction as to the degree of confidentiality; information is either confidential or not.[13]

D Exceptions to and Optional Derogations from the Duty of Professional Secrecy

7. Under Curaçao law, only limited exceptions exist to the attorney-client
privilege. The Dutch Supreme Court has ruled that in "highly exceptional
circumstances" exceptions apply to the privilege. These exceptions should
be construed narrowly.[14] If an exception applies, the attorney is required
to disclose the information that falls under the exception. The main
exceptions to the attorney-client privilege are discussed in the following
paragraphs.

[11] Dutch Supreme Court, June 7, 1985, NJ 1986, 174; Dutch Supreme Court, Jan. 13, 2006, NJ 2006, 480.
[12] Dutch Supreme Court, Nov. 17, 1967, NJ 1968, 164.
[13] Dutch Supreme Court, March 1, 1985, NJ 1986, 173; Dutch Supreme Court, June 16, 2009, ECLI:NL:2009:BH2678.
[14] Dutch Supreme Court, Oct. 12, 2013, ECLI: NL:HR:2013:1740.

8.   If police officers search an attorney's home or office, letters or documents are protected by the privilege, unless these are the object of the criminal act or have contributed to the commission of the criminal act (*corpora et instrumenta delicti*).[15] Examples are antedated documents, falsified documents or extortion letters.

9.   The second exception to the attorney-client privilege applies if the attorney is suspected of a serious crime. An example is an attorney who was suspected of forming a criminal organization with clients to launder money and commit forgery.[16] In such cases, a judge will accompany the police to decide which documents can be seized. The attorney may file a complaint against the seizure of the documents, and the documents will not be used until a decision on the complaint has been made and is final.

It is not entirely clear whether attorneys are required to report contemplated serious crimes by their clients to the authorities and thereby violate their duty of secrecy. It is unclear whether and how the authorities should be informed if an attorney learns that a client is planning to commit a serious crime. There seems to be consensus, however, that the attorney is required to inform the authorities in case there is an imminent threat to someone's life.

10.   The privilege can be waived only by the attorney. This must be done explicitly. The attorney, who is subject to the duty of secrecy, must obtain the consent of the client for waiving the privilege. The Dutch Supreme Court has ruled that, for correspondence with an attorney to be seized, the attorney must give explicit prior permission.[17]

E Law Firms

11.   It is customary for attorneys who work for a law firm to share among each other privileged information. It is generally accepted that no restrictions apply to this type of information sharing. When a client engages the services of a law firm, all the attorneys of the firm are deemed to be engaged by the client, unless there are indications to the contrary. The attorney-client privilege applies to all information provided by the client to the attorneys of the firm, whether they are partners or associates. The Dutch Supreme Court has confirmed that the attorney-client privilege applies to all attorneys who are employed by the law firm.[18]

---

[15] *See, e.g.*, Dutch Supreme Court, Jan. 24, 2006, NJ 2006, 109.
[16] Dutch Supreme Court, June 18, 2013, NJ 2013, 356; Dutch Supreme Court May 31, 2016, ECLI:NL:HR:2016:1017.
[17] Dutch Supreme Court, Nov. 25, 1986, NJ 1987, 513.
[18] Dutch Supreme Court, Dec. 6, 1955, NJ 1956, 22.

F Legal Assistants and Staff

12.   It is generally accepted that an attorney cannot handle most cases without the help of secretaries, paralegals or other support staff. Under Curaçao law, the duty to observe secrecy therefore does not apply only to the attorney but also to persons who perform services in furtherance to the handling of the matter by the attorney. These persons can benefit from a "derived" privilege and include secretaries, paralegals and other support staff. The Dutch Supreme Court has confirmed that the derived privilege applies to the secretary of the attorney.[19]

The Dutch Supreme Court has ruled that a consequence of the derived nature of the privilege is that the decision whether to invoke the privilege pertains to the attorney and not to persons who are granted a derived privilege.[20] The persons who enjoy a derived privilege are required to keep the privileged information confidential. The client also has a derived privilege and is not required to disclose privileged information.

G External Service Providers

13.   The derived attorney-client privilege can extend to external service providers. The Dutch Supreme Court has ruled that if an attorney deems it necessary, given the complexity of a matter, to request an expert to write an opinion (the case involved an accountant), the expert can claim privilege.[21] A similar derived privilege extends to a law student who works under the supervision of an attorney. Because a tax adviser cannot invoke the privilege, the attorney retained by the tax adviser cannot invoke privilege with respect to documents that were provided by the tax adviser, but that relate to a client of the tax adviser. However, correspondence between the tax adviser and the attorney is covered by legal privilege.

H Multidisciplinary Associations

14.   To the extent necessary for the proper handling of a case, the attorney can cooperate on a specific matter with a professional who is not an attorney, provided that privileged information is kept confidential. Attorneys in Curaçao can form professional associations with non-lawyers, such as tax advisers and accountants, who can benefit from the derived attorney-client privilege. Privileged information shared by attorneys with non-lawyers to prepare the client's case should be kept confidential.

---

[19] Dutch Supreme Court, Oct. 12, 2010, RvdW 2010, 1224.
[20] Dutch Supreme Court, March 29, 1994, NJ 1994, 552.
[21] Dutch Supreme Court, Feb. 12, 2002, NJ 2002, 440.

I In-House Counsel

15.   In Curaçao, it has long been assumed that attorneys can be employed by companies that are not law firms. In-house counsel can be admitted by the Court of Appeals for the Dutch Caribbean, although there is no requirement for in-house counsel to be admitted. A handful of in-house attorneys are indeed admitted to practice in Curaçao and are employed by banks, government entities and trust offices. The Dutch Supreme Court recently ruled in *X and Y/H9 Invest*[22] that admitted in-house attorneys can generally invoke the attorney-client privilege. This ruling is based on the assumption that in-house attorneys in the Netherlands are generally deemed to be independent because employers are under Dutch public law required to sign an agreement safeguarding the independence of in-house counsel. No similar requirement exists in Curaçao. However, in this author's view, this ruling of the Dutch Supreme Court also applies to attorneys admitted in Curaçao, unless it would become clear that they are not independent from their employer. If the employer wants to be sure that the attorney can invoke the privilege, it is recommended for the employer to sign an agreement safeguarding the independence of the attorney. In-house counsel who are not admitted by the Court of Appeals for the Dutch Caribbean are not afforded the privilege.

2 History of the Duty of Professional Secrecy in Curaçao

16.   The attorney-client privilege was formally introduced in Curaçao with the enactment of the Civil Code for Curaçao on May 1, 1869 (the "Old Civil Code"), which was subsequently amended numerous times before it was finally replaced in 2004. Prior to 1869, a labyrinth of laws was applicable to Curaçao that consisted of a myriad of statutes, ordinances, instructions and customs. Article 1928 of the Old Civil Code provided that all persons who are bound by a duty of secrecy pursuant to their status, profession or office could refuse to provide testimony, but only to the extent the testimony concerned knowledge that was entrusted to them in that capacity. This provision was copied from Dutch law and can be traced back to at least the Napoleonic Code Civil of 1804. As the famed Dutch legal scholar Johannes van der Linden expressed at the time, "an attorney can be discharged from its obligation to declare as a witness on matters that he has learned from his client in his profession."[23]

        Article 1928 of the Old Civil Code (and its Dutch equivalent) formed the basis for an extensive body of case law from the Dutch Supreme Court detailing to which professionals privileges apply and under which circumstances they

---

[22] Dutch Supreme Court, March 15, 2013, LJN BY6101.

[23] J. van der Linden, *Regtsgeleerd, practicaal en koopmans handboek*, Amsterdam, 1806, p. 181.

can invoke the privilege. It has never been in doubt that the privilege applies to attorneys. The privilege is today reflected in Article 144(1) of the Curaçao Code of Civil Procedure, which is almost exactly the same as Article 1928 of the Old Civil Code.

3 Supervision

A The Bar Associations

17.   Attorneys admitted in Curaçao are independent legal professionals who are free to determine how to best defend their clients and protect their rights and interests. Attorneys can accept and defend any case they consider in all honesty to be fair.

The Curaçao Bar Association was established in 1977 as a private association (*vereniging*). The Curaçao Bar Association therefore does not have authority to enact laws or legislation. However, in practice, the Code of Conduct for Attorneys that was adopted by the Curaçao Bar Association forms a keystone for the imposition of disciplinary sanctions by the Board of Supervisors. Attorneys are not required to be a member of the Curaçao bar to be able to practice as an attorney, although most of them are. Please note that a proposal is currently pending in Curaçao to replace the Curaçao Attorneys Act. Under the new Curaçao Attorneys Act, membership to the Curaçao Bar Association would become mandatory, and the Curaçao Bar Association would be given limited regulatory powers.

The Curaçao Bar Association cannot direct or instruct lawyers in the handling of their cases. The Curaçao Bar Association also cannot impose disciplinary sanctions if attorneys breach their ethical duties, provided that the attorneys can be discharged as members of the bar association in case of violation of the Code of Conduct for Attorneys or if there are other reasons to conclude that the attorneys are not in good standing (but the attorneys can subsequently still practice law in Curaçao).[24]

The duty of secrecy is also an ethical duty, the violation of which will result in the imposition of disciplinary sanctions.

B The Courts

18.   Attorneys admitted to practice in Curaçao must abide by Curaçao law. The Court of First Instance for Curaçao is competent to hear any claims for professional liability brought against an attorney by a client. The Curaçao Court of First Instance has jurisdiction over crimes committed by attorneys in the exercise of their profession. No special rules apply in this respect to attorneys.

---

[24] Section 9(1) of the bylaws (*huishoudelijk reglement*) of the Curaçao Bar Association.

4 Sanctions

A Proceedings and Sanctions

a Disciplinary Proceedings and Sanctions

19. Article 20 of the Curaçao Attorneys Act sets out that the purpose of disciplinary proceedings is to sanction improper acts of attorneys committed in their professional capacity or other behavior of attorneys that has tarnished the reputation of the legal profession. Although the Code of Conduct for Attorneys that was adopted by the Curaçao Bar Association does not constitute a law, the Court of Appeals (*Raad van Appel*) has confirmed that the Code represents an important standard to determine if attorneys have violated Article 20 of the Curaçao Attorneys Act.[25]

Unlike many other jurisdictions, the chair (*deken*) of the Curaçao Bar Association does not have a formal role in disciplinary proceedings. In practice, the chair can play an informal role when complainants have doubts as to whether to file a complaint. Please note that the chair of the Curaçao Bar Association will be granted a more extensive role in disciplinary proceedings if the new Curaçao Attorneys Act becomes law.

Everyone who has legal standing can file a complaint against an attorney for violation of the standard referenced above. Although the Curaçao Attorneys Act does not define which persons have legal standing, they should have a "direct interest" in submitting a complaint. The client or persons directly harmed by the acts of an attorney will usually have legal standing to file a complaint and, in exceptional circumstances, the chair of the Curaçao Bar Association has standing to file a complaint if it would be in the public interest.[26] Although not specified in the Curaçao Attorneys Act, it is generally understood that the complaint should be in writing. The Board of Supervisors will in most cases hear the complainant. The attorney must be properly called to testify at a public hearing. The attorney can be represented by another attorney. Except in highly exceptional circumstances, an attorney in disciplinary proceedings cannot refuse to produce documents that have been requested by the Board of Supervisors by invoking the duty of secrecy.[27]

Disciplinary sanctions are imposed in the first instance by the Board of Supervisors and on appeal by a Court of Appeals.[28] Both the Board of Supervisors and the Court of Appeals consist of two attorneys and one judge. The judge of the Board of Supervisors is its president, and the chair of the Court of Appeals for the Dutch Caribbean functions as the president of the Court of Appeals. The members of the Board of Supervisors and the Court of Appeals (other than the chair) are appointed by the Governor of Curaçao for

[25] Curaçao Court of Appeals, Dec. 18, 2003, case no. H 18/03.
[26] Curaçao Court of Appeals, March 10, 2015, case no. RvA 2/2015.
[27] Rule 54(2), Code of Conduct for Attorneys.   [28] Art. 20, Curaçao Attorneys Act.

a period of three years and can be discharged or suspended by the Governor of Curaçao, as well.[29] The deliberations of the Board of Supervisors and the Court of Appeals on the merits of the complaint are private and must be kept confidential.[30]

The following disciplinary sanctions can be imposed by the disciplinary courts: (i) a warning, (ii) a reprimand, (iii) a suspension to practice as an attorney for a period of up to one year or (iv) the termination of admission to practice as an attorney.[31] The disciplinary courts must give reasons for their decisions and, in case of the imposition of any sanctions other than a warning, publicly announce the imposition of these sanctions. The complainant and attorney can appeal judgments from the Board of Supervisors within three weeks after the judgment has been delivered to the attorney and complainant.[32]

20. The procedure described above for the Board of Supervisors also applies to proceedings before the Court of Appeals, provided that no further appeal is possible. If, following the imposition of a sanction that has become final, new evidence emerges that would have influenced the decision, then the attorney can request the Court of Appeals to revisit the decision and, if necessary, issue a new judgment.

b Criminal Proceedings and Sanctions

21. Pursuant to Article 2:232 of the Curaçao Criminal Code, the intentional noncompliance by an attorney of the duty of secrecy is punishable by imprisonment for a maximum period of one year or a fine of up to ANG 10,000 (USD $5,587). The Court of First Instance of Curaçao has jurisdiction over such proceedings, and appeal is possible to the Court of Appeals for the Dutch Caribbean and, finally, to the Dutch Supreme Court (on legal grounds only). Attorneys who disclose privileged information to defend themselves in disciplinary proceedings nonetheless violate Article 2:232 of the Curaçao Criminal Code, but they may be justified in doing so if it is necessary for their defense.[33]

c Civil Proceedings and Damages

22. Violation of the duty of secrecy by an attorney constitutes a breach of the contract with the client, and damages may be awarded if the breach caused harm to the client. The client bears the burden of proof in this regard. The Court of First Instance of Curaçao has jurisdiction over such proceedings, and appeal is possible to the Court of Appeals for the Dutch Caribbean and, ultimately, to the Dutch Supreme Court (on legal grounds only).

---

[29] Ibid., Art. 21.   [30] Ibid., Art. 28.   [31] Ibid., Art. 22(1).   [32] Ibid., Art. 25(1).
[33] Dutch Supreme Court, April 8, 2003, NJ 2004, 365.

B Relationship between Criminal Sanctions and Disciplinary Sanctions

23.   Disciplinary and criminal sanctions can likely be imposed independently because disciplinary sanctions are not deemed to be a part of criminal law. Therefore, under Curaçao law, the imposition of both criminal and disciplinary sanctions on the basis of the same facts probably does not violate the *ne bis in idem* principle. Please note that some Dutch legal authors have recently questioned this view and argue that imposition of both disciplinary sanctions and criminal sanctions may violate Article 6 of the ECHR, as disciplinary sanctions could constitute a criminal charge and have a punitive element.[34] In any event, the imposition of criminal sanctions against attorneys in Curaçao for violations of rules that are applicable only to attorneys is unusual, and disciplinary enforcement of such violations is more common in Curaçao.

5 Duty to Provide Information to the Authorities

24.   The Curaçao Act on the Reporting of Unusual Transactions (*Landsverordening Melding Ongebruikelijke Transacties*) obligates financial service providers who, in performing certain services in or from Curaçao, discover facts that indicate money laundering or financing of terrorism to report a contemplated or executed transaction relating thereto immediately to the Taskforce Unusual Transactions.[35] In addition, financial service providers (which may include attorneys, depending on the nature of the matter) are required to identify most of their clients pursuant to the Curaçao Act on the Identification of Financial Clients (*Landsverordening Identificatie bij Financiële Dienstverlening*).

The Act on the Reporting of Unusual Transactions also applies to attorneys. The list of services that are covered by the act is extensive. The duty to report unusual transactions conflicts with the attorney-client privilege and is therefore controversial. The Act on the Reporting of Unusual Transactions strikes a balance and applies only to attorneys to the extent that they render advice or legal assistance relating to (a) the sale or purchase of real estate; (b) managing monies, securities, coins, bank notes, precious metals, precious stones or similar valuables; (c) incorporating or managing companies; or (d) purchasing or selling companies.[36] The duty to report therefore does not apply to the traditional role of attorneys; attorneys are exempt from the reporting requirement if they represent a client in court or their advice relates in any way to potential or actual legal proceedings.[37] The reason for this exemption can be found in the reasoning behind the attorney-client privilege.

---

[34] T. Cleiren and J.W. Fokkens, "Tuchtrecht en het nemo tenetur-beginsel. Ontwikkelingen in de betekenis van het nemo tenetur-beginsel voor het wettelijk geregeld tuchtprocesrecht," in: Bleichrodt (e.a.), *Liber amicorum Hans den Doelder, Onbegrends Strafrecht*, 2013, at 202.

[35] Art. 11(1), Act on the Reporting of Unusual Transactions.   [36] Ibid., Art. 1a sub 15.

[37] Ibid., Art. 1(3).

A transaction is deemed "unusual" if it relates to money laundering or the financing of terrorism; if there are, in the view of the attorney, indications that it is the case; or the transaction involves a cash payment with a value of at least ANG 20,000 (USD \$11,175). The attorney must report the transaction within five business days following discovery or, in the event the reporting is triggered because the attorney believes there are indications that the transaction relates to money laundering or financing of terrorism, within two business days. Attorneys cannot inform their clients that they have reported an unusual transaction to the Taskforce Unusual Transactions. The attorney cannot be held liable under Curaçao law for any losses incurred by a client as a result of the notification, unless the client establishes on the basis of all facts and circumstances that the attorney could not reasonably have concluded that he or she ought to have made the notification.

The Taskforce Unusual Transactions has supervisory authority and can impose penalties and certain other administrative sanctions for violations of the Act on the Reporting of Unusual Transactions.[38] The Taskforce Unusual Transactions can request any information and review or request a copy of any books, documents or other data and enter any places, if and to the extent it is reasonably necessary to perform their supervisory tasks. The Act on the Reporting of Unusual Transactions does not explicitly exclude attorneys from the obligation to provide information or access, but in this author's view, the attorney does not need to cooperate with such a request if it relates to advice in connection with actual or contemplated legal proceedings.

6 Treatment of Attorneys' Documents and Correspondence in the Context of Judicial Investigations

25.　The Dutch Supreme Court has ruled that judicial authorities cannot in the course of a criminal investigation review correspondence between the attorney and client without the consent of the attorney, because such correspondence is privileged.[39] If the documents are found outside the attorney's office, the authorities can review the correspondence to confirm that it is privileged.[40] If that is the case, the privileged correspondence cannot be seized or used by judicial authorities and, if it has been seized incorrectly, the correspondence should be returned upon request of the interested parties. An exception applies for correspondence that is the object of a criminal act or has contributed to the committing of the criminal act, which correspondence is not privileged and can be seized by the judicial authorities.

---

[38] Ibid., Art. 22a–f, h.　[39] Dutch Supreme Court, Nov. 19, 1985, NJ 1986, 533.
[40] Dutch Supreme Court, Nov. 1, 1988, NJ 1989, 349.

7 Search of an Attorney's Office

26.   Article 125(2) of the Code of Criminal Procedure provides that judicial authorities can search an attorney's office or home only with the consent of the
attorney, where the search is limited to documents that fall outside the scope of
the attorney-client privilege or where the documents are the object of a criminal
act or have contributed to the commission of the criminal act.

Unless the attorney is suspected of a serious crime, or the circumstances are
otherwise highly exceptional, it is the attorney who decides whether documents
are protected by the attorney-client privilege. If it is clear that any of the
exceptions as set out in Article 128(2) of the Code of Criminal Procedure
apply, but the attorney nonetheless invokes the privilege, the attorney can be
overruled by the competent court.[41]

8 Tapping of Telephone Conversation with an Attorney

27.   Pursuant to Article 177r(1) of the Curaçao Code of Civil Procedure, the public
prosecutor can, in the case of suspicion of certain serious crimes, order the
police to intercept and record private telephone conversations. The supervisory
judge must approve the telephone tapping, and the duration of the order is
limited to a period of four weeks, which can each time be prolonged for another
four weeks. Telephone conversations must be documented in a police report
within three days of recording the conversation.

Article 177r(4) of the Curaçao Code of Civil Procedure provides that
telephone conversations of an attorney cannot be recorded, unless the attorney
is the suspect of a serious crime. Telephone conversations of the attorney can be
recorded where the alleged crime of the client relates to an act of terrorism. Any
telephone conversations of the attorney that fall under the privilege and that
have inadvertently been recorded must be immediately destroyed. Non-
privileged communications by the attorney can be added to the criminal file
only with the permission of the supervisory judge.[42] If these rules have been
violated, the communication is not admissible as evidence in court.

9 The Attorney as a Witness

28.   Article 144 of the Curaçao Code of Civil Procedure provides that everyone who
has been duly summoned to appear in court is required to appear and testify.
However, those who by virtue of their profession are under a duty of professional secrecy may refuse to testify with respect to information received in
a professional capacity. Attorneys who are called to testify cannot refuse to

---

[41] Dutch Supreme Court, April 20, 2010, NJ 2011, 222.
[42] Art. 177k(2), Curaçao Code of Civil Procedure.

appear, as not all of their knowledge may be privileged, and they should appear to invoke the privilege. After the privilege has been invoked, a court will assess whether the refusal to testify is reasonable. The Dutch Supreme Court has ruled that if it is immediately evident that the testimony of the attorney is privileged, the attorney may inform the court before the hearing and the court may accept that explanation and hold that the attorney does not need to testify.[43]

10 The Attorney and the Press

29. Pursuant to Article 8 of the ECHR, everyone has a right to free speech, including attorneys. However, attorneys' right to free speech is not absolute, as they should refrain from expressing themselves in a way that is unnecessarily hurtful and ensure that publicity is in accordance with the duty of care that applies to attorneys and does not harm the trust and respect attorneys have for one another.[44] Attorneys should refrain from making public statements in breach of their duty of secrecy. The Curaçao Board of Supervisors recently ruled that attorneys have large discretionary powers to freely express themselves in the press to properly defend their clients.[45] Therefore, the attorney can, with the client's consent, speak to the press to defend the client against allegations in the press. However, the attorney should refrain from conducting the case in the press rather than in the courtroom. If attorneys express themselves in the press for another purpose than defending a client, this discretionary power is more limited, and they should refrain from making public statements that could harm the reputation of the legal profession.

11 Powers of the Tax and Other Authorities

30. Pursuant to Articles 46(2) and 45 of the Curaçao General Taxation Act (*Algemene Landsverordening Landsbelastingen*), attorneys are not required to disclose information to the tax authorities that is protected by the attorney-client privilege. The Dutch Supreme Court has ruled that a trust office can benefit from a derived attorney-client privilege in the case the attorney has entrusted privileged information to the trust office. The trust office therefore does not need to disclose the privileged information to the Curaçao tax authorities.[46] If the trust office has received the information directly from the client and not from the attorney, it will need to disclose the information to the tax authorities.

As a general rule, clients subject to an investigation by Curaçao supervisory authorities may refuse to produce correspondence with their attorneys and

---

[43] Dutch Supreme Court, Sept. 19, NJ 2005, 454.   [44] Arts. 3, 34, Curaçao Code of Conduct.
[45] Curaçao Board of Supervisors, Dec. 19, 2014, case no. 66447/2014. The judgment was overturned on appeal for procedural reasons, but this part of the judgment remains relevant.
[46] Dutch Supreme Court, April 27, 2012, NJ 2012, 408.

other documents covered by the attorney-client privilege. This applies, for instance, to information requests made by tax and financial supervisory authorities.

12 National Security Issues

31. The State Security Service of Curaçao is governed by the Act on the State Security Service for Curaçao 2010 (*Landsverordening Veiligheidsdienst Curaçao*). The State Security Service of Curaçao has extensive powers to observe persons, enter locations and record private telephone conversations, provided that, in the latter two cases, prior written authorization from the Ministers of Justice and Internal Affairs has been obtained. The information gathered by the State Security Service is confidential and can only, with the prior approval of said ministers, be shared with other governmental agencies. Importantly, the security service can also collect information that would otherwise be protected by the attorney-client privilege. However, it is likely that information that has been collected in violation of the privilege cannot be used against a suspect in criminal proceedings.

18

Dominican Republic

LUIS RAFAEL PELLERANO
RICARDO PELLERANO
Pellerano & Herrera

Preliminary Note

1. In the Dominican Republic lawyers who are admitted to the bar are subject to a duty of professional secrecy.[1] Only lawyers who are admitted to the bar are entitled to appear in court, as established by the Judicial Organization Act (Art. 73). Such lawyers are self-employed, although they can be partners or associates in a law firm. They must comply with the bar's code of ethics. In the Dominican Republic, there is only one Bar Association for the whole country, and it is located in Santo Domingo. Law no. 91 of February 3, 1983, establishes the Bar Association of the Dominican Republic, which is presided over by a president.

   Lawyers who work for a company (in-house counsel) are also members of the bar and are legally allowed to provide legal assistance and consultation and can appear in the courts of the Republic. That is, in the Dominican Republic, to practice law, it is essential to be enrolled in the Bar Association of the Dominican Republic.

   It is important to point out that in January 2015 there was submitted to the Chamber of Deputies a draft of new legislation for the practice of law, which also would have established the duty of professional secrecy for lawyers. This draft was rejected on April 14 of the same year, but the provisions on professional secrecy were included in other legislation.

2. This chapter focuses on the professional secrecy of all lawyers who belong to the bar, as the term "lawyer" will refer to a member of the bar.

1 Scope of and Limitations on the Duty of Professional Secrecy/Attorney-Client Privilege

A Statutory Basis and Implications

3. Professional secrecy and confidentiality are both duties and at the same time rights of the lawyer. These principles only represent the realization of fundamental rights that the law recognizes for clients.

   Article 49.3 of Dominican Constitution of January 26, 2010, imposes a duty of professional secrecy on journalists: "The journalist's professional secrecy and his/her conscience clause are protected by the Constitution and the law."

   The statutory basis for professional secrecy in the Dominican Republic is found in the following legal provisions: (i) Law no. 821 on Judicial Organization of November 21, 1927; (ii) Law no. 172-13 on personal data of December 13,

---

[1] For some literature, see Angel Ossorio, "El alma de la Toga," *Editorial Futuro*, Santo Domingo, D. R. 186; Henri Lalou, "El secreto profesional de los notarios," *Gaceta Judicial*, 8(200): 39–40, Feb. 1, 2005; Juan Pellerano Gómez, *Guía del abogado*, Tome I, Volume I, Ca-Pel-Dom Editions, Santo Domingo, D. R. 1968; Pascal Peña, "Secreto profesional de periodista: péndulo entre el deber y el derecho," *Gaceta Judicial*, 7(159), May 23, 2003.

2013; and (iii) the Criminal Code of August 20, 1884, and the new Criminal Code of December 19, 2014, which entered into force in December 2015.

Article 78(b) of the Law on Judicial Organization establishes a duty for lawyers to proceed "in the exercise of their profession with honor and discretion," which is broadly understood to mean keeping a secret revealed by a client in the exercise of the legal profession.

Also, Article 6 of the law on personal data[2] provides:

> The person responsible for the personal data as well as those involved at any stage in the processing of personal data are obliged to professional secrecy regarding such data and also are subject to the duty of keeping it; obligations that will subsist even after ending its relations with the owner of the personal data file, or if applicable, with the person responsible for the same, unless the person is relieved of the duty of secrecy by a court decision and in cases where there are serious reasons relating to public security, national defense or public health.

For its part, the previous Criminal Code establishes in its Article 377 a duty of professional secrecy on doctors and other medical professionals and those who, pursuant to their profession, gain knowledge of secrets that are entrusted to them,[3] providing sanctions that include a prison term and a criminal fine.

Article 207 of the new Criminal Code of December 19, 2014, broadens the scope and therefore imposes a duty of professional secrecy on any person "who, pursuant to their status or profession, function or position, gain knowledge of secrets which are entrusted to them." Violation of this duty can be sanctioned by a prison term and a criminal fine, unless disclosure is made: (i) with the consent of the person affected, (ii) if the law expressly provides or authorizes the disclosure of the secret, or (iii) if disclosure is made before a court of law or the Public Prosecutor's Office. It is assumed that this provision also applies to lawyers, on the grounds that the guarantee of professional secrecy in the attorney-client relationship is a realization of the right to privacy, which is protected by the Constitution and international treaties.

This organic law establishes the limits on a fundamental and human right (the right to privacy)[4] by guaranteeing professional secrecy, while allowing access to information – or the supply of it – but only by compliance with certain

---

[2] Law no 550-14, published by the Official Gazette no 10788 and entered into force on Dec. 19, 2015.

[3] Note that in this case it may be data files in private ownership, as the law refers to personal data files in possession of individuals, companies or private entities, as well as public corporations. *See* Art. 6 of Law 172-13.

[4] The right to privacy is "the recognition of the existence of a proper scope and reserved against the action and knowledge of others; required by the standards of our culture to maintain a minimum quality of human life"(STC 207/1996; 209/1988; 117/1994) BJ no. 1237. Supreme Court. Dec. 18, 2013.

procedures.[5] Regarding this subject, recall that the Dominican Constitution explicitly provides in Article 74.2 that "only by law, on cases permitted by this Constitution, shall the exercise of fundamental rights and guarantees be regulated, respecting their essential content and the principle of reasonableness." And here it also should be noted that when the Constitution says "only by law," it means the law in a strict sense, that is, legislative acts that can be produced only by the National Congress.

4. When called to testify before a court, lawyers should exercise discretion and determine if disclosure is truly warranted. That is, the lawyer should consider whether the information in question is protected by professional secrecy, in which case the lawyer cannot reveal it.[6] In principle, a court or Public Prosecutor's Office cannot compel a lawyer to disclose confidential information.[7] This provision is apparently attenuated when analyzing the provisions of Law no. 137-11 on Constitutional Procedures, which states that "physical or moral persons, public or private, organ or agent of government to whom is addressed a request with the purpose of obtaining information or documents are required to provide them without delay within the period specified by judge."[8] In this case, the lawyer could invoke a qualification, professional secrecy being one of them, and refrain from providing information.[9]

    However, Articles 17 and 20 of the Bar Code of Ethics provide for an additional exception, that is, a lawyer can speak in self-defense when harassed or accused of wrongdoing by the client, and there may be other reasons[10] why an attorney cannot refuse to disclose information (see Section I.D of this chapter).

5. The French Court of Cassation, the cradle of law in the Dominican Republic, has emphasized the importance of lawyers' professional secrecy, unless this principle violates the right of defense.[11]

---

[5] Constitutional Court. Judgment TC / 0030 /14. Docket no. TC- 05-2011-0024, Feb. 10, 2014, at 33.

[6] Art. 197 of the Criminal Procedure Code of July 19, 2002, indicates who by law must keep professional secrecy. These persons cannot refuse to give testimony when they are released by the interested person of the duty of secrecy. Should they be summoned to appear at court, they must explain the reasons for their abstention.

[7] This is confirmed by Art. 15 and Art. 18 of the Code of Ethics, setting the professional secrecy of the lawyer as a right even before the judges.

[8] See paragraph I of Art. 87 of Law 137-11.

[9] Art. 58 of Law 834 of July 15, 1978, states "In case of difficulty, or if there is raised some legitimate impediment, the judge who has ordered the delivery or production may, on request without formality made, retract or modify the court's decision. Third parties can lodge an appeal regarding the new decision within fifteen days of the same."

[10] Art. 5(b) of Law 172-13 on personal data states, "when there are reasons relating to public security, national defense or public health."

[11] Cass. crim. June 5, 1995, no. 95-82.333, Bull. crim. no. 646, JCP 1976. II. 18243.

As already discussed, if lawyers disclose the information that constitutes part of the professional secret in their relation with the client, such lawyers will be deemed to have violated their duty of professional secrecy and will be subject to disciplinary sanctions before the Bar Association, without prejudice to other penalties previously described.

Articles 40.4 and 69 of the Dominican Constitution guarantee the right to legal assistance and effective judicial protection. However, this right can be effective only if clients can be sure that the information provided to their lawyers will not be disclosed by the latter to third parties and used against them. Also, Article 44 enshrines the right to privacy and personal honor, ensuring respect of and noninterference with one's privacy, family life, home and correspondence, including attorney-client correspondence, so that anyone who violates this provision is required to compensate or repair the damages caused.

The ultimate goal of the principle of professional secrecy is to defend the rights of the client in strict compliance with legal norms and moral law, which do not undermine the trust and good faith that should govern the relationship between lawyer and client.[12] Effective judicial protection of this principle will help to ensure respect for due process of law and an accessible and timely system of justice, which would lose all effectiveness if the client did not have the certainty that the confidences given to a lawyer might be revealed with impunity.

6.   In the contract for the provision of professional services, which regularly includes a mandate contract, the information provided by the client to the lawyer is confidential, so disclosure without consent entails the violation of such contract.

In principle, the lawyer should not accept a case in which the lawyer has an interest or in which the lawyer has been involved before. The lawyer is compelled to inform the potential client if the lawyer is subject to influences that are adverse to the interests of the client. If the client wants to hire the lawyer's services anyway, it should be with full knowledge of the facts and the risk that, should the lawyer be required to present testimony in court, the lawyer may reveal the facts of which the lawyer had knowledge prior to signing the contract for the provision of services to the client.[13]

B Scope

7.   Professional secrecy includes all information, whether written or oral, provided by the client or a third party to the lawyer (i) to prepare for litigation relating to the client's rights and obligations or (ii) in the course of soliciting advice

[12] (STC. 207/1996; 209/1988; 117/1994) BJ no. 1237. Supreme Court of Justice. Dec. 18, 2013.
[13] *See* Art. 25, Bar Code of Ethics.

regarding the client's legal rights and obligations, as well as information that comes to the lawyer's attention in this context, including information provided by the opposing party or counsel, a relative or a third party.

It is understood that professional secrecy includes everything that an attorney learns from the opposing lawyer or that the attorney knows from working together or in association with others or through employees or dependents of others.

As indicated by Article 16 of the Bar Code of Ethics, an obligation of secrecy extends to confidences made by third parties to legal professional by reason of the lawyer's profession. Attorneys must maintain confidentiality about the conversations held for a transaction that failed and about facts that became known only by such legal representation, including telephone conferences, consultations and pre- or post- litigation recommendations, including correspondence in physical, digital or electronic formats.[14] This fundamental duty remains in full force after the lawyer has ceased rendering services to the client. It is recognized by court decisions that the abovementioned secrecy embraces not only the lawyer but also the lawyer's office or firm where he or she operates and stores documents entrusted by the client.

The French Court de Cassation decided on May 24, 1962, that "professional secrecy does not cover all the facts and circumstances of the process, but only the ones that have intimate character, in relation to which there is a material or moral interest for the client to prevent its revelation."[15]

The lawyer not only receives information from the client, which is considered to be covered by professional secrecy, but must also consider confidential the information and discussions with the lawyer of the opponent regarding a case. The attorney must keep the professional secrecy for all cases known because of the lawyer's role, even if the client does not hire the lawyer for legal representation.

8.   Once the lawyer ends the relationship with the client, the lawyer must maintain the professional secrecy. Such is the case when the client entrusts information about a project, event or transaction to the lawyer, no matter whether it has been successful or not. The lawyer is also prevented, after accepting a case from a client and even if the representation has not yet been formalized, from serving a different client in the same case, the details of which the lawyer learned from the original client.

---

[14] Art. 44.3 recognizes, as part of the right to privacy, the inviolability of correspondence, documents or private messages in physical, digital, electronic or any other type of format. Also, Art. 187 of the Criminal Procedure Code states that medical diagnostic or tests covered by professional secrecy cannot be subject to sequestration, nor can communications between the accused and the defense counsel.

[15] Cass. Crim. May 24, 1862, D. P. 1862, 1. 545.

C Persons Subject to the Duty of Professional Secrecy

9. Lawyers through their actions and opinions are required to maintain the highest standards of conduct, to preserve intact the trust that society has placed in them. Given that the interests of others depend on their opinions, the attorney must maintain a constant independence of action and judgment in the client-lawyer relationship, keeping the strictest professional secrecy, because as indicated in previous sections, any breach of this duty constitutes a violation of the bar ethics code. The attorney is also subject to disciplinary sanctions by the Bar Association.

   The responsibility derived from professional secrecy depends, of course, on the fact that the lawyer signed a contract to provide professional services to a third party. In this case, we have a contractual responsibility, derived from the contract for the provision of professional services. In accordance with the Dominican Civil Code, the party that does not fulfill its obligations is subject to compensating the other party for damages.

   Such a strict position derives from the fact that the legally protected right in these cases is not only a client's right to personal privacy but also a matter of public policy requiring absolute safety of interests linked to the right to defense.

   In the collision of interests that may occur between the duty of professional secrecy and the obligation to cooperate with the justice system, the former should usually prevail, being the only way to safeguard the functionality of the profession, guaranteeing the client the freedom from any concern when hiring the services of an attorney. However, when the disclosure of information is enshrined as professional secrecy performed by a third party,[16] who is not part of the attorney-client relationship, it does not have enough weight to engage the responsibility of the person who benefits from said privilege.

D Exceptions to and Optional Derogations from the Duty of Professional Secrecy

10. One of the main obligations imposed by the Code of Ethics for Lawyers in the Dominican Republic is on professional secrecy. In the Dominican legal system, lawyers are unable to disclose, by any means, information regarding their clients that has been obtained from the client or third parties. The law currently in application[17] establishes that the "advocate will keep the strictest professional secrecy,"[18] and that "professional secrecy constitutes a duty from which they themselves can't be exempted . . . ."[19]

---

[16] This is without detriment to provisions of Art. 378 of the Criminal Code, which states that one who takes possession of another person's papers or letters and discloses them shall be punished with a judgment from three months up to a year in prison and criminal fine. The penalties do not apply to spouses, parents, guardians or their substitutes, or to the papers or letters from their spouses or minors under their guardianship or dependence.

[17] Decree No. 1290, which ratifies the Code of Ethics of the Lawyers of the Dominican Republic. G. O. 9616.

[18] Ibid., Art. 18.   [19] Ibid., Art. 15.

However, this prohibition is not absolute, since it has certain limitations and exceptions that allow legal professionals to discharge their obligations in specific cases listed expressly in the rule governing the matter. These exceptions and limitations are intended to provide for a client's protection to prevent information that has been provided to the client's legal representative, which in most cases is sensitive information, from being used against the client. An example of this is when the lawyer is harassed by the client in a non-judicial manner. Lawyers are released from professional secrecy in these cases, being able to reveal and present the documents entrusted to them to the extent necessary for their defense and to justify judicial action against former clients. This is provided in Article 17 of the Code of Ethics of the Lawyer[20] and has been upheld by the Supreme Court.[21]

Similarly, when clients judicially accuse lawyers of wrongdoing, lawyers are released from their secrecy obligation, within the limits necessary and indispensable to present a defense.[22]

Another exception is when the lawyer reveals the client's intent to commit a crime. In this case, the lawyer may violate professional secrecy by revealing what is necessary to prevent the commission of a crime. The Dominican Republic has not yet seen any cases of the type.

11. These scenarios do not give total freedom to the attorney to disclose the client's information, since the rule states that the lawyer should reveal only "the indispensable." The lawyer at all times should be careful with the information that the lawyer intends to reveal, limiting such disclosure to the essential elements, without disclosing information about other confidential aspects.

The prerogative of counsel to disclose information in limited circumstances is protected by the fundamental right of self-defense that applies to every citizen. As a constitutional right, it is above the obligation of professional secrecy of the lawyer. Similarly, the exceptions to professional secrecy safeguard the fundamental right to an effective judicial protection enshrined in the Dominican Constitution, as well as the right to "equal arms" in judicial trials, also a fundamental right.

12. The law provides expressly that the lawyer will reveal the secret "in accordance with his awareness," which means that the rule does not require that the attorney ignore his or her obligation, but it gives the possibility to do so, valuing the possible material or moral damages that might result from the commission of the crime.

---

[20] Ibid.

[21] Cass. Cam. Reun., April 30, 1908, D. P. 1910. I. 227. Aforementioned by Juan Manuel Pellerano Gómez, *Guía del abogado*, Tome I, Volume I, Ca-Pel-Dom Editions, Santo Domingo, D. R., 1968, at 23.

[22] Ibid., Art. 20.

In certain cases, the lawyer can be legally called to submit statements respecting the client. The law provides that, in this case, it is the sovereign discretion of the attorney to decide whether the lawyer may refuse to testify or decline to answer any questions involving the violation of confidential information provided by the client.[23]

The Dominican Criminal Procedure Code provides that any person summoned by court must appear and testify the truth of what is known and what is asked of the person, with certain exceptions provided by the law. Within these exceptions provided in Article 194 is the previously mentioned exception regarding the ability of the lawyer to testify against the client, as this would lead the lawyer to compromise the lawyer's penal responsibility.

13.   The exceptions to secrecy have their own exemptions. In Dominican legislation, there is no possibility of totally breaking attorney-client confidentiality. The revelation of professional secrets is sanctioned by Article 377 of the Dominican Penal Code, which punishes such violations with imprisonment consisting of a correctional prison term of one to six months and a fine of 10 to 100 Dominican pesos.

E Law Firms

14.   It is presumed that lawyers who work within the same company should not keep professional secrets among themselves. Ergo, it is not considered a violation of professional secrecy when talks are held with lawyers from the same firm. This is because it is understood that employees are governed by the same policies and standards as the company. However, when a firm wants to avoid such exchanges, firms should require employees involved in a case or transaction to sign a letter of confidentiality with respect to that case or particular transaction.

It is not considered a violation of professional secrecy to share information with colleagues, except in exceptional cases in which the lawyer has signed a preliminary confidentiality agreement. Therefore, the following maxim applies: *non licet nec quid*, which means "what is not forbidden is allowed."

F Legal Assistants and Staff

15.   It is common that law firms hire paralegals, secretaries, assistants and other administrative staff, who despite not having direct contact with the clients to which legal services will be provided may have greater or lesser access to such client's information.

---

[23] Decree No. 1290, which ratifies the Code of Ethics of the Lawyers of the Dominican Republic. G. O. 9616. Art. 18.

The obligation of professional secrecy is extended to legal assistants and staff, considering the provisions of Article 377 of the Dominican Penal Code, which states that the law applies to "all other persons who, because of their profession or trade are depositories of secrets of others . . .." Consequently, this includes the staff of the law firm. They too have an obligation to safeguard the professional secrecy.

G External Service Providers

16.   Because of the complexity or specialization of cases lawyers can handle, it is not unusual for them to make use of external consultants, legal translators and other experts who provide services outside the firm.

As is the case for administrative employees, the obligation of professional secrecy extends to external service providers, given that they handle the same sensitive and confidential client information.

Firm rules regarding confidentiality to clients apply not only within the company, but their policies should be applied at all times by all employees or partners of the company. If they do not respect and keep confidential client secrets, they can compromise their civil or criminal liability under the same conditions in which a lawyer does.

H Cooperation between Professionals from Different Disciplines

17.   It is possible and quite common for lawyers to work with professionals from different careers. Usually, these professionals will attend court to show or prove matters that require their technical knowledge. For example, a doctor will be asked to indicate how serious is the damage caused by the collapse of a 32-pound bag on a person's body from a height of 12 feet.

The lawyer is bound to ask the court to appoint the professional or expert who will be assisting during the case. Prior to making this request of the court, the lawyer should confirm with the client that the client agrees that an expert knows the details of the case. Once the client agrees and the court has granted the measure, the expert is committed to professional secrecy.

In many cases, considering the sensitivity of the information to be entrusted, lawyers will sign with the expert a confidentiality agreement to ensure the interests of the client. However, even when the expert does not sign the confidentiality agreement, if experts disclose information entrusted to them, they can be subject to the penalties that the norm establishes. It must be noted that the lawyer should not reveal to the collaborator more information than is necessary for the resolution of the case.

Every profession has a regulation regarding professional secrecy, so it will depend on the discipline exercised by the expert. As a result, there will be cases in which the exceptions and limitations applicable to a lawyer will apply to another professional, and vice versa.

I In-House Counsel

18. Many clients are cautious and demanding with the information they disclose to their lawyers. As a result, they specify in the letter of engagement which information is to be handled exclusively by contracted lawyers.

The section on "Law Firms" noted that it is not considered a violation of professional secrecy to share a client's information with colleagues who work together with the lawyer who handles the matter. The same rule would apply in principle for in-house lawyers.

However, the freedom of in-house lawyers to discuss or share information with other employees of the company for which they work, and even with external lawyers, may be limited or restricted by agreements between the in-house lawyer and the employer, either at the time of hiring, periodically, or on the occasion of particular issues or temporary assignments.

2 History of the Duty of Professional Secrecy in the Dominican Republic

19. Professional secrecy for lawyers in the Dominican Republic was implicit in the legislation until 1983 with Decree no. 1290, which ratifies the Ethics Code for the Bar Association in the Dominican Republic.

Decree no. 1290 provides in its second chapter that professional secrecy constitutes a duty that must be complied with by lawyers. Included as part of the professional secrecy are all the confidences made by third parties as a consequence of their profession.

However, the duty of professional secrecy yields to the needs of professional self-defense, when a lawyer is accused of wrongdoing by a client. In this case, the lawyer may reveal secret information to the extent necessary for the lawyer's defense.

Decree no. 1290 is still in force, although several laws containing provisions on professional secrecy have been enacted since then.

3 Supervision

A The Bar Associations

20. As per Law no. 91 of 1983, which creates the Dominican Bar Association, a lawyer who belongs to the bar is an individual who has obtained a law degree in the Dominican Republic. Furthermore, a lawyer shall comply with all the duties contained in Law no. 91 and the Ethics Code of the Bar Association, as well as any other provision adopted by the General Assembly of the Bar (Art. 4).

B The Courts

21. The criminal courts have jurisdiction to decide on any claim for breach of professional secrecy committed by lawyers, in which case lawyers may be brought to criminal courts by their clients.

4 Sanctions

A Proceedings and Sanctions

22. The Dominican Bar Association is entitled to investigate complaints concerning the behavior of its members in the exercise of the legal profession, to initiate proceedings and provide, by itself, sanctions in disciplinary jurisdictions under the relevant provisions of its code of ethics.

   However, breach of professional secrecy without the consent of the person concerned is also punishable by criminal sanctions of one day to one year in prison and a fine of one to two month's minimum wages of the public sector (Art. 207 of Law no. 550-14, which establishes the Dominican Criminal Code).

B Relationship between Criminal Sanctions and Disciplinary Sanctions

23. Disciplinary and criminal sanctions are imposed independently and have no effect on each other.

5 Duty to Provide Information to the Authorities

A Money Laundering and Terrorism

24. Article 13 of Law no. 72-00 on Money Laundering provides that professionals shall not invoke professional secrecy whenever it is demonstrated that there is a link between the professional and the individual or entity under investigation.

6 Treatment of Lawyers' Documents and Correspondence in the Context of Judicial Investigations

25. Any documentation that is obtained during the course of an investigation by a prosecutor or investigator, if legally obtained with a search warrant granted by a judge, can be presented in a court of law. The court will examine such evidence without making a decision whether such documents are or can be considered protected by the attorney-client privilege. In that sense, if disclosure occurs in this context, the lawyer cannot be subject to criminal sanctions.

   However, to obtain such evidence, the prosecutor must comply with the legal procedure established in Article 179 *et seq.* of the Dominican Code of Criminal Procedure. This legislative text states that a warrant must indicate:

(i) the specific place to be searched; (ii) the person designated to perform the investigation; and (iii) the reasons or motivation of the search with the exact indication of the objects and persons that are expected to be found. Furthermore, the search warrant must have an expiration date of 15 days from the date it was issued, taking into consideration that if the search occurs after this term expires, the evidence found shall not be taken into account by the judges.

7 Search of a Lawyer's Office

26. The Dominican Code of Criminal Procedure, specifically Article 180, states that the search of private places and homes can be performed only by request of a *Ministerio Público* (the Dominican equivalent to a district attorney in the United States) or prosecutor by a search warrant issued by a competent judge, duly motivated. In cases of urgency and in the absence of the *Ministerio Público*, the police can request such warrant directly.

The search warrant must be notified to the lawyer or person who lives in the house or the person in charge of the place to be searched, by issuing a copy of such warrant. The notified individual must be asked to observe the search. If nobody is present, the prosecutor can use force to enter into the location.

Nevertheless, if during the search the lawyer is questioned by the investigator, the lawyer should not disclose any information considered protected by the attorney-client privilege. Article 17 of the Dominican Attorney's Ethics Code states that the attorney must keep the most rigorous confidentiality. This fundamental duty remains in full effect after the lawyer has ceased to render services to the client. The lawyer has the right to refuse to testify against the client and may decline to answer any questions that involve the revelation of any information considered protected by the attorney-client privilege.

8 Tapping of Telephone Conversations with a Lawyer

27. The Dominican Code of Criminal Procedure establishes certain cases where a judge may authorize the tapping of telecommunications of third parties. Article 192 of the code expressly indicates that a judicial authorization is required to intercept, collect and record communications, messages, data, pictures or sounds transmitted through public or private telecommunication networks of the defendant or any other person who can provide reasonably relevant information to the determination of an offense, whatever the technical means used.

The communications interception measure is exceptional and must be renewed every 30 days, stating the justifications for the extension. The judicial decision authorizing the interception of communications or collection must indicate all the identified elements of the means to intercept and the facts that motivate such measures.

275

It is important to note that the interception applies only to the investigation of offenses with a maximum penalty of more than 10 years of imprisonment and cases processed under the special procedure for complex issues, pursuant to the Dominican Code of Criminal Procedure.

9 The Lawyer as Witness

28. As per the Dominican laws, there is no prohibition against making a lawyer testify in a court as a witness. As per Article 15 of the Dominican Attorney Ethics Code, if a lawyer is called as a witness, the lawyer must appear, and in the act and proceeding with absolute independence of judgment, the lawyer may refuse to respond to those questions whose answers, in the lawyer's opinion, would violate the attorney-client privilege. In addition, the court is not entitled to compel the lawyer to testify on issues protected by this privilege.

Additionally, a lawyer who is called to testify on matters in which the lawyer did not act as a lawyer can refuse to testify in the case where this lawyer has confidential information of the client of another lawyer, since Article 16 of the Dominican Attorney Ethics Code provides that the professional secrecy also covers confidences between colleagues.

On the other hand, the obligation of secrecy yields to the needs of the professional self-defense right, when accused of wrongdoing by a client. Lawyers can then reveal what is essential for their defense and provide, only with this purpose, the documents entrusted to them.

10 The Lawyer and the Press

29. Dominican laws do not refer to the release of information to the press by a lawyer. However, it is generally accepted that a lawyer can share information about a case with the press to defend the client against allegations publicly made, always with the client's express consent, without disclosing any privileged information.

11 Powers of the Tax Administration and Other Authorities

30. In principle, no entity has the authority to compel a lawyer to disclose information protected by the attorney-client privilege. If the tax authority suspects that the information provided by the client regarding the client's accounts is not truthful, it can initiate a formal investigation directly against the client.

12 National Security Issues

31. Pursuant to the authors' interpretation of the Dominican Attorney Ethics Code, in the case where a client expresses to the client's lawyer the intention to commit a crime, the lawyer has the obligation to make the necessary

disclosures to avoid the damages arising from the execution of the crime. Therefore, if a lawyer has knowledge that the client is going to commit a national security crime, the lawyer is under a duty to report such information.

In general terms, Law no. 172-13, regarding the Protection of Personal Data, indicates that any person who is responsible for a file of personal data is bound by professional secrecy. However, in cases where the national security is in jeopardy, such person is obligated to reveal such information as per a judicial resolution.

19

Ecuador

SEBASTIAN CAICEDO RICAURTE
BRUCE HOROWITZ

Paz Horowitz Robalino Garces Abogados

Preliminary Note

1.   In Ecuador, only lawyers duly incorporated in the Lawyers' Forum registry, which the National Judicial Council (NJC) maintains through its Regional Offices, have the right to practice the profession.[1]

The Constitutional Court of Ecuador[2] declared unconstitutional, for substantive reasons, all legal regulation concerning the requirement of membership to a professional body in order to practice a profession, including the prerequisite of lawyers to join a bar association[3] in order to practice law. Therefore, for a lawyer in Ecuador since 2008, it is not necessary to be or become a member of a bar association to practice law; rather, they must simply be incorporated into the Lawyers' Forum registry.

Despite the abovementioned decision of the Constitutional Court, bar associations still continue to exist in the different provinces[4] of the country, which, taken together, comprise the Ecuadorian Bar Association, regulated by the Law of the Ecuadorian Bar Association.[5] In this regard, it is worth noting that this law currently applies only to lawyers who are voluntarily affiliated with a bar association.

Ecuadorian law protects professional secrecy specifically between clients and lawyers, including communications concerning insider trading. Although there is no specific law or code governing the privilege of the "attorney-client" relationship, there are certain specific provisions in different legal bodies, discussed throughout this chapter, that ensure the protection and assurance, as well as the privilege, of confidentiality of information, communications, documents and instructions between the professional and the client.

1 Scope of and Limitations on the Obligation of Professional Secrecy/Attorney-Client Privilege

A Legal Basis and Implications

2.   There is no specific body of law governing privilege, focused only on the lawyer-client relationship.

---

[1] *See* Organic Code of the Judicial Function, Art. 324(3) and Eighth Transitional Provision.

[2] By Resolution no. 0038-2007-TC of March 5, 2008, published in Official Gazette no. 336 of May 14, 2008.

[3] Bar associations are constituted by province and represent their members before the Ecuadorian Bar Association.

[4] The Republic of Ecuador is divided into 24 provinces.

[5] Published in Official Gazette no. 507 of March 7, 1974.

Article 20 of the Constitution[6] recognizes the duty of confidentiality and professional secrecy, as follows: "The State shall guarantee the conscience clause to everyone, and professional secrecy and the confidentiality of sources to those who inform, or give their opinions through the media or other forms of communication, or work in any communication activity."[7]

"Professional" is not defined in the Constitution. However, it is clear from Article 20 that professionals in Ecuador have a duty to refrain from disclosing privileged or confidential information. Also, people have the right to keep their information confidential. Accordingly, Article 66(20)[8] of the Constitution recognizes and guarantees people the right to personal and family privacy.

The violation of this obligation is sanctioned by Article 179[9] of the Comprehensive Criminal Organic Code[10] (hereinafter "COIP"), which states that if someone discloses a "secret" entrusted to that person by virtue of his or her status or trade, employment, profession or art, and which disclosure could cause damage to another person, shall be sanctioned with a custodial sentence of six months to a year.

Similarly, Article 66(21)[11] of the Constitution states that the secrecy of all communications is guaranteed in general, recognizing the right to privacy and secrecy of physical and virtual correspondence, indicating that correspondence cannot be retained, opened or examined, except in cases provided by law, prior judicial intervention and with the duty to maintain secrecy of the affairs unconnected with the fact that encourages examination. This is in accordance with Article 5[12] of the Electronic Commerce, Signatures and Data Messages Act,[13] which indicates that all data messages are confidential and shall be considered inside information, including the information transmitted as a result of a professional-client relationship. The same article provides that

[6] Published in Official Gazette no. 449 of Oct. 20, 2008. [7] Unofficial translation.
[8] Unofficial translation: "It is recognized and guaranteed to persons: . . . The right to personal and family privacy."
[9] Unofficial translation: "Disclosure of secrets. The person who by having knowledge by reason of his or her status or trade, employment, profession or art, of a secret whose disclosure could cause damage to another person and reveals it, shall be punished with custodial sentence of six months to a year."
[10] Published in Official Gazette Supplement 180 of Feb. 10, 2014.
[11] Unofficial translation: "It is recognized and guaranteed to persons: . . . The right to inviolability and secrecy of physical and virtual correspondence; it cannot be retained, opened or examined, except in cases provided by law, prior judicial intervention and with the duty to maintain secrecy of the affairs unconnected with the fact that encourages examination. This law protects any type or form of communication."
[12] Unofficial translation: "Confidentiality and Reserves. The principles of confidentiality and reserve are set for data messages, whatever its form, medium or intent. Any violation of these principles, especially those related to electronic intrusion, illegal transfer of data messages or violation of professional secrecy shall be punished as provided in this Act and other regulations governing the matter."
[13] Published in Official Gazette Supplement 557 of April 17, 2002.

any violation of the principle of confidentiality and privacy of data messages will be punished in accordance with the relevant provisions and rules applicable to the matter.

The violation of the right of persons to inviolability and secrecy of physical and virtual correspondence is sanctioned by Article 178 of the COIP concerning the violation of privacy, which establishes that a person who, without the consent of another person or legal authorization, accesses, intercepts, examines, retains, records, reproduces, publishes or disseminates personal data, messaging data, voice, audio and video, postal items, information on media, private or reserved communications of such other person by any means, shall be punished with a custodial sentence of one to three years. It is worth noting that the same article states that the penalty does not apply to those who disclose audio and video in which they appear personally or when the disclosed information is of a public character.

Although Article 476[14] of the COIP provides certain exceptions for criminal judges in their ability to order the interception of communications or computer data, paragraph 5[15] of the same article states that it is strictly forbidden to intercept any communication that is protected by professional secrecy.

Article 424 of the COIP also provides certain exemptions from the duty to denounce to those who learn about the commission of a crime of public exercising.[16] Article 424 reads as follows "No one may be compelled to denounce his or her spouse, stable union partner or relatives to the fourth degree of consanguinity or second degree of affinity. The obligation will also not exist when knowledge of the facts is covered by professional secrecy."[17]

In addition, Article 503(2)[18] of the COIP sets the rules for hearsay evidence in a trial of criminal matters, noting that statements will not be received from persons holding a secret that they have known by virtue of their profession, trade or function, if these concern the matter of secrecy. If these individuals

---

[14] Unofficial translation: "Interception of communications or information data. The judge will order the interception of communications or computer data based on the request of the prosecutor if there are relevant signs for the purposes of the investigation . . . ."

[15] Unofficial translation: "The interception of any communication protected by the right to maintain professional and religious secrecy is prohibited. The procedural actions that violate this warranty lack evidence effectiveness, without prejudice of the respective sanctions."

[16] Art. 415 of the COIP indicates that the private exercise of criminal action is available only in the following offenses: slander, usurpation (taking by force), rape and injuries that generate disability or illness of up to 30 days, except for cases of violence against women or members of the household; in these cases, only the affected person is legally able to lodge a complaint.

[17] Unofficial translation.

[18] Unofficial translation: "Testimony from third parties. Third-party testimony is governed by the following rules: . . . Statements by persons holding a secret by virtue of their profession, trade or function will not be received if these are related to the matter of secrecy. In case they have been summoned, they shall appear to explain the reason from which the obligation arises and refrain from stating but only in regards to the secret or the confidential source."

have been summoned by the court to testify, they have the obligation to appear to explain the reason for which the obligation to refrain from disclosing information arises, maintaining discretion in regards to the secrecy or the confidentiality of the source. Likewise, for other matters, the general rule found in Article 175(2)[19] of the Organic Code of General Process[20] (hereinafter "COGEP") also provides that the declarant may refuse to answer any questions that violate the person's duty to keep information secret or confidential by reason of their status or trade, employment, profession, art or other express provision of the law.

Even the Organic Code of the Judicial Function[21] (hereinafter "COFJ") indicates that it is the duty of all lawyers to represent their clients subject to the principles of loyalty, honesty, truthfulness and good faith.[22]

3.   The right to privacy in Ecuador is also protected by international instruments, such as the International Covenant on Civil and Political Rights,[23] the Universal Declaration of Human Rights[24] and the American Convention on Human Rights.[25] It should also be noted that judges' obligation of professional secrecy in Ecuador is regulated by the Statute of the Libero-American Judge.[26]

Furthermore, the COIP states that a lawyer who in court reveals the secrets of a client to the other party or, after defending a party and becoming aware of the means of defense, leaves and defends the other party in interrelated proceedings, shall be sanctioned with custodial sentence of one to three years.[27]

Provisions have also been developed in different areas other than criminal responsibility. Thus, the COFJ prohibits lawyers from revealing secrets, documents or instructions from their clients as well as defending one party after having defended the other in related processes.[28] Therefore, any secret document or instruction provided by a client to the lawyer is protected. In the event that a lawyer violates these provisions, depending on the severity of the case, the attorney may be fined up to three minimum wages[29] or may be suspended from professional practice,[30] without prejudice of the corresponding criminal or civil liability.

---

[19] Unofficial translation: "Duty of the declarant. The declarant shall answer the asked questions. The judge may order the declarant to respond to what has been requested. The declarant can refuse to answer any questions that: ... Violate the duty to keep confidentiality or secrecy by reason of their status or trade, employment, profession, art or by express provision of the law."

[20] Published in Official Gazette Supplement 506, May 22, 2015.

[21] Published in Official Gazette Supplement 554 of March 9, 2009.   [22] *See* Art. 330(2), COFJ.

[23] *See* Art. 17(1)(2), International Covenant on Civil and Political Rights.

[24] *See* Art. 18, Universal Declaration of Human Rights.

[25] *See* Art. 11(1)(2)(3), American Convention on Human Rights.

[26] Adopted at the VI Summit by the president of the National Court of Justice in May 2001.

[27] *See* Art. 269, COIP.   [28] *See* Art. 335(1)(4), COFJ.

[29] The minimum wage for 2016 is USD $366.   [30] *See* Section 4(A)(a) in this chapter.

4.   In relation to the foregoing, it is worth noting that, under Article 76(4)[31] of the Constitution, any evidence or act performed in violation of professional secrecy or attorney-client privilege will not have validity and will lack evidentiary effect within any process. Even the Tax Code provides that in administrative procedures of this matter the competent authority cannot request information from professionals who have the right to invoke professional secrecy.[32]

B Scope

5.   The obligation of professional secrecy or client-attorney privilege usually covers all the secrets and confidences that lawyers, directly or indirectly, know by virtue of their professional practice.[33] The Constitutional Court has ruled on the context and scope of professional secrecy, even providing some specific examples – within the medical field – about what the protection of secrets against damaging disclosure means:

> In the case, the respondents alleged the inadmissibility of the habeas data because they cannot provide the requested information as they would be forced to engage in the conduct described in Article 284 of the Criminal Code, given the profession of medics or paramedics they practice they are repositories of professional secrecy and if they reveal it, even if declaring in trial, they could be penalized or punished with imprisonment. Well then, let us analyze what the protection of secrets against damaging disclosure means, and let us look to professional secrecy as such information that cannot be disclosed because it lies on knowledge related to the profession or business that can be leveraged by unfair competition, which does not constitute a good with intrinsic value, or the professional secrecy related to the duty of members of certain professions such as medics to not disclose to others facts that they have known under the exercise of their profession, as it would be the case of a congenital disease, injury, or the fact that a person suffers from HIV, information that shall be kept secret, and that in such cases does affect the privacy of individuals, their honor and reputation.[34]

Also, in accordance with the above statement, the same court in a similar case ruled on an important point by noting that the obligation of professional secrecy extends to protect those secrets that the medic knows directly or indirectly from the medic's practice, in the following terms: "professional secrecy is the ethical obligation of the medic to not disclose or enable others

---

[31] Unofficial translation: "In any process in which rights and duties of any type are determined, the right to due process shall be ensured, which includes the following basic guarantees: ...
Evidence obtained or acted in violation of the Constitution or the law will not be valid and will lack evidential effectiveness."

[32] *See* Art. 92, Tax Code.   [33] *See* Art. 13, Code of Ethics.

[34] Unofficial translation, Constitutional Court ruling of April 15, 2003, in case no. 046-2002-HD, published in Official Gazette Supplement 66 of April 22, 2003.

to know about the information obtained directly or indirectly during professional practice concerning the health and life of the patient."[35]

In relation to the previous statement, the Constitution provides that any exchange of communication between two or more people by any means is protected by the secrecy of communications,[36] meaning that everything communicated is secret. Therefore, all information that clients communicate to their lawyers shall be considered secret.

6.   Nevertheless, in criminal matters, such as in the Constitutional Court case discussed earlier in this section, the criminal law sanctions the damaging disclosure of secrets. Therefore, even though the lawyer has an obligation to keep all information that the client has provided confidential, the lawyer will be criminally responsible (with a custodial sentence of six months to one year) only in the event that the lawyer reveals a secret that may cause damage to another person. This in accordance with Article 179 of the COIP mentioned previously.

By virtue of what is stated in the previous paragraph, it is the lawyer who has to determine whether the disclosure of the information provided by the client could cause damage to the client or to a third party. The lawyer will not be criminally liable if the lawyer reveals information provided by the client that does not cause damage to the client or to a third party. In some other countries, damaging or deleterious information about the client that is received by the client's attorney from a third party is not considered to be privileged, confidential information. In contrast, in Ecuador, such damaging or deleterious information about the client that is received by the client's attorney from a third party is still considered to be a "professional secret" that attorneys and other professionals must not divulge.

7.   Similarly, for purposes of implementation and interpretation of the constitutional provisions regarding correspondence, it is worth citing the decision by the temporary judge in charge of the First Court of Childhood and Adolescence of Cuenca. In the trial of the National Council for Childhood and Adolescence against Mrs. Evelyn Vega Lisseth Mora, the judge ruled the following:

> Within the constitutional doctrine, the right to the inviolability of correspondence seeks protection from the danger of attacks against other rights in the same fundamental range. We are discussing the protection of freedom, both freedom to action and freedom to think and its extrinsic manifestations, which have two or more people communicating in this way in all its forms, namely the political, religious, sexual thoughts, belief, etc. Others believe that protects privacy, since in correspondence

---

[35] Unofficial translation, Constitutional Court ruling of June 23, 2008, in case no. 0018-2008-HD, published in Official Gazette Supplement 63 of July 11, 2008.

[36] *See* Art. 66(21), Constitution.

innermost feelings are printed, the stories of private life, family, secrets, the same if revealed could cause attacks on the honor and good name as well as great social upheavals for the individual who expressed them and even to the recipient. This right not only protects one person, but two or more people at one time, as due to the dynamics of letters and e-mail, it protects the sender and the recipient, in the exercise of their freedom or in the reservation of their privacy, which is why this right also protects other rights such as non-discrimination, economic rights, honor, image, etc. Therefore, the protected principle involves not only one right from my point of view, such as freedom or privacy only; but rather, it is a principle of intermediate protection because of the potential danger that could be faced in the violation of other rights that may be affected in the same mail content. This is because as we see, the contents are indeterminate for their protection; that is, no matter what it says or shows (as is in written language, images, sounds) meaning the information in a general sense for it to be inviolable or secret, but it is only protected against the danger that generates its violation or disclosure.[37]

Regarding the preceding paragraph, without neglecting the fact that everything communicated by whatever means is secret, it is clear that the Constitution guards and protects all correspondence without exception and regardless of its content because of the danger that could be caused by its violation or disclosure. This means that all information that lawyers know through correspondence is also secret; therefore, all the information that clients send to their lawyers through correspondence is also protected.

Nevertheless, the criminal law sanctions only the damaging disclosure of the correspondence. Therefore, even though the lawyer is obliged to maintain secrecy of all information that is known to the lawyer through correspondence, the lawyer will be criminally liable only in the event that the lawyer violates or discloses correspondence that causes damage to the client or to another person.

Notwithstanding the above, the COIP prescribes that people who, for their own benefit or on behalf of a third party, reveal proprietary information contained in archives, files, databases or the like, through or directed to an electronic system, computer, telematics or telecommunications, and willfully and intentionally violate the secrecy, intimacy and the privacy of individuals, shall be sanctioned with a custodial sentence of one to three years. If this behavior is committed by a public servant, employees of banking or popular economic institutions that perform financial intermediation, or contractors,

---

[37] Unofficial translation. Judicial Decision no 0318-2012 of Nov. 7, 2011, issued by the Temporary Judge in charge of the First Court of Childhood and Adolescence Cuenca City, in the case no. 0253-2012 *National Council for Childhood and Adolescence v. Lisseth Evelyn Vega Mora*. This judgment subsequently became known to the Court of the Specialized Chamber of Family, Children and Adolescents of the National Court, whose ruling was published in the Judicial Gazette. CXIII year. Series XVIII, no 13. P. 5432. (Quito, October 9, 2012).

these workers shall be sanctioned with a custodial sentence of three to five years.[38]

The notion that only damaging disclosures can be penalized relates to the "harmfulness principle" enshrined in the Constitution.[39] Only the disclosure by the lawyer of a secret whose disclosure could cause damage to another person and that affects the rights of another person can be criminally punished.

C Persons Subject to the Obligation of Professional Secrecy

8. One of the principles of the enforcement of rights is provided by Article 10(9) of the Constitution, which reads as follows: "The highest duty of the State is to respect and to enforce the rights guaranteed in the Constitution ...."[40] As mentioned previously, the Constitution guarantees confidentiality.[41] It is because of this that every professional has a duty to fulfill the obligation of professional secrecy at all times and to invoke the right to confidentiality when called to testify in court. Consequently, any person (including any government official) has the obligation to respect professional secrecy. Accordingly, the Constitutional Court has ruled that the protection of "the rights to keep ... reserve and professional secrecy ... is consistent with one of the highest duties of the State, namely to ensure the effective enjoyment of constitutional rights."[42]

    To extend the recognition that constitutional judges have granted to professional secrecy, it is worth noting that the Constitutional Court stressed that, in certain cases, confidentiality shall be regarded as a higher value that should prevail over other rights. This court took action, stating:

    > [T]he right to information coexists with other rights and duties that limit it such as the right to personal and family privacy and the reserve of professional secrecy that emerges from the performance of certain activities or businesses. This limitation also affects the guarantee mechanism, i.e. habeas data, because the legislator has considered higher values that prevail over the right to information, which if not respected would turn the exercise of this right into a clear case of abuse.[43]

D Exceptions to and Possible Exemptions from the Obligation of Professional Secrecy

9. The Ecuadorian legal system has established certain exceptions to and exemptions from the obligation of professional secrecy by the lawyer. However, such exceptions and exemptions apply to the lawyer as long as the constitutional

---

[38] *See* Art. 229, COIP. [39] *See* Arts. 66(5), 66(29)(d), Constitution.

[40] Unofficial translation. [41] *See* Art. 20, Constitution.

[42] Unofficial translation, Resolution of the Constitutional Court (Sept. 17, 2014), in case no. 003-14-SIN-CC, published in Official Gazette Supplement 346 (Oct. 2, 2014).

[43] Unofficial translation, Resolution of the Constitutional Court (April 15, 2003), in case no. 0001-2003-HD, published in Official Gazette Supplement 66 (April 22, 2003).

right to the defense of people – the same that is duly enshrined in Article 76(7)[44] of the Constitution – is not breached. In other words, under no circumstances can the lawyer be exempted from professional secrecy when, by omitting to comply with such an obligation, the client or the person who has requested the lawyer's services is left deprived of the right to defend oneself.

a Exceptions

10.   There are certain exceptions to the obligation of professional secrecy for professionals, generally, and for lawyers, specifically, as detailed below.

The Pichincha Bar Association's Court of Honor Rules of Procedure[45] states that lawyers are exempt from professional secrecy (i) when the client so authorizes it, (ii) in the case of the client's own defense, and (iii) in the case of the defense of the lawyer in an action brought against the lawyer by one of the lawyer's clients.[46]

Within this context, it is important to recall that the provision of the COIP that refers to the patterns of behavior indicates that not preventing an event when there exists a legal obligation to prevent it is equivalent to causing it.[47] In relation to this, Article 422 prescribes a duty to report only to those people who are forced to do so by express mandate of this code (as follows), and especially by order of the COIP: (i) public servants who, in the exercise of their duties, become aware of the commission of an offense against public administration efficiency; (ii) health professionals in public or private establishments who know of the commission of an alleged offense;[48] and (iii) the directors, teachers or other persons responsible for educational institutions, for alleged crimes committed in these centers.

Within the Ecuadorian judicial system there is no law that forces private attorneys to report on their clients about a crime that the client might have committed. This obligation to report is exclusively applicable to all public servants, under the obligation contained in Article 277 of the COIP.[49]

---

[44] Unofficial translation: "In all proceedings in which rights and obligations of whatever kind are determined, the right to due process shall be assured, which includes the following basic guarantees: . . . The right of persons to a defense that shall include the following guarantees: (a) No one may be deprived of the right to a defense in any stage or point in the proceeding."

[45] Available at: www.colabpi.pro.ec/index.php/tribunal-de-honor/reglamento-del-tribunal-de-honor.

[46] See Art. 4(a), Pichincha Bar Association's Court of Honor Rules of Procedure.

[47] See Art. 23, COIP.

[48] Unofficial translation. This in accordance with the provision of Art. 276 of the COIP: "Failure to denounce by a health professional. The professional or the medical assistant or other health-related branches that receive a person with signs of having suffered a serious violation of human rights, sexual and reproductive integrity or violent death and not denounces the fact shall be punished with custodial sentence of two to six months."

[49] Unofficial translation: "Failure to denounce. The person that serving as a public official on the basis of his or her position, that knows of any fact that could constitute an infraction and does not immediately denounces to the authority, shall be punished with custodial sentence of fifteen to thirty days."

The COIP provides that a person will be criminally responsible if the person threatens or injures, without just cause, a legal right protected by the COIP.[50]

b Exemptions

11.   Certain exemptions to the obligation of professional secrecy for lawyers have also been established.

Although the COFJ provides that lawyers must refrain from promoting public dissemination of confidential unresolved matters involved in the judicial process,[51] the Constitutional Court carved out exemptions for lawyers and judges as to making public statements. The court sustained that, in certain cases and in the exercise of the right to freedom of speech, it may become essential to both lawyers and judges to speak and report on matters of general interest. The court ruled:

> In regard to the subsequent imposition of responsibility, it should be pointed out that Ecuadorian legislation establishes prohibitions for lawyers and judges in relation to the matter they know. Thus, Article 10 of the Organic Law of the Judicial Function establishes: "Judges shall not: 1. Express their opinion or anticipate it in a case they are judging or that should be judged." Of course, the fact that judges or magistrates express their opinion or anticipate criterion concerning cases brought to their knowledge is malfeasance in office, and therefore subject to judicial responsibility. That rule is sufficient to establish the responsibility of judges; since it stresses that by prohibiting their freedom of expression in any criminal case would mean establishing a system of prior censorship that does not do merit to justice since it would establish in advance that their statements would always be cause for malfeasance in office, which is not necessarily true, and in some cases, on the other hand, it becomes indispensable in order to inform on matters of general interest; thereby, without violating the rights of others or promoting social imbalance. To accept otherwise would be tantamount to saying that because lawyers are not permitted to reveal the secrets of their clients they cannot make public statements since to do so would violate such secrecy. It may well be true, and in that case the legal professional will be subject to responsibilities, but it may be concerned with issuing public information of general interest, and in that case the right to freedom of speech takes full effect in a democratic state.[52]

E Law Firms

12.   Article 334 of the COFJ states:

> The lawyers that integrate collective law firms could substitute them interchangeably in the sponsorship of matters in their charge and they represent each other before the courts and corresponding tribunals. The creation of a collective law firm will be brought to the Judicial

---

[50] *See* Art. 29, COIP.   [51] *See* Art. 330(6), COFJ.

[52] Unofficial translation, Constitutional Court ruling of June 8, 2004, in case no. 001-2004 -DI, published in Official Gazette 374 of July 9, 2004.

Council, following the list of the members, with an indication of the date of joining the Forum and the respective registration number. The Judicial Council, through the Regional Offices, shall inform the courts and tribunals of the list of the law firm members. The omission of the duty of communication referred to by this rule shall prevent associated lawyers in collective law firms from practicing the profession under this modality. Lawyers from a collective law firm, who have either sponsored a cause, shall be jointly liable on conviction in procedural costs.[53]

In view of this article, it is generally accepted that there are no restrictions on the disclosure of the client's information among lawyers from the same law firm, provided that the client has hired the law firm.

The COIP establishes that legal persons can be subject to criminal liability,[54] indicating that legal persons, or in this case law firms, are criminally liable for the crimes committed on behalf of the law firm or its associates, by action or omission of: (i) those who exercise ownership or control; (ii) its governing or management bodies; (iii) authorized representatives; (iv) agents; (v) legal or conventional representatives; (vi) operators; (vii) factors; (viii) delegates; (ix) third parties who, contractually or not, interfere in management activity; (x) top executives or those who perform activities of management, discretion and supervision; and (xi) overall, those acting under orders or instructions of the said natural persons. The same article states that the criminal liability of the legal person is independent of the criminal liability of the natural persons who, through their actions or omissions, commit the offense. In accordance, Article 50 of the COIP provides:

> Concurrence of criminal responsibility. Criminal responsibility of legal persons is not extinguished or modified if there are concurrent responsibilities with natural persons in the realization of the facts as well as circumstances that affect or aggravate the responsibility or because such people have died or evaded the action of justice; because the criminal responsibility of the natural persons is extinguished, or dismissal is issued. The responsibility of legal persons is not extinguished when these have been merged, transformed, split, dissolved, liquidated or applied any other mode of modification established by the law.[55]

Therefore, in case of violation of the obligation of professional secrecy of lawyers and staff who make up a law firm, they may be punished individually or in conjunction with the law firm itself; applicable penalties for legal persons are set out in Article 71[56] of COIP.

---

[53] Unofficial translation.   [54] *See*, Art. 49, COIP.   [55] Unofficial translation.

[56] Unofficial translation: "Penalties for legal persons. Specific penalties that apply to legal persons are:
  1. Fine.
  2. Criminal forfeiture. The existing acts and contracts relating to the property subject to criminal forfeiture cease by full right, without prejudice to the rights of bona fide third parties, which are recognized, settled and paid as soon as possible, who will assert their

F Legal Assistants and Staff

13. The Constitutional Court in Resolution no. 0018-2008-HD on June 23, 2008, cited in Section I.B of this chapter, ruled that the principle of professional secrecy applies not only to medics but to all those who have access to "the patient's data at the various stages of treatment, that is to say the paramedical and auxiliary personnel or nursing or medicine students that perform the corresponding practices." By comparison, one can assume that professional secrecy not only applies to the lawyers of a law firm but also to the legal assistants or paralegals, administrative personnel, students who are doing their practices and, in general, all of the staff who have access to the client's information.

G External Service Providers

14. It may be that external service providers are neither lawyers nor professionals (people without professional degrees). However, under Article 179 the COIP, external service providers must also maintain the confidentiality of the information that they know by virtue of their status or trade, employment, profession or art, and whose disclosure could cause damage to another person.

As mentioned previously, under Article 4(a) of the Pichincha Bar Association's Court of Honor Rules of Procedure, a lawyer does not commit any offense (i) when the client authorizes the disclosure of information, (ii) when preparing the client's defense, and (iii) when acting in defense of the lawyer in an action brought against the lawyer by one of the lawyer's clients. If the lawyer does not seek the client's authorization for the disclosure, the lawyer must consider the client's interests so that the client does not suffer damages.

H Multidisciplinary Associations

15. In Ecuador, there is no prohibition for lawyers to form a professional association in conjunction with other professionals who are not lawyers.

> rights under the same judge of the criminal case. Declared assets of illicit origin are not eligible for protection of any property regime.
> 3. Temporal or permanent closure of the establishments, in the place in which the offense was committed, according to the severity of the infringement or the damage caused.
> 4. Conduct activities to benefit the community subject to monitoring and judicial review.
> 5. Comprehensive remediation of environmental damages.
> 6. Dissolution of the legal person, ordered by the judge, in the country in case of foreign legal entities and liquidation of its assets as provided by the law, in charge of the respective control body. In this case, there is no room for any form of rehiring or reactivation of the legal person.
> 7. Temporary or permanent ban to contract with the State, according to the severity of the infringement.

Under Article 179 of the COIP, all members of multidisciplinary associations are required to maintain confidentiality of the information they know by virtue of their status or trade, occupation, profession or art, and whose disclosure could cause damage to another person.

I In-House Counsel

16. All the provisions outlined in this chapter apply equally to in-house counsel.

However, there are specific cases provided by the law in which the in-house lawyer (as well as any other citizen) is required by law to denounce, for example (i) the case provided for in Article 72[57] of the Code of Childhood and Adolescence, (ii) the case provided for in Article 2[58] of the Law to Repress Money Laundering, or (iii) the case provided for in Article 356[59] of the Organic Monetary and Financial Code,[60] which states that the officials of the entities of the national financial system are required to report to the Prosecutor General's Office in the event that they become aware of evidence regarding the commission of a crime related to financial activities. The in-house lawyer must report to the authorities in these cases only if the lawyer was not hired by the company to prepare the defense in such cases. Otherwise, the lawyer must maintain professional secrecy (under no circumstances can the lawyer leave the client or the person who has requested the lawyer's services deprived of the right to defense).

2 History of the Obligation of Professional Secrecy in Ecuador

17. It is in Ecuador's 19th[61] Constitution of 1998[62] that the first constitutional reference was made to professional secrecy. Article 81 of this Constitution established: "The State ... ensures the conscience clause and the right to professional secrecy of the journalists and social communicators or of those who issue formal opinions as collaborators of the media."[63]

However, professional secrecy in Ecuador is not a new concept. The Criminal Code of 1837[64] (the first Criminal Code of Ecuador), in its Article 509 provided:

> Shall also be punished as guilty of public or private injury, depending on the circumstances, those who outside of the cases required by law,

---

[57] See Section 5(b) of this chapter.   [58] See Section 5(a) of this chapter.

[59] Unofficial translation: "Duty to Report. When the control bodies, the shareholders, administrators or the officials of the national financial system entities become aware of evidence of the commission of a crime related to the activities of financial institutions, they shall denounce immediately to the Prosecutor General's Office."

[60] Published in Official Gazette Supplement 332 of Sept. 12, 2014.

[61] Throughout history, Ecuador has had 20 constitutions; the first was created in the city of Riobamba on September 23, 1830.

[62] Published in the Official Gazette 1 of Aug. 11, 1998.   [63] Unofficial translation.

[64] Published in Original Gazette of April 14, 1837.

discover or reveal the secret that has been entrusted to them by someone else, as long as the discovery or revelation of the secret follows the person who trusted it with any damage in its honor, fame, character or reputation. FIRST. Shall be considered as violators of the secret, and comprised within the provision of this article, those who having removed, destroyed or illegally opened a sealed letter, addressed to another person, publish its content to the detriment of another.[65]

Related to this, Article 363 of the Criminal Code of 1837 stated:

The lawyer that in trial discloses the secrets of the client to the opposing party, after having undertaken to defend one party and finding out its claims and means of defense, then leaves and defends the other party, or otherwise knowingly damages the client to favor the opposing party, or to obtain a personal benefit, is also treacherous, infamous for the same offense and sentenced to disqualification for two to ten years, without prejudice of the corresponding compensation.[66]

Accordingly, Article 364 of the Criminal Code of 1837 also stated:

Any public, civil, ecclesiastical or military official who knowingly and without lawful order of the competent superior, discovers or reveals any writing of those who are entrusted, by reason of their destiny, and that according to the law should be kept in reserve or negotiates either way any document that they are responsible that should be kept in reserve, will lose employment or position, and shall suffer an imprisonment of two to ten years. FIRST. The provision of this article shall be understood without prejudice to the single article of the first title hereof, against those who violate secrets that jeopardize the security of the State.[67]

Also within the present context it is relevant to note that Article 104 of the Criminal Code of 1837 established the death penalty for those who revealed secrets that threaten the security of the state:

Whoever by emissaries or by correspondence, or in any other manner, informs the enemies of Ecuador, plans, instructions, knowledge, or news of the political and military situation of the Republic, or facilitate them, or procures any resources and means to make war or to occupy the Ecuadorian territory, or to give them any city, town, parade ground, strength, military post, arsenal, warehouse, park, forest, or munitions factories, is also a traitor, infamous and guilty of the death penalty.[68]

In addition, in judicial matters, the Organic Law of the Judicial Function of 1974[69] stated: "It is forbidden for jurisprudence doctors and lawyers to: 1. Reveal the secret, documents or instructions of the clients."[70]

---

[65] Unofficial translation. [66] Unofficial translation. [67] Unofficial translation.
[68] Unofficial translation. [69] Published in Official Gazette 636 of Sept. 11, 1974.
[70] Unofficial translation.

3 Supervision

A Bar Associations

18.   Lawyers who are voluntarily affiliated with a bar association are additionally covered by the Law of the Ecuadorian Bar Association, which states that every lawyer who is affiliated with a bar association is obliged to contribute to the improvement of the legal profession and to practice in accordance with the rules of professional ethics.[71]

Affiliated lawyers are also covered by the Code of Professional Ethics[72] of Avellán Ferrés, which states that professional secrecy is a duty and a right of lawyers in Ecuador. The same code provides that professional secrecy must be considered a duty toward the client – assuming it as a duty that will last over time, even after the lawyer has ceased providing services to the client – and as a right toward the judges or other authorities when lawyers are called to testify, as lawyers must refuse to answer questions that would require them to violate professional secrecy.[73] Indeed, this code also provides that lawyers should not even intervene in matters that may lead them to reveal the secrets known under the professional practice.[74]

B The Courts

19.   The civil courts have jurisdiction to process a lawsuit for civil liability brought by the client against a lawyer. Criminal courts also have jurisdiction to process a lawsuit for criminal liability brought by the client against a lawyer. There is no special process that applies to lawyers only.

4 Sanctions

A Procedures and Sanctions

a Disciplinary Proceedings and Sanctions

20.   If a lawyer who is voluntarily affiliated with a bar association violates professional secrecy,[75] without prejudice of the corresponding civil and/or criminal liability, the lawyer could also be judged by the competent Court of Honor.[76]

---

[71] *See* Art. 32(a), Law of the Ecuadorian Bar Association.

[72] Available at: www.colabpi.pro.ec/index.php/profesional-del-derecho/codigo-de-etica-profesional.

[73] *See* Art. 12, Code of Professional Ethics.   [74] *See* ibid., Art. 13.

[75] Unofficial translation, Law of the Ecuadorian Bar Association: "Art. 23. The Court of Honor shall hear and resolve the following matters relating to members of the Bar: . . . f) Violation of professional secrecy . . .."

[76] There is a Court of Honor in each Bar Association consisting of five affiliated lawyers with at least 10 years of professional practice, who are responsible for hearing and resolving the matters concerning the violation of professional secrecy. This is in accordance with Art. 22 of the Law of the Ecuadorian Bar Association.

The affected client has the power to report a violation of professional secrecy to the bar association to which the lawyer is affiliated.[77] The Court may sanction the affiliated lawyer with (i) a written warning, (ii) a monetary fine, (iii) censorship of the lawyer's professional conduct, or (iv) temporary suspension in the enjoyment of the rights of membership. In the event that the Court of Honor considers that the wrongdoing of the lawyer should be sanctioned with a suspension of professional practice, the Court must notify the respective Regional Office of the NJC. This office will analyze the case and determine the sanction.

However, affiliated or non-affiliated lawyers can be sanctioned *ex officio*, by a complaint brought[78] directly by the competent Regional Offices of the NJC for violating professional secrecy, depending on the severity of the case, (i) with a fine of up to three minimum wages, and if the lawyer defaults on the fine imposed during a period of three months, the lawyer will be suspended from the Lawyers' Forum and will remain suspended until the payment is made,[79] or (ii) with a suspension from professional practice of one month to six months.[80]

The decisions of the Regional Offices can be appealed to the Plenum of the Judicial Council; the decision of this Plenum cannot be appealed.[81]

b Criminal Procedures and Sanctions

21. The violation of professional secrecy is sanctioned under the aforementioned Article 179 of the COIP (six months to one year of a custodial sentence) plus a fine of three to four minimum wages.[82]

The Court of Criminal Guarantees has jurisdiction over these matters.[83] The decision of this court can be appealed to the competent Provincial Court.[84] The decision of the respective Provincial Court can be appealed to the National Court of Justice for violation of the law (for express contravention of the text of the law, for a misapplication of the law or for a misinterpretation of the law).[85]

Under Article 58[86] of the Organic Law for Jurisdictional Guarantees and Constitutional Control ("LOGJCC"), the decision of the National Court of Justice can be subject to an extraordinary protection action before the Constitutional Court for violation of a constitutional right or for violation of due process.

---

[77] Unofficial translation, Law of the Ecuadorian Bar Association: "Art. 27. The Court of Honor will act only on the basis of a written and recognized complaint, to be presented before the bar."
[78] *See* Art. 113, COFJ.   [79] *See* ibid., Art. 336.   [80] *See* ibid., Art. 337.
[81] *See* ibid., Art. 119.   [82] *See* Art. 70, COIP.   [83] *See* ibid., Art. 621.
[84] *See* ibid., Art. 653.   [85] *See* ibid., Art. 656.
[86] Unofficial translation: "Purpose. The extraordinary protection action is to protect the constitutional rights and due process in sentences, final judgments, resolutions with force of a sentence, which have violated by action or omission rights guaranteed under the Constitution."

c Damages and Civil Procedures

22.   Article 2214 of the Ecuadorian Civil Code[87] states: "Who has committed an offence or a quasi-offence that has inflicted damage to another is obligated to the compensation; without prejudice to the penalty imposed by laws for the offence or quasi-offence."[88] Therefore, the client is empowered to exercise the right to seek damages against the lawyer for violation of professional secrecy.

  The Civil Judicial Unit has jurisdiction over these cases. The decision of the Civil Judicial Unit can be appealed to the competent Provincial Court. The decision of the respective Provincial Court[89] can be appealed to the National Court of Justice on legal grounds only.[90]

  Similarly, in accordance with Article 58 of the LOGJCC mentioned in the preceding section, the decision of the National Court of Justice can be subject to an extraordinary protection action before the Constitutional Court for violation of a constitutional right or for violation of due process.

B Relationship between Criminal and Disciplinary Sanctions

23.   Criminal sanctions and disciplinary sanctions are independent of each other; the lawyer who violates professional secrecy can be criminally, civilly and/or administratively liable. In this regard, Article 76 of the Constitution states:

> In any process in which rights and obligations of any order are determined, the right to due process will be ensured, which includes the following basic guarantees: ... 7. The right of persons to defense include the following guarantees: (i) No one may be tried more than once for the same cause and matter. The cases decided by the indigenous jurisdiction shall be considered for this purpose.[91]

  The imposition of criminal, civil and administrative sanctions altogether for the same cause does not violate the general principle of *ne bis in idem* as the sanctions are imposed for the breach of different laws and matters.

5 Obligation to Provide Information to Authorities

A Money Laundering

24.   The Law to Repress Money Laundering[92] lists the entities that have a strict obligation to report to the Financial Analysis Unit ("UAF") concerning unusual and unjustified operations or transactions:[93] institutions of the financial and insurance system, stock exchanges and brokerage houses; fund and trusts managers; cooperatives, foundations and nongovernmental organizations;

---

[87] Published in Official Gazette Supplement 46 of June 24, 2005.   [88] Unofficial translation.
[89] *See* Art. 256, COGEP.   [90] *See* ibid., Art. 266.   [91] Unofficial translation.
[92] Published in Official Gazette 127 of Oct. 18, 2005.
[93] *See* enumerated article that follows Art. 3, Law to Repress Money Laundering.

natural and legal persons engaged in usual commercialization of vehicles, boats, ships and aircrafts; companies engaged in the service of national or international transfer of money or valuables, national and international transport of parcels, mail, including its operators, agents and agencies; travel agencies and tour operators; natural and legal persons engaged in usual investment and real estate brokerage and construction; pawnshops; jewelry, precious metals and stones negotiators; dealers of antiques and works of art; and public notaries.[94] In addition, the same article states that the UAF can request additional information from other natural or legal persons.

Furthermore, Article 2 of the Law to Repress Money Laundering states that, in addition to the abovementioned entities required to report, any person who knows facts related to unusual and unjustified operations or transactions must report them to the UAF. The same article states that unusual and unjustified economic operations or transactions are understood to be "economic movements, performed by natural or legal persons that do not correspond to the profile they have remained in the reporting entity and that cannot be sustained."[95]

Lawyers are not obliged to report to the UAF about unusual and unjustified operations or transactions. Also, in accordance with the preceding considerations, if a lawyer is hired to prepare the defense in a case in which the client has engaged in money laundering, the lawyer must keep the information confidential. Otherwise, it would mean a breach of professional secrecy, and the lawyer could be subject to civil and/or criminal liability.

B Protection from Mistreatment, Abuse, Sexual Exploitation, Trafficking and Loss of Children and Adolescents

25. Article 72 of the Code of Childhood and Adolescence[96] looks after the interests of children and adolescents, as follows:

> Persons obliged to denounce. The persons who due to their profession or trade become aware of a fact that presents characteristics of sexual abuse, mistreatment or exploitation, trafficking or loss which a child or teen has been victim of, shall denounce within twenty-four hours of such knowledge to any of the prosecutors, judicial or administrative competent authority, including the Ombudsman, as a guarantor of fundamental rights entity.[97]

---

[94] Unofficial translation. These people or entities can be sanctioned according to Art. 319 of the COIP: "Failure to control money laundering. A person who, being a worker of one of the entities required to denounce to the competent body and being in charge of the functions of prevention, detection and control of money laundering fails to comply with its obligations prescribed by law, shall be punished with custodial sentence of six months to a year."

[95] Unofficial translation.   [96] Published in the Official Gazette 737 on Jan. 3, 2003.

[97] Unofficial translation.

The requirement contained in the Article 72 does not apply to the lawyer who has been hired to prepare the defense of a person in such case. As it has been stressed, in Ecuador, under no circumstances can a person be left deprived of the fundamental[98] right to defense.

6 Treatment of Lawyers' Documents and Correspondence in the Context of Judicial or Police Investigations

26.   As mentioned previously, the COIP concerning the interception of communications or computer data indicates that the interception of any communication covered by professional secrecy or by the attorney-client privilege is prohibited. As such, any action in judicial or police investigations that violates the attorney-client privilege will be inadmissible at trial.[99]

7 Search of a Lawyer's Office

27.   Prior to a judicial order, a lawyer's office can be searched, and the items related to an offense can be seized.[100] However, no judge has the power to order a search of information that is protected by professional secrecy. Any information obtained from a search that violates the attorney-client privilege will be inadmissible at trial.

8 Interception of Telephone Conversations with a Lawyer

28.   Upon a request from the prosecutor, the judge can order the interception of telephone conversations, only if it is shown to be relevant for the purposes of the investigation. However, no judge has the power to order the interception of conversations that are protected by professional secrecy.

Thus, any information obtained from the interception of telephone conversations with a lawyer that violates the attorney-client privilege will be inadmissible at trial.

9 The Lawyer as Witness

29.   An attorney may be called to testify in court as a witness. However, as previously noted, no authority can force a lawyer to testify about what is protected by professional secrecy. The attorney who is duly called to testify has an obligation to appear before the court and explain the reason from which the obligation to refrain from testifying arises. The lawyer must not answer

---

[98] Unofficial translation. *See* Art. 424, Constitution: "The Constitution is the supreme norm and prevails over any other of the legal system . . .."
[99] *See* Art. 476(5), COIP.   [100] *See* ibid., Art. 478(1)(2).

questions that would require the lawyer to violate professional secrecy, and the court must respect the lawyer's right to invoke professional secrecy.

The lawyer can be subject to criminal and/or administrative sanctions and the client can sue for damages if the lawyer discloses privileged information before the court.

10 The Lawyer and the Press

30. As discussed in Section 1.D of this chapter and as stated in the Resolution of June 8, 2004, in Case no. 001-2004-DI of the Constitutional Court, it may well be the case that it becomes necessary for a lawyer or judge to speak to the media about issues of general interest where the right to freedom of speech prevails.

11 Powers of the Tax Administration and Other Authorities

31. The Ecuadorian legal system does not confer any competence to the tax authorities or other authorities to require the lawyer to testify about information that is protected by professional secrecy. This in accordance with Article 92 of the Tax Code.

12 National Security Issues

32. The security service of the Ecuadorian state must respect professional secrecy. The Public and State Safety Act[101] and its Regulation[102] do not provide any competence to the security agencies to compel a lawyer to report on issues that are protected by professional secrecy.

The Regulation states that public officials, civilian citizens and active members of the armed forces and the National Police shall be sanctioned in the event that they disclose information considered top secret, secret or reserved, of which the security agencies of the National Secretariat of Intelligence are in charge.[103]

---

[101] Published in Official Gazette Supplement 35 of Sept. 28, 2009.
[102] Published in Official Gazette Supplement 290 of Sept. 30, 2010.
[103] See Art. 29, Regulation of the Public and State Safety Act.

Preliminary Note

1. Often overlooked in El Salvador, the duty of professional secrecy is most likely the single most important source of trust between clients and attorneys. Clients need to trust that their attorneys will not breach this duty to provide them with the information needed for an effective and efficient legal representation. Clearly, a system of guarantees that this duty will be respected by attorneys is needed. This system, to a certain degree, exists in the Salvadoran legal framework, however diffuse and unclear it might be.

    Accordingly, rules that enforce the observance of this duty are the foundation of the trust clients choose to place in their lawyers. However, a lack of comprehensive, cohesive and exhaustive statutes and nonexistent case law effectively obscures the importance of this principle from the knowledge of clients. Questions regarding the basic aspects of the principle arise because of the system's diffuse nature. For example, clients do not generally know where to file complaints when their attorneys breach the attorney-client privilege. The foundation of trust thus is not strong enough. Additionally, the enforcement of such an important principle is not effective. Such a foundation needs to be first supported with knowledge of what is available.

2. This chapter, therefore, aims to achieve three main objectives: define the duty of professional secrecy, establish the scope of the duty and describe the sanctions and proceedings applicable when breaches to it occur. Practical examples of situations where attorneys are required to reveal certain information about their clients are also examined, to better illustrate how attorneys are required to cooperate with public authorities. With this knowledge, clients will be equipped with the essential tools to identify how they are protected, to what they are entitled, what exactly constitutes a breach of professional secrecy and how to defend themselves from it.

    Statutes ranging from the Salvadoran Constitution to the Criminal Code are studied in order to comply with the established objectives of this chapter. As will become evident, the scarce and uncertain rules pertaining to the duty of professional secrecy need to be reinforced to understand its practical effects.

This legal strengthening must be provided by an efficient judicial and administrative system that correctly applies the corresponding applicable rules. Consequently, what follows is a thorough examination of the most relevant applicable rules found in the Salvadoran legal system.

Most importantly, clients must know the answer to the following question: are your matters safe from disclosure in El Salvador? The intricate elements to the complicated answer are the basis of this chapter. Clients and their counsel outside of El Salvador are urged to pay close attention to the applicable rules found in our legal system.

1 Scope of and Limitations on the Duty of Professional Secrecy/ Attorney-Client Privilege

A Statutory Basis and Implications

a Defining Confidential Information

3.
Salvadoran law provides scarce statutory basis for analyzing attorney-client privilege; there is no clear legal definition. Rules pertaining to breaches of confidentiality are found only in the Criminal Code. Thus, before analyzing the legal rules applicable to this principle, it is essential to first define the term *confidential information*. However, it has to be highlighted that it is only possible to construe a working definition of the term based on various statutes and the Constitution.

To begin with, the closest approach to the aforementioned term is found in Article 187 of the Criminal Code, which describes the felony of "disclosure of professional secrets."[1] The term *secrets* is a first step toward approaching a definition for *confidential information*. *Secrets*, as found in the Criminal Code, refers to information regarding a client that becomes known to professionals who act on behalf of their clients as a consequence of engaging in their job or profession.

However, what makes this information secret? What kind of information is it? To answer these questions, Salvadoran constitutional jurisprudence has to be reviewed. The Constitutional Claims Chamber of the Salvadoran Supreme Court has provided enough elements to help determine what is *confidential information*. In this sense, the Chamber has defined the fundamental right to privacy because of the right to freedom, thereby establishing that it rests in the power that people have to keep certain information exclusively to themselves.[2]

---

[1] Art. 187 of the Criminal Code states in Spanish: El que revelare un secreto del que se ha impuesto en razón de su profesión u oficio, será sancionado con prisión de seis meses a dos años e inhabilitación especial de profesión u oficio de uno a dos años.

[2] Final decision rendered by the Constitutional Chamber of the Salvadoran Supreme Court for *Amparo* 118-2002 Sentencia March 2, 2004.

This information is directly related to their own existence, and it may refer to their ideas, values, principles, status and the like – ultimately any information relating to them.[3] People, in accordance with the Chamber, have the right to choose to whom they want to disclose this kind of information.

An additional element of our working definition can be found in the Civil Code, with regard to two important institutions: the *mandato* and contractual obligations. *Mandato* is the civil law equivalent of the legal institution known as power of attorney in common law jurisdictions. Regarding the *mandato*, one of the agent's legal obligations is to protect the interests of principals and to abstain from executing actions contrary to them.[4] Therefore, any information that if disclosed may harm the principal's interests can be considered confidential. Specifically, information regarding the legal status of a client is to be considered confidential, as its disclosure to third parties may negatively affect the client. On the other hand, pertaining to contractual obligations, parties may enter into agreements in which one of them accepts the obligation not to disclose certain information therein described.[5] In this last case, the parties themselves define what is confidential information.

In the end, a working definition for *confidential information* in attorney-client relations can be construed by combining all of the aforementioned elements. This leads to the term being defined as all information regarding the legal status of clients or any information entrusted by a client to the client's attorney, which if revealed could cause damage to the client, or information specifically defined as confidential by the client and expressly prohibited from being disclosed by the client's attorney.

---

[3] Final decision rendered by the Constitutional Chamber of the Salvadoran Supreme Court for Habeas Corpus 135-2005, 32-2007 on May 16, 2008.

[4] Art. 1875 of the Civil Code states in Spanish: El mandato es un contrato en que una persona confía la gestión de uno o más negocios a otra, que se hace cargo de ellos por cuenta y riesgo de la primera.

    Art. 1889 of the Civil Code states in Spanish: El mandatario responde hasta de la culpa leve en el cumplimiento de su encargo. Esta responsabilidad recae más estrictamente sobre el mandatario remunerado.

[5] Art. 1309 of the Civil Code states in Spanish: Contrato es una convención en virtud de la cual una o más personas se obligan para con otra u otras, o recíprocamente, a dar, hacer o no hacer alguna cosa.

    Art. 1316 of the Civil Code states in Spanish: Para que una persona se obligue a otra por un acto o declaración de voluntad es necesario:

    1 Que sea legalmente capaz;

    2 Que consienta en dicho acto o declaración y su consentimiento no adolezca de vicio;

    3 Que recaiga sobre un objeto lícito;

    4 Que tenga una causa lícita.

La capacidad legal de una persona consiste en poderse obligar por sí misma, y sin el ministerio o a autorización de otra.

b Applicable Law

4.   The regulation of the attorney-client privilege is spread throughout the Salvadoran legal system, with rules found in laws ranging from the Criminal Code to the Judiciary's Organic Law and the Civil Code. Thus, three genres of rules apply: criminal, civil and disciplinary.

First, criminal rules define what is legally considered to be a breach of confidentiality, define the scope of the duty to withhold confidential information and establish the penalty for breaching confidentiality. Second, civil rules provide criteria to determine damages arising from a breach of confidentiality, which actions can be deemed to be breaches of confidentiality and the remedies available to affected clients. Third, disciplinary rules establish the foundation for a legal mechanism that allows for professional negligence, arising from breaches of confidentiality, to be punished. A practical consequence of the composition of this system is that a breach of confidentiality can give rise to civil, criminal and professional liability.

Following the particular construction of the abovementioned system, a coherent analysis of the statutory basis will conform to the following structure: (i) a definition of what is the duty to withhold confidential information, (ii) a definition of what constitutes a breach of confidentiality, (iii) the scope of the confidentiality duty and available exceptions, and (iv) remedies and penalties.

c The Rules That Form the Duty of Confidentiality

5.   It is necessary to collect elements from all applicable legal rules to define the content of the duty of confidentiality with which attorneys must comply. As a consequence, criminal, civil and disciplinary rules will all be analyzed.

(i) Criminal Rules

6.   Pursuant to Article 187 of the Criminal Code, professionals who because of the nature of their profession obtain knowledge of confidential information can be sentenced to two years' imprisonment and barred from practicing their profession from one to two years if they reveal this information to third parties. Specifically, the revealing party discloses confidential information without authorization to do so. Commentary to this rule has led to its interpretation as applying only to those professionals who execute actions on behalf of other persons:[6] a definition entirely applicable to attorneys. Having established the prohibited actions, it is evident that the duty of confidentiality is complied with when attorneys simply do not disclose any confidential information regarding their clients.

---

[6] Francisco Moreno Carrasco and Luis Rueda García, *Código Penal Comentado*, Consejo Nacional de la Judicatura, San Salvador.

(ii) Civil Rules

7. From the civil rules applying to attorney-client privilege, it is possible to extract additional elements to construe the content of the duty of confidentiality. First, concerning the *mandato*, an attorney is prohibited from revealing any information that when disclosed could harm a client's interests or negatively affect the client's legal status quo. Second, pertaining to contractual obligations, an attorney does not have to disclose any information the client has forbidden the attorney to reveal. Therefore, civil rules can be classified into legal rules and contractual rules.

(iii) Disciplinary Rules

8. Article 182 of the Salvadoran Constitution[7] establishes the professional responsibilities that attorneys have to comply with, albeit in a very broad manner. In accordance with this provision, attorneys must "comply with their professional obligations," "act diligently" and have "good professional and private conduct" to avoid being suspended from practicing law up to a maximum of five years. The duty of confidentiality can be construed as both "good professional conduct" and as a "professional obligation" of attorneys. Thus, the obligation to uphold it has its main statutory basis in Article 182 of the Constitution, as it is part of an attorney's professional responsibilities. The reason for this is that both the civil rules regarding the *mandato* and the criminal rule extracted from Article 187 of the Criminal Code oblige attorneys not to disclose their clients' confidential information, making it "a professional obligation" that, when breached, is contrary to "good professional conduct." Therefore, the main disciplinary rule regarding attorney-client privilege can be constructed from both Article 182 of the Constitution and Article 51 of the Judiciary's Organic Law[8] in the following sense: attorneys who breach their duty of confidentiality are professionally liable to be suspended from the practice of law from one to five years.

---

[7] Art. 182 of the Salvadoran Constitution states in Spanish: Son atribuciones de la Corte Suprema de Justicia:

12ª: Practicar recibimientos de abogados y autorizarlos para el ejercicio de su profesión; suspenderlos por incumplimiento de sus obligaciones profesionales, por negligencia o ignorancia graves, por mala conducta profesional, o por conducta privada notoriamente inmoral; inhabilitarlos por venalidad, cohecho, fraude, falsedad y otro motivos que establezca la ley y rehabilitarlos por causa legal. En los casos de suspensión e inhabilitación procederá en la forma que la ley establezca, y resolverá con sólo robustez moral de prueba. Las mismas facultades ejercerá respecto de los notarios ....

[8] Art. 51 of the Judiciary's Organic Law states in Spanish: Son atribuciones de la Corte Plena las siguientes:

3ª: Practicar recibimientos de abogados y autorizarlos para el ejercicio de su profesión y para el ejercicio de la función pública del notariado, previo examen de suficiencia para esta última, ante una comisión de su seno; inhabilitarlos por venalidad, cohecho, fraude o falsedad, y suspenderlos cuando por incumplimiento de sus obligaciones profesionales, por negligencia o ignorancia graves, no dieren suficiente garantía en el ejercicio de sus funciones; por mala conducta profesional, o privada notoriamente inmoral; y por tener auto de detención en causa por delito doloso que no admita excarcelación o por delitos excarcelables.

d The Duty of Confidentiality Defined

9.   This set of rules makes it possible to define the specific content of the duty of confidentiality that attorneys in El Salvador are legally required to uphold. The resulting working definition can be construed as the professional obligation that bars attorneys from revealing to third parties confidential information that clients have entrusted to their attorneys, that the latter have gained knowledge about, or that lawyers have expressly been prohibited from disclosing.

B Scope

10.   The scope of this professional obligation has two objective dimensions: what it protects and when it is applicable. As understood from the definition, under no circumstance can an attorney disclose clients' confidential information, unless the clients' consent is obtained. Thus, the scope of this duty applies to any situation in which attorneys may find themselves involved, particularly because the applicable rules examined do not establish limits to the corresponding duty of confidentiality.

    An apparent limit to the scope of attorney-client privilege can be found whenever an attorney is called to testify. This situation, however, is not a limit to the scope of attorneys' professional duty of confidentiality. For example, Article 205 of the Criminal Proceedings Code[9] expressly establishes an obligation for attorneys to abstain from revealing facts constituting confidential information when testifying during criminal procedures. Likewise, Article 370(1) of the Civil and Commercial Proceedings Code[10] provides an express exemption for attorneys who are called to testify in civil or commercial proceedings to excuse themselves from testifying when such testimony can result in a breach of confidentiality. In the end, attorneys must make sure that no action they take results in a breach of confidentiality.

C Persons Subject to the Duty of Professional Secrecy

11.   Aside from applying to attorneys, the duty of professional secrecy also applies to other professionals or service providers who, as a consequence of their profession or job, become acquainted with an attorney's clients' confidential information. This can be extracted from Article 187 of the Criminal Code,

---

[9] Art. 205 of the Criminal Proceedings Code states in Spanish: No podrán declarar sobre los hechos que han llegado a su conocimiento en razón del propio estado, oficio o profesión, bajo pena de nulidad, los ministros de una iglesia con personalidad jurídica, los abogados, notarios, los profesionales y auxiliares de las ciencias relacionadas con la salud, según los términos del secreto profesional, y los funcionarios, empleados y demás servidores públicos sobre secretos de Estado. Si el testigo invoca erróneamente ese deber, se procederá a interrogarlo.

[10] Art. 370 of the Civil and Commercial Proceedings Code states in Spanish: Las partes y sus abogados tendrán la facultad de negarse a declarar o a facilitar documentación en un proceso respecto de una comunicación sostenida entre ellos.

Article 372 of the Civil and Commercial Proceedings Code[11] and Articles 205 and 206 of the Criminal Proceedings Code, since these provisions expressly extend either a right or an obligation to abstain from disclosing clients' confidential information to a broader ensemble of professionals or service providers. For example, physicians and accountants are professionals who come to know confidential information about their clients' medical or accounting status and records and thus are barred from disclosing it to third parties.

D Exceptions to and Optional Derogations from the Duty of Professional Secrecy

12. There are currently no relevant exemptions to the duty of professional secrecy, except when disclosure is expressly and exceptionally required by certain criminal rules, as studied in another section of this chapter. However, clients may expressly authorize their attorneys to disclose certain or all of their confidential information to third parties, for the protection or benefit of their interests. In this sense, it is important to take into account that the disclosure of confidential information, a corollary of the fundamental right to privacy, is a right to which the client, not the attorney, is entitled. Hence, for example, a client may expressly allow an attorney to disclose financial information to attain a particular objective, such as being credited with a loan. In that case, if the attorney discloses the information the attorney was authorized to reveal, that action cannot be considered a breach of confidentiality but rather an exception to the rule.

Careful consideration has to be taken when weighing an attorney's professional obligation to protect and further the client's interests, against the attorney's other responsibility to avoid disclosing confidential information to third parties. As mentioned previously, the client is the only party entitled to freely disclose his or her own confidential information. Thus, for an attorney to reveal it to third parties, the attorney needs the client's express authorization to do so. Consequently, even if an attorney considers that disclosure of certain confidential information may benefit a client, it is

---

[11] Art. 372 of the Civil and Commercial Proceedings Code states in Spanish: Un sacerdote tiene derecho a rehusar dar testimonio o revelar el conocimiento obtenido en la confesión; y cualquier ministro religioso tendrá el mismo derecho en lo tocante a asuntos de conciencia.

La comunicación entre un contador público y su cliente, o entre un auditor y su cliente, estará sujeta a lo dispuesto por la ley de la materia. Esta información podrá ser divulgada por mandato de ley o por orden judicial.

El dueño de un secreto comercial o de negocio y el propietario de una patente o su licenciatario tienen la facultad de negarse a revelarlo. También tienen el derecho de impedir o evitar que lo divulgue uno de sus empleados. Sin embargo, se admitirá testimonio sobre dicho secreto cuando fuere necesario para probar un fraude de ley, un delito, una violación a la legislación sobre propiedad intelectual o industrial o para resolver cualquier otra controversia, a juicio prudencial del juez o tribunal en función de descubrir la verdad sobre los hechos en disputa.

Lo mismo se aplica a aquellas personas que en razón de su profesión u oficio tengan obligación de guardar secreto.

a breach to reveal it, unless previously authorized by the client to do so. In addition, what happens if an attorney accidentally reveals confidential information about a client? Because there was no intent to disclose that information, it cannot be considered a breach of confidentiality. However, it also cannot be considered an exception to the rule.

E Law Firms

13. In essence, a law firm is an entity that provides legal services to its clients by assigning attorneys to represent clients in the solution of their legal issues. In Salvadoran practice, law firms are generally established as corporate entities, a matter of importance for the duty of professional secrecy. The reason for this is that the legal representative of a law firm, or any of its agents or delegates, acting in that capacity, cannot reveal clients' confidential information on behalf of the firm. The legal basis for this statement is found in Article 187 of the Criminal Code, wherein no differentiation is made between individuals and corporate entities regarding the felony of disclosing confidential information. Thus, both individuals and corporate entities can be found guilty of committing said felony, and, in turn, both are obliged to uphold professional secrecy. Moreover, Article 372 of the Civil and Commercial Proceedings Code prohibits corporate entities from disclosing confidential information when their agents or legal representative are called to testify on their behalf. This provision is also devoid of any differentiation as to whom it applies, being that it literally applies to any "person" who is obliged to keep another party's confidential information secret.

In addition, it is also common practice to contractually oblige law firms, as legal service providers, to abstain from disclosing a client's confidential information. A breach of this contractual obligation makes the firm responsible for civil liability and entitles the affected client to file a claim for damages against the firm. It also makes the firm criminally liable.

F Legal Assistants and Staff

14. Legal assistants and staff are also bound by law to abstain from disclosing clients' confidential information. All of the aforementioned applicable rules found in the Criminal Code and the Civil and Commercial Proceedings Code oblige any person who, because of their job, attain knowledge of another person's confidential information to abstain from disclosing that information to third parties. The general formulation of these rules makes the duty of confidentiality derived from them entirely applicable to legal assistants and staff, since the nature of their job may put them in contact with clients' confidential information. Consequently, if they do come into contact with confidential information, legal assistants and staff are legally bound to abstain from disclosing it to third parties.

G External Service Providers

15. Regarding external service providers, such as firms that provide outsourced accounting or data processing, they are also obliged to uphold the duty of professional secrecy. This legal obligation stems from the general formulation of the applicable rules, as previously shown. The reason for this is that external service providers, be they individuals or corporate entities, as a result of their profession or job, gain knowledge about an attorney's clients' confidential information. For instance, accounting firms may gain knowledge about a lawyer's clients' financial and tax status as a practical result of providing outsourced services. The same can be said for firms that offer data management or processing services. It is also possible to contractually bind external service providers to an obligation requiring them to abstain from revealing information expressly deemed confidential by an attorney's clients.

H Multidisciplinary Associations

16. Professionals providing different kinds of services to a law firm's or attorney's client are bound by the duty of professional secrecy in two ways. First, the applicable rule derived from Article 187 of the Criminal Code binds the individual providing the multidisciplinary service. Consequently, if the individual service provider gains knowledge about the firm's or attorney's client's confidential information, such provider is personally responsible for not disclosing it to third parties. For example, a private investigator working for a law firm is bound to abstain from disclosing confidential information about a client that such investigator comes to know about, as a result of his or her job.

   Second, professionals providing such services within a firm to an attorney's client can be reputed to be acting on behalf of the firm or attorney when rendering said services for the benefit of the client. In this case, such professional is bound by the same legal and contractual obligation that binds the firm or attorney to uphold the duty of confidentiality. Specifically, should the professional breach said duty, the professional is personally responsible for criminal liability, and the firm for civil liability. For instance, a public relations adviser working for a law firm is barred from revealing information regarding the marital status of a client.

I In-House Counsel

17. Attorneys hired as internal legal counsel for a particular individual or entity are legally bound to abstain from disclosing their employer's confidential information. In this case, an in-house counsel's job results in such counsel acquiring confidential information about the counsel's employer. Failure to maintain confidentiality makes the employee criminally liable.

In addition, the employer may also contractually bind its in-house counsel to refrain from revealing information expressly deemed to be confidential. Thus, all of the rules previously shown as applicable to attorneys apply to attorneys hired as in-house counsel. However, unless given power of attorney, the civil rules for the *mandato* do not apply to internal legal counsel, making it advisable for employers to enter into non-disclosure agreements (NDAs) with their in-house counsel. An NDA makes it easier for employers to file civil claims seeking to remedy an in-house counsel's breach of confidentiality, since the instrument itself is a direct source and proof of the duty of confidentiality. Also, Salvadoran contract law allows for the quantum of damages, resulting from a breach of confidentiality, to be contractually defined in the NDA by means of a liquidated damages clause.

In addition, because in-house counsel are employees, they are bound by the Salvadoran Labor Law. Thus, pursuant to Article 50(4) of the Salvadoran Labor Law,[12] employees are liable to be terminated, without liability to their employer, when they disclose their "employer's secrets" or "information about administrative aspects that can harm the employer." Moreover, as a means to easily identify which information is confidential, employers can also bind their in-house counsel to comply with the NDA in their work contracts, allowing them to legally terminate an attorney's employment for breach of the NDA. A provision in this sense gives cause to terminate employment contracts on the basis of Article 50(4) of the Labor Law. It also allows employers to terminate their in-house counsel's employment, since disobeying an employer's direct orders legally allows the former to do so.

2 History of the Duty of Professional Secrecy in El Salvador

18. A correct historical overview of how the duty of professional secrecy has been legally established in El Salvador requires the examination of how certain statutes have evolved. First, it is essential to study the constitutional evolution of the fundamental right to privacy. Second, a complete overview requires that the criminal and disciplinary rules establishing the duty of confidentiality are also traced down to their roots. Thus, the end result will be a historical study of how the most important elements of the definition of the duty of professional secrecy came into existence in El Salvador's legal system and how they have been developed ever since.

---

[12] Art. 50 of the Labor Law states in Spanish: El patrono podrá dar por terminado el contra- to de trabajo sin incurrir en responsabilidad, por las siguientes causas: 4) Por revelar el trabajador secretos de la empresa o aprovecharse de ellos; o por divulgar asuntos administrativos de la misma que puedan causar perjuicios al patrono.

A The Fundamental Right to Privacy in the Salvadoran Constitution

19.   The Salvadoran Constitution of 1824, when the country was part of the Federal Republic of Central America, established the first statute protecting Salvadoran citizens' right to privacy. In this sense, in accordance with Article 66 of the 1824 Constitution,[13] the search of a person's house, books and correspondence was prohibited, with limited exceptions. Similarly, Article 168 of the 1824 Constitution of the Federal Republic of Central America[14] further regulated the search of a person's household, establishing that it would only be allowed when a competent authority rendered a written order to that effect. Moreover, under Article 169[15] of that same Constitution, a person's private documents could not be searched, disclosed or used in judicial proceedings, unless treason was suspected.

The Salvadoran Constitution of 1841 established in Article 84[16] the protection of only letter correspondence, prohibiting its seizure and invasion, except for when permitted by any legislative statute. Articles 90 and 166 of the Salvadoran Constitution of 1864 and 1871, respectively, borrowed the same wording as Article 84 of the 1841 Constitution.

Until 1886,[17] no Salvadoran Constitution had protected the privacy of all types of correspondence. It was not until 1886 that all correspondence was protected from unauthorized seizures and searches, with further Constitutions keeping this more general rule. A particular constitutional provision was included in the 1939 Salvadoran Constitution, as its Article 38[18] was the first

---

[13] Art. 66 of the Salvadoran Constitution states in Spanish: de 1824. La casa de todo ciudadano y sus libros y correspondencia serán un sagrado, y no podrán registrarse sino como ordene la ley.

[14] Art. 168 of the Salvadoran Constitution states in Spanish: Federal de Centroamérica de 1824. Ninguna casa puede ser registrada sino por mandato escrito de autoridad competente, dado en virtud de dos disposiciones formales que presten motivo al allanamiento, el que deberá efectuarse de día. También podrá registrarse a toda hora por un agente de la autoridad pública. 1o. En la persecución actual de un delincuente: 2o. Por un desorden escandaloso que exija pronto remedio: 3o. Por reclamación hecha del interior de la casa. Mas hecho el registro se comprobará con dos disposiciones que se hizo por alguno de los motivos indicados.

[15] Art. 169 of the Salvadoran Constitution states in Spanish: Federal de Centroamérica de 1824. Solo en los delitos de traición se pueden ocupar los papeles de los habitantes de la República; y únicamente podrá practicarse su examen cuando sea indispensable para la averiguación de la verdad, y a presencia del interesado, devolviéndosele en el acto cuantos no tengan relación con lo que se indaga.

[16] Art. 84 of the Salvadoran Constitution states in Spanish: de 1841. La correspondencia epistolar es inviolable y no podrá interceptarse ni abrirse, sino en los casos expresamente determinados por la ley, y cuando lo exija la seguridad y salud pública; pero bajo las formas y requisitos que la misma ley establece. Fuera de estos casos la interceptación y registro, no presta fe en juicio ni fuera de él, contra alguna persona.

[17] Art. 30 of the Salvadoran Constitution states in Spanish: de El Salvador de 1886. La correspondencia epistolar y telegráfica es inviolable. La correspondencia interceptada no hace fe ni podrá figurar en ninguna especie de actuación.

[18] Art. 38 of the Salvadoran Constitution states in Spanish: de El Salvador de 1939. Solamente podrá practicarse el registro o la pesquisa de la persona para prevenir o averiguar delitos o faltas.

such rule to clearly and directly protect Salvadorans' households from unwarranted searches.

20. However, the most significant developments happened in 1950, when Article 165[19] of that year's Constitution established that a person's property, not only the household, was to be protected from unwarranted searches and invasions. This extended the protection to other venues different from homes, as it effectively protected other establishments from unauthorized trespassing. Another important change was found in Article 159[20] of the 1950 Constitution, which allowed exceptions to the secrecy of correspondence in cases of bankruptcy, allowing authorities to intercept it.

Previous Salvadoran Constitutions did not directly protect or recognize the right to privacy. In the past, only certain specific varieties and attributes of that right were protected: the secrecy of correspondence and the protection of a person's property from trespassing. The reason for this apparent lack of regulation was that the corresponding Constituent Legislative Assemblies considered that the only manifestations of the right to privacy were those two examples. It was not until 1983 that the fundamental right to privacy found direct and clear constitutional recognition and protection. Article 2(2) of the 1983 Salvadoran Constitution expressly establishes that "the right to persons' and their family's privacy is guaranteed."

Article 24 of this Constitution also built on the right to privacy as it established exceptions to the privacy of telecommunications. Prior to this reform, there were no exceptions to this variety of the right to privacy, and only telephone communications were protected from unlawful interventions. This is the reason why Article 24 had to be reformed in 1983: to protect the privacy of all genres of telecommunications and to allow for only the authorized intervention of them. Therefore, Article 24[21] had to be amended to read as follows:

> El domicilio es inviolable; únicamente podrá decretarse el allanamiento para la averiguación de los delitos, persecución de los delincuentes o para fines sanitarios, en la forma y en los casos que determine la ley.

[19] Art. 165 of the Salvadoran Constitution states in Spanish: de El Salvador de 1950. Sólo podrá practicarse el registro o la pesquisa de la persona para prevenir o averiguar delitos o faltas. La morada es inviolable; únicamente podrá efectuarse el allanamiento en caso de incendio u otros análogos, para la averiguación de delitos y persecución de delincuentes, y para fines sanitarios, en la forma y circunstancias que determine la ley.

[20] Art. 159 of the Salvadoran Constitution states in Spanish: de El Salvador de 1950. La correspondencia de toda clase es inviolable; interceptada no hará fe ni podrá figurar en ninguna actuación, salvo en los casos de concurso y quiebra.

[21] Art. 24 of the Salvadoran Constitution states in Spanish: La correspondencia de toda clase es inviolable, interceptada no hará fe ni podrá figurar en ninguna actuación, salvo en los casos de concurso y quiebra.

Se prohíbe la interferencia y la intervención de las telecomunicaciones. De manera excepcional podrá autorizarse judicialmente, de forma escrita y motivada, la intervención

The interference and intervention of telecommunications is prohibited. Exceptionally, through a written and reasoned judicial warrant, any kind of telecommunication can be temporarily intervened, without violating the secrecy of irrelevant content. Information resulting from an unlawful intervention shall lack legal validity.

B Historical Overview of the Duty of Professional Secrecy

21.   Because the duty of professional secrecy stems from criminal, civil and disciplinary statutes, it is essential to examine the historical roots of those rules. However, because the Civil Code has remained virtually unchanged since it came into force in 1860, it is not necessary to trace the statutory evolution of the *mandato*. Therefore, only disciplinary and criminal rules will be historically analyzed.

a Disciplinary Rules

22.   Perhaps the oldest statutory regulation establishing the duty of professional secrecy for attorneys is found in the 1880 Salvadoran Constitution. Article 104[22] of the 1880 Salvadoran Constitution establishes that attorneys could be "suspended" from practicing law or have their university degree "revoked," by the Supreme Court, if they were found to be responsible for "bribing," "receiving bribes" or "fraud." Therefore, the disciplinary rule that can be derived from that provision is that attorneys who knowingly pay bribes, accept bribes or act fraudulently can be either suspended from practice or have their university degree revoked. The common denominator of the prohibited conduct is that the attorney acts with deceit, dishonestly or harming good faith, thus the term "fraud." As a consequence, it can be established that the duty of professional secrecy fits within the scope of this constitutional provision, albeit implicitly. Of important

temporal de cualquier tipo de telecomunicaciones, preservándose en todo caso el secreto de lo privado que no guarde relación con el proceso. La información proveniente de una intervención ilegal carecerá de valor.

La violación comprobada a lo dispuesto en este artículo, por parte de cualquier funcionario, será causa justa para la destitución inmediata de su cargo y dará lugar a la indemnización por los daños y perjuicios ocasionados.

Una ley especial determinará los delitos en cuya investigación podrá concederse esta autorización. Asimismo señalará los controles, los informes periódicos a la Asamblea Legislativa, y las responsabilidades y sanciones administrativas, civiles y penales en que incurrirán los funcionarios que apliquen ilegalmente esta medida excepcional. La aprobación y reforma de esta ley especial requerirá el voto favorable de por lo menos las dos terceras partes de los Diputados electos.

[22] Art 104 of the Salvadoran Constitution of 1880 states in Spanish: Corresponde a la Corte Plena: 6o. Practicar el recibimiento de abogados y escribanos, suspenderlos y aún reiterarles sus títulos por venalidad, cohecho o fraude, con conocimiento de causa. 7o. Conocer de los recursos de fuerza.

consideration is that university degrees could be revoked because they were issued only by the state university.

The formulation of this provision did not change significantly until 1939. The reform to the Constitution moved Article 104 of the 1880 Constitution to Article 112[23] and modified its text. The text of this provision was modified to suppress the Supreme Court's ability to revoke attorneys' law degrees. Therefore, the court was empowered only to suspend or disqualify attorneys for committing felonies such as prevarication, forgery of documents, fraud and bribing. In addition, the same penalty applied to attorneys found to be responsible for acting with "notorious immorality." As was the case with the 1880 Constitution, the duty of professional secrecy found only an indirect and still unclear basis in Article 112 of the 1939 constitutional reform.

However, an important development was the succinct establishment of the particular features of the summary disciplinary proceeding for the disqualification or suspension from practicing law for attorneys. Apart from the summary nature of said proceeding, the 1939 constitutional reform also established the applicable evidentiary rules. Analysis on this issue is included in Section 4 of this chapter.

23. The next major development happened 11 years later, when the 1950 Salvadoran Constitution included more general genres of sanctioned conduct in the applicable provision. Article 89[24] of the 1950 Salvadoran Constitution enacted suspension and disqualification as penalties for attorneys who "breached their professional obligations," who acted with "negligence or grave ignorance" or whose "professional conduct" was deemed to be "bad." With that formulation, the duty of professional secrecy found its first direct disciplinary basis as a result of the 1950 Constitution. The 1983 Salvadoran Constitution did not modify this provision. Consequently, the current statutory basis for the duty of professional secrecy, as described in this chapter, has been in force for six decades.

[23] Art. 112 of the Salvadoran Constitution of 1939 states in Spanish: Son atribuciones de la Corte Suprema de Justicia: 6a. Practicar recibimientos de Abogados, inhabilitarlos o suspenderlos y rehabilitarlos en el ejercicio de su profesión por los delitos de prevaricato, cohecho, fraude, falsedad o por conducta notoriamente inmoral, con solo robustez moral de prueba, procediendo sumariamente para establecer los hechos. Igual facultad ejercerá respecto de los notorios y de los procuradores . . ..

[24] Art. 89 of the Salvadoran Constitution of 1950 states in Spanish: Son atribuciones de la Corte Suprema de Justicia: 11. Practicar recibimientos de abogados y autorizarlos para el ejercicio de su profesión; suspenderlos por incumplimiento de sus obligaciones profesionales, por negligencia o ignorancia graves, por mala conducta profesional, o por privada notoriamente inmoral; inhabilitarlos por venalidad, cohecho, fraude o falsedad, y rehabilitarlos por causa legal. En los casos de suspensión e inhabilitación procederá en forma sumaria, y resolverá con solo robustez moral de prueba. Las mismas facultades ejercerá respecto de los notarios y de los procuradores.

Before 1984, however, there were no entities with the authority to investigate the professional conduct of attorneys. A regulation for the corresponding legal proceeding was also nonexistent. These statutory voids were solved in 1984 when the Judiciary's Organic Law came into force and the Professional Investigation Unit was established within the Supreme Court, giving it the power to investigate attorneys' and notaries' professional conduct. This law, additionally, established other features of the applicable disciplinary proceedings, as will be described below.

b Criminal Rules

24.   On the other hand, the applicable criminal rules do not present much of an evolution. The three milestones for these rules are found in the 1904 Criminal Code, and the 1973 and 1998 Criminal Codes. In 1904, criminal rules for the duty of professional secrecy were applicable only to professionals whose job required them to have obtained a degree. Article 297 of the 1904 Criminal Code thus punished professionals who disclosed "secrets" that they came to know about as a result of their job. The penalty depended on certain criteria: imprisonment for up to one year if the disclosure of information causes harm to the disclosed party; if no harm was caused, six months of prison time. In all cases, Article 298 provided for professional suspension for the duration of the prison sentence.

Later on, the 1973 Criminal Code regulated the felony of revealing professional secrets following the general statutory tradition established by Spanish Criminal Law since 1848. Specifically, Article 236[25] of the 1973 Criminal Code punished the act of disclosing secrets that the revealing party came to know as a result of such party's job, profession or status, whenever that disclosure may cause harm and the information was not a "commercial" or "industrial" secret. The penalty for this felony was six months to one year of prison time. This provision excluded commercial and industrial secrets from protection and suppressed the suspension of professional practice in place since 1904.

Compared to the 1973 statute, Article 187 of the current Criminal Code punishes any professional who discloses any information considered to be confidential. This is similar to the original formulation of the felony enacted in 1904. There are currently no requirements for possible harm as a result of disclosing confidential information, and it does not matter if that information is industrial or commercial. In addition, the current statute punishes the disclosing party by barring such party from exercising his or her profession or job for up to two years. Basically, the change between both statutes is that the one in force

---

[25] Art. 236 of the Criminal Code of 1973 states in Spanish: El que indebidamente revele un secreto que no fuere comercial o industrial, que se le ha impuesto por razones de su estado u oficio, empleo, profesión o arte y cuya divulgación pudiere causar daño, será sancionado con prisión de seis meses a un año.

lowers the standard for the determination of the criminal conduct, and it also includes another penalty in addition to prison time. It would seem, therefore, that the current provision has its most immediate source in the 1904 Criminal Code, given the similarities between Article 187 of the 1998 code and Article 297 of the 1904 statute.

3 Supervision

25. Because there is no bar association in El Salvador, supervision of attorneys' professional conduct is handled by the courts and the Professional Investigations Unit (PIU) of the Salvadoran Supreme Court. Disciplinary rules are enforced by the Professional Investigations Unit, while civil and criminal rules are enforced by the corresponding tribunals when claims are filed.

A The Bar Associations

26. In the absence of bar associations, the supervision of lawyers' professional conduct is carried out by the PIU. The following is an overview of how the basic enforcement of professional duties is carried out in El Salvador.

27. When the Judiciary's Organic Law was enacted in 1984, an office charged with the investigation of attorneys' and notaries' professional conduct was established as a unit within the Supreme Court. This unit was empowered with investigative authority, allowing the officer in charge of it to take witness depositions and issue subpoenas. The officer in charge of the PIU has to comply with the same personal and professional requirements applicable to judges in order to be appointed. Investigations may begin as a result of a complaint made by any interested person to the unit or *ex officio* by the unit itself.[26] In cases pertaining to attorneys breaching the duty of confidentiality, given the nature of this conduct, it is more likely that investigations will commence only if a complaint is made. The reason for this is that the nature of a breach of the professional duty of confidentiality is not an event readily known by the PIU, and thus investigations are feasible only if a complaint is made by the affected

---

[26] Art. 115 of Judiciary's Organic Law states in Spanish: Habrá en la Corte Suprema de Justicia una Sección encargada de investigar la conducta de los abogados, notarios, estudiantes de derecho con facultad de defender o procurar, jueces ejecutores y demás funcionarios de nombramiento de la Corte. Esta Sección estará a cargo de un Jefe, que deberá reunir las condiciones que se exigen para ser Juez de Primera Instancia, quien actuará con un Secretario que nombrará la Corte, y podrá actuar de oficio o a solicitud de cualquier interesado.

El Jefe de la Sección sustanciará la información, pudiendo tomar declaraciones, ordenar comparendos y librar las esquelas correspondientes, a nombre del Presidente de la Corte. Al estar concluida la información, y después de oír la opinión del Fiscal de la Corte, dará cuenta con ella al Presidente, quien, si la considera depurada, la someterá a conocimiento de la Corte Plena.

client. The investigation's results are ultimately submitted to the Supreme Court, which then decides if the attorney in question has to be sanctioned.

B The Courts

28. Salvadoran courts do not actively supervise the professional conduct of attorneys. However, whenever breaches to criminal or civil rules of the duty of confidentiality are included as part of claims, tribunals act as a supervising entity. The reason for this is that tribunals become an authority in determining if a breach of the duty of confidentiality really occurred and thus sentencing the offending attorney with the corresponding criminal or civil penalty.

Specifically, criminal tribunals will act as supervising entities when offended clients prosecute an attorney charged with committing the felony of disclosing confidential information. These tribunals will, in other words, examine evidence and enforce criminal rules when such cases are argued before them. Civil tribunals will act in a similar capacity when clients file claims for either a breach of an NDA or *mandato* against attorneys who fail to comply with the duty of professional secrecy. Relief is provided by ordering the defendant to remedy the damages suffered by the plaintiff.

4 Sanctions

29. Applicable sanctions for attorneys who breach the duty of professional secrecy stem from the rules that regulate it. As a result, attorneys are subject to disciplinary, criminal and civil sanctions. Accordingly, the Salvadoran legal system provides similarly natured proceedings to punish attorneys who disclose their clients' confidential information.

A Proceedings and Sanctions

a Disciplinary Proceedings

30. The legal basis for these proceedings is composed of several disaggregated provisions found in the Constitution and the Judiciary's Organic Law. Therefore, a correct understanding of applicable disciplinary proceedings requires an individual examination of each of its procedural elements. Before illustrating the proceeding, it is important to take into account that Article 182 of the Salvadoran Constitution establishes that the Supreme Court has to proceed "pursuant to applicable law" in order to disciplinarily sanction attorneys for professional misconduct. The applicable law is not found in a single statute, and since the proceeding is an administrative proceeding, the Supreme Court acts in an administrative capacity. This allows for the specific procedural steps of the proceeding to be structured by the investigating entity to some degree.

First, the Constitution provides the basic framework applicable to all administrative proceedings in Articles 2, 11, 12, 14 and 18.[27] The elements extracted from these provisions are the basic building blocks of the applicable disciplinary proceedings for attorneys who breach the duty of confidentiality. Basically, the Constitution requires that any administrative proceeding has to respect due process. As a consequence, individuals who are subject to administrative proceedings, such as attorneys, have to be subjected to proceedings based on enacted statutes, which guarantee their right to be heard, provide evidence and receive a lawful ruling. Therefore, the disciplinary proceeding that determines whether an attorney breached the duty of professional secrecy, and thus is professionally liable, has to be tailored to those specifications.

Second, Article 182 of the Salvadoran Constitution establishes the basic elements of the disciplinary proceeding. This provision establishes that the Supreme Court is the entity empowered to disbar or suspend attorneys who breach the duty of confidentiality. In order words, the Supreme Court magistrates are the judging authority, who on the basis of presented evidence decide whether to apply sanctions to investigated attorneys. The Supreme Court analyzes and weighs evidence presented against attorneys based on how effective the evidence is at convincing the magistrates that a breach of professional secrecy was committed.

Third, a legal corollary of due process is that an attorney suspected of being responsible for such a breach has the right to be tried by an impartial and independent judging authority. For that reason, the Supreme Court cannot be the same entity that both investigates professional conduct and applies the corresponding penalties. Therefore, the Judiciary's Organic Law provides the legal basis for the existence of the PIU and empowers this office with investigating breaches of professional duties by attorneys.

[27] Art. 2(1) of the Salvadoran Constitution states in Spanish: Toda persona tiene derecho a la vida, a la integridad física y moral, a la libertad, a la seguridad, al trabajo, a la propiedad y posesión, y a ser protegida en la conservación y defensa de los mismos.

Art. 11(1) of the Salvadoran Constitution states in Spanish: Ninguna persona puede ser privada del derecho a la vida, a la libertad, a la propiedad y posesión, ni de cualquier otro de sus derechos sin ser previamente oída y vencida en juicio con arreglo a las leyes; ni puede ser enjuiciada dos veces por la misma causa.

Art. 12(1) of the Salvadoran Constitution states in Spanish: Toda persona a quien se impute un delito, se presumirá inocente mientras no se pruebe su culpabilidad conforme a la ley y en juicio público, en el que se le aseguren todas las garantías necesarias para su defensa.

Art. 14 of the Salvadoran Constitution states in Spanish: Corresponde únicamente al Órgano Judicial la facultad de imponer penas. No obstante, la autoridad administrativa podrá sancionar, mediante resolución o sentencia y previo el debido proceso, las contravenciones a las leyes, reglamentos u ordenanzas, con arresto hasta por cinco días o con multa, la cual podrá permutarse por servicios sociales prestados a la comunidad.

Art. 18 of the Salvadoran Constitution states in Spanish: Toda persona tiene derecho a dirigir sus peticiones por escrito, de manera decorosa, a las autoridades legalmente establecidas; a que se le resuelvan, y a que se le haga saber lo resuelto.

317

Article 115 of that law describes the procedural steps of the disciplinary proceeding. First, the officer in charge of the PIU begins investigating the possible breach of the duty of confidentiality. This can begin either as a response to a claim presented to the unit by any person or *ex officio*. Second, the unit's officer can subpoena witnesses and exercise ample investigative prerogatives enabling the officer to gather the necessary information. Third, after compiling that information, the officer in charge further complements it with the Court Attorney's opinion on the matter. Fourth, afterwards, the officer in charge of the unit submits the information to the president of the Supreme Court. Fifth, if the president of the Supreme Court finds the information to be adequate, the president submits the case to the other magistrates when the court is in session.

The aforementioned elements give an idea of how the applicable process is to be practically structured. It is important to consider that, as a result of the nonexistent specific statutory basis for this administrative proceeding, the PIU has the limited power to procedurally structure it within the bounds of due process and the constitutional mandate that justice must be served swiftly and sufficiently.

b Judicial Proceedings

31. Civil and criminal proceedings, which seek to enforce the applicable civil and criminal rules of professional secrecy, are exhaustively established and structured in enacted statutes. Therefore, they are much more straightforward than disciplinary proceedings.

On one hand, criminal proceedings that are intended for the investigation and possible sentencing for felony breach of professional secrecy begin when an affected client files a claim with the competent sentencing tribunal. Afterwards, the accused attorney is served process and ordered to appear before the tribunal for a conciliation hearing. If this hearing ends without a settlement, the tribunal will set the date for another hearing. In this other hearing, the tribunal will examine evidence submitted by the parties and either admit or dismiss them, setting the date for the public hearing. Closing arguments are rendered by the parties and evidence is examined by the tribunal in the public hearing. Immediately afterwards, the tribunal deliberates on the facts and evidence presented to it and renders a decision either convicting or absolving the attorney. The sentence is then notified to the parties, after which the hearing is closed.

On the other hand, the applicable civil proceedings seek to determine if either a breach of an NDA has been committed by an attorney or if the *mandato* was breached. In either case, the correct civil proceeding is a declarative proceeding for breach of contract. The proceeding starts when a client files a civil suit against an attorney who unlawfully disclosed confidential information. The attorney is notified by the tribunal of the suit filed

318

against him or her and given 20 working days, after being notified, to respond or file a counterclaim. Once the defendant files a response, within a maximum of 60 working days, the tribunal must hold a preparatory hearing. The purpose of this hearing is mainly to allow the court and both parties to set the terms of the dispute, correct any formal defects of the suits filed, offer new evidence and set a date for the evidence hearing. In this last hearing, the parties present evidence to the judge, examine witnesses and orally submit their closing arguments. After a recess, the judge announces the ruling. Fifteen days after the conclusion of this hearing, the judge must render the decision either ruling that the sued attorney has breached the NDA or *mandato*, or that no such breach occurred.

Additionally, the judge can also decide on any claims asking for damages, holding that the remedy has to be paid to the plaintiff. For damages to be quantified, the plaintiff has to file a motion for a summary proceeding, for the quantification of damages. The result of this proceeding is an injunction for a determined amount to be paid as remedy for damages arising from a breach of an NDA or *mandato*.

B Relationship between Criminal and Disciplinary Sanctions

32.   Because disciplinary rules are of an administrative nature, they are not mutually exclusive with criminal rules. This means that attorneys can be both sentenced to prison time, as a consequence of disclosing their clients' confidential information, and be disbarred or suspended by the Supreme Court, for the same breach. The relationship between both genres of rules is, in essence, complementary: criminal penalties can be reinforced by disciplinary sanctions. Article 187 of the Criminal Code prohibits convicted attorneys from practicing law for up to two years only; however, the Supreme Court can disbar or suspend attorneys for up to five years. Consequently, the PIU can begin investigating a convicted attorney *ex officio*, after the attorney has been sentenced by a criminal tribunal, for example.

5 Duty to Provide Information to the Authorities

33.   Certain statutory mandates require attorneys to reveal some of their clients' confidential information, during special types of criminal investigations and some civil procedures. From a criminal point of view, disclosing such information under those circumstances exempts attorneys from criminal liability. The compliance with orders issued by authorities, pursuant to specific statutory rules, suppresses the unlawfulness of disclosing confidential information. Likewise, complying with such rules also excuses attorneys from civil liability, as it is not of their own negligence or will that they disclose confidential information in those circumstances.

A Money Laundering and Terrorism

34. Article 2 of the money and asset laundering law[28] establishes that attorneys must disclose to the competent authorities information regarding transactions over USD $10,000 in which their clients partake. Article 9[29] of that law specifies that this obligation arises when such transactions are cash-based, giving counsel five working days to notify the Financial Investigations Unit of the Attorney General's Office. Pursuant to Article 2, attorneys are only required to disclose the existence of the transaction. Disclosure of other confidential information is not required. Failure to disclose information related to cash transactions in excess of USD $10,000 makes the attorney criminally liable.

    The Salvadoran anti-terrorism law establishes in Article 44[30] the duty to disclose information about the importation of firearms, explosives and chemical weapons to the Attorney General or the National Civil Police. Because this obligation applies to every person in El Salvador, attorneys are required to disclose this kind of information, even if it is considered to be confidential.

    Similarly, Article 309 of the Criminal Code[31] obliges any person in El Salvador to disclose information to the public authorities regarding the planned

---

[28] Art. 2 of the Law Against Money and Asset Laundering states in Spanish: La presente Ley será aplicada a toda persona natural o jurídica aún cuando esta última no se encuentre constituida legalmente, quienes deberán presentar la información que les requiera la autoridad competente, que permita demostrar el origen lícito de cualquier transacción que realicen.
 Sujetos obligados son todos aquellos que habrán de, entre otras cosas, reportar las diligencias u operaciones financieras sospechosas y/o que superen el umbral de la Ley, nombrar y capacitar a un Oficial de Cumplimiento y demás responsabilidades que esta Ley, el Reglamento de la misma, así como el Instructivo de la UIF les determine.
 Se consideran sujetos obligados por la presente Ley, los siguientes:
 Así mismo los abogados, Notarios, Contadores y Auditores tendrán la obligación de informar o reportar las transacciones que hagan o se realicen ante sus oficios, mayores de Diez Mil Dólares de los Estados Unidos de América, conforme lo establece el Art. 9 de la presente Ley.

[29] Art. 9 of the Law Against Money and Asset Laundering states in Spanish: Los sujetos obligados deberán informar a la UIF, por escrito o cualquier medio electrónico y en el plazo máximo de cinco días hábiles, cualquier operación o transacción de efectivo, fuere individual o múltiple, independientemente que se considere sospechosa o no, realizada por cada usuario o cliente que en un mismo día o en el término de un mes exceda los Diez Mil Dólares de los Estados Unidos de América o su equivalente en cualquier moneda extranjera. El plazo para remitir la información se computará a partir del día siguiente de realizada la operación o transacción. Igual responsabilidad tendrán si se trata de operaciones financieras que se efectúen por cualquier otro medio, si esta fuere superior a Veinticinco Mil Dólares de los Estados Unidos de América o su equivalente en cualquier moneda extranjera.

[30] Art. 44 of the Law Against Terrorist Acts states in Spanish: Toda persona natural o jurídica está obligada a informar a la Fiscalía General de la República o a la Policía Nacional Civil acerca de la introducción al territorio nacional o existencia de armas de las mencionadas en la presente Ley, que puedan suponer una amenaza grave a la salud y la seguridad del país.

[31] Art. 309 of the Criminal Code states in Spanish: El que teniendo conocimiento cierto, de que se fuere a cometer un delito contra la vida o la integridad personal, la seguridad colectiva, la salud pública, la libertad individual o sexual y no existiendo peligro o daño para sí o para sus

or impending perpetration of terrorist acts. Failure to do so gives rise to criminal liability, including prison time for up to six months or one year, if the terrorist act's execution is under way. It is important to take into account that the same obligation and penalty apply for felonies affecting an individual's basic rights, as well as public health and security, thus extending to acts of terrorism. Attorneys are also bound by this legal obligation.

B Collective Settlement of Debts

35. No statutory rules specifically require that attorneys reveal confidential information during collective settlements of debts. Under Salvadoran constitutional law, limitations on fundamental rights, such as the right to privacy, are lawful only when statutorily established. For example, correspondence can only be intercepted and seized in cases of collective settlement of debts. Considering that the basis of the duty of professional secrecy is the fundamental right to privacy, and no specific statute allows attorneys to disclose their client's confidential information even during the collective settlement of debts, attorneys should not reveal such information under those circumstances. As previously established, attorneys and their clients may decline to reveal correspondence and communications of any kind between them during any civil or commercial proceeding.

6 Treatment of Lawyers' Documents and Correspondence in the Context of Judicial or Police Investigations

36. Documents and correspondence are legally protected from seizures and searches, and only in specific circumstances is that protection waived. Similar rules protect both types of documents. During judicial investigations, both the Criminal Proceedings Code and the Civil and Commercial Proceedings Code protect attorneys' documents. Additionally, the Criminal Code protects documents and correspondence from unlawful interventions, searches and disclosure by establishing a felony for executing such actions.

To begin with, Article 286 of the Criminal Proceedings Code[32] prohibits the seizure of documents and correspondence kept in a criminal defense attorney's office. These documents and correspondence have to be intimately related to the attorney's job, thus the protection effectively applies to documents and correspondence containing clients' confidential information. Documents that come to

---

parientes, no lo pusiere en conocimiento del amenazado o de la autoridad, será sancionado con prisión de seis meses a un año, si el delito hubiere comenzado a ejecutarse.

Si las conductas anteriores se realizaren respecto de los delitos de extorsión o secuestro la sanción será de cuatro a ocho años de prisión.

[32] Art. 286 of the Criminal Proceedings Code states in Spanish: No se podrán secuestrar las cosas o documentos que se envíen o entreguen a los defensores o que ellos posean en su oficina, para el desempeño del cargo. La protección no alcanzará a los instrumentos o productos del delito.

exist as a result of a felony, however, are not protected from seizure. The practical consequence of this rule is that neither the police nor a criminal judge or tribunal are permitted to confiscate or order the seizure of such documents.

The Criminal Code complements that procedural rule. First, Article 301 of the Code[33] makes it a felony, punishable by one to three years of prison, for police officers and any public authority to unlawfully open sealed private correspondence. This rule has an exemption, found in Article 24(1) of the Salvadoran Constitution, which permits the interception of private correspondence, during judicial proceedings, only if those proceedings are centered on the collective settlement of debts. Therefore, sealed correspondence found in an attorney's office cannot be opened by way of a judicial order or during a police investigation.

Second, Article 184[34] of the Criminal Code expressly punishes gaining possession of a person's document if it is not addressed to the perpetrator. The same exception applies if the perpetrator is not mentioned in such documents. The penalty is a fine, which is increased when the person additionally discloses the information contained in the documents.

On the other hand, a civil or commercial tribunal cannot order an attorney to submit such documentation regarding communications with his or her client. Additionally, Article 336 of the Civil and Commercial Proceedings Code[35] establishes that documents that contain information related to issues debated in a civil or commercial proceeding must be submitted to the corresponding

---

[33] Art. 301 of the Criminal Code states in Spanish: El funcionario o empleado público, agente de autoridad o autoridad pública que fuere de los casos previstos por la of the Salvadoran Constitution states in Spanish: y en el transcurso de una investigación policial o judicial, violare correspondencia privada, o lo ordenare o permitiere, será sancionado con prisión de uno a tres años e inhabilitación especial para el ejercicio del cargo o empleo respectivo por igual tiempo.

[34] Art. 184 of the Criminal Code states in Spanish: El que con el fin de descubrir los secretos o vulnerar la intimidad de otro, se apoderare de comunicación escrita, soporte informático o cualquier otro documento o efecto personal que no le esté dirigido o se apodere de datos reservados de carácter personal o familiar de otro, registrados en ficheros, soportes informáticos o de cualquier otro tipo de archivo o registro público o privado, será sancionado con multa de cincuenta a cien días multa.

Si difundiere o revelare a terceros los datos reservados que hubieren sido descubiertos, a que se refiere el paragraph anterior, la sanción será de cien a doscientos días multa.

El tercero a quien se revelare el secreto y lo divulgare a sabiendas de su ilícito origen, será sancionado con multa de treinta a cincuenta días multa.

[35] Art. 336 of the Civil and Commercial Proceedings Code states in Spanish: Las partes tienen la obligación de exhibir los instrumentos que se encuentren en su poder y de cuyo contenido dependa algún elemento del objeto del proceso. Se podrá solicitar al juez que ordene la exhibición del mismo, so pena de ser sancionado el que incumpla con una multa cuyo monto se fijará entre cinco y diez salarios mínimos urbanos, vigentes, más altos.

La exhibición se deberá producir en el plazo que indique el Juez, que será el más breve posible atendidas las circunstancias.

Si el documento que deba exhibirse se encontrare en poder de tercero, se le intimará para que lo presente. Si lo acompañare, podrá solicitar su oportuna devolución dejando testimonio o copia autenticada en el expediente.

tribunal by whoever holds them, including third parties. Consequently, if an attorney has such documents in his or her possession, such attorney is required to surrender them to the tribunal ordering their submission.

Outside of the established exceptions for Article 301 of the Criminal Code, correspondence and documents addressed or belonging to an attorney cannot forcibly be obtained for their incorporation as evidence in criminal proceedings. However, if correspondence addressed to an attorney is intercepted during a proceeding for the collective settlement of debts, no felony is committed and the correspondence can be admitted as evidence. It is important to bear in mind that no statute establishes a similar exception for other documents in an attorney's possession.

7 Search of a Lawyer's Office

37.   It is generally only during criminal proceedings and police investigations that the search of a person's office is allowed. An attorney's office is not exempted from such searches. However, it is of the utmost importance to take into account that searches can either be permitted by the office's owner or ordered by a search warrant issued by a judge, pursuant to Articles 192 and 193[36] of the Criminal Proceedings Code. In either case, the final paragraph of Article 198[37] of the Criminal Proceedings Code establishes that fundamental rights, of which the right to privacy is one, have to be respected during searches. Thus,

---

[36] Art. 192 of the Criminal Proceedings Code states in Spanish: Cuando el registro deba practicarse en una morada o local habitado o en sus dependencias cerradas, se hará la prevención de allanamiento, si no da el permiso correspondiente, dicha prevención podrá ser omitida cuando exista grave riesgo para la vida o la seguridad de las personas.
Formalidades para el registro.
Art. 193 of the Criminal Proceedings Code states in Spanish: La orden judicial de registro, se notificará al que habite el lugar, o cuando esté ausente, a su encargado y, a falta de éste, a cualquier persona mayor de edad que se encuentre en el lugar. Al notificado se le invitará a presenciar el registro. Cuando no se encuentre a nadie ello se hará constar en el acta.
Practicado el registro, se consignará en el acta, su resultado con expresión de las circunstancias útiles para la investigación y en su caso, las razones por las cuales se omitió la prevención de allanamiento. El acta será firmada por los concurrentes. Si alguien no lo hace se dejará constancia de ello.

[37] Art. 198 of the Criminal Proceedings Code states in Spanish: No podrán ser utilizados en la investigación o el proceso, los documentos y objetos encontrados en el registro que se refieran a:
1) Las comunicaciones entre el imputado y sus defensores.
2) Las comunicaciones escritas entre el imputado y las personas que están facultadas para abstenerse de declarar.
3) Los archivos de las personas indicadas en los numerales precedentes que contengan información confidencial relativa al imputado. Este apartado comprende también los documentos digitales, videos, grabaciones, ilustraciones y cualquier otra imagen que sea relevante a los fines de la restricción.
La exclusión no tendrá lugar cuando se obtenga autorización expresa de su titular o cuando se trate de personas vinculadas como partícipes o coautoras del delito investigado o de uno conexo.

documents containing confidential information regarding communications between defendants and their attorneys, written communications between defendants and people who are obliged to abstain from testifying, and documents belonging to the attorney, the defendant and persons not allowed to testify pertaining to the defendant.

Documents and correspondence containing confidential information about clients of an attorney cannot be used during investigations and judicial proceedings. As a consequence, such documents cannot be seized and searched during those kinds of proceedings. Ultimately, the same rules regarding the protection given to documents during police or judicial investigations described in Section 6 of this chapter also apply when an attorney's office is being searched.

Regarding civil and commercial proceedings, the corresponding procedural law provides for a type of evidence called judicial inspection evidence, pursuant to Articles 390 and 392[38] of that law. This kind of evidence consists of having a judge visually inspect an object, person or place to determine the truth about facts alleged by the parties to a dispute. Because any kind of judicial activity is required to uphold constitutional rights, judicial inspections of an attorney's office are limited to the verification of the perceptible traces left by the facts alleged by the parties. However, judges are bound by the same rules protecting an attorney's documents examined in Section 6 of this chapter. In addition, Article 44 of the Competition Law[39] allows the Competition Authority to search the venues where evidence regarding an anticompetitive

El registro y allanamiento deberá realizarse en todo caso con respeto a la dignidad, a la propiedad y demás derechos constitucionales. Los abusos o excesos de autoridad darán lugar a la responsabilidad penal correspondiente.

[38] Art. 390 of the Civil and Commercial Proceedings Code states in Spanish: Si para el esclarecimiento de los hechos es necesario que el juez reconozca por sí a una persona, un objeto o un lugar, se podrá proponer este medio de prueba.

Art. 392 of the Civil and Commercial Proceedings Code states in Spanish: Cuando se pretendiere el reconocimiento de una persona o de un objeto, deberá llevarse a cabo en la audiencia; y se procederá sin más al examen correspondiente, debiéndose describir en forma ordenada e inteligible el estado en la persona o en que el objeto se encuentren. Cualquiera de las partes podrá objetar en todo momento la descripción referida.

Si el reconocimiento se refiriera a un inmueble, se señalará día y hora para su práctica, la cual se realizará antes de la audiencia probatoria, con cita previa de las partes.

El juez podrá ordenar de oficio el reconocimiento judicial cuando lo considere necesario para dictar sentencia.

[39] Art. 44 of the Competition Law states in Spanish: El Superintendente, en el ejercicio de sus atribuciones, podrá requerir los informes o documentación relevante para realizar sus investigaciones, así como citar a declarar a quienes tengan relación con los casos de que se trata.

El Superintendente podrá realizar las investigaciones necesarias para la debida aplicación de esta Ley. En el curso de las inspecciones podrá examinar, ordenar compulsas o realizar extractos de los libros, documentos, incluso de carácter contable, y si procediere a retenerlos por un plazo máximo de diez días. En sus inspecciones podrá ir acompañado de peritos en las materias en que versen las investigaciones.

practice are located. The objective is for the Competition Authority to acquire the evidence it needs to conduct its investigation into the actions of economic agents. Therefore, an attorney's office can be searched, but the only evidence that can be extracted is that which is related to the facts of the investigated anticompetitive conduct.

8 Tapping of Telephone Conversations with a Lawyer

38.   A special law regulates the judicial authorization for the tapping of telephone conversations with an attorney. This and other similar limitations to the fundamental right to confidentiality of telecommunications are constitutionally allowed by paragraphs 2, 3 and 4 of Article 24 of the Salvadoran Constitution. Article 1 of the special law establishes the limit of such interventions: it is only temporarily allowed with a sufficiently reasoned judicial authorization, and it can only affect information related to a police investigation or criminal proceeding.[40]

Moreover, Article 5 of the same special law[41] provides for such phone interceptions only when certain felonies are being investigated or prosecuted. These felonies include homicide and aggravated homicide; limitations to

---

Cuando se trate de registros o allanamientos, en la solicitud que se haga al Juez, el Superintendente deberá incorporar, entre otros, los siguientes elementos:
a) El objeto del procedimiento en el que se desarrollaría la diligencia solicitada;
b) La indicación de las personas que participarán en el registro o allanamiento;
c) La dirección del inmueble o inmuebles en donde se realizará la diligencia;
d) La fecha y hora en las que se realizaría la misma;
e) Los elementos probatorios que pretenden recabarse a través de la diligencia;
f) La relación de los elementos probatorios que pretenden recabarse con el objeto del procedimiento;
g) Las razones que justifiquen que el registro o allanamiento es el medio idóneo y necesario para recabar los elementos probatorios.
El Juez deberá resolver lo solicitado y notificar al Superintendente la orden de registro o allanamiento concedida en un plazo de veinticuatro horas contadas a partir de la presentación de la solicitud.
La ejecución del registro o allanamiento será realizada por el Superintendente y/o las personas autorizadas para ese efecto, quienes podrán auxiliarse de la fuerza pública. La diligencia deberá iniciar en horas hábiles.

[40] Art. 1 of the Law for the Intervention of Telecommunications states in Spanish: Se garantiza el secreto de las telecomunicaciones y el derecho a la intimidad. De manera excepcional podrá autorizarse judicialmente, de forma escrita y motivada, la intervención temporal de cualquier tipo de telecomunicaciones, preservándose en todo caso el secreto de la información privada que no guarde relación con la investigación o el proceso penal. La información proveniente de una intervención ilegal carecerá de valor.

[41] Art. 5 of the Law for the Intervention of Telecommunications states in Spanish: Únicamente podrá hacerse uso de la facultad de intervención prevista en esta Ley en la investigación y el procesamiento de los siguientes delitos:
1) Homicidio y su forma agravada.
2) Privación de libertad, Secuestro y Atentados contra la Libertad Agravados.

personal freedom, kidnapping and aggravated damage to personal freedom; pornography, the use of minors, legally incompetent persons and the mentally ill in pornography, and possession of pornography; extortion; criminal negotiations; taking and paying bribes; criminal associations; sale and trafficking of people; international criminal associations; terrorist and drug felonies, money and asset laundering; organized crime; felonies punished by the applicable law; and felonies related to any of these.

Additionally, Article 302(2) of the Criminal Code[42] allows for the interception of telephone communications, in this case without the need for a judicial authorization, when a criminal court or the Attorney General is conducting an investigation. It is required that the victims of a felony, or other offended

3) Pornografía, Utilización de personas menores de dieciocho años e incapaces o deficientes mentales en pornografía, y Posesión de pornografía.
4) Extorsión.
5) Concusión.
6) Negociaciones Ilícitas.
7) Cohecho Propio, Impropio y Activo.
8) Agrupaciones Ilícitas.
9) Comercio de Personas, Tráfico Ilegal de Personas, Trata de Personas y su forma agravada.
10) Organizaciones Internacionales delictivas.
11) Los delitos previstos en la Ley Reguladora de las Actividades Relativas a las Drogas.
12) Los delitos previstos en la Ley Especial contra Actos de Terrorismo.
13) Los delitos previstos en la Ley contra el Lavado de Dinero y de Activos.
14) Los delitos cometidos bajo la modalidad de crimen organizado en los términos establecidos en la ley de la materia.
15) Los delitos previstos en la presente Ley.
16) Los delitos conexos con cualquiera de los anteriores. A los efectos de este numeral se entiende como conexo aquel delito cometido para perpetrar o facilitar la comisión de otro de los previstos anteriormente o para procurar al culpable o a otros el provecho o la impunidad.

En ningún caso la intervención procederá cuando el delito investigado sea menos grave, salvo en caso de conexidad.

[42] Art. 302 of the Criminal Code states in Spanish: El que interceptare o interviniere las comunicaciones telefónicas o usare artificios técnicos de escucha o grabación de dichas comunicaciones o lo ordenare o permitiere, será sancionado con prisión de dos a cuatro años, e inhabilitación especial para el ejercicio del cargo o empleo por igual tiempo, si fuere funcionario o empleado público.

En el marco de una investigación judicial o de la Fiscalía General de la República, no se considerará como interferencia o intervención telefónica, ni violación al derecho de intimidad, cuando se estuviere recibiendo amenazas, exigiendo rescate de una persona que estuviere privada de libertad o secuestrada o se pidiere el cumplimiento de determinados hechos a cambio de la liberación de dicha persona, o a cambio de no intentar ninguna acción penal o se trate de delitos de crimen organizado, y la víctima, el ofendido o su representante, en su caso, solicitaren o permitieren por escrito a la Fiscalía General de la República, la escucha y grabación de las conversaciones o acciones en que se reciban tales amenazas o exigencias. La escucha y grabación así obtenida podrá ser utilizada con fines probatorios en juicio y, en este caso, deberá ser valorada por el juez.

parties, request it of the Attorney General or authorize it. The limited circumstances in which this can occur all deal with the urgent need to preserve life and personal security: when threats are received, ransoms for kidnapping are demanded and in case of organized crime. If any of such telephone conversations include one between an attorney and a client, they can be lawfully intervened.

Outside of those parameters, intercepting telephone conversations of an attorney lack legal validity. Failure to comply with this regulation may also result in criminal liability for the perpetrating agents of the authorities. Article 302(1) of the Criminal Code punishes this conduct with prison time from two to four years and job suspension for the same period of time.

9 The Lawyer as Witness

39.   Attorneys are legally required to withhold from disclosing confidential information about their clients when testifying during criminal and civil proceedings, mentioned in Section 1 of this chapter. The provisions applicable to civil and commercial proceedings also apply to any kind of proceedings established in other Salvadoran laws, in accordance with Article 20 of the Civil and Commercial Proceedings Code.[43] In consideration of this, attorneys are therefore barred from disclosing their clients' confidential information in civil, commercial, criminal, labor and administrative proceedings.

10 The Lawyer and the Press

40.   Unless expressly released by their clients from the duty of professional secrecy, attorneys are not entitled to disclose their clients' confidential information to the press. Failure to do so will result in a breach of the duty of confidentiality as previously examined in Sections 1 and 4 of this chapter. Under the rules of the *mandato*, a lawyer cannot communicate with the press, unless the lawyer has an express authorization or request by the client to do so.

11 Powers of the Tax and Other Authorities

41.   In El Salvador, public authorities are able to do only what the Constitution or laws empower them to do. For this reason, the Salvadoran tax authority is not entitled to oblige attorneys to disclose their clients' confidential information, since no law expressly allows them to do so.

---

[43] Art. 20 of the Civil and Commercial Proceedings Code states in Spanish: En defecto de disposición específica en las leyes que regulan procesos distintos del civil y mercantil, las normas de este código se aplicarán supletoriamente.

However, attorneys are expressly required to disclose information about certain felonies, as described in Section 5 of this chapter, to the Attorney General's Office and the National Civil Police. Also, Article 36 of the Financial System Supervision Law[44] requires that any person providing services to institutions participating in the financial system are required to notify the Financial System Superintendence concerning certain information regarding their clients. This information, regarding transactions between financial institutions and their shareholders or managers, can be expressly requested by the Superintendence. Apart from these provisions, no additional relevant rules empower other public authorities to order that attorneys disclose their clients' confidential information.

12 National Security Issues

42.   As analyzed in Section 5 of this chapter, attorneys are not exempted from the legal duty to inform the authorities about the planned or impending perpetration of terrorist acts or those acts that would threaten public safety. In addition, Article 29 of the Salvadoran Constitution[45] establishes that the prohibition against authorities intercepting correspondence and tapping telecommunications does not apply when a state of emergency is declared. This can happen during wartime, when the country's territory is invaded, or when acts of rebellion or sedition are being perpetrated, for example.

---

[44] Art. 36 of the Law for the Regulation and Supervision of the Financial System states in Spanish: Sin perjuicio de otras obligaciones legales, reglamentarias y normativas que les correspondan, el auditor externo deberá opinar, ante la junta general de accionistas u órgano superior de administración y ante la junta directiva u órgano de gobierno del integrante del sistema financiero de que se trate, sobre la integridad, adecuación y eficacia de los sistemas de control interno.
    Los directores, administradores, gerentes, auditores internos y externos, otros funcionarios y demás personas que presten servicios a cualquier integrante del sistema financiero, deberán reportar a la Superintendencia las operaciones que ésta les haya requerido, en particular aquellas que se realicen o se hayan realizado entre aquel y sus accionistas o administradores y las relacionadas con el conglomerado financiero a que pertenezca si fuere el caso. La forma, periodicidad y circunstancias en las que se deberán reportar estas operaciones se establecerán en las normas técnicas que para tal efecto se emitan.

[45] Art. 29 of the Salvadoran Constitution states in Spanish: En casos de guerra, invasión del territorio, rebelión, sedición, catástrofe, epidemia u otra calamidad general, o de graves perturbaciones del orden público, podrán suspenderse las garantías establecidas en los artículos 5, 6 paragraph primero, 7 paragraph primero y 24 de esta Constitución, excepto cuando se trate de reuniones o asociaciones con fines religiosos, culturales, económicos o deportivos. Tal suspensión podrá afectar la totalidad o parte del territorio de la República, y se hará por medio de decreto del Órgano Legislativo o del Órgano Ejecutivo, en su caso.
    También podrán suspenderse las garantías contenidas en los Arts. 12 paragraph segundo y 13 paragraph segundo de esta Constitución, cuando así lo acuerde el Órgano Legislativo, con el voto favorable de las tres cuartas partes de los Diputados electos; no excediendo la detención administrativa de quince días.

In a different context, when an attorney is representing the government of El Salvador, the attorney is required not to reveal classified information. Therefore, these attorneys are not empowered by Article 19 of the Law of Access to Public Information[46] to disclose information regarding secret military plans and political negotiations in which the president participates. Other information that must not be disclosed includes that which endangers national defense and public safety, may affect international relations or diplomatic negotiations, or endanger a person's life.

13 Conclusion

43. Attorney-client privilege is neither sufficiently nor clearly defined or regulated in the Salvadoran legal system. As a result, the diffuse statutory rules have to be compiled to produce a cohesive body of law needed to understand what the duty of professional secrecy is in El Salvador, what it protects and how it is enforced. This leads to certain inconsistencies that are not apparent or readily understandable to clients.

An example of such inconsistencies is found in the Law Against Money and Asset Laundering, which requires that attorneys reveal certain information about specific cash transactions of their clients to the Attorney General's Office. This would appear to conflict with the felony prohibiting the disclosure of clients' confidential information. However, the solution to this apparent conflict is explained by means of a structural analysis of the felony penalized in Article 187 of the Criminal Code: it excludes the attorney from criminal liability since conduct different from disclosing information is not legally expected. For a principle of the utmost importance for clients, this kind of

---

[46] Art. 19 of the Public Information Access Law states in Spanish: Es información reservada:

Los planes militares secretos y las negociaciones políticas a que se refiere el artículo 168 ordinal 7o de la Constitución.

La que perjudique o ponga en riesgo la defensa nacional y la seguridad pública.

La que menoscabe las relaciones internacionales o la conducción de negociaciones diplomáticas del país.

La que ponga en peligro evidente la vida, la seguridad o la salud de cualquier persona.

La que contenga opiniones o recomendaciones que formen parte del proceso deliberativo de los servidores públicos, en tanto no sea adoptada la decisión definitiva.

La que causare un serio perjuicio en la prevención, investigación o persecución de actos ilícitos, en la administración de justicia o en la verificación del cumplimiento de las leyes.

La que comprometiere las estrategias y funciones estatales en procedimientos judiciales o administrativos en curso.

La que pueda generar una ventaja indebida a una persona en perjuicio de un tercero.

No podrá invocarse el carácter de reservado cuando se trate de la investigación de violaciones graves de derechos fundamentales o delitos de trascendencia internacional.

solution is too complicated: clients generally are not attorneys trained in legal interpretation.

What this means is that, as opposed to other countries, El Salvador is in need of a binding Code of Ethics for attorneys, with a corresponding system for its enforcement. Such a statute will need to clearly define the nature and scope of attorney-client privilege and establish penalties that incentivize the observance of the duty, something not done by the current system.

First, applicable felonies are less stringent than the disciplinary rules, since the Supreme Court can suspend attorneys for up to five years or disbar them. Second, even if rules are enforceable, they do not provide a real incentive for attorneys to respect their duty of professional secrecy: a) the prison sentence can be commuted for domestic arrest or community service; b) breaches of the applicable civil rules require the process of long proceedings with complicated evidentiary rules; and c) the corresponding disciplinary rules do not include monetary sanctions for lawyers responsible for breaching confidentiality. Third, clients are effectively left alone, with no substantial assistance from the state, when proceeding against attorneys who have breached their professional duty of secrecy, since the Attorney General does not have jurisdiction over the corresponding felony. Fourth, the Salvadoran court system has a heavy caseload, with the result that civil or criminal actions will not be processed expediently. Fifth, no special tribunals are charged with the sole responsibility to know about cases of professional responsibility.

This long list of problems with the current system can be solved with the aforementioned Code of Ethics, which would contain rules, proceedings and sanctions and an entity specifically tasked with investigating and punishing breaches of attorney-client privilege. Comprehensive rules, specific proceedings, adequate sanctions and a single enforcing entity will make an effective incentive not to breach the duty of professional secrecy. However, a first obstacle has to be overcome: a bar association needs to be established in El Salvador. A consequence of not having a bar association is the lack of a Code of Ethics and the subsequent dispersal of applicable rules throughout the whole Salvadoran legal system.

Are your secrets safe in El Salvador? This question, which begs for a simple answer, unfortunately cannot be answered in such a way. Instead, a complicated answer has to be rendered: it depends. Are there established rules that seek to enforce respect for the duty of professional secrecy? Yes. Are they effectively applied? Not frequently. One way to remedy this situation is to include a nondisclosure clause in the *mandato* or for clients to agree to a sufficiently robust NDA with their attorneys. Clients and their counsel are thus urged to protect themselves contractually as best as possible.

21

Guatemala

ALFONSO CARRILLO M.

Carrillo y Asociados

Preliminary Note

1.   All professionals who practice in the Republic of Guatemala are subject to general professional secrecy laws. Regardless of whether they have their own practice; belong to a law firm as partners or associates; or are in-house lawyers for private corporations, for the state or public institutions, lawyers are bound, in addition, by attorney-client secrecy laws under a different body of law.

        Professional secrecy and attorney-client privilege are protected by civil law, and their infringement is penalized by criminal law. General oversight, compliance and the imposition of sanctions are entrusted to the Bar Association and the civil and criminal courts.

        Recent legislation has restricted the absolute character that attorney-client privilege used to have. Exceptions to attorney-client privilege may include affairs relating to terrorism, money laundering and national security.

1 Scope of and Limitations on the Duty of Professional Secrecy/Attorney-Client Privilege

A Statutory Basis and Implications

2.   The duty of professional secrecy and attorney-client privilege both have a statutory basis in Guatemala.

a Professional Secrecy

3.   Civil law establishes that professionals are responsible for the damages and losses they cause by willful misconduct, fault or inexcusable ignorance, and for the disclosure of the secrets of their clients. Any reserved or confidential information to which professionals become privy as a result of the practice of their profession would be deemed a secret for the purposes of professional secrecy laws.[1] The law does not distinguish between the circumstances or persons from whom the professional obtains such information, for instance, the client or a third party (e.g., a family member interviewed by a physician), and all such information could be considered subject to professional secrecy laws.

        Ethical codes issued by professional associations also include disciplinary provisions on duties of professional secrecy.

---

[1] Arts. 1668, 2033, Civil Code of Guatemala (Decree-Law 106).

Criminal law penalizes the disclosure of professional or any other secrets or private and confidential communications and documents with imprisonment and fines.[2]

4. For the purposes of the duties of professional secrecy, a person is deemed to be a professional when he or she holds an academic degree issued by a university, is an active member of the corresponding professional association, abides by the applicable ethical rules and is legally authorized to practice.[3] Academic degrees and titles to practice must be issued or recognized by a Guatemalan university.[4]

The Political Constitution of the Republic of Guatemala recognizes the right of free association with the sole exception of professional association, which is mandatory.[5] Professional association refers to the association of university graduates of related professions, in professional entities, in accordance with the provisions of the Law of Mandatory Professional Association.[6] The goals of professional association are the moral, scientific, technical and material improvement of the professionals and the supervision of their practice. All professionals must abide by the norms of the professional association and observe the resolutions of its authorities.[7] All professionals must render their services with full dedication and diligence, observing the prescriptions of the corresponding science or art and maintaining professional secrecy in connection to the secrets of their clients.[8] Each professional association issues its own rules and ethical code to which its members are bound.

b Attorney-Client Privilege

5. The Law of the Judicial Body of Guatemala and the Code of Professional Ethics of the Guatemalan Bar Association contain specific regimes on professional secrecy for lawyers.[9]

---

[2] Arts. 222, 223, Criminal Code (Decree 17-73).
[3] Contreras Ortiz, Rubén Alberto, *Obligaciones y Negocios Jurídicos Civiles (Parte Especial: Contratos)*, Universidad Rafael Landívar, Guatemala, 2008, at 485.
[4] Art. 90, Political Constitution of Guatemala; Art. 1, Law of Mandatory Professional Association (Decree no. 72-2001); Art. 196, Law of the Judicial Body (Decree 2-89).
[5] Art. 34, Political Constitution of Guatemala.
[6] Art. 1, Law of Mandatory Professional Association (Decree no. 72-2001).
[7] Art. 90, Political Constitution of Guatemala; Art. 1, Law of Mandatory Professional Association (Decree no. 72-2001).
[8] Arts. 87, 89, Political Constitution of Guatemala.
[9] An *academic* degree in legal and social sciences (*Licenciatura en Ciencas Jurídicas y Sociales*) from a law school of a university in the Republic of Guatemala, which is generally issued together with the *professional* titles to practice as an attorney-at-law and notary public, is required to practice law in Guatemala. In addition, lawyers must be active members of the Bar Association (*Colegio de Abogados y Notarios de Guatemala*) and should be registered at the Supreme Court of Justice.

The first prohibits attorneys-at-law from disclosing the secrets of their clients[10] and holds them responsible for any damages they may cause due to proven ignorance, fault, willful misconduct, carelessness, negligence or bad faith.[11] As in the case of professionals, in general, the law does not distinguish between the circumstances and persons from whom the lawyer obtains reserved or confidential information, that is, the client, the counterparty or a third party (e.g., a potential witness). All such information obtained by the attorney in the practice of the legal profession could thus be considered a secret.

The Guatemalan Bar Association approved the Professional Ethics Code currently in force in 1994. Loyalty is one of the principles set forth by the code and involves faithfulness to the interests of justice and the client. It entails the rigorous observance of professional secrecy, honorable conduct in litigation, and a respectful and considerate demeanor in relation to judges, the authorities and the counterparty.[12] Even though the code was not issued by the legislative branch, it is mandatory for its members by virtue of their membership in the association.

B Scope

6.   In accordance with the Professional Ethics Code of the Guatemalan Bar Association, attorney-client privilege is both a lawyer's duty and an unwaivable right that survives the relationship between the lawyer and the client. It comprises all reserved and confidential information revealed by the client or otherwise made known by a counterparty or a third party to the lawyer in the course of the lawyer's professional practice.

Article 5 of the Professional Ethics Code of the Guatemalan Bar Association establishes that:

> Observing professional secrecy is a duty and a right for lawyers. Regarding their clients, it is a duty that remains in force even after the rendering of services has finished. Before the judges and other authorities, it is an unwaivable right. The obligation to observe professional secrecy includes all confidences related to the matter.

On March 24, 2004, a lawyer filed an action for the protection of constitutional rights before an appellate court. He was challenging the ruling of a civil judge who had subpoenaed the attorney to render a sworn statement regarding aspects of a professional services agreement that he had executed with a client. In his opinion, said subpoena violated the professional secrecy obligation set forth in Article 2033 of the Civil Code and Article 223 of the Criminal Code, the object of which is to protect individuals from the damages that may be caused by the disclosure of secrets that they have entrusted to a professional.

[10] Art. 201(3), Law of the Judicial Body (Decree 2-89).   [11] Ibid., Art. 202.
[12] Arts. 198, 200, Law of the Judicial Body.

The appellate court rejected the action because it considered that he should have filed an appeal remedy against the ruling. The professional appealed the ruling of the appellate court. In that appeal, the Court of Constitutionality reversed the appellate court ruling, granted the requested constitutional protection, stated that the attorney did not have to appeal the ruling and confirmed that the rights of the lawyer had been breached because the judge intended him to reveal the secrets of his client through the subpoena.[13]

C Persons Subject to the Duty of Professional Secrecy

7.   All professionals who practice in Guatemala are subject to the duty of professional secrecy, and all lawyers are bound by the rules of attorney-client privilege.[14] See no. 5 of this chapter regarding the specific provisions applicable to attorneys-at-law.

D Exceptions to and Optional Derogations from the Duty of Professional Secrecy

8.   Even though professional secrecy may be considered a waivable right of the client, attorney-client privilege is not waivable.[15] The provisions of the Judicial Branch Law that impose the obligations of secrecy on lawyers are a matter of public law and thus may not be waived.

Express provisions regarding the nonwaivable character of professional secrecy are contained only in the Code of Professional Ethics. The provisions of civil law, which entitle a client to damages and reimbursement of losses in the event of breach of the duties of professional secrecy, are a matter of private law, the provisions of which are generally considered waivable, subject to the autonomous will of the parties. Breach of professional secrecy provisions is penalized by criminal law, however, so any waiver agreed on under private law could be questioned on the grounds of public interest.

In addition, the law provides certain exceptions to the duties of secrecy of a lawyer when specific crimes are being investigated, which will be discussed below.

E Law Firms

9.   All professionals who are members of law firms must observe professional secrecy. This obligation includes lawyers and all other university graduates, regardless of their field of specialization or practice.

Guatemalan author Rubén Alberto Contreras Ortiz states that, due to its *intuitu personae* nature, a professional service agreement can be executed only

---

[13] Action for the Protection of Constitutional Rights (*Amparo*) no. 1638-2004.

[14] Arts. 1668, 2033, Civil Code of Guatemala (Decree-Law 106).

[15] Art. 5, Professional Ethics Code of the Guatemalan Bar Association.

between an individual and a client.[16] In 1992, a thesis analyzed the feasibility of institutionalizing law firms as companies to render professional legal services to clients. The author's conclusions include the following: (i) lawyers should specialize in specific areas and should get together to offer legal services as a group; (ii) institutionalization is achieved through the joining of various professionals in an organized and permanent manner; (iii) institutionalization allows clients to receive continuous legal services regardless of the physical presence of a specific attorney, since they receive services from specialists through an organization that has technical, material and human resources; (iv) it is feasible to incorporate a company to mediate the rendering of legal services between the professional and the client; the agreement between the client and the company is not a professional services agreement but an agreement of intermediation of professional services; (v) the intermediation carried out by the company does not imply the depersonalization of the professional services, since the professionals involved have a direct relationship with the client to render the services; (vi) the company should have professionals who are specialists in the corresponding fields of law; (vii) the professionals remain liable to the client and the company, and the client has a double security, since in case of negligence, the client could file a claim against both the professional and the company; (viii) the professionals who render their services through the company, regardless of whether they are partners or not, will always be bound to the company through an employment or professional services agreement.[17]

Since Guatemalan law protects clients and the privileged information that they entrust to professionals, attorneys-at-law would be deemed included, regardless of whether the professional has his or her own practice; is a member of a law firm as a partner, associate, or employee; or in any other capacity.

The legal representatives of a law firm who are not lawyers could none-theless be held criminally responsible for any public disclosure of private documents, correspondence, papers, photographs and the like that the firm should hold secret under general criminal law, which requires secrecy of information delivered upon conditions of confidentiality.[18]

F Legal Assistants and Staff

10.   There are no specific civil or professional legal provisions applicable to legal assistants and staff. Thus, in practice, professional secrecy is protected through

---

[16] Contreras Ortiz, Rubén Alberto, *Obligaciones y Negocios Jurídicos Civiles (Parte Especial: Contratos)*, Universidad Rafael Landívar, Guatemala, 2008, at 485.

[17] Rodolfo Alegría Toruño, *Consideraciones Sobre la Intermediación de la Sociedad Mercantil en la Prestación de Servicios Profesionales*, Tesis de Graduación para Obtener el Grado de Licenciado en Ciencias Jurídicas y Sociales y los Títulos de Abogado y Notario, Universidad Francisco Marroquín, Guatemala, 1992, at 125-29.

[18] Art. 222, Criminal Code of Guatemala (Decree 17-73).

the execution of confidentiality agreements with all the personnel who are part of work teams and have access to privileged information and documentation.

Those who have personnel under their authority, which would be the case of the employers of the legal assistants, paralegals and clerical staff, are liable to the client for the damages or losses caused by such employees and workers in the performance of their duties. The law provides that employers and persons who have someone else under their authority are liable for the damages and losses caused by such employees and other workers in the performance of their duties. They are also liable for the acts of third parties if they deliver or transfer to the third parties objects or elements of any kind in their possession or with which they have been entrusted, if such third parties do not provide the necessary guarantees to handle them.[19]

Law firms organized as legal entities are juridical persons and, as such, are civilly liable for the damages or losses caused by their legal representatives in the exercise of their duties.[20] The law allows the responsible party who pays for damages and losses to claim reimbursement from the person who actually caused such losses, unless it can be proved that the individual followed instructions received from the person in charge.[21]

G External Service Providers

11.   If external service providers are professionals, professional secrecy provisions are applicable. If they are not professionals, confidentiality agreements should be executed to guarantee nondisclosure of privileged information.

H Multidisciplinary Associations

12.   Each professional of a multidisciplinary association is bound to observe professional secrecy as set forth by the law. If the group includes individuals who are not professionals, they should execute confidentiality agreements to protect the client's confidential information.

I In-House Counsel

13.   In-house lawyers who work for private corporations, for the state or for public institutions are bound by attorney-client secrecy laws. Guatemalan law does not draw distinctions between employed lawyers and outside counsel.

Attorney-client secrecy would cover advice given by the in-house lawyer on legal issues affecting the corporation or any other employer.

Breach of attorney-client privilege in the case of lawyers who are public officers or public servants found liable for the disclosure of facts, acts or documents known to them by virtue of their post, which must remain secret

---

[19] Art. 1663, Civil Code of Guatemala (Decree-Law 106).   [20] Ibid., Art. 1664.
[21] Ibid., Art. 1666.

by law, would be sanctioned with a one- to three-year imprisonment term, a fine and special disqualification.[22]

2 History of the Duty of Professional Secrecy in Guatemala

14.   Professional services agreements and professional secrecy were first regulated by the current Civil Code of Guatemala, Decree-Law 106, which entered into force on July 10, 1964.

The explanatory memorandum issued by the committee in charge of drafting the Civil Code stated that it was necessary to have a special section (*título*) in connection with professional services contracts, since it was distinct from other personal services agreements, such as employment and personal "lease" agreements. The committee included the obligations of professionals to render services with due diligence and observing professional secrecy.

Articles 1668 and 2033 of the Civil Code were thus drafted to establish that professionals are liable for the damages and losses they cause by the disclosure of their clients' secrets. Article 2033 provides:

> The professional is required to render the services with full dedication and diligence and in accordance with the prescriptions of the corresponding science or art, and is responsible for the damages and losses he/she causes by willful misconduct, fault or inexcusable ignorance, or as the result of disclosure of the secrets of his/her client.

Prior to the current Civil Code, Decree number 1932 of the Legislative Assembly of the Republic of Guatemala was the applicable law.[23] It referred to the "lease of services" (*locación de servicios*). Article 1754 stated, "A person may undertake the obligation to render his/her personal or industrial service, to a person or entity, during a certain period of time." It did not specifically mention anything regarding professional secrecy.

15.   Article 201(3) of the Law of the Judicial Body, Decree 2-89, currently in force, provides that attorneys are forbidden from disclosing the secrets of their clients. The previous Law of the Judicial Body, Decree 1762,[24] contained a similar provision. Article 201(3) provided that attorneys were forbidden from revealing the secrets of their clients.

3 Supervision

A The Bar Associations

16.   All lawyers must belong to the Guatemalan Bar Association to practice law. Guatemalan legal practice does not distinguish between solicitors and barristers.

---

[22] Art. 422, Criminal Code of Guatemala (Decree 17-73).   [23] Issued on May 13, 1933.
[24] Issued on June 11, 1968.

One of the goals of professional associations is to oversee the ethical and efficient practice of the professions for the benefit of the community.[25]

Professional associations, including the Bar Association, have a Disciplinary Court (*Tribunal de Honor*), which is in charge of handling disciplinary cases whenever a complaint is filed against one of its members. Once the proceeding has been completed, the applicable penalty is set by the Disciplinary Court, the Board of Directors or the General Assembly, in accordance with the severity of the case.[26]

B The Courts

17.   Civil courts have jurisdiction to hear and resolve claims involving damages and losses arising from the breach of a professional service agreement or tort law claims.

Criminal courts may resolve both criminal claims and civil liability claims if the latter arises from violation of criminal law on matters of professional secrecy.

4 Sanctions

A Proceedings and Sanctions

a Disciplinary Proceedings and Sanctions

18.   In the event a member of the Bar Association is accused of having acted unethically or against the honor, decorum and prestige of the legal profession, the matter must be handled by the Disciplinary Court, which is in charge of carrying out the investigation, issuing an opinion and determining the penalty.[27]

The procedure starts with the filing of a written complaint before the Disciplinary Court, through the Secretary of the Board of Directors of the Guatemalan Bar Association. It must contain a detailed explanation of the facts and offer the necessary evidence. The secretary must inform the president of the Disciplinary Court, who shall immediately call the members of the Disciplinary Court so they are made privy to the facts of the case, within a three-day term.

If there are sufficient grounds to warrant an investigation, the accused must be given a hearing within nine days for the purpose of arguing whatever is relevant for the defense and of presenting exculpatory evidence. A 30-day evidence period follows the hearing. If any evidence is to be collected abroad,

---

[25]   Art. 3(c), Law of Mandatory Professional Association (Decree 72-2001).

[26]   Ibid., Art. 19; Arts. 24, 42, 45, Articles of Association of the Guatemalan Bar Association.

[27]   Art. 19, Law of Mandatory Professional Association (Decree 72-2001); Arts. 24, 28–41, Articles of Association of the Guatemalan Bar Association.

the Disciplinary Court will grant an extraordinary six-month term. The Disciplinary Court will receive the evidence offered by the parties and will carry out all the necessary proceedings to clarify the facts during this period. The file will then be made available to the parties for a period of five days for review and for their final allegations.

The Disciplinary Court may have an extraordinary eight-day period to carry out any further proceedings it may deem appropriate to issue a better judgment. It will then have an additional eight days in which to issue an opinion, which will be notified in writing to the parties. The parties then have a 24-hour period to request a clarification if the terms of the opinion were unclear, ambiguous, contradictory or need amplification, if an issue was left out of the analysis.

All the resolutions of the Disciplinary Court must be decided by an absolute majority of votes. A certified copy of the opinion issued by the Disciplinary Court will be sent to the Board of Directors so that it, or the General Assembly, as the case may be, can issue a resolution.

Any events unforeseen by the Articles of Association shall be resolved through the application of the civil and commercial litigation provisions, as applicable, as well as the principles of equity and justice.

19. The following penalties may be imposed: (i) fines, (ii) private admonishment, (iii) public admonishment, (iv) temporary suspension (minimum of six months and maximum of two years),[28] and (v) definitive suspension. Definitive suspension implies deprivation of active membership in the professional association. The decision must be made by two-thirds of the Disciplinary Court and ratified by the General Assembly of the Professional Association, with the vote of at least 10 percent of the total number of active members of the professional association.

The constitutional right of defense and due process must be observed. The principles of oral procedures, continuity and procedural economy are applicable.[29]

It is up to the Board of Directors to determine whether admonishment will be public or private.

Temporary and definitive suspension may be applied only by the General Assembly. Any suspension, either temporary or definitive, must be recorded in the Book of Registry.[30]

The penalties decided upon by the Disciplinary Court are definitive and are subject to appeal only before the Assembly of Presidents of the professional associations, in accordance with the appeal regulation of said body.[31]

---

[28] Art. 26, Law of Mandatory Professional Association.   [29] Ibid., Art. 26.
[30] Arts. 42, 45, Articles of Association of the Guatemalan Bar Association.
[31] Art. 27, Law of Mandatory Professional Association.

b Civil Proceedings and Liability

20.   If an attorney-at-law or a notary public, who is rendering professional services, breaches the obligation to observe professional secrecy, causing damages or losses to the client, the client is entitled to file a civil liability claim against the professional before a civil court.[32]

c Tort Proceedings and Liability

21.   In case a third party, other than the client, suffers damages and losses arising from the disclosure of secrets known by a professional by virtue of his or her practice, such third party is entitled to file a civil liability claim before a civil court.[33]

d Criminal Proceedings and Sanctions

22.   A professional who breaches the obligation to observe professional secrecy is also criminally liable.

Article 223 of the Criminal Code of Guatemala establishes that individuals who, without having just cause, revealed or used for their own or someone else's benefit a secret known by them by virtue of their state, occupation, job, profession or art, if by doing so they cause or may cause losses, will be penalized with prison from six months to two years or a fine of 100 to 1,000 quetzals (between approximately USD $13 and USD $130, or €11 and €115).

B Relationship between Criminal Sanctions and Disciplinary Sanctions

23.   Criminal sanctions are independent from disciplinary sanctions. This does not contradict the principle *ne bis in idem*.

The Guatemalan Constitutionality Court has ruled that the Disciplinary Court is a disciplinary body the function of which is to judge the conduct of the members of a professional association. It must investigate claims of dishonorable conduct, issue an opinion and recommend the corresponding penalty. The right of defense and due process must be observed in any such proceedings. Said dishonorable actions may or may not be crimes.

Disciplinary action does not infringe on the principles of legal certainty or the jurisdiction of the courts. The primary purpose of the disciplinary proceeding is the moral, scientific, technical and economic betterment of the university professions and the supervision of their practice. That is, the Disciplinary Court issues administrative penalties the purpose of which is to maintain the scientific and moral quality of its association's members, and it is thus entirely different from the purpose and content of a civil or criminal procedure.[34]

---

[32] Art. 2033, Civil Code of Guatemala (Decree-Law 106).   [33] Ibid., Art. 1668.
[34] Judgment of case no. 1892-2001 of June 12, 2002.

The Constitutionality Court has held that the need for a body with the power to supervise the correct practice of professional activities and of penalizing any unethical conduct of the members of the professional association was unquestionable.

Because disciplinary actions brought by professional associations have a different nature and purpose, it also judged that the principle *ne bis in idem* is not violated and that its resolutions do not oppose the *ius puniendi* of the state. The power to discipline dishonorable or unethical conduct of the members of a professional association does not imply a revision of what is judged in judicial cases, since they are proceedings of different nature.[35]

24.   A judgment of disqualification, whether temporary or definitive, issued by an authority of the Judicial Body must be communicated to the appropriate professional association for registration. The Disciplinary Court of the professional association must also hear the case and fulfill the duties set forth in Article 19 of the Law of Mandatory Professional Association and the Articles of Association of the appropriate professional association.

5 Duty to Provide Information to the Authorities

A Money Laundering and Terrorism

25.   The Law to Prevent and Repress the Financing of Terrorism, Decree 58-2005, created a special regime against terrorism. It is applicable to those who, due to the nature of their activities, must provide the Superintendence of Banks, through the Special Verification Intendence, upon request, with information, reports and free access to their sources of information and information systems, for the purpose of verification or amplification of the information necessary for the analysis of terrorism financing. Article 18(e) of the law mentions notaries public among the persons to whom this special regime is applicable. Unlike other persons subject to the special regime, notaries are not required to report suspicious transactions to the authorities, except upon request.

The Law Against the Laundering of Money and Other Assets, Decree 67-2001, also contains provisions of particular importance to professionals. In accordance with Article 19 of this law, certain people have the legal obligation to adopt, develop and execute appropriate programs, norms, procedures and internal controls to prevent the undue use of their services and products for the laundering of money and other assets. They are also required to provide information to the authorities, upon request.

Lawyers and notaries could be subject to disclosure requirements in certain cases, in accordance with the provisions of Governmental Decree 118-2002 that develop the Law Against the Laundering of Money and Other Assets.

---

[35]   Judgment of case no. 2346-2014 of Dec. 2, 2014.

If a person carries out any of the activities mentioned in Article 5(ñ), the person would be required to fulfill the legal obligations established by the law and to provide the authorities with the information requested as per the applicable procedures. The activities refer to individual or juridical persons who render services upon instructions or in favor of their clients or third parties when such persons: i) act by themselves or through third parties, as holders of nominative shares, partners, associates or founders of juridical persons; ii) act by themselves or through third parties, as directors, members of the administration board or board of directors, administrators, attorneys-in-fact or legal representatives of juridical persons; and iii) provide a physical address as tax domicile or headquarters of juridical persons.

If attorneys-at-law or notaries public carry out any of the activities listed above, the legal obligations set forth by the Law Against Money Laundering and Other Assets would be applicable to them. They would not be entitled to invoke the violation of any confidentiality provisions regarding the information, whether set forth in the law or entered upon agreement.[36]

The obligated persons, their owners, directors, managers, administrators, officers, legal representatives and duly authorized employees who provide information in compliance with the law are held harmless from any criminal, civil or administrative liability for disclosure.[37]

B Collective Settlement of Debts

26.   There are no specific provisions regulating professional secrecy in these cases.

6 Treatment of Lawyers' Documents and Correspondence in the Context of Judicial or Police Investigations

27.   The Political Constitution of Guatemala states that every person's correspondence, documents and books are inviolable. They can be reviewed or confiscated only by virtue of a court order. The secrecy of correspondence and communications is guaranteed. Tax documents may be reviewed by the competent authorities. Documents or information obtained in violation of this constitutional article are not valid and cannot be used as evidence in a trial.[38]

All administrative acts are public, with the exception of data provided by individuals under guarantees of confidentiality.[39]

Article 22 of the Law of Access to Public Information, Decree 57-2008, includes professional secrets among information deemed confidential. Article 29 of said law sets forth that reserved or confidential information must be made available to the authorities in charge of the administration of justice whenever

---

[36] Art. 28, Law Against the Laundering of Money and Other Assets (Decree 67-2001).
[37] Ibid., Art. 30.   [38] Art. 24, Political Constitution of Guatemala.   [39] Ibid., Art. 30.

they request it, through a court order, as long as it is indispensable and necessary for a court proceeding, provided that such information is of a public character.

Therefore, an attorney would have to comply with a court order to deliver attorney-client privileged information if such information fulfills the criteria set forth by law to be considered public information.

7 Search of a Lawyer's Office

28.   Article 199 of the Criminal Procedural Code, Decree 51-92, provides that written communications between a defendant and the persons who may abstain from declaring as witnesses by reason of professional secrecy cannot be seized. These include the notes taken regarding communications confided by the defendant regarding any circumstance. The limitation is applicable only when the communications are in the possession of authorized persons, such as attorneys-at-law.

8 Tapping of Telephone Conversations with a Lawyer

29.   Decree 71-2005 contains the Law of the Directorate of Civil Intelligence. Article 4 of said law provides that the cases in which there is evidence of organized criminal activities, with an emphasis in narco-activity and common delinquency that could pose a threat against the life, integrity, liberty and assets of certain persons, the Public Prosecutor's Office may request, as an urgent measure, the authorization of a Court of Appeals to temporarily tap telephone, radio, electronic and similar conversations. This request will be evaluated regarding its grounds and must be resolved within a maximum 24-hour period, under absolute reserve.

9 The Lawyer as Witness

30.   In accordance with the Criminal Proceedings Code, counselors, attorneys-at-law and attorneys-in-fact of the defendant are not required to render statements regarding the facts to which they are privy due to their legal capacity and that comprise a professional secret.[40]

If the court considers that a witness is erroneously invoking the right to refrain from giving a statement or regarding the reserve of secrecy, it will order the statement to be given.[41]

The documents, objects and other elements of conviction that in accordance with the law must be kept secret, or that are directly related to secret facts, will be examined by the competent court or by the judge who controls the

---

[40] Art. 212(2) of the Criminal Proceedings Code (Decree 51-92).   [41] Ibid., Art. 214.

investigation. If they are considered useful to the investigation, they will be incorporated into the proceedings under reserve. During the preparatory proceeding, the judge will expressly authorize the exhibits in the presence of the parties to guarantee the right of defense. The persons who obtain knowledge of these elements are obliged to keep them secret.[42]

10 The Lawyer and the Press

31.   Article 21 of the Code of Professional Ethics of the Guatemalan Bar Association states that lawyers may not publish or discuss writs regarding an ongoing matter in publications unless justice and morality demand rectification.

Once litigation has concluded, publications may be made for the purposes of a juridical exposition of the case, while at the same time keeping professional secrecy and due respect to the courts, the authorities, the parties and interested persons, and using a moderate and decorous language.

11 Powers of the Tax and Other Authorities

32.   The Political Constitution of Guatemala provides that the competent authorities may review tax documents.[43] The Tax Code, Decree 6-91, sets forth the obligation of individuals and entities to provide the tax authorities with information for tax verification purposes. The tax administration shall receive the information subject to duties of confidentiality. If the information is protected by virtue of professional secret, the tax administration will observe the legally established provisions and procedures.

12 National Security Issues

33.   The Framework Law of the National Security System, Decree 18-2008, contains provisions concerning internal and external national security and intelligence. National security is defined by the Law of Access to Public Information, Decree 57-2008, as:

> All those affairs that are part of State policy in order to preserve the physical integrity of the Nation and of its territory for the purpose of protecting all elements that conform the State, from aggressions originating from foreign or national belligerent groups, and those concerning the survival of the Nation-State, in the face of other States.

National security information is defined by Article 23 as confidential information for the purposes of the Law of Access to Public Information.

---

[42] Ibid., Art. 244.   [43] Art. 24, Political Constitution of Guatemala.

Article 29 of the Law of Access to Public Information sets forth that confidential information must be made available to the authorities in charge of the administration of justice whenever they request it, by means of a court order, as long as it is indispensable and necessary for a court proceeding.

In consequence, an attorney would have to comply with a court order to deliver attorney-client privileged information if it pertains to national security.

22

Honduras

J. HUMBERTO MEDINA ALVA

MARCELA AGUILAR

Central Law Honduras

Preliminary Note

1. Lawyers have the duty and the right to maintain professional secrecy of all facts and news that they know because of their professional performance, and lawyers may not be compelled to testify about these.

    Professional secrecy is justified because of the need for absolute trust between legal professionals and the clients who seek their services. Thus, a person accused of a crime should be able to tell the whole truth to the lawyer, without fearing that the lawyer could be forced to testify against the accused person in the future.

    At present, the attorney-client privilege is continuously protected. However, it is important to note that the standard is not absolute; special situations may be considered in which it is not mandatory for the lawyer to maintain professional secrecy. Indeed, in many cases, those exceptions are explicitly stated in Honduran law.

1 Scope of and Limitations on the Duty of Professional Secrecy/Attorney-Client Privilege

A Statutory Basis and Implications

2. In Honduras, professional secrecy is governed by the following regulations: (i) the Organic Law of the Honduran Bar Association, (ii) the Code of Ethics of the Honduran Legal Profession, (iii) the Criminal Code, (iv) the Special Law Against Money Laundering, (v) the law to regulate the activities of the designated non-financial professions, (vi) the Code of Civil Procedure and (vii) the Constitution of the Republic of Honduras.

    The Code of Ethics of the Honduran Legal Professionals, in its fourth chapter, provides the following guidelines:

    (i) The lawyer must not use broadcast or written press to discuss issues as assigned or publicize portions of the case in any pending lawsuits, unless this is necessary to correct errors when justice or morality so require.
    (ii) Once a legal process is completed, the lawyer may publicize documents and proceedings with the lawyer's comments, observing the corresponding fairness and professional restraint.
    (iii) Any press publication – except for studies or reviews in professional publications, which are allowed – should be guided by the general principles of ethics. Should the aforementioned publication hurt any person's honor and good name, that person's name should be omitted.
    (iv) Counsel should keep the strictest professional secrecy, even after having ceased serving the client.

(v) The ban on lawyers disclosing to others privileged information extends to information they learn as a result of their profession or of their judicial or administrative functions.

(vi) Everything that the lawyer does in dealing with the opposing party is considered "professional secrecy."

(vii) The duty of professional secrecy extends to confidences made by third parties to the lawyer by virtue of the lawyer's profession and even confidences derived from discussions needed to reach a settlement that never took place. The secret must also include the confidences of colleagues.

(viii) The lawyer must not intervene in matters that may lead the lawyer to reveal a professional secret or to use for the lawyer's own benefit any confidences received in the exercise of the lawyer's profession, unless the lawyer obtains prior written consent from the client. This prohibition extends to the secrets that lawyers know through their associates, employees or the dependents thereof.

B Scope

3. In the collision of interests that may occur between the duty of keeping a professional secret and the obligation to collaborate with justice, the first should normally prevail, as the only way to protect the functionality of the profession is by guaranteeing to every person the freedom to share with the lawyer any and all relevant information and to do so with confidence and free of any concern.

However, the Code of Ethics of the Honduran Legal Professional sets a limitation on that scope by stipulating that: "Should a lawyer be judicially charged by a client, he shall be released from keeping professional secrecy within the limits necessary for his self-defense."

C Persons Subject to the Duty of Professional Secrecy

4. Lawyers, in the execution of their profession, are subject to the obligation of professional secrecy when providing services to all people who come to them. This duty includes the performance of the lawyer and in the lawyer's various roles in the legal system, such as procurator, manager, conciliator, arbitrator, curator, adviser, consultant and notary public.

D Exceptions to and Optional Derogations from the Duty of Professional Secrecy

5. The following exceptions can be found in Honduran law.

In the Code of Ethics of the Honduran Legal Professional, Article 23 provides that "The lawyer has the right to refuse to testify against his client and may decline to answer any question involving the revelation of the secret or violation of confidences of his client." Furthermore, Article 25 releases the legal professional from keeping professional secrecy if the client judicially charges the lawyer, in which case the lawyer is entitled to reveal professional secrets within the limits necessary for the lawyer's self-defense.

6. The Criminal Code establishes the right of legal professionals to refuse to testify in matters in which their clients are being charged.

To further clarify, the foregoing provisions also apply to ministers of any religious faith and professionals (including lawyers) authorized to operate in the country regarding the confidences or secrets that have come to their knowledge by reason of the performance of their ministry or profession.

This does not excuse the lawyer from appearing before the authority and informing the authority at the time of such appearance and before the lawyer's deposition that the lawyer has a right to refrain from speaking about the client's secrets. And if the lawyer determines to do so, the lawyer may refrain from answering the questions that the lawyer chooses not to answer.

The Criminal Code also states that communications between lawyer and client cannot be subject to sequestration (that is, at the request of the Public Prosecutor in case of investigation):

> Written communications that occurred between the accused and his counsel or between the former and the people who, in accordance with Article 228, may lawfully refrain from testifying as witnesses by reason of kinship or who should not be obliged to do so due to professional secrecy.

7. The Special Law against Money Laundering provides in Article 47 that, provided a legal mandate, and as part of an investigative diligence, individuals or entities may break their promise to keep secret confessions of others. The law states as follows:

> For purposes of the applicability of said law, notwithstanding the safeguard of the fundamental rights of the people; bank, professional or tax secrecy may not be invoked.

8. The law regulating the activities of designated non-financial professions also contains exceptions to the duty of professional secrecy.

The purpose of this act is to establish the measures that, in accordance with the level of risk, should be implemented by individuals or entities engaged in designated non-financial businesses and professions, among whom are lawyers (Article 3(12)), to prevent such persons from being used by or participate directly or indirectly in the crime of money laundering or terrorist financing.

As far as professional secrecy is concerned, Article 19 of the act states: "For purposes of application of this Act and safeguarding the fundamental rights of the person, professional secrecy may not be invoked."

The provisions of both laws (Special Law against Money Laundering and the law for the regulation of activities of designated non-financial professions) have been the subject of discussion in the legal community in Honduras, as these clearly contradict the provisions regarding the Professional Secret Code of Ethics for Honduran Legal Professionals.

E Law Firms

9. In Honduras there are many law firms specializing in different subjects and areas for the implementation of effective law in accordance with the needs of clients. It is their performance of tasks entrusted to them that serves as a reference for the growth of these firms.

At present, we have observed an intense development regarding the actions of Honduran law professionals, as they have received recognition for their knowledge and application thereof, with results that influence the growth of the country.

At this stage of development, an emerging approach to the duty of professional secrecy is being acknowledged in Honduras. Aware of their obligations to clients and society, the best structured legal firms have emphasized the use of measures to govern professional secrecy.

This focus on the attorney-client privilege is being recognized by some firms through the (i) establishment of rules of internal conduct requiring the firm's members to abide by the requirements of professional secrecy; (ii) implementation of mechanisms to effectively comply with these standards; and (iii) dissemination of appropriate ethics manuals to the law office's staff, so that the staff understand their responsibilities as members of the law office and be governed by them.

F Legal Assistants and Staff

10. To ensure that every legal firm has well-trained support personnel to assist the lawyers in the performance of their activities, staff should be well versed in professional secrecy issues to promote the teamwork required for the operation of the law firm.

As mentioned previously, upon the initiative of some firms, lawyers, paralegals and support staff are instructed in a timely and systematic manner on how their actions within the firm must be in accordance with ethical standards. As respect for professional secrecy is one of the most relevant rules for the legal practice, so is the firm's fulfillment of that duty of primary importance.

G External Service Providers

11. It is common practice that the various entities or companies that do not require ongoing services of a professional in a particular specialty to outsource delivery

of that service. In hiring such external service providers, it is recommended to take special care in the preparation of agreements governing these relations and to always provide for confidentiality clauses to have clear guidance where the professional secrecy is concerned.

However, the absence of a general agreement or the inclusion of these clauses does not exempt the service provider from compliance with the obligation to maintain the secrecy of the information obtained in the course of the service for which the service provider was hired. This is indicated by the Organic Law and the Code of Ethics governing Honduran lawyers.

H In-House Counsel

12. When in-house counsel are involved in the operations of a company or institution, it is implicitly established that such employees should have care with information related to the execution of assigned functions. Thus, the obligation of professional secrecy remains for any field in which the internal advocate may have access to privileged information within the company or institution.

The Code of Ethics of Honduran Legal Professionals "gives equal treatment" to in-house lawyers, outside counsel and internal attorneys. Therefore, in-house counsel are obliged to observe the law, and, in addition to the internal rules and regulations that companies or institutions impose on internal lawyers, they must meet every provision of general application concerning professional secrecy.

2 History of the Duty of Professional Secrecy in Honduras

13. Since ancient times, professional secrecy has been applied in a range of different settings. In the Hippocratic Oath, it is mentioned: "everything I see or hear in my profession or outside it, I will keep it with utmost secrecy." The Hebrew Oath of Asaph, dating from the third century, says, "You will not reveal secrets that have been entrusted to you." And Catholic tradition provides a special place for confidentiality in the sacrament of reconciliation or confession (confession secret).

In fact, broadly speaking, professional secrecy in Honduras has its roots in these doctrines, which are generally applicable to the various professions that require prudent management of the information that clients provide to their service providers for the effective delivery of such service.

In a strict sense, the Corpus Juris of Roman Law, Digest (Act 25 of Test. XXII, V), contains a clear reference to the obligation for lawyers, prosecutors and legal clerks not to divulge secrets. In particular, for the legal professional, this principle, which is rooted in the Roman doctrine, has significant weight in the applicable law in this country.

This right is provided for and protected for all people, for securing the constitutional right to defense, and for the client to have the security and confidence to convey information and to obtain further guidance on how to proceed in situations of conflict.

Since the creation of the Code of Ethics of Honduran Legal Professionals in 1966, professional secrecy between attorney and client is directly provided for.

3 Supervision

14. The Court of Honor of the Bar of Attorneys is the body responsible for monitoring the conduct of people subject to the authority of the Bar Association who violate the Code of Professional Ethics, laws, regulations and resolutions issued by its organs and imposing the established sanctions.

Among the powers this court holds is that of hearing and managing complaints against bar members and persons subject to the authority of the Bar Association. It also imposes penalties or acquittals in accordance with the Organic Law of the Bar of Attorneys, administering appropriate sanctions starting from private reprimand up to temporary suspension of professional practice.

The Interagency Commission for the Prevention of Money Laundering and Financing of Terrorism (CIPLAFT) is responsible for the prevention, control and fight against crimes of money laundering. CIPLAFT reports to the presidency of the republic and is under the command of the National Council of Defense and Security.

A The Bar Association

15. In Honduras, there is a single Bar Association with national jurisdiction. The Bar Association of Honduras is required to monitor the performance of legal professionals in any sphere they act and of any hierarchy they are, to make the necessary arrangements, either in private or public affairs, to stop wrongdoing and, if necessary, suspend the offender from the practice of law.

As such, the Bar Association of Honduras is the ultimate body that oversees and sets guidelines that legal professionals must follow in the performance of their functions and services, regardless of whether their practice of law is public or private.

The enforcement of these disciplinary rules is rare in Honduras. Being a Court of Honor, composed of other attorneys who make up the union, there is no real guarantee of impartiality in the handling of cases between clients and lawyers. On the other hand, there are major limitations in the case-assignment process; hence, many filed complaints remain unresolved.

B The Courts

16. The Code of Ethics of Legal Professionals establishes that the lawyer must support the judiciary and keep a respectful attitude before it, but without undermining the lawyer's own independence and autonomy in professional practice. Such obligation implies that professionals conduct themselves ethically and with a collaborative attitude in the pursuit of justice.

    The code also states that when there is a serious reason for complaint against a judicial officer, the lawyer must submit the complaint to the Bar Association so that it can impose sanctions as it deems necessary or convenient. The provisions of this article are also applicable to other officials with whom the lawyer acts while serving as a lawyer.

    If lawyers serve as judicial officers, such lawyers may not accept cases in which they may have participated as officers, except in criminal trials in which they may have participated. Nor may they sponsor such matters as those in which they may have issued adverse opinions when acting in their official capacity, as long as they have not satisfactorily justified their change of opinion.

4 Sanctions

A Proceedings and Sanctions

17. The Organic Law of the Bar Association of Honduras states that the bar authorities may impose on its members the following sanctions: (i) private reprimand from the board for gross negligence or inexcusable ignorance in the execution of the profession; (ii) public reprimand before the General Assembly for having failed to observe professional ethics or for causing a grievance against the decorum and prestige of the profession; (iii) disqualification from elected and appointed positions within the Bar Association, for up to two years, in cases of serious offenses not included in previous portions of this article; (iv) through disciplinary proceedings, a fine of 5 to 25 Lempiras for absences of members to meetings of the Board of Directors or the Ordinary and Extraordinary Assemblies or for lack of compliance with the performance of commissions or duties assigned to them by this act or entrusted to them by the bar authorities; and (v) temporary suspension from the practice of their profession, from six months to three years.

    Suspended bar members must continue their financial obligations to the Bar Association.

    If the acts that caused the sanction of public reprimand occur for a third time, a subsequent sanction, consisting of suspension for up to one year of execution of the rights pertaining to the members of the Bar Association, will be imposed.

18. The procedure before the court may be initiated *ex officio*, upon request or by the Prosecutor of the Bar Association. This procedure will be broad to

guarantee the principles of defense, the evaluation of evidence based on sound judgment, and independence of judgment to allow the court to establish the truth of the facts.

If there is sufficient evidence to initiate an investigation, the court will order the legal professional to appear personally or by proxy to receive a statement of objections.

This citation shall be effected by the court through the Bar Association Secretariat, using the assistance of jurisdictional bodies operating in the place of domicile of the defendant. In any case, the costs of completing the citation will be borne by the complainant.

The defendant's answer and relevant evidence must be submitted within a period of eight days. Once the proposed evidence is provided, the court will review the facts and issue the appropriate decision within the next five days.

Once the charges have been answered, the trial proceedings may not take more than 20 days, unless the standard of proof demands a longer period, in which case the court may extend it no longer than 20 days. The court may issue orders for other arrangements. Should the summoned person not appear, the complaint will continue to be reviewed in absentia.

The decision issued by the court will be held by secret ballot, with the assistance of all its members and by majority vote. The secretary will personally notify the parties concerning the decision, if the parties attend the court proceedings. If they do not concur or reside in the departments, notification shall be effected by means of communication sent to the representative of the Bar Association.

B Relationship Between Criminal Sanctions and Disciplinary Sanctions

19. As stated earlier, disciplinary sanctions range from verbal reprimand to temporary suspension from the practice of the profession for up to three years. Suspended bar members must continue their financial obligations to the Bar Association notwithstanding. And, in case of recidivism, subsequent suspensions for up to one additional year may be imposed on top of the previous suspension imposed.

Meanwhile, the penalties imposed by the Penal Code are more severe in that they impose penalties of imprisonment, in accordance with the following:

> Article 215. Anyone who reveals without just cause, or uses for their own or someone else's behalf a secret that he has learned by virtue of office, employment, profession or art, and thus causes harm to anyone, shall be punished with imprisonment of three (3) to six (6) years.
>
> Article 381. Is punishable by imprisonment of two to four years, plus special disqualification for twice the duration of the detention, to the notary, lawyer, graduate in law and social sciences or prosecutor that abuses the fulfilling of his mandate or because of inexcusable negligence

or ignorance that harms his client or discloses the secrets he has known through the practice of his profession.

This last article, in addition to imposing a sentence of imprisonment, imposes on wrongdoing lawyers the disqualification of practicing their profession for twice the duration of their detention.

5 Duty to Provide Information to the Authorities

A Money Laundering and Terrorism

20. The Special Law against Money Laundering was created to prevent, control and combat money laundering and the financing of terrorism.

This act restricts the scope of professional secrecy, since Article 47 provides that, for purposes of the application of the act and to always safeguard the fundamental rights of the person, bank, professional (including attorney-client), and tax secrecy may not be invoked.

The act also determines that all provisions concerning the institutions supervised by the National Commission on Banking and Insurance related to the crime of money laundering are equally applicable to certain "designated non-financial professional activities," be they natural or legal persons, who perform the following activities:

> The Lawyers, Notaries Public and Accountants, when performing operations for their clients through the following activities: buying and selling of real estate; money management, securities and other assets; organization of contributions for the creation, operation, management or purchase and sale of commercial companies; and, the creation, operation or management of legal structures.

It is clear that a conflict of interest occurs, which is not easy to solve. The lawyer is subject to two kinds of obligations that contradict each other: on the one hand, to keep confidential any facts or news such lawyer knows through the execution of any functions the lawyer performs, and on the other hand, the lawyer must report to the Financial Intelligence Unit concerning the evidence or certainty of money laundering that the lawyer learned in his or her work for a client.

6 Treatment of Lawyers' Documents and Correspondence in the Context of Judicial or Police Investigations

21. The Criminal Code provides that, in investigative processes, any written communications between the accused and his or her counsel, or between the lawyer and all persons who are not required to testify against the accused, may not be disclosed, as stipulated in the code.

Therefore, the law enforcement and police authorities may not require such documents from lawyers in the course of pending cases.

7 Search of a Lawyer's Office

22. Lawyers' offices can be searched as long as there is an order or request from a competent authority in the legitimate exercise of its powers.

All agents of authority or public officials may search a law office only if they have previously completed all the formalities prescribed to carry out such action.

8 Tapping of Telephone Conversations with a Lawyer

23. In Honduras, the Special Law on the Intervention of Private Communications establishes the legal framework of procedural regulation to intercept communications as an exceptional mechanism of investigation to be used only as an essential tool in the fight against crime, while guaranteeing the human rights of people to communicate.

The act authorizes intervention in the investigation and prosecution of crimes in which the use of this special technique is required. Therefore, lawyers' telephones may be wiretapped, always within the indicated parameters and with previously obtained legal authorization.

However, Article 11 of the act provides that the interception of communications between a defense attorney, legally constituted in a criminal proceeding, and the person being investigated or charged, is prohibited, when such communication is executed on the basis of the individual's right of defense.

9 The Lawyer as Witness

24. As stated previously, lawyers have the right to refuse to testify against their clients and must refrain from answering any question involving the disclosure of a trade secret or violation of confidences from the client. It is further stressed that, if summoned, the lawyer must appear in court, and the declaration of professional secrecy must be made at the precise moment so the legal professional may decide how to act.

Article 304 of the Civil Procedure Code states: "When, because of his status, profession or occupation, the witness has a duty to maintain the secrecy of facts for which he is questioned, he will manifest it reasonably and the Court, considering the basis of the refusal to testify, will settle it by providence, as appropriate in law."

If the witness is released from responding, it shall be recorded in the minutes as so.

357

10 The Lawyer and the Press

25.   As mentioned previously, the Organic Law of the Bar Association limits the interactions that take place between counsel and the press and other media concerning the information obtained in the processes for which a client hires the lawyer. That law orders the lawyer not to use written or broadcast press to discuss the matters entrusted to the lawyer, nor release records of pending trials publicly, unless this is necessary for the correction of errors where justice or morality so require.

Once the representation ends, lawyers may publicize documents and proceedings with their comments, as prudent restraint and fairness require.

11 Powers of the Tax and Other Authorities

26.   Honduras, as part of its major effort in the fight against organized crime, corruption and tax evasion, has approved a series of laws and regulations that seek to address more effectively the criminal offenses that are related to these criminal activities.

In pursuit of these objectives, the laws governing tax matters as well as money laundering and corruption, as discussed in this chapter, impose on the lawyer a duty to disclose professional secrets, in cases and under the circumstances prescribed by such laws. Moreover, it also obliges the lawyer to provide information in other areas that would remain otherwise confidential between the lawyer and client.

All of the above is clear evidence of the power that the country's authorities are executing through such legislation on lawyers regarding issues of professional secrecy and confidential information.

23

Jamaica

PETER S. GOLDSON

RENÉ C.K. GAYLE

Myers, Fletcher & Gordon

Preliminary Note

1. Jamaica's legal system is based on the English common law. The London-based Judicial Committee of the Privy Council sits at the pinnacle of Jamaica's court hierarchy. Consequently, decisions of that court on appeal from Jamaica are binding on lower courts in Jamaica, while other Privy Council decisions are considered highly persuasive. Considerable guidance is also taken from cases from other English courts, such as the Supreme Court and the former House of Lords, as well as from the superior courts of other common law jurisdictions. References in this article to non-Jamaican cases are therefore made to the extent that they form part of the common law.

    In Jamaica, professional secrecy and attorney-client privilege are more often referred to as "legal professional privilege," which is the nomenclature ascribed by the common law. However, the modern view is that professional secrecy is distinguishable from attorney-client privilege. The former is a duty of confidentiality that attaches to a range of professions, including the legal profession. On the other hand, privilege, which prevents disclosure of certain communications, is unique to the attorney-client relationship and is a right that belongs to the client. In this chapter, therefore, references to an attorney's duty of confidentiality are equivalent to the obligation of professional secrecy, which is enshrined in statute in Jamaica. On the other hand, references to legal professional privilege relate to both legal advice privilege and litigation privilege, which arise by virtue of the common law. Both confidentiality and legal professional privilege are important in the legal context of Jamaica, as information relating to a client's affairs that is in the possession of an attorney is usually privileged as well as confidential.[1]

1 Scope of and Limitations on the Duty of Professional Secrecy/ Attorney-Client Privilege

A Statutory Basis and Implications

2. The governing statute for the legal profession in Jamaica is the Legal Profession Act, 1971 and its attendant rules and regulations, one of which is the Legal Profession (Canons of Professional Ethics) Rules, 1978.[2] These rules stand as a codification of the professional code of ethics to which each attorney licensed to practice in Jamaica is bound to uphold.

    Canon IV(t) provides:

    > [A]n Attorney shall not knowingly – (i) reveal a confidence or secret of his client, or (ii) use a confidence or secret of his client – (1) to the client's disadvantage; or (2) to his own advantage; or (3) to the advantage of any

---

[1] *Prince Jefri Bolkiah v. KPMG (A Firm)* [1999] 1 All ER 517, 526.
[2] Referred to hereinafter as the "Canons" and individually as "Canon *x*."

other person, unless in any case it is done with the consent of the client after full disclosure.

This Canon therefore gives statutory force to the common law duty of an attorney to keep his client's confidences.

The Canons, however, do not replace the attorney's common law duty. Section 5(1) of the Legal Profession Act, 1971 indeed provides that every attorney, when acting as a lawyer, shall be subject to "all such liabilities as attach by law to a solicitor." This essentially means that the Act preserves all pre-existing duties of an attorney under the common law, which includes the duty of confidentiality or professional secrecy, as well as, that of attorney-client privilege.

Some of the Canons are denoted by an asterisk, which signifies that their breach shall constitute professional misconduct; Canon IV(t) is one such Canon.[3] By virtue of Section 12(4) of the Legal Profession Act, 1971, an attorney who is adjudged guilty of professional misconduct may be struck off the Roll, suspended from practice, fined, reprimanded, ordered to attend pre-scribed courses of training, ordered to pay all or part of a party's costs, ordered to pay a sum by way of restitution or any combination of the foregoing.

Additionally, the duties of confidentiality and attorney-client privilege also arise from the contract of retainer between the attorney and client. This applies whether the retainer is written or oral, and even when written, whether the duty is expressly stated in the retainer or not. Consequently, a breach by an attorney of a client's confidence or privilege may also amount to a breach of contract and may thereby give rise to contractual remedies.

B Scope

3.   The scope of the duty of confidentiality is as expressed in Canon IV(t). That is, an attorney should not reveal or use the confidential information of a client without the client's consent after full disclosure. The scope of the duty is expressly limited to instances where the use or revelation by the attorney is done intentionally and where it results in a disadvantage to the client or an advantage to the attorney or some third party.

As first drafted, Canon IV(t) contained a proviso that permitted an attorney to "reveal confidences or secrets necessary to establish or collect his fee or to defend himself or his employees or associates against an accusation of wrongful conduct." By an amendment in 2014, this proviso was expanded to also permit attorneys to reveal their client's confidences or secrets where required by the Proceeds of Crime Act or Terrorism Prevention Act,[4] and in instances where the

---

[3]   See the full list of those Canons at Legal Profession (Canons of Professional Ethics) Rules, 1978, Canon VIII(d).

[4]   *See* Section 5 of this chapter.

attorney is required by law to disclose knowledge of all material facts relating to a serious offence that has been committed. This amendment codifies the common law rule (albeit the common law remains extant) that an attorney could reveal a client's confidences where required by law already existed at common law. However, it was felt that the prevention of money laundering and terrorism is of such importance in modern society that it warrants an explicit statutory exemption.

Despite the foregoing limitations, it is considered that "the duty to preserve confidentiality is unqualified."[5] Its scope extends to former clients and may operate to prevent an attorney from acting against a former client, where doing so might give rise to a real risk of disclosure of that client's confidential information.[6] The onus lies on the former client to establish that his former attorney possesses confidential information that might be relevant to the attorney's new or proposed engagement and that the client has not consented to the disclosure of such confidential information.[7] The burden then shifts to the attorney to show that there is no risk of disclosure or that adequate measures have been taken to prevent disclosure. A fanciful risk of disclosure or an allegation that the disclosure may occur inadvertently will not suffice. If a real risk is established, the client may be able to obtain an injunction restraining the attorney from accepting the new engagement or ordering the attorney to put in place proper safeguards to prevent disclosure of the former client's confidential information. In instances where the confidential information arises from a joint retainer, or where the same attorney acted for two clients in related matters in which they had a common interest, the attorney is unlikely to be found in breach of confidence for disclosure of one client's confidential information to the other client, as a waiver of confidentiality will be implied in such circumstances.[8]

Unlike with attorney-client privilege, there is no common law principle that protects documents from disclosure solely on the grounds that they contain confidential information.[9] Rather, confidentiality will constitute only one of the factors a court or tribunal will consider in the exercise of its discretion whether to order discovery. The considerable limitation imposed on the duty of confidentiality, by virtue of the rule that the duty does not apply where such an exception is required by law or where ordered by a competent court, is perhaps what necessitates the existence of a separate and absolute obligation of attorney-client privilege, which prevents disclosure of certain communications.

4. There are two types of attorney-client privilege recognized by the common law: legal advice privilege and litigation privilege. Legal advice privilege protects from disclosure communications that comprise legal advice from the attorney

---

[5] *Prince Jefri Bolkiah v. KPMG (A Firm)* [1999] 1 All ER 517, 527. [6] Ibid., 526–28.

[7] *Koch Shipping Inc. v. Richards Butler (A Firm)* [2002] EWCA Civ 1280.

[8] *Winters v. Mishcon de Reya* [2008] EWHC 2419 (Ch).

[9] *Science Research Council v. Nassé* [1980] AC 1028, 1065.

to his client. Litigation privilege, on the other hand, protects from disclosure communications between an attorney and his client (as well as third parties in some circumstances) that were made in contemplation of actual or potential litigation. Together, legal advice privilege and litigation privilege encompass what is known under the common law as "legal professional privilege."[10]

Legal advice privilege is broader in scope than litigation privilege, as it covers communications that constitute legal advice, whether or not litigation is contemplated.[11] For this type of privilege to apply, the advice must be given by the attorney in the attorney's professional capacity and not merely as someone having legal knowledge.[12] Therefore, advice given by an attorney to friends, family members or members of the public with whom the attorney does not have a contract of retainer is not privileged.[13] Additionally, information given by an attorney to a client that does not constitute legal advice – that is, it is not "advice as to what should prudently and sensibly be done in the relevant legal context"– will not be covered by legal advice privilege.[14]

Despite its seemingly narrow nature, the definition of what is considered legal advice has been given a broad interpretation. It is understood that legal advice is "not confined to telling the client the law."[15] For example, communications between a bank's inquiry unit and its lawyers regarding the presentation of its case to an inquiry for the purpose of persuading the inquiry that the bank had properly discharged its obligations under the Banking Act of the United Kingdom. were considered to constitute legal advice. Such communications were, therefore privileged, even though the advice related only to the form of presentation of the bank's case and not the bank's legal rights and obligations.[16]

Litigation privilege, on the other hand, attaches only to communications that had as their dominant purpose pending or contemplated litigation. As a result, where this privilege is asserted, the party is required to give a full report of how the document was prepared. As early as the 1800s, Cotton, LJ, observed that, for privilege to attach to communications between an attorney and a third party or a client and a third party, there must be a definite prospect of litigation and not mere vague anticipation of it. However, it is not necessary that a basis for a claim has arisen or that the third party should also anticipate litigation.[17] In the

---

[10] *Three Rivers District Council v. Governor and Company of the Bank of England (no 6)* [2005] 1 AC 610, 677.

[11] *Minet v. Morgan* (1873) 8 Ch App 361.

[12] *See Greenough v. Gaskell* (1833) 1 My & K 98, 104.   [13] Ibid.

[14] *Balabel v. Air India* [1988] 1 Ch 317, 330, approved by the House of Lords in *Three Rivers District Council v. Governor and Company of the Bank of England (no 6)* [2005] 1 AC 610, 651.

[15] *Balabel v. Air India* [1988] 1 Ch 317, 330.

[16] *Three Rivers District Council v. Governor and Company of the Bank of England (no 6)* [2005] 1 AC 610.

[17] *See Wheeler v. Le Marchant* (1881) 17 Ch. D 675; *Cross & Tapper on Evidence*, 9th ed., at 452.

case of *Waugh v. British Railway Board*,[18] the appellant sued the British Railway Board under the English Fatal Accidents Act for the death of her husband. She sought discovery of an internal inquiry report made by two officers of the Railway Board two days after the accident, but the Railway Board refused discovery on the ground of legal professional privilege. The House of Lords held that, since the purpose of obtaining the legal advice in anticipation of litigation appeared to have been of no more than equal rank and weight with the purpose of assessing railway operation and safety, the Board's claim for privilege failed, and disclosure of the report was ordered.[19]

Despite its name, legal professional privilege has also been extended to other binding forms of dispute resolution, such as arbitration.[20]

The protection from disclosure afforded to privileged communications is said to be absolute.[21] It was held in *R v. Barton*[22] and *R v. Ataou*[23] that public interest considerations, such as assisting with the defense of an accused, may in some instances outweigh a client's right to rely on privilege. However, both cases were overruled by the House of Lords in *R v. Derby Magistrates' Court, Ex parte B*,[24] in which it was held that legal professional privilege was not an interest that could be balanced against competing public interests.[25] According to Taylor, CJ, the rationale for such a broad and unqualified rule is that "a man must be able to consult his lawyer in confidence, since otherwise he might hold back half the truth. The client must be sure that what he tells his lawyer in confidence will never be revealed without his consent."[26] Taylor, CJ, went on to observe that:

> "legal professional privilege is thus much more than an ordinary rule of evidence, limited in its application to the facts of a particular case. It is a fundamental condition on which the administration of justice as a whole rests ... It is not for the sake of the appellant alone that the privilege must be upheld. It is in the wider interest of all those hereafter who might otherwise be deterred from telling the whole truth to their solicitors."[27]

Similarly, the Privy Council in *B v. Auckland District Law Society*[28] held that legal professional privilege was a fundamental condition of the administration of justice that could not be overridden at common law by, or balanced against, any competing public interest or right to compel production. Rather, it could be overridden only in a statute by clear words or necessary implication. Legal professional privilege has even been expressed to be a human right. Hoffman, LJ, for example, (speaking in the context of England,

[18] [1980] AC 521.   [19] Ibid., 531–35.
[20] *See Alfred Crompton Amusement Machines Ltd. v. Customs and Excise Commissioners (no 2)* [1974] AC 405.
[21] *R v. Derby Magistrates' Court, Ex parte B* [1995] 4 All ER 526, 541.
[22] [1972] 2 All ER 1192.   [23] [1988] 2 All ER 321.   [24] [1995] 4 All ER 526, 526.
[25] Ibid., at 541.   [26] *R v. Derby Magistrates' Court, Ex parte B* [1995] 4 All ER 526, 540.
[27] Ibid., 540.   [28] [2004] 4 All ER 469.

which has an unwritten constitution and no enumerated bill of rights) considered it "a fundamental human right long established in the common law."[29]

There are several principles that emanate from the absolute nature of legal professional privilege. First, legal professional privilege, whether in respect of oral or written communications, continues indefinitely. It survives the death of the client,[30] as well as the termination of the retainer.[31] Second, it is a right that belongs to the client, and therefore any waiver or limitation of the right can be done only by the client.[32] Third, a client cannot be compelled to waive the privilege, even where it may assist with a criminal conviction or is otherwise in the public's interest.[33] Additionally, a client's refusal to waive the privilege, for whatever reason, or for no reason, cannot be questioned or investigated by the court.

C Persons Subject to the Duty of Professional Secrecy

5. Legal professional privilege is unique to the attorney-client relationship. This does not mean, however, that the courts will in all instances order disclosure of confidential but non-privileged information, which is held by a professional other than an attorney. In *Attorney-General v. Mulholland & Foster*, the English Court of Appeal stated: "[t]he only profession that I know which is given a privilege from disclosing information to a court of law is the legal profession, and then it is not the privilege of the lawyer but of his client."[34] The English Court of Appeal then illustrated this by saying:

> Take the clergyman, the banker or the medical man. None of these is entitled to refuse to answer when directed to by a judge. Let me not be mistaken. The judge will respect the confidences which each member of these honourable professions receives in the course of it, and will not direct him to answer unless not only it is relevant but also it is a proper and, indeed, necessary question in the course of justice to be put and answered.[35]

Unlike legal professional privilege, which only attaches to the attorney-client relationship,[36] the duty of confidentiality is not unique to the legal profession. Many professions have the duty expressly included in their code of ethics, such as the Hippocratic Oath of the medical profession, or in their governing legislation.Section 145 of the Banking Services Act, for example,

---

[29] *R (on the application of Morgan Grenfell & Co Ltd) v. Special Commissioner of Income Tax* [2002] 3 All ER, at para. 7.

[30] *Bullivant v. Attorney-General for Victoria* [1901] AC 196.

[31] *Allison v. Clayhills* (1907) 97 LT 709; *Prince Jefri Bolkiah v. KPMG (A Firm)* [1999] 1 All ER 517.

[32] *R v. Derby Magistrates' Court, Ex parte B* [1995] 4 All ER 526, 538.   [33] *See* ibid., 538.

[34] [1963] 2 QB 477, 489.   [35] [1963] 2 QB 477, 489.

[36] *R v. Special Commissioner of Income Tax and another* [2013] UKSC 1.

imposes an obligation of professional secrecy on bank officials in Jamaica in relation to the confidential information of their customers. A similar provision also exists in Section 59B of the Securities Act, 1993, in relation to officials and employees of the Financial Services Commission. Even where no such express duty exists in a statute, the duty may still arise at common law. Judicial decisions, for example, have acknowledged the duty with respect to other professionals, such as accountants,[37] arbitrators[38] and mediators.[39]

Furthermore, the duty of confidentiality may also arise outside of a contractual or professional context. This was illustrated in *Attorney General v. Guardian Newspapers (no 2)*,[40] where it was observed that:

> the right can arise out of a contract whereby one party (the confidant) undertakes that he will maintain the confidentiality of information directly or indirectly made available to him by the other party (the confider) or acquired by him in a situation, e.g. his employment, created by the confider. But it can also arise as a necessary or traditional incident of a relationship between the confidant and the confider, e.g. priest and penitent, doctor and patient, lawyer and client, husband and wife.[41]

Any person may therefore become subject to the duty of confidentiality at common law. In the words of Goff, LJ:

> a duty of confidence arises when confidential information comes to the knowledge of a person (the confidant) in circumstances where he has notice, or is held to have agreed, that the information is confidential, with the effect that it would be just in all the circumstances that he should be precluded from disclosing the information to others.[42]

Goff, LJ, considered that "the existence of this broad general principle reflects the fact that there is such a public interest in the maintenance of confidences, that the law will provide remedies for their protection."[43]

The equitable duty of confidentiality, which applies to confidants generally, is limited by three principles: (i) the information must have the quality of confidence, (ii) the information must not be useless or trivial and (iii) there must not be any countervailing public interest that out-weighs its nondisclosure.[44]

---

[37] *Prince Jefri Bolkiah v. KPMG (A Firm)* [1999] 1 All ER 517.

[38] *Ali Shipping Corporation v. Shipyard Trogir* [1999] 1 WLR 314.

[39] *Farm Assist Ltd v. Secretary of State for the Environment, Food and Rural Affairs (no2)* [2009] EWHC 110.

[40] [1988] 3 All ER 545.

[41] [1988] 3 All ER 545, 597 and, in particular, the judgment of Sir John Donaldson MR in the Court of Appeal.

[42] *Attorney General v. Guardian Newspapers (no 2)* [1988] 3 All ER 545, 658.   [43] Ibid.

[44] Ibid., 658–59.

D Exceptions to and Optional Derogations from the Duty of Professional Secrecy

6. Though the duty of confidentiality is said to be unqualified[45] and legal professional privilege is regarded as absolute,[46] exceptions do apply.

   As it pertains to legal professional privilege, it was stated in *R v. Special Commissioner of Income Tax and Another*[47] that:

   > where legal professional privilege attaches to a communication between a legal adviser and a client, the client is entitled to object to any third party seeing the communication for any purpose, unless: (i) the client has agreed or waived its right, (ii) a statute provides that the privilege can be overridden, (iii) the document concerned was prepared for, or in connection with, a nefarious purpose, or (iv) one of a few miscellaneous exceptions applies (e.g. in a probate case where the validity of a will is contested).

   In relation to the duty of confidentiality, the common law exceptions are now contained in the proviso to Canon IV(t), which was expanded in 2014 to now read that:

   > an Attorney may reveal confidence or secrets in the following circumstances – (i) where it is necessary to establish or collect his fee; (ii) to defend himself or his employees or associates against an accusation of wrongful conduct; (iii) in accordance with the provisions of the Proceeds of Crime Act and any regulations made under that Act; (iv) in accordance with the provisions of the Terrorism Prevention Act and any regulations made under that Act; or (v) where the attorney is required by law to disclose knowledge of all material facts relating to a serious offence that has been committed.

7. The exceptions that apply to both confidentiality and privilege, therefore, are: (i) where the client consents to the disclosure (waiver), (ii) where the communication is to facilitate the commission of fraud or a crime, (iii) where the information is relevant to fee disputes between attorneys and their clients and (iv) where specifically required by statute. Each is discussed in turn.

   There is little debate that clients have the authority to waive privilege or to consent to the disclosure of their confidential information. However, as the right to privilege or confidence belongs to the client, the authority to waive these rights vests in the client only.[48] A client's waiver may be implied in some circumstances, such as where the client chooses to disclose communications that he or she is at liberty not to disclose due to privilege.[49] However, a mere

---

[45] *Prince Jefri Bolkiah v. KPMG (A Firm)* [1999] 1 All ER 517, 527.

[46] *R v. Derby Magistrates' Court, Ex parte B* [1995] 4 All ER 526, 541.

[47] [2013] UKSC 1, at para. 17.

[48] *R v. Derby Magistrates' Court, Ex parte B* [1995] 4 All ER 526, 538; *R v. Special Commissioner of Income Tax and another* [2013] UKSC 1, at para.

[49] *Paragon Finance v. Freshfields* [1999] 1 WLR 1183, 1188.

reference to the existence of such communications, without disclosing details, will not suffice to waive the privilege.[50]

Where an attorney faces a claim of wrongful conduct or a dispute as to their remuneration, the shield of privilege or confidentiality will be lifted from the client. This exception exists for the benefit of the attorney, so that a client may not insist on the obligation of secrecy owed to him by his attorney in instances where that client has made claims against his attorney.[51] In such situations, a waiver of the duty is implied to allow the attorney to properly defend himself.

Similarly, derogations from the duty of confidentiality may be allowed where the information will allow the accused to adequately defend himself against allegations of serious offences, or where it will assist with the prosecution of serious offences. This exception, however, does not apply to privileged communications, as seen in *R v. Derby Magistrates' Court, ex p B*,[52] which overruled *R v. Barton*[53] and *R v. Ataou*[54]. In *R v. Derby Magistrates' Court, ex p B*, the House of Lords ruled that a client cannot be compelled to waive the privilege, even where it may assist with a criminal conviction or is otherwise in the public's interest.[55]

Nevertheless, neither privilege nor confidentiality will be upheld where the communication had as its purpose the facilitation of a crime or fraud. This ensures that neither will be used to further criminal aims, especially money laundering and terrorism. Therefore, if a client seeks the advice of an attorney to guide the client in the commission of a crime or fraud, the communication between the two will not be privileged, regardless of whether the attorney was aware of the client's criminal aims.[56] This was illustrated in the case of *R v. Cox & Railton*, where the court took the view that a communication in furtherance of a criminal purpose does not come within the ordinary scope of professional employment and that protection of such communications cannot possibly be otherwise than injurious to the interests of justice. Accordingly, only communications given in the legitimate course of the professional employment of the attorney will be covered by privilege.[57] However, if the crime or fraud has already been committed and the client seeks the attorney's advice to assist with a defense, then the communications will be privileged.

---

[50] See *Osland v. Secretary of State to the Department of Justice* [2008] HCA 37.

[51] *See Cross & Tapper on Evidence*, 9th ed., at 460.   [52] [1995] 4 All ER 526, 526.

[53] [1972] 2 All ER 1192.   [54] [1988] 2 All ER 321.

[55] *R v. Derby Magistrates' Court, Ex parte B* [1995] 4 All ER 526, 538.

[56] See *R v. Cox and Railton* (1884) 14 QBD 153; *R v. Bullivant* [1900] 2 QB 163; *O'Rourke v. Darbishire* [1920] AC 581; *Butler v. The Board of Trade* [1971] 1 Ch 680; *Jamaican Bar Association and others v. the Attorney General and the Director of Public Prosecutions and others* (delivered Dec. 14, 2007), at para. 17.

[57] *R v. Cox and Railton* (1884) 14 QBD 153.

The main modern statutory exceptions are those found in statutes dealing with anti-money laundering and the prevention of terrorism. These are discussed later in this chapter.

E Law Firms

8. One of the main issues that arises in relation to law firms and the duty of confidentiality is where one attorney possesses confidential information of a client that ought to be withheld from another attorney within the same firm, owing to a conflicting retainer of that attorney. The case of *Bolkiah v. KPMG*[58] is instructive on this point, though it involved a firm of accountants and not attorneys.[59] In that case, KPMG had acted as auditors of the Brunei Investment Agency (BIA) since its creation in 1983. Prince Jefri Bolkiah acted as the chairman of BIA until he was removed from office in March 1998, following a dispute with his brother, the Sultan of Brunei. He engaged KPMG between 1996 and 1998 to provide support services in litigation in which he was personally involved. KPMG thereby acquired a substantial amount of confidential information concerning his financial affairs. After the litigation was settled in March 1998, BIA asked KPMG to assist it with an investigation into the withdrawal of assets from BIA. Although realizing that the investigation might be contrary to Prince Bolkiah's interests, KPMG accepted the engagement, on the basis that it had put in place "ethical walls" within the firm to protect the confidential information obtained from Prince Bolkiah. Prince Bolkiah appealed a Court of Appeal ruling[60] that found he was not entitled to an injunction restraining KPMG from carrying out BIA's investigation. The House of Lords allowed his appeal.

The basis of their Lordships' decision was that, unless special measures are taken, information moves within a firm, and the court ought to intervene unless it is satisfied on clear and convincing evidence that effective measures have been taken to ensure that no disclosure will occur, rather than merely that reasonable steps will be taken to do so. In this regard, although "ethical walls" or other similar arrangements are not in principle insufficient to eliminate the risk of disclosure, they have to be an established part of the organizational structure of the firm and not just implemented *ad hoc*.

The approach taken by the House of Lords in *Bolkiah v. KPMG*[61] was stricter than that previously taken by the Court of Appeal. In *Rakusen v. Ellis Munday & Clarke,*[62] for example, the Court of Appeal discharged an injunction restraining a partner of a small firm of solicitors from acting for a client who

---

[58] [1999] 1 All ER 517.
[59] The House of Lords held that the duty of an accountant in providing litigation support services ought to be considered similar to that of a solicitor.
[60] *See Bolkiah v. KPMG* [1998] EWCA Civ 1564.   [61] [1999] 1 All ER 517.
[62] [1912] 1 Ch 831.

was on the other side of the same matter for which his partner had been previously engaged. It may have been that the circumstances of the *Rakusen* case were considered unusual in that the firm had only two partners who carried out separate practices, each with his own clients, while sharing support staff. However, such arrangements are not unusual in the Caribbean, where many attorneys share chambers but do not act in partnership. The decision in *Bolkiah* means that even in such situations, an attorney might be restrained from acting adverse to a client of his or her chamber-mate, where it presents a risk of disclosure of either client's confidential information.

F Legal Assistants and Staff

9.   Legal support staff, such as secretaries, paralegals and document processors, are essential to the performance of an attorney's duties to a client. In this regard, an attorney may have an implied authority to disclose a client's affairs not only to his partners and associates but also to members of his staff. In doing this, an attorney must impress upon his staff the weight and importance of the duty of confidentiality and legal professional privilege. In *Bolkiah v. KPMG*,[63] Lord Hope of Craighead pointed out that a client is entitled to insist that measures be taken by his attorney that will ensure that the client is not exposed to the risk of disclosure of confidential information, not only by the attorney, but also by "his partners in the firm, its employees or anyone else for whose acts the solicitor is responsible."[64] This suggests that while the professional duty of confidentiality and privilege is owed to a client by the attorney directly, an attorney also has a responsibility to ensure that there are no indirect breaches of the duty through his colleagues and those in their charge, or else an attorney may be found vicariously liable for his employee's actions. It is therefore prudent for an attorney to include a confidentiality clause in the employment contracts of his staff or have his staff execute a separate nondisclosure agreement. Such a clause or agreement will not only evince that the attorney has taken steps to advise his or her employees of the duty, but it will also give rise to an express contractual obligation on the part of the employee to uphold the duty. It would, in turn, be feasible for the attorney to bring a claim against the employee for breach of that contractual duty.[65]

While an attorney may be vicariously liable for breaches of the duty by his employees, legal support staff may also have an independent duty of confidentiality to the client in equity, though not of legal professional privilege. Such a duty may arise if the requirements set out in *Attorney General v. Guardian Newspapers (no 2)*[66] are met, that is, "where one party (the confidant) undertakes that he will maintain the confidentiality of information directly or

---

[63] [1999] 1 All ER 517.   [64] *Prince Jefri Bolkiah v. KPMG (A Firm)* [1999] 1 All ER 517, 520.
[65] See, for example, *Lister v. Romford Ice and Cold Storage Co.* [1957] AC 555.
[66] [1988] 3 All ER 545.

indirectly made available to him by the other party (the confider) or acquired by him in a situation, e.g. his employment, created by the confider."[67] It is foreseeable that these criteria will easily be met in relation to legal support staff in most instances.

G External Service Providers

10. External service providers are likely to be independent contractors and, therefore, not agents or employees of the attorney by whom they are hired. In such instances, therefore, the attorney may not be vicariously liable for any breach of a client's confidence that is done by the external service provider. However, it is doubtful whether an attorney has a similar implied authority to disclose their client's affairs to external providers as they do with his internal staff. As such, the very disclosure of a client's confidence to an external service provider may amount to a breach of the client's confidence. It would therefore be advisable for an attorney to ensure that they obtain his client's express consent prior to making such a disclosure.

External service providers may also have an independent duty of confidentiality to the client in equity, where the circumstances are such that they can be said to have undertaken (whether explicitly or implicitly) to maintain the confidentiality of the information directly or indirectly made available to them.[68]

H Multidisciplinary Associations

11. In situations involving multidisciplinary associations, each member will be required to abide by all of the professional duties to which they are bound. Where the association is responsible for the members, the association will also need to ensure that all obligations are met, both individually and collectively. For example, in some jurisdictions, multidisciplinary practices involving lawyers and accountants have emerged. In such instances, each will be individually bound by their professional duties as an attorney and as an accountant, respectively, and will be answerable to their relevant disciplinary bodies. On the other hand, the firm or association itself may be responsible for the individual and collective breaches of those in its employ.

I In-House Counsel

12. The regulation of the legal profession in Jamaica does not differentiate between in-house or salaried attorneys and other attorneys. Therefore, in-house counsel in Jamaica, are subject to the same privileges and duties as any other attorney in

---

[67] See Section 1(C) of this chapter.   [68] See Section 1(C) of this chapter.

Jamaica.[69] They are accordingly also governed by the Legal Profession Act, 1971 and the Canons, which impose a duty of confidentiality in Canon IV(t).

In-house counsel are also subject to the same privileges and duties under the common law as external lawyers.[70] This was confirmed by the English Court of Appeal in *Alfred Crompton Amusement Machines v. Customs & Excise Commissioners*.[71] In that case, the Court of Appeal overturned a decision of the English High Court, which held that only communications passing between an organization and external counsel are subject to privilege. In allowing the appeal, Lord Denning, MR, observed in relation to in-house counsel that:

> [t]hey are regarded by the law as in every respect in the same position as those who practise on their own account. The only difference is that they act for one client only, and not for several clients. They must uphold the same standards of honour and of etiquette. They are subject to the same duties to their client and to the court. They must respect the same confidences. They and their clients have the same privileges.[72]

2 History of the Duty of Professional Secrecy in Jamaica

13.   The history of the duty of professional secrecy in Jamaica is grounded in Jamaica's application of the English common law. As early as the 1800s it was stated in England that "the first duty of an attorney is to keep the secrets of his client."[73] This belief was arguably adopted from early Roman law traditions.[74] The primary rationale for legal professional privilege, as expressed in 1833 by Lord Brougham LC in *Greenough v. Gaskell*,[75] was that:

> The foundation of this rule is not difficult to discover. It is out of regard to the interests of justice, which cannot be upholden, and to the administration of justice, which cannot go on, without the aid of men skilled in jurisprudence, in the practice of the Courts, and in those matters affecting rights and obligations which form the subject of all judicial proceedings. If the privilege did not exist at all, everyone would be thrown upon his own legal resources; deprived of all professional assistance, a man would not venture to consult any skillful person, or would only dare to tell his counsellor half his case.

This rationale continues to form the basis of the doctrine in the present day.

---

[69] In-house counsel are, however, understood as being exempted from some disclosure obligations under anti-money laundering legislation, which is discussed later in this chapter.

[70] *Alfred Crompton Amusement Machines v. Customs & Excise Commissioners (no 2)* [1972] 2 QB 102, 129.

[71] Ibid., 102.   [72] Ibid., 102, 129.   [73] *Taylor v. Blacklaw* (1836) 3 Bing 235.

[74] *McCormick on Evidence*, 3rd ed., West Publishing, St. Paul, Minn., 1984, at 205.

[75] (1833) 1 My & K 98, 103.

3 Supervision

A The Bar Associations

14. The Jamaican Bar Association is a representative body for attorneys-at-law in Jamaica. Its membership is voluntary, and it does not perform any supervisory or disciplinary functions in relation to the legal profession. Nevertheless, the Jamaican Bar Association has been very active in representing the profession in matters related to legal professional privilege, such as the search and seizure of attorneys' offices[76] and opposing the imposition of new legislation that might impinge on legal professional privilege.[77]

    Supervisory and disciplinary functions are carried out by the General Legal Council ("GLC"), which is a statutory body established under the Legal Profession Act, 1971. As part of its mandate, the GLC is charged with "upholding standards of professional conduct."[78] In discharging this role, the GLC will ensure that attorneys abide by the Canons, including Canon IV(t), which sets out the duty of confidentiality.

B The Courts

15. By virtue of section 5(1)(b) of the Legal Profession Act, 1971, all attorneys who are entered on the Roll are deemed officers of the Supreme Court. The Supreme Court is consequently responsible for all attorneys, though disciplinary matters are undertaken by the GLC. The Supreme Court will therefore consider breaches of confidence or privilege that are brought as a civil action rather than as a disciplinary proceeding. The Court of Appeal will have jurisdiction to hear any appeals of a decision of the Supreme Court,[79] as well as of the Disciplinary Committee of the GLC.[80]

4 Sanctions

A Proceedings and Sanctions

16. A Client who considers that his former or current attorney has breached a confidence or privilege may institute civil proceedings against his attorney for breach of contract or disciplinary proceedings for breach of the Canons. A civil claim in most instances will be brought before the Supreme Court, whereas disciplinary proceedings will be first heard by the GLC.

---

[76] See *Jamaican Bar Association and others v. The Attorney General and the Director of Public Prosecutions and others* SCCA Nos. 96, 102 and 108 of 2003, delivered Dec. 14, 2007.

[77] See *Jamaican Bar Association v. Attorney General & General Legal Council,* 2014 HCV 0772 (heard March 23–26, 2015).

[78] Section 3(1)(b), Legal Profession Act, 1971.

[79] Section 42, Judicature (Supreme Court) Act, 1955.

[80] Section 16(1), Legal Profession Act, 1971.

B Disciplinary Proceedings

17.   Complaints related to professional misconduct (which includes a breach of a client's confidence in contravention of Canon IV(t)) should be made to the GLC to be heard by a Panel of the Disciplinary Committee. The GLC is responsible for constituting the Disciplinary Committee, which is made up of a minimum of 15 people who are either current or former members of the GLC, have held high judicial office, are attorneys who have been members of a former disciplinary body or have been in practice for not less than 10 years. The Disciplinary Committee has discretion to issue a wide range of orders. In relation to a breach of Canon IV(t), the possible orders that may be issued include that the attorney may be struck off the Roll, suspended from practice, fined, reprimanded, ordered to attend prescribed courses of training, ordered to pay all or part of a party's costs, ordered to pay a sum by way of restitution or any combination of the foregoing. Orders issued by the Disciplinary Committee may be appealed to the Court of Appeal by way of a rehearing at either the instance of the attorney or the client.[81] Unless otherwise directed by the Court of Appeal, the lodging of an appeal does not operate as a stay of the orders made by the Disciplinary Committee.[82]

C Relationship between Criminal Sanctions and Disciplinary Sanctions

18.   As it pertains to the conduct of attorneys in Jamaica, criminal proceedings and disciplinary proceedings may run concurrently. The Disciplinary Committee, however, may postpone hearing and determining a disciplinary matter for which criminal proceedings are also pending, where in the opinion of the committee the disciplinary hearing would be prejudicial to the fair hearing of the pending criminal proceedings.[83] Alternatively, where the Disciplinary Committee proceeds with hearing the disciplinary matter while criminal proceedings are ongoing, the Disciplinary Committee may, if it thinks fit, on its own initiative or at the request of the attorney, delay the filing of any orders it issues until the criminal proceedings have concluded.[84]

5 Duty to Provide Information to the Authorities

A Money Laundering and Terrorism

19.   Jamaica is a party to several international conventions related to anti-money laundering, such as the United Nations Convention Against Illicit Traffic in Narcotic Drugs and Psychotropic Substances, 1988; the United Nations Convention against Transnational Organized Crime and the Protocols Thereto,

---

[81] Ibid., Section 16(1).   [82] Ibid., Section 16(2).   [83] Ibid., Section 12B(1).
[84] Ibid., Section 12B(2).

2003; and the United Nations Convention against Corruption, 2005. Jamaica is also a member of the Caribbean Financial Action Task Force on Money Laundering. Pursuant to these international obligations, Jamaica has enacted domestic legislation, in particular, the Proceeds of Crime Act, 2007 ("POCA"), to thwart money laundering.

POCA provides that where persons (including attorneys) know, believe, or have reasonable grounds to know or believe that another person is engaged in a transaction that could constitute money laundering and the information on which that state of mind is based came to such persons in the course of their business, such persons have a duty to make a report of that suspicion. This provides a statutory exception to the rule that an attorney must obey a client's confidence or privilege. The rationale is that legal professional privilege must not be used as a cloak for the commission of crimes, and where this may be the case, legal professional privilege will be lifted.

There are provisions in POCA, however, that demonstrate a respect for legal professional privilege. For example, Section 94(5)(b) states that a person does not commit an offence in relation to nondisclosure if such person is an attorney-at-law and the information or other matter came to him or her in privileged circumstances. Section 94(8) further provides that information or other matter comes to an attorney-at-law in privileged circumstances if it is communicated or given to the attorney (a) by, or by a representative of, a client in connection with the giving by the attorney-at-law of legal advice to the client; (b) by, or by a representative of, a person seeking legal advice from the attorney-at-law; or (c) by a person in connection with legal proceedings or contemplated legal proceedings. Section 94 follows with a proviso that the foregoing will not apply where the information was given with the intention of furthering a criminal purpose.

The obligations on attorneys under POCA were generally accepted by the legal fraternity in Jamaica, until their obligations were enlarged by an amendment to the legislation in 2013. These amendments sought to extend certain reporting obligations under POCA to attorneys carrying out certain activities[85] on behalf of clients, to prescribe an annual declaration by attorneys,[86] and to establish a competent authority in relation to the anti-money laundering obligations of the legal profession (which was later designated to be the GLC).[87]

---

[85] These activities include (a) purchasing or selling real estate; (b) managing money, securities or other assets; (c) managing bank accounts or savings accounts of any kind, or securities accounts; (d) organizing contributions for the creation, operation or management of companies; (e) creating, operating or managing a legal person or legal arrangement; or (f) purchasing or selling a business entity.

[86] This does not cover in-house counsel.

[87] *See* Proceeds of Crime Act, 2007; Proceeds of Crime (Money Laundering) Regulations, 2013, as extended by the Proceeds of Crime (Designated Non-Financial Institution) (Attorneys-at-Law) Order, 2013.

Pursuant to the new regulations, attorneys (as designated non-financial institutions, or "DNFIs") may be held liable for money laundering where they (i) know or believe or have reasonable grounds for knowing or believing that another person has engaged in a transaction that could constitute or be related to money laundering; (ii) the information or matter on which the knowledge or belief is based or which gives reasonable grounds for such knowledge or belief came to them in the course of business in the regulated sector; and (iii) they fail to report suspected cases of money laundering.

a) In reaction to the new obligations, the Jamaican Bar Association, on behalf of its members, instituted a constitutional motion challenging the constitutionality of the new obligations. Essentially, the Jamaican Bar Association sought a declaration that Sections 91A, 94 and 95 of POCA and its regulations, insofar as they apply to attorneys-at-law, are unconstitutional and of no force and effect and that their application ought not to extend to attorneys. The constitutional challenge was heard by the full court March 23 to 26, 2015, but the judgment is yet to be delivered.

B Collective Settlement of Debts

20. The Insolvency Act, 2014 was recently introduced in Jamaica to, among other things, consolidate the law relating to bankruptcy, insolvency, receiverships, provisional supervision and winding up. It provides far-reaching powers of the trustee, which includes the power (a) to examine under oath any person: (i) reasonably thought to have knowledge of the affairs of the bankrupt or (ii) who is or has been an agent, clerk, servant, officer, director or employee of the bankrupt; and (b) to require any person liable to be so examined to produce any books, documents, correspondence or papers in his or her possession or power relating in whole or in part to the bankrupt, the bankrupt's dealings or property.[88] Where a person fails to supply the information requested, the trustee may apply to the court for an order to obtain such information. Section 135 further provides that any person subject to being examined by a court "is bound to answer all questions relating to the business or property of the bankrupt, to the causes of his bankruptcy and the disposition of his property." The broad language of these provisions means that attorneys may well be captured and be requested to provide information on a client facing insolvency or bankruptcy proceedings. The legislation is, however, still in its nascent stages, and, consequently, there is yet to be any judicial pronouncements on its provisions. Nevertheless, given that Jamaican courts have closely guarded legal professional privilege in previous cases, it is quite possible that a court will consider that these provisions do not override legal professional privilege, in cases

---

[88] Section 131(1).

where it applies. However, as it relates to information that is confidential, but not privileged, the statutory provisions might prevail.

6 Treatment of Lawyers' Documents and Correspondence in the Context of Judicial or Police Investigations

21. Legal professional privilege is given much deference in Jamaica, and so, even in the context of judicial or police investigations, privilege is expected to be respected. This was illustrated in the case of *Jamaican Bar Association and others v. The Attorney General and the Director of Public Prosecutions and others*, where the Canadian authorities requested the assistance of Jamaica in obtaining information on a Canadian national who was a resident in Jamaica at the time and facing extradition.[89] The Jamaican Court of Appeal held that the seizure by the Jamaican police of privileged documents was unconstitutional.

7 Search of a Lawyer's Office

The case of *Jamaican Bar Association and others v. The Attorney General and the Director of Public Prosecutions and others*[90] also involved the search of an attorney's office. In this case, the police examined and removed information from an attorney's client file during a search of the attorney's premises. In allowing an appeal from the Constitutional Court, the Jamaican Court of Appeal held that in the absence of any allegation of criminal conduct occurring on the premises, or by the attorneys or their clients in the attorney-client relationship, the searches of the attorney's offices and the seizure of privileged client documents amounted to a breach of legal professional privilege. This case was, however, decided in relation to the Mutual Assistance Act, which did not have any express provisions in relation to legal professional privilege. On the other hand, the respect for legal professional privilege is expressed in Section 117 of the Proceeds of Crime Act, which states that a search and seizure warrant does not confer the right to seize any information or material that a person would be able to refuse to produce on the grounds of legal professional privilege in proceedings in the Supreme Court. The GLC has also published in its *Anti-Money Laundering Guidance for the Legal Profession* that, pursuant to the POCA regulations, the files of attorneys may be periodically inspected. The guidance, however, noted that the powers of the GLC to examine and take copies of documents and information in the possession or control of any attorney do not extend to information or advice that is subject to legal professional privilege or was obtained in privileged circumstances.[91] The GLC, therefore, encouraged attorneys to keep privileged

---

[89] SCCA Nos. 96, 102, 108 of 2003, delivered Dec. 14, 2007.   [90] Ibid.

[91] *See* Section 91A(4), Proceeds of Crime Act, 2007.

documents separate from other documents and information that are to be made available for inspection and disclosure to prevent any inadvertent breach of their clients' privilege.

Further to an application made by the Jamaica Bar Association, the Supreme Court granted an injunction restraining the GLC from exercising its mandate as the competent authority for attorneys-at-law pursuant to Section 91A of the Proceeds of Crime (Amendment Act), 2013. As a result of the injunction, attorneys in Jamaica are presently exempted from complying with the new obligations related to being designated as a DNFI, pending the outcome of the constitutional motion. The continued existence of the injunction does not, however, exempt attorneys from prosecution for money laundering offences under the general money laundering provisions in Sections 92 and 93 of POCA.

8 Tapping of Telephone Conversations with a Lawyer

22.   There are no known instances of the tapping of an attorney's telephone conversations in Jamaica. Taking guidance from the Court of Appeal's decision in *Jamaican Bar Association and others v. The Attorney General and the Director of Public Prosecutions and others*,[92] it is likely that such activities would be considered unconstitutional and in breach of legal professional privilege, unless the conversations were in furtherance of a criminal aim.

9 The Lawyer as Witness

23.   An attorney can be called to testify as a witness, where appropriate. However, an attorney is unlikely to be compelled by the courts in Jamaica to act as a witness against a client in circumstances where doing so would amount to a breach of the client's privilege. This follows the common law notion that "the loyalty owed by the lawyer to his client disables him from being a witness in his client's case."[93] Nevertheless, in the unlikely event that an attorney is called as a witness, such attorney will be expected to express when he or she is unable to answer a particular question or disclose certain information on the grounds of attorney-client privilege.

The position is different in relation to the duty of confidentiality, as Canon IV(t) provides exceptions that may be relevant where an attorney is called as a witness. These include that attorneys may reveal a confidence of a client where it is necessary to establish or collect their fee or to defend themselves or their employees or associates against an accusation of wrongful conduct, or where attorneys are required by law to disclose knowledge of all material facts relating to a serious offence that has been committed.

---

[92] SCCA Nos. 96, 102, 108 of 2003, delivered Dec. 14, 2007.
[93] *McCormick on Evidence*, 3rd ed., at 204.

10 The Lawyer and the Press

24.   Attorneys in Jamaica are often contacted by the press to provide their comments on newsworthy matters, including cases in which the attorney may be involved. When dealing with the press, an attorney is expected to decline to answer questions that may result in a breach of a client's confidence or privilege. Additionally, attorneys are not expected to comment on matters in which they are involved that are still pending determination by a court.

11 Powers of the Tax and Other Authorities

25.   The tax authorities cannot compel an attorney to provide relevant information on a client in circumstances where doing so might amount to a breach of the client's privilege. However, in circumstances where the information is confidential, but not privileged, the need for its disclosure will be weighed against the need to respect its confidential nature.

12 National Security Issues

26.   Jamaica maintains the common law position that legal professional privilege is not an interest to be balanced against other competing interests.[94] Consequently, legal professional privilege will not be trumped by national security issues. This is illustrated, for example, in the respect for privilege afforded by Jamaica's anti-money laundering legislation.[95] Confidentiality, on the other hand, may be outweighed by a countervailing public interest, including national security issues.[96]

---

[94] See *R v. Derby Magistrates' Court, Ex parte B* [1995] 4 All ER 526, 541.
[95] Section 94, Proceeds of Crime Act, 2007; Section 91A(4), Proceeds of Crime (Amendment) Act, 2013.
[96] *See Attorney General v. Guardian Newspapers (no 2)* [1988] 3 All ER 545, 658.

24

Mexico

SAMUEL GARCÍA-CUÉLLAR
MICHEL NARCIA MARTÍNEZ
Creel, García-Cuéllar, Aiza y Enríquez, S.C.

Preliminary Note

1. Under Article 5 of the Political Constitution (Constitución Política; the "Constitution") of the United Mexican States ("Mexico"), all persons are free to practice any licit profession, industry, commerce or job. The Regulatory Law of Article 5 of the Mexican Constitution, related to the Professions in the Federal District (*Ley Reglamentaria del Artículo 5o. Constitucional, relativo al Ejercicio de las Profesiones en el Distrito Federal*; "Professions Law") establishes which professions require a title or degree and the conditions to obtain such title. The Professions Law establishes the requirements that need to be satisfied by any college to issue a degree. The degrees must be registered with the Ministry of Education, which will issue a practice license known as *Cédula Profesional*, which is required by a lawyer to practice law and appear in court.

   The Professions Law does not require that lawyers be members of a bar association or other association of professionals to practice.

   Lawyers may join any of the existing bars or associations in Mexico. The *Ilustre y Nacional Colegio de Abogados de México* (the "INCAM") was created in 1760, while Mexico was a Spanish colony. The Mexican Bar (*Barra Mexicana, Colegio de Abogados*; the "BMA") was created in 1922. The National Association of Corporate Lawyers (*Asociación Nacional de Abogados de Empresa*, the "ANADE") was created in 1970. The BMA, the INCAM and the ANADE each have a Code of Ethics, which contains provisions on professional secrecy, which is both a duty and a right of the member lawyers. It is a duty to the clients and a right of a lawyer, who may refuse to reveal confidential information or release documents to a court or authority.

   There are two bills before the Senate in Mexico, one to amend several articles of the Constitution, including Article 5, and the other to enact a new Professions Law (the "New Professions Law"), which will establish the obligation to join a bar or an association to practice and the obligation of professionals to be certified every five years. The bills were submitted to the Senate in February 2014 and have been extensively discussed by lawyers and members of the existing bars and associations of professionals in Mexico.

   The New Professions Law also provides that bars or associations will have to adopt a Code of Ethics and be responsible for enforcing disciplinary measures on their members if they breach their obligations under the Code of Ethics.

2. Article 41 of the New Professions Law establishes several obligations of professionals, one of which is not to reveal or use any reserved or secret communications that they came to know or receive in the performance of the professional services, except (i) when they have the express authorization of their client, (ii) to stop a crime that could cause the death or harm the health of any persons, or (iii) when the professional has an obligation to reveal the

information under any other laws. Another obligation is that professionals should not provide services at the same time to clients who have conflicting interests in any transaction, unless they have the consent of all parties to perform services in the common interest of all those involved.

Under Article 42 of the New Professions Law, a professional will be disbarred when a final court order is issued disqualifying the professional to practice law or the bar issues a final order expelling the professional for a breach of the Code of Ethics.

The violations to the New Professions Law could result in fines, warnings, temporary suspension to practice law or disqualification from the practice of law.

The Ministry of Education (*Secretaría de Educación Pública*) is responsible for enforcing the New Professions Law.

3.   We are confident that the bills before the Senate, as may be amended, will be approved in the near future. When that happens, Mexico will have regulations on professional secrecy similar to many other jurisdictions and will have professional associations in charge of imposing disciplinary sanctions to those professionals who breach their obligations under a Code of Ethics.

1 Scope of and Limitations on the Duty of Professional Secrecy/ Attorney-Client Privilege

A Statutory Basis and Implications

4.   There are separate isolated statutory provisions governing the professional secrecy obligation (rather than a "privilege") in Mexico that is binding on all types of persons carrying out professional activities in Mexico, including lawyers.

Throughout the Mexican legal framework, the following statutes contain references to professional secrecy: the Constitution; the Professions Law; the National Code of Criminal Procedures (*Código Nacional de Procedimientos Penales*; "National Criminal Code");[1] the Federal Code of Criminal Procedures (*Código Federal de Procedimientos Penales*; "Criminal Procedures Code"); the Federal Criminal Code (*Código Penal Federal*; "Federal Criminal Code"); the

---

[1] On December 29, 2014, the National Criminal Code was published in the Official Gazette of the Federation. The statute was created with the purpose of establishing a uniform oral, adversarial criminal trial process (and provides rules for the various stages of investigation, prosecution and punishment of crimes). In principle, each of Mexico's 32 independent local jurisdictions must publish amendments to their local criminal legal framework and begin implementing the National Criminal Code (this was meant to take place by June 2016). Once all of Mexico's local jurisdictions adopt these measures, the National Criminal Code will derogate all local codes of criminal procedures, as well as the Federal Criminal Code. As of November 24, 2015, 7 out of Mexico's 32 local jurisdictions have adopted these measures, and the National Criminal Code became binding as of November 30, 2015. For purposes of this chapter, both the National Criminal Code and the Federal Criminal Code will be analyzed, as both statutes contain provisions governing the professional secrecy obligation.

Federal Code of Civil Procedures (*Código Federal de Procedimientos Civiles*; "Civil Procedures Code"); the Federal Civil Code (*Código Civil Federal*; "Civil Code"); the Federal Labor Law (*Ley Federal del Trabajo*; "Labor Law"); the Industrial Property Law (*Ley de la Propiedad Industrial* "Industrial Property Law"); as well as very few decisions issued by Mexican courts.

As the provisions governing the professional secrecy obligation (also known as the attorney-client privilege) contained in the above statutes are isolated, it would be advisable to standardize each of these statutory provisions to properly regulate the professional secrecy obligation in Mexico.

Article 16 of the Constitution contains specific rules for disclosing and protecting communications exchanged between detainees and lawyers during criminal procedures.[2] In accordance with such provision, all private communications are inviolable, and it is considered a crime to perform any act hindering the independence and secrecy of such communications, except in those cases whereby such communications are voluntarily offered by the participants involved. Accordingly, no communication may be admitted as evidence if its submission amounts to a breach of a confidentiality duty.

The above provision has the purpose of ensuring that detainees have a proper defense by their lawyers. All detainees have a right to legal assistance. To be effective, detainees must be sure that the information provided to their lawyers will not be disclosed in any procedure. It may be interpreted that such rights arise once a procedure has initiated; however, it may also be argued that such rights could also be applicable to all types of communications exchanged between lawyers and clients, even those exchanged before the procedure has been initiated.

Because there are no specific rules to confirm that all communications between lawyers and clients are protected under Article 16 of the Constitution, such analysis would require an assessment of the specific circumstances surrounding a particular situation. It would be advisable that future amendments to Article 16 of the Constitution provide that all communications between clients and lawyers are protected by the professional secrecy obligation.

5.   In principle, all persons providing professional services in Mexico have a professional secrecy obligation. Article 24 of the Professions Law provides that professional services comprise any type of habitual undertaking, for

---

[2] Art. 16 of the Constitution provides the following: "The federal judicial authority, prior request by a federal authority entitled by law or the head of the corresponding local Prosecutor's Office (Ministerio Público), may authorize the intervention of any private communication. For these purposes, the relevant authority shall express the applicable statutory provisions and rationale for such request, specifying the type of intervention, subjects and duration related thereto.
The federal judicial authority may not grant these authorizations when it involves electoral, tax, commercial, civil, labor or administrative matters, or communications between detainees and lawyers."

consideration or without payment, of all acts or services rendered that are characteristic of each of the professions, even when it is a simple consultation.

In Mexico, to be entitled to provide professional services, you need to have obtained a certificate or degree, and, in certain cases, you need to obtain a license to practice (known as *cedula profesional*). These specific requirements are also applicable to lawyers.

In accordance with Article 36 of the Professions Law, all professionals are bound to keep in strict confidence the information confided to them by their clients, except for certain mandatory reports required by law.[3] It is important to mention that this provision is applicable only in Federal District (Mexico City), but the same obligation has been replicated by the majority of local state laws in Mexico. Article 36 of the Professions Law is defined as an "obligation" that is binding on all professionals in order to maintain as confidential all information provided by their clients.

It must be noted that, as an exemption, professionals will have to reveal confidential information of their clients when other laws require such reports.[4]

In a recent decision issued by a Mexican Federal Collegiate Tribunal for civil matters,[5] professional secrecy was upheld even in cases where laws or courts require lawyers to disclose their clients' information. In this decision, it was resolved that the professional secrecy obligation applies to medical doctors, lawyers, financial institutions, accountants and priests, among others. Persons bound by the professional secrecy obligation cannot disclose any information provided by their clients during their business relationship, nor can they be compelled to give witness testimony unless clients provide express authorization to do so. The objective of such rule is to provide that all types of professionals, including lawyers, should have the right to refuse to provide witness testimony, information and documentation to courts and authorities when those individuals are bound by a professional secrecy obligation.[6]

Similarly, the National Criminal Code, the Federal Criminal Code and the Civil Procedures Code contain specific statutory provisions establishing a list of persons who may refuse to provide witness testimony in connection with information provided by their clients or with any person with whom they have a personal relationship.

The Civil Code also prohibits lawyers and those acting as attorneys-in-fact of a corporation or individual from disclosing information or documents that

---

[3] Art. 36 of the Professions Law provides: "All professionals are bound to keep strict confidentiality of all matters entrusted by their clients, except for those mandatory reports required by the applicable laws."

[4] *See* Sections 1(B) and 5 of this chapter.

[5] *See* Tribunal's decision I.3o.C.698 C, *Semanario Judicial de la Federación y su Gaceta, Novena Época*, t. XXVIII, September 2008, at 1411.

[6] *See* Section 9 of this chapter.

may be used against their representatives.[7] Any breach of this obligation could give rise to a claim against the lawyer to cover damages and losses.

In addition, the Labor Law contains a specific regulation restricting employees from divulging confidential information of their employers that, if disclosed, may constitute a crime under the Federal Criminal Code.[8]

Furthermore, trade secrets and confidential information are protected under the Mexican legal framework. The Industrial Property Law contains specific statutory provisions regarding the protection of trade secrets. Article 82 of the Industrial Property Law defines trade secrets as any and all information of industrial or commercial application kept by an individual or entity as confidential, that allows the owner to obtain or maintain a competitive or economic advantage in performing certain economic activities and, with respect to which, the individual or entity has adopted sufficient measures or systems to preserve its confidential nature and to restrict access to it.[9]

As explained previously, it would be advisable to revise the different statutes governing the professional secrecy obligation to have a consistent legal framework.

B Scope

6.   Based on an analysis of the statutory provisions governing the duty of professional secrecy, it can be argued that all types of information exchanged between clients and lawyers, regardless of whether such information was disclosed prior to or once a judicial procedure has initiated, are covered under the secrecy obligation applicable throughout different statutes of Mexican legislation.[10]

Disclosure of confidential information or information that has been acquired as a result of someone's employment or position, if such disclosure causes harm to the employer and it is made without the employer's consent and without a just cause, may constitute a crime. Thus, it is essential that, if a person is subject to a professional secrecy obligation, disclosure of information to any person (including to the authorities) be authorized by the person who entrusted the information to the individual.

Professional secrecy may be breached only under extreme circumstances, such as the commission of a crime. Lawyers are bound by the professional

---

[7] *See* Art. 2590, Civil Code.   [8] *See* Arts. 47, 134, Labor Law.
[9] The Industrial Property Law does not consider as a trade secret any information that (i) is publicly available, (ii) is known to a technician because of his or her previous experience, (iii) must be disclosed by operation of law or a court order when such information is furnished to and held by a person as a trade secret in order to obtain licenses, permits, authorizations, registrations or any other acts of a government authority.
[10] *See* Section 1(A) of this chapter.

secrecy duty even after they provide legal services to their clients. Information obtained by a lawyer when acting as a director or as a trustee is not protected by the professional secrecy duty.

C Persons Subject to the Duty of Professional Secrecy

7.   In general, the professional secrecy obligation, as provided in the Mexican legal framework, is binding for anyone carrying out professional activities in Mexico. Article 36 of the Professions Law is applicable to a large number of people, including architects, accountants, medical doctors, psychologists, lawyers, engineers and notaries public, among others.

As it will be further explained,[11] both the Criminal Procedures Code and the Civil Procedures Code contain very similar provisions establishing a list of people, including religious ministers, journalists, medical doctors, lawyers, notaries and other professionals, who cannot be compelled to give witness testimony in court if the laws governing their respective profession impose a duty of confidentiality. Both statutes contain provisions that identify those individuals who may refuse to provide witness testimony in connection with their clients or with any person with whom they have a personal relationship.

In addition, Articles 47 and 134 of the Labor Law[12] provide specific obligations for employees to maintain confidential information of their employer and entitles the latter to terminate an employee in case of any disclosure that causes harm to the employer. Additionally, the disclosure of confidential information by employees is considered a crime under the Federal Criminal Code.[13]

Notwithstanding the above provisions and limits for employees to disclose confidential information of their employers, there are no precedents or case law on the refusal by an employee to either provide information or give witness testimony.

Furthermore, as it will be explained,[14] the Industrial Property Law establishes both civil and criminal sanctions for individuals who breach confidentiality obligations.

---

[11] *See* Section 9 of this chapter.

[12] Art. 47 of the Labor Law provides: "The following correspond to causes of termination in which no liability shall be attributed to employers: . . . IX. In case an employee reveals trade secrets or discloses information of reserved matters, causing harm to his employer." Art. 134 of the Labor Law establishes the following: "Employees' obligations are the following: . . . XIII. Maintain strict confidentiality of technical, commercial and manufacturing secrets of all products in which such employees participate, directly or indirectly, in their manufacturing process, or of which they have any knowledge as a consequence of their position; as well as any managerial matter which, if disclosed, may harm its employer."

[13] Art. 210, Federal Criminal Code.   [14] *See* Section 4(A) of this chapter.

D Exceptions to and Optional Derogations from the Duty of Professional Secrecy

8.   A lawyer may disclose confidential information when the life or health of a person is at stake. Article 15, Section V, of the Federal Criminal Code provides that no crime will be committed if the lawyer discloses a professional secret to save a person from real, actual and imminent crime, as long as there are no other means to stop the crime. The lawyer must disclose only the information that is absolutely necessary to stop the crime. The same exception applies if lawyers disclose the information to defend an act of aggression or attack against themselves or others, if such disclosure is inevitable for the defense. Also, the lawyer may defend against an unjustified claim from a client and disclose confidential information if that is absolutely necessary, to have a fair trial.

A lawyer may not use the duty of professional secrecy to cover up a crime in which the lawyer has participated.

Article 400, Section V, of the Federal Criminal Code refers to the crime of concealment. All persons have an obligation to stop or impede any crime that is to be committed or that is being committed. This obligation needs to be complied with even if it implies the disclosure of information protected by the duty of professional secrecy. There is no obligation if the crime has already been committed.

E Law Firms

9.   The Mexican legal framework described above[15] makes no reference to lawyers working as employees, associates or partners in law firms, and it does not regulate the activities of law firms. All references to professional secrecy are to individual lawyers. The duty of secrecy does not apply to attorneys who engage in activities that do not constitute legal advice to clients.

In Mexico, many lawyers practice in law firms. In these cases, the clients retain a law firm to provide legal services. In such cases, the confidential information received by the law firm is shared by all members of the law firm. There are no rules on professional liability in cases where lawyers practice in a law firm. In exceptional cases, a client may wish to retain a partner and not a law firm, in which case the partner must not share the confidential information with other members of the law firm and must keep separate files.

The client must be assured that all the employees working in the law firm understand the obligation to maintain the confidentiality of the information and not to reveal such information to third parties.

As explained previously,[16] Article 36 of the Professions Law establishes that all professionals are bound to keep strict confidence of all matters entrusted to them by their clients. In the case of lawyers practicing in law firms, this

---

[15] *See* Section 1(A) of this chapter.   [16] Ibid.

obligation is imposed on all of them. Law firms frequently have a Code of Ethics that deals with this and other issues, such as professional liability of the lawyers and partners of the law firm.

There are other law firms that operate under a cost-sharing structure, in which case the lawyers must keep separate files and not share the confidential information with the other members of the law firm.

F Legal Assistants and Staff

10.   The Professions Law does not apply to non-lawyers. All employees of the law firm could have access to confidential information received from the clients. Such employees are considered representatives of the law firm for which they work. Law firms must take all necessary measures to explain to their employees the nature and extent of the obligation to maintain all information received from the clients as confidential, and they must explain the consequences of any breach of this obligation.

Any disclosure of any confidential information by any employee of the law firm could result in liability to the partners of the law firm. Sanctions may be imposed on the partners of the law firm, including civil liability.

In this regard, Article 71 of the Professions Law provides that all professionals are responsible for the civil liability arising out of any professional activity carried out by their assistants or employees when those professionals failed to provide adequate instructions or those instructions resulted in harm.

Under the Federal Criminal Code, employees may incur criminal liability for revealing secrets or information known as a result of their employment.

G External Service Providers

11.   In Mexico, law firms do not generally outsource services to external service providers. Practically all legal services are handled by members and employees of the law firm.

One exception is the use of translators. The Professions Law is not applicable to translators. It is generally understood that translators should not reveal or disclose information obtained from their clients. Any disclosure by the translator of confidential information received in connection with the services provided could constitute a criminal offense under the Federal Criminal Code. The translator will have to pay for the damages and losses resulting from the breach of the secrecy duty.

Law firms use public notaries who are lawyers and are subject to the same or more strict obligations of secrecy.

On occasion, law firms may, with the consent of the client, retain other lawyers or law firms to perform professional services in special areas of practice. The obligation to maintain as confidential the information received from the client also applies to such professionals. Any breach of the secrecy obligation could result in civil or criminal liability.

H Multidisciplinary Associations

12. The Professions Law does not regulate a multidisciplinary association.

There are no legal impediments to the formation of multidisciplinary associations, which could include lawyers and other professionals. Lawyers may form a multidisciplinary association with non-lawyers.

The Professions Law applies to other professionals such as accountants, economists, engineers and others. In Mexico many accounting firms have lawyers to provide legal services in the area of taxation.

All of the members of the multidisciplinary association have the obligation to maintain the confidentiality of the information and documentation of the clients. Any breach of professional secrecy will result in civil or criminal liability.

I In-House Counsel

13. In-house counsel are subject to the professional secrecy duty, based on Article 36 of the Professions Law, in their capacity as lawyers.

In-house counsel provide legal advice to management in public and private entities and must comply with legal and ethical rules that govern the activities of the legal profession. In-house counsel may not disclose or reveal to third parties any information they learn within the organization.

As individuals, they may incur criminal liability if they divulge confidential information. In-house counsel, as employers of public or private entities, are not bound to provide reports or information in regards to money laundering or organized crime. In-house counsel could disclose confidential information to stop a crime.

In-house counsel may refuse to provide testimony on any confidential information protected by the duty of professional secrecy.

As explained, in-house counsel, as employees of public or private entities, are also subject to the obligations imposed under the Labor Law.

2 History of the Duty of Professional Secrecy in Mexico

14. The first recorded statutory provisions in Mexico regarding lawyers' professional secrecy was published in the 1800s. The Civil Code of the Federal District (Mexico City) of 1870 included a specific provision to regulate the professional secrecy obligation. Article 2520[17] of that statute mirrored the regulation regarding the breach of professional secrecy obligation contained

---

[17] Art. 2520 of the Civil Code of the Federal District (1870) provided that any lawyer disclosing a secret to a counterparty, as well as exchanging documents or information causing harm to

in the Seven Laws (*Siete Partidas*) of Spain, which were in force during the Spanish conquest of Mexico.

Specifically, the Seven Laws provided that any lawyer who discloses to a counterparty a secret confided by a client would be considered a person with poor reputation and would be suspended from acting as a lawyer in any matter, as well as being subject to the penalties to be determined by a judge. Such provision remained in the Civil Code of the Federal District (Mexico City) of 1884, as well as the Civil Code currently in force, which no longer contains the suspension from acting as a lawyer as a sanction.

In addition, the "Criminal Code of the Federal District and Baja California regarding local crimes, and for all the Republic regarding crimes against the Federation of 1871" (*Código Penal para el Distrito Federal y Territorio de la Baja California sobre delitos del fuero común, y para toda la República sobre delitos contra la Federación de 1871*; the "Criminal Code of 1871") included a specific statutory provision governing the disclosure of secrets.

Specifically, Article 767 of the Criminal Code of 1871 provided criminal penalties between two and six years' imprisonment and occupational prohibitions to individuals disclosing a secret known as a consequence of their employment, professional activity or position.

Article 768 of the Criminal Code of 1871 established that confessors, medical doctors, surgeons, midwives, apothecaries, lawyers and attorneys-in-fact, notaries, and other professionals cannot be compelled to disclose secrets entrusted to them as a consequence of their employment or professional activity, including any crime known as a consequence of their position.

Afterwards, in 1945, the year in which the first version of the Professions Law entered into force, Article 24, which identifies the specific activities considered to be professional services in Mexico, and Article 36, governing the professional's secrecy obligation, were the first statutory provisions explicitly regulating the lawyer's secrecy obligation.[18] Such provisions remain in force in the Professions Law currently in force.

3 Supervision

A The Bar Associations

15.   As explained in the Preliminary Note, in Mexico today professionals, including lawyers, are not required to join a bar or other association to practice law. They only need to obtain a degree from a recognized college and register the degree with the Ministry of Education.

---

a client, would be liable for all damages and losses resulting from such conduct, in addition to any criminal penalty that may be applicable.

[18] *See* Section 1(A) of this chapter.

Lawyers may voluntarily join a bar or other association. Such bars or associations have Codes of Ethics, which contain articles on the duty of professional secrecy. The bar or association has the authority to oversee compliance with the Codes of Ethics of the legal profession. The bar or association may impose disciplinary sanctions on its members who breach the obligations established in the Codes of Ethics. Only the lawyer has the authority to decide how to defend his or her clients. The bar cannot direct the lawyer on how to defend the client's case.

INCAM, BMA and ANADE[19] each have a disciplinary body that investigates and imposes disciplinary sanctions on the members who violate the Code of Ethics.

16.   Professional secrecy is an ethical duty of the member lawyers, the violation of which will result in disciplinary sanctions.

The Code of Ethics of the BMA provides that maintaining professional secrecy is a duty and a right of the lawyer. It is a duty to the client that survives the term of the professional services. It is a right of the lawyer to not reveal confidential information to courts and other authorities. When asked to appear as a witness, the lawyer should appear before the court or other authorities and must refuse to respond to the questions relating to any matters covered by professional secrecy. The obligation to keep the professional secret includes any information known to the lawyer as a result of the professional services rendered.

The lawyer should not participate, without the consent of the client, in any other case in which the lawyer could be forced to reveal or use the confidential information.

If a client files an unjustified claim against a lawyer, the lawyer may reveal any information that is necessary to defend him- or herself. If the client informs the lawyer that the client plans to commit a crime, such information would not be covered by professional secrecy, and the lawyer must reveal such information to prevent the crime or to protect innocent persons.

The breaches of the Code of Ethics must be submitted to the Honor Board (*Junta de Honor*) of the BMA, which has the authority to impose disciplinary sanctions.

The bylaws of the BMA contain the provisions that govern the Honor Board. The Honor Board must investigate any complaints received by the BMA. If the complaint is admitted, the Honor Board will follow the procedure described in the bylaws and will give the defendant the opportunity to participate in a defense and offer whatever evidence he or she deems appropriate.

The Honor Board may impose one or more of the following disciplinary sanctions: (i) admonition and (ii) suspension of the rights of the member and expulsion from the BMA.

---

[19] *See* the Preliminary Note of this chapter.

Because the lawyer may practice without being a member of the BMA, in many cases the lawyers who are facing a complaint resign from the BMA.

B The Courts

17. The legal profession, and other professions in Mexico, are governed by the Professions Law and other related laws and codes.[20] The Ministry of Education supervises the legal profession. The Ministry of Education is the authority that hears complaints against lawyers. The legal profession is not self-regulated.

The Civil Courts have jurisdiction to hear and decide any claims brought by clients against lawyers for professional liability. If lawyers are found guilty, they are obliged to indemnify the clients for any direct damages and losses suffered. Decisions of the Civil Courts can be appealed. An appeal on legal grounds is possible to the Supreme Court.

Criminal Courts have jurisdiction to preside over crimes committed by lawyers, including the disclosure of professional secrets. Decisions of the criminal courts can be appealed, including an appeal to the Supreme Court.

4 Sanctions

A Proceedings and Sanctions

18. The breach of a professional secrecy obligation may result in criminal sanctions. Article 210 of the Federal Criminal Code provides penalties between 30 and 200 days of community service to any person who, without reasonable cause, in prejudice of another and without prior authorization, discloses any type of "secret" or reserved communication known as a consequence of the person's employment or position. Secrets and confidential information shall be maintained as confidential as long as such information is not publicly available.

The Industrial Property Law establishes both civil and criminal sanctions for individuals who breach confidentiality obligations. Under the Industrial Property Law, the following constitute criminal offenses:[21]

1. Disclosing to a third party a trade secret that is known to individuals by virtue of their job, position, work, profession, business relationship or the granting of a license, without the consent of the owner of the trade secret and after having been warned of its confidentiality, to either (i) obtain an economic benefit for themselves or for a third party, or (ii) cause damage to the owner of the trade secret.
2. Misappropriation of a trade secret without the consent of the owner of the trade secret (or its authorized user) to use or disclose to a third party the trade secret for the purpose of either (i) obtaining an economic benefit for

---

[20] *See* Section 1(A) of this chapter.   [21] Art. 223, Industrial Property Law.

oneself or for a third party, or (ii) causing damage to the owner of the trade secret (or to its authorized user).

3. Using the information contained in a trade secret, where that information was either (i) known to individuals by virtue of their job, position, work, profession or business relationship, without the consent of the owner of the trade secret (or its authorized user), or (ii) disclosed to them by a third party, knowing that the third party did not have the consent of the owner of the trade secret (or its authorized user) to disclose the information, with the purpose of obtaining an economic benefit or causing damage to the owner of the trade secret (or its authorized user).

Pursuant to Article 224 of the Industrial Property Law, any of the above-mentioned actions may result in criminal penalties of between two and six years' imprisonment and a fine of between USD $424 to USD $42,400. Both imprisonment and a fine can be imposed at the same time. Irrespective of these penalties, under the Industrial Property Law, the victim or offended party has the right to receive compensation for damages, which, in any case, will not be less than 40 percent of the retail price of each product or service implicated.[22]

In addition, Article 211 of the Federal Criminal Code includes certain situations in which the above criminal penalties are increased. In this regard, if the breach of secrecy is carried out by a person providing professional or technical services or a public officer, or if the revealed information corresponds to a trade secret, the Federal Criminal Code provides penalties between one to five years of community service, a minimum monetary fine, and suspension from participating in the individual's profession for a period between two months and one year.

More importantly, Article 211 Bis of the Federal Criminal Code provides penalties between six and twelve years' imprisonment and a fine of between 300 to 600 days' salary[23] to those individuals who reveal, disclose or unlawfully use, with the purpose to cause harm to others, any type of information or images obtained through the interception of any private communication.

19. It is important to mention that professionals carrying out or participating in criminal activities will also be liable for breaching their professional responsibility. In case of breach of professional responsibility, Article 228 of the Federal Criminal Code provides temporary suspension of professionals for a period between one month and two years, in case of repetition of the same offense as well as the payment of any damages and losses resulting from their conduct (including those damages resulting from the conduct of their assistants or employees).

---

[22] Art. 221 Bis, Industrial Property Law.

[23] Pursuant to the Federal Criminal Code, a day's salary will be calculated pursuant to the daily net income of the individual at the time of the infringement.

In addition, Article 2590 of the Civil Code provides that any attorney-in-fact or lawyer who discloses or provides to a counterparty (a) secrets or information, and/or (b) documents or data that could be used against a client will be liable of all damages and losses arising out of such conduct, in addition the criminal penalties that may be applicable.

B Relationship between Criminal Sanctions and Disciplinary Sanctions

20.   In Mexico, criminal sanctions are independent from any disciplinary sanction that may be imposed by a Mexican bar or association. In this regard, lawyers who breach their professional secrecy obligation may be subject to criminal sanctions, together with any disciplinary sanction that may be imposed by a Mexican bar. The principle that no one can be tried twice for the same matter does not stop a lawyer who breached the professional secrecy obligation from being subject to both criminal sanctions and disciplinary sanctions.

For instance, if a lawyer reveals a secret confided to him or her by a client, the lawyer may be subject to the criminal and civil penalties explained above, together with any disciplinary sanction that may be determined by the Board of Honors of a Mexican bar (such as admonition or suspension of lawyer's rights as a member of the bar).

Nevertheless, because professionals (including lawyers) currently are not required to join a bar or association to practice law in Mexico, criminal and civil sanctions are enforced in Mexico when lawyers breach their professional secrecy obligation. This situation, as explained previously,[24] will change once the New Professions Law is approved by the Mexican Congress.

5 Duty to Provide Information to the Authorities

A Money Laundering and Terrorism

21.   On October 17, 2012, the Federal Law on the Prevention and Identification of Operations from Illicit Sources (*Ley Federal para la Prevención e Identificación de Operaciones con Recursos de Procedencia Ilícita,* "Anti-Money Laundering Law") was published, which became effective on July 17, 2013. This statute includes specific obligations to disclose information to Mexican authorities regarding activities considered to be "vulnerable," due to their likelihood of involving money laundering and organized crime.

The underlying purpose of the Anti-Money Laundering Law is to establish new measures and procedures, including mandatory reports to be provided to the Mexican Ministry of Finance and Public Credit (*Secretaría de Hacienda y Crédito Público*), to prevent and detect acts or transactions carried out with funds obtained from illicit activities. However, the required disclosures may

---

[24] *See* Section 3(A) of this chapter.

result in a breach of the professional secrecy obligation. These are the types of exemptions from liability for breaches of the professional secrecy obligations referenced in Article 36 of the Professions Law.[25]

Among a substantial list of activities, it is mandatory to disclose activities involving the provision of independent professional services where no labor relationship with the client exists (such as the type of business relationship between clients and lawyers), and only if the following operations are prepared for a client or are performed in the client's name and on the client's behalf: (i) purchase, sale or assignment of real estate properties; (ii) administration and management of resources, securities or any other client assets; (iii) management of bank accounts, savings or securities accounts; (iv) equity contributions or any other resource for the incorporation, operation and management of companies; and (v) incorporation, spin-off, merger, operation and administration of companies or corporate vehicles, including trusts and the purchase or sale of mercantile entities.[26]

Due to the nature of the activities mentioned in the preceding paragraph, we may conclude that in-house lawyers are not bound to disclose information in terms of the Anti-Money Laundering Law, since such individuals typically perform their activities under a labor relationship with their employers; thus, their professional activities are not provided in an independent manner, as required by the statute.

22. Based on the above, the mandatory reports required to be submitted to the Mexican authorities in terms of the Anti-Money Laundering Law will certainly require disclosure of information that, in many cases, contains confidential information handled by lawyers, thus also covered by the professional secrecy obligation. In these cases, lawyers will require authorization from their clients to submit those reports. If the authorization is not obtained, the professional secrecy obligation would be breached. Article 36 of the Professions Law provides that the professional must comply with obligations established in other laws and must deliver the corresponding reports.

Similar arguments were discussed in a recent *amparo* proceeding initially analyzed by a federal district judge and confirmed by the Mexican Supreme Court of Justice on May 13, 2015.[27] In this proceeding, the applicant argued that, among other provisions, Article 17 of the Anti-Money Laundering Law violates the applicant's constitutional human rights to labor, specifically in connection with the professional secrecy obligation; to privacy; and to due process.

In response, the Supreme Court of Justice stated that the professional secrecy obligation expressly provides that, except for the procedures provided

---

[25] *See* Section 1 of this chapter.   [26] Art. 17, Anti-Money Laundering Law.

[27] *Amparo* procedure with file number 177/2015. Names and information of applicants to that procedure are not publicly available.

by the Mexican legal framework, no third party may be provided with the information handled by professionals. In addition, it stated that the information reported in accordance with the Anti-Money Laundering Law does not violate the professional secrecy obligation as it will not be publicly available but used only by the authorities to ensure that Mexico enforces its legal framework to combat money laundering activities, as well as organized crime.

Although the Mexican Anti-Money Laundering Law represents a major step in combatting organized crime, it also conflicts with other statutory provisions of the Mexican legal framework, such as the right of lawyers to refuse to provide witness testimony and information of their clients during criminal procedures.[28]

B Collective Settlement of Debts

23. Any lawyer providing advice to a distressed debtor is protected by the duty of professional secrecy. These lawyers cannot be forced by an order of a judge or other authority to disclose confidential information of their clients. The professional secret prevails over the assistance to a bankruptcy court in locating asserts of a distressed debtor.

6 Treatment of Lawyers' Documents and Correspondence in the Context of Judicial or Police Investigations

24. Lawyers' documents and correspondence with their clients should be protected by the duty of professional secrecy and must not be admitted as proof in an investigation.

In accordance with Article 16 of the Constitution, any seizure of privileged information requires a seizure warrant specifying the type of information to be seized, the type of seizure, the identity of the subjects involved, as well as the duration of the seizure. As mentioned previously,[29] no court may grant these authorizations when they involve electoral, tax, commercial, civil, labor or administrative matters, or communications between detainees and lawyers. There are other cases in which the documents and correspondence of lawyers may be the subject of a seizure warrant in cases of national security, as explained in Section 12 of this chapter.

7 Search of a Lawyer's Office

25. The search of the office or home of a lawyer is not contemplated in the law. Because of the existence of privileged information of several of the clients of lawyers, a search warrant should be specific on the type of documents or

---

[28] *See* Section 9 of this chapter for further information.   [29] *See* footnote 2.

information that may be searched and the measures to be taken to protect the secrecy of the clients involved.

During the search, the lawyer must not disclose any protected information. Should the lawyer disclose protected information, the client may sue for damages.

8 Tapping of Telephone Conversations with a Lawyer

26.   Under Article 16 of the Constitution, private communications are inviolable. In no case may private communications protected by the professional secrecy be admitted as evidence.[30]

Only a federal judicial authority, at the request of the Public Prosecutor, may authorize the intervention into private communications. The judicial authority must give solid legal reasons to justify the intervention. The order must specify the type of intervention, the persons involved and the duration. The federal judicial authority will not grant the authorization in connection with taxes; government elections; mercantile, civil, labor or administrative issues; or communications between detainees and their lawyers.

9 The Lawyer as Witness

27.   The Mexican legal framework contains statutory provisions that entitle certain people to refuse to provide witness testimony when it involves disclosing information from clients.

For instance, Article 362 of the National Criminal Code[31] contains a specific rule for giving no value to witness testimonies rendered by any person who is protected by a professional secrecy obligation. In addition, it is provided that, if a person obliged under this duty is subpoenaed, the person will be entitled to

---

[30] Art. 16 of the Constitution also provides the following: "All private communications are inviolable and any act hindering its independency and secrecy will be considered as a crime, except in those cases whereby such communications are voluntarily offered by the participants involved thereto. Courts will analyze the evidential value of the communications voluntarily offered, as long as such evidence contains information related to a crime. No communication shall be admitted as evidence if its submission amounts to a breach of a confidentiality duty established by law."

[31] Art. 362 of the National Criminal Code provides: "No witness testimony will be admitted when it is rendered by persons who have a duty to maintain the secrecy of the information they hold as consequence of their activities or profession, such as religious ministers, lawyers, inspectors of human rights, medical doctors, psychologists, pharmacists and nurses, as well as public officials regarding information that it is not subject to be disclosed pursuant to the applicable laws. However, these professionals will not be allowed to refuse to give witness when clients provide authorization to disclose the relevant information. In case of being subpoenaed, such individuals shall appear and explain the motives under which the secrecy obligation arises and refuse to give witness."

explain the specific relation through which the professional secrecy obligation derives and refuse to give witness testimony.

The above rule is also followed by Article 243 Bis of Criminal Procedures Code, which provides that, among a list of persons (including religious ministers, journalists and medical doctors), lawyers, notaries and other professionals cannot be compelled to give witness testimony in court if the laws governing their respective profession impose a duty of confidentiality. The above rule is not applicable when clients provide authorization to lawyers, notaries or others professionals to disclose or provide information to courts.

A similar rule is contained in Article 90 of the Civil Procedures Code.[32] Specifically, it provides that third parties not related to a procedure are bound to assist courts in conducting their procedures, including to reveal related documents and information. It is also provided that Mexican courts are entitled to compel third parties to assist in their duties. Nevertheless, such provision provides that relatives, spouses and any person bound under a secrecy obligation cannot be compelled to give witness testimony, nor to provide documents.

If lawyers are asked to testify on matters in which they did not act as a lawyer, they cannot refuse to testify.

10 The Lawyer and the Press

28.   In Mexico, it is generally accepted that a lawyer can, with the consent of a client, speak to the press to dispute any arguments made in the press against the client. Nevertheless, the lawyer under no circumstances should divulge any information protected by professional secrecy or that is not publicly available.

Any violation of professional secrecy could result in a criminal offense or could give a right to the client to file a claim for damages. The lawyer should never litigate the case through the press.

It is relevant to mention that on September 11, 2014, the Law of Journalists' Professional Secrecy (*Ley del Secreto Profesional del Periodista en el Distrito Federal*; the "Journalists Law") was published in the Official Gazette of Mexico City. Such statute is applicable only in the Mexico City and no other local jurisdiction in Mexico has enacted a similar statute.

In general, the purpose of the Journalists Law is to provide journalists and sources protection regarding the confidentiality of the information exchanged between them.

In accordance with the Journalists Law, a journalists' right to maintain as confidential the identity of their sources is limited only in specific situations,

---

[32] Art. 90 of the Civil Procedures Code establishes the following: "Third parties are bound, any time, to assist courts in finding the truth. Such persons shall, without delay, provide documents they hold when such information is requested. ... Relatives, spouses and any person bound under a secrecy obligation shall not be bound under this provision, when a court requests to provide information in connection with the person with whom they have a relationship."

when a prior order is issued by a Mexican court. Such judicial order shall be in accordance with international treaties for human rights' protection.

The Journalists Law includes a list of rights and protections in favor of journalists and their sources. For instance, Article 4 of the Journalists Law provides the right to journalists and their sources to refuse to disclose information of their sources, when a tribunal subpoenas them to provide a witness statement in a proceeding (either criminal, civil, administrative or in the form of a trial).

The above right also covers the cases where an authority requests a journalist to provide information regarding an ongoing investigation. In such cases, journalists will be entitled to refuse to disclose information. In addition, no authority is entitled to obtain or use journalists' and sources' notes, personal and professional documents, digital files and audio that may lead to the discovery of the identity of a source.

11 Powers of the Tax and Other Authorities

29.   Generally, any breach of the tax laws is not considered a criminal offense except in the case of a fraud.

Tax authorities cannot compel a lawyer to disclose protected information or to provide testimony related to the taxes of the lawyer's client.

The tax authorities have no power to obtain a search order from a court against the lawyer regarding information protected by professional secrecy. Specifically, Article 16 of the Constitution protects the professional secret.

If the lawyer discloses protected information to the tax authorities, the lawyer could face criminal charges or civil claims for damages, filed by the client.

12 National Security Issues

30.   Mexican security issues are regulated by several legal statutes, including the National Security Law (*Ley de Seguridad Nacional*), the Federal Law Against Organized Crime (*Ley Federal contra la Delicuencia Organizada*), the National Criminal Code and the Criminal Procedures Code.

Among the statutes governing national security issues, there are no specific references regarding the professional secrecy obligation. Notwithstanding, other statutes, including international treaties adopted by Mexico, provide that a breach of a professional secrecy obligation where information revealed is required as a matter of national security is not a criminal offense.

For instance, the International Treaty of Civil and Political Rights (*Pacto Internacional de Derechos Civiles y Políticos*), adopted by Mexico in 1981, which remains in force, contains a specific provision limiting those situations in which certain rights and obligations, including the professional secrecy obligation, may be suspended.

Article 19 of the Treaty of Civil and Political Rights provides that a right may be restricted or suspended if required by law and if necessary to (a) ensure the protection of rights or reputation of others or (b) to protect the national security, the public order, health or public morality. As this treaty forms part of the Mexican legal framework, we may conclude that national security issues prevail over professional secrecy.

Article 16 of the Constitution does not provide that the courts should not issue an order to search for information protected by professional secrecy where an investigation by the federal security forces is petitioned to the courts.

Notwithstanding the above, any information obtained must be kept confidential to protect the clients' privacy, when such clients are participating in any activities that constitute a potential threat to national security.

25

Panama

JOSÉ AGUSTÍN PRECIADO M.
MARIO A. PRECIADO MIRÓ

Fabrega Molino Mulino

Preliminary Note

1. Panamanian law is based on the civil law system (Romano-Germanic or Continental) as a consequence of the Spanish and Colombian influence on the country. The Constitution of Panama provides that the country shall have a unitary form of government, so the law applies uniformly within the whole country. The state is divided into three main branches: legislative, judicial and executive.

    To practice law in the Republic of Panama, a law degree must be attained at the University of Panama, Santa María La Antigua University or any other accredited university in Panama that offers a law degree with a curriculum approved by the National Assessment and Accreditation System for the Improvement of University Education Commission. For a law degree obtained abroad to be recognized, it must be validated by the University of Panama, except in the case of an international agreement that waives this requirement.

    The legal profession is reserved for Panamanian nationals.

1 Scope of and Limitations on the Duty of Professional Secrecy/Attorney-Client Privilege

A Statutory Basis and Implications

2. The concept of the personal privacy of communications and documents is provided for in the Panamanian Constitution as a fundamental right (Political Constitution, Art. 29):

    > Correspondence and other private documents are inviolable and shall not be searched or seized except by warrant of a competent authority, for specific purposes and in accordance with the legal formalities. In any case no notice shall be taken of matters alien to the object of the search or seizure.
    >
    > The registration of letters and other documents or papers shall always take place in the presence of the person concerned or of a member of his/her family, or, in their absence, of two honorable neighbors living near the place.

    The consent of the subject is required for the transfer of any personal information, in accordance with Article 42 of the Constitution of the Republic of Panama:

    > Every person has a right of access to his/her personal information contained in data banks or public or private registries and to request their correction and protection, as well as their deletion in accordance with the provisions of the law.
    >
    > This information may only be collected for specific purposes, subject to the consent of the person in question or by order of a competent authority based on the provisions of the law.

    Attorney-client privilege is set forth in Article 13 of Chapter II of the Code of Ethics and Attorney's Professional Responsibility, adopted in Plenary

General Assembly under the Tenth National Congress of Lawyers, January 27, 2011, Official Gazette no. 26796 of May 31, 2011:

> Lawyer's duty to keep secrets and confidences of his client. This duty remains even after the termination of services and extends to employees of the lawyer and neither he nor those employees may be forced to disclose such confidences, unless it is authorized by the customer. The lawyer who is the subject of an accusation by his client, can reveal the secrets that his accuser has entrusted in him if necessary for his defense.

This Code of Ethics has its legal basis in Article 18 of Law 9 of April 18, 1984, whereby the practice of law in the Republic of Panama is regulated:

> The breach of the rules in the Code of Ethics and Professional Responsibility of the Panama Bar Association and any legal provision in effect with respect to a particular matter shall be a violation of ethics.

3. Panamanian law also governs privilege in regard to the relationship between legal entities and their resident agents. Law No. 32 of February 26, 1927, on Corporations established the resident agent as one of the essential requirements of the articles of incorporation. The resident agent enjoys no authority to bind the corporation or to enter into contracts on its behalf. The sole function of the resident agent is to serve as a link between authorities or third parties and the client, without this constituting governing authority or granting the resident agent powers of representation or management of the corporation. Also, the resident agent is not an agent to receive notifications for the corporation; it is simply a facilitating entity.

Article 2 of Law 2 of February 1, 2011, under which the measures to know your customer by registered agents of existing corporations organized in accordance with the laws of the Republic of Panama are governed ("Law 2"), defines the resident, or registered, agent as "Lawyer or law firm providing services as such and who shall keep the records required by this Law on behalf of corporations organized under the laws of the Republic of Panama and with whom they have an existing professional Relationship."

Article 8 of Law 2 sets forth the confidentiality obligations of resident agents and even establishes sanctions:

> The information furnished by the customers to the registered agent, in regards to the requirements of this Law, shall be strictly confidential and only be furnished to competent authorities in strict compliance with the procedures and formalities to that end.
>
> The officials and natural or juridical persons in the private sector that due to the positions they discharge have access to the information resulting from the implementation of this Law shall be bound to maintain due confidentiality when they cease their posts, unless that said information is kept in official records of public nature.

The offender of the provisions of this Article will be punished with a penalty from one thousand Balboas (B/.1,000.00) to twenty five thousand Balboas[1] (B/.25,000.00), without prejudice of civil or criminal sanctions that may be applied.

In the same spirit, Article 14 of Law 2 specifically addresses the issue of professional secrecy:

In regards to professional secrecy of the lawyer-customer relationship, the lawyer is not bound to provide any information or documents required by this Law on which he has legitimate right of professional secrecy, unless that information is limited strictly to the one required by his duties on the measures to know your customer.

The right the competent authority has to request information is not considered as an authorization to search the offices of the registered agent or to confiscate files or archive means, as computers and databases. These actions by the competent authorities shall be made in due compliance with the concerning rules to that end, established in the Panamanian ordinary legislation.

Aspects of criminal law also address these issues. Chapter III of Title II of the Penal Code (Crimes against Secrecy and Inviolability of the Right to Privacy) states in Article 166:

Anyone legitimately coming into possession of private or personal mail, recordings or documents – not intended for publication, even if addressed to that person who makes them public without the required permission and which results in harm, will be punished by 200 to 500 day-fines[2] or

---

[1] Panama does not have a central bank that regulates monetary policy, and it has been a Panamanian sovereign decision since 1904 not to adopt national paper currency of forced tender. This is supported by constitutional restrictions on forced tender and legal provisions placing the Panamanian nominal currency (the Balboa) and the U.S. dollar at par and making the U.S. dollar legal tender in Panama. However, Panama's principal state-owned bank, the National Bank of Panama, serves as the compulsory depositary of all funds of the central government, the municipalities and all governmental entities. By law, the National Bank is also the clearinghouse for all settlements of the Panamanian banking system. The National Bank is organized by Law 20 of 1975, as amended, as an autonomous entity having its own independent legal personality and patrimony. It operates as a commercial and mortgage lending bank, taking deposits not only of state funds but from private persons and lending to the general public, as do other private banks with general licenses to operate in Panama.

[2] The penalty of day-fines is an obligation to pay the state a sum of money, to be determined in accordance with the economic situation of the accused, in view of their income, livelihoods, level of expenses or other aspects accredited in trial.

When the sentenced person's livelihood is the product of his or her daily work, the day-fine shall not exceed 50 percent of his or her daily income. The minimum is 50 days' fine, and the maximum is 500 days' fine.

Verifying the economic situation of the sanctioned, the judge may establish a maximum period of 12 months for the payment of the penalty imposed. If these fines are not paid, equivalent jail time will be ordered.

weekend imprisonment. The disclosure of documents necessary for the understanding of history, science and the arts shall not be considered a crime. Forgiveness by the victim will result in the dismissal of the case.

4.   To conform to the pressures that it had been receiving from international bodies such as the Organization for Economic Cooperation and Development (OECD), Panama has, by means of Law 47 of August 6, 2013, introduced a custody system applicable to bearer shares. This law created a process known as "immobilization of bearer shares," which is achieved by means of a custody method. This regime still allows for the existence of bearer shares, but the transfer of such shares will not take place by the mere delivery of share certificates, since such shares must be kept by an authorized custodian, who has to be notified of the transfer of bearer shares to any new owner.

Banks with a general banking license and trusts established in the Republic of Panama and regulated by the Superintendency of Banks of Panama, as well as brokerage houses and securities firms established in the Republic of Panama and regulated by the Superintendency of the Securities Market of Panama, are covered by the law. Likewise, all attorneys registered with the Fourth Chamber of General Business of the Supreme Court of Justice in a special registry kept for such purposes may act as authorized local custodians.

Article 10 of Law 47 deals with the obligations of the authorized custodian:

> Obligations of the authorized local custodian. 4. Provide the information referred to in this Law at any time it is required by the competent authorities. The provision of information at the request of the competent authority shall not be considered as a failure to comply with the obligation to keep the information strictly confidential or as a violation of the duty of confidentiality or the right to privacy.

5.   Finally, Panama's National Assembly enacted Law no. 23 of April 27, 2015, adopting Measures for the Prevention of Money Laundering, Terrorism Financing and Financing of Proliferation of Weapons of Mass Destruction and other provisions. This law includes lawyers within the professions subject to supervision by the Regulatory Body of Supervision and Regulation for Non-Financial Subjects, in any of the following cases:

> Activities performed by professionals subject to supervision. Lawyers, certified public accountants and notaries will only be subject to supervision when in the execution of their professional Activities they perform on behalf of a customer or customers, the following Activities:
>
> 1. Sales of property.
> 2. Administration of money, market capitalization or other assets of the customer.
> 3. Management of bank, savings or securities accounts.
> 4. Organization of inputs or contributions for the creation, operation or management of companies.

5. Creation, operation or management of legal persons or legal structures, such as: Private Interest Foundations, Corporations, Trusts and others.
6. Sale of legal persons or legal structures.
7. Performing or arranging for a person paid by the lawyer or law firm, to act as proxy director of a company or a similar position in relation to other legal persons.
8. Provide a registered office, business address or physical space, correspondence or administrative address for a company, corporation or any other legal person or structure that is not of his or her property.
9. Perform or arrange for a person, paid by the lawyer or law firm, to act as a figurehead shareholder for another person.
10. Perform or arrange for a person, paid by the lawyer or law firm, to act as a member of an express trust or perform an equivalent function for another form of legal structure.
11. Those of a Resident Agent of legal entities incorporated or existing under the laws of the Republic of Panama.

But the following provision of the same law provides for the protection of the attorney-client privilege:

> Protection of Professional Secrecy. Lawyers and certified public accountants that while performing their professional activities, are classified as activities performed by professionals subject to supervision, are not required to report suspicious transactions if the relevant information was obtained in circumstances in which they are subject to professional secrecy or legal professional privilege, or confession that his client makes for proper defense.

B Scope

6. The confidentiality extends to all information concerning the affairs of the client that the lawyer has come to know in the exercise of the lawyer's profession. All communications between client and lawyer are protected by the laws of the republic that regulate professional secrecy, and they cannot be disclosed without explicit consent of the client. The right and the obligation of professional secrecy cover the information provided by the client and all the facts and documents that have been disclosed to the lawyer on the basis of the performance of legal services, as well as subject matters related to the private life of the client. This obligation extends to other lawyers, trainees and other employees in the case of a law firm. It also includes any electronic communication, digital media or any other means of communication.

Duties that comprise the duty of confidentiality are:

(i) Prohibition of disclosure: lawyers must refrain from disclosing information covered by the duty of confidentiality and from providing, displaying or granting access to materials, electronic or otherwise, containing such information and that are in their custody.

(ii) Duty of care: attorneys must take reasonable steps to ensure that the conditions under which they receive, obtain, retain or disclose information subject to a duty of confidentiality are such that they safeguard the confidentiality of such information. It is understood that allowing a third party access to this information (i.e., by omission) also violates due confidentiality. This is a consequence of the duty of care.

(iii) Duty of care concerning the actions of collaborators: lawyers must take reasonable steps to ensure that client confidentiality is maintained by those who collaborate with them. In cases of transmission of information under confidentiality from the attorney to another person, that is, a chain of secondary insiders, the lawyer must take precautions so that, during the transmission of confidential information, it is not accessible to outsiders.

C Persons Subject to Professional Secrecy

7.   All of these laws are applicable to all lawyers, whether they are freelance professionals, partners or associates of a law firm, in-house counsel working for companies, lawyers for the state or otherwise.

Professional secrecy also binds the employees of the lawyer, the law firm, and any personnel of a company that come in contact with information related to the activities of an in-house lawyer.

D Limitations on and Derogations from the Duty of Professional Secrecy

8.   Prior to the privilege's existence, there must be an attorney-client relationship. In general, the attorney-client privilege does not start to have an effect until the parties have reached an agreement on the representation of the client.

In most instances, the establishment of the attorney-client relationship takes place simply when the attorney has expressly acknowledged representation of the client. This express recognition may be confirmed by an engagement letter, a contract setting forth the professional fees, or even an oral agreement as to the type of services to be rendered by the attorney or law firm.

Lawyers who are the subject of an accusation by their clients can reveal information that their accusers have entrusted to them, if necessary for their defense.

Pursuant to Law 47 of August 6, 2013, adopting a custody regime applicable to bearer shares, the supply of information at the request of the competent authority shall not be considered a failure to comply with the obligation to keep the information strictly confidential or as a violation of the duty of confidentiality or the right to privacy, for example, the issuance of certificates stating the identity of the owner of the bearer shares whenever they are required via judiciary orders by the owner or a secured creditor.

407

No breach of the duty of confidentiality exists with explicit or tacit consent by the client. At any time the client can withdraw such explicit consent. Tacit consent means that the client consents to the disclosure if it is suitable for the successful provision of the professional services of a lawyer to the client, unless the client instructs otherwise. In case of doubt, the lawyer must protect confidentiality.

Duty to disclose: Attorneys must disclose information subject to confidentiality to prevent the commission of a crime. The lawyer must disclose information subject to confidentiality to prevent serious danger of death or serious bodily injury to a person or persons. Attorneys are authorized to disclose such information subject to confidentiality only when the harm that it prevents is substantially greater than the harm it causes. The Panamanian Criminal Code (Art. 33) further protects such disclosure under the Principle of Defense of Necessity:

> [One] acts in a state of need [when] the person who, in a situation of danger, or to prevent harm to himself or a third party, infringes the legal rights of another, provided that the following conditions are met: (i) the danger is serious, current or imminent; (ii) [the danger is] not otherwise avoidable; (iii) the danger was not caused voluntarily by the officer or the person who is protected; (iv) the agent has a legal duty to take the risk; and (v) the harm produced is less severe than the one avoided.

The lawyer may disclose information subject to confidentiality for professional advice from another lawyer, provided that the other lawyer is subject to confidentiality. In this case, one of the lawyers is the client, and the other is providing a service and thus is bound by the duty of confidentiality.

Attorneys may disclose information about a client to collect fees owed to them.

The foregoing scenarios authorize attorneys to make the disclosure only when necessary to achieve those purposes, provided also that the lawyer has no other practicable means that are less harmful to the client.

E Law Firms

9. Law firms, like any other enterprise, handle personal information in the exercise of their activities and therefore are subject to the regulatory regime for the protection of personal information. A distinction must be made between the professional confidentiality obligations of attorneys and general data protection and privacy regulations derived from constitutional principles.

The attorney-client privilege is a manifestation of the right to counsel, which gives attorneys the right and the obligation not to disclose information entrusted to them by their clients.

The duty of confidentiality on data protection concerns the custody of files within the offices of and data processing by lawyers and other professionals.

F Legal Assistants and Staff

10.   As stated previously, professional secrecy also binds the employees of the lawyer, the law firm, or any personnel of a company who come in contact with information related to the activities of an in-house lawyer. Any breach of this obligation by members of the staff who are not lawyers may result in civil liabilities for the attorneys or law firm.

G External Service Providers

11.   There are no provisions in Panamanian law with respect to external service providers besides the aforementioned privacy rules. Attorneys and law firms should exercise caution when choosing outside contractors such as translators, messenger services and the like, because any breach of confidentiality by these providers may result in civil liability.

H Multidisciplinary Associations

12.   Lawyers and law firms in Panama frequently seek advice and services from a variety of professionals on behalf of their clients. Many law firms have accountants, economists, financial experts and other professionals as part of their staff, and there are no legal restrictions on this. Any needed transfer of information for these purposes is protected by the aforementioned privacy protection regulations.

I In-House Counsel

13.   Panamanian legislation does not specifically address in-house lawyers, but they are bound and protected by the same attorney-client duties and protections discussed above. In this case, the client is the attorney's employer. In addition, in-house counsel are constrained by the general privacy protection laws and regulations that arise from the fundamental right to privacy that is enshrined in Panama's Constitution.

   In-house lawyers have an employment relationship with the employer and thus are covered by extensive Panamanian labor laws, which in Panama are considered "social laws," since they provide one of the parties of the relationship, the employee, more safeguards and protections than to the other party, the employer. The employee is considered the weaker part of the relationship, and hence Panamanian labor laws provide a preferential protection for the employee that aims to level the inequalities between the employee and the employer.

2 History of the Duty of Professional Secrecy in Panama

14.   Attorney-client privilege in Panama corresponds to the Roman law legal tradition. The confidentiality of certain activities has its origin in Roman times.

Of course, the principle was generally applied first and then more specifically to certain professions. At that time, there were two ways to explain the existence of this professional secret: First was *conmiso*, under which the obligation of secrecy was imposed due to the existence of an agreement preceding the confidence, which made the act of confidence and reception in a kind of pact. The other way was the *promiso*, which, unlike *conmiso*, supposed that first a confidence was delivered and then immediately received, and the depositary became bound to secrecy by the mere fact of confidence. In the *Corpus Juris* of Roman law, Digest (Act 25 Test. XXII, V), reference is made to the obligation not to divulge secrets regarding lawyers, prosecutors and clerks.

Currently all professions have established in different ways and on an ongoing basis the right of individuals to confidentiality of information obtained because of a professional relationship. Modern codes consider that this rule is not absolute, that is, it is considered that there are particular situations where it is not mandatory to adhere to professional secrecy, and in many cases those exceptions are explicitly set forth.

3 Supervision

15.   The National Bar Association of Panama has an Honor Tribunal to investigate violations of ethics that are reported by interested parties or public servants of the Judicial Branch, the Prosecution or the Administrative Branch, who know of the case in which the breach took place. The Honor Tribunal is composed of five lawyers, elected in accordance with the Bylaws of the National Bar Association, for a term of four years.

If the Honor Tribunal considers that a hearing is warranted, it will request that the General Business Chamber of the Supreme Court of Justice decree a citation to judge the accused attorney.

4 Sanctions

A Proceedings and Sanctions

16.   Law 9 of April 18, 1984, whereby the practice of law is regulated, sets forth the proceedings and sanctions for supposed violations by lawyers.

The breach of the rules in the Code of Ethics and Professional Responsibility of the National Law Society and related legal provisions shall be a violation of ethics (Art. 18).

If the material facts in a disciplinary hearing are, additionally, a criminal act that may be prosecuted without complaint, the disciplinary tribunal must make these facts known to the prosecutor's office (Art. 19).

The existence of a criminal complaint regarding the same material facts will not result in the suspension of the disciplinary hearing.

The sanctions that apply to lawyers who violate the law that regulates the practice of law, the Code of Ethics and Professional Responsibility of the National Law Society, or any legal provisions in effect regarding the practice of law and legal ethics include the following: (i) a private admonishment, which consists of a private reprimand made to the accused for the breach committed; (ii) a public admonishment, which consists of a public reprimand made to the accused for the breach committed; (iii) for first offences, a suspension of the license to practice law for a period of more than one month and less than one year; (iv) for subsequent offences, a suspension of the license to practice law for a minimum of two years (i.e., disbarred from practicing (Art. 20)). The sanctions contemplated in (iii) and (iv) shall apply only where there is no criminal sentence issued by a Criminal Court with a similar effect (Art. 20-A).

17. The National Bar Association of Panama shall create an Honor Tribunal to investigate violations of ethics that are presented by interested parties or public servants of the Judicial Branch, the Prosecution or the Administrative Branch, who know of the case in which the breach took place (Art. 21).

The Honor Tribunal shall be composed of five lawyers, elected in accordance with the Bylaws of the National Law Society, for a term of four years (Art. 22). The Bylaws of the National Law Society provide for a rotating election of these five members.

The members of the Honor Tribunal must fulfill the following requirements: (i) have at least 10 years' experience in practicing law; (ii) have good moral and professional standing; and (iii) not be a public servant in the Public Administration, Judicial Branch or Prosecutor's Office.

Each member has one deputy, who will replace the member in case of sickness or temporary or permanent absence. The Honor Tribunal elects its president and secretary from its members, and its internal regulations are established in accordance with the Bylaws or special regulations of the National Law Society. For the following election, three members are elected for a period of two years. In the following biennial elections, each group of members are elected for a complete term of four years.

When the Supreme Court of Justice advises that there have been acts that constitute a violation of professional ethics or when a complaint is received from an interested party, the Honor Tribunal will be asked to conduct the corresponding investigation. The tribunal will proceed immediately to investigate the facts resulting in the alleged violation of professional ethics, and the investigation will be limited to the facts indicated in the complaint. The investigation must be concluded within 15 days following the receipt of the communication from the Supreme Court of Justice (Art. 23).

The investigation is undertaken for the following purposes: (i) to confirm whether the act constitutes a violation as presented, through the practice of any hearings and investigations required to arrive at the truth; (ii) to establish the circumstances that gave rise to the act and those that justify, mitigate or amplify it; (iii) to verify that the person against whom the complaint is laid is licensed to practice law, how long the person has been practicing law and whether the person has been subject to any prior disciplinary hearings; and (iv) to determine if there are any other participants in addition to the principal person accused. Accused lawyers have the opportunity to recount, in writing, to the tribunal the circumstances that, in their view, release them from responsibility of the acts of which they are accused (Art. 24).

The Honor Tribunal must reject the accusation and order the filing of the investigation when it is patently obvious that the alleged violation did not take place, where the act in question does not actually meet the requirements for a violation of ethics, or where judgment will not ensue for lack of merit (Art. 25).

The resolution that endorses the filing of the investigation must be well-reasoned and is not subject to appeal.

If the Honor Tribunal considers that a hearing is warranted, it will request that the General Business Chamber of the Supreme Court of Justice decree a citation to judge the accused (Art. 26).

The hearing must include the personal details of the accused lawyer, or those necessary to identify the lawyer, and a clear, precise, circumstantial and specific narration of the facts that constitute the violation of ethics and the legal description. A resolution must be adopted by a majority vote of the Honor Tribunal and be signed by those members of the Tribunal who approve it (Art. 27). Upon receiving the request from the Honor Tribunal, the General Business Chamber of the Supreme Court of Justice must notify the accused, who may, in the following five days: (i) present exceptions and (ii) contest the hearing, requesting the filings of the proceedings (Art. 28).

When the term indicated in the preceding article has expired or upon deciding the pleadings, the Chamber of the Supreme Court of Justice will order the dismissal of the case for lack of merit or declare that a hearing be held, as appropriate (Art. 29). This order shall close the investigation.

If it is not possible to find the accused to notify them of the requirement of the Honor Tribunal, they will be summoned by public notice posted in the Secretarial Section of the Supreme Court of Justice for 10 days, and a copy of the notice will be sent by regular mail to the professional address or domicile that is available. If within the three days after the notice is removed the accused has not appeared, a public defender will be appointed to represent the accused in the proceedings (Art. 30).

The resolution that transforms the investigation into a hearing must specify the requirements of Article 27 of this law and, additionally, must include the name and general details of the complainant or the indication of the authority or public office that presented the accusation (Art. 31).

In this same resolution that initiates the hearing, a date is set for an oral hearing to occur in no less than 10 days and no more than 15 days; at the hearing, evidence will be presented by the parties (Art. 32). At the hour established for the hearing, the presiding justice will declare the hearing open, the secretary will read the resolution that lists the charges and the evidence will be presented. Immediately thereafter, the accused or their counsel will be heard (Art. 33). Once the hearing is finished, the members of the General Business Chamber of the Supreme Court of Justice will meet in a private session to deliberate. The decision will be given immediately and, if the justices condemn, they shall indicate the corresponding sanction to the accused. Only when the Chamber of the Supreme Court of Justice considers that a longer period is required to decide will the sentence not be pronounced at the hearing.

In any proceeding for professional misconduct, the Attorney General was heard as a party (Art. 34); however, that is no longer the case, after the Supreme Court found that provision unconstitutional.[3]

Given the disciplinary character of these rules, the Supreme Court of Justice is given wide discretion to impose sanctions, taking into account the nature, severity and type of breach, and the personal and professional background of the accused, without prejudice to other actions and civil and criminal sanctions that may be available (Art. 35). Only when the sanction imposed is the suspension or disbarment from the practice of law may the sentence may be petitioned for reconsideration, within three days of notification (Art. 36).

B Relationship between Criminal Sanctions and Disciplinary Sanctions

18. Only within the general rules concerning the protection of confidentiality are there criminal sanctions. As mentioned in Section 1(A) of this chapter, the Panamanian Penal Code contains provisions that make it a crime to divulge confidential information and establish that unauthorized release of information is subject to criminal prosecution.

5 Duty to Provide Information to the Authorities

A Money Laundering and Terrorism

19. Law no. 23 of April 27, 2015, which adopts measures to prevent money laundering, financing of terrorism and proliferation of weapons of mass

---

[3] This article was declared unconstitutional by a Supreme Court ruling on October 30, 1996. The court considered that participation by the Attorney General in the process would be an invasion of the disciplinary proceedings of independent professionals, which are carried out through their peers. Article 34 was declared to be in violation of Article 40 and Article 217 of the Constitution, which enshrine the rights of independent professionals.

destruction and other provisions, includes the legal profession within the activities subject to supervision.

Attorneys are monitored by the Intendancy for Supervision and Regulation of Non-Financial Subjects, provided that in the exercise of their professional activities on behalf of a client or customer, the following activities are performed: sale of property; managing money, securities or other assets of the client; management of bank, savings or securities accounts; organization of contributions for the creation, operation or management of companies; creation, operation or management of legal persons or structures; and actions of resident agents for legal entities existing under the laws of the Republic of Panama.

Lawyers shall maintain, in their operations, due diligence and care to reasonably prevent these operations from being carried out with funds derived from activities related to the crimes of money laundering, terrorism financing and the financing of the proliferation of weapons of mass destruction.

The mechanisms for customer or final beneficiary identification, as well as the verification of information and documentation, will depend on the risk profile of the financial reporting entities, the non-financial reporting entities and activities performed by professionals subject to supervision, by considering the types of customers, products and services offered, the distribution or commercialization channels used, and the geographic location of their facilities and of their customers or final beneficiaries. These variables, either separately or in combination, can increase or decrease the potential risk posed, thus affecting the level of due diligence measures. In this sense, there are circumstances where the risk of money laundering, terrorism financing and the financing of the proliferation of weapons of mass destruction is higher, and stricter measures must be taken. In other circumstances, the risk is lower. Provided that there is an appropriate risk analysis, simplified due diligence measures may be applied.

Attorneys must communicate directly with the Financial Analysis Unit for the Prevention of the Crimes of Money Laundering and the Financing of Terrorism the existence of any fact, transaction or operation in which there is a suspicion that it may be connected to the crimes of money laundering, terrorism financing or the financing of the proliferation of weapons of mass destruction, regardless of the amount of the transaction that cannot be justified or supported, as well as financial control weaknesses. The reports should be submitted to the Financial Analysis Unit within 15 calendar days from the detection of the event, transaction, operation or control failure. Nevertheless, reporting entities may request an extension of 15 more calendar days to send the supporting documentation where there is a complexity in the collection. But lawyers and certified public accountants who, while performing their professional activities, are classified as professionals subject to supervision, are not required to report suspicious transactions if the relevant information was obtained in circumstances in which they are subject to professional secrecy or legal professional privilege, or confession that the client makes for proper defense.

B Sexual Abuse

20. The duty to disclose crimes was discussed in Section 1(D) of this chapter. Those same principles apply here. Article 189 of the Panamanian Criminal Code (Corruption of Minors, Commercial Sexual Exploitation and other behaviors) additionally penalizes anybody not reporting sexual abuse of a minor:

> Anyone who has knowledge of the use of minors in the execution of any of the offenses referred to in this Chapter, and that this knowledge has been obtained by reason of his office, function, business or profession, or any other source, and fails to report it to the competent authorities shall be punished with imprisonment from six months to two years.
>
> If the offense is not proven, the complainant shall be exempt from any liability in respect of the complaint referred to in this Article, except in cases of a manifestly false report.

6 Treatment of Lawyers' Documents and Correspondence in the Context of Judicial and Police Investigations

21. This chapter has covered the general principles of privacy of communications derived from Panama's Constitution, as well as attorney-client privilege, or professional secrecy, pursuant to Panamanian regulations.

Evidentiary issues arising from judicial investigations must follow the aforementioned principles and regulations; otherwise, any evidence gathered in violation of fundamental rights enshrined in the Constitution may be deemed illegal evidence.

Concerning the possession of evidence that could be considered illicit, treatment should be the same regardless of who carries out the work of seeking and obtaining sources of evidence. For these purposes, the nature of the person (public official or private person) is irrelevant given the *erga omnes* effectiveness of fundamental rights.

Continuing along these same lines, Panama's Judicial Code sets forth in Article 783:

> Evidence should adhere to the subject matter of the process and evidence which does not relate to the facts discussed, as well as legally ineffective, will be inadmissible.
>
> The judge may reject outright evidence prohibited by the law, notoriously dilatory or proposed in order to hinder the progress of the process; the judge may also reject the taking of obviously irrelevant or ineffective evidence.

7 Search of a Lawyer's Office

22.   A search of a lawyer's office is allowed for the purposes of seizure of assets subject to attachment, up to USD $5,000 chosen by the debtor.

Any items vital to the defense of a client or subject to the attorney-client privilege are immune from search, requisition, attachment or execution.

8 Tapping of Telephone Conversations with a Lawyer

23.   Article 29 of the Constitution allows wiretapping by order of a judicial authority. The rule is based on the principle of respect for the privacy of private communications, including fax, email, personal conversations and any other kind of communication of a private nature. Article 29 provides:

> Correspondence and other private documents are inviolable and shall not be searched or seized except by warrant of a competent authority, for specific purposes and in accordance with the legal formalities. In any case no notice shall be taken of matters alien to the object of the search or seizure.
>
> The registration of letters and other documents or papers shall always take place in the presence of the person concerned or of a member of his/her family, or, in their absence, of two honorable neighbors living near the place.
>
> All private communications are inviolable and may not be intercepted or recorded unless authorized by judicial warrant.
>
> The non-compliance with this provision means that the results [of the interception] cannot be used as evidence, without prejudice to the criminal liability incurred by its authors.

In addition, Panama's Criminal Code, Article 167, criminalizes the following unauthorized activities: "Whoever, without the authorization of the judicial authority, intercepts telecommunications or uses technical devices for listening, transmission, recording or reproduction of conversations not for the public shall be punished by two to four years in prison."

Having said this, this constitutional provision cannot supersede the fundamental right to legal defense, and thus any interception of telephone conversations between an attorney and the client is not permissible.

9 The Lawyer as Witness

24.   Those who, because of their profession or position have familiarity or affinity with the accused, come to know facts relative to the subject matter of the proceeding, may not be ordered to testify, and these persons may not reveal any such information without violating the secrecy they are required to keep. Any forced deposition would violate ethical and moral principles that are the foundation of a profession, position or endowment.

Article 912 of the Judicial Code establishes this exception to the general rule that every person has the duty to testify:

> The following are not required to testify:
> 1. A lawyer or agent, of the confidences they have received from their clients and the advice they have given with regard to the proceeding they are handling.
> 2. The confessor about the revelations made by the penitent.
> 3. The doctor regarding the confidences made by their patients.
> 4. The judge in charge of the proceeding.
> 5. The son against father or mother, nor them against him. One spouse against another, except in proceedings between them.
> 6. The spouse or permanent cohabitant against the other, except in a process between them.

In the context of the lawyer-client relationship, and as part of the confidence that the client places in the lawyer to defend the client's interests, the client makes revelations and may even make confessions in the privacy of the conversation. This trust may not be betrayed by counsel, because such trust is the cornerstone on which rests the right to legal assistance and representation. For this purpose, an accreditation of power of attorney for the lawyer is not required; just an interview in confidence is enough to activate the exception set forth in Article 912(1) of the Judicial Code.

10 The Lawyer and the Press

25.   The attorney's Code of Ethics states:

> A lawyer should avoid any statement or publication in the media regarding its causes or pending or future litigation, unless the other party does not comply with this requirement, provided you exercise their right of reply or clarification of the terms set out in paragraph 22 of Article 37 of this Code, when a media referencing the case or litigation misrepresented the facts.

Notwithstanding the foregoing, lawyers frequently speak to the press in Panama in relation to clients' cases, although this situation is more prevalent in high-profile cases of a criminal nature. Lawyers must refrain from revealing any information that clients have not cleared for release.

11 Powers of the Tax and Other Authorities

A Corporate Veil

26.   "Corporate veil" establishes a separation between the assets of the corporation and its shareholders. The doctrine of piercing the corporate veil has been applied in exceptional situations to prevent evasion of the responsibility by natural persons hiding behind it. It may be exercised only in exceptional

circumstances, when there is simulation, involving the incorporation or use of a corporation, with the intent to conceal assets that are the result of criminal activities. The piercing of the corporate veil is an exceptional measure applicable only provisionally to effect economic precautionary measures related to illegal acts under investigation in the Republic of Panama. Panama does not allow the piercing of the corporate veil for tax matters.

B Other Authorities

27.   Authorities cannot require lawyers to turn over any information that they may have about their clients that was obtained under conditions subject to professional secrecy or attorney-client privilege, or confessions that their clients make for proper defense.

26

Paraguay

ROSA ELENA DIMARTINO

Berkemeyer Law Firm

Preliminary Note

1. The exercise of the legal profession in Paraguay is regulated from the professional, civil, criminal and administrative perspectives.

   Professional associations do not have sanctioning power in the country, nor is compulsory licensing required in order to maintain ethical sanctions, but these sanctions will not affect the exercise of the profession.

   It is essential to distinguish between the two major legal professions that exist in Paraguay: attorneys-at-law and notaries public.

   To practice as a lawyer, a person must graduate from a university in which the applicant completed five or six years of higher education. After obtaining a degree, the Supreme Court grants the authorization to practice as a lawyer for life. The authorization is called *matricula* in Paraguay.

   To practice as a notary public, a person must graduate from a university in which the applicant completed four years of higher education. After obtaining a degree, the professional must pass a competitive examination provided by the Supreme Court, and, if the person succeeds, the Supreme Court grants the authorization to practice as a notary public somewhere in the Paraguayan territory for life. The authorization is called *registro*.

   Of these two legal professions, the notarial profession is much more regulated than the legal profession. However, the responsibilities are similar, and, with regard to the obligation of professional secrecy, they both must observe the common law.

1 Scope of and Limitations on the Duty of Professional Secrecy/ Attorney-Client Privilege

A Statutory Basis and Implications

2. The Paraguayan Penal Code contains the most important rule relating to professional secrecy: Section 147 criminalizes the disclosure of a secret by a lawyer.

   The law stipulates that revealing a secret to a third person, when such secret came to the knowledge of the one who reveals it in his or her role as physician, dentist or pharmacist, lawyer, notary public, defender in criminal cases, auditor or financial consultant, or a professional helper or trainee of any of these, or when required by law to remain silent, will be punished with imprisonment of up to one year or a fine.

   This same penalty applies to anyone who discloses a secret that was received from a responsible party, in accordance with criminal law. If the secret has an industrial or business character, the sentence of imprisonment may be increased to three years. It will also be punished if there is only an attempt to reveal the secret.

The criminal prosecution of the act will depend on the request of the victim.

A "secret" for purposes of the law means any fact, data or knowledge that, if disclosed to third parties, would have harmful consequences.

Section 192 of the Criminal Code establishes that this breach of trust by a lawyer or notary public is a crime. The breach of trust occurs when a person, through a law or a contract, assumes the responsibility to protect an important proprietary interest of another person and causes, within the scope of the established protection, a financial loss to the other person.

For especially serious cases, imprisonment may be increased to 10 years. From the moment a sentence of imprisonment is established as a sanction, the action is considered a very serious crime.

B Scope

3. Professional secrecy covers all information, written or oral, provided by the client to the lawyer to prepare a case. It also covers a client's financial Information and personal data, in accordance with the Information Privacy Law of 2001.

In Paraguay since 2001, personal data is protected by law, which imposes civil penalties (fines) in case of dissemination of sensitive data without authorization. These sanctions, combined with criminal sanctions for disclosure of personal data without the owner's consent by legal professionals, results in a very serious combination, with respect to the offender.

Protection of sensitive personal data, which cannot be disseminated without consent of its owner, is established by law and combined with the obligation of professional secrecy, to the extent that this obligation is made stronger by (i) its application to professionals affected by government regulations and (ii) the fact that the secret being revealed is personal data.

Protected personal data appears in a 2001 law, which is replicated in several subsequent regulatory provisions, meaning that the penalties for careless or unauthorized dissemination of professional secrets are taken seriously; applying this provision to professionals, sanctions are no longer civil and become criminal.

C Persons Subject to the Duty of Professional Secrecy

4. As noted previously, under Paraguayan law, it is stipulated that revealing a secret to a third person, when such secret came to the knowledge of the one who reveals it in his or her role as physician, dentist or pharmacist, lawyer, notary public, defender in criminal cases, auditor or financial consultant, or professional helper or trainee of any of these, or if required by law to remain silent, will be punished with imprisonment of up to one year or a fine.

421

This same penalty applies to anyone who discloses a secret that has been received from a responsible party, in accordance with criminal law.

D Exceptions to and Optional Derogations from the Duty of Professional Secrecy

5.   There are no exceptions or derogations from the duty of professional secrecy. The only circumstance that can lift the veil of secrecy is the law itself.

Professional secrecy may not override the duty of collaboration with justice that all people have in Paraguay.

There are also administrative provisions relating to financial institutions that impose on legal professionals a duty to provide information to the government under certain circumstances.

E Law Firms

6.   Law firms operate on an equal footing with independent professionals, with the same rights and obligations. The obligation of professional secrecy applies to all of the lawyers in the law firm.

F Legal Assistants and Staff

7.   The obligation of professional secrecy applies to all employees within a law firm, even to those who are not lawyers.

G External Service Providers

8.   There are no specific provisions under Paraguayan law or practice relating to external service providers.

H Multidisciplinary Associations

9.   There are no specific provisions under Paraguayan law relating to multidisciplinary associations.

I In-House Counsel

10.   In-house counsel are subject to the same legal and administrative provisions that outside counsel are.

2 History of the Duty of Professional Secrecy in Paraguay

11.   There is no tradition of regulation of professional secrecy in Paraguay. The provisions of criminal law are those that have always maintained this duty with penalties or fines, which have never been applied.

In Paraguay, professional secrecy is a matter of morality and ethics rather than law.

3 Supervision

A The Bar Associations

12. Neither the *Colegio de Abogados del Paraguay* nor the *Colegio de Escribanos del Paraguay* monitor violations of loyalty on the part of professionals, despite both organizations having ethical courts. Professional associations in Paraguay have no power to impose penalties and licensing.

B The Courts

13. No relevant court cases on the lack of loyalty to clients are recorded.

4 Sanctions

A Proceedings and Sanctions

14. There is no specific procedure to determine the guilt of a legal professional with regard to a lack of loyalty to the client. The rules applied are the rules that govern all judicial proceedings.

B Relationships between Criminal Sanctions and Disciplinary Sanctions

15. In all cases, sanctions are determined with fines (fines are mandatory, while imprisonment is not). There is no difference between a criminal sanction and an administrative penalty.

5 Duty to Provide Information to the Authorities

A Money Laundering and Terrorism

16. In Paraguay, prevention of money laundering has gained unprecedented momentum in recent years, thanks to recent actions taken by the government. These actions resulted in laws that, since 1997, have been adjusted in the most sensible way possible to the needs of this type of action.

    The obligation to report suspicious transactions is done online, through a secure server, Secretariat for the Prevention of Money Laundering (SEPRELAD). In principle, regulations of that agency affect the public notaries, who are forced quarterly to report suspicious activity without breaking the duty of professional secrecy.

B Collective Settlement of Debts

17. There are no specific provisions under Paraguyan law or practice regarding this matter.

6 Treatment of Lawyers' Documents and Correspondence in the Context of Judicial or Police Investigations

18.   All criminal investigations should be carried out by prosecutors, who are obliged to maintain the secrecy of the investigation, regardless of what type of documents are subject to the investigation.

7 Search of a Lawyer's Office

19.   Lawyers' offices can be searched if such search is authorized by the government.

8 Tapping of Telephone Conversations with a Lawyer

20.   The validity of the recordings of telephone calls can be invoked only if the recording had been authorized by the authorities. Otherwise, the recordings are invalid.

9 The Lawyer as Witness

21.   Law professionals are considered qualified in their witness statements, meaning the value of their testimony in matters within their competence are superior to those of any other witness. They cannot normally be required to testify concerning their clients' or their secrets.

   In addition, both lawyers and notaries may issue legal opinions regarding the exercise of their legal practice, as experts.

10 The Lawyer and the Press

22.   The same rules on secrecy and confidentiality apply to lawyers and notaries in their interactions with the press. While there is absolute freedom of press in Paraguay, it cannot take precedence over professional secrecy.

11 Powers of the Tax and Other Authorities

23.   In Paraguay, the Treasury has extensive powers, but not over confidentiality. Confidentiality will be respected, and all required reports are submitted in a protected manner.

12 National Security Issues

24.   There are no provisions under Paraguayan law regarding national security issues affecting professional secrecy.

27

Peru

JEAN PAUL CHABANEIX

LUIS BEDOYA

Rodrigo, Elías & Medrano Abogados

Preliminary Note

1.   In Peru, lawyers who enter a *Colegio de Abogados* (bar association) must abide by a duty of professional secrecy (also known as attorney-client privilege). The lawyer's Code of Ethics provides strict guidance for professional secrecy, including its limitations, exceptions and duration. Admitted lawyers are independent and self-employed, although they can be partners or associates in a law firm or work for companies. In total, there are 21 bar associations in Peru, each presided over by an elected dean.

    Lawyers must be members of a bar association to be able to appear in court, provide legal counsel or advice, and work in law firms or companies regarding matters of law. Although it is possible for law school graduates to provide some legal advice prior to their registration, they are also bound by professional secrecy, as it is regulated in the Constitution and in the Penal Code. This chapter will focus on professional secrecy, or attorney-client privilege, of lawyers who belong to a bar association in Peru and who must therefore comply with the Code of Ethics regarding the legal matters they handle.

1 Scope of and Limitations on the Duty of Professional Secrecy/Attorney-Client Privilege

A Statutory Basis and Implications

2.   The 1993 Political Constitution is the first Constitution in Peru to fully mention professional secrecy, in Article 2(18). This article states that every person has the right "to maintain in private their political, philosophical, religious or any other type of convictions, as well as to maintain professional secrecy." It should be noted that the Penal Code is broader than the Constitution, as it takes into account that persons without a professional degree may receive privileged information. Article 165 of the Code of Ethics provides that any person who, on the basis of the person's employment, job, profession, ministry or state, acquires information that can cause harm or damage due to its publication or revelation without consent, must keep it private. If breached, the sanction is no more than two years of jail time and from 60 to 120 days of fines. There is no formal list of "professions" that fall under the category of the article. However, several statutes of the pertinent bar associations include specific regulations to affirm their duty of professional secrecy and impose the corresponding sanctions. In accordance with these regulations, the Criminal Procedure Code protects the disclosure of information obtained through professional secrecy by acknowledging the right to remain silent under interrogation, which is evidenced in Article 165(2)(a).[1]

---

[1] Those who are bound by law to professional or state secrecy must abstain from testifying, following the provisions contained in Article 165:

This new Criminal Procedure Code is set to replace the Code of Criminal Procedures by 2016 and is being introduced slowly throughout the provinces in Peru. The new code puts in place a more thorough regulation on professional secrecy, and although it is only enforceable in some provinces, it is accepted that it can be used as an analogy when the Code of Criminal Procedures does not provide a specific regulation for the matter at hand. This would be true in the case of professional secrecy.

Lawyers and other professionals who are subject to the abovementioned articles must protect their clients' well-being, as well as their clients' wishes, regarding which information is disclosed. This not only reflects the Code of Ethics but also the disclosure of confidential information (breach of the duty to maintain professional secrecy), which can lead to a criminal procedure. In a 2005 ruling, the Constitutional Court[2] stated that secrecy is a duty of the lawyer. Therefore, if a lawyer reveals the information during an interrogatory without being subject to violence or coercion, such lawyer cannot demand that the information revealed be discarded. It is also assumed that if the lawyer willingly supplies the information, there is a breach of professional secrecy, showing both sides of the rule. On one hand, no court of law or authority can force lawyers to reveal confidential information. On the other, it is the lawyers' duty not to disclose confidential information and to use the articles mentioned previously to protect their clients. In case of unauthorized disclosure, the fault for this breach lies with the lawyer and not with the authority.[3]

The Penal Code of Peru sanctions the disclosure of information protected by professional secrecy, but it does not mention its limits. It is normally assumed that it refers to any disclosure of information that may cause damage to the client, whether said revelation occurs inside a court of law or outside (public statements, for example).

3.   Professional secrecy must oppose the interest of the authorities, including the court of law. No authority can force the revelation of information protected under professional secrecy. It is from this fact that it can be concluded that the right to professional secrecy is preferred over others, as it matters more than the interest

---

"Those who are bound by professional secrecy cannot be compelled to testify on the subject matter known by reason of their profession, except in cases where they have the obligation to report it to the judicial authorities. Among them are lawyers, ministers of religious organizations, notaries, medics and sanitary personal, journalists and other professions expressly exempted by law. Nevertheless with the exception of ministers of religious organizations, the aforementioned may not deny their testimony when they are released by the interested party of their duty to maintain confidentiality."

[2]   The Constitutional Court is an independent body from the judiciary. It has the final say in constitutional cases.

[3]   Tribunal Constitucional Peruano. EXP. No. 7811-2005-PA/TC.

of the justice system.[4] It is important to mention that the Constitutional Court has ruled in several cases that there is no "absolute right," and as such it is understood as a coexistence of rights. Therefore, in specific situations, the authorities should ponder and decide what right to prefer. Professional secrecy is subject to such interpretation, and the judge can authorize access to documentation that was produced as part of a professional service. This exception is justified by the understanding that disclosure may be necessary to protect a more important right. For example, if a law firm had been created for the purpose of aiding a criminal organization and it is hiding relevant information under professional secrecy, it is safe to assume that a judge would order relevant documents to be retrieved.

One of the purposes of professional secrecy between a lawyer and a client is to allow the client to provide the lawyer with all the relevant information to help in the client's case without being concerned about it being shared without the client's approval. In other words, it provides the possibility to receive the best possible legal advice. As it is recognized as a constitutional right, clients are further assured that their private information will remain so. If this was not the case, the information provided to lawyers by clients would not be enough to provide sound legal advice, and this could result in less than positive results for the client.

Contracts between the client and the lawyer incorporate professional secrecy. The disclosure of information would be a breach of contract. In accordance with the Code of Ethics of the Bar Association, the professional secrecy for the subject matter discussed is permanent, although the client can free the lawyer from this obligation.[5] This means that the lawyer, in accordance with the rules of professional secrecy, cannot take another client whose case is against the same subject the lawyer previously handled with another client, as is shown in Article 41 of the Code of Ethics.[6] Lawyers must reject clients who pose a threat of causing a breach of professional secrecy, in order to preserve their legal duty.

B Scope

4. Professional secrecy in Peru covers all the information lawyers receive from clients as a result of their professional relationship, in accordance with Article 30 of the Code of Ethics.[7] This would contain all types of information,

---

[4] R. Gamarra Herrera, R. Uceda Pérez and G. Gianella Malca, *Secreto Profesional: Análisis y perspectiva desde la medicina, el periodismo y el derecho*, PROMSEX, Lima, 2011.

[5] Art. 33. "Professional secrecy is permanent. It subsists after the professional relationship has concluded, although the client can relieve the lawyer from his or her obligation."

[6] Art. 41. "A lawyer cannot accept a case when it is related with a previous one of another client with which it maintains conflicting interests on the subject matter discussed, unless they have prior and written consent of both parties. The lawyer can accept the client if the subject matter is unrelated, and when there is no risk of being limited in his or her duties to the first client."

[7] Art. 30. "Professional secrecy is the duty of a lawyer to protect and maintain in strict confidentiality the facts and information of a client or potential client which they have received on account of the professional relationship between them."

including written and oral, that would supply the lawyer with background or support to face trial or prepare legal counsel for the client. It also includes information that is not relevant to trial or counsel but is also revealed during the work done by the lawyer. The work performed by the lawyer must be kept secret to protect the clients' wishes and their well-being, and also to avoid a criminal procedure. The lawyer must hold this information in the highest secrecy possible to avoid exposing it.

The information may be of varying natures, as it can be facts, deductions or projections that can be made through the inquiry or knowledge of the work done, and that are obtained or known due to a certain profession.[8] Professional secrecy also includes data, consultations, proposals, documents received and mail (or email). It even includes information the lawyer may acquire without the participation of the client, including matters of which the client could be unaware.[9]

Due to the vast amount of information that is protected by the duty of professional secrecy, it may be difficult to maintain confidentiality of some aspects of it. The lawyer or law firm must be extremely careful when reviewing and discussing the evidence they receive from the client. The messages sent between the lawyer and the client are confidential and require special authorization from the court to be used.

There is an interesting point that must be mentioned, regarding whether professional secrecy applies when a client divulges information to a lawyer who later rejects the legal representation. In Peru, it is generally accepted that the pillar of this right (professional secrecy) rests on the trust the lawyer must provide to a client to obtain the information needed to defend a case, and even if the lawyer does not take the case or the client chooses not to engage the lawyer's services, the information provided beforehand must be kept secret.[10] Such information was provided to the lawyer on account of the lawyer's profession; therefore, the fact that the lawyer was not employed does not affect the nature and reason as to why the lawyer received the information.

Professional secrecy, in accordance with the Criminal Procedure Code, also gives lawyers the possibility not to report clients concerning information they receive.[11] In this case, if a lawyer is given information that would entitle the lawyer to make a formal report to the authorities, possibly regarding a crime, the lawyer is entitled to maintain silence and cannot be charged with obstruction of justice or as a collaborator of the committed crime. There are certain

---

[8] Tribunal Constitucional Peruano. Sentencia 7811-2005-PA/TC, Fundamento Jurídico No. 8.
[9] R. Gamarra Herrera, R. Uceda Pérez and G. Gianella Malca, *Secreto Profesional: Análisis y perspectiva desde la medicina, el periodismo y el derecho*, PROMSEX, Lima, 2011.
[10] E. Cortés Bechiarelli, *El secreto profesional del abogado y del procurador y su proyección penal*, at 94.
[11] Art. 327(2). "There is no obligation when the knowledge of the facts is protected by professional secrecy."

exceptions to this provision, as there are certain times when lawyers must divulge the information given.

C Persons Subject to the Duty of Professional Secrecy

5.   As stated previously, the Penal Code grants a broad vision of professional secrecy, including those who receive information on account of their profession, employment, ministry or state. Regarding lawyers, their duty has been regulated throughout the legal system, from the Code of Ethics of the Bar Association to the Constitution and Penal Code. Lawyers who violate professional secrecy are subject to different sanctions, as it is would imply a breach of both the Code of Ethics and the laws of Peru.

The attorney-client privilege must be respected by the court, public prosecutor's office, the police and any party involved in the proceedings. As an exception, authorities may have access to privileged documents.

Professional secrecy also applies to interrogations held by authorities, such as the police or district attorney, and declarations made to the press.[12] Information, such as documents, that are obtained in the course of an investigation that breaches professional secrecy cannot be used when the breach is made by the authorities. As already mentioned, if the professional voluntarily hands over privileged information, it can be used despite the breach. Regarding documents obtained by the authorities, the prosecutor is entitled to review and decide whether the information is indispensable for the case and ask for its admission. The decision on this is made by the judge.[13]

As we can see from a ruling from the Constitutional Court, lawyers can be summoned to testify in an ongoing investigation, and they must exercise their right to professional secrecy.

In no case can the lawyer divulge the information during the interrogation and later claim a breach in professional secrecy by the prosecutor's office and the police.[14] As already mentioned, the lawyer's claim can be accepted only if the interrogation involved intimidation or coercion. If the lawyer is summoned to make a statement and does not mention professional secrecy, any information the lawyer reveals that causes damage to the client and breaches the secrecy is entirely the lawyer's fault, and the lawyer must face the corresponding sanctions.

Regarding tax administration, Peru has not managed to settle proper limitations that protect professional secrecy. Tax administrators can require information for fiscal searches, and this information contains transactions, files, documents, registers and assets of any nature. From this they obtain information not only from the searched party but also from all who have contracted or

---

[12] R. Chanamé Orbe, *Comentarios a la Constitución*, Jurista Editores, Lima, 2006, at 124.

[13] Art. 224, Criminal Procedure Law Code.

[14] Tribunal Constitucional Peruano. EXP. No. 7811-2005-PA/TC.

traded with them. It could even mean that emails or information exchanged between the lawyer and the person investigated could be revealed. Due to this, tax administrators usually have access to privileged information, undermining the professional secrecy between the lawyer and the client, as the lawyer could have presented an analysis or comment regarding economic decisions made by the client.[15]

6. Professional secrecy is a matter of public interest. Clients have the right to defend themselves in the best possible way, and it is the responsibility of lawyers to provide the best defense they can offer.

Clients can, indeed, allow lawyers to reveal matters that are confidential, but lawyers cannot decide this for themselves. Nevertheless, there are some cases in which lawyers are obligated to inform the authorities.

D Exceptions to and Optional Derogations from the Duty of Professional Secrecy

7. The right to professional secrecy is subject to a number of exceptions and derogations. If there is an exception, the lawyer must disclose the information. In case of derogation, the lawyer must decide whether the information should be disclosed or not. These exceptions and derogations are narrowly considered because they pose a threat of limiting due process and the ability to properly defend a client in trial, as any information disclosed can be used against them.

If the client reveals information to the lawyer that indicates the client's plans to commit a crime in the future, the lawyer has the duty to report this to the authorities.[16] The Code of Ethics, which clearly states that the lawyer is obligated to divulge the information in case it threatens the physical or psychological integrity or the life of a person,[17] supports this statement. In this case, if the client has confided plans to harm or damage a person or has targeted a specific location that would cause harm or damage to a number of people, the lawyer is obligated by the Code of Ethics to act upon this knowledge and inform the authorities, with the aim of preventing the event from taking place. This is an example of when professional secrecy may be considered a lesser right in comparison with the rights protected by the disclosure. Any kind of violence against children or women, which typify a specific crime in the Penal Code, must be reported immediately, even if it constitutes a breach of

---

[15] C. J. D. Villanueva Faustor, "La información Tributaria y el Secreto Profesional: ¿Cómo Lograr el Equilibrio Deseado?," *Derecho & Sociedad* 35, 318.

[16] R. Gamarra Herrera, R. Uceda Pérez and G. Gianella Malca, *Secreto Profesional: Análisis y perspectiva desde la medicina, el periodismo y el derecho*, PROMSEX, Lima, 2011, at 19.

[17] Art. 37. "The lawyer must reveal to the authority information protected by professional secrecy when necessary, to prevent the client from causing strong damage to the physical/ psychological integrity, or the life of a person."

professional secrecy. The exception also applies if the lawyer gains evidence of the client's involvement in the propagation of diseases or infections that pose a threat on a national level. The basis of this exception is the protection of national security and health matters concerning fast-acting diseases or infections, and it aims at protecting public and even private health. The lawyer (or other professionals entrusted with the information) should inform the client's spouse or other family members in case the disease threatens them in any sort of way. Should it be possible for the disease to become a matter of public concern, the relevant information must be communicated to the authorities.[18]

As we can see, the exceptions presented need the correct analysis of the lawyer, who must evaluate the case in its entirety and realize that the higher value that is protected is the life or integrity of other people who might suffer due to the actions the client plans to initiate or due to a health risk that might expand.

It should be noted that the limits presented above do not apply if the lawyer has information of a crime already committed by the client that is under investigation, as this is protected by professional secrecy, and the client has the right to maintain confidentiality of this information to ensure the best defense possible.[19]

Lawyers cannot hide information under professional secrecy when they have helped or collaborated with the client to commit a crime. In this case, they are collaborators and are prosecuted as such. To be able to abide by the Code of Ethics and the law, the lawyer must abstain from participating in the crime the client has perpetuated. This includes, as it can be understood, making suggestions to the client to perform actions that go against the law.[20] Lawyers should always provide the client with the best possible defense, but the lawyer cannot go against the law by participating with the client in illegal conduct.

Any information that proves the lawyer's involvement in the client's crime is admissible in an investigation, and as the prosecutor has the power to enforce the search, the prosecutor can decide if there is enough suspicion of the lawyer's involvement to allow the analysis of the documents.

8.   The Code of Ethics presents certain situations that allow lawyers to disclose the information they have received or discovered about a client. In these cases, lawyers must decide whether they choose to divulge the information and must select which information to disclose, as the protection of the client is essential.

    The client can release the lawyer from the professional secrecy that binds the lawyer. From this moment forward, the lawyer would be allowed to divulge

---

[18] R. Gamarra Herrera, R. Uceda Pérez and G. Gianella Malca, *Secreto Profesional: Análisis y perspectiva desde la medicina, el periodismo y el derecho*, PROMSEX, Lima, 2011, at 21.

[19] S. Abad Yupanqui, "Tribunal Constitucional y Secreto Profesional," *Compendio De Jurisprudencia*, 2008.

[20] Ibid., 49.

publicly and privately the information given by the client beforehand.[21] This permission from the client must be granted, as stated in Article 36 of the Code of Ethics, in an "express and prior" manner. The client must be aware of the consequences of this permission, and in any case the lawyer must be sure to mention the implications of the client giving consent. It must be a previous authorization. The lawyer cannot divulge the information relying on the permission the client may give after the event.

In case of inquiry by the prosecutor's office or an authority, lawyers can reveal information protected by professional secrecy to help their own personal case.[22] This is also included in Article 36 of the Code of Ethics and presents a justification for breach of professional secrecy. In these cases, the lawyer must face an inquiry by an authority. It does not matter if it is a judicial process or not. If the lawyer sees the necessity to present information protected by professional secrecy to help the lawyer's interests against an authority, the lawyer is entitled to do so.

Both derogations from professional secrecy must follow a strict analysis where the lawyer must decide what information can be revealed without causing substantial harm to the client. It does not mean that just because the lawyer is questioned by an authority, the lawyer can release all the information confided by the client. The lawyer must determine that some of the knowledge or data the lawyer has acquired would help his or her case, and in that case divulge it in defense of the lawyer's own cause.

Another derogation included in the Code of Ethics refers to the lawyer who decides to reveal the information given by the client in a book or article. The lawyer is entitled to do so but must ensure that the information released does not allow the case or the person involved to be recognized, although this is possible if the lawyer has the consent of the client.[23]

E Law Firms

9.   In Peru, lawyers who work for a law firm work together on cases, share and discuss information regarding the clients, and ask advice from others. The Code of Ethics clearly states that sharing information within the law firm proves no breach of professional secrecy.[24]

---

[21] Art. 36. "The lawyer is allowed to reveal information protected by professional secrecy when: a) The lawyer has the express and prior consent of the client, which must be in writing."

[22] Art. 36. "The lawyer is allowed to reveal information protected by professional secrecy when: . . . b) It is necessary for the defense of his or her legitimate interests against an authority, inside or outside of a sanctioning process."

[23] Art. 35. "The lawyer can publish articles regarding information he or she has received on account of his or her profession when the case or the persons involved cannot be identified, unless he or she has the prior, written and express consent of the client."

[24] Art. 34. "When the lawyer gives professional services as part of a group, the professional secrecy binds all the lawyers who are involved and who work in the institution."

The privilege applies to all information that is provided by the client to the lawyers of the law firm, who analyze the data and assess the information, in some cases dividing the job to work effectively. This would not mean a violation of professional secrecy, as it is allowed in the Code of Ethics.

Independent lawyers cannot share their clients' files with other lawyers, as this is not supported in the Code of Ethics and would constitute a breach of professional secrecy.

F Legal Assistants and Staff

10. Law firms employ numerous workers who do not practice law, such as secretaries, support staff and legal assistants. As they are not members of a bar association, they cannot practice law and cannot offer their services as lawyers. However, they have access to the information shared by the client and have been included inside the professional secrecy rights in accordance with the Constitutional Court.[25] Moreover, as mentioned before, the criminal code punishes the disclosure made not only by professionals but also by whosoever received information on account of their work. That being said, this "non-attorney" worker is subject to the same duties.

G External Service Providers

11. In cases where a law firm employs service providers outside of its offices, such as document reviewers, secretaries and translators, or even legal services for purposes such as a due diligence review, it is assumed that the duty of professional secrecy is extended to these outside workers. Messengers who deliver confidential documents are also included inside the duties of professional secrecy, and if the documents are handed to the wrong person or revealed, they could be charged with breach of professional secrecy. Nevertheless, it is common to request these service providers to execute a confidentiality agreement, providing extra security for the information traded.

H Multidisciplinary Associations

12. Some cases may require the lawyer to share information with professionals of other areas outside the law to be able to form a defense or have a better understanding of the case. There is no mention of this in the Code of Ethics or in the regulations made by the government. But many professions have their own codes of ethics, and as was mentioned beforehand, other professions have the same right and duty to professional secrecy as lawyers. Taking this into

---

[25] Tribunal Constitucional Peruano Sentencia 7811-2005-PA/TC, Fundamento Jurídico no. 8: "The protection clause includes, and therefore also enforces, the duty to maintain secrecy, not only to the professionals who have been entrusted with the secret, but also his or her collaborators, helpers, assistants and even the service personal that could have access to them."

account, a lawyer who consults a doctor regarding a case can be assured that the doctor is bound by the same professional secrecy as the lawyer is, and as such it is assumed that the information cannot be revealed.

I In-House Counsel

13.   In-house counsel are common in Peru. Companies have their own legal professionals, who work full time inside the company regarding the legal matters that are required. In-house counsel follow the same logic as the law firms and must protect the information they handle. Professional secrecy applies to them in the same way as it applies to lawyers in law firms.

Companies hire the services of law firms even when they have in-house counsel, as they sometimes require specific help on a complex subject. In such cases, professional secrecy binds both the law firm hired and the in-house counsel, who share information in order to provide the best service and response to the needs of the company.

2 History of the Duty of Professional Secrecy in Peru

14.   The first Constitution of Peru to mention the right to professional secrecy was published in 1993, in Article 2(18). Nevertheless, mention of this right can be traced throughout the history of the law schools in Peru. This can be seen from Peru's different Codes of Ethics, which mention the right the client has to due process and to have the best service provided by the lawyer, whose duty must be to protect the client's wishes. The Code of Criminal Procedure of 1939 mentions the right individuals have to abstain from declaring secrets obtained through the exercise of their profession (Art. 141).

An article from 1966 provides an in-depth analysis of professional secrecy before its inclusion as a constitutional right. Taking into account the aforementioned article, Garcia Rada is keen to mention the importance of professional secrecy as a way of maintaining a society at peace, as he stated that "Justice administrators must respect the secrecy that binds the medic, the lawyer . . . as this duty is a matter of social need. It is not done to free certain persons from the obligation to testify as it only applies to specific professions. It is not a privilege, but the recognition of a necessary element of society."[26] Its importance lies in that it was recognized and applied even before it was mentioned in the Constitution of Peru.

The development of professional secrecy has not changed much since those years, as it maintains the idea that the professional who receives information regarding a client is entitled and obligated to keep it a secret

---

[26] D. García Rada, *El Secreto Profesional y el Proceso Penal*, Themis 3, 1966, at 20.

and can refuse to give testimony on that information. It also shows that professional secrecy is rather subjective, as it proposes the idea that it is the duty of the lawyer or professional to decide which matters fall into the category of secrets, and if they are not secrets, they can be revealed. It also presents the idea that public administrators have the duty to provide any information regarding a crime, even if it is given by a client at a given moment, as they are not bound by professional secrecy. This idea is criticized by Garcia Rada, who believes that public administrators or workers have the duty to research and give notice of anything suspicious but are also bound to professional secrecy as it means that they cannot release the information they have without a proper justification.[27]

Throughout the years, the duty and right of professional secrecy has been preserved, and there are very few cases that see this right being questioned.

3 Supervision

A The Bar Associations

15.   Through the Code of Ethics, the bar associations have enumerated the limits and derogations that apply regarding professional secrecy. In 2012, all the bar associations of Peru held a conference that proposed that the same Code of Ethics be used for all of them, and it concluded with the release of the Code of Ethics referred to throughout this chapter.

As well as its scope, the Code of Ethics presents the sanctions that can apply in case of breach of professional secrecy.

B The Courts

16.   Outside the bar associations, lawyers must, of course, abide by the law. As mentioned before, the Penal Code presents, in its Article 165, the sanction that corresponds to the breach of professional secrecy.[28] The Civil Code makes no mention of professional secrecy, but through the Code of Ethics we understand that any breach of professional secrecy results in the lawyer being obligated to pay the client in the form of civil damages.

As has been stated previously, the Criminal Procedure Law Code determines situations in which the lawyer can refuse to report and to appear in court, and the protection given to documents.

---

[27] Ibid.

[28] Art. 165. "The person who, due to his or her state, employment, profession, ministry or office, has access to secrets that can cause harm if they are published, reveals them without consent, is subject to imprisonment for no longer than two years and from sixty to a hundred and twenty fine days."

4 Sanctions

A Proceedings and Sanctions

17.   Article 81 of the Code of Ethics establishes what constitutes an act against professional ethics that is subject to sanction.

Every bar association has an Ethics Council, which can review cases on its own initiative or from a complaint made by a person with a legitimate interest (Arts. 80 and 83 of the Code of Ethics[29]). The complaint must be in writing. During the time of investigation, the Council is responsible for the correspondent inquiry and research of documents, as well as setting the date for the hearing. The hearing brings both parties together to discuss the matter in question, as well as settling the admission and rejection of evidentiary material (Art. 97 of the Code of Ethics[30]). The Council then has 20 days to settle its decision and verdict, which can be appealed. In the second instance, the Honor Court views the case (Arts. 99 and 100 of the Code of Ethics[31]).

The sanctions vary depending on the sentence. Article 102 of the Code of Ethics determines the different sanctions that may apply. In case the Council determines guilt and sentences, the lawyer may be charged with a written warning or fines, both of which are registered and saved in the bar archives for a certain period (three and six months, respectively). Also,

[29] Art. 80. "Bar Associations in Peru, through their Ethics and Directing Organs, investigate on their own initiative or through a complaint the acts against professional ethics involving lawyers, and impose the corresponding sanctions to those held responsible."

Art. 83. "The administrative organ of every Bar Association is the Ethics Directory, with the functions regulated by the code. The Ethics Council and the Honor Tribunal are the disciplinary organs of the Bar Association."

[30] Art. 97. "Throughout the disciplinary procedure the Ethics Council will perform the necessary diligences to verify the facts: acting proofs, establishing extenuating circumstances, mitigations or aggravations of the facts: verify the records of the lawyer and determining the author or coauthor depending on the case.

The Ethics Council will set a unique hearing, where the involved parties will be cited to establish the controversy and to admit, reject and present the evidence.

The parties or their representatives can ask for speaking time.

During the disciplinary procedure the parties can supply evidentiary material until the Council is ready to sentence."

[31] Art. 99. "The Council will issue its opinion within twenty business days from the hearing. An appeal presented before the deadline suspends the effects of the verdict until it is resolved in a second instance. If the deadline for appeal passes, the decision from the Ethics Council is consented."

Art. 100. "Against the Council's decision, the parties can present an appeal before the Honor Tribunal, with a deadline of five business days from the time they are notified. The appeal presented before the deadline suspends the effects of the decision until it is resolved in a second instance."

lawyers can be charged and forced to stop their practice for a period of two years or less, as well as being suspended from the bar for up to five years. The highest punishment permitted is the permanent expulsion from the bar association.

Expulsion, in accordance with Article 104, is applicable in cases where the lawyer causes or promotes violations of constitutional rights and liberties. Analyzing this, it can be concluded that, as professional secrecy has been regulated as a constitutional right under Article 2(18), a lawyer who violates it could be subject to this level of sanction by the bar association.

All the sanctions, in accordance with the Code of Ethics, must be reasonably justified in the verdict, and they must take into account the event, the circumstance and the harm done.[32] This secures the right to due process.

18.   The Penal Code provides that the crime regarding the release of confidential information is sanctioned with a prison term of up to two years and a fine (Art. 165 Penal Code). The criminal court has jurisdiction in these matters. No case can be accepted in which the lawyer revealed information under the protection of the limitations discussed previously. The process would follow the legal steps determined in the Criminal Procedure Law Code.

B Relationship between Criminal Sanctions and Disciplinary Sanctions

19.   Disciplinary and criminal sanctions are applied independently and have no effect on each other. Nevertheless, when a criminal process is opened against a lawyer, the bar association is informed, which would result in a disciplinary process being initiated.

In Peru it is perfectly possible for both criminal and disciplinary sanctions to be held on the basis of the same facts. This has been shown not to violate the general principle of *non bis in idem*, as the sanctions are imposed under the violation of different rules.[33]

C Claims for Damages

20.   As a general rule, whoever causes damage to another person is obligated to indemnify them. Therefore, if lawyers breach their duty to maintain professional secrecy, the affected party will be entitled to claim for damages. This is an independent claim from the criminal or administrative proceedings that can also be followed.

---

[32] Art. 103. "Sanctions established in Subsections a), b), c) and d) of the preceding article will apply taking into account the seriousness of the event and the damage caused."

[33] C. Aliaga Castillo, *Principio non bis in idem: independencia entre el proceso administrativo y el proceso judicial*, Jurisprudencia Constitucional, RAE Jurisprudencia, 2008, at 215.

5 Duty to Provide Information to the Authorities

A Money Laundering and Terrorism

21. There are some cases in which the government, through its administration, can require the lawyer to provide certain information regarding a client, as the government could suspect the client's involvement in money laundering, terrorism or other crimes. This would mean a breach of professional secrecy but is justified as it aims to prevent the commission of a serious crime.

    To help in this scenario, lawyers who acquire information that connects their clients to a crime that threatens the integrity or the life of a person are obligated to report it (Art. 407 of the Penal Code, in correspondence with Article 37 of the Code of Ethics). For example, tax lawyers who handle delicate information of their clients must be careful to be aware of any indications that may show the clients' involvement in a crime regarding the funding of terrorism. If they continue to represent the client, they might end up facing trial as co-defendant. It should be mentioned that lawyers must maintain the secrecy of information clients provide or information they find through research, but they can never conceal a future crime or help the client commit a crime. If the lawyer finds information on his or her client that reveals the client's involvement in a financial crime, the lawyer must report it, because failing to do so would mean that the lawyer is covering up for the client, which is in itself a crime.

    The Tax Administration can require a lawyer to provide documents in an investigation regarding money laundering, and in these cases the lawyer must provide the documents, even if that constitutes a breach of professional secrecy. Through this, lawyers fulfill their duty of providing information in relation to a crime (or clearing the client's name) and also avoid becoming an accomplice in said crime.

    In 2002 the Financial Intelligence Unit (UIF, for its acronym in Spanish) was created through Law no. 27693. It aims to reduce money and asset laundering. Article 8 of this law states that civil law notaries must inform the UIF of any client who engages in suspicious activities or transfers. The same law provides a list of actions that should be considered suspicious, but it makes no mention of other branches of lawyers.

    Lawyers must also be careful when handling their clients' personal information, as indications of money laundering or terrorism funding may appear. In that case, it can be assumed that professional secrecy is not possible, as it would also mean the covering up of a crime. The lawyer must therefore report the activities to the relevant authorities and provide the documents that evidence the crime.

B Collective Settlement of Debts

22.　As mentioned previously, the Tax Administration is entitled to review the financial situation of different individuals to gain evidence to prove different crimes.[34] In the cases where they require information that is protected by professional secrecy in order to prove the financial debts of the clients, the prosecutor can review the information and decide whether they are admissible in the investigation, and then require the judge to accept the evidence.[35]

This means that information that is of vital importance for the case may be accepted in the trial, even if that means a breach of professional secrecy. This would mean that in cases of collective settlement of debts, the debtors' accounts could be checked thoroughly, releasing the professional secrecy that binds different files and data of extreme importance in the case.

6 Treatment of Lawyers' Documents and Correspondence in the Context of Judicial or Police Investigations

23.　In the Criminal Procedure Law Code, there are two important articles that apply to search and seizure. First is Article 224, which refers to non-private documents. In this case, the law indicates that documents seized during an investigation can be exhibited, unless it is a matter of state secrecy. If someone is in possession of the documents required during an investigation, the person is bound by law to hand them in, unless the person claims to be protected by professional secrecy. The prosecutor must be diligent in deciding whether the information is protected correctly and if it is indispensable for the case, and after that formulate a petition to the judge to accept the documents. If the judge deems it appropriate, the judge orders the confiscation of the documents. In this case, professional secrecy is only a barrier during an investigation, as the judge can deem disclosure necessary for the case, requesting the documents.

Second, we also have Articles 232 and 233 of the Criminal Procedure Code regarding private documents. It is important to mention that, in Peru, a private document is described as one that does not contain the characteristics of a public document. To understand this, we must look at Articles 235 and 236 of the Civil Procedure Code,[36] which define both private and the public documents.

---

[34] C. J. D. Villanueva Faustor, "La Información Tributaria y el Secreto Profesional: ¿Cómo lograr el equilibrio deseado?," *Derecho & Sociedad* 35, 2011, at 317.

[35] Art. 224, Criminal Procedure Law Code. "2. When professional secrecy is invoked, the prosecutor will realize the correspondent investigations when it is of utmost importance, and if the prosecutor considers it necessary to revoke it, he or she will urge for judicial involvement. The judge of the preliminary investigation can consider the allegations founded and, with a previous hearing, order the seizing of the information."

[36] Art. 235. "A public document is:
　1. The one given by a public official in performance of their duties;

Article 232 of the Criminal Procedure Code refers to a situation in which authorities involved in an investigation, research or an inspection find private documents on site or in the possession of a person subject to inquiry. In this case, they must have a search warrant that allows for said documents to be examined. If not, they must be kept by the authorities but are not examined until the judge has determined that they are necessary for the case. This formality is regulated by Article 233 of the Criminal Procedure Code, and although it does not mention professional secrecy, when it is claimed by the subject inquired, it could be a factor that would help the judge to sentence against evaluating or examining the documents. The judge would have to consider the prosecutors' claim on one side and professional secrecy and its importance on the other in order to make a fair decision.

7 Search of a Lawyer's Office

24.   The search of a lawyer's office or home is allowed through the search warrants discussed above. If the prosecutor deems it necessary, the prosecutor can ask the judge of the preliminary hearing to allow the investigation to involve the lawyer's office or home, in order to seize documents regarding the client under scrutiny. It is important to mention that during this search the authorities should avoid opening or looking at files regarding other clients not subject to investigation. Professional secrecy applies individually to each lawyer's clients, and if one is being investigated, the others should remain protected.

8 Tapping of Telephone Conversations with a Lawyer

25.   There are certain cases where the prosecutor is empowered to access telephone lines and hear and record a conversation. This is regulated through the Criminal Procedure Code, which in its Article 230 states that the prosecutor, when he or she suspects the existence of a crime with a determined jail time, and it is absolutely necessary, can solicit for the tapping of a telephone line. This is also regulated through Law no. 27697, which applies when there are indications that a specific crime has been committed (Art. 1 of the aforementioned law provides a list).

Tapping into telephone conversations of a lawyer is admissible only in the cases where there is an ongoing investigation, and the lawyer or the client is

---

2.   A public writing or other document given by a public notary, in accordance with the law; and

3.   All which are given said condition through special laws.

A copy of a public document has the same value as the original if it is certified by an auxiliary court, public notary or notary."

Art. 236. "A private document is the one which does not contain the characteristics of a public document. The legalization or certification of a private documents does not turn it into a public document."

a suspect of one of the crimes enumerated in Article 1 of Law no. 27697. There is no mention of professional secrecy in said law, to which it must be assumed that any information that is not related to the specific crime investigated is inadmissible, as that information is protected through others laws and through the Constitution.

9 The Lawyer as Witness

26. Lawyers can be called to testify in court as witnesses. If they are called, they must raise the subject of professional secrecy when refusing to answer, and it is a valid ground to avoid a question.[37] This is supported by Article 165 of the Criminal Procedure Law Code, as it is clear to mention that those bound by professional secrecy cannot reveal the information acquired through the exercise of their profession. This is further stated in Article 141 of the Code of Criminal Procedure, as it includes the same information regarding professional secrecy and trial. The limit set through these articles resides on information acquired through the profession. It can be argued then that any information possessed by the lawyer that has not been received on account of the lawyer's profession is admissible in trial. Disclosing this type of information would not breach professional secrecy and would therefore not constitute a crime or a violation of the Code of Ethics.

10 The Lawyer and the Press

27. Lawyers, with the client's consent, can speak to the press regarding the case in order to defend the client against allegations made before, during or after the case. They should refrain from narrating the case in public and from disclosing privileged information. In Peru, it is common for criminal lawyers to appear in the press commenting on their clients' cases, defending them against allegations made by the press or the public.

11 Powers of the Tax and Other Authorities

28. Tax Administrators have the power to obtain and analyze the data of selected individuals to determine their tax obligations. Due to the scope of the tax audit, it is likely that it will include the verification of a specific service that was provided or received by a professional worker. Through this, the Tax Administration has a flexible limit regarding the access to documents protected by the professional secrecy. Some authors even consider that this power manages to "break" professional secrecy, as it makes them immune to it.[38] Files in the possession of an

---

[37] A. Medina Otazú, *El Derecho de Defensa de los Testigos en el Proceso Penal*, Instituto de Ciencia Procesal Penal.

[38] C. J. D. Villanueva Faustor, "La Información Tributaria y el Secreto Profesional: ¿Cómo lograr el equilibrio deseado?," *Derecho & Sociedad* 35, 2011, at 318.

attorney can be seized by the Tax Administration and can be revealed. As already mentioned, in some cases where there is presumption of a crime regarding the funding of terrorism, money laundering or tax evasion, the Tax Administration can obtain the files and data of the suspect (Art. 62 of the Tax Code).

The Tax Administration's power is justified by the idea that Tax Administrators would never be allowed to do a thorough search if the information is not provided completely.[39] Lawyers who are asked to present their accounts must do so in accordance with the law. In a 2008 ruling, the Constitutional Court dictated that fundamental rights have limits, and that it's the duty of the Tax Administrators to do a detailed investigation to determine if there is a serious imbalance that might lead to the discovery of a crime.[40]

In the cases where they are investigating the lawyer for tax-related imbalances, information regarding clients could also be included but would probably be ignored by the Tax Administration. In any event, it is protected by Article 85 of the Tax Code, which states that information given may be used and seen only by the Tax Administration, and it should not be disclosed, although there are some exceptions stated in the article.

As stated above, authorities investigating a crime can, through the prosecutor, request permission to access documents covered by professional secrecy, and the judge decides whether to allow it or not.

12 National Security Issues

29. During the investigation of state security matters, the authorities responsible must also act in accordance with the professional secrecy laws. They cannot coerce or intimidate lawyers to reveal information protected by professional secrecy. As has been mentioned elsewhere in this chapter, lawyers must disclose information in cases involving matters of national security. In cases in which the lawyer refuses to reveal the evidence, the prosecutor can ask the judge of the preliminary hearing to allow the prosecutor to search through documents protected by professional secrecy to prevent a threat to the country. If such evidence is found, the lawyer could be charged with obstruction of justice due to the lawyer's unwillingness to provide the information (Art. 407 of the Penal Code).

If there is a threat to national security, and with the proper authorizations, the relevant authorities can exercise different actions with the aim of reducing the threat, which could include tapping phones, searching offices or houses of the suspect or the lawyer, accessing bank accounts and tax information, or even checking computers.

---

[39] E. Gonzales, *Requerimiento y Uso de la Información en Materia Tributaria*, Revista Peruana de Derecho Tributario, Universidad de San Martín de Porres, 2007.

[40] EXP. No. 04168-2006-PA/TC.

28

Puerto Rico

RICHARD GRAFFAM-RODRÍGUEZ

McConnell Valdés LLC[1]

---

[1] The author acknowledges the contribution of Yahaira de la Rosa, an attorney of the firm.

Preliminary Note

1. Puerto Rico is one of the few mixed jurisdictions in the world: its local judiciary is grounded in the centuries-old Spanish civil code system (based on the Napoleonic Code) and yet since 1898, it is also part of the United States of America's federal judicial system, with a constitutional federal common and statutory law, as if it were a state of that republic. Puerto Rico is a territory of the United States; therefore, the U.S. Congress has plenary powers over all laws in Puerto Rico, and the U.S. Constitution is the supreme law of the land. In 1950, the U.S. Congress passed The Puerto Rico Federal Relations Act, allowing Puerto Rico to write and ratify its own Constitution and elect its own local government, but Puerto Rico still has no federal vote nor international treaty power, as the United States maintains sovereignty over the island. In 1917, the U.S. Congress conferred U.S. citizenship on all Puerto Rico residents.[2] In 1967, it converted the United District Court for the District of Puerto Rico from an Article I (territorial) court to a full-fledged Article III (constitutional) court.[3] Currently, Puerto Rico is the only U.S. territory to have such a U.S. constitutional court.

    The legal field today is the following: all federal (U.S.) constitutional and federal statutes usually apply equally to Puerto Rico as if it were a state and are enforced by a federal prosecutorial department and an Article III court with tens of judges and Article I magistrates and bankruptcy judges to aid them.[4] All proceedings in these federal courts are in English and governed by the Federal Rules of Civil Procedure and the American Bar Association (ABA's) Model Rule of Ethics, which are enforced by the federal judges. Conversely, all proceedings in the local, or "state" court, are in Spanish, ruled by Puerto Rico's hundreds-year-old Civil Code. Puerto Rico's ethical system regarding lawyers has its own Canon of Ethics, enforced by the Puerto Rico Supreme Court.

---

[2] Jones Act of 1917, HIST L.P.R.A. § 5.

[3] 1966 U.S.C.C.A.N. 2786–90; *Examining Bd. of Engineers, Architects and Surveyors v. Flores de Otero*, 426 U.S. 572, 595, 96 S. Ct. 2264, 49 L.Ed.2d 65 (1976). Article 1 courts do not enjoy the independence of life tenure and no diminishment of salaries that Article III judges have and that form the bedrock of the U.S. separation of powers control on its three branches of government.

[4] While beyond the scope of this paper, it is important to note that "Congress which is empowered under the territory clause of the Constitution . . . to make all needful rules and regulations respecting the territory . . . belonging to the United States, may treat Puerto Rico differently from states, so long as there is a rational basis for its actions." *Franklin California v. Commonwealth of P.R., et al.*, 1st Cir. July 6, 2015, 15-1218, Hon. Judge Torruella concurring, at 51 (citing *Califano v. Torres*, 435 U.S. 1, 5 (1978)). This power of Congress over Puerto Rico has been used to provide disparate treatment to Puerto Ricans, and the commonwealth itself, on an array of matters ranging from disallowance of Puerto Rico municipalities and corporations to file for federal bankruptcy (*Franklin California, supra*), to reduced health and welfare benefits (see *Jusino-Mercado v. P.R.*, 214 F.3d 34 (1st Cir. 2000), to denial of protection of Puerto Rico-based seamen under the Jones Act and the LHWCA (see Hon. Gustavo A. Gelpí Jr., "Maritime Law in Puerto Rico and Anomaly in a Sea of Federal Uniformity," 26(2) *Revista Jurídica de la Universidad Interamericana de P.R.*, 1992.

In terms of ethics and privileges or secrets, both systems are generally similar, with some exceptions, such as that the local canon of ethics does not allow conflicts of interest to be cured by consent of the parties,[5] and attorneys are held to a higher standard of "appropriate" conduct under its rules. That is, they can be sanctioned for improper conduct in public even though such conduct was outside their functions as lawyers.[6]

The other significant difference, and one that raises innumerable ethical issues, is that many Puerto Rico lawyers are also notaries at law. The seal, signature and individual script of a notary is essential for all documents in a commercial, probate, marriage, or other similar transaction. Unlike the concept of a notary in the United States, a notary in Puerto Rico requires a lawyer's license and a separate bar admission.[7] Also, notaries represent the public faith in all transactions in which they are involved; thus, they can have no interest with either party to a transaction or to the commercial subject itself.[8] Notaries are bound under *both* the Canon of Ethics for all lawyers and the Puerto Rico Notarial Act and Regulations.[9]

Because some notaries often combine both roles in one transaction, the ethical violations and corresponding rulings are rife. In many cases of breaches of contract and the like, the notary involved will be made a party (although recently the Supreme Court of Puerto Rico has lessened this practice).[10] In short, to practice in both federal and local court, you must pass the state general law exam, the notary bar exam and the federal bar exam of the U.S. District Court for the District of Puerto Rico.[11] Notaries are required to maintain a public bond and a fireproof protocol of all notarizations with their corresponding stamps of payments of the notarial tax for each transaction.[12]

2.   In sum, both lawyers in federal practice and those in local practice are bound by the attorney-client privilege, as it is best known in the United States, and the duty of professional secrecy, with the exception that local ethics rules and those for notaries are much more stringent than the federal rules.

This chapter focuses on such privileges.

---

[5] Canon 21, Puerto Rico Canons of Professional Ethics, PR ST T. 4 Ap. IX; *In re Carrera Rovira y Suárez Zayas*, 15 P.R. Offic. Trans. 1027 (1984).

[6] Canon 38, Puerto Rico Canons of Professional Ethics, PR ST T. 4 Ap. IX.

[7] Rule 7, Regulations of the Board of Bar Examiners, PR ST T. 4 Ap. VII-B.

[8] Section 2003, Notarial Act, PR ST T. 4.

[9] *In re Vargas Velázquez*, 190 D.P.R. 730, 734 (2014).

[10] *García Colón v. Sucn. González*, 178 D.P.R 527, 556, 567 (2010).

[11] It is interesting to emphasize that the U.S. District Court for the District of Puerto Rico is the only district court that requires the applicant to pass a comprehensive exam on federal practice and procedure. There were two other districts that previously required passing a federal bar exam: one was the Southern District of Ohio, which replaced the exam with a seminar, and the other was the Northern District of Florida, which replaced the exam with an Internet tutorial.

[12] *In re Ribas Dominicci*, 131 D.P.R. 491, 495–96 (1992).

1 Scope of and Limitations on Professional Secrecy

A Statutory Basis and Implications

3.   The duty of confidentiality set forth in the Puerto Rico Canons of Professional Ethics can be found in Canon 21. All attorneys have an obligation not to divulge the secrets or confidences of their clients and to adopt adequate measures to avoid disclosure thereof.[13] As a result, an attorney should not accept the representation of a client in matters adversely affecting any interest of a current or former client, nor should the attorney be an arbitrator, especially when the former client has made confidences to the attorney that may affect one or the other client, even though both clients consent. It will be highly improper for a lawyer to use the confidences of a client to the latter's prejudice.[14]

An attorney-client relationship arises when a client resorts to an attorney to seek professional services for advice or legal representation in a legal matter.[15] The attorney-client relationship is of a fiduciary nature and is anchored in the most absolute honesty, loyalty and fidelity.[16]

It is the duty of the attorney to represent the client with fidelity, and the attorney is forbidden from divulging the secrets and confidences given to him or her by the client. Nor can the attorney accept employment from others in matters consulted or entrusted to the attorney by a former client and which affect adversely the interest of the former client with respect to which confidences have been shared.[17] There is a non-rebuttable presumption that confidential information will be used by an attorney who represented a client and subsequently takes a position against the client's interests.[18] An intention of not using confidential information against the former client is not sufficient to avoid the conflict of interest, as every attorney has the duty to avoid the *appearance* of professional impropriety established explicitly in Canon 38.[19] Nonetheless, both federal and local ethical rules are now focusing on whether the new client the attorney is representing has a dispute regarding material matters involving the representation of another client.

To prove a violation of Canon 21, it is not necessary to present evidence that attorneys have communicated the secrets or confidences in question and that they divulged them. It is sufficient to show that the attorney had the opportunity to do so.[20]

---

[13] Canon 21, Puerto Rico Canons of Professional Ethics, PR ST T. 4 Ap. IX.   [14] Ibid.

[15] *In re Belén Trujillo*, 126 D.P.R. 743 (1990).

[16] *López de Victoria v. Rodríguez*, 13 P.R. Offic. Trans. 341 (1982).

[17] *In re Guzmán*, 80 P.R.R. 689 (1958).

[18] *In re Carrera Rovira y Suárez Zayas*, 15 P.R. Offic. Trans. 1027 (1984).

[19] *In re Concepción Suárez*, 11 P.R. Offic. Trans. 599 (1981).

[20] *In re Monge García*, 173 D.P.R. 379, 388 (2008).

4.   Insofar as a legal proceeding is concerned, Rule 503 of the Puerto Rico Rules of
     Evidence for the General Court of Justice establishes when the disclosure of an
     attorney-client privilege, also known as professional secrets, can occur. Under
     this rule, the client, whether or not a party to the action, has an absolute duty to
     refuse to disclose, and to prevent another from disclosing, a confidential com-
     munication between client and attorney. The privilege may be claimed not only
     by the holder of the privilege, that is, the client, but also by a person who is
     authorized to do so on behalf of the client or by the attorney who received the
     confidential communication if the privilege is claimed in the interest of the
     client.[21]

     A client is defined under this rule as any natural or juridical person who,
     directly or through an authorized representative, consults an attorney for the
     purpose of retaining the attorney or securing legal service or advice from the
     attorney in a professional capacity.[22] This includes an incompetent person who
     directly consults the attorney or whose guardian so consults the attorney on
     behalf of the incompetent.[23]

     The attorney is understood to be a person authorized or reasonably believed
     by the client to be authorized to practice law.[24] This includes such person and
     his or her partners, aides and office employees.[25] However, only the attorney
     can practice before the court.

5.   In federal court, the ABA model rules apply and are similar, except for the
     aspect of "appearance" (that is, conduct) outside the profession or practice and
     for consent to waive conflicts of interest among clients. If two or more clients
     retained or consulted an attorney on a matter of common interest, none of them
     may waive the attorney-client privilege without the other clients' consent.
     The concept is that the owner of the privilege is the client, not the attorney.
     Therefore, the attorney cannot make such a waiver.

B Scope

6.   The duty of confidentiality encompasses all secrets or confidences made by
     a client to an attorney.[26] However, confidentiality does not equal privilege if the
     communication does not contain legal advice or opinion, or is just factual.

     Under the attorney-client privilege, confidential information is that trans-
     mitted between a client and an attorney in the course of that relationship and in
     confidence by a means that does not disclose the information to third persons
     other than those to whom disclosure is necessary for the accomplishment of the
     purposes for which it is transmitted. Consequently, a lawyer's staff are covered
     under the privilege.

---

[21] Rule 503, Puerto Rico Rules of Evidence for the General Court of Justice, PR ST T. 32 Ap. VI.
[22] Ibid., Rule 503(a)(2).   [23] Ibid.   [24] Ibid., Rule 503(a)(1).   [25] Ibid.
[26] *Pueblo v. Fernández Rodríguez*, 183 D.P.R.770 (2011).

Recently, there have been several cases in which both federal and local courts have held that wireless communications, such as with cell phones, are *not* confidential and thus not privileged since they can be captured from transmission in the public airwaves. Another example is that recently the Puerto Rico Supreme Court held that an opposing attorney cannot speak to the client of the opposing party without that client's attorney being present, even if such conversation was agreed to by the opposing attorney.[27]

C Persons Subject to the Duty of Professional Secrecy

7. Only attorneys who have an attorney-client relationship with a client are subject to the duty of confidentiality imposed by Canon 21. The lack of an attorney-client relationship does not allow the imposition of disciplinary sanctions for a violation of Canon 21.[28] The protection of Canon 21 and its ABA counterpart extends to the situation when a client turns to an attorney for legal advice and, for any reason, the attorney-client relationship does not materialize. In this type of situation, the attorney has an obligation to keep the confidences made by the client. Again, the protection is for legal advice or consultation by an attorney at the request of the client. The *facts* of such conversation are not protected.

D Exceptions to and Optional Derogations from the Duty of Professional Secrecy

8. No attorney-client privilege will be recognized in five prescribed situations: (1) when the services of the lawyer were sought or obtained to enable or aid anyone to commit or plan to commit a crime, a tortious act or a fraud; (2) if the communication is relevant to an issue between the heirs of a deceased client, regardless of whether the claims are by testate or intestate succession or by *inter vivos* transaction; (3) the communication is relevant to an issue or breach by the attorney of a duty arising out of the attorney-client relationship; (4) the communication is relevant to an issue of a document drawn by the attorney in his or her capacity as notary public; and (5) the communication is relevant to a matter of common interest between two or more clients of an attorney, in which event none of them may claim a privilege under this rule against another such client.[29]

9. The Puerto Rico Rules of Evidence allow the waiver of the attorney-client privilege. For instance, the voluntary disclosure of protected information under the attorney-client privilege constitutes a waiver. However, the waiver does not extend to non-disclosed communications or information about the same subject matter.[30]

---

[27] *In re Guzmán Rodríguez*, 167, at 3.   [28] *In re Belén Trujillo*, 126 D.P.R. 743 (1990).
[29] Rule 503, Puerto Rico Rules of Evidence for the General Court of Justice, PR ST T. 32 Ap. VI.
[30] Ibid., Rule 505(b).

449

The attorney-client privilege can also be waived by stipulation. The parties in a litigation can stipulate to waive the privilege. This waiver will only bind the parties to the litigation, unless the stipulation is incorporated in a judicial order.[31]

An order issued by a court as part of a judicial proceeding in the Commonwealth of Puerto Rico that states that the attorney-client privilege should not be considered waived by disclosure of information done in said judicial proceeding obligates every person or entity to comply with the order in all judicial or administrative proceedings in Puerto Rico, independently of whether those persons or entities have been parties in the judicial proceeding if: (1) the order incorporates the stipulation of the parties before the court and (2) if any controversy arises between the parties over the existence of a privilege or of its waiver in the case of inadvertent disclosure, the rules state that there was no waiver. If a waiver of the privilege existed as a result of a disclosure, the order rules that there was no waiver.[32]

A person who would otherwise have an attorney-client privilege waives the right to claim such privilege if the court finds that such person, or any other person who was the holder of the privilege, is bound by word given to another not to claim the privilege, or that, without coercion and having full knowledge of the privilege, said person disclosed or permitted disclosure by another of any part of the privileged matter.[33]

An implicit waiver of the attorney-client privilege can be found by the judge presiding over a case when the judge makes a determination that the conduct of the holder of the privilege constitutes a waiver because the communication was not done confidentially or did not include lawyer-sought advice.[34] These same principles apply in federal court.

10. In both federal and local court, there are issues with electronically stored information (ESI) and its "claw back" provision for privileged documents. (See Rule 26 of the Federal Rules of Civil Procedure.) Nonetheless, that practice has been relatively limited. Still, in Puerto Rico, the federal rules, imitated by the revised rules of the local ("state") courts in 2009, are identical to the requirements in the federal rules that no doubt will be amply discussed by our colleague from the United States in his chapter in this book.

E Law Firms

11. All staff employed by an attorney or client to produce legal advice is covered by the privilege; however, sanctions can be levied only on the lawyer and the law firm.

---

[31] Ibid., Rule 505(d).   [32] Ibid., Rule 505(e).   [33] Ibid., Rule 517(a).   [34] Ibid., Rule 517(b).

F Legal Assistants and Staff

12. Information received by legal assistants and staff working for the law firm benefits equally from the attorney-client privilege.

G External Services Providers

13. Documents and information handled by third-party providers exclusively on behalf of an attorney for one party is confidential and subject to nondisclosure due to privilege or attorney work-product doctrine.

H Multidisciplinary Associations

14. Multidisciplinary associations are allowed in Puerto Rico and can be subject to different secrets or privilege protections; for example, there is an accountant-client privilege in Puerto Rico, as well. Otherwise, disclosure of information to consultants or experts is *not* privileged.

I In-House Counsel

15. Canon 33 of the Puerto Rico Canon of Professional Ethics has been recently amended to allow out-of-state attorneys to practice as in-house counsel in Puerto Rico without having to seek bar admission from the Puerto Rico Supreme Court.[35] However, for any outside lawyer to practice in local, federal, or arbitration proceedings, the lawyer has to be sponsored by a locally admitted attorney. Regarding in-house counsel, the issues are similar to those in the U.S. jurisdictions, that is, to what extent did the in-house counsel actively participate in the legal advice that constitutes the privilege. If the in-house counsel was either acting as a representative of the client and obtaining legal advice from outside counsel or if such counsel was actively involved in the preparation or trial of a case involving the company for which the lawyer works, such actions and communications may be considered privileged or covered under the work-product doctrine.

2 History of the Duty of Professional Secrecy in Puerto Rico

16. The attorney-client privilege was the first privilege recognized under the federal common law, and it is a bedrock principle of the Puerto Rico Canon of Ethics and the ABA rules. It is one of the most enduring and respected privileges in Puerto Rico.[36]

Its protection is enforced by the courts.

[35] Canon 33, Puerto Rico Canons of Professional Ethics, PR ST T. 4 Ap. IX, Canon 33.
[36] E.L. Chiesa, *Tratado de Derecho Probatorio*, República Dominicana, Publicaciones J.T.S., 1998, T.I, at 218.

3 Supervision

A The Bar Associations

17.   For hundreds of years, membership in the local bar association (*Colegio de Abogados*) was compulsory, and the bar association had responsibility over ethical complaints against its members.[37] However, in 2011 the Puerto Rico Supreme Court eliminated the compulsory requirement and severely limited the bar association's powers.[38] Today, all local ethical complaints against lawyers are dealt with exclusively by the Puerto Rico Supreme Court, normally with the investigative aid of the Puerto Rico Department of Justice.[39] Likewise, all federal complaints are handled by the federal judges at the district court level and are subject to appeal to the First Circuit Court of Appeals in Boston, Massachusetts.

B The Courts

18.   In the local courts, grievances against attorneys for ethical violations can be initiated by the court *sua sponte*, especially for offensive conduct in court proceedings; by opposing attorneys; or by current or former clients. Beyond the monetary discovery and exclusion of evidence that all courts (whether local or federal) can impose for violations in their courts, any attempt to otherwise sanction attorneys or disbar them triggers constitutional issues of due process and, thus, requires ulterior proceedings, namely evidentiary hearings and a right to appeal.

   In local court, any severe sanction against an attorney requires a formal complaint or referral to the Puerto Rico Supreme Court. The court then normally refers the complaint or referral to the Puerto Rico Department of Justice for factual findings and a recommendation. Thereafter, a three-judge panel of the court decides whether to accept or modify such recommendation and the appropriate sanction, which can range from a reprimand to suspension or disbarment. These final resolutions are published.

   In the federal court, the procedure is somewhat different. Following the ABA model rules and federal precedent, especially as regards the "inherent" (constitutional) power of all federal courts to manage their affairs and the conduct of attorneys before them, the disciplinary procedure is more complicated. A grievance or complaint for disbarment can be filed by an attorney in or outside any particular proceedings.

   If the complaint regards misconduct by an attorney in a specific case, the judge in charge of the case will independently impose sanctions, short of disbarment. For example, very recently a judge imposed a public, heavy reprimand and fine to an attorney who said in a deposition, on the record,

---

[37] *Colegio de Abogados de P.R. v. Schneider*, 112 D.P.R. 540 (1992).
[38] *Rivera Schatz v. ELA y C. Abo. PR II*, 191 D.P.R. 791, 821 (2014).   [39] Ibid., 806.

that a female opponent's complaint about the room temperature being too hot to be due to her menopausal status. But the court did not grant the request for disbarment.[40]

In more expansive cases, the federal court will do the following: (1) the federal judge assigned the complaint will hold an evidentiary hearing with the full participation of the aggrieved attorney to determine if there is cause for further procedures. If so, (2) the judge will refer the case to a panel composed of two attorneys and a magistrate judge. (3) Once the judge receives the report, the judge will comment extensively and issue a recommendation that (4) then goes to a panel of six judges to accept or decline such recommendation.[41]

4 Sanctions

19.   The sanctions applicable to lawyers for violations of client confidentiality, as described in more detail in Section 3(B) of this chapter, can include disbarment, fines and reprimands (both public and private).

5 Duty to Provide Information to the Authorities

A Money Laundering and Terrorism

20.   All money laundering and terrorism activity is covered by federal law, especially the Patriot Act.[42] Though confidentiality of secrets is maintained, a lawyer must divulge confidential information if ordered by a court.

B Collective Settlement of Debts

21.   In Puerto Rico, a lawyer can divulge certain secrets to defend against an action by a former client or to collect a debt. Such disclosures, however, are normally handled "under seal," depending on their sensitivity.

6 Treatment of Lawyers' Documents and Correspondence in the Context of Judicial or Police Investigations

22.   Although confidentiality is maintained, no privilege or work-product doctrine can prevent a court from examining documents or secret/confidential information obtained by an attorney who is either the subject of a criminal investigation or materially related to a criminal investigation.

---

[40] Memorandum and Order of Aug. 17, 2015, *Eliezer Cruz-Aponte et al. v. Caribbean Petroleum Corporation et al.*, Civil no. 09-2092 (FAB).
[41] *Romero-Barceló v. Acevedo-Vilá*, 275 F. Supp. 2d 177 (2003); *In re Pagán Ayala*, 15 P.R. Offic. Trans. 1078, 1080 (1984).
[42] USA Patriot Act of 2001, Pub. L. 107–56, Oct. 26, 2001, 115 Stat 272.

453

7 Search of a Lawyer's Office

23.   The search of a lawyer's office is allowed with proper court subpoenas.

8 Tapping of Telephone Conversations with a Lawyer

24.   The Constitution of Puerto Rico prohibits tapping or recording of conversations without complete consent. Nonetheless, some attorneys have circumvented this prohibition by initiating and recording such conversations from states that allow recording as long as one of the two parties consents. Otherwise, federal law, especially the National Security Act, the Patriot Act and general federal prosecutorial actions, allow for such tapping of conversations regardless of whether they are privileged. But all of these in Puerto Rico require a court-issued subpoena. And many times they are regulated by strict confidentiality and nondisclosure to the general public.

9 The Lawyer as Witness

25.   The Puerto Rico Canons of Professional Ethics also limit severely the attorney's ability to act as a witness. Specifically, Canon 22 establishes that, except when essential to the ends of justice, the lawyer should avoid testifying in court on behalf or in support of a client. When a lawyer is a witness for a client, except as to merely formal matters, such as the attestation or custody of a tangible or intangible good, the lawyer should leave the trial of the case to another counsel. Likewise, a lawyer should withdraw from the representation of a client when the lawyer finds out that the lawyer him- or herself, one of the lawyer's partners or a lawyer in his or her firm may be called to testify against the client.[43]

Canon 22 discourages the participation of an attorney as an evidentiary element in a suit. It seeks to avoid a mix-up between the duty of the attorney and the role of a witness.[44] The same is true in federal proceedings.

10 The Lawyer and the Press

26.   In Puerto Rico, attorneys must refrain from publishing or in any manner facilitating the publication in newspapers, or through other means of divulging information, the details or opinions concerning pending or anticipated criminal cases, or pending or anticipated litigation, since such publications may interfere with an impartial trial and prejudice the due administration of justice.[45]

---

[43] Canon 22, Puerto Rico Canons of Professional Ethics, PR ST T. 4 Ap. IX.

[44] *Ades v. Zalman*, 15 P.R. Offic. Trans. 675 (1984)s.

[45] Canons 13, 14, Puerto Rico Canons of Professional Ethics, PR ST T. 4 Ap. IX.

Under this principle, the Puerto Rico Supreme Court has sanctioned conduct from an attorney who brought outside the court proceedings documents and discussion over a pending case to the press and to a hearing at the Puerto Rico Senate Judiciary Committee.[46]

However, the court has declined to sanction the conduct of an attorney who issued a press release over the matters of a judgment in a case that was final and unappealable. The court expressed that the attorney was only requesting with his action the fulfillment of the judgment issued by a lower court.[47]

To avoid the filtration of information in criminal cases that could prevent an impartial process, the Department of Justice, as representative of the government, should be especially careful when guarding all evidence and information related to a criminal case to ensure that its premature publication doesn't undermine the constitutional guarantees that protect the accused.[48]

If the extreme circumstances of a particular case justify a statement to the public, it is unprofessional to make it anonymously. A unilateral or *ex parte* reference to the facts of a case should not go beyond quotation from the records and papers on file in the courts. But even in extreme cases, it is better to avoid such statements.[49]

In criminal cases, when actual extraordinary circumstances justify statements to the public, such statements should be limited to the records on file in the court, without reference to the evidence they have at their disposal or to the witnesses to be used, nor to the content of their testimonies.[50]

The counsel for the defense, as well as the prosecuting attorney, should avoid, insofar as possible, appearing in photographs for publicity purposes, and it is improper for a lawyer or a prosecuting attorney to appear in photographs in connection with criminal cases in which the lawyer participates or has participated.[51]

11 Powers of the Tax and Other Authorities

27.   The local tax authorities need a court subpoena to inspect a lawyer's records.

12 National Security Issues

28.   All national security issues are handled by the federal government through its designated agencies, especially the National Security Agency, Immigration and Customs Enforcement, Homeland Security, FBI, CIA, U.S. federal prosecutors and the like.

---

[46] *In re Clavell Ruiz*, 131 D.P.R. 500 (1992).
[47] *In re Nogueras Cartagena*, 150 D.P.R. 667 (2000).
[48] *Pueblo v. Rivera Nazario*, 141 D.P.R. 865 (1996).
[49] Canon 14, Puerto Rico Canons of Professional Ethics, PR ST T. 4 Ap. IX.
[50] Ibid., Canon 13.   [51] Ibid.

In Puerto Rico, as in the rest of the United States, there has been a lot of criticism of the undermining of the privileges and secrets discussed above, as well as of the criminal system in general with the surveillance procedures and laws put into effect after the terrorist attacks of September 11, 2001. Some attorneys, scholars and organizations have argued that the U.S. government has intentionally violated the attorney-client privilege in the name of national security.[52]

13 Conclusion

29.   Given Puerto Rico's unique mixed jurisdiction and status as a territory of the United States, issues of privileges or professional secrecy can be quite complex. But complexity in the law is an inviting challenge for all jurists in all jurisdictions.

---

[52] See, for example, Nicolás Niarchos, "Has the NSA Wiretapping Violated the Attorney-Client Privilege?," *The Nation*, Feb. 4, 2014; Marjorie Cohn, "The Evisceration of the Attorney-Client Privilege in the Wake of September 11, 2001," 71 *Fordham Law Review*, at 1233 (2003).

29

Trinidad and Tobago

MARK JAMES MORGAN

Fitzwilliam Stone, Furness – Smith & Morgan

Preliminary Note

1.   This chapter focuses on professional secrecy, or attorney-client privilege in Trinidad and Tobago. Unless otherwise provided for by statute, the system of law observed in Trinidad and Tobago is the English common law and doctrines

of equity.[1] Consequently, decisions of the British Commonwealth courts, though not binding on the Trinidad and Tobago courts, are accorded great respect. In the course of this chapter, reference therefore will be made to Trinidad and Tobago statutes,[2] decisions of the Trinidad and Tobago courts and decisions of the British Commonwealth courts, in particular the English courts.

In Trinidad and Tobago, the criminal and civil law is administered through the Trinidad and Tobago court system. Apart from certain specialized tribunals that deal with industrial relations, tax and environmental matters,[3] the local court system comprises the Magistrates' courts, the High Court and the Court of Appeal. Trinidad and Tobago has retained the Privy Council in London as its final appellate court.

Attorneys-at-law who are the holders of a valid practicing certificate have the right of audience before any court[4] and are members of the Law Association of Trinidad and Tobago.[5] Except for litigants in person (that is, unrepresented parties), other individuals have a right of audience before the courts in only very restricted cases.[6]

There is no distinction between attorneys-at-law in private practice and in-house lawyers, whether in the employment of the state or otherwise, save that law officers (i.e., state attorneys) are exempt from paying certain fees.[7]

1 Scope of and Limitations on the Duty of Professional Secrecy/Attorney-Client Privilege

A Statutory Basis and Implications

2. Schedule 3 of the Legal Profession Act contains rules constituting the Code of Ethics for the professional practice, etiquette, conduct and discipline of attorneys-at-law. By Section 35(2) of that act, a breach of the rules in Part A may constitute a breach of professional conduct, while a breach of the rules in Part B will constitute a breach.

Legal professional privilege is dealt with in both Part A and Part B.

---

[1] Section 12, Supreme Court of Judicature Act Chap. 401.
[2] Trinidad and Tobago statutes can be accessed at www.legalaffairs.gov.tt/Laws_listing.html.
[3] The Industrial Court, Tax Appeal Board and Environmental Commission, respectively.
In addition, the Chief Immigration Officer is empowered under the Immigration Act, Chap. 18:01, to hear and determine certain specified immigration offenses.
[4] Section 21, Legal Profession Act, Chap. 90:03, available at http://rgd.legalaffairs.gov.tt/Laws2/Alphabetical_List/lawspdfs/90.03.pdf.
[5] Section 6, Legal Profession Act.
[6] For example, under Section 57 of the Summary Courts Act, Chap. 4:20, in the magistrates court in the exercise of its criminal jurisdiction, a person may, with leave of the court, assist his or her child, parent, sibling, wife or domestic servant in the conduct of his or her case.
[7] Section 27, Legal Profession Act.

In Part A, Rule 23(2) of the Code of Ethics provides that: "An attorney at law shall scrupulously guard and never divulge his client's secrets and confidences."

More significantly, Rule 15 of Part B provides:

> An Attorney-at-law shall never disclose, unless lawfully ordered to do so by the Court or required by statute, what has been communicated to him in his capacity as an Attorney-at-law by his clients and this duty not to disclose extends to his partners, to junior Attorneys-at-law assisting him and to his employees provided however that an Attorney-at-law may reveal confidences or secrets necessary to establish or collect his fee or to defend himself or his employees or associates against an accusation of wrongful conduct.

In its decision in *Dexter Brown v. Lomas Dass*,[8] the court stated that the High Court is required to be cognizant of those provisions and to monitor compliance as their observance is fundamental to the administration of justice and the protection of litigants, the public and the rule of law, and that it is a fundamental aspect of the attorney-client relationship that attorneys do not disclose their client's confidences.

It is clear from the decided cases that the local courts treat the above statutory provisions as one aspect of the English common law position, and in their decisions refer extensively and adopt the positions of the English courts.

3.   At common law, there are two aspects to legal privilege. The first is privilege from revealing confidential information, which now finds statutory force in the abovementioned prohibitions under the Code of Ethics. The second protects either party from being liable for defamation in respect of such communication should the privileged information be disclosed.[9]

At common law, there are two broad heads of privilege that may be claimed by the attorney-at-law on behalf of the client or by the client itself (and, if not claimed by the client, may still be recognized by the court[10]). The first is legal advice privilege, which covers confidential communications passing between the attorney-at-law and the client. It has been given a very broad and liberal meaning in the English and Commonwealth courts and covers all forms of advice and communications passing between the attorney and the client for the purpose of obtaining legal advice or which falls within the scope of the advice given by the attorney in the course of the attorney's employment. It extends to

---

[8] (Unreported) Case No. Cv 2011–03614, Rajkumar J, at paras. 55–57 ("*Dexter Brown*").

[9] *Regan v. Taylor* [2000] EMLR 549.

[10] Thus, in *Dexter Brown, supra*, the defendant's former attorney gave evidence for the claimant as to certain advice that he had given to the defendant. The court, having noted that this was evidence that was protected by privilege, rejected it and ordered that the Registrar of the High Court refer the attorney to the Disciplinary Committee.

situations where no litigation was contemplated at the time the advice was sought or given.

The second head of privilege is "litigation privilege," this covers a narrower set of circumstances in that it only pertains to communications that are made where litigation is contemplated,[11] pending or in existence, and the contemplated, pending or existing litigation was the dominant purpose for which the communication came into existence. "Dominant purpose" is a matter of fact, and though the litigation need not be the sole purpose of the communication, it is not sufficient to establish that the litigation was one of a number of purposes of equal importance.[12]

B Scope

4. In Trinidad and Tobago, the attorney-client privilege attaches to confidential written or oral communications between a professional legal adviser and the client or any person representing the client, in connection with and in contemplation of, and for the purposes of, legal proceedings or in connection with giving legal advice.[13] Such privilege ensures that the confidential communications made between the client and attorney are inadmissible as evidence, except in clearly defined exceptional circumstances.[14]

Mere communication between the attorney and client will not by itself attract legal professional privilege. The communication between the client and the attorney will fall within the scope of legal professional privilege only if it is directed at obtaining advice or representation in relation to a particular matter or a series of matters that are within the contemplation of the parties.[15]

The principle is that a client should be free to consult with an attorney without fear of such communications being revealed,[16] that the client must be able to consult with a lawyer in confidence and more importantly that the client must be sure that what is communicated to the lawyer in confidence will never be revealed without the client's consent.[17]

Therefore, an attorney who breaches this privilege and does not respect the client's confidences or even the client's alleged confidences must justify any disclosure of them.[18]

The obligation of secrecy being a statutory obligation, an improper disclosure of confidential material is a breach that would make the attorney liable to

---

[11] Meaning whether litigation is reasonably in prospect. *Three Rivers (no. 6)* [2005] 1 AC 610, per Lord Carswell, at para. 83 (*"Three Rivers"*).

[12] *Waugh v. British Railways* [1980] AC 1.

[13] *The State v. Bakhorie* TT 2007 HC 234, Boodoosingh J, at para. 7.   [14] Ibid., para. 8.

[15] Ibid., para. 17.

[16] *The State v. Roland Doorgarden* (unrep.) HC Crim no. 115 of 2001, Volney J at 2.

[17] *Dexter Brown, supra,* at para. 67 (quoting *Three Rivers, supra*).   [18] Ibid., para. 63.

a claim for an injunction to restrain further disclosure.[19] In addition, the attorney may be subject to disciplinary action that could result in sanctions, including, in serious cases, being disbarred.[20] Clearly it would also be a breach of contract.

An attorney's obligation of secrecy is not displaced or lost by reason of the death of the client.[21]

C Persons Subject to the Duty of Professional Secrecy

5. The prohibition in the Code of Ethics applies only to lawyers who have been entered onto the roll of attorneys-at-law and are therefore legally entitled to practice law in Trinidad and Tobago. This includes in-house lawyers.[22]

However, privilege extends only to communications between clients and their lawyers when the latter are acting in their capacity as professional legal advisers. This is generally more important in the case of in-house lawyers, but it can extend to external lawyers as well. Thus, in *Bakhorie*, the court held that communications between an accused and a policeman-lawyer with respect to a homicide allegedly committed by the accused were not privileged simply because the accused had consulted the policeman-lawyer previously for advice on a divorce and custody matter.

In England it has been held that, at common law, the privilege that attaches to communications between a client and a lawyer applies equally to communications with the client's foreign lawyers.[23] Though there was no detailed discussion on this point, in the local decision of *Ferguson and Galbaransingh v. A.G.*,[24] the High Court accepted without question that advice given by an English Queens Counsel to the attorney general on a question of Trinidad and Tobago law was protected by legal professional privilege.

English and Commonwealth courts have refused to extend the privilege beyond lawyers and their staff to personal consultants,[25] accountants giving tax advice,[26] consultants in the construction industry when they are giving advice of a legal nature[27] and union representatives.[28] Similarly, it is thought that

---

[19] In Trinidad and Tobago, the test for the grant of an interlocutory injunction is, assuming that there is a serious issue to be tried, whether, when all relevant circumstances are considered, the balance of justice favors of the grant of the injunction. *East Coast Drilling and Workover Services Ltd v. Petroleum Co. of Trinidad and Tobago Ltd* (2000) 58 WIR 351.

[20] *See* Section 4 of this chapter.   [21] *Bullivant v. A.G. for Victoria* [1901] AC 196 ("*Bullivant*").

[22] *Alfred Crompton Amusement Machines Ltd v. Commissioners of Customs and Excise (No. 2)* [1972] 2 All ER 353.

[23] *International Business Machines Corp. v. Phoenix International (Computers) Ltd.* [1995] 1 All ER 413.

[24] (2011) CV no. 4144 of 2010.   [25] *New Victoria Hospital v. Ryan* [1993] ICR 201.

[26] *Prudential PLC v. Special Commissioner of Income Tax* [2013] UKSC 2010.

[27] *Walter Lilly and Company Ltd v. Mackay* [2012] EWHC 649 (TC).

[28] *Wood v. Commonwealth Bank of Australia* (1996) 67 IR 46.

a litigant in person cannot claim privilege for work done that falls outside the protection of litigation privilege because there is no communication between lawyer and client,[29] and the prevailing view is that the privilege does not extend beyond communications between clients and their lawyers or lawyers' agents. However, where a client in good faith deals with an individual believing the individual to be a lawyer, those communications are privileged notwithstanding that the individual was not in fact a qualified lawyer.[30]

D Exceptions to the Duty of Professional Secrecy

6.   There are many circumstances in which privilege may be lost or frustrated. These include the following: (i) where the communication is a material fact; (ii) material in the public domain or otherwise available; (iii) fraud or illegality; (iv) waiver by the client; and (v) a party having a right to the information.

Where the privileged material constitutes a material fact in the proceedings, it can be disclosed. Thus, for example, in *Conlon v. Conlons Ltd*,[31] privilege was held not to extend to a communication from a client to a solicitor authorizing the solicitor to offer terms of settlement. Similarly, Rule 15 provides that an attorney-at-law may reveal confidences or secrets necessary to establish or collect a fee or to defend the attorney or the attorney's employees or associates against an accusation of wrongful conduct.

Legal professional privilege does not extend to documents that are in the public domain.[32] This is sometimes described as a waiver of privilege, but in *Mohammed v. Ministry of Defence*,[33] it was stated that it was more accurate to say that the privilege could not be claimed because the confidentiality had been lost. Accordingly, if a third party comes into possession of privileged material by any means, and even if without the knowledge or consent of the other party, the receiving party is free to use such material, subject to the equitable jurisdiction of the court to restrain a breach of confidence.[34]

Communications that are in themselves parts of a criminal or unlawful proceeding are not privileged.[35] To bring a case within this limitation, a definite charge of fraud or illegality must be present, and a *prima facie* case must be made out: "there must be something to give color to the charge."[36] However, legal advice on how to stay on the right side of the law[37] or warning against the results of a proposed action[38] remain privileged.

---

[29] *Lydell v. Kennedy* (1883) 27 Ch.D. 1.
[30] *Dadourian Group International Inc & Ors v. Paul Simms & Ors* [2006] EWHC 2973.
[31] [1952] 2 AER 462.   [32] *Goldstone v. Williams* [1899] 1 Ch 47.
[33] [2013] EWHC 4478, at para. 14.   [34] Ibid., para. 14.   [35] *Bullivant, supra*, at 201.
[36] *O'Rourke v. Darbishire* [1920] AC 581, per Viscount Findlay, at 604.
[37] *Bullivant, supra*, at 207.   [38] *Butler v. Board of Trade* [1971] Ch. 680.

What might be called a "true" waiver occurs if one party either expressly consents to the use of privileged material by another party or chooses to disclose the information to the other party in circumstances that imply consent to its use. Such a waiver may be either general or limited in scope.[39] Where a party waives privilege in the above sense by deliberately deploying material in court proceedings, the party also loses the right to assert privilege in relation to other material relating to the same subject matter.[40] Privilege can be waived by the client but not by the lawyer,[41] and the waiver may be express or implied. Waiver may be unintentional; thus, in *Joint Consultation Council for the Construction Industry v. The Minister of Planning and Sustainable Development*,[42] a statement made by a minister in Parliament that advice received from the ministry's legal unit and the attorney general to the effect that a request for proposals with respect to the development of certain state lands was not subject to the Central Tenders Board Act, was sufficient for the court to hold that the privilege had been waived and should be disclosed in accordance with the Freedom of Information Act. However, in England it has been held that a mere reference to a privileged communication will not amount to a waiver.[43]

No privilege can be claimed against a party who has an independent right to the information, for example, partners in a business relationship,[44] a joint client,[45] a company's shareholders[46] or a *cestui que* trust.[47]

E Law Firms

7. Communications between lawyers acting jointly for a client are protected.[48] The practice in Trinidad and Tobago is for lawyers in the same firm to share client information without it being considered to be a breach of the Code of Ethics, and this is implied from the language of the prohibition in Rule 15. It would, however, be otherwise if there was a specific arrangement to the contrary with the client.

F Legal Assistants and Staff

8. Communications to an attorney's assistants or staff are protected at common law on the footing that they are the attorney's agents.[49] It is implied from the

---

[39] *Mohammed v. Ministry of Defence, supra*, at para. 14.   [40] Ibid., para. 14.
[41] *Dexter Brown, supra.*   [42] CV 2012-04538 ("*JCC*").
[43] *Rubin v. Expandable Ltd* [2008] EWCA Civ 59.
[44] *BBGP Managing Partner v. Babcock* [2011] Bus. L.R. 466.   [45] Ibid.
[46] *Re Hydrosan Ltd* [1991] BCLC 418 (save that a company may claim litigation privilege in a dispute with shareholders).
[47] *In re Londonderry's Settlement* [1964] Ch. 594.
[48] *Mostyn v. West Mostyn Coal and Iron Co.* (1876) 34 L.T. 531.
[49] *Wheeler v. Le Marchant* (1881) 17 Ch. D. 675.

language of the prohibition in Rule 15 that a proper communication of confidential information by an attorney to legal assistants and staff for the purpose of carrying out the client's business would not be considered to be a breach of the Code of Ethics. Again it would, however, be otherwise if there was a specific arrangement to the contrary with the client.

G External Service Providers

9. A lawyer may engage a third party to provide information and, depending on the circumstances, such information may attract legal advice or litigation privilege. Thus, in *Wheeler v. Le Marchant*,[50] a report from surveyors that was delivered directly to the client's lawyers attracted privilege.

H Multidisciplinary Associations

10. Rule 9, Part A, of the Code of Ethics prohibits a lawyer from entering into a partnership or fee-sharing arrangement concerning the practice of law with non-qualified bodies.

I In-House Counsel

11. In-house lawyers enjoy the same privilege as external lawyers, but only when they are acting in their capacity as professional legal advisers[51] and not otherwise. Thus, in *JCC*, the High Court held that in-house advice given to the Minister by the Office of the Attorney General was privileged.

2 History of the Duty of Professional Secrecy in Trinidad and Tobago

12. Attorney-client privilege is not a new concept; it has existed in English law for more than 400 years. The House of Lords' survey on the development of the principle in *R. v. Derby Magistrates Court Ex. P. B.*[52] refers to decisions in 1577 and 1579 establishing the existence of litigation privilege and then to the decision of *Greenough v. Gaskell* in 1833,[53] which extended the principle to legal advice privilege. As set out above,[54] as a common law principle, this principle of attorney-client privilege is incorporated into the laws of Trinidad and Tobago by Section 12 of the *Supreme Court of Judicature*, and the Trinidad and Tobago courts rely heavily on the English decisions for guidance in this respect.[55]

---

[50] Ibid.

[51] *Alfred Crompton Amusement Machines Ltd v. Commissioners of Customs and Excise (No. 2)* [1972] 2 All ER 353.

[52] [1996] AC 487.   [53] (1833) 1 M & K 98.   [54] *See* note 1.

[55] For example, in *Dexter Brown, supra*, the court quoted extensively from the judgment in *Three Rivers, supra*, in coming to its decision.

3 Supervision

13.   A breach of the Code of Ethics can result in the attorney being referred to the Disciplinary Committee of the Law Association either by the client or the court, as was done in *Dexter Brown*, and in serious cases suspension and removal from the roll by the courts.[56]

4 Sanctions

14.   Under Section 37 of the Legal Profession Act, complaints can be made to the Disciplinary Committee by the client, the Registrar of the High Court on instructions from the court, or any other person alleging an act of professional misconduct by an attorney-at-law (other than the attorney general or a law officer). Under Section 39, on the hearing of the application, the Disciplinary Committee may impose a fine on the attorney, reprimand the attorney, order the attorney to pay costs or compensation, and in cases where it considers that a more severe sanction should be imposed, forward a copy of the proceedings and its findings to the chief justice and the attorney general.

Under Section 41 of the Legal Profession Act, the High Court sitting as a full court of three judges may suspend an attorney-at-law from practice or disbar an attorney by removing the attorney's name from the roll of attorneys entitled to practice as attorneys-at-law, in addition to ordering costs against an attorney and such further or other order as the circumstances of the case require.

Breach of privilege is not an offence. However, a lawyer who communicates a confidential communication to others without the client's authorization could be sued by the client for damages. A third party who had accidentally seen the contents of a lawyer's file could be prohibited by injunction from disclosing them.[57]

5 Duty to Provide Information to the Authorities: Money Laundering and Terrorism

15.   Under Trinidad's money-laundering and anti-terrorism legislation, an attorney-at-law who is engaged in a listed business (buying and selling of real estate property; managing of client money, securities and other assets; management of banking, savings or securities accounts; organization of contributions for the creation, operation or management of companies, legal persons or arrangements; and the buying or selling of business entities)[58] is required to report that funds being used for the purpose of a transaction are the proceeds of a crime or a transaction or an attempted transaction; is related to the commission or

---

[56] *See* Section 4 of this chapter.   [57] *Carter v. Northmore Hale Davy & Leake* (1995) 183 CLR
[58] First Schedule of the Proceeds of Crime Act, Chap. 11:27.

attempted commission of a money laundering offence; or that funds are linked or related to, or to be used for, terrorism, terrorist acts or by terrorist organizations or those who finance terrorism.[59] However, it is not an offence for a professional legal adviser to fail to disclose any information or other matter that has come to the adviser in privileged circumstances.[60] Further reporting requirements for listed businesses are stipulated in regulation 8 of the Financial Obligations Regulations 2010.[61] However, regulation 9 provides that regulation 8 does not apply where a listed business is a legal professional adviser and the knowledge or suspicion is based on advice or information or other maters that came to the legal adviser in privileged circumstances. These privileged circumstances include those communicated or given to a legal adviser (a) by the client or a representative of the client, in connection with the provision of legal advice, (b) by another person or representative seeking legal advice from the adviser, or (c) in connection with legal proceedings or contemplated legal proceedings, that is, in the traditional circumstances where legal advice and litigation privilege exist.

6 Treatment of a Lawyer's Documents and Correspondence in the Context of Judicial Investigations

16.   A lawyer's privileged documents and correspondence will be respected by the courts.

7 Search of a Lawyer's Office

17.   In Trinidad and Tobago, the police authorities must respect attorney-client privilege.[62] This common law position is specifically enacted in some statutes, for example, Section 33(5) of the Proceeds of Crime Act.

8 Tapping of a Telephone Conversation with a Lawyer

18.   Section 6 of the Interception of Communication Act (Chap. 15:08) prohibits the interception of communications across a telecommunications network without a warrant. Though legal professional privilege is not specifically mentioned, on the basis of the common law position, privileged communications will be respected.

---

[59] This summary is taken from the Financial Intelligence Unit's Guidance for Attorneys-at-Law, available at: www.fiu.gov.tt/content/AML%20CFT%20Guidance%20for%20Attorneys%20at %20Law.pdf.

[60] Section 52, Proceeds of Crime Act.

[61] Available at: www.fiu.gov.tt/content/The%20Financial%20Obligation%20Regulations%20-% 202010.pdf.

[62] *A.G. v. Northern Construction Ltd.* TT 2009 CA 8.

9 The Lawyer as a Witness

19.   An attorney-at-law can be called to testify in court as a witness but must respect attorney-client privilege in the course of testifying.[63]

10 The Lawyer and the Press

20.   Lawyers are not prohibited from speaking to the press on client matters, but they must remain within the limits of their client's authority and the dignified and courteous conduct required of a lawyer by the Code of Ethics.

11 Powers of the Tax Administration

21.   The tax authorities in Trinidad and Tobago must respect legal professional privilege.

12 National Security Issues

22.   In Trinidad and Tobago, issues of national security do not provide an exception to legal professional privilege.

13 Freedom of Information Act

23.   Under Section 29(1) of this act, a document is an exempt document and is therefore not subject to disclosure if it is of such a nature that it would be privileged from production in legal proceedings on the ground of legal professional privilege.

---

[63] *Rajcoomar v. McNicholls* TT 2006 HC 107.

30

United States

GERRY SILVER

Sullivan & Worcester LLP

Preliminary Note

1.   In the United States, the legal protection afforded to communications between
       lawyers and their clients is known as the attorney-client privilege. The attorney-
       client privilege protects communications between attorney and client for the
       purpose of giving or receiving legal advice. These communications are gen-
       erally covered by an absolute privilege, whether or not litigation is contem-
       plated or in progress.

       The attorney-client privilege is the oldest privilege for confidential commu-
       nications recognized by the common law. The privilege is intended to encou-
       rage full and frank communication between attorneys and their clients and
       protects not only the provision of legal advice but also the giving of information
       to the lawyer to enable the lawyer to give sound and informed advice.
       Recognizing that reliable legal advice and effective advocacy depend on the
       lawyer being fully informed by the client, the attorney-client privilege provides
       clients with the confidence to share with their attorney all information relevant
       to the representation.

       Legal protection is also afforded under the attorney work product doctrine.
       The attorney work product doctrine protects documents and communications
       prepared by a lawyer, as well as communications between a lawyer (or client)
       and a third party, provided that they are prepared in anticipation of litigation.
       In contrast to the attorney-client privilege, the work product doctrine protects
       attorneys' mental impressions, conclusions, opinions or legal theories created
       in anticipation of litigation. The work product doctrine is rooted in the under-
       standing that proper client representation requires that a lawyer work with
       a certain degree of privacy, free from unnecessary intrusion by opposing parties
       and their counsel.

1 Scope of and Limitations on the Duty of Professional Secrecy/Attorney-Client Privilege

A Statutory Basis and Implications

2.   A lawyer's duty of client confidentiality has historical roots in the common law.
       It remains a common law duty, but today it is also codified in the rules of
       professional conduct of every jurisdiction in the United States, in essentially
       the same form as in the ABA Model Rules of Professional Conduct ("Model
       Rules").[1] The duty of confidentiality protects all information relating to the
       representation, even if that information has been otherwise disclosed in public
       documents. The Model Rules provide narrow exceptions that permit, but do not

---

[1] *See* ABA Model Rules of Professional Conduct (2016), available at www.americanbar.org
/groups/professional_responsibility/publications/model_rules_of_professional_conduct/mod
el_rules_of_professional_conduct_table_of_contents.html.

require, lawyer disclosure of confidential client information. Such exceptions include, but are not limited to, when the lawyer reasonably believes disclosure is necessary to prevent reasonably certain death or serious bodily harm, to prevent the client from committing a crime or fraud that is reasonably certain to result in substantial financial injury to another and for which the client has used or is using the lawyer's services, to consult with another lawyer about the lawyer's compliance with the Model Rules, and to comply with another law or a court order.[2] Courts often rely on and utilize case law precedents in interpreting the Model Rules and state statutes.

While there may be subtle variations from state to state, such as with regard to the duty of disclosure for certain particular crimes or fraud, and attorneys are advised to check the law of the applicable state, the attorney-client privilege and work product laws are generally similar across the 50 states.

B Scope

3. Most U.S. evidentiary and discovery rules are aimed at enhancing the fact-finding process for the purpose of leading to the discovery and determination of the truth based on reliable evidence at trial. The attorney-client privilege, however, is intended to foster full and frank communication and uninhibited dialogue between attorney and client, without fear of subsequent disclosure. This exchange between attorney and client is viewed as necessary for effective representation. Because there is tension between the United States' truth-finding process and the attorney-client privilege, the burden of establishing the attorney-client privilege is on the party asserting it. Courts will therefore narrowly construe the attorney-client privilege.

Generally, the attorney-client privilege allows a client, or potential client, to refuse to disclose, and to object to the disclosure by others of, a confidential communication made by the client or client's representative to or from a lawyer (or lawyer's representative) who is acting with respect to a legal matter for the purposes of rendering professional legal services to the client. The privilege belongs to the client, not the lawyer, and can be claimed or waived only by the client.

In particular, the attorney-client privilege "applies to communications from the client to the attorney when the communication is 'made for the purpose of obtaining legal advice and directed to an attorney who has been consulted for that purpose.'"[3] "By analogy, for the privilege to apply when communications are made from attorney to client – whether or not in response to a particular

---

[2] *See* Model Rules R. 1.6(b) (2015).

[3] *The People of the State of New York v. Greenberg*, 50 A.D.3d 195, 200, 851 N.Y.S.2d 196, 200 (1st Dep't 2008) (quoting *Rossi v. Blue Cross & Blue Shield of Greater New York*, 73 N.Y.2d 588, 593, 542 N.Y.S.2d 508, 511 (1989)).

request – they must be made for the purpose of facilitating the rendition of legal advice or services, in the course of a professional relationship."[4]

> As is plain from a mere statement of the principles, whether a particular document [or communication] is or is not protected is necessarily a fact-specific determination. ... The critical inquiry is whether, viewing the lawyer's communication in its full content and context, it was made in order to render legal advice or services to the client.[5]

It is irrelevant for purposes of determining whether the privilege applies whether the attorney was paid a fee.[6] Moreover, "[s]o long as the communication is primarily or predominantly of a legal character, the privilege is not lost merely by reason of the fact that it also refers to certain nonlegal matters. ... Indeed, the nature of a lawyer's role is such that legal advice may often include reference to other relevant considerations."[7] Further, "[i]t is not unusual for attorneys and their clients to be friends. The mere fact that an attorney is a friend, even a close friend, does not mean that he ceases to act as an attorney in providing assistance to the client."[8]

Moreover, "[c]ommunications from an attorney to a client dealing with the substance of imminent litigation generally will fall into the area of legal rather than business or personal matters."[9] The attorney-client privilege applies when an attorney is "exercising a lawyer's traditional function in counseling his client regarding conduct that had already brought it to the brink of litigation," and "any content that reveals the motive of the client in seeking representation, litigation strategy, or the specific nature of the services provided, such as research particular areas of law, fall[s] within the privilege."[10]

The attorney work product doctrine protects from disclosure those materials prepared by an attorney or the attorney's representatives that contain mental impressions, conclusions, opinions or legal theories. The burden of establishing the work product privilege rests on the party asserting it. Work product consists

---

[4] *Rossi*, 73 N.Y.2d at 593, 542 N.Y.S.2d at 511; *Spectrum Systems International Corporation v. Chemical Bank*, 78 N.Y.2d 371, 377, 575 N.Y.S.2d 809, 814 (1991) ("[a]lthough typically arising in the context of a client's communication to an attorney, the privilege extends as well to communications from attorney to client").

[5] *Spectrum*, 78 N.Y.2d at 379, 575 N.Y.S.2d at 815; *The People of the State of New York v. O'Conner*, 85 A.D.2d 92, 95, 447 N.Y.S.2d 553, 556 (4th Dep't 1982) ("whether the relationship exists or not is determined by the client's purpose in contacting the attorney").

[6] *O'Conner*, 85 A.D.2d at 95; 447 N.Y.S.2d at 556 (internal citations omitted) ("the relationship is not established because one pays a legal fee or lost because the client does not pay a fee").

[7] *Rossi*, 73 N.Y.2d at 594, 593, 542 N.Y.S.2d at 511.

[8] *United States v. Burnett*, 1996 WL 1057161, *7 (E.D.N.Y. March 11, 1996).

[9] *Rossi*, 73 N.Y.2d at 594, 542 N.Y.S.2d at 511.

[10] *Newmarkets Partners, LLC v. Sal. Oppenheim Jr. & Cie*, S.C.A., 258 F.R.D. 95, 101 (S.D.N.Y. 2009) (internal quotation omitted).

471

of interviews, statements, memoranda, correspondence, briefs and reports about pending litigation or litigation about to commence. It also includes an attorney's dealings with expert witnesses, including observations and information disclosed by the attorney to the witness.

The work product doctrine is narrowly construed and is limited to material prepared by an attorney relating to legal analysis and strategy and does not pertain to items such as bills, names and addresses of witnesses, or other non-legal information. An attorney's observations of a client's demeanor, physical characteristics and mental capacity may not be protected because a non-lawyer can make these observations. Reports relating to the routine operation of a business, or related to drafting corporate agreements, are generally not viewed as being prepared in anticipation of litigation, although they may still be covered by the attorney-client privilege. The attorney work product doctrine, unlike the attorney-client privilege, is qualified, meaning that if the adverse party can show substantial need and undue hardship in obtaining the substantial equivalent of the information by other means, a court may order disclosure. However, courts construe this exception extremely narrowly.

C Persons Subject to the Duty of Professional Secrecy

4. The attorney-client privilege applies to communications with a lawyer or the attorney's direct employees or representatives, regardless of whether the lawyer is external, such as with an outside firm, or is in-house counsel at a corporation. The attorney-client privilege applies not only to communications with officers or executives of a corporation but also to low- and mid-level employees. The lawyer should exercise reasonable care to prevent the lawyer's employees, and others whose services are used by the lawyer, from disclosing confidential information (except as permitted under the rule).

Generally, U.S. courts have found communications with foreign in-house counsel providing legal advice on U.S. matters to be privileged only when presented with proof of the existence of a specific legal privilege governing in-house counsel under the law of the applicable foreign jurisdiction. The absence of such proof has led to the rejection of claims of attorney-client privilege with regard to foreign in-house lawyers in numerous countries, including France, India, the Netherlands, China and Russia. To help ensure that a communication with foreign in-house counsel will be protected by the attorney-client privilege during U.S. litigation, the communication should include at least one attorney who is unequivocally within the privilege, particularly U.S. counsel. The presence of foreign external or outside counsel may help preserve the privilege as well, so long as the communications would be privileged under applicable foreign law.

D Exceptions to and Optional Derogations from the Duty of Professional Secrecy

5.   Rule 1.6 of the Model Rules provides that a lawyer shall not knowingly reveal confidential information of a client. Nor may the attorney use such information to the disadvantage of a client or for the advantage of a lawyer. However, there are numerous exceptions to the attorney's duties of secrecy. These include where the client gives informed consent or where the disclosure is implicitly authorized to advance the best interest of the client and is reasonable under the circumstances. Other exceptions are where the disclosure is necessary to prevent reasonably certain death or substantial bodily harm, to prevent the client from committing a crime, to withdraw a prior opinion or representation previously given, to secure legal advice about compliance with the rules of professional conduct, to defend the lawyer against accusations of wrongful conduct, or to establish or collect a fee.[11]

The crime-fraud exception "assure[s] that the seal of secrecy ... between a lawyer and client does not extend to communications made for the purpose of getting advice for the commission of a fraud or crime."[12] An adverse party seeking to overcome the attorney-client privilege through the crime-fraud exception must introduce *prima facie* evidence that (1) the client was committing or intending to commit a fraud or crime, and (2) the attorney-client communications were in furtherance of the alleged fraud or crime. For the crime-fraud exception to apply, the attorney is not required to possess knowledge of the alleged criminal or fraudulent scheme. All that is necessary is that the client misuse, or intend to misuse, the attorney's advice in furtherance of a crime. It is the client's intent that is relevant, not the intent of the attorney. If the attorney is unaware of the client's illegal activity, the work product doctrine may still apply.

6.   The privilege may be waived as a result of various events or circumstances. The privilege may be waived if confidentiality is breached. For example, the unnecessary presence of third parties or voluntary disclosure of attorney-client communications to a third party may waive the privilege. Once the privilege is waived in one context or legal proceeding, it is deemed waived in other contexts or legal proceedings. Courts do not allow a party to treat communications in an inconsistent manner.

Further, a client's testimony that the client acted in reliance on the advice of counsel may place counsel's advice in issue and may waive the attorney-client privilege. Courts prohibit the use of the attorney-client privilege as both a sword and a shield and seek to prevent the inherent unfairness that arises from selective or partial disclosure of selected communications solely for self-serving purposes, while retaining privileged status for related damaging

---

[11] *See* Model Rule 1.6.
[12] *United Sates v. Zolin*, 491 U.S. 554, 563, 109 S. Ct. 2619, 2626 (1989).

communications. For example, when a client brings civil proceedings against his or her lawyer, alleging negligence or malpractice, the client implicitly waives the attorney-client privilege with respect to all matters relevant to the client's claim and any defenses the lawyer may have. However, merely disclosing that there was consultation between attorney and client on a general subject does not waive the attorney-client privilege.

Nevertheless, if an attorney or client realizes that he or she inadvertently disclosed to an adversary privileged documents or communications, he or she can avoid waiver and successfully assert the privilege if he or she proves: (1) the disclosure was inadvertent or unintentional, (2) an intent to keep the document or communication confidential, (3) that the disclosure occurred despite the existence of reasonable precautions to prevent disclosure, (4) a prompt objection to the use of the document or communication was made and (5) reinstating the privilege will not prejudice the adverse party.

7. The United States has also adopted the joint defense privilege, sometimes referred to as the common interest privilege. It is an exception to the general rule that confidentiality is breached when communicating with a third party or the third party's counsel. In particular, when parties who are represented by separate counsel engage in a joint defense or common interest, communications made and documents exchanged remain privileged and protected from disclosure. However, the mere existence of a common interest is not sufficient. The parties must actively decide and agree to cooperate toward a common legal goal. A written joint defense agreement is recommended, even if done through an informal email exchange.

Like the attorney-client privilege, the attorney work product doctrine can be waived by express consent, or implicitly by production of documents to third parties. Unlike the attorney-client privilege, waiver is limited to the specific document turned over and is not a blanket waiver over all related documents. Work product protection, however, is not absolute. To the extent an attorney's work product contains relevant and non-privileged facts, it is discoverable upon a showing of substantial need for the information and an inability to obtain the substantial equivalent without undue hardship. However, work product composed of an attorney's opinions, mental impressions and legal theories is typically undiscoverable.

E Law Firms

8. Lawyers who work in law firms often share privileged information. It is generally accepted that no restrictions apply to sharing information in this way. When a client engages the services of a law firm, all the lawyers of the firm are deemed engaged, so the privilege applies to all lawyers of the firm, whether they are partners, of counsel or associates.

F Legal Assistants and Staff

9. Communications with non-attorney employees or other support staff of a lawyer or law firm, including secretaries, paralegals, interns or summer associates acting under the direction of a lawyer are privileged.[13]

G External Service Providers

10. The attorney-client privilege and work product doctrine apply if a law firm uses outside independent contractors, such as document copy services to copy privileged communications.[14] "[A]ttorneys often must rely on the assistance of investigators and other agents in the compilation of materials in preparation for trial. It is therefore necessary that the doctrine protect material prepared by agents for the attorney as well as those prepared by the attorney himself."[15]

H Multidisciplinary Associations

11. Under Model Rule 5.8, multidisciplinary associations between lawyers and non-lawyers are incompatible with the core values of the legal profession, and therefore a strict division between services provided by lawyers and those provided by non-lawyers is essential to protect those values. Thus, in the United States, lawyers will instead have a contractual relationship with a non-legal professional service firm. The attorney-client privilege with respect to such non-legal professional service firm applies as set forth above with regard to external service providers.

I In-House Counsel

12. As noted in Section 1(C) of this chapter, communications with in-house counsel are protected under the attorney-client privilege.

2 History of the Duty of Professional Secrecy in the United States

13. The attorney-client privilege is the oldest common law privilege for confidential communications, dating to 16th-century England. It is a privilege the underlying purpose of which is to enable persons to seek and retain lawyers to provide candid legal advice through unfettered communication between lawyer and client without fear that those communications will be disclosed to others. The availability of the privilege is considered indispensable to effective

---

[13] *See generally,* Jack B. Weinstein and Margaret A. Berger, *Weinstein's Federal Evidence* § 503.07[1], at 503–26 (2d ed. 1997) (attorney-client privilege protects communications made to attorney's staff, consultants and other agents employed in rendering services).

[14] *Compulit v. Bantech, Inc.,* 177 F.R.D. 410, 412 (W.D. Mich. 1997).

[15] *United States v. Nobles,* 422 U.S. 225, 238–39 (1975).

lawyer advocacy on behalf of clients in every representation, both before tribunals and elsewhere. In a landmark case regarding attorney-client privilege, the Supreme Court noted, "full and frank communication between attorneys and their clients" also "promote[s] broader public interests in the observance of law and administration of justice."[16]

3 Supervision

A The Bar Associations

14. The governing entity enforcing disciplinary rules varies from state to state. In certain states, power has been bestowed upon mandatory bar associations. In others, the state bar or disciplinary board enforces disciplinary rules. A court also has the power to enforce disciplinary rules for violations occurring before it. The violation of an ethical rule does not, per se, give rise to a cause of action by a client. The governing entity will determine what penalty, if any, to impose if it finds an ethical rule has been violated.

B The Courts

15. The civil courts have jurisdiction to hear any claim for professional liability brought against a lawyer by a client (unless there is an agreement to arbitrate). Civil courts in the United States have jurisdiction to hear any claims for professional liability, such as negligence or malpractice, brought against a lawyer by a client. Criminal courts have jurisdiction over crimes committed by lawyers in the exercise of their profession.

4 Sanctions

A Proceedings and Sanctions

16. The state bar associations and disciplinary committees may issue sanctions, including fines and disbarment.

B Relationship between Criminal Sanctions and Disciplinary Sanctions

17. Generally, disciplinary sanctions are imposed, unless the attorney has also committed a crime, which is in the jurisdiction of law enforcement, as opposed to the state bar associations or disciplinary committees.

The form and severity of sanctions depends on a number of factors, such as the materiality of the offense, the harm imposed, and whether the attorney is a repeat offender. Sanctions may take the form of fines, restitution,

---

[16] *Upjohn Co. v. United States*, 449 U.S. 383, 389 (1981).

requirements that the attorney take continuing legal education courses, reprimands, admonitions, probation, suspensions and even disbarment.

5 Duty to Provide Information to the Authorities

A Money Laundering and Terrorism

18. As set forth above, a lawyer may disclose client confidences when necessary to prevent reasonably certain death or serious bodily harm and to prevent the client from committing a crime or fraud that is reasonably certain to result in substantial financial injury to another and for which the client has used or is using the lawyer's services. To the extent federal statutes require disclosure of potential money laundering or terrorism, the best course may be for the attorney to exercise the attorney's right to disclose.

B Collective Settlement of Debts

19. An attorney's action to recover a fee owed from the client may permit the attorney to reveal client confidences, but the attorney should attempt to do so narrowly and consider filing documents under seal to protect unnecessary disclosure to third parties.

6 Treatment of a Lawyer's Documents and Correspondence in the Context of Judicial or Police Investigations

20. Unless an exception applies, the attorney-client privilege and attorney work product doctrine apply even in the context of government or law enforcement investigations. However, there may be certain benefits for a client to cooperate by waiving the attorney-client privilege in government investigations, such as to discourage or reduce charges or obtain potential leniency. However, waiver of the attorney-client privilege in a government investigation will most often constitute a waiver in subsequent litigation involving third parties with respect to the events at issue in the government investigation. Accordingly, in sharing documents or communications with the government, the attorney and client may consider attempting to limit such disclosure to factual documents, as opposed to documents containing legal advice, requests for legal advice or attorney work product.

7 Search of a Lawyer's Office

21. The Fourth Amendment of the U.S. Constitution protects against warrantless search and seizure. Law enforcement may be able to search an attorney's office if a warrant is obtained, but the attorney should insist on care being taken to

avoid discovery and disclosure of attorney-client communications and attorney work product, as well as that the search be narrow and that it comply strictly with the warrant. Law enforcement is often required to use "minimization procedures," such as avoiding review of materials clearly covered by the attorney-client privilege or work product doctrine or using a "clean" team of investigators not associated with the investigation for which the search is being conducted to first review for privileged communications. Unless an exception applies, attorney-client communications and attorney work product uncovered in the search would not be admissible at trial.

8 Tapping of Telephone Conversations with a Lawyer

22.   The U.S. Supreme Court has held that the Fourth Amendment protection applies to all conversations with a "reasonable expectation of privacy." This includes phone calls, thereby setting forth the rule that wiretapping for a criminal investigation without a warrant violates the U.S. Constitution.

    Significantly, Title III of the Omnibus Crime Control Act of 1968 (the "Wiretap Act")[17] and the Foreign Intelligence Surveillance Act (FISA) provide protection for communications covered by the attorney-client privilege. While law enforcement may monitor communications that could be covered by the attorney-client privilege or work product doctrine, law enforcement bodies attempt to honor legal privileges such as attorney-client communications through "minimization procedures." Minimization procedures include refraining from monitoring conversations clearly covered by the attorney-client privilege or work product doctrine. The minimization procedures do not necessarily prohibit the government's acquisition of privileged communications, but they may prevent such communications from being introduced in court as evidence. If the government fails to insulate, seal and protect privileged communications between a client and the client's attorneys, not only may the privileged communications be suppressed but also the evidence derived from the wiretap.

9 The Lawyer as Witness

23.   An attorney may be called to testify in court as a witness. However, the lawyer is not permitted to disclose the confidences of the client or matters protected by the attorney-client privilege (unless an exception applies). The lawyer may be required to testify as to whether the lawyer has a document in his or her possession, or the date or time the attorney conferred with the client, but the lawyer may not reveal attorney-client privileged communications, unless the client consents or an exception applies.

---

[17] 18 U.S.C. § 2510.

However, a lawyer who is testifying as a witness or likely to be a witness may not continue to represent the client unless the matter relates to an uncontested issue or a matter of formality, the testimony relates solely to the nature and value of legal services rendered, the disqualification of the lawyer would convey a substantial hardship on the client, or a court orders otherwise. Further, a lawyer may not act as an advocate if another lawyer from the firm will be testifying in a manner prejudicial to the client.

10 The Lawyer and the Press

24. Attorneys are permitted to discuss matters with the press, but as a practical matter they should obtain client consent before doing so. Lawyers should be careful not to disclose client confidences or attorney-client communications in discussions with the press. Civil lawyers are permitted to discuss generally their legal standpoint on a given issue.

Under Model Rule 3.6, a lawyer who is participating in a civil or criminal matter shall not make any public statement that has a substantial likelihood of materially prejudicing the adjudication of the proceeding. Such statements include those relating to the character, credibility, reputation or criminal record of a party or a witness, as well as information that the attorney knows would be inadmissible at trial. Lawyers in criminal proceedings must be particularly careful not to give any opinion as to guilt or innocence of a defendant or suspect and should consult Model Rule 3.6 for numerous other restrictions and regulations.

11 Powers of the Tax and Other Authorities

25. Unless an exception applies, the attorney-client privilege and work product doctrine apply to investigations by the tax administrations and other similar authorities.

12 National Security Issues

26. The U.S. National Security Agency has expressed the agency's commitment to attorney-client privilege, stating that it has afforded and will continue to afford appropriate protection to privileged attorney-client communications acquired during lawful intelligence missions, in accordance with U.S. law.[18] However, it remains unclear how often privileged information is collected or reviewed in investigations or matters pertaining to national security. In cases where national security may be implicated, attorneys may take special precautions to protect client confidences, such as face-to-face meetings with witnesses and clients.

[18] *See* NSA letter to James R. Silkenat, President of the American Bar Association, March 10, 2014, available at: www.americanbar.org/content/dam/aba/images/abanews/nsa_re sponse_03102014.pdf.

31

Uruguay

SANTIAGO GATICA
JOSÉ JUAN GARI
JUAN BONET
SANTIAGO MURGUÍA
DANIEL MOSCO
CAMILA UMPIÉRREZ

Guyer & Regules

entitled to invoke attorney-client privilege when they are under criminal investigation for concealment of their client, criminal partnership with the client, obstruction of justice or deception toward the court.[5]

4. In the case of attorneys who work as public officers, the duty of professional secrecy conflicts with the anticorruption legislation, which imposes the duty to report the irregularities and crimes committed by their superiors in the office where they work. In this case, attorney-client privilege cannot be invoked to avoid reporting corruption, as the public office cannot be considered a client in the same way as in private practice.[6]

    In the case of attorneys who also act as representatives or figureheads of their client, or as directors of a company, the declarations made or information given in the context of such activities shall not be covered by the attorney-client privilege.

    In the case of notaries at law, the duty of professional secrecy covers the declarations made and information given by the client prior to, during and after the execution of a notarized document.[7]

5. Finally, professional secrecy must also be respected after the professional relationship between the attorney and the client has concluded. This duty must be respected even after the death of the client, unless there are no heirs or the heirs have no interest in the maintenance of the secrecy, as no prejudice can be caused in these cases.[8]

C Persons Subject to the Duty of Professional Secrecy

6. The term "client" covers not only those who resort to a permanent professional assistance but also any individual or legal entity who requires a professional service (even accidentally), including those who merely exchange general information of a confidential nature with the attorney in the context of a preliminary consultation.[9]

    The term "attorney" covers lawyers who have graduated from a certified university and who have sworn before the Supreme Court of Justice. The same requirements must be met by notaries at law.

    Professional secrecy must be enforced against any public authority and cannot be waived against the decision of the attorney, as recognized by scholars and the Code of Ethics of the Uruguayan Bar Association (Art. 3.9.3).

D Exceptions to and Optional Derogations from the Duty of Professional Secrecy

7. In accordance with Article 302 of the Criminal Code, professional secrecy is not applicable when a valid "justified cause" for disclosure exists.

---

[5] R. Cervini and G. Adriasola, *supra*, at 176.   [6] Ibid., at 162.
[7] J. F. Delgado de Miguel, *supra*, at 37.   [8] F. Bayardo Bengoa, *supra*, at 340.
[9] R. Cervini and G. Adriasola, *supra*, at 155.

Regarding professional secrecy in general, a justified cause for disclosure exists when: (i) the interested party freely grants consent; (ii) a real state of need exists and the disclosure is required to avoid a greater wrong; (iii) the disclosure is needed to defend or protect a legitimate right of the professional (e.g., protection against an unfair offense or the danger of severe, actual damage against the professional); or (iv) a legal provision obliges the professional to disclose certain information.[10]

Regarding attorney-client privilege in particular, lawyers are exempted from respecting the privilege when: (i) a conflict exists between the lawyer and the client, in which case the lawyer may disclose only the information necessary to his or her own defense; (ii) a client communicates his or her intention of committing a crime, in which case the lawyer may make the necessary disclosures to prevent the crime and protect other endangered persons; (iii) the client has waived the privilege; or (iv) the disclosure prevents the conviction of an innocent party or unfair damages to the community.[11] Article 3.9.4 of the Code of Ethics adopted by the Uruguayan Bar Association provides the same exceptions to attorney-client privilege as stated in (i) and (ii) of the preceding paragraph.

For example, scholars understand that attorneys may disclose privileged information to seek payment of their professional fees. Attorneys may not be denied their right to be compensated for their services, so if this right depends on the disclosure of privileged information, then it is understood that such disclosure is legal.[12]

If the declarations or information covered by the privilege relates to more than one client, the consent for its disclosure must be granted by all of them. If all of the clients involved do not grant their consent, then the attorney is not entitled to disclose the privileged information.

In addition, even when a client waives the privilege regarding certain information, the attorney will not be obliged to proceed with its disclosure, unless judicially requested. In this sense, the attorney may still have a valid reason not to disclose the information, such as the protection of the attorney's reputation or the avoidance of a harmful disclosure.

The party entitled to determine whether a declaration or information is covered by professional secrecy, or whether a valid justified cause for disclosure exists, is the professional him- or herself, in accordance with the professional's own ethical principles.[13] If the decision of the professional to disclose or not to disclose is judicially reviewed, then the standard under

---

[10] F. Bayardo Bengoa, *supra*, at 333–40.

[11] G. Ordoqui Castilla, *Responsabilidad Civil del Abogado y del Escribano*, 2007, at 165.

[12] F. Bayardo Bengoa, *supra*, at 338.

[13] B. Puga, "La Ética Profesional. Relaciones del Abogado con su cliente. El Secreto Profesional," *Revista Técnico Forense*, 1991, at 61.

which it is reviewed is whether the professional made an "honestly possible judgment."[14]

E Law Firms

8. Regarding the collective exercise of the legal profession, the information provided to one member of a law firm can be distributed among the rest of the attorneys involved in the rendering of the advice. Therefore, the duty of professional secrecy is extended to all of the members of the firm, whether associates or partners.[15]

    However, in case of mere cost-sharing structures, the duty of professional secrecy covers only the information provided to the attorney representing the client, as the legal profession is not exercised collectively.

    The offices and domiciles of legal professionals are inviolable, and any documents or communications with clients found therein cannot be seized.

F Legal Assistants and Staff

9. Although professional secrecy relating to legal assistants and staff is not specifically regulated in Uruguay, it is considered that the information shared with paralegals, secretaries and other staff is in principle covered by professional secrecy, if such information was obtained by virtue of their employment.

G External Service Providers

10. When services are outsourced by an attorney or a law firm (e.g., translations), professional secrecy is extended to those external service providers for the information provided by virtue of their professional employment, even when they are not attorneys.

H Multidisciplinary Associations

11. Multidisciplinary associations are not specifically regulated in Uruguay, but attorneys can form a professional association with non-lawyers, in which case the information provided to the non-lawyers by virtue of their profession will still be covered by professional secrecy.

I In-House Counsel

12. In the case of attorneys who work as in-house counsel, it can be understood that the duty of professional secrecy covers the declarations made or information given or made available by virtue of their employment.

---

[14] F. Bayardo Bengoa, *supra*, at 337; 2nd Criminal Court of Appeals, Feb. 11, 2010, Decision no. 16/2010.

[15] G. Ordoqui Castilla, *supra*, at 166.

2 History of the Duty of Professional Secrecy in Uruguay

13. The current Criminal Code, which includes the abovementioned Article 302, was approved in 1934. Although precedents of professional secrecy can be found in the Roman Digest and the 1810 French Criminal Code, in Uruguay only disperse regulation existed prior to 1934.

   For example, Article 227 of the 1879 Criminal Instruction Code (repealed in 1980) stipulated that all those aware of an alleged offence could be called to testify, notwithstanding their gender or age, except for lawyers and doctors regarding facts that may have been related to the services offered in the exercise of their respective professions. Also, under the 1889 Criminal Code (repealed in 1934), law professionals who betrayed the trust of their clients by revealing secrets provided in the course of their defense would be guilty of the crime of prevarication and therefore could be sanctioned with a fine and suspension of two to four years.

   The Criminal Procedure Code currently in force, including Article 220 on the duty of lawyers to refrain from disclosing secrets, was approved in 1980. The Civil Procedure Code currently in force, including Article 156.2 on the duty of professionals to refrain from answering questions before the court that may violate their client's confidentiality, was approved in 1988.

   The American Convention on Human Rights was ratified by Uruguay in 1985 by Law No. 15.737, thereby formalizing the commitment to respect clients' right to communicate freely and privately with their attorneys.

   Finally, the Uruguayan Bar Association approved its Code of Ethics in 2003 and expressly recognized the attorneys' duty to rigorously respect professional secrecy (Art. 3.9).

3 Supervision

A The Bar Associations

14. Affiliation with the bar association is not mandatory for attorneys in Uruguay, so only those professionals who are affiliated with the bar may be subject to its authority.

   The Uruguayan Bar Association's board of directors is in charge of supervising compliance with its Bylaws and Code of Ethics. But its authority is limited to the imposition of sanctions when a member lawyer fails to comply with these regulations, including Article 3.9 of the Code of Ethics, which provides the attorneys' duty to rigorously respect professional secrecy (Art. 3.9).

B Judicial Power

15. Civil courts have jurisdiction over professional liability actions filed by clients seeking compensation against legal professionals who breached their duty of professional secrecy.

Criminal courts have jurisdiction over crimes committed by legal professionals in the exercise of their profession, including the illicit disclosure of declarations and information covered by attorney-client privilege. General provisions and rules apply to these kinds of crimes.

4 Sanctions

A Civil Proceedings

16. Although Uruguayan case law shows few examples of civil claims related to the breach of the duty of professional secrecy, and those few cases mainly relate to professionals other than attorneys, the breach of this duty may result in a lawsuit against the professional on the grounds of contractual liability and damages as a consequence of the breach of the attorney-client service agreement.

    The competent courts to hear these kinds of disputes will be determined by the amount of the claim. If the amount of the claim is higher than Uruguayan pesos 500,000 (approximately USD $17,500), the Civil Courts of First Instance will have jurisdiction over the claim. If the amount of the claim is lower than Uruguayan pesos 500,000, the Courts of Peace will have jurisdiction over the claim.

    The losing party may appeal the first instance decision before a Civil Court of Appeals. A third instance before the Supreme Court will be available only when the amount of the claim is higher than 6,000 readjustable units (approximately USD $170,000) and the two prior decisions differ.

B Criminal Proceedings

17. Breach of the duty of professional secrecy may be subject to the criminal sanction provided for in Article 302 of the Criminal Code, which is exclusively monetary (no jail time): a fine from 100 to 600 readjustable units (approximately USD $2,850 to USD $17,000).

    Criminal Courts of First Instance will have jurisdiction over the alleged breach of professional secrecy. Criminal Courts of Appeals will have jurisdiction over an appeal filed by the losing party, and an eventual third instance will be heard by the Supreme Court of Justice if the second instance decision departs from the law either on the merits or in formal aspects.

C Disciplinary Sanctions

18. Although, as previously mentioned, affiliation with the bar association is not mandatory for attorneys in Uruguay, in accordance with the Uruguayan Bar Association's Bylaws, the following sanctions may be applied to its members: (i) warning by the president of the board of directors, either privately or in the

presence of the other members of the board; (ii) censorship; (iii) partial or total suspension of the rights of the member; or (iv) expulsion.

While the first sanction (warning) may be imposed solely by the president, the remaining sanctions can be imposed only by the board of directors. In addition, the affirmative vote of the absolute majority of the members of the board of directors is required to apply the last sanction (expulsion of a member).

Once a sanction of censorship, suspension or expulsion is imposed, the sanction is served to the member of the bar by certified telegram or any other authentic means of notification. The sanction may be appealed before the bar's general assembly of members (the bar's supreme and primary body) within a period of 20 days from the date the member was served. The appeal must be filed in writing and will not suspend the effects of the sanction. The board of directors will call for a meeting of the general assembly, which must be held not later than 30 days from the date when the appeal was filed. The record of the case will be remitted to the general assembly, which will only confirm or revoke the appealed sanction, and no deliberation will take place.

D Relationship between Criminal Sanctions and Disciplinary Sanctions

19.   Criminal and disciplinary sanctions are not related in any way and are imposed independently, especially taking into account that the affiliation with the bar association is not mandatory for attorneys in Uruguay.

5 Duty to Provide Information to the Authorities

20.   Law professionals (whether attorneys or notaries at law) may be required to provide information to the authorities as representatives of their clients or by themselves when directly liable. Following is a description of the latter case.

A Money Laundering and Terrorism

21.   Money laundering and terrorism are mainly governed by Law No. 17.835 (Empowering of Legal Instruments against Money Laundering and Financing of Terrorism) and its regulatory Decrees.

The main office fighting against money laundering and financing of terrorism in Uruguay is the Financial Information and Analysis Unit (*Unidad de Información y Análisis Financiero*, UIAF) of the Uruguayan Central Bank. The UIAF receives reports from parties compelled to file information on suspicious activities and proceeds with any necessary investigation. Reports are confidential and may be done anonymously. If the UIAF considers that an operation may be linked to criminal activities, notice will be given to the competent criminal court.

Attorneys with a private practice are not covered by the provisions of Law No. 17.835. Attorneys who work for financial institutions or other entities controlled by the Uruguayan Central Bank must report suspicious activities to the UIAF, not due to their status as law professionals but due to their status as employees of such financial entities. The reported information will not be covered by attorney-client privilege, as it will concern operations of the financial entities' clients, not the entity itself.

However, notaries at law are covered by Law No. 17.835 due to the nature of their activities: they are legal professionals and officers who participate in the execution of public deeds, transactions, and registration of movable assets or real estate, and they give public faith (*fe pública*) regarding the signatures of the documents, origin of assets, lawful provenance of properties and former owners, powers of representatives to purchase or pay, condition of the goods and so on. Under Law No. 17.835, notaries at law are required to investigate their clients' backgrounds and must report suspicious activities to the UIAF when hired to participate in the following transactions: (i) purchase or sale of real estate; (ii) money, securities or asset administration; (iii) bank account administration; (iv) capitalization and contributions for incorporation, transaction or management of companies; (v) creation, transaction or management of legal entities or other instruments; and (vi) purchase or sale of business premises.

B Collective Settlement of Debts

22.   There is no regulation and there have been no cases on this matter in Uruguay.

6 Treatment of Lawyers' Documents and Correspondence in the Context of Judicial or Police Investigations

23.   Lawyers' documents and correspondence cannot be violated, even in the context of judicial or police investigations.

Article 28 of the Uruguayan Constitution stipulates the secrecy of correspondence in general terms, while Article 213 of the Criminal Procedure Code currently in force recognizes the inviolability of letters or documents sent or delivered to lawyers in the context of their duties. This inviolability is interpreted broadly by including both judicial and extrajudicial documents and correspondence. The new Criminal Procedure Code, recently enacted by Law No. 19.293 and which will enter into force on February 1, 2017, respects this solution and provides the same protection to the communications exchanged between attorneys and clients by considering them privileged (Art. 205.2). This protection is also supported by the Code of Ethics of the Uruguayan Bar Association (Art. 3.9.2).

Hence, any document delivered or correspondence sent by a client to an attorney is privileged. Attorneys have no duty to disclose documents or correspondence entrusted by their clients or related to their clients. When, in the course of an investigation, judicial or police authorities come across communications to or from a lawyer, or documents prepared by a lawyer, they must consider these communications and documents privileged information.

Finally, Article 8 of the American Convention on Human Rights, ratified by Law No. 15.737, recognizes the right to a fair trial, stipulating in its paragraph (d) that every client has the right to communicate freely and privately with an attorney.

7 Search of a Lawyer's Office

24. An attorney's office can be subject to judicial inspection only when the person subject to the investigation is the attorney herself or the attorney has helped others to commit the crime that is being investigated. Otherwise, an attorney's office is inviolable, even when one of the attorney's clients is under criminal investigation.

8 Tapping of Telephone Conversations with a Lawyer

25. In principle, the inviolability of attorney-client communications is absolute, and Article 5 of Law No. 18.494 expressly forbids tapping telephone conversations between an attorney and a client.

However, Article 208.3 of the new Criminal Procedure Code enacted by Law No. 19.293, which will enter into force on February 1, 2017, provides that the competent criminal court may authorize the tapping of telephone conversations between a client and an attorney when there are serious indications that such attorney is also criminally liable. This court authorization must indicate the name of the person subject to this measure, as well as its scope and duration.

9 The Lawyer as Witness

26. In principle, courts cannot compel an attorney to testify on matters protected by the attorney-client privilege.

Regarding criminal proceedings, Article 220 of the Criminal Procedure Code establishes the duty of lawyers (among others) to refrain from disclosing secrets that have reached their knowledge by virtue of their profession, but it also states that they cannot refuse to give testimony when they are "formally relieved from the duty to keep secrecy." This legal provision does not stipulate, however, who can relieve them from the obligation to keep the secrets: whether only the client or the criminal judge as well. Some scholars understand that, since Article 302 of the Criminal Code refers to "justified cause," criminal judges are allowed to relieve lawyers from the obligation to keep the secrets. On the other hand, other commentators understand that even criminal judges are not empowered to relieve attorneys from such obligation.

Regarding civil proceedings, Article 156.2 of the Civil Procedure Code establishes that those who have the duty to preserve professional secrecy can refrain from answering questions before the court that may violate their duty of confidentiality. Therefore, in the context of civil and commercial suits or actions, there is no doubt that only the client would be able to relieve the lawyer from the attorney-client privilege obligation. This has been confirmed by the 7th Civil Court of Appeals, which held that a judge cannot compel a lawyer to disclose privileged information when testifying in court as a witness.[16]

10 The Lawyer and the Press

27. Attorney-client privilege is still applicable with relation to the press. Attorneys are not entitled to disclose privileged information to the press, and it is generally accepted that an attorney can speak to the press to defend the client only with the latter's consent.

11 Powers of the Tax and Other Authorities

28. Under Uruguayan law, the tax authorities cannot obtain information protected by attorney-client privilege for tax purposes.

Additionally, the vast majority of the International Exchange Agreements or Double Tax Treaties with an exchange of information clause (Art. 26) stipulate that the provisions of the Agreements shall not impose on Uruguay an obligation to obtain or provide information that would reveal confidential communications between a client and an attorney, or other admitted legal representative, when such communications are (i) produced for the purposes of seeking or providing legal advice, or (ii) produced for the purposes of use in existing or contemplated legal proceedings.

Uruguay's Administrative Litigation Court (*Tribunal de lo Contencioso Administrativo*, TCA) understands that the scope of the term "professional" is in principle limited only to attorneys and medical doctors.[17] Other professions should be analyzed on a case-by-case basis.

12 National Security Issues

29. Under the Uruguayan constitution and international treaties ratified by Uruguay, such as the American Convention on Human Rights and the International Covenant on Civil and Political Rights (Law No. 15.737), the rights of citizens may be temporarily limited or suspended in three situations:

---

[16] 7th Civil Court of Appeals, Feb. 16, 2000, Decision no. 10/2000.
[17] Administrative Litigation Court, Dec. 18, 2014, Decision no. 725/014.

(i) declaration of a state of war by the executive branch with the prior approval of the Parliament, under which military jurisdiction applies and military court trials can be held for civilians; (ii) declaration of an emergency due to a natural disaster; and (iii) declaration of emergency security measures by the executive branch in case of internal commotion or external attack (which do not imply a declaration of war) that must be informed to the Parliament.

Scholars have not given an opinion on whether the state could limit professional secrecy in the abovementioned cases. If the attorney-client privilege is considered part of the judicial guarantees needed for defense in trial, then this privilege will be covered by the American Convention on Human Rights as a right that cannot be limited in such cases. However, the only specific provision on this matter included in the American Convention on Human Rights is found in Section 8(d) regarding the right of clients to freely and privately communicate with their attorneys.

In any case, Uruguay has not declared war on another state since the end of World War II in 1945, and the last declaration of emergency security measures was made in 1968.

32

U.S. Virgin Islands

XAVERIE L. BAXLEY-HULL

Dudley Rich Davis LLP

Preliminary Note

1.   In the Virgin Islands, lawyers are required to keep information relating to the representation of a client confidential. Client confidentiality is addressed in the Virgin Islands Rules of Professional Conduct[1] and via statute.

While there are exceptions, lawyers practicing in the Virgin Islands must have taken and passed the bar exam given in the Virgin Islands. The bar exam consists of a local section and a multistate section. In addition, lawyers are required to take the professional responsibility examination prior to being licensed to practice law in the Virgin Islands. To continue to hold an active license, Virgin Island attorneys are required to attend continuing legal education requirements annually.

The Supreme Court of the Virgin Islands governs the admission of all attorneys to the Virgin Islands Bar and has exclusive jurisdiction over members of the legal profession. The court regulates the conduct of attorneys by overseeing the Virgin Islands Bar Association and approving the rules governing the discipline of attorneys and the practice of law in the Virgin Islands. In addition, where an attorney faces serious discipline, a petition for discipline will be filed in the Supreme Court by the Ethics and Grievance Committee, and the court will determine the appropriate sanction.

The Virgin Islands Bar Association and its standing Ethics and Grievance Committee work alongside the Supreme Court and the Office of Disciplinary Counsel to regulate the practice of law. The Ethics and Grievance Committee considers whether a complaint involves attorney misconduct, conducts hearings and may impose sanctions on attorneys who have violated their professional duties. The committee may reprimand or admonish an attorney and may order the payment of restitution. Where the recommended sanction is probation, suspension or disbarment, the committee submits its recommendation to the Supreme Court.

The members of the Office of Disciplinary Counsel are employees of the Supreme Court and are responsible for investigating and prosecuting complaints against attorneys. With respect to attorney discipline, the Disciplinary Counsel receives and screens grievances, conducts investigations, notifies parties about the status of pending cases, and makes recommendations to the Ethics and Grievance Committee of the Virgin Islands Bar Association regarding the disposition of pending cases.

Prior to February 1, 2014, Supreme Court Rule 203 provided that the ABA's Model Rules of Professional Conduct governed the conduct of members of the Virgin Islands Bar. However, effective February 1, 2014, Supreme Court Rule 211, which establishes the Virgin Islands Rules of Professional Conduct,

---

[1] The Virgin Island Rules of Professional Conduct are found in Virgin Islands Supreme Court Rule 211, effective Feb. 1, 2014.

governs the conduct of Virgin Islands attorneys. The Virgin Islands Supreme Court, through Rule 211, adopted the Virgin Islands Rules of Professional Conduct, which include a duty of client confidentiality.

2. This chapter focuses only on Virgin Islands statutory and common law and rules and regulations promulgated by the Virgin Islands Legislature and the Virgin Islands Supreme Court. This was to focus on Virgin Islands law and not to discuss the rules and statutory construction of the federal courts of the United States.

1 Scope of and Limitations on the Duty of Professional Secrecy/Attorney-Client Privilege

A Statutory Basis and Implications

3. The statutory basis for the attorney-client privilege is found in Title 5 of the Virgin Islands Code (V.I.C.) §852, aptly named the lawyer-client privilege and codified for the first time in 2011.

Section 852 provides definitions on who is a client and what communications are confidential. Clients include people, public officers or corporations, associations, or other organizations or entities, either public or private, who receive professional legal services from a lawyer, or who consult with a lawyer with a view toward obtaining professional legal services from the lawyer.

Communications are confidential if they are not intended to be disclosed to third parties other than those to whom disclosure is made in furtherance of the rendition of professional legal services to the client, or those reasonably necessary for the transmission of the communication.

A client has a privilege to refuse to disclose and to prevent any other person from disclosing confidential communications made for the purpose of facilitating the rendition of professional legal services to the client (1) between the client or the client's representative and the client's lawyer or the lawyer's representative, (2) between the client's lawyer and the lawyer's representative, (3) by the client or the client's representative or the client's lawyer or a representative of the lawyer to a lawyer or a representative of a lawyer representing another in a matter of common interest, (4) between representatives of the client or between the client and a representative of the client, or (5) among lawyers and their representatives representing the same client. This privilege exists whether or not the person actually retains the lawyer or law firm to render professional legal services to him or her.

The privilege may be claimed by the client; the client's guardian or conservator; the personal representative of a deceased client; or the successor, trustee or similar representative of a corporation, association or other organization, whether or not in existence. A person who was the lawyer or the lawyer's representative at the time of the communication is presumed to have authority to claim the privilege – but only on behalf of the client. A lawyer is obligated to assert the privilege to protect a client who cannot assert it for a valid reason such as incapacity or death. The privilege continues even after the death of either the client or the attorney.

4.   In addition, the Virgin Islands Supreme Court promulgated the Virgin Islands Rules of Professional Conduct, wherein lawyers are subject to Section 211.1.6 on confidentiality of information, which provides:

> A lawyer shall not reveal information relating to the representation of a client unless the client gives informed consent . . . .
>
> A lawyer may reveal information relating to the representation of a client to the extent the lawyer reasonably believes necessary: (1) to prevent reasonably certain death or substantial bodily harm; (2) to prevent the client from committing a crime or fraud that is reasonably certain to result in substantial injury to the financial interests or property of another and in furtherance of which the client has used or is using the lawyer's services; (3) to prevent, mitigate or rectify substantial injury to the financial interests or property of another that is reasonably certain to result or has resulted from the client's commission of a crime or fraud in furtherance of which the client has used the lawyer's services; (4) to secure legal advice about the lawyer's compliance with these Rules; (5) to establish a claim or defense on behalf of the lawyer in a controversy between the lawyer and the client, to establish a defense to a criminal charge or civil claim against the lawyer based upon conduct in which the client was involved; and (6) to comply with other law or a court order.

B Scope

5.   Attorney-client privilege includes all communications whether written or oral relating to the representation of a client, with certain exceptions. The attorney work product doctrine is defined in 5 V.I.C. §852 and called work product immunity.

Work product immunity may protect an attorney from disclosing to a third party some of the information the attorney creates or acquires while preparing for litigation (qualified immunity). Work product materials may be subject to discovery if the party requesting them proves (i) a substantial need for the materials and (ii) an inability to obtain a substantial equivalent of those materials by another method.

Attorneys possess absolute immunity from disclosing work product when they divulge the attorneys' "mental impressions, conclusions, opinions, or legal theories regarding litigation."

C Persons Subject to the Duty of Professional Secrecy

6.   Besides attorneys, the Rules of Professional Confidentiality apply to all members of the law firm, employees, legal assistants and staff members. Attorneys

would expect that all external service providers, such as copy service companies, not divulge any confidential documents.

Attorneys must ensure that any outside service provider, whether it be a copy service or a contract attorney, maintain client confidences, or the attorney could be found in violation of the duty of attorney-client confidentiality and subject to sanctions by the Supreme Court, whether it be through the Office of Disciplinary Counsel or the Board of Professional Responsibility.

D Exceptions to and Optional Derogations from the Duty of Professional Secrecy

7.   The exceptions to the duty of client confidentiality are spelled out in both the statutory authority and the Rules of Professional Conduct.

There are no privileged communications between the client and the attorney when the services of the lawyer were sought or obtained to enable or aid anyone to commit or plan to commit what the client knew or reasonably should have known to be a crime or fraud.

Other exceptions include communications relevant to (i) an issue between parties who submit claims through the same deceased client, regardless of whether the claims are by testate or intestate succession or by *inter vivos* transaction; and (ii) an issue of breach of duty by the lawyer to the client or by the client to the lawyer.

If a client makes an accusation against an attorney and revealing a communication is necessary for the lawyer to defend him- or herself in a legal proceeding wherein the lawyer is accused of assisting a client in criminal or fraudulent conduct, the lawyer is able to reveal the communication.

Section 852 has several other exceptions to attorney-client privilege, but very few have been addressed by the courts. One that is pending in the Superior Court is the exception regarding communications between an attorney and a "public client," or what is better known as a government client.

There is no privilege as to a communication between a public officer or agency and its lawyers unless the communication concerns a pending investigation, claim or action and the court determines that disclosure will seriously impair the ability of the public officer or agency to process the claim or conduct a pending investigation, litigation or proceeding in the public interest.

E Law Firms

8.   Attorneys who work in law firms tend to share privileged information amongst each other, and this is considered an acceptable practice. Law firms tend to assign cases to different attorneys, sometimes due to time constraints, but more often than not due to knowledge and experience in a particular type of matter. The privilege applies to all of the lawyers in the firm.

F Legal Assistants and Staff

9.   Legal assistants and staff are not allowed to practice law, since only attorneys admitted to the bar can practice law. Despite that, as discussed previously, legal assistants and staff, as spelled out in the Rules of Professional Conduct, are bound by the Rules, but the supervising attorney is directly responsible for the actions of the support staff.

G External Service Providers

10.   For external service providers, client confidentiality applies. It has become a regular practice for some firms to hire contract attorneys or have attorneys "of counsel" to perform certain legal work. The supervising attorney is the person with the ultimate responsibility to ensure that client confidentiality is protected when outsourcing any work.

H Multidisciplinary Associations

11.   Attorneys cannot fee share with a non-lawyer. However, an attorney may need to consult with accountants, medical experts, causation experts and other non-lawyers. Privileged and confidential client information with non-lawyers will remain protected. Case law is lacking within the Virgin Islands regarding this particular issue, but the Supreme Court would evaluate this by looking at federal and state common law to come to the best conclusion.

I In-House Counsel

12.   On June 1, 2015, the Virgin Islands Supreme Court amended Rule 202, allowing an attorney who has been admitted to the practice of law in a state, commonwealth or territory of the United States other than the Virgin Islands, or the District of Columbia ("U.S. jurisdiction"), who is or will be employed as a lawyer by an organization, the business of which is lawful and consists of activities other than the practice of law or the provision of legal services and who will have a systematic and continuous presence in the Virgin Islands, may apply for a Virgin Islands Certificate of Limited Practice as In-House Counsel.

All attorneys who obtain the certificate of limited practice must abide by the Virgin Islands Rules of Professional Conduct. A lawyer certified under this rule is subject to all laws and rules governing the practice of law in the Virgin Islands, including the Virgin Islands Rules of Professional Conduct and the Virgin Islands Rules for Attorney Disciplinary Enforcement. The Supreme Court, the Office of Disciplinary Counsel, the Board of Professional Responsibility and the Board on the Unauthorized Practice of Law have jurisdiction over the certified in-house counsel with respect to the conduct of the lawyer in this or another U.S. jurisdiction to the same extent as they have over lawyers regularly admitted in the Virgin Islands. This jurisdiction will continue whether or not the lawyer retains the Virgin Islands Certificate of Limited Practice as In-house Counsel and irrespective of the lawyer's continued presence in the Virgin Islands.

2 History of the Duty of Professional Secrecy in the U.S. Virgin Islands

13. Until 1984, the District Court (a court of federal jurisdiction) possessed both appellate jurisdiction and the authority to promulgate rules for the Superior Court of the Virgin Islands. The Superior Court would look to the District Court and the 3rd District Court of Appeals for case precedent. Attorney-client privilege then and even today is evaluated using federal case law.

The Superior Court, as the sole local court, exercised the power for the first time in 1994. In addition, on January 29, 2007, the Supreme Court of the Virgin Islands assumed its role as the court of last resort in the Virgin Islands. The Supreme Court now exercises general oversight of the judicial branch of the government of the Virgin Islands.

Section 21(c) of the Revised Organic Act provides that "[t]he rules governing the practice and procedure of the courts established by local law . . . shall be governed by local law or the rules promulgated by those courts."[2]

The Supreme Court of the Virgin Islands has previously held that the above-referenced provision vests the Virgin Islands Judiciary and the Virgin Islands Legislature with authority to promulgate procedural rules, while permitting only the Legislature to establish substantive rules.[3]

The Supreme Court has admonished the Superior Court several times when it uses merely the Federal Rules to determine Virgin Islands issues. Recently, in *Vanterpool v. Government of Virgin Islands*, 2015 WL 4723651 (Aug. 2015), the Virgin Islands Supreme Court opined:

> Such uncritical application of the rules of another court to a proceeding in the Superior Court is wholly inconsistent with our admonition that "the Federal Rules of Civil Procedure, the Federal Rules of Criminal Procedure, and the Local Rules of the District Court should represent rules of last resort rather than first resort, and should be invoked only when a thorough review of applicable Virgin Islands statutes, Superior Court rules, and precedents from this Court reveals the absence of any other [applicable] procedure."[4]

In that capacity, the Supreme Court has questioned whether Superior Court Rule 7 comports with the Revised Organic Act's requirement that the court

---

[2] 48 U.S.C. § 1611(c).

[3] *Phillips v. People*, 51 V.I. 258, 275 (V.I. 2009); *Gov't of the V.I. v. Durant*, 49 V.I. 366, 373 (V.I. 2008) (citing *In re Richards*, 213 F.3d 773, 783–84 (3d Cir. 2000)).

[4] *Vanterpool* (quoting *Sweeney v. Ombres*, 60 V.I. 438, 442 (V.I. 2014)).

rules employed in proceedings before Virgin Islands courts actually be promulgated by the Virgin Islands judiciary.

On its face, Superior Court Rule 7 appears to incorporate the Federal Rules of Civil Procedure, the Federal Rules of Criminal Procedure, the Local Rules of Civil Procedure and the Local Rules of Criminal Procedure into Superior Court proceedings as promulgated and amended by the U.S. Supreme Court and the U.S. District Court of the Virgin Islands. While apparently intended to make local and federal practice as similar as possible, *Gov't of the V.I. v. Thomas*, 32 V.I. 64, 66–68 (V.I. Super. Ct. 1995), the wholesale adoption by reference of four sets of rules promulgated by courts outside of the Virgin Islands judiciary to govern proceedings in the Superior Court may be problematic, given that Congress provided in Section 21(c) of the Revised Organic Act that "[t]he rules governing the practice and procedure of the courts established by local law ... shall be governed by local law or the rules promulgated by those courts."

The Court further opined:

> [W]e must also note that while Rule 7 was intended to make practice in Virgin Islands courts less complex, the practical application of Rule 7 requires litigants to be intimately familiar with the Superior Court Rules, the Federal Rules of Civil Procedure, the Federal Rules of Criminal Procedure, the Local Rules of Civil Procedure, the Local Rules of Criminal Procedure, and every provision of the Virgin Islands Code dealing with judicial proceedings in order to know when a federal rule or District Court rule is not "inconsistent" with a Superior Court Rule or local statute, and therefore applies to Superior Court proceedings. The sheer volume of case law from this Court, the Superior Court, the Appellate Division of the District Court, and the Third Circuit attempting to figure out which rule applies speaks to the complications inherent in Rule 7, and underscores the fact that Rule 7 has done exactly the opposite of what it was intended to do.[5]

---

[5] The court in *Thomas* illustrates its point by citing the following cases: *see, e.g., Estick v. People*, S. Ct. Crim. no 2013–0070, —— V.I. ——, 2015 WL 1777884, at *6 n.7 (V.I. Apr. 15, 2015); *Bryan v. Fawkes*, 61 V.I. 201, 239 n.30 (V.I. 2014); *Sweeney*, 60 V.I. at 442–43; *Joseph v. People*, 60 V.I. 338, 344–50 (V.I. 2013); *Fuller v. Browne*, 59 V.I. 948, 953–56 (V.I. 2013); *Benjamin v. People*, 59 V.I. 572, 576 (V.I. 2013); *DeGroot v. People*, S. Ct. Civ. no 2008–0107, 2013 WL 1792825, at *2 n.1 (V.I. Apr. 29, 2013) (unpublished); *Chciuk–Davis v. People*, 57 V.I. 317, 324–25 (V.I. 2012); *Santiago v. V.I. Housing Auth.*, 57 V.I. 256, 275–78 (V.I. 2012); *Tindell v. People*, 56 V.I. 138, 149–50 (V.I. 2012); *Terrell v. Coral World*, 55 V.I. 580, 590–91 & n.12 (V.I. 2011); *Blyden v. People*, 53 V.I. 637, 659 (V.I. 2010); *Corraspe*, 53 V.I. at 482; *Phillips v. People*, 51 V.I. 258, 273–76 (V.I. 2009); *Gov't of the V.I. v. Durant*, 49 V.I. 366, 373–74 (V.I. 2008); *People v. Velasquez*, Super. Ct. Crim. no. 063/2012 (STX), 2014 WL 495534, at *5–6 (V.I. Super. Ct. Feb. 6, 2014) (unpublished); *Bertrand v. Cordiner Enters.*, 55 V.I. 247, 254–57 (V.I. Super. Ct. 2011); *In re Richards*, 213 F.3d 773, 786 (3d Cir. 2000); *Gov't of the V.I. v. Greenidge*, 41 V.I. 200, 208 n.5 (D.V.I. App. Div. 1998).

The opinions of the Virgin Islands Supreme Court reveal how in flux the law is as it relates to many different issues, including the attorney-client privilege. The Supreme Court's history is short compared to other jurisdictions, and different issues are continually being determined. Presently, there is very little case law on attorney-client communications and confidentiality, but it is believed that the Virgin Islands courts will continue to do a thorough analysis of case law before deciding the best rule of law for the territory.

3 Supervision

A The Bar Associations

14. The Virgin Islands Bar Association and its standing Ethics and Grievance Committee work alongside the Supreme Court and the Office of Disciplinary Counsel to regulate the practice of law.

B The Courts

15. The Virgin Islands Supreme Court, as the highest court, possesses statutory authority to regulate the practice of law in the Virgin Islands.[6] The Supreme Court has the authority to discipline attorneys and may refer matters to the Ethics and Grievance Committee.

4 Sanctions

A Proceedings and Sanctions

16. With oversight by the Supreme Court, there is an Office of Disciplinary Counsel, members of which are appointed by the Supreme Court, a Preliminary Review Committee and the Board of Professional Responsibility. They are charged with oversight to consider matters in violation of the rules of professional responsibility, conduct hearings, and make findings of fact and conclusions of law.

The board will file its findings of fact and conclusions of law and make recommendations to the court. The board chair must designate the members of the Hearing Panel and its chair. Decisions of the Hearing Panel on the merits of discipline or disability matters require the concurrence of at least two votes. The Hearing Panel chair will decide scheduling, administrative, procedural and evidentiary matters. If the Hearing Panel chair is not available to rule on an administrative, procedural or evidentiary matter, the parties may address the matter to the remaining lawyer on the Hearing Panel or the chair or vice chair of the board.

---

[6] 4 V.I.C. §32(e).

B Relationship between Criminal Sanctions and Disciplinary Sanctions

17. Sanctions against an attorney found in Virgin Islands Supreme Court Rule 207 include (i) disbarment by the court; (ii) suspension by the court for an appropriate fixed period of time not in excess of three years; (iii) immediate interim suspension by the court, pending final determination of disciplinary sanctions, or suspension by the court as a result of "show cause" proceedings under Rule 207.17 or on a *sua sponte* basis; (iv) public probation by the court; (v) public reprimand by the court; (vi) private admonition by the court or, with the consent of the respondent, by the Preliminary Review Committee; (vii) private probation by the court or, with the consent of the respondent, by the Preliminary Review Committee; (viii) conditional diversion by the court or, with the consent of the respondent, by the Preliminary Review Committee; (ix) court-ordered restitution to persons financially injured; and (x) limitation by the court on the nature and extent of the respondent's future practice.

5 Duty to Provide Information to the Authorities

A Money Laundering and Terrorism

18. The Virgin Islands Supreme Court has not opined on whether there is a duty to provide information to the authorities. None of the issues regarding money laundering, terrorism or the searching of an attorney's office has reached the local courts. In a matter that seeks information related to any of these items, this author believes the court would look to federal court decisions to determine what is the best rule of law for the Virgin Islands.

B Collective Settlement of Debts

19. There is no current law on this topic in the Virgin Islands.

6 Treatment of Lawyers' Documents and Correspondence in the Context of Judicial or Police Investigations

20. In may be suggested that the Superior Court would look to federal and state courts to determine how to rule on an attorney's documents in the context of judicial or police investigations when it shapes Virgin Islands common law. In this jurisdiction, case law is lacking as to this particular issue.

7 Search of a Lawyer's Office

21. Whether an authority of the Virgin Islands government has the right to search an attorney's office has not been specifically reviewed or discussed by the Virgin Islands Superior Court or Supreme Court.

8 Tapping of Telephone Conversations with a Lawyer

22.   Whether an authority of the Virgin Islands government has the right to tap
        telephone conversations of lawyers has not been specifically discussed or
        reviewed by the Virgin Islands Superior Court or Supreme Court.

9 The Lawyer as Witness

23.   In *Browne v. Virgin Islands*, 56 V.I. 307, a 2012 case, the Supreme Court of the
        Virgin Islands reviewed several U.S. circuit court opinions, state appellate
        decisions and the Third Restatement to discuss whether an attorney should
        have been allowed to testify after the client asserted a privilege. Their review
        suggests that, without case law on the specific issue, it would look to the federal
        courts of the United States and individual state cases to determine how this
        issue would be decided.

        In a footnote, the court stated: "The attorney-client privilege protects commu-
        nications between attorneys and clients from compelled disclosure. In order for the
        attorney-client privilege to attach to a communication, 'it must be '(1)
        a communication (2) made between privileged persons (3) in confidence (4) for
        the purpose of obtaining or providing legal assistance for the client.'"[7] In this case,
        attorney Schrader-Cooke's proposed testimony concerned a communication made
        between the government, the person claiming the privilege and herself.

        However, the Supreme Court did not reach the issue on whether the attorney
        would be allowed to testify when it stated: "However, we need not reach that
        issue today because even if the trial court erred in excluding Attorney
        Schrader-Cooke from testifying, its error was harmless beyond a reasonable
        doubt."

10 The Lawyer and the Press

24.   There is no prohibition against attorneys in the U.S. Virgin Islands speaking to
        the press. There is an expectation that licensed attorneys would not violate the
        rules of professional conduct and reveal privileged information to the press.

        As far as statements to the press during a trial, the Virgin Islands Supreme
        Court has promulgated a rule (Rule 211.3.6) that attorneys must not make
        statements that will have a substantial likelihood of materially prejudicing an
        adjudicative proceeding.

        Attorneys can make statements regarding the claims, offense or defense
        involved; the identity of the persons; and any information contained in a public
        record. Additionally, attorneys may make a statement that a reasonable lawyer

---

[7] *Browne*, 56 V.I. 307 (citing *In re Teleglobe Commc'ns Corp.*, 493 F.3d 345, 359 (3d Cir. 2007)
(quoting Restatement (Third) of the Law Governing Lawyers § 68 (2000))).

would believe is required to protect a client from the substantial undue pre-judicial effect of recent publicity not initiated by the lawyer or the lawyer's client. A statement made pursuant to this paragraph must be limited to such information as is necessary to mitigate the recent adverse publicity.

There are no opinions by any Virgin Islands court interpreting this rule to date.

11 Powers of the Tax and Other Authorities

25. An older District Court opinion from 1987, *Olive v. Isherwood, Hunter & Diehm*, 656 F. Supp. 1171, 23 V.I. 168 (1987) contains the only opinion regarding the powers of the tax authorities. Again it is believed the Supreme Court of the Virgin Islands would do the same analysis as the District Court did and come to the same conclusion. The District Court, when it evaluated a tax summons and whether the attorney-client privilege applied to the escrow account records of attorneys, stated:

> The summons power is not absolute and is limited by the traditional privileges, including the attorney-client privilege. ... Whether material is privileged is a matter of federal law and is governed by F.R.E. [Federal Rules of Evidence] 501. ... The essential elements of the privilege are:
>
> (1) the asserted holder of the privilege is or sought to become a client; (2) the person to whom the communication was made (a) is a member of the bar of a court, or his subordinate and (b) in connection with this communication is acting as a lawyer; (3) the communication relates to the fact of which the attorney was informed (a) by his client (b) without the presence of strangers (c) for the purpose of securing primarily either (i) an opinion of law or (ii) legal services or (iii) assistance in some legal proceeding and not (d) for the purpose of committing a crime or tort; and (4) the privilege has been (a) claimed and (b) not waived by the client. ...
>
> The financial aspects of the attorney-client relationship are generally not privileged because fees and awards seldom involve the pursuit of legal counseling. Thus, the privilege excludes a lawyer's record of fees collected from a specific client. ...
>
> In response to a tax summons, therefore, a lawyer must reveal both the nature of and remuneration for legal services. ... Moreover, the privilege does not immunize the contingency fee contract and statement of distribution from a tax summons.
>
> The courts are in accord that the fact that money passes through an attorney's escrow account does not privilege an otherwise unprivileged transaction. Factually, the most similar case is *United States v. Tratner*, 511 F.2d 248 (7th Cir. 1975). Tratner, a lawyer, invoked the attorney-client privilege when asked to identify the payee of a $10,000 check drawn on his escrow account. The Seventh Circuit held that no *per se* privilege attached to the account and, therefore, Tratner was required to demonstrate that

either the account or the transaction was privileged or else comply with the summons.

In *United States v. Dickinson*, 308 F. Supp. 900 (D.Ariz.1969) *aff'd*, 421 F.2d 702 (9th Cir.1970), an attorney whose accounts receivable records were summoned to determine his individual tax liability attempted to invoke the privilege on the theory that production would expose the identities of his clients. The court rejected this argument on the authority of the well-established rule that absent a "compelling reason to protect the identity of the client . . ., the identity of the client is not a communication protected by the privilege." *Id.* at 901.

Nor can the attorney or client claim the privilege to prevent the bank holding the escrow account from producing its records.

Finally, the Third Circuit has unequivocally stated that local laws requiring lawyers to establish escrow accounts add nothing to the federal common law privilege. . . .

The sole grounds advanced in support of the claim of privilege is the firm's bald statement that the documents are entitled to protection merely because they pertain to the escrow account. A finding in favor of the firm would require us to rule that escrow records are privileged per se, a result that is contrary to the established rule. . . . We hold, therefore, that if privilege is to attach to any of the approximately 1,600 escrow transactions, the firm must prove each one individually.[8]

12 National Security Issues

26. While not addressed in any Virgin Islands case law, Virgin Islands attorneys would be subject to the U.S. federal court decisions and U.S. Attorney General opinions regarding confidentiality issues that deal with national security.

---

[8] *Olive v. Isherwood, Hunter & Diehm*, 656 F. Supp. 1171, 23 V.I. 168 (1987) (internal quotations and citations omitted).

33

Venezuela

FERNANDO PELÁEZ-PIER
ALEJANDRO GALLOTTI

Hoet Peláez Castillo & Duque

Preliminary Note

1.   The Venezuelan legal system regulates the professional practice of lawyers through different regulations, such as the Code of Professional Ethics of the Venezuelan Lawyer (CPE), the Statute of Lawyers, the Criminal Code and the Code of Civil Procedure (CCP), among others. These regulations aim at protecting and monitoring the behavior of professionals and also at protecting their clients and the correct development of the justice administration system.

    Among the parameters expressly provided in the abovementioned legal regulations is professional secrecy, which is understood in Venezuelan doctrine as the duty "imposed on all persons who are entrusted with secrets because of their status, profession or position."[1] This parameter placed on professional conduct may entail several implications, depending of the profession under examination. In the legal environment, professional secrecy will mostly refer to the confidentiality of information provided by clients (whether they are natural or legal persons) to lawyers when seeking their advice, representation or defense.

    Professional secrecy is then an obligation of the legal professional that would entail, in turn, the client's right to keep confidential all disclosures made to lawyers during the course of a professional services relationship.

1 Scope of and Limitations on the Duty of Professional Secrecy/ Attorney-Client Privilege

2.   One must first understand what exactly the practice of the legal profession is in Venezuela. Article 11 of the Statute of Lawyers defines it as the "development of activities inherent in the law profession or work entrusted because of a special law to a holder of a law degree, or occupations that necessarily require legal knowledge." In addition, the statute provides that this professional practice is understood as "the regular work or rendering of professional services for profit or for free inherent in the law profession, with no need for any official appointment or designation."

A Statutory Basis and Implications

3.   While the duty of professional secrecy is described in and regulated by several Venezuelan statutes and regulations, as stated previously, there is no doubt that the Code of Professional Ethics of the Venezuelan Lawyer (CPE) is the primary instrument that describes this concept. Article 25 of the CPE reads as follows:

---

[1] Excerpt translated from M. Espinoza Melet, *"El Secreto Profesional* [Professional Secrecy]," 36 *Anuario*, 2013, at 16–32.

> Lawyers shall maintain strict professional secrecy. This secrecy shall extend to their files and documents even after the lawyers have ceased to provide services for the clients. Lawyers may refuse to testify against clients and refrain from answering any question that entails the disclosure of any secret or the violation of confidences made.
>
> Moreover, lawyers cannot discuss with third parties any information that such lawyers may come to know because of their profession. Professional secrecy shall also encompass all matters that attorneys may discuss with the representative of the opposing party.

The parameters that address professional secrecy of lawyers are quite extensive, including detailing the means or locations where information may be kept, such as files and documents, which are protected even after the professional relationship has ended, so that professional secrecy survives the professional services relationship. In this regard, the term "documents" has a broad meaning, including papers produced by the client and papers that may have been obtained or prepared by the lawyer insofar as they require professional secrecy.

Pursuant to the article quoted above, professional secrecy logically involves third parties. Professional secrecy is violated not only by disclosing information to several individuals or collectively but also by disclosing it to a single individual.

Moreover, any meetings, discussions or conversations that may be held with the lawyer of the opposing party are also under the umbrella of professional secrecy. This raises several matters to be considered: (i) lawyers should not disclose any information to the opposing party's lawyer, except information that the client has clearly consented to provide; and (ii) any new information that the lawyer may obtain in such conversations or meetings, whether involving the client or the opposing party, are also protected by professional secrecy in the terms analyzed above.

4.   Article 26 of CPE provides other matters that must be considered in connection with professional secrecy of lawyers.[2] Matters involving legal opinions, consultancy services, advice and other services are also covered by professional secrecy, so as to make sure that the information the lawyer has obtained during the course of the professional relationship and that requires professional

---

[2] Translation of Art. 26 of CPE: "The duty of professional secrecy shall also encompass any information disclosed or discovered when the lawyer's opinion, advice or defense is required, and, in general, any information that the lawyer may come to know because of the nature of the profession. Lawyers must not participate in affairs that may lead them to disclose secrets or use, for their own benefit or that of their client, any confidences made during the practice of their profession, except when they get prior, express and written consent of the person who made the confidence. The obligation to keep professional secrecy also covers any matters that the lawyers may come to know due to common or associated work with other lawyers or through employees or persons who are dependent workers or employees of lawyers or other professionals."

secrecy is not limited only to that of the judicial field or the representation of the client before public authorities, but also includes any information lawyers obtain because of their profession and that must be protected.

Furthermore, Article 26 provides that lawyers must not intervene in matters that may lead them to disclose a secret. This could refer not only to potential conflicts of interest but also any other matters that, because of their connection, may eventually drive lawyers to disclose the information that they have obtained and that may have an impact on that new case. This applies not only to the information that relates to the specific matter that the lawyer handled but also any industrial, trade, corporate or personal secret of the client.

B Scope

5. The lawyers' duty to maintain professional secrecy surely has its origins in the constitutional right to defense and due process granted to all citizens, and provided in the Constitution of the Bolivarian Republic of Venezuela ("Constitution") and in the American Convention on Human Rights (ACHR),[3] which was signed and ratified by Venezuela. Article 49(1) of the Constitution provides that "Defense and legal assistance are inviolable rights in any state and during any stage of the investigation and any stage of the process." It is understood that, to guarantee legal assistance that allows proper defense, the attorney-client relationship must be confidential, so that it is as honest as possible, which allows the lawyer to know the real circumstances of the case and which would make the lawyer's work easier, whether it is consultancy and advice or developing a strategy to defend the client before the justice administration institutions.

   Concerning ethical behavior of the lawyer, professional secrecy is one of the main tenets that must be upheld. Espinoza Melet,[4] when referring to Tomás Liscano, states that professional secrecy must involve "all those [secrets] that, once disclosed, may tarnish the honor of the subjects, harm their interests and persons, or destroy or lessen any esteem that such subjects may have within society."

C Persons Subject to the Duty of Professional Secrecy

6. First and foremost, those who practice the legal profession are bound to maintain professional secrecy vis-à-vis the client or matters that they have come to know because of their professional activity. In general terms, obligations and duties of lawyers apply, in a broad sense, to all those who practice the profession, including the following:

   > The following lawyers are subject to this law, and, consequently, to the
   > same rights and obligations: Professors in universities of the country,

---

[3] Also known as the Pact of San Jose.
[4] M. Espinoza Melet, "*El Secreto Profesional* [Professional Secrecy]," 36 *Anuario*, 2013, at 22.

Justices of the Supreme Court of Justice or Judges of the Republic, court clerks, defenders, Public Prosecutors, Registrars, Notaries, consultants or legal advisors of public or private individual or collective persons and, in general, lawyers who, while conducting a task and because of their special legal knowledge, advise third parties publicly or privately.[5]

In this regard, lawyers in general must comply with the rights and duties described in the Statute of Lawyers, and this is also evidenced in Article 1 of the CPE, which provides that "Compulsory compliance with the norms in this Code is required for all lawyers in their public and private life." It also provides that the application thereof will correspond to the professional associations provided in the law, in the understanding that "the provisions thereof cannot be rendered ineffective or be relaxed by agreements of any kind." This leads to Article 25 of the CPE quoted previously that provides that "[l]awyers shall maintain strict professional secrecy."

As per the preceding, one of the duties of lawyers is to maintain secrecy and protect the information obtained in the course of the practice of the legal profession.

D Professional Secrecy Exceptions and Optional Derogations

7.   Article 26 of the CPE provides certain exceptions for the duty to maintain professional secrecy. While it is true that, as stated previously, lawyers must not participate in affairs that may lead them to disclose secrets or use them for their own benefit or that of other clients, the exception is that they may do so if they obtain the client's "prior, express and written consent."

In addition, there are other scenarios where a lawyer is allowed to make disclosures as provided in Article 27 of the CPE,[6] which stipulates that a lawyer may disclose confidential information of the client if the client has filed a claim or complaint against the lawyer before the relevant authorities. However, it is necessary to point out that such claim or complaint does not enable the lawyer, by operation of law, to disregard professional secrecy entirely; this exception applies only to the information that is necessary for the defense of the lawyer. Lawyers must continue to maintain professional secrecy over all other matters.

Moreover, Article 28 of the CPE[7] provides another scenario where lawyers are released from their duty to maintain professional secrecy, namely, when

---

[5] Art. 11, Statute of Lawyers.

[6] Art. 27: "Lawyers who are the subject of claims or complaints initiated by a client before the Disciplinary Court of the bar, will not be required to maintain professional secrecy within the necessary and indispensable limits of their own defense."

[7] "If the client lets the lawyer know of his intention to commit a crime, the latter shall do as necessary in order to persuade the client and, if unsuccessful, the lawyer may make the disclosures that may be necessary so as to prosecute such action or protect the persons and assets under threat."

clients intend to commit a crime. In this case, lawyers may set aside professional secrecy, provided that the crime is to be committed in the future.

E Law Firms

8. Article 26 of the CPE provides that "The obligation to keep professional secrecy also covers any matters that the lawyers may come to know due to common or associated work with other lawyers or through employees or persons who are dependent workers or employees of lawyers or other professionals."

    Consequently, professional secrecy encompasses not only the information obtained directly from advising or representing a client but also the information obtained through colleagues, associates, employees, subordinates or other professionals. The main examples of the foregoing are law firms, where all members of a firm must maintain professional secrecy, even when one of them has not participated in that particular case or the client is not part of that member's client portfolio. In addition, any colleague who does not belong to the firm and who may have been consulted in connection with a particular case is also bound by professional secrecy.

F Legal Assistants and Staff

9. As explained in the preceding section, Article 26 of the CPE provides for the confidentiality of matters that the lawyers may come to know due to common or associated work with other lawyers or through employees or persons who are dependent workers or employees of lawyers or other professionals, which clearly refers to staff and legal assistants of the lawyer who maintain a direct professional relationship with the client.

G External Service Providers

10. Professionals such as outside counsel, consulting partners and others are also considered in Article 26 of the CPE. It is common for a law firm or an interdependent lawyer to require certain external services that are not necessarily in the legal area. They may need an accountant or a particular specialist for the purposes of solving certain litigation or consultation matters. In these cases, the confidentiality of the lawyer-client relationship must be maintained in connection with any information that the external service providers may handle.

H Multidisciplinary Associations

11. Similarly, in the course of representing a client, a lawyer may require the expertise of other professionals, which is completely accepted. In fact, the "expert's assessment" and "expert witness" are mentioned in the Code of Civil

Procedure (CCP) and the Civil Code, acknowledging the concept of turning to other professionals for the purposes of resolving litigation.

Logically, for these specialized professionals to be able to contribute, it is necessary for them to know certain details of the case, which would entail that, under the provisions of Article 26 of the CPE, professional secrecy also applies to them.

I In-House Counsel

12.   The provisions of Article 26 of the CPE also apply to in-house counsel.

2 History of the Duty of Professional Secrecy in Venezuela

13.   In 1788, the Caracas Bar Association was established in Venezuela. Then, on March 2, 1863, a decree ordered the foundation of a bar association per district, formed by the lawyers inhabiting such areas. Twenty years later, by means of decree dated February 7, 1883, the then-president of the republic, Antonio Guzman Blanco, created the Bar Association of the Republic with its office in Caracas. Afterwards, the Statute of Lawyers and Prosecutors appeared on June 30, 1894; this statute provides for the possibility of establishing bar associations in the Federal District and any other state where there are at least five lawyers willing to form them.[8]

The Code of Professional Ethics of the Venezuelan Lawyer[9] was published in 1956 by the Bar Association of the Federal District, exercising the power given to bar associations by Article 42(10) of the Statute of Lawyers, in the ordinary session of October 18, 1956. Thus, Article 23 of the Code of 1956 provides that "Lawyers shall maintain strict professional secrecy … this secrecy also applies to confidences made by third parties to the lawyer because of his profession, and those deriving from conversations necessary to reach an agreement that was not perfected. Secrecy shall also encompass the disclosures of colleagues." This Code has since been repealed.

The 1956 Code may be considered the first formal regulation of professional secrecy in Venezuela. Until then, there were only provisions concerning the internal affairs of the law profession and the corresponding professional associations. As it may be observed, while this provision was substituted by the CPE of 1985, the content and scope of application of the duty of professional secrecy of lawyers remains almost intact vis-à-vis its predecessor of 1956.

---

[8] Bar Association website, available at: www.ilustrecolegiodeabogadosdecaracas.com /HISTORIA.htm.

[9] Publicaciones del Colegio de Abogados del Distrito Federal No. 8: "Código de Ética Profesional del Abogado Venezolano" [Publications of the Bar Association of the Federal District no. 8: "Code of Professional Ethics of the Venezuelan Lawyer"]. Caracas 1956. Editorial El Cojo.

3 Supervision

14. Pursuant to the CPE and the Statute of Lawyers, the Federation of Bar Associations, the regional bar associations (each formed by an assembly, board of directors, secretary and disciplinary courts) and the Lawyer Social Welfare Institute (*Inpreabogado*) are the bodies in charge of supervising the lawyers' professional practice.

    In accordance with Article 18 of the Statute of Lawyers, lawyers must comply with the regulations, agreements, resolutions and further decisions of the Federation of Bar Associations, the bar associations of the location where they practice and the Lawyer Social Welfare Institute.

A The Bar Associations

15. In accordance with Article 7 of the Statute of Lawyers, any person who has obtained a law degree in the Republic must register with a bar association. This is a requirement to legally practice the profession. Every state of the country has a bar association.

    Under Article 10 of the Statute of Lawyers, a lawyer registered in a bar association may legally practice in the entire territory of the Republic. In case the lawyer were to practice in a state that, because of its territory, corresponds to another bar association, or if the lawyer were to change his or her residence because of the duties performed, the lawyer must join the corresponding bar association within 30 days.

B The Courts

16. Illegal actions within the parameters of the practice of the legal profession may be subject to penalties in the disciplinary courts of the bar associations, and may even be subject to criminal sanctions in the criminal courts of the Judicial Power, which depends on the illegal action committed.

    As specified in Article 3 of the CPE, the disciplinary breaches that entail the sanctions provided in the law are those violations of the duties established in Title II of the Code (that is, the duty of professional secrecy). Also, Article 61 of the Statute of Lawyers provides that disciplinary courts of bar associations will hear, in the first instance, matters involving violations of this law and the regulations thereof. Article 61 expressly mentions norms of professional ethics, including "the violation of professional secrecy, except that it occurs in order to prevent or denounce the commission of a crime." However, it must be noted that Article 61 mentions the possibility of waiving the duty of secrecy only for the purposes of preventing a crime, but other exceptions should be added, such as when claims are filed by the client against the lawyer, when lawyers need to disclose confidential information for their own defense, or when lawyers are called to give a deposition or testimony before a judge.

4 Sanctions

A Proceedings and Sanctions

17. Article 63 of the Statute of Lawyers and the following articles describe the procedure to initiate disciplinary procedures, emphasizing violation of ethical and professional duties (Art. 61). However, concerning sanctions for infringements or breaches of lawyers' obligations, the law is a little ambiguous as it relates to professional secrecy. There is no specific penalty for violation of the duty of professional secrecy or at least for the scenarios provided in Article 61 of the Statute of Lawyers. Moreover, if the actions of the lawyer are considered prevarication, a criminal process will be initiated, and it may conclude with a custodial sentence, as explained later in this chapter.

Article 70(e) of the Statute of Lawyers provides the sanction for those who violate the duty of professional secrecy, which reads as follows:

> Lawyers who fail to heed admonishments and those who incur *serious breaches of ethics*, honor and professional discipline will be penalized with suspension from professional practice ranging from one month to one year, depending on the severity of the breach.   (Emphasis added.)

Failure to observe the duty of professional secrecy may be considered a severe ethics violation, but the rules are not clear, nor do they define the concept of "serious breaches." This makes it difficult to subsume the professional secrecy violation within any of the scenarios provided in Article 70.

The above would be the scenario for decisions that the disciplinary court of the bar association may render against one of its members; however, it is necessary to take into account the description and regulation provided in the Criminal Code in connection with these professional actions. Article 250 and the following articles establish the crime of prevarication, providing that lawyers who affect the case entrusted to them through collusion with the opposing party or through any other fraudulent means, or lawyers who represent opposing interests in the same case, will be sanctioned with imprisonment from 45 days to 15 months, and they will be suspended from professional practice for the same time. Also, in the case of lawyers who defend one party and also defend the other party without the consent of the former, they will be imprisoned from one to three months.

In addition to the conflict of interests, it is important to protect all information and knowledge that the client has provided to the lawyer. Therefore, representing opposing interests is banned in the Criminal Code, as well as acting on behalf of both parties, due to the fact that this entails handling confidential information that is logically protected by professional secrecy and that requires good judgment and discretion.

B Relationship between Criminal Sanctions and Disciplinary Sanctions

18.   There is the possibility of imposing disciplinary sanctions on legal profes-
        sionals before the courts of the bar associations, but there are also certain
        behaviors that are regulated and prohibited in the Criminal Code, such as
        those where lawyers who disclose information of a client and cause damages
        may be sentenced to prison.

        Applicability of the sanctions will depend on the action or omission of the
        legal professional; that is, not all breaches committed by lawyers concerning
        professional secrecy will be simultaneously penalized by the Bar Association
        and by the criminal courts of the Judicial Power. The specific actions of the
        lawyer must be examined for the purposes of establishing if only disciplinary
        sanctions would apply or if such behavior requires a criminal sanction in
        a correlative manner. In any case, it is important to note that lawyers sanctioned
        with imprisonment "shall be suspended from professional practice for the
        entire time of their sentence and starting from the moment when the decision
        is final," pursuant to the provisions of Article 70(G) of the Statute of Lawyers.

5 Duty to Provide Information to the Authorities

A Money Laundering and Terrorism

19.   The Organic Law against Organized Crime and Terrorism Financing (OLOC)
        primarily regulates operations in the financial area, particularly those concern-
        ing banks, insurance activity, the stock market and real estate. However, it also
        applies to lawyers engaged in independent practice when they perform transac-
        tions for a client involving the following activities: (i) purchase or sale of real
        estate; (ii) administration of money, securities and other assets pertaining to the
        client; (iii) management of bank accounts, whether savings or securities; (iv)
        organization of contributions for the creation, operation or management of
        companies; and (v) creation, operation or management of legal persons or
        structures, and purchase and sale of business entities.

        In those scenarios, lawyers will have several obligations that may infringe
        on professional secrecy, such as providing clients' information to state entities
        during the course of an investigation in connection with organized crime or
        terrorism financing. Lawyers may, therefore, have to report cash transactions,
        report suspicious activities of the client, and identify the client and any third
        party who may be participating in such transactions and operations (see Art. 10
        and following articles of the OLOC).

        In addition, pursuant to Article 63 and following articles of the OLOC, the
        Public Prosecutor's Office is empowered, with the authorization of a judge, to
        arrange or apply special measures, such as the "interception of communica-
        tions, e-mails and correspondence" (Art. 64.1). Article 64(4) of the OLOC
        provides that state entities have completely subjective powers to order "[a]ny

other similar measure that favors prevention, prosecution and sanction of the crimes established in this Law."

As a result, certain restrictions concerning privacy and disposition of assets and accounts are relaxed in light of the severity of the crimes that were allegedly committed and are under investigation or already subject to a criminal process, which clearly may affect lawyers' duty of professional secrecy, subject to the OLOC.

B Collective Settlement of Debts

20. Corporation liquidation processes, whether through bankruptcy or others, are primarily developed in the Code of Commerce. Articles 41 and 42 of the code provide the possibility that the judge, during the course of a trial, may ask to see the books to confirm or clarify certain facts. However, there is no reference to the duty of professional secrecy or any scenario that may compromise lawyers' duty to maintain confidentiality, which is why a potential obligation to provide information would have to be linked to organized crime or any other exceptions mentioned in the preceding sections of this chapter.

Nevertheless, the Public Prosecutor's Office has the capacity to ask a criminal court to seize documents, titles, securities and sums of money available in bank accounts or safe-deposit boxes in banks or held by third parties, when there is reasonable basis to believe that they are related to the crime under investigation (Art. 204 of the Organic Code of Criminal Procedure (OCCP)). This rule does not specifically mention professional secrecy, so it should be interpreted in favor of keeping the principle of confidentiality between client and lawyer in the terms provided in Article 48 of the Constitution, which guarantees the secrecy and inviolability of private communications, in the understanding that they may be intercepted only under the order of a court but always "preserving the secrecy of private matters that are not related to the corresponding process."

6 Treatment of Lawyers' Documents and Correspondence in the Context of Judicial or Police Investigations

21. Professional secrecy extends to "files and documents even after the lawyers have ceased to provide services for the clients" (Art. 25 of the CPE). However, Article 6 of the Communications Privacy Protection Law (CPPL) of 1991 provides that police authorities have the power to "prevent, interrupt, intercept or record communications" solely for the purposes of investigating the following: (i) crimes against national security or independence, (ii) crimes established in the Organic Law for the Preservation of Public Assets, (iii) crimes established in the Organic Law of Narcotics and Psychotropic Substances, and (iv) crimes of extortion and kidnapping.

This statute does not list exceptions, as may be the case for professional secrecy between lawyer and client. However, it is understood that this has to be consistent with Article 48 of the Constitution, which provides that private communications "cannot be intercepted but with an order of the jurisdictional court, upon compliance of the legal requirements, and always preserving the secrecy of private matters that are not related to the corresponding process."

In addition, Article 8 of the CPPL provides that all authorized recordings "will be exclusively used by the police and judicial authorities in charge of the investigation and processing thereof, and, consequently, officers cannot disclose the information obtained." Moreover, Article 204 of the OCCP establishes that criminal investigative police bodies are empowered, in urgent cases, to directly ask the judge, with prior authorization (through any means) of the Public Prosecutor's Office, to order the seizure of documents, securities, bank accounts and similar instruments, when they are believed to be involved in the crime under investigation.

7 Search of a Lawyer's Office

22.　As mentioned, professional secrecy extends to "files and documents even after the lawyers have ceased to provide services for the clients" (Art. 25 of the CPE), which logically involves lawyers' offices, as that is where they keep most of the documents for cases that they are currently handling or that they handled in the past.

In accordance with Article 204 of the OCCP, during the investigation of a crime, the Public Prosecutor's Office, with the authorization of the judge, may "seize the correspondence and other documents that are believed to be produced by the author of the crime or that such author may have sent, and that may be related to the events under investigation," as well as "titles, securities and sums of money available in bank accounts or safe-deposit boxes in banks or held by third parties."

8 Tapping of Telephone Conversations with a Lawyer

23.　As explained previously, Article 48 of the Constitution guarantees secrecy and the inviolability of private communications, which can be intercepted only with an order of the jurisdictional court "upon compliance of the legal requirements, and always preserving the secrecy of private matters that are not related to the corresponding process."

Article 205 of the OCCP establishes the possibility of intercepting and recording private communications, whether they are in person, via telephone or through any other means, for the purposes of a criminal investigation. These communications may not be used as evidence in a trial because, in accordance with Article 207 of the OCCP, all recordings authorized in accordance with the law shall be exclusively used by the authorities in charge of the investigation and trial. Therefore, it is prohibited to disclose the information obtained.

Such investigation powers of the entities that help the justice administration system do not make any reference to lawyers, which suggests that recordings of phone conversations with lawyers may be included. However, the provisions of Article 48 of the Constitution should be observed, that is, any interception must preserve the secrecy of private matters that are not related to the corresponding process.

9 The Lawyer as Witness

24.   The Venezuelan legal system provides that lawyers have the option to refuse to serve as a witness against a client and refrain from answering questions that may lead to the disclosure of a secret or the violation of confidences. This rule was not drafted to be interpreted as an absolute prohibition or obstacle to testify against the client. The legislation provides that the lawyers "have the option to refuse," that is, legal professionals may decide if they are to testify against a client or not. Hence, it can be inferred that this discretionary power may even cover choosing to refrain or not from disclosing confidential information in the testimony.

Article 25 of the CPE means that the possibility of disclosing professional secrets is limited to situations in which the lawyer is called as a witness in an administrative procedure, in a judicial procedure, or in any other means of dispute resolution, strictly subject to the provisions of Article 49 of the Constitution, Article 395 and following articles of the CCP, and any other procedural provisions that may apply in accordance with the nature of the procedure.

The provisions of the CPE match the provisions of the CCP concerning evidence. Article 408 thereof provides: "The persons who, under the law, are released from the obligation to appear to declare as witnesses are not obligated to appear before court to make depositions. In these cases, evidence shall be brought in observance of the provisions concerning witnesses, as they may apply." Article 481 of the same law establishes that "All persons capable of serving as witness must give declaration. The following may, however, excuse themselves: ... 2. Those that due to their status of profession must keep professional secrecy in connection with the matter at hand." As per the foregoing, there are no obstacles to give depositions or testify in light of the legal provisions or the profession, but it is a possibility or power of the legal professionals to decide if they will give depositions or testify.

10 The Lawyer and the Press

25.   In principle, any Venezuelan citizen has freedom of speech as established in Article 57 of the Constitution, which provides that any person has the right to

"freely express any thoughts, ideas or opinions aloud, in writing or through any other means, and use any means of communication and broadcasting to this end, and no censorship may be applied." However, Article 9 of the CPE stipulates that lawyers must not use mass media "to discuss matters entrusted to them, or publicize the files of matters that have not been decided yet, unless it is necessary for the purposes of correcting concepts when justice and morality so require."

Even after a case has ended, lawyers' comments may be published, but only for exclusive scientific purposes and in professional publications that "shall follow the professional principles of ethics." In addition, the rule provides that "proper names shall be omitted if the publication may damage the honor and reputation of any person. Moreover, mass media cannot be used to make threats related to judicial actions or force anyone to reach an agreement."

Therefore, even though lawyers may turn to mass media to expose certain circumstances related to cases or litigation that they handle, their statements must be limited to elements that do not lead them to disclose professional secrets, the merits of the case or the files of matters "unless it is necessary for the purposes of correcting concepts when justice and morality so require."

11 Powers of the Tax Authorities and Others

26.   In the Organic Tax Code, there are certain provisions in connection with the obligation to provide information to tax authorities that may eventually limit professional secrecy. Article 134 establishes that civil, political, administrative and military authorities of the Bolivarian Republic of Venezuela, state and municipal authorities, bar associations, professional associations, trade and production associations, unions, banks, financial institutions, insurance and capital market institutions, taxpayers, responsible parties, third parties, and, in general, any individual or organization "are obligated to collaborate with all tax administration entities and officers, and occasionally or periodically provide the general or specific information that the officers may require." The foregoing also encompasses the obligation of such subjects to report any actions that constitute violations of the tax rules.

Such disclosed information can be used only for tax purposes. The article also establishes that "[s]ubjects under a dependency relationship with the taxpayer or responsible party cannot rely on professional secrecy." That is, when lawyers are dependent employees of the taxpayer, they will be obligated to disclose the information obtained during the rendering of their professional services.

12 National Security Issues

27.   Article 6 of the CPPL provides that police authorities have the power to "prevent, interrupt, intercept or record communications" only for the purposes

of investigating certain crimes, including "crimes against national security or independence."

In addition, the applicable law in this case is the Organic Law of National Security, which establishes the obligation to provide data or information to national or foreign natural or legal persons, as well as public officers, when it may be necessary for national security purposes (Arts. 7, 38.7 and 54). However, the law is not specific in connection with the limits of this obligation, nor does it make any reference to professional secrecy.

Index

ABA. *See* Anguilla Bar Association
Act on the Reporting of Unusual
    Transactions (Curaçao), 258–259
advice privilege
  in Anguilla, 13
  in Barbados, 80, 87–88
  in Bermuda, 115–117
  in BVI, 161–162
  in Jamaica, 362–363
  in Trinidad and Tobago, 459–460
American Bar Association, 6–7
AML laws. *See* Anti-Money Laundering
  laws
Anderson v. Bank of British Columbia, 16,
  35
Anguilla
  advice privilege in, 13
  AML legislation in, 18
  attorney-client privilege in, 3
    breach of contract for, 3
    limitations of, 16–18
    scope of, 13–15
    after search of lawyer's office, 25
    statutory basis of, 11–13
    after voluntary or unintentional
      disclosures, 17–18
  CFT legislation in, 18
  under Common Law (Declaration of
    Application) Act, 11, 20
  CRA in, 11, 22
  duty of confidentiality in, 11–13
  duty to provide information to authori-
    ties, 23–24
    for collective settlement of debts, 24
    for money laundering, 23–24
    for terrorism, 23–24
  ECSCA in, 10
  external legal service providers in, 19
  in-house counsel in, use of, 19–20
  law firms in, 19
    legal assistants in, 19
  lawyers in
    office searches of, 25
    press disclosures by, 27
    as trial witnesses, 26–27
  legal documents and correspondence
    in, treatment of, 24
  legal supervision in, 20–21
    through bar associations, 10–11,
      20–21
    through courts, 21
  litigation privilege in, 2–3, 13
    scope of, 15
  multidisciplinary associations in, 19
  national security issues in, 28
  OECS BA in, 10–11, 20–21
  under POCA, 23–24
  powers of tax authorities in, 27
  proceedings and sanctions in, 21–23
    civil, 22–23
    criminal, 22, 23
    disciplinary, 21–22, 23
  professional secrecy in
    exceptions for, 16–18
    history of, 20
    limitations of, 16–18
    optional derogations for, 16–18
    persons subject to, 15–16
  tapping of phone conversations in,
    25–26
Anguilla Bar Association (ABA), 10–11,
  20–21